Nancy Hart and the Tories

History
of
Hart County Georgia

By:
John William Baker

Southern Historical Press, Inc.
Greenville, South Carolina

This volume was reproduced from
An 1935 edition located in the
Publisher's private Library

All rights reserved. No part of this publication may be reproduced,
stored in a retrieval system, transmitted in any form, posted
on to the web in any form or by any means without
the prior written permission of the publisher.

Please direct all correspondence and orders to:

www.southernhistoricalpress.com
or
SOUTHERN HISTORICAL PRESS, Inc.
PO BOX 1267
375 West Broad Street
Greenville, SC   29601
southernhistoricalpress@gmail.com

Originally published: Georgia, 1935
ISBN #0-89308-933-8
All rights Reserved.
Printed in the United States of America

INDEX

History of Hart County	I
Copyright	II
A Brief Auto-Biography of J. W. Baker	VII
Preface	IX
A Resolution of General Assembly	X
Election and Appointment of J. W. Baker County Historian	XI
A Jug Factory	274
Avery, Rev. Asa	311-12
Alford, D. C.	414-15
Boundary, Name, When Created, From What Territory Laid out, Full Text of Acts of Legislature Creating County	14-20
Benson, John Blassingame	49-50
Brief History	54-59
Brown, Leroy C.	318
Bobo, Solomon M.	305-6
Bowersville	320-25
Bailey, John C.	411-12
"Cateechee of Keowee"	4-9
County Divided Into Militia Districts	34-5
Charter of the Town of Hartwell	48-49
Carnes, Thomas P.	126-129
County Farm	53-54
County Officers	85-6
Congressional Districts	88
Cornog, W. L.	286-7
Cobb, Ransom A.	297-8
Chapman, Elijah	298
Craft, Captain J. F.	412

CHURCHES

Providence Methodist Church	359-61
Cokesbury Methodist Church	366
Mount Zion Methodist Church	366-7
Hartwell Methodist Church	369
Hartwell Camp Ground	369-70
Hartwell Presbyterian Church	371-2
Pleasant Hill Presbyterian Church	374-5
Harmony Presbyterian Church (abandoned and gone)	375-77
New Hope Methodist Church (abandoned and gone)	377
Hartwell Baptist Church	378-9
Holly Springs Baptist Church	380-5
Hendrys Baptist Church	385
Sardis Baptist Church	385-7
Shoal Creek Baptist Church	389-91
Reed Creek Baptist Church	391-4
Line Baptist Church (abandoned and gone)	395-6
Bio Baptist Church	396-8
Milltown Baptist Church	398-400
Cross Roads Baptist Church	400-2

Cedar Creek Baptist Church	402-4
Oak Bower Baptist Church	404
City Court	89
"Center of the World"	98-99
Creswell, David Survey	100
"Cedar Crest"	187-8
First Court House	37
Second Court House	46
Third Court House	51
First Term of Court	38
First Jail	39
Second Jail	52
Third Jail	52
Fourth Jail	53
First Buildings in Hartwell	39-42
Flood, Drought, Freeze, Quake and Storm	288-294
Frost, Amaziah	233

FAMILY HISTORY

Looney Family History	138
Elias Sanders Family History	141-5
Harbour Family History	175-6
Skelton, John, Family History	176-8
McMullan Family History	178-184
Richardson Family History	184-6
Stowers Family History	186-7
Carter Family History	188-194
McCurry, John, Family History	195-7
McCurry, John G., Family History	197-202
McCurry, Daniel E., Family History	202
Jones Family History	203-208
Sadler Family History	208-212
Teasley Family History	212-218
Burton Family History	218-221
O'Barr Family History	221-224
Henry Farmer Chandler Family History	224-228
Obadiah Wright Family History	232-233
Robert Black Family History	233-4
Bobo Family History	234-236
Brown, Nicholas, Family History	236-7
Brown, Levi, Family History	237-9
Dyar Family History	239
White, John Martin, Family History	244-247
William Glover Family History	248
Bowers Family History	248-258
Jackson, Joseph, Family History	252-260
Haynes Family History	260-62
Herndon Family History	263-66
Hunt Family History	267-8
Skelton, Noel, Family History	268-9
McCurry, John, Family History	269-71
Dooly, William, Family History	272-3
Barron, Barnabas, Family History	273-4

INDEX—Continued

Ayers, Moses, Family History	275-6
Gordon, John, Esq., Family History	278-9
Stowers, Hon. F. C., Family History	279-80
Peek Family History	281-2
Thornton Family History	283-4
Maret Family History	287-8
Myers, William, Family History	294-5
Myers, James R., Family History	295-6
Fleming, Peter, Family History	301
Fleming, Peter Lewis, Family History	301-2
White, Samuel, Family History	306-8
Pearman Family History	308-9
Parker, Lewis, Family History	308
Cleveland Family History	341-8
Redwine Family, Redwine Church, Lorenzo Dow, Mrs. Corra Harris, Major Durkee, Families of the Redwine Community	348-359
Ledbetter Family History	361-3
Fisher Family History	363-5
Johnson, Daniel M., Family History	372-4
Sanders, William A., Family History	409-11
Geology of Hart County	59-61
Gibson, Walter M.	387-9
Historical and Geographical Background	1-4
Hart, Nancy	24-31
Hartwell Messenger	43-45
Hartwell Fifty Years Ago	45-6
History of Hart County Board of Education	404-409
Hodges, Hon. F. B.	312-313
Hodges, Mrs. F. B.	313
Hartwell School History	329-32
Hodges, Walter L.	414
History of Public Roads	61-73
Hall, Joel T., Mail Carrier, R. F. D. No. 2	79
Holland, Jefferson	310
Historic Old Andersonville	110-120
History of Old Linder Farm	228-230
Indian Dancing Mound	99
Isaac Briggs Survey	101
Intoxicating Liquors	339-40
Judges Superior Court, N. J. Circuit	88-89
King's Bench	124-126
Kay, John R.	313-14
King's Mount Goldmine	287
Knox's Bridge	145-6
Ledbetter, George M.	361
Meetings at "Center of the World"	21-24
Murder Most Foul, Henry Hill Kills T. V. Skelton	332-8
Matheson, Julius D.	413
Magill, John H.	413-14
MUSTER ROLLS OF COMPANIES GEORGIA VOLUNTEERS, C. S. A. HART COUNTY	
Company "B," 24th Georgia Regiment, Phillip E. Devant, Captain	151-3
Company "C," 16th Georgia Regiment, J. H. Skelton, Captain	153-6
Company "H," 15th Georgia Regiment, Wm. R. Poole, Captain	156-8
Company "F," 38th Georgia Regiment, John C. Thornton, Captain	158-62
Company "D," 37th Georgia Regiment, John G. McMullan, Captain	162-4
Company "C," 5th Georgia Regiment, D. G. Johnson, Captain	165-6
Company "E," 4th Georgia Regiment, B. D. Johnson, Captain	166-8
Montevideo, John McDonald, James Patterson, Montevideo Post Office, Montevideo Manufacturing Co., Col. Richard J. D. Durrett, Rice's Store	230
Nancy Hart	24-31
New Town, Shockley's Ferry, etc.	106-110
Organization of the County and Election of Officers	20-21
Physical Features of the Town of Hartwell	32
Purchase of Land for County Site, Survey of the Area Into Lots, Squares and Streets	37
Prison Bounds	39
Post Offices, Star Routes, Rural Free Delivery	74-79
Political Parties	90-5
Powder Mill Branch	100
Peek, Captain John	282
Poole, Judge Wm. R.	302-4
Partial List of Names of Doctors of Hart County	325-9
Parkertown	129-130
Parker Brothers	130-131
Parker, Lewis, Wm. H. and J. Hubbard	131
Parker, John D., Obituary	132
Parker, Rev. Benjamin B., Obituary	133
Parker, Jacob, Obituary	134
Parker, Hon. B. B.	135-6
Parker, Morgan L.	136
Parker, Howell B.	138
Parker, Rev. John R.	138
Perry and Bynum Duel on Island at Hatton's Ford	120-4
Representatives and State Senators from Hart County	84
Railroad History	79-83
"Reminiscences From Away Back"	95-8

iv

INDEX—Continued

Red June Apple Orchard on Whinnery's Creek	233	Old Court House	47
Statistics	168-175	John Blassingame Benson	49
Shoal Creek Factory	285-6	Map Geology of the County	60
Stephenson, Hon. F. C.	296-7	Marker at "Center of the World"	99
Sanders, Rev. Samuel B.	309-10	Homes of J. D., B. B. and Jacob Parker, and Old Store Post Office	137
The Beaufort Treaty	10-13	Knox's Bridge	146
Tugaloo River	101-106	Sinclair McMullan Old Mill	183
The "Big Sawmill"	147-8	Micajah Carter Home	192
The War Between the States	149-151	John G. McCurry	201
Tamar Escapes from the Indians	266-7	James Patterson Home	207
Tyler, Rev. Henry	367-8	Old Burton Home	220
The John Benson Chapter, D. A. R.	416-17	Old Home of Henry Farmer Chandler	227
The Hartwell Chapter, U. D. C.	417-18	Job Bowers Old Home	257
Ussery, Mumford	377-8	Herndon Coat of Arms	265
Vanna	318-20	Home of Hon. F. G. Stowers	280
Vernon, Rev. J. T. W.	298-301	Photo of Hon. F. C. Stephenson	297
Williams, James Wesley	314-17	Photo of James Wesley Williams	314
World War Veterans	418-428	Redwine Methodist Church and Corra Harris	356
		Old Pleasant Hill Presbyterian Church	375
ILLUSTRATIONS		Reed Creek Baptist Church	394
Nancy Hart and the Tories	Frontispiece	Milltown Baptist Church	399
Photo of J. W. Baker	VI	Cross Roads Baptist Church	401
Nancy Hart Monument	33	Photo of D. C. Alford	415
John A. Cameron, First County Surveyor	35		

v

J. W. BAKER

A Brief Auto-Biography of John William Baker, Author of the Hart County History

WHILE I do not consider my life as being in any ways illustrious or worthy of special mention, yet for the benefit of those who may be curious to know more about the author of the Hart County History, than elsewhere referred, I will give this brief sketch of myself.

I was born in Reed Creek District, Hart County, Georgia, September 22, 1858.

My father was James Cullen Baker, who married Rhoda C. Pinson, December 14, 1857. To this union were born myself and one sister, Mariah, born May 11, 1861.

James Cullen Baker, my father, son of John Baker and Sarah Suit Baker, was born in Lancaster County, South Carolina, December 22, 1832, and came with his father and the other members of the family to Georgia, crossing the Tugaloo River at Pullen's Ferry, January 1, 1852.

My father enlisted in the service of the War Between the States and died of disease at Petersburg, Va., March 2, 1863.

My mother, Rhoda C. Pinson Baker, daughter of Sterling Pinson and wife, Mary Burton Pinson, was born February 14, 1834, and died October 27, 1861.

After the death of my father and mother, my grandfather, John Baker, and wife, Sarah Suit Baker, took me and sister, orphans, into their home, cared for and raised us to manhood and womanhood, and like many others, perhaps, we never fully realized the gratitude we were due for the fatherly and motherly care and teaching received from our gracious grandparents.

My paternal grandfather, John Baker, was born in Lancaster County, South Carolina, December 18, 1808, married Sarah Suit ...., came to Georgia in 1852, as already stated, died December 30, 1896, at the age of 88 years, buried at Reed Creek Baptist Church.

My paternal grandmother, Sarah Suit Baker, was born in North Carolina July 26, 1810, moved with her people in her girlhood to Lancaster County, South Carolina, married John Baker,—died May 29, 1875, buried at Reed Creek Baptist Church of which she and her husband, John Baker, were members.

My maternal grandfather was Sterling Pinson, who came in young manhood from Virginia to Franklin County, Georgia, born in 1795—married Mary (or Polly) Burton, daughter of John and Mary Hudson Burton, March 4, 1827, settled in Reed Creek section Franklin (later Hart) County, Ga., taught school for a part of the time, engaged in farming, owning several tracts of land, which by his will he bequeathed to his children. He was a member of Reed Creek Baptist Church, being a charter member when the church was constituted May 7, 1830. Was quite prominent and active in the affairs of the church, serving as clerk and trustee of the church, and for a number of years represented the church as a delegate in the Tugaloo Baptist Association. He died November 27, 1857, buried at Reed Creek Church, his grave marked by a rock vault.

My maternal grandmother, Mary (or Polly) Pinson, daughter of John Burton and Mary Hudson Burton, as already mentioned, died May 14, 1841, and is buried in the family grave-yard at the old Burton homestead.

During my boyhood days I attended school in the community, later entered the Hartwell High School under the efficient tutelage of Prof. M. V. Looney, and later attended the same school under Professors S. W. Peek and Solomon M. Bobo.

Joined the Baptist Church at Reed Creek September 1, 1876, at the age of eighteen years. Later served the church as deacon and clerk.

My sister, Mariah, was twice married, first to L. T. Wright, to which union were born four sons and one daughter. Three of the sons survive. After the death of her first husband she married E. A. Caldwell, to which union were born one daughter who is still living. My sister, Mariah, died October, 1924.

On January 24, 1884, I was married to Miss Fannie A. Sanders. A full record of marriage, names and number of children and date of death of wife is given in the William A. Sanders Family History which will be found elsewhere in this history.

On October 4, 1894, I married Miss Martha L. Martin of Reed Creek, and to us have been born ten children, six sons and four daughters, five of the sons and three of the daughters are still living.

Engaged in teaching for a couple of years, one year in 1879 and in 1888. Settled on farm near Reed Creek church and engaged in farming for a part of the time. Established the first cannery in the country, raised crops of vegetables, notably tomatoes which were pronounced the finest and best in the market at the time. Also, canned fruits of various kinds. While I did not succeed very well in a financial way in the canning industry, my experiment has proven of great benefit to the people of the country, as the people are now taking care of their fruits and vegetables by the process of canning, both for home use and for sale, as a result of the dissemination from my experiment.

Acted as Notary Public ex-officio Justice of the Peace in Reed Creek District for several years.

Have been a practical surveyor for many years, acting as county surveyor a part of the time, and in 1889 made a survey of Hart County and published a county map, and have published two revisions of the map since.

Superintended and financed the survey and publishing of a map of Elbert County in 1905.

On January 28, 1904, I was elected to the office of Clerk of the Superior Court of Hart County, Ga., which position I held for twelve years and eleven months.

Am now serving as Clerk of the Board of Commissioners of Roads and Revenues of Hart County, Ga.

My career has been more or less chequered and not very successful, in the common acceptation of the term, yet I trust that my efforts have and will continue to contribute to the best interest of Hart County and her people on all progressive lines.

PREFACE

WE HAD conceived the idea, years ago, of writing a history of Hart County at sometime or other, but did not get active until some seven or eight years ago, when we began to collect data looking to the project, not realizing at the time the stupendous amount of work and time required to bring it to a successful consummation; so weeks lengthened into months, and months into years before we could complete the work in anything like a satisfactory way.

In the meantime we were elected by the Grand Jury of Hart County, and commissioned by the Judge of the Superior Court, as the legal historian of Hart County, the proceedings of which appear further on.

In the matter of research we have consulted about all the files of the newspapers published since the county was created.

We have written scores of letters to various parties in different parts of the country, asking for information of one character or another of an historical nature relative to the county, and in most all instances received courteous replies with valuable information and the kindest of wishes expressed for our success.

We have interviewed many of the older citizens of the county with reference to certain facts, and in most cases received valuable information that we, perhaps, would not have received otherwise.

As to matters of a more remote date, we have consulted various historical publications dealing with the history of our country in the dim and distant past.

Having been born soon after the organization of the county, and having a fairly retentive memory, and having had occasion to travel over the county many times during the years, we have written a good portion of the history from memory and observation.

The result of our work is only a partial history, as the source of data seems to be inexhaustible and it would require volumes to record a full and complete history of our county.

We have mentioned many of the pioneer families and men of prominence who have lived in our county, but have left unwritten any account of many more who were just as eligible and deserving of mention, all for the lack of time and space.

To all who have so generously aided us in any way in our undertaking, we are sincerely grateful.

In conclusion will say, as has been said by other county historians of our State, the writing of this history has been a labor of love—love for those who have lived, toiled and passed on, and love for those who are carrying on, as well as for those who may come after us.

Respectfully,

J. W. BAKER.

A Resolution of General Assembly

WHEREAS, the founding of the Colony of Georgia by General James Oglethorpe occurred in 1733 and the two hundredth anniversary of that venturesome, political and philanthropic event will occur in 1933 and should be marked in some way proper to its historic character, so as to perpetuate for our posterity and the records of the State and Nation the facts of the evolution and progress of the commonwealth that became a constituent State of the Federal republic of the United States, and

Whereas, no provision has been made by the State Government to celebrate and memorialize the momentous establishment of the colony and subsequent sovereign State, and

Whereas, there is not in existence today a comprehensive and contemporaneous history of the State, therefore, be it

Resolved, by the General Assembly of Georgia, both houses thereof concurring herein, that the Judges of the Superior Courts of the State are hereby earnestly requested to give in charge to the grand jury of each county in their several circuits, at the next term of the court, the urgent consent of some competent person in their county to prepare between now and February 12th, 1933, being Georgia Day, as nearly a complete history of the formation, development and progress of said county from its creation up to that date, together with accounts of such persons, families and public events as have given character and fame to the County, the State, and the Nation. And that said county histories be deposited on Georgia Day in 1933 in the State's Department of Archives and History, there to be preserved for the information of future citizens of the State and prospective biographers and historians. And this action is recommended to the judges, grand juries, and the people of all the counties of the State, for early procedure because delay will leave action in this behalf too short a time for the necessary research and accumulation of data to make the county histories as full and accurate as they should be for full historic value.

Resolved, Further, that the Governor of the State is respectfully requested to transmit an officially certified copy of these resolutions to each of the Judges of the Superior Courts of the State.

> W. CECIL NEILL,
> *President of Senate.*
>
> D. F. MCCLATCHEY,
> *Secretary of Senate.*
>
> RICHARD B. RUSSELL, JR.,
> *Speaker of House.*
>
> E. B. MOORE,
> *Clerk of House.*

Approved: L. G. HARDMAN, *Governor.*
This 23rd day of August, 1929.

Election and Appointment of J. W. Baker, County Historian

October 15, 1929.

We, the Grand Jury chosen and sworn to serve at the August Adjourned Term, Hart Superior Court, 1929, make the following Presentment:

We unanimously recommend that Hon. J. W. Baker be appointed County Historian, and feel that with the knowledge he already possesses this work will be full and complete.

W. B. McMullan, *Foreman*	S. L. Thornton
	D. M. Shiflet
I. S. Haley, *Clerk*	J. O. Banister
Grover Heaton	F. O. Mauldin
A. M. Pruitt	J. S. Craft
R. P. Robertson	W. L. Hunt
A. M. Teasley	C. W. Rice
Geo. W. Richardson	J. A. Martin
E. P. Ayers	Will G. Roe
L. A. Pruitt	Stewart Bowers
A. L. Baker	I. N. Scott
G. P. McGarity	D. B. Alford

At Chambers, Hartwell, Georgia,
October 26, 1929.

It appearing to the undersigned that the General Assembly of Georgia adopted a resolution at its regular session in 1929, and approved by the Governor on August 23, 1929, the object of which is to secure the consent of some competent person in the respective counties of this State to prepare, between now and February 12, 1933, as nearly a complete history of the formation, development and progress of the various counties from their creation up to that date, together with the accounts of such persons, families and public events as have given character and fame to the counties, the State and the Nation, and for other objects named in such resolution:

And it further appearing that the Grand Jury of Hart County at its recent August Adjourned Session, 1929, named John W. Baker, Esq., to prepare said work, and that he has consented thereto:

Whereupon, it is ordered and adjudged that the said John W. Baker, Esq., be and is hereby appointed to prepare a complete history of the formation, development and progress of said county from its creation up to February 12, 1933, together with the account of such persons, families and public events as have given character and fame to said County, the State and the Nation.

Let this order be entered upon the Minutes of the Superior Court of Hart County by the clerk thereof.

W. L. HODGES,
Judge Superior Courts, Northern Circuit.

GEORGIA, HART COUNTY.

I, Jno. G. Richardson, Clerk Superior Court, said State and County, hereby certify that the above and foregoing is a true and correct extract from the Presentments of the Grand Jury of Hart Superior Court at the August Adjourned Term, 1929, dated the 25th day of October, 1929, and the order of the Court therein; appointing Hon. John W. Baker, Esq., as Historian of Hart County, Georgia.

This the 25th day of November, 1929.

JNO. G. RICHARDSON,
Clerk Superior Court, Hart County, Georgia.
(Official Seal.)

HISTORICAL AND GEOGRAPHICAL BACKGROUND

THE history of our country, of which Hart County is but a small unit, may be divided into five periods:

The Aboriginal, Voyage and Discovery, Colonial, Revolution and Confederation, and the Great National period, and for the sake of convenience, the Great National period may be divided into first and second, or ante-bellum and post-bellum, the first covering the time from the end of the period of Revolution and Confederation to the War Between the States, and the second, from the close of the War Between the States to the present time.

The Aboriginal period was from remote antiquity to the coming of the white man, by which we mean the voyage and discovery of Christopher Columbus in the year 1492, as it is well authenticated history that the land, later known as America, had been discovered many centuries before the coming of Columbus, by the Norsemen who lived in Norway, Sweden and Denmark, who were daring and skillful sailors.

The first people to inhabit our country, so far as we have any account were the Mound Builders, about whom very little is known, and so far as the territory embraced in Hart County is concerned, it is not definitely known that they ever lived in any part of it, while it is quite evident that they were pretty generally distributed over North America.

The Indians who occupied our country after the Mound Builders seemed to know nothing of them, and with the exception of some crude engravings upon the rocks on the mountainsides and along the streams, which have never been deciphered and are yet unintelligible, together with mounds built in the dim, distant and misty past, nothing is known of them; from whence they came and when, and whither and when they went is yet unknown.

After the discovery by Columbus, and when it became known that there was a new world beyond the Atlantic, voyages began to be made by the English, French and other people of the old world.

The King of England, Henry VII, sent out an Italian sailor, John Cabot, who sailed westward in the spring of 1497. After sailing many weeks he came to land, which was the mainland of our continent, somewhere in the neighborhood of Cape Breton Island, at the entrance of the Gulf of St. Lawrence, which he took possession of in the name of the King of England.

The next year John Cabot and his son, Sebastian, explored the coast of North America all the way from Novia Scotia to North Carolina. Upon the voyages of the Cabots, England laid claim to all the mainland of North America; however, after adjustment with other claimants, the territory of England, so far as related to that part of North America, which later became the United States, was restricted to the Atlantic seaboard, and extending to the Mississippi River.

In 1663, Charles II, King of England, selected eight of his friends, conspicuous among them was Charles' prime minister, the Earl of Clarendon; another was the Duke of Albemarle, who had done more than any other man to make Charles king; and these eight was given a charter to all of the territory, including the present states of North and South Carolina, Georgia, Alabama and Mississippi, which boundary was known as Carolina, named in honor of Charles II and of his father, Charles I, and included all the territory from 31° to 36° North Latitude, and from sea to sea, and later was increased to 29° to 36° 30' North Latitude, the Mississippi River being the western limit.

The Lord Proprietors, as the owners in England were called, did not care for the colonies which had been planted in that part of their possessions east of the Savannah River, except to get as much money out of them as possible. Their rule was very unpopular with the people who came into the land. After more than fifty years had passed, and Carolina had became well settled and established, these proprietors turned over their government to the crown. The two Carolinas were then divided into North Carolina and South Carolina, or rather the territory east of the Savannah River was so divided, and each became a separate royal province. This was in 1729.

The King of England, George II, bought from the proprietors all the land west of the Savannah River granted them under the charter from Charles II.

In 1732, James Edward Oglethorpe and twenty trustees obtained a charter for the founding of a colony for the relief of the debt-ridden people of England and to give them the chance of a new start in life.

King George II signed the Charter of the Colony of Georgia on June 9, 1732, conveying all territory west of the Savannah River, and being all of the territory purchased from the eight Lords Proprietors. The name "Georgia" was adopted in honor of the reigning monarch.

The right of discovery did not give right of possession and ownership to the lands of America, as it was occupied by native Indians of various tribes, however the right of discovery carried with it the right of pre-emption of the soil of the native Indians which, as we understand it, meant a prior right of those making the discovery to that of others to purchase from the owners or occupants.

The lands embraced in Hart County were originally owned by the Cherokee Indians, the boundary of their possessions being described as follows:

From the confluence of the Wateree and Congeree rivers to the Cherokee Corner, crossing the Savannah River at or near the mouth of Broad River where it empties into the Savannah, and from the Cherokee Corner on in the same direction to the most southerly branch of the Oconee River, thence up said branch or tributary to its source, thence to a point near the present town of Cedartown, Ga., thence to the Tennessee River, thence down said river to where it empties into the Ohio River, thence up the Ohio River to the mouth of the Great Kanawha River, thence up said river to its source, thence along the Blue Ridge Mountains to the source of the Wateree River, thence down said river to the point of beginning.

At this juncture perhaps it would be proper to give some history of the occupancy and activities of the Cherokee Indians in this part of the country, however we have but meager historical data upon the subject. As a matter of fact they did occupy the entire territory now included in Hart County, which is evidenced by arrow heads, pieces of pottery and various other relics which are encountered in all parts of the country. There are quite a number of traditions and accounts of the Indians which we will mention incidentally in connection with other subjects, but the sketches are so disconnected that

HISTORICAL BACKGROUND

it is not practical to give them all in narrative form or rather to relate them all in one continuous story.

The Cherokees were, perhaps, the most intelligent of all the tribes, more graceful in form and figure, more beautiful in feature, due perhaps in a measure to environment, as the territory they occupied was, and is still, the most picturesque and romantic of that occupied by any of the other tribes.

The names given by the Cherokees to the mountains, rivers and other objects of nature are the most beautiful in their significance, while their legends and lore are superior in beauty and interest to that of other tribes.

Many treaties were made with the Cherokee Indians from time to time by which they conveyed their lands to the colonies and later to the states.

In 1783, a treaty was entered into by the Cherokees with the representatives of Georgia at Augusta, by which they conveyed a certain boundary of their lands, described as follows:

Beginning at Savannah River, where the west line of Wilkes County strikes the same; then along the said line to the Cherokee Corner; from thence on in the same direction to the south branch of the Oconee River; thence up the said river to the head or source of the most southern stream thereof; thence along the temporary line separating the Indian hunting-ground to the northern branch of the Savannah River, known by the name of Keowee, and thence down said river to the beginning.

In 1784, the county of Franklin was created and included all of the territory conveyed by the said treaty.

The territory south of the line of Franklin to the original line separating the Cherokee and Creek lands, included in Wilkes County, later Elbert, had been conveyed by a former treaty with the Cherokees in 1773.

Wilkes County was created in 1777. It formerly included all the lands north of the Ogeechee, acquired by treaty from the Cherokees and the Creeks, at Augusta, 1st June, 1773.

It was named in honor of John Wilkes, who, as a member of the English Parliament, strenuously opposed the measures which produced the war with America.

On the motion in parliament to bind the colonies and people of America, in all cases whatsoever, Mr. Wilkes said, "that he considered the designs of the ministry to be the shortest compendium of slavery ever given. It is the broadest basis of tyranny. Three millions of people to be taxed at the arbitrary will and pleasure of this house, without a single person present to represent them! If the Americans could tamely submit to this, they would deserve to be slaves."

Ebert County was laid in 1790 from territory taken altogether from Wilkes County, and included all of that part of Wilkes County north of Broad River, all of which originally belonged to the Cherokees.

The county was named for Major-General Samuel Elbert, who was a distinguished officer of the War of the Revolution, and Governor of Georgia at the close of hostilities. He was born of English parents in the State of South Carolina, 1740, but engaged in mercantile pursuits in Savannah. Partial to military life, he became one of the King's soldiers. But he resented the oppressive measures of the British Parliament and identified himself with the Colonial patriots.

He was a member of Georgia's first Council of Safety, a delegate to the Provincial Congress on July 4, 1775, and, when the Georgia Battalion of Colonial troops was organized he was commissioned Lieutenant-Colonel. On the departure of General McIntosh from Georgia, subsequent to an unfortunate duel with Button Gwinnett, the supreme command of the Continental forces in Georgia devolved upon General Elbert.

There is quite a lot of interesting history in connection with General Elbert and his achievements, military and otherwise, but space forbids that we make further mention of it here.

Franklin County was created by Act of the General Assembly February 25, 1784, and included all of the lands conveyed by the Cherokee Indians in a treaty entered into at Augusta, Ga., in 1783, as already described. The county was named for the celebrated New England philosopher and patriot, Benjamin Franklin, who in various important matters acted as Georgia's agent in London on the eve of the Revolution.

The boundary of Franklin County included a large part of the lands between the Tugaloo and Seneca rivers. The Savannah River to the source of the most northerly branch or tributary was designated as the line between the Colony of South Carolina and the Colony of Georgia, by the charter of George II, King of England, and after the colonies became states after the close of the War of the Revolution, it remained the line until 1787, when by a treaty entered into by and between representatives of the two states, known as the Beaufort Treaty, the line was shifted from the Seneca to the Tugaloo River. A copy of the Beaufort Treaty is hereinafter reproduced and hereby referred to for a fuller account and description.

In 1784, a few months after ratification of the treaty of peace, by which our national independence was acknowledged, the Legislature, again in session at Savannah, passed an act appropriating 40,000 acres of land for the endowment of a college or university. The lands so appropriated were surveyed into lots of 5,000 acres each, located in different parts of the State, and one such lot known as the Keowee Lot was located in Franklin County between the two rivers, Tugaloo and Seneca, and when the Beaufort Treaty was entered into the State lost all of the country between the two rivers and the university lost the 5,000 acres which had been appropriated to it.

"CATEECHEE OF KEOWEE"

JUST here we will intersperse with the beautiful story of "Cateechee of Keowee," and other items of history connected with Keowee River, which was formerly the line between the two states, with a mention of its tributaries, their names and the part they played in the "muddying of the waters."

"In 1750 Capt. James Francis and his two sons, Allen and Henry, in company with two other pioneers, Messrs. Cowdy and Savage, came to the vicinity of Ninety-Six, S. C., formerly known as Fort Cambridge, and established a trading post with the Cherokees. Allen Francis, with his father, frequently visited the Cherokee country on trading expositions. During these visits he became acquainted with Cateechee, Issaqueena, as she is sometimes called.

She was a slave to the old chief, Kuruga, and a captive Choctaw maiden, hence the two names by which she is known in tradition. The former is Cherokee and the latter Choctaw. The names mean the same thing—"The Deer's Head." She was a beautiful girl, and Allen Francis became enamored with her personal charms. A few years after the establishment of the trading post Kuruga determined to massacre the traders and appropriate their effects. The plot was betrayed by Cateechee, who rode through the forest from Keowee, a famous Cherokee town located on the Keowee River, in what is now the northwestern part of Pickens County, S. C., to Ninety-Six, in what is now Greenwood County, and revealed Kuruga's dark designs to her lover, Allen Francis. The betrayal of the plot thwarted the designs of the old chief. Cateechee did not return to Keowee, but became the wife of Allen Francis. Some years after this event, young Francis and Cateechee were captured by Cherokee braves and carried into the Cherokee country, where they remained for nearly two years. Finally they escaped, as related in the poem written by Dr. J. W. Daniel, South Carolina's highest authority on Indian lore, and came back to the old trading post where they lived and died.

Stump-House Mountain, the scene of their escape, is six miles north of Walhalla, S. C., and around its base flows Issaqueena Creek; and the falls down which it is said Issaqueena leaped are at the southern entrance of the somewhat famous (locally) tunnel of the Blue Ridge railroad partly excavated through Stump-House Mountain.

* * *

The place-names—Ninety-Six; Six Mile, a creek in Pickens County; Twelve-Mile, a small river in Pickens County; Eighteen Creek, constituting a lengthy portion of the line between Pickens and Anderson counties; Three-and-Twenty and Six-and-Twenty creeks in Anderson County—were all named in commemoration of Cateechee's famous and heroic ride.

These streams crossed her path, and were respectively six, twelve, eighteen, twenty-three and twenty-six miles at the point where she crossed them from the Cherokee town, Keowee; and Ninety-Six, the terminus of her ride, is just ninety-six miles from Keowee.

In the story it is related that Allen Francis and his wife, Cateechee, were captured, as already mentioned, and were carried back to Keowee, together with the baby girl that had been born to them, and that Cateechee and her baby were returned to Kuruga and liberated and that Allen Francis, bound, was arraigned before the council to answer such charges the Indians saw fit to accuse him and await his fate, and that his stoic demeanor was such that Kuruga was determined to adopt him as his son, and that the little family was reunited, but very carefully guarded. After some two years had passed, during which time Allen Francis became a very expert archer and went on hunting expeditions with the braves, the women went on a nutting expedition, or as related by others, went on a berry hunting, Cateechee and her baby went with them and there arose a terrific storm, the women scattered, each running for home, and nobody guarding Cateechee, who had her little girl with her. The fleeing women met Francis coming in search of his wife and child, and they told him she was coming after them, being delayed by the weight of the child, or as said in the poem, "Papoose makes her weary, papoose makes Deer's Head droop."

When they met they decided this was their opportunity—so they fled to the mountain. They knew better than to attempt to return to their friends at once, so far a time they dwelt in a hollow tree on the top of the mountain.

The Indians suspecting that they had returned to Fort Cambridge, or Ninety-Six as it was called after Cateechee's run of ninety-six miles, so messengers were sent to spy and find out where they were. The messengers stated that the couple certainly had not returned to their friends. Then most of the Indians settled into the belief that they had been struck dead by lightning during that dreadful storm, and that wild beasts had devoured their bodies. But there was one wise old medicine man, Salooe, who did not feel sure of their fate, and he determined to seek for them in the mountain fastnesses. Taking with him some young Indians, they made a thorough search, and finally arrived at the big hollow tree which had been the couple's shelter. Salooe scornfully called it a "stump house" and by this incident the mountain became and is still known as Stump-House Mountain.

Francis had just completed a boat, and he and his family were about ready to trust themselves to flight down the river. Francis was in the woods completing his arrangements, and Cateechee, with the child, was walking about the river's brink. The Indians saw and rushed to capture her. She snatched the child in her arms and plunged into the shallow stream down which she fled, the Indians on the bank running after her. Finally she reached the head of a swift high fall, and there she hesitated, but a shout from her pursuers made her plunge over, preferring death to capture. Seeing her make the awful plunge, they were sure she and the child were dashed to pieces and carried down the river, so they returned to the "Stump House" to wait for the return of Francis. But Cateechee had not been dashed to pieces. With her little girl in her arms, she landed on a shelf of rock about ten feet below the brink of the fall and there she slipped behind the vail of the falling water.

The cataract now bears the name "Issaqueena Falls." Francis, on the opposite side of the river, had seen the whole thing, and when the coast was clear, with thongs of leather he helped Cateechee to climb to the brink, then together they took their places in the little boat and rowed down stream until they reached the Savannah, then they abandoned the boat and went through the woods back to Ninety-Six.

A few extracts from the poem mentioned:

> "Lovely Keowee's vale stretched,
> Far north, while the sable shadows
> Of approaching night fell o'er it.
> 'Twas dark here and light there—spotted
> As a leopard, flecked with light,
> Dappled with spots by the pale moon,
> Which, now and then, peeped through clouds
> And bedecked the vale with shadows,
> Like a silver thread the river
> Flowed through the beautiful vale—
> Murmured sweetly—whispered secrets
> To the stars, and gurgled sweet songs

*To the moon, which peeped through clouds
Quickly to steal silent kisses
From the sparkling waters, chatting
With stones, toying with the bobbing
Boughs of alder, beech, and willows;
Drooping to lave their arms, or tips
Of their tiny fingers, in that
Clear stream, flowing fresh from the womb
Of the towering blue mountains.
Keowee, where mulberries grow—
Place of Mulberries, whose ripe fruit
Crowned the board of the red man,
In its season, every year;
Whose roots, beaten to pulp and cast
Into the still waters, made drunk
The fish, which, thus drugged, floated,
Stupid, on the eddy water,
Easy for the angler to take.
Keowee, Cateechee's wild home,
Was the jewel of Kuruga's
Possession of crags and vales,
Lying like a diamond rare
At the bottom of a blue lake,
Barricaded with crags and rocks,
Standing up like pickets on guard,
Keeping vigil o'er the jewel,
Which lay at their bases, as safe
As a daughter with her bosom
Bared, sleeping by her sire's couch.
The town perished in days long past,
But the laughing river murmurs
Still the red man's beautiful name—
Bears the Cherokee word as soft
As the ripple of its waters;
And enshrines forever noble
Memories of Issaqueena,
Choctaw maid and lovely captive—
A slave girl to savage masters—
Whose name, Deer's Head, they translated
Into Cherokee "Cateechee."*

In a conversation reputed to have been between John H. Magill and Prof. Solomon M. Bobo several years ago, Mr. Magill mentioned the Savannah River and Mr. Bobo said that it was originally called "Isudigia." We have made some inquiry of the Bureau at Washington, D. C., as to the meaning of the word, and received the following reply:

"We are informed by the Bureau of American Ethnology that the word Isudigia is possibly a corruption of I'su nigu, an important Cherokee settlement, commonly known to the whites as Seneca, formerly on Keowee River in Oconee County, South Carolina."

It may be possible there was a misprint in the account of the conversation between Magill and Bobo, and it is possible that Mr. Bobo gave the word "Isunigu."

It is a matter of conjecture that the stream which we now know as Whitewater, further down as Keowee, and still further down as Seneca and then Savannah, may have been at one time in the remote past known all the way by the Indians as "Isunigu." Of course this is but conjecture, and more or less confusing, however, as it is an historical statement, we give it here and the reader can consider it for what it is worth.

The names which the river bears today in its several reaches are as follows:

First it is Whitewater, which rises in the mountains of North Carolina and flows in a southerly direction for a ways, its crystal waters tumbling over beautiful falls in the spray of which rainbows flash in the sunshine. When it reaches to where a tributary known as Toxaway River, also known as Horse Pasture, enters, the name changes to Keowee, which in the Cherokee Indian dialect means "River of Mulberries." From this point to the mouth of Twelve Mile Creek it is known as Keowee, and from the mouth of Twelve Mile to where it converges with the Tugaloo River to form the Savannah it is known as Seneca, which name in the Indian language or dialect means "muddy water."

From the mouth of Twelve Mile for the balance of the way the waters are turbid, due to the fact that the Twelve Mile, the Eighteen Mile, the Three-and-Twenty and Six-and-Twenty and other tributaries are "muddy" or turbid. Like the Yellow Sea, which is so called because its waters are thus colored by soil washed from the hillsides and mountains of China, so it is with the waters of the tributaries of the Seneca River which are colored by the erosion of the red or brown soil of the territory which they drain.

The Keowee-Seneca river is quite historic in many respects. The old Indian town of Keowee and Fort Prince George were located on the Keowee. Not far below the mouth of Twelve Mile River on the east side of the Seneca and overlooking the same, was the magnificent home of John C. Calhoun, South Carolina's illustrious son. His place was known as "Fort Hill," and at which today is located Clemson College, one of the leading educational institutions of the South.

Right near this place and on the east or left side of the Seneca, near the Blue Ridge Railroad trestle, is where General Pickens made a treaty with the Cherokee Indians in the spring of the year 1785, whereby the Indian chiefs conveyed the Washington District, embracing the whole of what is now Anderson, Greenville, Pickens and Oconee counties, and which were thrown open to colonization. The gaunt old tree, "Treaty Oak," under which the agreement was made stood for a number of years, but was blown down a few years ago. The spot is now marked by a stone slab.

Another interesting item of history which we will give in connection with the Seneca River is an account of a fort erected in time of the War of the Revolution which stood near the river. We wrote the Professor of History of Clemson College, S. C., for some information with reference to this old fort and herewith give in part his reply to same:

"Mr. J. W. Baker,   "Clemson College, S. C., Sept. 21, 1931.
"Hartwell, Ga.

"Dear Mr. Baker: Fort Hill was the name John C. Calhoun gave to his plantation. The small estate to which he came to live about 1826 had been called Clergy Hall. Some time after Calhoun acquired the estate, he enlarged the house, added other lands to the estate and changed its name to Fort Hill. He gave this name to his estate because on this estate, or the lands of this estate, stood an old Revolutionary War fort, known as Fort Rutledge, named in honor of South Carolina's President or Governor, John Rutledge. This fort, a rude, temporary stockade affair, was erected about August, 1776, by Gen. Andrew Williamson as a protection against the Indians and Tories in the campaign of that year. Evidences of the fort have disappeared, but a marker placed by the Clemson College board at the request of the Daughters of the American Revolution stands near the original site. This stands on a high bluff on the east side of the Seneca River in the extreme southeastern corner of Oconee County, S. C. It is about one mile directly south of the Calhoun mansion, which is the property of Clemson College and near the college buildings.

"The site of the old fort is also on the property of the college estate. The site of the old fort is probably 200 to 300 yards from the Seneca.

"In Revolutionary War times this stream was called the Keowee. Today we speak of the Seneca as made by the confluence of the Keowee and Twelve Mile Creek. These streams come together just above where the main line of the Southern Railway crosses. This point is about two miles up stream from the location of the old fort."

There is another important tributary of Seneca which flows in from the west side of the river, known as Conneross Creek, and was so named from the fact that a wild duck built its nest under a cliff—or rather, under a great rock that projected over the creek from a perpendicular cliff on its banks. When the duck flew from her nest she was compelled to drop downward until she cleared the rock, and then she arose. Hence the name Kawanurasui in the dialect of the Lower Cherokees, and Kawanulassui in the Upper Cherokee, abbreviated by the Indians to Kawanuras. This creek traverses for most of its course Oconee County, crossing the Oconee and Anderson County line near its mouth where it flows into Seneca River. It will be remembered that this creek, before the change in the state line, lay in Franklin County, Georgia.

One other matter in connection with Seneca River is that a short way above Earle's Bridge there is a noted shoal, known as Portman's Shoals, and at which several years ago there was built a dam and a hydro-electric plant installed, the power of which is transmitted to Anderson and used for industrial purposes. At or near the bridge there is, or was in the days before the building of bridges across the streams and installation of ferries, a ford where all traffic crossed the river.

From an old map published in 1800 we have an account of an old post road which was on a line of march through South Carolina into Georgia by Spartanburg, Greenville, Pendleton, Hatton's Ford and on to Carnesville, Georgia, and which to the best of our information crossed the Seneca River at the ford mentioned near Earle's Bridge.

THE BEAUFORT TREATY

Convention Between South Carolina and Georgia, Concluded at Beaufort, 1787

TO ALL whom these presents shall come. The underwritten Charles Cotesworth Pinckney, Andrew Pickens, and Pierce Butler, Esqs., commissioners appointed by the State of South Carolina, of the one part, and the underwritten John Habersham and Lachlan McIntosh, Esqs., a majority of the commissioners appointed by the State of Georgia, of the other part—send greeting:

Whereas, the State of South Carolina did heretofore present a petition to the United States, in Congress assembled, and did therein set forth, that a dispute and difference had arisen and subsisted between the states of South Carolina and Georgia concerning boundaries; and the states claiming respectively the same territory, and that the case and claim of the State of South Carolina was as follows, that is to say: "Charles the Second, King of Great Britain, by charter dated the twenty-fourth day of March in the fifteenth year of his reign, granted to eight persons as therein named, as lords proprietors thereof, all the lands lying and being within his dominions of America between thirty-one and thirty-six degrees of north latitude, in a direct line to the south seas, styling the lands so described 'the province of Carolina;' that on the thirteenth day of June, in the seventeenth year of his reign, the said king granted to the said lords proprietors a second charter, enlarging the bounds of Carolina, viz., from twenty-nine degrees of north latitude to thirty-six degrees thirty minutes, and from those points on the sea-coast west in a direct line to the south seas; that seven of the said proprietors of South Carolina sold and surrendered to George the Second, late king of Great Britain, all their title and interest in the said province, and the share of the remaining proprietor was separated from the king's, and allotted to him in north part of North Carolina; that Carolina was afterwards divided into provinces, called North and South Carolina; that by a charter, dated the ninth day of June, one thousand seven hundred and thirty-two, George the Second, King of Great Britain, granted certain persons therein named, all the lands lying between the rivers Savannah and Altamaha, and between lines to be drawn from the heads of those rivers respectively to the south sea, and styled the colony 'Georgia'; that by treaty of peace concluded at Paris on the tenth day of February, one thousand seven hundred and sixty-three, the river Mississippi was declared to be the western boundary of the North American colonies; that the Governor of South Carolina, in the year one thousand seven hundred and sixty-two, conceiving that all the lands southward of the Altamaha still belonged to South Carolina, granted several tracts of the said lands; that the government of Georgia complained to the King of Great Britain respecting those grants as being for lands within its limits, and thereupon his majesty, by proclamation dated the seventh day of October, one thousand seven hundred and sixty-three, annexed to Georgia all the lands between the rivers Altamaha and St. Mary's, the validity of the grants passed by the Governor of South Carolina as aforesaid remaining however acknowledged and uncontested, and the grantees of the said land, or their representatives still holding it as their legal estate; that South Carolina claims the lands lying between the North Carolina line, and the line run due west from the mouth of Tugaloo River to the Mississippi, because as the said state contends the river Savannah loses that name at the confluence of Tugaloo and Keowee rivers, consequently that spot is the head of Savannah River. The State of Georgia, on the other hand, contends that the source of the Keowee River is to be considered as the head of Savannah River; that the State of South Carolina also claims all the lands lying between a line to be drawn from the head of the river St. Mary's, the head of the Altamaha, to the Mississippi and Florida, being, as the said state contends, within the limits of its charter, and not annexed to Georgia by the said proclamation of one thousand seven hundred and sixty-three. The State of Georgia on the other hand contends that the tract of country last mentioned is a part of that state. The State of South Carolina did, therefore, by their said petition, pray for a hearing and determination of the difference and dispute subsisting as aforesaid, between the said state and Georgia, agreeable to the article of confederation and perpetual union between the United States of America. And whereas, the State of Georgia was duly notified of the said petition, and did by their lawful agents appear in order to establish their right to the premises, in manner directed by the said articles of confederation, and proceedings were therein had in Congress in order to the appointment of judges to constitute a court for hearing and determining the said matter in question; and whereas, it appeared to be the sincere wish and desire of the said states of South Carolina and Georgia, that all and singular the differences and claims subsisting between the said states, relative to ooundary, should be amicably adjusted and compromised; and whereas, the Legislature of the State of South Carolina did elect the above named Charles Cotesworth Pinckney, Andrew Pickens, and Pierce Butler, Esqs., commissioners, and did invest them, or a majority of them, with full and absolute power and authority in behalf of that state, to settle and compromise all and singular the differences, controversies, disputes and claims, which subsist between the said state and the State of Georgia, relative to boundary, and to establish and permanently fix a boundary between the two states, and the said State of South Carolina did declare that it would at all times thereafter ratify and confirm all and whatsoever the said commissioners, or a majority of them, should do in and touching the premises, and that the same should be forever binding on the said State of South Carolina; and whereas, the Legislature of the State of Georgia did appoint John Houston, John Habersham, and Lachlan McIntosh, Esqs., commissioners, and did invest them with full and absolute power and authority, in behalf of that State, to settle and compromise all and singular the differences, controversies, disputes and claims which subsist between the said State and the State of South Carolina, relative to boundary, and to establish and permanently fix a boundary between the two states; and the said State of Georgia did also declare that it would at all times thereafter ratify and confirm all and whatsoever the last mentioned commissioners, or a majority of them, should do in and touching the premises, and that the same should be forever binding on the said State of Georgia:—Now, therefore, know ye, that the underwritten commissioners on the part of the states of South Carolina and

Georgia respectively, having by mutual consent assembled at the town of Beaufort, in the State of South Carolina, on the twenty-fourth day of this present month of April, in order to the due execution of their respective trusts, and having reciprocally exchanged and considered their full powers, and declared the same legal and forever binding on both states, and having conferred together on the most effectual means of adjusting the differences subsisting between the two states, and of establishing and permanently fixing a boundary between them, have agreed, and by these presents for and in behalf of their respective states, do mutually agree to the following articles, that is to say:

Article I. The most northern branch or stream of the river Savannah, from the sea or mouth of such stream to the fork or confluence of the rivers now called Tugaloo and Keowee; and from thence, the most northern branch or stream of the said Tugaloo, till it intersects the northern boundary line of South Carolina, if the said branch or stream of Tugaloo extends so far north, reserving all the islands in the said rivers Savannah and Tugaloo to Georgia; but if the head spring or source of any branch or stream of the said Tugaloo does not extend to the north boundary line of South Carolina, then a west line to the Mississippi, to be drawn from the head spring or source of the said branch or stream of Tugaloo River, which extends to the highest northern latitude, shall forever hereafter form the separation, limits and boundary between the states of South Carolina and Georgia.

Article II. The navigation of the river Savannah at and from the bar and south, along the northeast side of Cockspur Island, and up the direct course of the main northern channel along the north side of Hutchinson's Island, opposite the town of Savannah, to the upper end of said island, and from thence up the bed or principal stream of the said river to the confluence of the rivers Tugaloo and Keowee, and from the confluence up the channel of the most northern stream of Tugaloo River to its source, and back again by the same channel to the Atlantic Ocean—is hereby declared to be henceforth equally free to the citizens of both states, and exempt from all duties, tolls, hinderance, interruption, and molestation whatsoever attempted to be enforced by one state on the citizens of another; and all the rest of the river Savannah to the southward of the foregoing description, is acknowledged to be the exclusive right of the State of Georgia.

Article III. The State of South Carolina shall not hereafter claim any lands to the eastward, southward, southeastward or west of the boundary above established, but hereby relinquishes and cedes to the State of Georgia all the right, title and claim which the said State of South Carolina hath to the government, sovereignty, and jurisdiction in and over the same, and also the right of pre-emption of the soil from the native Indians, and all other the estate, property, and claim, which the State of South Carolina hath in or to the said land.

Article IV. The State of Georgia shall not hereafter claim any lands to the northward or northwestward of the boundary above established, but hereby relinquishes and cedes to the State of South Carolina all the right, title, and claim which the said State of Georgia hath to the government, sovereignty, and jurisdiction in and over the same, and also the right of preemption of the soil from the native Indians, and all other the estate, property, and claim which the State of Georgia hath in or to the said lands.

Article V. The lands heretofore granted by either of the said states between the fork of Tugaloo and Keowee shall be the private property of the first grantees, and their respective heirs and assigns; and the grantees of any of the said lands under the State of Georgia shall, within twelve months from date hereof, cause such grants or authentic copies thereof, ratified under the seal of the State of Georgia, to be deposited in the office of the Secretary of the State of South Carolina, to the end that the same may be recorded there; and after the same shall have been so recorded, the grantees shall be entitled to receive again from the said secretary their respective grants, or the copies thereof, whichsoever may have been so deposited, without any charge or fee of office whatsoever, and every grant which shall not, or which the copy certified as above mentioned shall not be deposited, shall be judged void.

Article VI. The commissioners on the part of the State of South Carolina do not, by any of the above articles, mean to cede, relinquish, or weaken the right, title, and claim of any of the individual citizens of the State of South Carolina to any lands situated in Georgia, particularly to the lands situated to the south of the river Altamaha, and granted during the administration of Governor Boone in the year one thousand seven hundred and sixty-three; and they do hereby declare, that the right and title of the said citizens to the same is, and ought to remain, as full, strong, and effectual as if this convention had not been made. The commissioners on the part of the State of Georgia do decline entering into any negotiation relative to the lands mentioned in this article, as they conceive they are not authorized so to do by the power delegated to them.

In testimony whereof, the said Charles Cotesworth Pinckney, Andrew Pickens, and Pierce Butler, for, and in behalf of the State of South Carolina, and the said John Habersham and Lachlan McIntosh for, and in behalf of the State of Georgia, have to these presents and a duplicate thereof, both indented, interchangeably set their hands and affix their seals. Done at Beaufort, in the State of South Carolina, the twenty-eighth day of April, in the year of our Lord one thousand seven hundred and eighty-seven, and in the eleventh year of the Independence of the United States of America.

                        CHARLES COTESWORTH PINCKNEY (L. S.)
                        ANDREW PICKENS (L. S.)
                        PIERCE BUTLER (L. S.)
                        JOHN HABERSHAM (L. S.)
                        LACHLAN MCINTOSH (L. S.)

The above and foregoing was adopted as an amendment to the Constitution of the State of Georgia.

Boundary—Name—When Created—From What Territory Laid Out—Full Text of the Act of the Legislature Creating the County—And Various Other Acts Relative to Other Territory Added

Hart County is bounded on the north by the Tugaloo River; on the east by the Savannah River, and separated from the State of South Carolina by said rivers; on the south by Elbert County, and on the west by Madison and Franklin counties.

The county was named for Nancy Hart, a Revolutionary heroine, several sketches of whose life, patriotism and deeds of daring appear further on in these pages.

Hart County was created by Act of the Legislature, dated December 7th, 1853, and was laid out in 1854 from territory taken from Franklin and Elbert counties.

Other territory was added from time to time and several changes made in its boundary lines.

Full texts of the various Acts of the General Assembly, relative to the creation and organization of the county and the various changes in its boundary lines are herewith given, and are as follows:

"(No. 226)"

"An Act to lay out and organize a new county from the counties of Franklin and Elbert, and to provide for the organization of the same.

"Section I. Be it enacted by the Senate and House of Representatives of the State of Georgia, in general assembly met, and it is hereby enacted by the authority of the same, That from and after the passage of this Act, a new county shall be laid out from the counties of Franklin and Elbert, to be included within the following limits, to wit:

"Beginning at Stowers' Ferry, on Savannah River, formerly known as Brown's Ferry, and running in a straight line to the residence of Middleton G. Hickman, in Elbert County, including said residence in the new county, thence in a straight line to the corner of Madison County nearest to the Little Holly Springs, thence along the boundary line of Madison County to the corner of Elbert, Franklin and Madison counties, near the residence of Angus Johnson, thence in a straight line to the nearest cross roads to the residence of Job Bowers, not including the residences of Moses and Joseph Manley, in Franklin County, between said residences and Carnesville, on the road leading from Carnesville to Ruckersville, thence in a straight line to a place sometimes called the Negro's old store place, now owned by Leonard Bonds, of Franklin County, thence in a straight line to the mouth of Gum Log Creek, on Tugaloo River, thence along the eastern boundary of the State of Georgia to the beginning.

"Sec. II. And be it further enacted by the authority aforesaid, That the new county described in the first Section of this Act shall be called and known by the name of Hart, and shall be attached to the Northern Judicial

Circuit, to the Sixth Congressional District, and to the First Brigade of the Fourth Division of the Georgia Militia.

"Sec. III. And be it further enacted by the authority aforesaid, That the persons included within the said new county entitled to vote, on the first Monday in February next, elect five Justices of the Inferior Court, an Ordinary, a Clerk of the Superior and a Clerk of the Inferior Court, a Sheriff and Coroner, a Tax Collector and Receiver of Tax Returns, and County Surveyor, for said county, and that the election of said county officers shall be held at the Line Meeting House, and shall be conducted and superintended in the manner prescribed by law, and the Governor, on the same being certified to him, shall commission the persons elected for the terms prescribed by law; and that Justices of the Inferior Court, after they shall have been commissioned, shall proceed to lay off said county into militia districts; and to advertise for the election of the requisite number of Justices of the Peace in said districts, and the Governor on being duly certified of the election of such Justices of the Peace, shall commission them according to law.

"Sec. IV. And be it further enacted by the authority aforesaid, That the Justices of the Inferior Court, after they shall have been duly commissioned, shall have full power and authority to employ some competent person or persons, at the expense of said new county, to run off and plainly mark the boundary lines of said new county, also, the boundary lines of said militia districts, also, they shall have full power and authority to select and locate a site for the public buildings in said new county, to purchase a tract of land for the location of the county site, to divide the same into lots and sell each lot at public sale for the benefit of said new county, and to make such other arrangements or contracts concerning the county site or location of the public buildings as they may think proper, and to establish election precincts in said new county, not exceeding seven in number, one of which shall be at the Court House.

"Sec. V. And be it further enacted by the authority aforesaid, That the elections of the county generally, and the public business thereof shall be held and transacted at the Line Meeting House aforesaid, until the public site shall be located by the Inferior Court as aforesaid, and until the establishment of the election precincts as aforesaid.

"Sec. VI. And be it further enacted by the authority aforesaid, That all officers now in commission, who shall be included within the limits of said new county, shall hold their commissions, and exercise the duties of their several offices within the said county, until their successors shall have been elected and commissioned.

"Sec. VII. And be it further enacted by the authority aforesaid, That all mesne process, executions, and other final process, in the hands of the Sheriff, Coroners, and Constables, of the counties of which the said new county is formed, and which property belongs to said new county, and which may have been levied, or in part executed, and such proceedings therein, not finally disposed of at the time of passing this Act, shall be delivered over to the corresponding officers of said new county, and such officers are hereby authorized and required to proceed with the same, and in the same manner as if such process had been originally in their hands, and all such process which properly belongs to the counties out of which said new county is formed, which may be in the hands of the officers of said new county, shall in like manner be delivered over to the officers of said counties out of which said new county is formed, to be by them executed in manner herein prescribed.

"Sec. VIII. And be it further enacted, That the Superior Courts of said county shall be held on the third Mondays in March and September, and the Inferior Courts on the third Mondays in June and December.

Sec. IX. And be it further enacted by the authority aforesaid, That all laws and parts of laws militating against this Act, be and the same are hereby repealed.

"Approved December 7th, 1853." Acts 1853-4, page 302-304.

"(No. 61)"

"An Act to change the lines of certain counties therein mentioned. Approved March 6th, 1856.

"45. Sec. II. And be it further enacted, That the line between Elbert and Hart be changed so as to run from Stowers' Ferry along the old Brown's Ferry road (now Stowers' Ferry road), about four miles, near John S. Corry's, thence with the line as now run or laid out between said counties, to the line of T. J. Teasley's land, thence to said Teasley's spring, thence in the same direction to Cold Water Creek, thence up said creek till it intersects line, also to change the residence of John E. Teasley from the county from the county of Hart, to that of Elbert.

"46. Sec. III. And be it further enacted, That the line between Hart and Franklin, be so altered and changed as to run from the Cross Roads, west of and near Job Bowers, to the former residence of Jeptha A. Bowers on the Carnesville road, thence to the western corners of William R. Poole's land known as Poole's and Burrough's corner, thence a straight line to the Negro's old store, as described in the act laying out the county of Hart."

Acts General Assembly of Georgia, 1855-6, page 129.

"(No. 25)"

"An Act to change the line between the counties of Elbert and Hart, so as to include one hundred and seven acres of land and the residence thereon of Allen S. Turner, now of the county of Elbert, and add the same to the county of Hart.

"69. Sec. I. Be it enacted, &c., That the line between the counties of Elbert and Hart be so changed as hereinafter to run and include one hundred and seven acres of land and the residence thereon of Allen S. Turner, now of the county of Elbert, and add the same to the county of Hart, commencing at the Savannah River on the line dividing the counties of Elbert and Hart, thence along said line two miles and nine tenths to a red oak tree, thence south $56\tfrac{3}{4}°$ west 20.30 chains to a red oak tree, thence north $52°$ west 10.30 chains to the said county line.

"70. Sec. II. Repeals conflicting laws.

"Assented to Dec. 11, 1858." Acts General Assembly 1858, page 41.

"Elbert and Hart."
"9, Line between Elbert and Hart changed."
"(No. 244)"

"An Act to change the line between the counties of Elbert and Hart.

"9. Sec. I. Be it enacted, &c., That the county line between the said counties of Elbert and Hart, be changed to run as follows: Beginning at Thomas T. Teasley's spring, running thence south 47 deg. W., two and one half miles to a rock corner, near the residence of F. C. Davis, including said residence in Hart County, thence running north 78 deg. W., three and five eighths miles to a persimmon tree corner, on the present line of Hart County, near Big Holly Spring; that all the citizens residing within said boundary are truly made citizens of Hart County, and that territory included in said boundary, be and the same is hereby added to the county of Hart.

"Sec. II. Repeals conflicting laws.

"Assented to, December 13th, 1859." Acts General Assembly 1859, page 269.

"An Act to change the line between the counties of Madison and Hart.

"5. Section I. The General Assembly of the State of Georgia do enact, That the county line between the counties of Madison and Hart, be changed as follows: Beginning on the line between the counties of Elbert and Madison, at a point south of, and nearest to the residence of Robert Caruthers, and running northwest so as to include the residence of said Robert Caruthers in Hart County, to the road leading from Daniel's Ferry to Hatton's Ford, near the residence of R. W. Berryman, then along said road till it strikes the Hart County line at Angus Johnson's; and that portion of territory lying east of said line be added to, and become a part of the county of Hart.

"Sec. II. Repeals conflicting laws.

"Assented to April 4, 1863." Acts General Assembly 1862-3, page 207.

The above described part of Madison County cut off to Hart County was surveyed by W. A. Stone, surveyor, August 5 and 6, 1863, for which services he received sixteen dollars, including six dollars for services of his chainmen.

"No. CCLII=(O. No. 242)"

"An Act to change the county line between the counties of Elbert and Hart, so as to include the residence and lands of John B. Maxwell, of Elbert County, and for other purposes.

"Section I. Be it enacted by the General Assembly of the State of Georgia, That from and after the passage of this Act the county line between the counties of Elbert and Hart be so changed as to include within the county of Hart the residence and lands of John B. Maxwell, now of the county of Elbert, the line to commence on the lands of said John B. Maxwell where it joins the counties of Hart and Elbert, and run around his land until it reaches the Hart County line."

"Sec. II. Repeals conflicting laws.

"Approved March 2, 1875." Acts General Assembly 1875, page 271-2.

At the time the act of the Legislature of Georgia was passed, December

7, 1853, creating Hart County from portions taken from Elbert and Franklin counties, all of the Savannah River counties were entitled to one senator and two representatives.

Col. Wm. B. White was the senator and L. H. O. Martin and E. M. Rucker the representatives from Elbert County, and Wm. R. Poole was senator and Jefferson Holland representative from Franklin County.

Wm. H. Mattox, a young man at the time, was the private secretary of Col. White, and we herewith give a copy of a letter written by him many years afterwards giving an account of the preparation and passage of the act.

"Heardmont, Ga., June 14, 1887.

"Editor of *Sun:* In the last issue of *The Sun,* in your 'Historical Sketches of Hart County,' we note an error, which, with your permission, we will correct. It is true we were but a boy at the time of which we write, but we appeal to the record if the correctness of our statement is questioned.

"At the time of Hart's organization, each county in the State had a representative or senator in the upper branch of the Legislature, and the majority of the then existing counties had two members in the lower house. All of the Savannah River counties (excepting Lincoln) from Richmond to Habersham, furnished two representatives, and as we have already stated every county in the State had a senator.

"After the organization of Hart, the three counties being reduced to one representative, it was a loss to northeast Georgia of one member. This fact caused some objection to the act, as the old Whig and Democrat lines had not at that time been obliterated, and every move giving one party any advantage was fought by the other. Elbert was a strong Whig county—Franklin was Democratic. They so framed Hart as to give a small Whig majority, and thereby retained the two Whig members and gain a Whig senator. Franklin lost one Democrat representative, and hence some opposition from that party, which was then in a small majority in the Legislature.

"In 1853—the year Hart was formed, or rather the year in which the Legislature that organized Hart was elected, for the bill though introduced in December, 1853, did not become a law until February, 1854. L. H. O. Martin and E. M. Rucker, and in the Senate by Wm. B. White—an abler trio the grand old county never furnished before or since.

"Col. White, with the aid of several friends and advisers, drew the bill laying out the county, and introduced it in the Senate. And if the original manuscript as offered by Col. White is still in existence, it will show the boyish impress of your humble correspondent's chirography. On the night previous to its introduction next day by Col. White, in the Senate, a parcel of friends met in Col. White's room in the old Brown hotel in Milledgeville and perfected the bill. Elbert's two representatives, Martin and Rucker, Poole of Franklin, Clark of Oglethorpe, and some few others were present as members of the Legislature, besides Judge T. W. Thomas, Col. W. M. McIntosh, and perhaps one or two others as interested outside advisers.

"The writer was clerk and did the writing, and under the instructions of Col. White, after the caucus adjourned, wrote up the bill for him.

"The line between Elbert and the new county was a question of prolonged discussion, we well remember, but the differences in the views of the various friends we do not remember. We only know that on the last night of the caucus, Judge Thomas contended for the Gary-Teasley line and Col. White for the Patterson-McCurry line. Judge Thomas' counsel prevailed and the White party acquiesced in giving up, as they said, too much of Elbert's territory."

As to the Gary-Teasley line mentioned, we are not sure just where it was any more than the present county line runs near the Van D. Gary old homestead, and as first run before there was some additional territory added from Elbert County, ran near the residence of John Easton Teasley.

The Patterson-McCurry line was evidently from or near the residence of James Patterson, now the home of Rev. J. D. Turner, and by the place formerly owned by John McCurry, afterwards known as the A. W. McCurry place near Bethesda Church.

At the time Elbert County was created it was divided into 12 militia districts, numbered from 1 to 12.

The description of district No. 7, is as follows:

"Beginning at the mouth of Big Creek, thence up the North Fork of Broad River to the line of Franklin County, thence along the said line to the North Fork of Beaverdam Creek, thence down the Beaverdam to William Higginbotham's, thence in a direct line to the upper boundary of district No. 4."

It is evident that part of this district is now included in Madison County, and a portion from the Madison County line to North Beaverdam Creek is now included in Hart County, and in the 1113th militia district, known as Ray's District, that is to say, the upper or northern portion of said district No. 7, is so included.

The description of district No. 9, is as follows:

"Beginning at the north corner of district No. 7, on the North Fork of Beaverdam Creek, thence along the line of Franklin County to Coldwater Creek, thence down the said creek to Cunningham's road, thence along the said road to the Beaverdam, thence up the Beaverdam to the beginning."

It will be seen from this description that the northern portion of district No. 9 is now included in Hart County, and for the most part in the 1118th militia district, known as McCurry's District.

The description of district No. 10, is as follows:

"Beginning at the north corner of district No. 9, thence along the line of Franklin County to Savannah River, thence down the said river to Cedar Creek, thence up said creek to Cunningham's road, thence along the said road to Coldwater Creek, thence up the said creek to the beginning."

All of district No. 10, as above described, is now included in the 1112th, 1114th, 1118th and 1119th militia districts of Hart County, and known, respectively, as Town, Smith's, McCurry's, and formerly Dooley's, now Alford's districts. As to the location of the precinct or lawground of district No. 10, we have never learned.

The description of district No. 11, is as follows:

"Beginning on Savannah River at the mouth of Cedar Creek, thence down the said river to the mouth of Coldwater Creek, thence up the said creek to Cunningham's road, thence along the said road to Cedar Creek, thence down the said creek to the beginning."

About all if not quite, of district No. 11, north of the present line of Hart and Elbert counties is embraced in Hart County, and in the 1114th and 1118th districts, known as Smith's and McCurry's districts.

The portion taken from Franklin County, which embraces all of the territory of Alford's and Town districts north of Big Lightwoodlog Creek, all of Reed Creek district, and most, if not all, of Shoal Creek district, was known as district No. 214 of Franklin County, and one time was designated as Capt. Conner's district, with the court or lawground and company muster ground at "King's Bench," a history of which place will be found elsewhere in this record.

The remaining portion taken from Franklin County is included in Hall's, Ray's, and possibly a portion of Shoal Creek district, originally included in No. 370, adjoining No. 214, on the west, and known as Manley's district, with the court ground, for possibly some of the time, near where the town of Bowersville is now located, as we have a statement made by a man who lived in the early days of Franklin County, to the effect that there was a court ground located about four hundred yards northeast of where the depot in Bowersville stands and it in all probability was at one time the court ground of No. 370.

Here it is proper to state that in the plan of the organization of the State militia, the counties were divided into militia districts and each district was supposed at the time of its creation to contain one hundred men subject to military duty, and as the country at the time was sparsely settled, the districts contained a much larger area than at the present time.

The districts took the name of the captain of the company, and as a matter of course when there was a change made the district took the name of the new or succeeding officer, consequently the name was changed from time to time, but officially the number remained the same, as in the case of Captain Conner's district, which was so named and known during his term of office as captain, but when a successor was elected the name was changed to that of the successor, while the official number 214 remained the same during the time it was included in Franklin County.

The captains of the districts of Elbert County, numbers 7, 9, 10 and 11, at the time they were organized, were respectively John Collins, Esq., Joseph Blackwell, Esq., Hugh McDonald, Esq., and Hezekiah Bailey, Esq.

ORGANIZATION OF THE COUNTY AND ELECTION OF OFFICERS

IN PURSUANCE of the provision made in the act, creating the new county, there was, on Monday, February 6, 1854, an election held at Line Church, which was located about two miles north of where the town of Hartwell was later located, for five Justices and a Clerk of the Inferior Court, an Ordinary, Clerk of Superior Court, Sheriff, Tax Receiver and Collector, Surveyor and Coroner, which resulted in the election of Henry F. Chandler, Micajah Carter, Clayton S. Webb, Daniel M. Johnson and

James V. Richardson, as Justices, and Frederic C. Stephenson, Clerk of the Inferior Court.

James T. Jones, Ordinary; Burrell Mitchell, Clerk of the Superior Court; William Myers, Sheriff; W. C. Davis, Tax Receiver; Richard Shirley, Tax Collector; John A. Cameron, County Surveyor; and Richmond Skelton, Coroner.

Samuel White was appointed County Treasurer by the Justices of the Inferior Court on March 27th, 1854.

After the various officers had been commissioned by Herschel V. Johnson, Governor, it became the duty of the Justices of the Inferior Court, among other things, to locate the county seat, and in order to obtain the center of the county, John A. Cameron, County Surveyor, and Wm. C. Davis, Surveyor, were authorized to make surveys to determine the central point.

When the survey was completed it developed that the central point was at, or near, "Joe's Patch," which was a patch of ground that Joel H. Dyar, son-in-law of Elias Sanders, had cleared and is located not far northwest of the present residence of Mr. I. N. Scott, and about equal distance from the present location and a point about three miles southwest of the town and known as the "Center of the World."

The citizens of the county were divided on the question—some wanted the town at the "Center of the World," while others were in favor of the present site. The two factions could not agree and the party favorable to the "Center of the World," proceeded to hold meetings at the "Center of the World," to take action in the matter.

The proceedings of the first meeting, so far as we have any record, were as follows:

"Meeting in Hart County"

"A meeting of a large portion of the citizens of Hart County, Ga., was held at the 'Center of the World,' on Saturday, 27th May, 1854. The meeting was called to order by calling Job Bowers, Esq., to the chair, and requesting James E. Henderson to act as secretary. The object of the meeting being explained by Asa Duncan, when, on motion, B. A. Teasley, Asa Duncan and Robert Henderson were appointed a committee to report resolutions for the action of the meeting. The committee retired for a short time, and reported the following preamble and resolutions, which were unanimously adopted.

"Georgia, Hart County. Whereas, a majority of the Justices of the Inferior Court of said county have, in our opinion, agreed and determined to locate the county site at a point ineligible, inconvenient and destructive to the permanent interest of the people; and whereas, we believe a large majority of them are utterly opposed to the location fixed upon by the court, we, a portion of the people, therefore feel it not only a right, but our duty, to protest against the improper, unjust and ill-advised action of the court, and to publish our opinions to our fellow citizens, who think and will act with us, and invite their co-operation.

"1st. Be it therefore resolved, That the county site ought to be fixed at the place which will best serve the interest and convenience of the greatest number, without undue influence or favor, and without partiality to anybody.

"2d. Be it further resolved, That the Justices of the Inferior Court, in this matter, are the agents of the people, their servants in fact, and bound by good faith and republican principles, to respect and abide the wishes of a majority in the location of the county site.

"3d. Be it further resolved, That in the action of a majority of justices, in locating the county site, they have disregarded the public interest, not less than the public will.

"4th. Be it further resolved, That against this action we respectfully but earnestly protest, and request the Inferior Court to suspend further proceedings until the public voice can be heard and the public will consulted, and if they can not do this consistently with their own sense and views of right, then we respectfully ask them to resign their trust into the hands of those who gave it and allow the people to elect other agents, who are neither above nor below consulting the public voice in the management of the public affairs.

"5th. Be it further resolved, That all present, in favor of these resolutions, be, and they are hereby requested to sign a copy of them, and that the chairman appoint a committee of three in each militia district, whose duty it shall be to procure the signatures of such as may be favorable to the views herein expressed, and who are now absent.

"6th. Be it further resolved, That another meeting of the people be called, to be held at this place (the Center of the World) on the 1st Saturday in June, and that the citizens of Hart County, without distinction of party, are invited and earnestly requested to attend, who are in favor of the county site being located in obedience to a vote of the majority of the people.

"7th. Be it further resolved, That we notify all bidders for lots at the location, now fixed upon by the court, that we shall persevere in our attempts to remove the county site from said location, by all lawful and fair means, and that if we can not get our interest respected by the court, we shall appeal to the next Legislature, and nothing but the will of the people, fairly expressed, shall induce us to desist.

"8th. Be it further resolved, That the secretary of this meeting furnish each of the Justices of the Inferior Court with a copy of the foregoing preamble and resolutions and that he forward a copy of the same to the *Chronicle and Sentinel* and *Constitutionalist and Republic*, at Augusta, Ga.; *Southern Banner*, Athens, Ga.; and *Southern Rights Advocate*, Anderson, C. H., S. C., for publication.

"On motion, Thomas J. Teasley, Francis S. Roberts and Abner C. Walters were appointed a committee to procure a speaker to address our next meeting."

"JOB BOWERS, *Chairman*.

"JAMES E. HENDERSON, *Secretary*."

Following is reproduced the proceedings of what appears to have been the next meeting of the party who wanted the county seat located at the "Center of the World."

"Public Meeting in Hart County"

"'A few malcontents' (?), 'a few factionists' (?), 'a few senseless rebels' (?), 'a miserable squad' (?), 'a small mob' (?), as those who live on the 'soil in proximity to the Savannah River' are wont to call us, met at the Center of the World June 24, 1854, called Job Bowers, Esq., to the chair, and Dr. J. E. Henderson to act as secretary. The object of the meeting was stated by Wm. T. O. Cook.

"On motion the district committees were requested to present the names of the signers to the resolutions adopted on the 27th ult., to Neal Johnson, J. H. Skelton, and J. A. Bowers, to be examined. Jas. E. Henderson, J. H. Skelton, J. A. Bowers, L. W. Rice and B. A. Teasley were appointed to draft some further resolutions. Mr. Thomas, Esq., was then called for to address the 'miserable squad' (?), which he did in a gentlemanly style.

"The committee appointed to report matter for the action of the meeting, think proper to report only the following facts: We find that 463 legal voters of Hart County have signed the resolutions adopted on 27th May, last, not counting those names obtained by several of the committee-men, and not reported here to-day. We further add, that at the last county election, 759 voters were polled; taking this for a basis, a majority of 167 voters have sustained our action, and condemned the action of the court as unjust, ill-advised, and, destructive to the permanent interest of the county.

"We further recommend the adoption of the following resolutions:

"1. Resolved, That we approve the resolutions adopted on 27th May, last, and are resolved not to be turned from our purpose either by abusive language or the forms of unjust and despotic power.

"2. Resolved, That the committee appointed at last meeting are hereby requested to continue their exertions to procure signatures to the resolutions passed at said meeting, and that the executive committee be empowered to fill any vacancy that may occur in any of said district committees.

"3. Resolved, That Beverly Teasley, Jeptha A. Bowers, Leonard W. Rice, John H. Skelton, and Dr. Jas. E. Henderson, be and they are hereby appointed an executive committee to call meetings and manage generally the cause we have in hand.

"4. Resolved, That we highly approve the conduct of Daniel M. Johnson, who offers to resign his seat at any time when the other justices will do so, and thereby give the people an opportunity to be heard in a new election.

"5. Resolved, That the secretary forward a copy of the proceedings and resolutions for publication to the *Chronicle and Sentinel, Constitutionalist and Republic*, Augusta, Ga.; *Southern Banner*, Athens, Ga.; and *Southern Rights Advocate*, Anderson, C. H., S. C.

"6. Resolved, That we tender our hearty thanks to Mr. Thomas, Esq., for his services."

"JOB BOWERS, ESQ., *Chairman.*
"DR. JAS. E. HENDERSON, *Secretary.*"

The party that wanted the county seat located at the "Center of the World," filed quo warranto proceedings against the Justices of the Inferior

Court and employed Thomas R. R. Cobb of Athens, Ga., to represent them, and the Judges of the Inferior Court employed Howell Cobb, brother of Thomas R. R. Cobb, as their attorney, and after a strong legal battle, the question was decided in favor of the present location.

The Judges of the Inferior Court paid Howell Cobb the sum of $428 as his fee, which amount was paid out of the county funds, while the opposition paid their attorney with funds of their own.

The main street in the town of Hartwell was named Howell in honor of Howell Cobb. It was suggested at first that the street be called Cobb street, but upon reflection, it was evident that if it was named Cobb street that it would be a question as for which of the Cobbs the street was named; so in order that there should never be any doubt as to which one of the Cobbs the name referred, it was named simply Howell.

Some of the Physical Features of the City, Formerly the Town, of Hartwell

There is a watershed line that traverses the city, formerly the town, of Hartwell dividing the waters of Lightwoodlog Creek from those of Big Cedar Creek.

The rain water that falls on the north side of the court house, as well as that which falls on the north side of the town, is carried off by the Cleveland branch to Big Lightwoodlog Creek, while that which falls on the south side of the court house, as well as that which falls on the south side of the town, is carried off by Coody, now known as Tanyard, branch and other tributaries to Big Cedar Creek.

A Marvelous Mountain View

The city of Hartwell is so situated as to enjoy a marvelous view of the story-famed Blue Ridge Mountains, sufficiently remote that the "distance lends enchantment to the view."

The prospect occupies a quadrant of the horizon, extending from north to west, the beautiful intervening landscape of green rises by a succession of grades and is silhouetted against the mountains of blue, which in turn are silhouetted againset the luminous sky beyond, forming a panorama of grandeur and scenic beauty.

NANCY HART

NANCY HART, the Revolutionary heroine, for whom Hart County and the town of Hartwell were named, was a native of North Carolina. Her maiden name was Nancy Morgan before her marriage to Captain Benjamin Hart, a native of Kentucky. Soon after their marriage they came to Georgia and settled on Wahatchee Creek, in what is now Elbert County, a short distance from where said creek empties into Broad River.

The great ancestor of the Hart family in the United States emigrated from London about A. D. 1690, and settled in Hanover County, Virginia, where he died, leaving an only son, Thomas Hart, who was about 11 years of age when his father arrived in Virginia. Of the elder Thomas Hart, little is known, except that he was a merchant and, probably late in life, a blind man.

Thomas Hart, the son, married Susanna Rice of Hanover, the aunt of Rev. Daniel Rice, of the Presbyterian church, who settled in Kentucky in the year 1781. Thomas Hart, Jr., died in Hanover about the year 1755, leaving six children: Thomas, John, Benjamin, David, Nathaniel and Ann, all of whom with their mother migrated to Orange County, North Carolina, about 1760.

Benjamin Hart, third son of Thomas Hart, of Hanover, and Susanna Rice, accompanied his mother to North Carolina, where he married Nancy Morgan, daughter of Thomas Morgan of the Revolution Army.

Mrs. Hart was a woman of remarkable strength and decision of character, and she exhibited as much, if not more, courage and heroism as any woman during that great drama of American liberty—the War of the Revolution. History recounts many deeds of daring achieved by her during the war, and we herewith reproduce a few of the many accounts given of the life and activities of Nancy Hart.

In Historical Collections of Georgia, by the Rev. George White, M.A., 1855, he says:

One among the most remarkable women that any country has ever produced resided in Elbert.

The clouds of war gathered, and burst with a dreadful explosion in this State. Nancy's spirit rose with the tempest. She declared and proved herself a friend to her country, ready "to do or die."

On one occasion, when information as to what was transpiring on the Carolina side of the river was anxiously desired by the troops on the Georgia side, no one could be induced to cross the river to obtain it. Nancy promptly offered to discharge the perilous duty. Alone, the dauntless heroine made her way to the Savannah River; but finding no mode of transport across, she procured a few logs, and, tying them together with a grapevine, constructed a raft, upon which she crossed, obtained the desired intelligence, returned, and communicated it to the Georgia troops.

Once more, when Augusta was in possession of the British, the American troops in Wilkes, then under the command of Col. Elijah Clarke, were very anxious to know something of the intentions of the British. Nancy assumed the garments of a man, pushed on to Augusta, went boldly into the British camp, pretending to be crazy, and by this means was enabled to obtain much useful information, which she hastened to lay before the commander, Colonel Clarke.

In Memorials of Dixieland, by Lucian Lamar Knight, M.A., LL.D., the author writes:

It was during the troublesome days of Toryism in upper Georgia that Nancy Hart performed the courageous feat which has since carried her name to the ends of Christendom. There is perhaps no exploit in our annals richer in the thrilling elements of the drama. It was staged in a little cabin in the backwoods.

The Hart family, into which she married, an aristocratic one, gave a wife to the illustrious Henry Clay, while it flowered again in the great Thomas

Hart Benton, of Missouri. Her own maiden name was Nancy Morgan, a name which honorably connects her with one of the best families of the Old Dominion. She has left us no mound to bedew with our tears, to bedeck with our garlands; but she has left us an immortal memory.

In the Women of the Revolution, by Elizabeth F. Ellett, written in 1848, the authoress writes:

At the commencement of the Revolutionary War a large district in the State of Georgia, extending in one direction from Newsons Ponds to Cherokee Corner near Athens and in the other from the Savannah River to Ogeechee River and Shoulderbone, had been already organized into a county which received the name of Wilkes, in honor of the distinguished English politician. At the commencement of hostilities so great a majority of the people of this country espoused the Whig cause that it received from the Tories the name of the "Hornet's Nest." In a portion of this district, near Dye's and Webb's ferries on Broad River, now in Elbert County, was a stream known as "Warwoman's Creek," a name derived from the character of an individual who lived near the entrance of the stream into the river.

This person was Nancy Hart, a woman entirely uneducated and ignorant of all conventional civilities of life, but a zealous lover of liberty and of the "liberty boys," as she called the Whigs.

On the occasion of an excursion from the British camp at Augusta a party of loyalists penetrated into the interior, and, having savagely massacred Colonel Dooley in bed in his own house, proceeded up the country with the design of perpetrating further atrocities. On their way a detachment of five from the party diverged to the east and crossed Broad River to examine the neighborhood and pay a visit to their old acquaintance Nancy Hart. When they arrived at her cabin they unceremoniously entered it, although receiving from her no welcome but a scowl, and informed her that they had come to learn the truth of a story in circulation that she had secreted a noted rebel from a company of "king's men," who were pursuing him, and who, but for her interference, would have caught and hung him. Nancy undauntedly avowed her agency in the fugitive's escape. She had, she said, at first heard the tramp of a horse and then saw a man on horseback approaching her cabin at his utmost speed.

As soon as she recognized him to be a Whig flying from pursuit, she let down the bars in front of her cabin and motioned him to pass through both doors, front and rear, of her single-roomed house—to take to the swamp, and secure himself as well as he could. This he did without loss of time; and she then put up the bars, entered the cabin, closed the doors, and went about her usual employments. Presently some Tories rode up to the bars, calling vociferously for her. She muffled up her head and face, and opening the door, inquired why they disturbed a sick, lone woman. They said they had traced a man they wanted to catch near to her house, and asked if anyone on horseback had passed that way. She answered no, but she saw someone on a sorrel horse turn out the path into the woods some 200 or 300 yards back. "That must be the fellow," said the Tories; and asking her direction as to the way he took, they turned about and went off, "well fooled," concluded Nancy, "in an opposite course to that of the Whig boy; when, if they had not been so lofty minded, but had looked on the ground inside the bars, they would have seen his horse's tracks up to that door, as plain as you can see the tracks on this here floor, and out of t'other door down the path to the swamp."

This bold story did not much please the Tory party, but they would not wreck their revenge upon the woman who so unscrupulously avowed the cheat she had put upon the pursuers of a rebel. They contented themselves with ordering her to prepare them something to eat. She replied that she never fed traitors and kinsmen if she could help it—the villians having put it out of her power to feed even her own family and friends by stealing and killing all her poultry and pigs "except that one old gobbler you see in the yard." "Well, and that you shall cook for us," said one who appeared to be leader of the party; and raising his musket he shot down the turkey, which another of them brought into the house and handed to Mrs. Hart to be cleaned and cooked without delay. She stormed in protest, but seeming at last disposed to make a merit of necessity, began with alacrity the arrangements for cooking, assisted by her daughter, a little girl 10 or 12 years old, and sometimes by one of the party, with whom she seemed in a tolerably good humor—now and then exchanging rude jests with him. The Tories, pleased with her freedom, invited her to partake of the liquor they had brought with them—an invitation which was accepted with jocose thanks.

The spring—of which every settlement has one near by—was just at the edge of the swamp, and a short distance within the swamp was hid among the trees a snag-topped stump, on which was placed a conch shell. This rude trumpet was used by the family to convey information, by variations in its notes, to Mr. Hart or his neighbors who might be at work in a field, or "clearing," just beyond the swamp, to let them know that the "Britishers" or Tories were about, that the master was wanted at the cabin, or that he was to keep close, or "make tracks" for another swamp. Pending the operation of cooking the turkey, Nancy had sent her daughter, Sukey, to the spring for water, with direction to blow the conch for her father in such a way as should inform him there were Tories in the cabin, and that he was to "keep close" with his three neighbors who were with him until he should again hear the conch.

The party had become merry over their jug, and sat down to feast upon the slaughtered gobbler. They had cautiously stacked their arms where they were in view and within reach; and Mrs. Hart, assiduous in her attentions upon the table and to her guests, occasionally passed between the men and their muskets. Water was called for; and our heroine having contrived that there should be none in the cabin, Sukey was a second time dispatched to the spring, with instructions to blow such a signal on the conch as should call up Mr. Hart and his neighbors immediately. Meanwhile, Nancy had managed, by slipping out one of the pieces of pine which forms a "chinking" between the logs of a cabin, to open a space through which she was able to pass to the outside two of the five guns. She was detected in the act of putting out the third. The whole party sprang to their feet, when quick as thought Nancy brought the piece she held to her shoulder, declaring she would kill the first man who approached her. All were terror struck, for Nancy's obliquity of sight caused each to imagine himself her destined victim. At length one of them made a movement to advance upon her and true to her threat she fired and shot him dead. Seizing another musket she leveled it instantly, keeping the others at bay. By this time Sukey had returned from the spring, and taking up the remaining gun carried it out of the house, saying to her mother, "Daddy and them will soon be here."

This information much increased the alarm of the Tories, who perceived the importance of recovering their arms immediately; but each one hesitated, in the confident belief that Mrs. Hart had one eye on him at least for a mark. They proposed a general rush. No time was to be lost by the bold woman; she fired again, and brought down another of the enemy. Sukey had another musket in readiness, which her mother took, and posting herself in the doorway, called upon the party to surrender "their Tory carcasses to a Whig woman." They agreed to surrender, and proposed to "shake hands upon the strength of it." But victor, unwilling to trust their word, kept them in their places for a few minutes, till her husband and his neighbors came up to the door. They were about to shoot down the Tories, but Mrs. Hart stopped them, saying they had surrendered to her; and her spirit being up to boiling heat, she swore that "shooting was too good for them." This hint was enough; the dead man was dragged out of the house; and the wounded Tory and the others were bound, taken out beyond the bars and hung.

Extracts From a Newspaper Account of Nancy Hart as Related by Rev. Mr. Snead of Baldwin County, Georgia

One among the most remarkable women that any country has ever produced resided in Elbert. We give our readers various particulars concerning her, derived from conversations which we have had with persons who were acquainted with her, and from notes kindly furnished by the Rev. Mr Snead, of Baldwin County, Georgia, a connection of the Hart family. We are also under obligations to the Hon. Thomas Hart Benton, to whom we addressed a letter asking for information in regard to the relationship existing between the family of the Harts and himself, who promptly favored us with all that we desired.

Nancy Hart's maiden name was Morgan. She was married to Benjamin Hart, and soon afterwards came to Georgia. Her husband was a brother of the celebrated Colonel Thomas Hart of Kentucky, who married a Miss Gray of Orange County, North Carolina. This gentleman was the father of the wife of Henry Clay, and maternal uncle of the Hon. Thomas Hart Benton. The family of Mr. Snead removing to Georgia, in consequence of the relationship between them and the Harts, Aunt Nancy, as she was usually called, came to see them. Mr. Snead says he well remembers her appearance, and many anecdotes related of her. He describes her pretty much as she is made to appear in the Yorkville sketch, but says she was positively not cross-eyed. He represents her as being about six feet high, very muscular, and erect in her gait; her hair light brown, slightly sprinkled with gray when he last saw her, being at that time about sixty years of age. From long indulgence in violent passion, her countenance was liable, from trivial causes, to sudden changes.

In dwelling upon the hardships of the Revolution, the perfidy of the Tories, and her frequent adventures with them, she never failed to become much excited.

Among the anecdotes remembered by Mr. Snead is the following:

On one evening, she was at home with her children, sitting around the log fire, with a large pot of soap boiling over the fire. Nancy was busy stirring the soap and entertaining her family with the latest news of the war.

The houses in those days were all built of logs, as well as the chimneys. While they were thus employed, one of the family discovered some one from the outside peeping through the crevices of the chimney, and gave a silent intimation of it to Nancy. She rattled away with more and more spirit, now giving exaggerated accounts of the discomfitures of the Tories, and again stirring the boiling soap, and watching the place indicated for a reappearance of the spy. Suddenly, with the quickness of lightning, she dashed the ladle of boiling soap through the crevice full in the face of the eavesdropper, who, taken by surprise, and blinded by the hot soap, screamed and roared at a tremendous rate, whilst the indomitable Nancy went out, mused herself at his expense, and, with gibs and taunts, bound him fast as her prisoner.

Mrs. Wyche, an aged Elbert County lady, who was an intimate friend of Mrs. Hart, once related to the author of an article, entitled "History of Nancy Hart," several incidents.

On one occasion Nancy met a Tory, entered into conversation so as to divert his attention, seized his gun, marched him to the American fort, and delivered him to the commander.

On still another occasion, Nancy was left in a fort with several other women and some small children, the men having gone for provisions, when a party of Tories and Indians attacked the fort. Nancy was unable to handle the one cannon alone. Looking about she saw a young man hiding under a cowhide. She quickly pulled him out, and threatened him with instant death unless he helped her to fire the cannon. He obeyed, and helped. The cannon was fired. The enemy fled.

From Governor George R. Gilmer's History of Georgia, 1853, is the story that Nancy captured three Tories, single handed. To deliver them to the Whigs she had to cross the Broad River. She gathered her skirt high under one arm, grabbed a gun in the other and waded the river at a shallow place, marching the Tories before her to the Whig camp.

In The Life and Times of William H. Crawford, by J. E. D. Shipp, A.B., 1909, he says, in part:

On the north side of Broad River at a point about 12 miles from the present city of Elberton, Ga., and 14 from historic Petersburg, in what is now Elbert County, was situated the log house in which Benjamin Hart and his wife, Nancy Morgan Hart, lived at the commencement of the Revolution.

The State records show that Benjamin Hart drew 400 acres of land on Broad River, and afterwards another body of land in Burke County. He was a brother to the celebrated Col. Thomas Hart of Kentucky, who was father of the wife of Henry Clay.

Nancy Hart, alone with six boys—Morgan, John, Thomas, Benjamin, Lemuel, and Mark, and her two girls, Sally and Keziah—presents a unique case of patriotic fervor, courage and independence of character unparalleled in history.

In the story of Georgia and Georgia people, by George Gillman Smith, D.D., 1900, he says:

In her old age the governor says she became a shouting Methodist and was recognized by all as a good woman. She married an uncle of Thomas Hart Benton, the famous senator, and the sterling old statesman was always proud of his connection with her.

Letter From Nearest Living Relative of Nancy Hart to Mrs. Z. W. Copeland. Mrs. Mary C. Dixon, Age 93, of Henderson, Ky., Writes About Her Great Grandmother

The letter below, never before published, and the property of Mrs. Z. W. (Edna Arnold) Copeland, of Elberton, is of great interest to not only the people of Hartwell and Hart County but the State in general.

It is a great granddaughter of Nancy Hart, famous Revolutionary War heroine, and for whom Hart County was named. Mrs. Copeland, who has spent several years in tracing the genealogy and history of the Hart family, recently received the letter from Mrs. Mary C. Dixon, of Henderson, Ky., who is now 93 years of age, and Nancy Hart's nearest living descendant.

The *Sun* is greatly indebted to Mrs. Copeland for this courtesy. The letter in full follows:

March 18th, 1928.

My dear Mrs. Copeland: I received and read with pleasure your letter. At your request I will tell you what relation I am to "Nancy Hart": My mother's maiden name was Kexia Hart; her parents were Patience Lane (sister of Gen. Joe Lane) and John Hart, second son of Nancy Hart. My mother was born in Georgia. Her home was on the banks of the Oconee River. She, with her mother and family and grandparents and a number of other families, moved in covered wagons through a wilderness inhabited by Indians; some were kind, others hostile; at night when they camped they drove their wagons around in a circle—they did this in order to prevent the Indians from stealing them. After a long, tedious journey they arrived in Henderson County, Ky., not far from the city which was home.

There is a monument to Nancy Hart's memory in the Hart grave yard.

Stiles A. Martin, in an article in the Atlanta *Constitution* in 1928, says in part: "It was through Mrs. John D. Hart, Sr., and Miss Anie Floyd that I located the grave of Nancy Hart, 12 miles out from Henderson, Ky.

"The finding of this grave rewarded a search of several years. This grave has recently been marked."

While perhaps it would not be possible for Hart County, the State of Georgia or the United States, to be as loyal to the memory of Nancy Hart as her noble character was true to American liberty, however, in a measure her memory has been revered and perpetuated in several very substantial ways.

The people of Hart County was loyal to her to the extent that they named their county Hart and their county seat Hartwell in honor of the famous Revolutionary heroine.

The first locomotive engine on the Hartwell Railroad was named Nancy

Hart, and in construction and style was about as unique in appearance as the personality of the heroine for whom she was named, and performed many very remarkable stunts as she pulled long and heavily loaded trains from Bowersville to Hartwell and vice versa, up heavy grades down steep inclines and around various curves, from 1879 for a number of years.

One of the splendid consolidated schools of Hart County bears the name "Nancy Hart."

One of the leading highways of the State, Route No. 77, extending from Hartwell to Augusta, is known as the Nancy Hart Highway, and on the little park in the City of Hartwell, at the intersection of Carter and Benson streets, stands a granite marker, which, with appropriate exercises, was on July 19, 1928, unveiled to the memory of Nancy Hart, which bears the following inscription:

"NANCY HART HIGHWAY
NAMED BY GA. D. A. R.
JOHN BENSON CHAPTER,
MARCH, 1928."

Along the route at a number of places splendid other like markers have been erected in memory of Nancy Hart.

On the Bankhead National Highway, State Route No. 8 and U. S. Route No. 29, a little more than a mile east of the City of Hartwell, at the intersection of the Smith & McGee Bridge road with the highway, stands a very imposing granite monument, erected at a cost of $1,650 appropriated by the U. S. Government, which was unveiled on November 11, 1931, with very appropriate and impressive exercises, witnessed by a crowd estimated at 5,000 people.

It was indeed an auspicious occasion and will ever remain a green spot in the memory of all whose good fortune it was to be present and witness the ceremonies.

The program, which was carried out in a most excellent and befitting manner, is given herewith:

PROGRAM

UNVEILING EXERCISES
NANCY HART MEMORIAL

HARTWELL, GEORGIA,
November 11, 1931

Auspices: JOHN BENSON CHAPTER, D. A. R.

MRS. GUY H. NORRIS
Master of Ceremonies

FIRING OF SALUTE
Hdq. Co. 3d. Bn. 122nd Inf., Ga. N. G.
Co. "M" 122nd Inf., Ga. N. G.

SCRIPTURES
DR. S. H. BENNETT

INVOCATION
REV. FRANK E. JENKINS

SALUTE TO THE FLAG
Led by MRS. JULIUS Y. TALMADGE
Ex-Vice President, General National Society, D. A. R.

SONG: "AMERICA"
Led by U. S. ARMY BAND

GREETING
MAYOR J. C. JENKINS

REPRESENTING SECRETARY OF WAR HURLEY
BRIGADIER-GENERAL GEO. H. ESTES
Commanding General 81st Division, U. S. A.

REMARKS
CONGRESSMAN CHAS. H. BRAND

PRESENTATION OF MEMORIAL
CAPTAIN RICHARD T. EDWARDS, U. S. A.

UNVEILING
DR. JUANITA H. FLOYD
Great-Great Granddaughter of Nancy Hart

ACCEPTANCE OF MEMORIAL
For D. A. R.—MRS. BUN WYLIE
State Regent
For Hart County—MR. FRED S. WHITE
Chairman, County Board of Commissioners

ADDRESS
GOVERNOR RICHARD B. RUSSELL, JR.

BENEDICTION
REV. R. E. TELFORD

Music Interspersed Throughout the Program
by the U. S. Army Band from Ft. McPherson

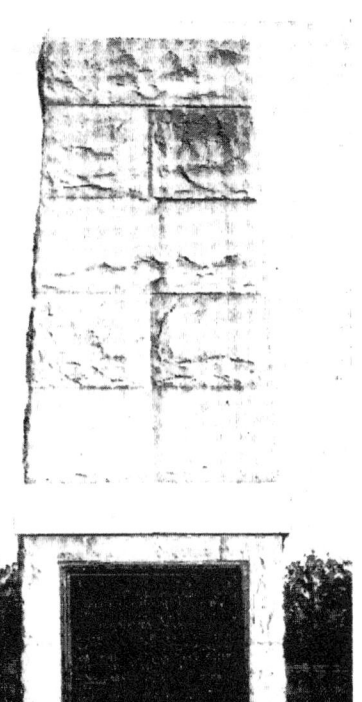

The following inscription is on the bronze tablet:

ERECTED BY THE GOVERNMENT OF THE UNITED STATES IN YEAR 1931
TO COMMEMORATE THE HEROISM OF

NANCY HART

DURING THE AMERICAN REVOLUTION A
PARTY OF BRITISH TORIES CAME TO
HER HOME. SINGLE HANDED, SHE KILLED
ONE AND WOUNDED ANOTHER. THE REMAINDER
OF THE PARTY SURRENDERED
AND WERE LATER HANGED BY HER
AND A FEW OF HER NEIGHBORS.

County Divided Into Militia Districts

AFTER the county lines had been determined in accordance with the description as designated in the act creating the county, it was then divided in eight militia districts by John A. Cameron, County Surveyor, in pursuance of an order of the Inferior Court, issued at the regular meeting on March 24, 1854. The districts were numbered from 1112 to 1119 and named as follows:

Town District............No. 1112th   Hall's District ....No. 1116th
Ray's District............No. 1113th   Shoal Creek District..No. 1117th
Smith's District ....No. 1114th   McCurry's District....No. 1118th
Reed Creek District..No. 1115th   Dooley's District.........No. 1119th

It will be observed that the districts were numbered alternately, as to location and not consecutively, apparently to aid the memory in locating the districts as to their relative position.

The 1112th was named Town District for the reason that the county seat was in the district.

The 1113th was named Ray's District for Mr. Washington Ray, who was a very wealthy, prominent and influential citizen of the county at the time it was created and lived in the district named for him.

The 1114th was named Smith's District for an old citizen by the name of Smith who lived near where Cokesbury Church is located and, if we have been correctly informed, it was at or near his residence the law ground was formerly located.

The 1115th District was named Red Creek District for the stream by that name which traverses its territory.

The 1116th was named Hall's District for Mr. John Hall for the reason that the law ground was at first located on his land. Later the court ground was moved up on the road at a point not far east of Cannon Church, and still later, after the town of Bowersville was established, the court ground was moved to Bowersville where it still remains.

The 1117th was named Shoal Creek District for the stream by that name which traverses the district.

The 1118th was named McCurry's District, because it included the settlement of the McCurry family, John McCurry being the forefather and his sons, namely, Daniel E., and John Gordon McCurry, who were very prominent in the county affairs in its first years, as elsewhere mentioned.

The 1119th was named Dooley's District, presumably for the reason that it included the home of William Dooley, who during his lifetime was quite prominent as a man of wealth and also for his moral and religious life.

In the year 1861 there was a petition presented to the Inferior Court for the establishment of a precinct in the 1119th District, G. M., and the following is the order of said court:

"Whereupon, It is ordered by the court, the same be established in said district at the grocery house of Lodwick Alford in said district, and that the Clerk notify the Justices of the Peace in said district of the same."

When the precinct was established at said place the name was changed from that of Dooley's to Alford's District, which name it still retains. For a part, if not all the time, from the creation of the county up until the precinct was established at the above named place the citizens of Dooley's, later Alford's District, voted at the county seat, and it is probable that the Justices' courts of the district were held at the county town until the establishment of the precinct at Lodwick Alford's place.

Purchase of Land for County Site and Survey of the Area Into Lots, Squares and Streets

THE Judges of the Inferior Court, on May 12th, 1854, purchased 100 acres of land from the heirs of James Vickery, on which to locate the town or county seat, for the sum of $200, same being a portion of a tract of land granted to said Vickery heirs, and proceeded to have it laid off by John A. Cameron, County Surveyor, into streets, squares and lots.

The land adjoined a tract of land, known as the Fortson lands, on the south, and the line between the two tracts was and still is known as the "Fortson Line," and at the time had a bearing of about N. 79 W., or the reverse, S. 79 E.

Howell Street was laid off parallel with the "Fortson Line," and borders upon the south side of the public square and was named Howell, as already explained.

JOHN A. CAMERON
First County Surveyor. Photo taken at the age of 90 while on a visit to the county after an absence of fifty years.

Franklin Street is parallel with Howell Street, and borders the public square on the north, and named Franklin for the reason, presumably, that it led out towards Franklin County.

The street north of and parallel with Franklin Street was named Johnson Street for Daniel M. Johnson, one of the Judges of the Inferior Court.

The street bordering on the west side of the public square runs at right angles with Howell, Franklin and Johnson streets, and at the time had a bearing of practically N. 11 E., or the reverse, S. 11 W., and was named Carolina for the reason that it led out in the direction of South Carolina.

The street bordering on the east side of the public square runs parallel with Carolina Street and was named Elbert Street for the reason that it led out towards Elberton and Elbert County.

The street east of Elbert Street, and which has the same direction, was named Carter Street for Micajah Carter, one of the Judges of the Inferior Court.

The street east of and parallel with Carter Street was named Richardson Street for James V. Richardson, one of the Judges of the Inferior Court.

The street east and parallel with Richardson was named Hodges Street for F. B. Hodges, who did considerable work in surveying and laying out the streets and lots of the town.

The street west of Carolina Street, and which has the same direction, was named Jackson. Why it was so named we have never learned.

The street west of and parallel with Jackson Street was named Webb Street for Clayton S. Webb, who was one of the Judges of the Inferior Court.

The street west of and parallel with Webb Street was named Chandler Street for Henry F. Chandler, one of the Judges of the Inferior Court.

The four streets bordering on the public square are eighty feet in width, all the other streets mentioned are sixty feet in width with the exception of Hodges Street, which is forty-seven feet in width.

The above mentioned streets were laid out in the original plan of the town of Hartwell.

An interesting item of history that should be mentioned in connection with the streets of Hartwell and their width, is an account as related by Hon. Wm. R. Poole, as appears in the old files of *The Hartwell Sun* of September 24, 1881, which in substance is about as follows:

It appears that Hon. Wm. R. Poole and Hon. Jefferson Holland were members of the Legislature while measures were pending to make the new county, and they stopped over at Madison, Morgan County, Ga., for the night. It was a beautiful moonlight night, and the town presented a lovely appearance with its broad streets. Judge Poole suggested that they measure the streets, and when the new county should be made, have the streets surveyed in the same manner. They stepped the streets off that night, and the result is broad, capacious streets in Hartwell, the prettiest town of its size in the State.

Upon the margin of the map of Hart County, which we published in 1889, there appeared the following reference to the location of the town:

"The place selected for the location of this town was originally a prominent deer stand, and the old hunters and trappers of former days often felled the fleet-footed buck on this spot of ground."

With reference to the spot once being a hunting ground, will say that on the sidewalk along Benson Street, and about opposite the residence of Mrs. J. W. Williams, there used to stand a large chair-shaped flint rock, and in passing it several years ago in company with Mr. William Myers, he pointed it out and said that he had often sat on it waiting and watching for deer to pass as they were routed and chased by the hounds. It was perhaps common to rout deer on the streams which furnished feeding grounds, and as they made their way in the chase from one stream to another across the ridges they were often felled by the hunter who was stationed at the stand where it was pretty well known that the deer would pass. The rock referred to has of late years been blasted or leveled flush with the surface of the ground.

In making the survey of the streets and public square of the town of Hartwell, it is related that James E. Scott cut down the first bush in a wilderness of black-jacks for the surveyors to run the lines.

The Justices of the Inferior Court had the area divided into 139 lots, numbered from 1 to 139.

Lot No. 1 was donated as a lot for the site of the court house, and located at the S. E. corner of Franklin and Elbert streets.

Lot No. 57 was donated as a site for the Methodist Church, however it was later sold or exchanged for other property, as the Methodist Church was erected at the S. W. corner of Howell and Webb streets, the present location.

Lot No. 91 was donated as a site for the Male Academy, however it was never used for the purpose for which it was donated. It now belongs to A. N. Alford, on which is located the Hartwell Roller Mill.

Lot No. 94 was donated as a site for the Presbyterian Church, but the Presbyterian Church is located on a part of Lot No. 60, and the lot left for it was bought by Dr. A. J. Mathews and is now the property of Dr. W. I. Hailey.

Lot No. 112 was donated as a site for the Baptist Church, located at N. W. corner of Howell and Chandler streets.

Lot No. 113 was donated as a site for the Female Academy and on which the school building stood for a number of years, after which it was sold and the school moved to the present location. Lot No. 113 is now occupied by the residence of C. I. Kidd.

Lot No. 122 was donated for the cemetery of the town.

F. B. Hodges, Wm. R. Poole, John McDonald, John B. Benson and James T. Jones composed the committee appointed by the Inferior Court to select the lots donated as above indicated.

The remaining 132 lots were advertised for sale in the *Keowee Courier*, Walhalla, S. C., and in the *Southern Banner*, Athens, Ga.

J. H. Chappellear, Sheriff of Franklin County, Ga., was paid $20.00 as auctioneer for three days' services in selling the lots, which sale was on July 6 and September 5, 1854.

First Court House, First Court

The first court house built for the county was located on Lot No. 1, according to the original plan of the town of Hartwell, and for which purpose the said lot was donated, as already stated.

The contract for the building of the court house was let on May 18, 1854, to Noel Skelton for the price or sum of $499. On completion of the house, there arose some complaint about the house not being built according to the plan and specifications, and the Justices of the Inferior Court and Mr. Skelton compromised the matter of dispute by a reduction of $35, thus making the cost $464.

The building was a two-story wooden structure, the lower story being one large room and used as a court room. The upper story was divided into a number of small rooms and used as offices, etc.

The contract for pillowing the court house was let to S. B. Sanders at the price of $10.

C. L. Scott was paid $63.18¾ for painting the court house.

The first court held in the building was in September, 1854, and was the first Superior Court to be held in the new county.

The terms of the Superior Court for the new county were fixed to convene on the third Monday in March and September of each year.

The March term of the Superior Court, and the first court which was to have been held at the Line Church in March, 1854, was, on account of the cold weather and the inadequacy of the building, adjourned over till September, 1854, and in the meantime the wooden court house was built, and the first court was held in September, 1854, Judge Garnett Andrews, presiding.

The first case on the minutes of the court is: Griffin Bailey vs. Jas. A. Conwell, Assumpsit.

The first Grand Jury was composed of the following named citizens:

W. B. Sadler, Foreman	David Carter	Sterling Pinson
Daniel M. Johnson	Rowland Cheek	Francis Hubbard
Wyly H. Brown	Jas. S. Cunningham	Thos. J. Teasley
Moses H. Adams	Joseph Caldwell	Lemuel Scott
Aaron Risener	Wm. McConnell	Leonard W. Rice
E. G. Brown	Wm. C. Ray	Moses Roberts
Ansel Strickland	Moses Davis	John Stephens, Bailiff
Jas. M. Carter	John G. McMullan	

First Petit Jury:

William Brown	Marcus Carter	John L. Duncan
Samuel A. Moore	Henry Dunn	Richmond Wooten
Wm. Dawson	Elihu Rodgers	Joseph Burden, Bailiff
Wm. Adkins	John P. Shiflet	
Thos. C. Moore	Larkin Brown	

From the General Presentments of the Grand Jury we herewith give a few paragraphs, all of which were very timely and appropriate.

"We recommend the Inferior Court to urge upon the Commissioners the necessity of opening and thoroughly working all the public roads; and further that they have each road measured, posted, and post painted, especially those leading to the court house, after the permanent location of the same.

"In view of the prevailing vice of drinking ardent spirits and of gambling among slaves, we urge the Justices of the Peace to have the patrol laws strictly and rigidly enforced, as it would certainly redound to the welfare of the slaves and the good of the county.

"In consideration of furthering the character and prosperity of our county, now in its infancy, we would most respectfully recommend that all those in authority see to it that our laws are respected and rigidly enforced, as nothing in our opinion would tend more to secure our peace and prosperity and elevate us to an honorable position than a prudent but strict enforcement of law."

There was no local bar at the time of the holding the first court in the new county, and following are the names of the visiting attorneys:

Thomas Morris, Temple F. Cooper, Capt. Milligan, T. R. R. Cobb, Howell Cobb, Thomas W. Thomas, J. R. Sanford, G. Nash, Robert Hester, W. T. VanDuzer, L. J. Gartrell, Judge Dougherty, Amos T. Akerman,........ Glenn,......... Overby.

First Jail

The first jail for the county was a wooden two-story building, located on Lot No. 6, in the original plan of the town of Hartwell, which lot was bought by the Judges of the Inferior Court from Micajah Carter, for the sum of $50.57.

The contract for the building of the jail was let by the Justices of the Inferior Court to Judge Noah Looney, for the contract price of $905.00 on 13th day of April, 1855, and for the faithful performance of carrying out the contract Judge Looney executed a bond payable to the Justices of the Inferior Court in the sum of $1810.00 and gave John D. Parker as security on said bond.

As stated this jail was a two-story building, weatherboarded and painted on the outside. We have no record of the inside structure or how the walls and the other parts were arranged.

On December 17, 1855, Judge Looney was given an extension of time in which to complete the contract which prolonged until March 1st, 1856.

Prison Bounds

In connection with the history of the first jail, it is proper to state that there were prison bounds laid off, which bounds contained an area of fifty acres, and in accordance with the law in force at that time, persons placed in prison for debt, could have the privilege of staying outside anywhere within the limits of the prison bounds, which of course was during the daytime.

The prison bounds as laid off cornered on a rock on the "Fortson Line," and ran thence N. 10 E. about parallel with Elbert Street, 22.36 chains to a rock corner, thence N. 80½ W. 22.36 chains to a rock corner, thence S. 10 W. about parallel with Carolina Street, 22.36 chains to a rockcorner on the "Fortson Line," thence along said line 22.36 chains to the beginning rock corner, which boundary included the court house and jail.

First Buildings in Hartwell

THE first house built in Hartwell was made from pine logs, split in halves, close fitting and chinked.

This house John B. Benson had built, not on the street, but on the lot near the present residence of Mrs. I. L. McCurry.

It was occupied by Pick Cole, a carpenter in the employ of J. B. Benson in building frame houses, with other carpenters under Samuel McGukin, foreman.

To Mr. and Mrs. Cole was born the first baby in Hartwell and he was named William Hartwell Cole. Mr. J. B. Benson suggested the middle name in honor of the new town.

Mr. Benson knew he would buy lots at the first sale, so ordered lumber to have in readiness for building immediately after the sale which he did.

The store building located on the public square, corner of Carolina and Howell Streets, where the Pan-Am Filling Station is now located, was the first frame house in the town.

J. B. Benson opened the first stock of goods in Hartwell in that building.

Burrell Mitchell, the first Clerk of the Superior Court of Hart County was also his first clerk.

In connection with the first stock of goods opened by J. B. Benson, we herewith relate the story of an aged pocket knife, as the same was published in The Hartwell Sun in 1904, which is as follows:

Mr. Eppy W. White was in Hartwell one day this week. He showed in E. B. Benson & Son's store a pocket knife that is a curiosity, by reason of its age and history. His father, Mr. Thomas H. White, and Mr. F. S. Roberts were at the store of Mr. John B. Benson in 1854, when he was opening up his first stock of goods here. Mr. White bought this knife, which was the first one ever sold in Hartwell, and Mr. Roberts bought one of the same kind, being the second. Fifty years is a long time to keep the same pocket knife in a family. That is what has been done in this instance. Mr. Thomas H. White gave the knife to his son, Mr. E. W. White, with this story and he kept it until this week, when Mr. E. B. Benson gave him a new I. X. L. knife of the same pattern for it. The old knife shows service and the blades of the same are nearly worn out, but still show their good metal in their keen edges.

"This knife will be handed down with several other relics and curios which Mr. Benson possesses."

J. B. Benson was the first postmaster in Hartwell, having the postoffice in his store, the same building. He was postmaster at Fairplay, S. C., the first quarter and at Hartwell the latter part of the same quarter.

There was a slot or opening in the front door and a box or receptacle inside the door for drop letters.

Mr. Benson soon resigned the office of postmaster and F. B. Hodges was the second postmaster. Hodges and Holland kept a hotel where Dr. B. C. Teasley now lives, in fact, part of that building, since remodeled.

They had a store in the south room fronting the public square and kept the postoffice in the store.

On the southwest corner of the public square, I. N. Reeder built a hotel and operated it, where Hailey's Drug Store No. 2 now stands.

J. B. Benson's first residence was where Hotel Hartwell is now located and that building remodeled to the rear of the lot, the hotel taking its place. The house was remodeled by Capt. J. F. Craft when owned by him. J. B. Benson had a tin shop on Howell Street, occupying parts of lots now the residence lots of T. G. Craft and Mrs. I. L. McCurry.

J. B. Benson sold his first residence and built fronting the public square between his store and the Holland & Hodges hotel. This building Dr. I. L. McCurry had remodeled and moved to its present location, fronting Howell Street.

J. R. Kay's first residence was on the lot where F. T. Kidd formerly lived, now owned by Dr. W. E. McCurry, in front of Hotel Hartwell.

Coming back to the public square, Gus Patterson built a two-story house with a store room where the McCurry building now stands. A little grocery store was there.

The first brick building, where the McMullan building now stands, was erected before the Civil War by I. N. Reeder, with the masonic hall up stairs and two offices and a store room below. One of these offices was occupied as a law office by John G. McMullan, Esq.

When General Brown's raid of Federal troops (Yankees) were crossing Savannah River, coming to Hartwell, Mrs. E. G. Murrah was teaching school in the store room. There was a sudden closing of the school when news reached the town of the approach of the enemy.

The next building adjoining this was a two-story frame, built and owned by Sampson Bobo, and occupied first by James T. Jones for a residence and store. The site is now occupied by the First National Bank and A. N. Alford's building.

Afterwards, Jas. T. Jones built the store occupied by J. B. Benson at the beginning of the Civil War, and the location southeast of the public square, Elbert and Howell streets, by the brick store of J. B. and E. B. Benson and E. B. Benson & Son until a few years ago. Since this building burned J. A. W. Brown, the present owner, converted it into a filling station and garage.

The Hartwell Bank building is on the corner of a lot on which Dr. Jas. M. Webb built a residence which was burned during the Civil War, then the property of James Allen who was one of the early traders in Hartwell real estate.

J. H. Skelton's store room adjoining the bank and Hailey's Drug Store, are on the same lot. Dr. Webb's office was in a little brick building where Hailey's Drug Store, No. 1 stands.

The next building on east side of the public square where J. D. Matheson & Sons' building was a frame building, a bar in one of the rooms before the war, but the building was used for a Confederate commissary during the war.

The first court house, a temporary wooden structure, stood where the Matheson & Kidd building is.

After the brick court house, in the center of the square was completed, the wooden building was rented for various purposes. The Hartwell Messenger, the first newspaper published in the town, had its printing office up stairs in this building.

During the Civil War, the building was used as a wood repair shop by Shaw & South. They also made horn combs and pewter buttons there. The first preaching services in the town were held in this building. Then after the completion of the brick court house, for a short time, preaching and a union Sunday School were had in it. Then when the school house was built on the lot now occupied by the C. I. Kidd residence, it was used for the purpose, instead of the court house.

The Methodist Episcopal Church, South, was organized in 1854, with Rev. Howell Parks as senior pastor and Rev. Wm. S. Turner, junior pastor. The first revival services were held in the school house, Rev. John Knight doing the preaching. The meeting has been remembered as a great one, with some notable conversions.

When the Methodist Church was erected on the ground now occupied by the present splendid brick building, at the corner of Webb and Howell streets, fronting Howell Street, all denominations were invited to hold services there. Being on a circuit with only one day for each month, the other Sundays were used by other denominations as wanted.

There was no other church building in the town, though Line Church, two miles distant from the court house was an old established Baptist church. A great revival was held there, people attending from the town. Rev. J. T. W. Vernon was pastor. J. R. Kay and Jas. T. Jones, Methodist laymen of the Hartwell Methodist Church took active parts with him. It is said that the conversion of four Baptist preachers date from that meeting, viz.: Rev. B. J. McLeskey, Rev. W. J. Vickery, Rev. Jas. P. Vickery and Rev. A. J. Cleveland.

The friendship and brotherly love of Vernon, Kay and Jones continued through life.

Where the bottling plant of A. F. Bell now is, stood the "red top grocery" —a bar room and some others adjoining, fronting on Franklin Street. In those days bar rooms abounded, but Hart County declared against them and voted them out, in advance of our State and other Southern States.

The two-story residence, northside public square, now Mrs. M. L. Blackwell, was built by J. P. Gulley before the Civil War, but has been remodeled since.

Sampson Bobo erected a large two-story frame building for a hotel on the lot now owned by Dr. W. I. Hailey, adjoining lot of Mrs. Blackwell. The building was used for offices and rooms to lodges and a deguerotype gallery, and after the war, as a residence, when it was burned.

On the northwest corner of the square, part of lot now owned by Dr. B. C. Teasley, J. P. Gulley built a store and stocked it with family groceries before the war. This was the store occupied by A. M. Holland & Son (T. J. Holland) just after the war and afterwards by W. H. Stephenson for several years. Torn away many years ago.

Adjoining the present Hartwell Hotel property, erected on lots of Mrs. Nimqui Smith's residence, Mrs. Mary Scott owned lots and had her residence on corner of Webb and Howell streets. She was the mother of C. L. Benjamin, William, James E. and J. H. Scott, and Mrs. J. A. Vickery and Mrs. Eliza Moseley. Friends bought and presented to Mrs. Scott the first sewing machine in Hart County. That was before the Civil War. It had a round top and in appearance, the table looked like a candle stand. It proved to be better for that than a satisfactory sewing machine.

A residence was built by F. B. Hodges on Howell Street, opposite the Methodist Church, now owned and occupied by Mrs. J. C. Linder.

F. C. Stephenson built his first residence on lot, now owned by Leard & Massey, south end of Carolina and at the present northwest corner of Carolina and Depot streets. He afterwards bought a residence where the "Oaks" now stands.

T. J. Cason built and occupied, while Clerk of the Superior Court, before and during the war the residence at the corner of Benson and Carter streets.

C. P. Pressnell had his residence and shops on the lot, now owned by Dr. G. S. Clark, corner of Carter and Howell streets.

John Brown, called tanner John Brown, built his residence on the lot, now occupied by E. E. Satterfield on Howell Street and he had a tanyard on Coody Branch, now known as Tanyard branch, on road leading out by Factory Chapel, all torn away with nothing left to tell the tale except in the name of Tanyard branch.

Hartwell Messenger

During the latter part of the year 1859, and the first part of the year 1860, there was a weekly newspaper published in Hartwell, called "Hartwell Messenger," which was owned and edited by a man named Edward Symmes, formerly of Pendleton, S. C.

Following are a number of clippings and extracts gleaned from its columns:

PROFESSIONAL AND BUSINESS ADS.

W. J. Roberts, Grocer and Confectioner,
Southwest of public square,
Hartwell, Ga.

Dr. William A. Skelton, Surgeon and Mechanical Dentist,
All Work Done in a Superior Manner and Warranted.
Hartwell, Ga.

---

100 NEGROES WANTED.

The subscriber will pay the highest cash price for One Hundred Negroes, girls and boys, from 12 to 25 years old. Those having such property to dispose of will please call on or address me at this place.

October 19, 1859.   W. S. Smith, Anderson, S. C.

HARTWELL ACADEMY.

The Trustees of the above named Institute have procured the services of Mr. J. L. Mize, as Principal. Mr. Mize is a thorough scholar and a gentleman of good moral character, and has had a great deal of experience in teaching. The school will open on the 2nd Monday, January, 1860. Board can be obtained in respectable families at moderate rate.

Hartwell is unsurpassed for health.

The rates of Tuition are: For the Rudimental Branches $12.00, and for the higher branches $16.00 per year.

J. B. Benson, John Brown and T. J. Cason, Trustees. Nov. 9, 1859.

MORRIS HOTEL, SOUTHWEST CORNER PUBLIC SQUARE,
Hartwell, Ga.,

Is in good repair, and well furnished for the accommodation of the traveling public. No pains will be spared to make the patrons of the House comfortable in every respect. All I ask is a fair trial.

Charges quite moderate.   July 20, 1859.   William Morris.

HERMON LODGE, No. 189 A. F. M.

The regular communication of this Lodge will take place on Friday Evening, the 10th February, in Hartwell, Georgia.

J. L. Mize, Secty.

Jan. 21, 1860.   F. B. Hodges, W. M.

Hymeneal.

Married—On the 15th of December, 1859, Mr. F. M. Cook and Miss Sarah L. Ray, all of Hart County, Ga.

Also, on the 1st day of January, 1860, Miss Julia Carolina Holland and Rufus J. Morris, all of Hartwell.

E. J. BROWN, Attorney at Law,

Will Practice in the Courts of Elbert, Madison, Franklin, Banks, Rabun, Habersham and Hart.   July 13, 1859.

BUSINESS DIRECTORY, HART COUNTY.

Judiciary.

Thomas W. Thomas, Judge Superior Courts, N. C.
Thomas M. Daniel, Solicitor-General, N. C.

Judges Inferior Court.

James V. Richardson, Wm. R. Poole, John Gordon McCurry, James M. Webb, Wm. Bowers.

Sittings of Inferior Court, Third Monday in March, June and December.

County Officers 1860.

Clerk Inferior Court—F. C. Stephenson.
Clerk Superior Court—Thomas J. Cason.
Ordinary—F. B. Hodges.
County Surveyor—Hugh McLane.
Sheriff—Wm. A. Neese.
Deputy Sheriff—Berry Moore.
Coroner—Allen McGee.

Board of School Commissioners.

Robert I. Gordon	F. B. Hodges	J. M. Bradley
B. B. Parker, Jr.	R. S. Hill	

James T. Jones, Died March 23, 1860. Was Ordinary from 1854 to 1860. Was a Master Mason.

SAD ACCIDENT.

A very serious accident took place in our town on Saturday afternoon last. It seems that a couple of lads, one a son of Mrs. Holland and the other a son of Mr. Benson, were playing with a pistol in the possession of young Sam Holland, when the pistol was accidently discharged, lodging the contents in young Berry Benson's breast. The pistol seems to have not been heavily charged, or immediate death must have been the result. As it is, we are happy to state that little Berry is in a fair way of recovery. Drs. Webb and Turner probed the wound and extracted the shot. They pronounced the wound not necessarily dangerous.

This should be a warning to all parents to keep firearms out of the hands of their children until they come to the years of discretion.

NOTICE.

The Andersonville Mills will grind for the fifteenth, until the new crop of wheat comes in.   February 7, 1860.

Board of Commissioners of the town of Hartwell, Ga., 1860. James T. Jones, C. P. Pressnell, John Brown, King Jaster Skelton, Wesley Washington.
John Hamilton Skelton, Clerk.
Elias Sanders Dyar, Marshal, James Benjamin Scott, Deputy Marshal.

The year 1859 was a dry year in Hart County, and there were hard times in 1860 for lack of provisions. There was no corn to be had in the county and people hauled corn from the mountains at $1.25 per bushel.

Statistics of Hartwell, June 29, 1860.

The U. S. Deputy Marshal, John G. McCurry, has just completed taking the census of Hartwell. Through his kindness we have been put in possession of the following statistics, which we think speaks well for a five-year-old town, under the circumstances:

White inhabitants	200	Sunday School	1
Slaves	33	Carriage shop	1
Free persons of color	2	Wagon shop	1
Lawyers	5	Blacksmith shops	2
Doctor	1	Shoe shop	1
Merchants	3	Hotels	2
Drayman	1	Groceries	3
Painters	2	Tannery	1
Resident mechanics	7	Masonic lodge	1
Brick masons	2	Church societies	3
Silversmith	1	Value of real estate	$54,000
School	1		

"HARTWELL FIFTY YEARS AGO."

Under the above caption Rev. Ebenezer G. Murrah wrote an article which gives a description of the town of Hartwell, as it appeared about the year 1857, some three years after it was laid out.

Mr. Murrah was a cousin of C. L. Scott, James E. Scott, and the other children of Lemuel Scott, his mother being before her marriage a Miss McDaniel and sister to Mrs. Lemuel Scott. Mr. Murrah was a Methodist preacher and was by profession a dentist. Following are reproduced some extracts from the article written March 1, 1907.

"The hamlet, fifty years ago, nestling in its quiet seclusion away from the storms of the large commercial centers, has grown like the palm tree and is flourishing like a cedar of Lebanon. She is and has been for half a century, beautiful for situation, the joy of her enterprising citizens, as well as those that live contiguous to her.

"Hartwell is very dear to me, because when I was just entering my young manhood the little handful of Methodists in an old hull of a school house that stood opposite the Methodist church, gave me license to preach, and sent me on my itinerate career of fifty years as an itinerate preacher.

"Hartwell had no streets in those halcyon days, and all her roads were new. Every one of them, if I remember correctly, were rooty and stumpy. They were known as the roads that led to the different churches in the county. The one running north went to the Line and Reed Creek Baptist churches. The one running east, went to Sardis Baptist and Mt. Zion Methodist churches. The one going south led to Bethesda church, the one southwest went to Hendry's church; the one going west would carry you to Providence or Parkertown. We had mail by the stage line from Anderson, S. C., to Athens, three times per week. The advent of the stage, which was always preceded by the blowing of the bugle, was hailed with more delight than any extra excursion train that ever came to Hartwell. There were two stores in the town, one of them on the corner opposite the Bobo house, run by John B. Benson, and one where Berry Benson now holds forth, or did the last time I was in Hartwell, kept by two brothers, James and Russell Jones. There were no churches in town, but the Methodist had organized one and held services in the school house before alluded to.

"The next year (1858) the brick court house was built and all denominations worshipped in the court room. We had one carpenter in town, John R. Kay; one boot and shoe maker, James Scott; one doctor, J. M. Webb (whom the Federals killed in 1865 when they passed through the town); county surveyor, F. B. Hodges; three brick masons, William Morris and his two sons, William and Thomas; three lawyers, James Elbert Skelton, Henry Cleveland, John Justice; one painter, Chesley Scott; F. C. Stephenson was postmaster. There were two boarding houses, one called the Holland house run by Thomas Holland, one (now the Bobo house), run by William Morris.

"There were three families, in which were four young ladies, at that time in town, their names were Eliza Scott, Eliza Morris, and Ellen and Carrie Holland. There were only eight children that I remember that were out of the cradle, these were Berry and Myra Benson, three Holland children, and Wesley and Fletcher Kay and Bob Stephenson.

"John W. Knight and John McGee were the itinerate Methodist preachers, Van Gary and Henry Tyler and Uncle Johnny Wade were the local ministers of the Methodist Church, Calvin and Sammie Sanders, J. T. W. Vernon, James McMullan, L. W. Stephens and the four Goss brothers, James, Isom, Bennie and William, were the Baptist ministers that preached in the house, all of whom lived in the country. The gospel, as we had it preached to us in those days, was in simplicity and with the power of the Holy Ghost.

"I have many friends in Hartwell. They are the children of those I knew and loved in the long ago, as well as those I knew when I was junior preacher on that work in 1862, and that belonged to the work when I was preacher in charge in 1865."

Second Court House

On February 5th, 1856, William Morris, as principal, and John B. Benson, Francis G. Stowers and Barnabas J. Dooley, as securities, entered into an obligation with H. F. Chandler, C. S. Webb, Micajah Carter, Jas. V. Richardson and D. M. Johnson, Justices of the Inferior Court, in and for such said county and their successors in office, in the just and full sum of Eleven Thousand Dollars.

The condition of the above obligation was such that the said William Morris should build a court house in the town of Hartwell according to the specifications and dimensions as attached to the bond. There was no date, so far as we have found, when the work was to be completed and the contract price, as will be seen from the amount of the bond, was $5,500.00, half the amount mentioned in the bond.

The court house was located on the present site and was a two-story brick structure, with four chimneys, with four fireplaces down stairs and four upstairs.

Old Court House

The lower story was divided into six rooms with a hall running full length through the middle. The room on the S. W. corner was used for the most of the time the building stood as the ordinary's office. The room on the S. E. corner was used as the Clerk of Court office. The other rooms were used for various purposes. The middle room between the clerk of court office and the room at the N. E. corner was used a part of the time by the county school commissioner. In the year 1894 vaults were placed in this room, the one facing the office of the clerk of court was used for his records, while the one facing the room at the N. E. corner was used for the records of the ordinary's office, the office of the ordinary being moved at the time from the S. W. to the N. E. corner room, and thus the middle room, which had been used by the county school commissioner, was eliminated, the vault occupying all the space of said room.

The room between the S. W. and the N. W. corner was for a short while used as a dispensary. It had been used before that perhaps as a lawyer's office and perhaps for some time after the dispensary was discontinued, which was in the year 1897.

The room at the N. W. corner was used for several years before the house was destroyed by fire as the post office.

The upper story, which was reached by a flight of steps built on the outside at the south end of the house, was composed of one large room, which was the court room, and two smaller rooms at the north end of the building were used for jury rooms.

There was no grand jury room, and the clerk's office, for the most of the time, was used by the grand jury.

There was a portico at the south end of the house supported by four brick pillars, and the roof of the portico was supported by four pillars which extended from the floor or platform of the portico. The portico was the landing for the steps and back of the floor of the platform was the main entrance to the court room.

This house stood from the time it was built until December 25, 1900, when it was destroyed by fire.

Charter of the Town of Hartwell

The town of Hartwell was incorporated by Act of the Legislature of the State of Georgia, approved February 26, 1856, which Act is herewith given in full, and is as follows:

"An Act to incorporate the town of Hartwell in the county of Hart, and for other purposes therein named.

"Section I. Be it enacted &c., That from and after the passage of Act, the town of Hartwell, in the county of Hart, be, and the same is hereby incorporated and that the corporate limits shall extend four hundred yards in every direction from the public square in said town of Hartwell, and that James T. Jones, John G. Justice, F. B. Hodges, I. N. Reeder and John B. Benson be, and they are hereby appointed a board of commissioners who shall hold their term of office until the second Monday in January, eighteen hundred and fifty-seven.

"Section II. And be it further enacted, That on each and every second Monday in January thereafter, all citizens residing within the corporate limits of said town, who shall be entitled to vote for members of the Legislature of the State, shall be entitled to vote for five commissioners, at which election any two freeholders of said town may preside as managers of said election, and the five persons receiving the highest number of votes shall be declared elected, and that the managers of said election shall give a certificate of the election which shall be sufficient authority for said commissioners to enter upon the discharge of their duties, and in case no election should be held by the legal voters as aforesaid, that then at any time thereafter on a written notice of the time and place of holding said election, be posted at the court house door ten days previous to holding said election, the citizens of said town may proceed to elect the said board of commissioners in the same manner as though the same had been held on the second Monday in January.

"Section III. And be it further enacted, That said commissioners shall have power and authority to pass all ordinances and by-laws for the government of said town corporation, not in conflict with the constitution and laws of this State, and of the United States.

"Section IV. And be it further enacted, That said commissioners shall be authorized to grant license for the retail of spiritous liquors within the corporate limits of said town, under such regulations and restrictions as they may prescribe.

"Section V. And be it further enacted, That the commissioners of said town corporation shall appoint a Marshal and a Clerk, who shall be Treasurer with such compensation as shall be determined on by said commissioners, and such other officers as may be necessary to carry this act into effect.

"Section VI. And be it further enacted, That all persons liable to road duty by the laws of this State who reside within the corporate limits of said town shall be compelled to work the streets and public square of said town and that they shall be exempt from all other road duty.

"Section VII. And be it further enacted, That the said board of commissioners of the said town of Hartwell, by their corporate name shall have power to sue and be sued, plead and be impleaded, and do all other acts relating to corporate capacity, and shall use and have a common seal, any law to the contrary notwithstanding."

The charter of the town of Hartwell, later the city of Hartwell, has been changed several times for certain purposes.

The corporate limits were extended to one mile in every direction from the center of the town, and the line of corporation was surveyed and established by the writer in 1889.

The form of government, which was formerly by a board of commissioners, was later changed to a mayor and board of aldermen.

John Blassingame Benson

John B. Benson

SON of Enoch Berry and Esther Blassingame Benson, born at Pendleton, S. C., September 2, 1822. Died at Hartwell, Ga., January 27, 1892.

He married Miss Elizabeth Arlesa Norton, daughter of Jeptha and Elizabeth Moore Norton, Pickens, S. C., September 2, 1847.

Mrs. Elizabeth Arlesa Benson died June 6, 1881.

Their children: Myra Postell, married Dr. C. A. Webb; an infant son died soon after birth; Enoch Berry Benson; Fannie Norton, married A. G. McCurry; Mattie Cater, married S. W. Peek; and Mary Eliza; of whom only E. B. Benson and Mrs. Fannie N. McCurry are now living.

Enoch Berry Benson, born May 19, 1852, married Miss Alice Elizabeth Adams, daughter of Moses H. Adams and Lavinia McMullan Adams, May 21, 1873.

The children of E. B. Benson and Alice E. Benson: John Berry; Lavinia Norton (both died in childhood); Paul Edwin, married Miss Lola Josephine Cox; Alice Elizabeth (died in childhood); Grace, married J. Loyd Teasley; Ethel, married Charles E. Matheson; Myra Edna; Enoch Blassingame, married Miss Christine Sanders of Birmingham, Ala.

Children of Paul E. and L. Josephine Benson: John Berry (deceased); Paul Edwin.

Children of J. Loyd and Grace Benson Teasley: Elizabeth Benson, Alice Benson, Grace Benson and James Benson (deceased).

Children of Charles E. and Ethel Benson Matheson: Charles Edward, Berry Benson and Julius Daniel.

Child of Enoch Blassingame and Christine Sanders Benson: Beverly Sanders Benson.

John Blassingame Benson married Miss Martha A. Ethridge June 25, 1882. No children by this marriage. Mrs. Martha A. Benson died August 12, 1911.

Tracing the line of forbears of the Bensons, who came from Virginia to South Carolina: Thomas Benson, who married Miss Martha Prince; their son, Enoch Berry Benson, married Miss Esther Blassingame, daughter of John Blassingame. These were the parents of John Blassingame Benson, and grandparents of Enoch Berry Benson, now living in Hartwell.

Thomas Benson and John Blassingame were both Revolutionary soldiers. Jeptha Norton, father of Mrs. John B. Benson, was a captain under General Andrew Jackson in the war of 1812. He and his company fought the British in the battle of New Orleans, the last battle of that war, fought, in fact, after terms of peace were agreed upon, but in those days of slow communication the news had not reached New Orleans. In that battle, bales of cotton were used as breastworks by our troops.

The different lines of the Benson family have their Enochs and Berrys, the latter having been a surname on the mother's side several generations back.

John B. Benson built the first house in Hartwell and had the first stock of goods in the beginning of the town, in 1854. He was the first postmaster here. He had been postmaster at Fairplay, S. C., before moving to Hartwell. Acted in that capacity in both places parts of the same quarter.

He served this district, then Hart, Franklin and Habersham, as State Senator during the Civil War and represented the county in the Legislature one term since.

He was engaged in the mercantile business as Benson & Justice when the War Between the States began.

At his death the firm name was J. B. & E. B. Benson. Succeeding that business, E. B. Benson operated in his own name several years, followed by E. B. Benson and Son—the son being Paul E. Benson.

In 1877 J. B. and E. B. Benson bought *The Hartwell Sun* and printing outfit from R. E. Belcher who, with John H. Magill, established it in Hartwell in 1876.

For several years the Bensons, in connection with John H. Magill, published the paper. J. B. Benson was an interesting writer and noted for his wit and store of jokes.

E. B. Benson was business manager while connected with the paper and established a free delivery for *The Sun* which served the communities of Ford's Store, Parker's Store, and Kings Bench, and people along the route. This was continued until a mail route from Toccoa to Hartwell was established.

This, perhaps, was the first and only free delivery ever operated by a country newspaper.

Third Court House

EARLY in the year 1901, after the court house was destroyed by fire on December 25, 1900, preparations were made for the erection of a new court house, and by order of Hon. J. M. Thornton, Ordinary, an election was held in the county on April 27, 1901, for court-house bonds, at which the requisite majority voted favorably for bonds, which were issued in the aggregate sum of $25,000, in denominations of $1,000 each and to run for a period of twenty-five years. The last installment of $1,000 was paid June 22, 1926.

The contract for the building of the court house was let on March 26, 1901, to W. W. McAfee, of Atlanta, Ga., at the price of $25,469.

The cost of the court house to Hart County, complete, was $28,627.04. The contractor did not realize any profit on the job, but rather lost considerably, and his securities had to come to his rescue and finish up the contract.

The building is quite an up-to-date court house, conveniently arranged in all its several departments, and at the present time would perhaps cost double the amount of the original cost to duplicate.

The corner-stone of the court house at Hartwell was laid by the Masonic fraternity on Wednesday, August 7, 1901, which was witnessed by a large concourse of people of the town and county.

The ceremonies were interesting and impressive, and were participated in by the following officers composing the Grand Lodge:

Grand Master, J. R. Stephens.	Grand Marshal, W. H. Cobb.
Deputy Grand Master, Park Clark.	Grand Architect, J. R. Meredith.
Grand Senior Warden, D. C. Alford.	Grand Chaplain, J. T. W. Vernon.
Grand Junior Warden, A. N. Alford.	Grand Steward, A. J. Cleveland.
Grand Senior Deacon, L. E. Meredith.	Grand Secretary, D. B. Brown.
Grand Junior Deacon, D. A. Perritt.	Grand Treasurer, J. M. Thornton.

Dr. J. W. Oslin, of Gainesville, Ga., was the orator of the occasion and his remarks were heartily appreciated by his hearers.

In the vault of the stone were deposited many relics, among them Confederate bills, a Cuban 5c bill, silver coins, names of the officers of the local bank, town and county, a copy of *The Hartwell Sun*, and many other articles "of the time in which the stone was laid."

From all the neighboring towns large numbers came, among them prominent Masons from Royston, Elberton and Lavonia.

The following inscription appears upon the corner stone. On east face of stone:

"ERECTED 1901-2,
J. M. THORNTON, ORDINARY,
J. W. GOLUCKE, ARCHITECT,
J. D. MATHESON, } INSPECTORS,
D. C. ALFORD,
W. W. MCAFEE, BUILDER."

On north face of the stone:

"PLACED BY MASONS, AUG. 7, A. D. 1901. A. L. 5901.
J. R. STEPHENS, ACTING G. M."

At a late valuation the court house and the property connected therewith was placed at the following figures:

Grounds	$ 27,000.00
Building	66,000.00
Equipment	14,000.00
Total	$107,000.00

Second County Jail

The first jail, which was built by Judge Noah Looney during the year 1855-6, was destroyed by fire some time prior to December 4, 1866, as it appears of record that the Justices of the Inferior Court on that date contracted with John A. Johnson for the erection of a new jail.

The price paid Mr. Johnson, according to the record of payments received by Mr. Johnson, was about $550.00.

This jail was built on the site of the first jail, which was on Lot No. 6 in the original plan of the town of Hartwell, and was constructed of large hewed or split logs, with an outer and an inner wall, and filled with rock between the two walls, and was a one-story building.

This, the second jail built for the county, stood until the year 1877, when a new jail was built, being the third jail built for the county.

The lot on which the old jail stood, together with the old jail building, was sold to John B. Benson, who moved it to near his residence and converted it into a barn. A part of it is still standing and now owned by Mr. D. C. Alford.

Third County Jail

The committee, appointed in March, 1877, to let the contract for the building of the new jail, it being the third jail built for the county, and to have supervision during its construction, was composed of John R. Kay, J. T. W. Vernon, Jas. W. Williams, T. E. Vickery and D. C. Alford, they to act in conjunction with F. C. Stephenson, Ordinary.

The lot on which this jail was built was known as Lot No. 2 in the original plan of the town of Hartwell, located at the S. W. corner of Franklin and Carter streets, and was bought by F. C. Stephenson, Ordinary, acting for the county, from John Linder for the sum of $100.00.

The said building committee let the contract to B. M. McGinty at the price of $2,991.00, and on completion of the jail was allowed $20.00 for extra work, making the cost $3,011.00.

This jail was a two-story building of brick and wood, and at the time was considered to be safe and to fill all requirements of a jail.

In this jail Henry Hill killed Thomas V. Skelton, the jailor, on February 23, 1881, a full account of which is given elsewhere in these pages.

On January 30, 1893, this jail was destroyed by fire. Jim Cornog and

Berry Bradley, two negroes, were in jail at the time and evidently set the jail on fire by trying to burn a hole in the wall to make their escape, but lost control of the fire and came very near being burned to death, and would have been if it had not been for the timely and heroic work on the part of several men who came up just in time to rescue them.

Several escapes and attempts to escape had been made before this, and, as stated, the jail when it was built was considered safe and one of the best in the country, but by the several escapes and attempts to escape, brought it into contempt and the people were quite indifferent to its untimely fate.

Fourth County Jail

The next jail, and the one now in use, located at the N. E. corner of Johnson and Jackson streets on Lot No. 89 in the original plan of the town of Hartwell, which was purchased from J. R. Myers & Co., at the price of $120.00.

The old jail lot at the S. W. corner of Franklin and Carter streets was sold by J. L. Johnson, Ordinary, for $300.00.

With one exception, the same committee was appointed to let the contract as of the jail just described, to wit: John R. Kay, J. W. Williams, T. E. Vickery, J. D. Matheson and D. C. Alford.

The committee was empowered to formulate the plans and specifications, let the contract, and have supervision of construction, to look after the class of all material out of which the jail was to be built, and as stated, to have entire supervision of the work.

On May 20, 1893, the contract was let by the building committee to Will L. Landrum, contractor for the Pauly Jail Building & Manufacturing Company of St. Louis, Mo., at the contract price of $5,897.50, but on completion was allowed $150.00 in addition to the contract price, for some extra work done by the contractor, making the total cost of $6,047.50.

Since the building of this jail, an annex has been added, costing somewhere in the neighborhood of $2,000.00.

A few years after the jail was built, a wooden building was erected in connection with the jail and is used for a kitchen, the cost of which we have not learned, but estimate that was about $600.00.

The jail at present is considered one of the best in the country, safe and secure, and modern in all respects.

At a recent valuation, the jail building, equipment and grounds have been placed at the following figures:

Lands	$ 700.00
Building	8,500.00
Equipment	1,070.00
Total	$10,270.00

County Farm

On October 15, 1867, John G. McCurry, R. A. Cobb, C. P. Pressnell, C. L. Scott and D. G. Johnson, Justices of the Inferior Court, purchased from J. H. Skelton, surviving partner of the firm of James E. & J. H.

Skelton, and Littleton Skelton, 201½ acres of land for a site for a county farm, same being a part of a tract of land granted to Reuben Bramlett, for the consideration of $300.00. The deed recorded in Book C, page 365, Clerk's Office, Superior Court, and plot and survey made by J. H. Warren, Surveyor, dated January 7, 1914, and recorded in Book V, page 141, in said office.

On December 9, 1867, the Justices of the Inferior Court entered into a contract with R. A. Cobb, as superintendent or keeper of the poor farm, at the price of $100.00 per annum, in which said R. A. Cobb bound himself with security on a bond in the sum of one thousand dollars, to well and truly perform all the duties incumbent upon him as keeper of the poor farm for the next ensuing year from date of the contract, his duties specified as follows:

"1st, Superintend all the buildings and improvements of any kind and purchase provisions and take charge of the home and distribute the necessities and visit the poor house at least twice per week during the year and see that the poor are properly cared for and have medical attention when necessary; also, to cause each inmate to labor according to their physical ability."

Following is a partial list of the names of those who have served as stewards:

R. A. Cobb, Simeon Shiflet—who perhaps served as an overseer under Mr. Cobb, Thomas Sanders, Ira F. Myers, W. Clayton Myers, Benjamin Risener, Asa M. Pruitt, W. W. Hicks and W. H. Herring, the last named being the present steward.

At a late valuation of the county farm, it was placed as follows:

205 acres of land	$ 8,530.00
Buildings	8,000.00
Live stock	750.00
Equipment	475.00
	$17,755.00

Brief History

HART COUNTY is located in northeast Georgia, between 34 and 35 degrees north latitude, and longitude 83 degrees west from Greenwich, or 6 degrees from Washington, D. C., the 83rd meridian passing through the county about midway between the east and west boundaries.

The area is practically 246 square miles; the boundary of the county is correctly represented by the county map published by the writer in 1889, and revised editions published later. Population 15,173, U. S. Census 1930.

The county is ideally situated in the famous Piedmont Belt, not too far from the highlands on the north nor too near the coastal plain on the south, with a mild and salubrious climate, fanned by the bracing breezes of the Blue Ridge Mountains, with an average temperature of about 60 degrees, not too hot in the summer nor too cold in the winter.

The topography of the county is for the most part undulating, with several large areas nearly level, with steeper grades adjacent to the rivers and other streams. The average altitude is about 750 feet above sea level with some peaks above 900 feet.

The slope of the country is northerly and easterly towards the Tugaloo and Savannah rivers, with a southerly slope along the course of Coldwater and Beaverdam creeks, and with a gradual slope from north to south along and parallel with the course of the rivers.

The soils of the county are of various classifications, the gray sandy and brown predominating, and with proper cultivation are capable of producing abundant crops of all the agricultural crops commonly grown in this part of the country.

For a more complete and comprehensive knowledge of the physical features, geology, soils and other allied and kindred subjects with reference to Hart County, the reader is hereby referred to the splendid, interesting and instructive article, together with the map therewith, prepared by Mr. Glenn L. Fuller, who made a soil survey of the county during the years 1928-9, which appear in following pages.

The territory embraced in Hart County was very sparsely settled up to the time of the War of the Revolution; in fact we have no record of any settlements that had been made prior to that time, however it is reasonable to suppose that there were perhaps some few white people who lived in the county at the time; nevertheless, it was all at or immediately before the beginning of hostilities included in the Cherokee Indian possessions, they by treaty conveyed a portion just before the time of the Revolutionary War, and the remainder soon after.

After the war and after the treaties with the Indians, when the territory was opened for colonization, emigrants began to move in from Virginia, North Carolina, South Carolina, and some perhaps from other states, and acquired titles to the lands, some by bounty warrants in consideration of their services in the war, and others by headright titles.

The pioneers, or first settlers, were English, Scotch-Irish, Welsh and other nationalities, the English predominating.

Many of the first settlers owned slaves and the most of the work done in the clearing and cultivation of the lands was by slave labor. As a result large plantations were cleared and put into cultivation.

Magnificent homes, for that day, were erected—large, commodious, comfortable and conveniently located.

The first and most important settlements were made along and adjacent to the Tugaloo and Savannah rivers and along the larger creeks, which lands were considered the most fertile and better suited for crop production, as well as for the convenience to the streams.

The back country, a great portion of which was dubbed "blackjack ridges," was not considered of much value for agricultural purposes, so consequently the settlements were made on what was at the time the most fertile lands; however, the back country of ridge uplands were thinly settled with less pretentious homes and farms less productive.

Large crops of corn, wheat, tobacco and other crops were grown; cattle, hogs, sheep, horses and all animals were raised sufficient for the needs of the farm, and a surplus for sale. The farms were in every way self-sustaining. But very little cotton was cultivated until many years after the first settlements were made in the territory. The methods of farming were more or less primitive.

In the course of time, after the cotton gin had been invented and proven a success, most every large farmer erected a gin house on his estate and installed a gin, which was propelled by horse power, and cotton began to be profitably grown. The same was true with machinery for threshing small grain. A threshing machine was installed in most all of the gin houses and, like the cotton gin, was propelled by horse power.

Markets in the early days were remote from the farms in our part of the country. The Tugaloo and Savannah rivers were used by the people as arteries of commerce. Pole boats plied the rivers from our part of the country to Hamburg, S. C., and Augusta, Ga., and all surplus crops and products, consisting of corn, wheat, bacon and other produce, and later cotton, were floated down the rivers to market and sold, and such merchandise as was needed by the people was brought up on the return trip.

This condition applied more particularly to the farms along the rivers. The people who lived remote from the river transported their produce by wagons to market, which required considerable time as the roads in those days were not so good as at the present time and the travel was necessarily slow.

Later railroads were built to Anderson, S. C., and to Athens, Ga., and other points, which greatly reduced the time and expense of travel, and a better profit realized upon such produce as the people had for sale. River freightage was eventually entirely dispensed with, the last trips down the river were in about the year 1879 or soon after.

The War Between the States, which terminated in 1865, very materially changed farming conditions of our country, and all other conditions as well. One result of the war was the emancipation of the slaves, which has become universally accepted as the best solution of the slave question. Many of the slaves after freedom remained on the farms as tenants or hired help, while some moved to the towns and cities.

At the last census taken before the war the number of colored people was about 25% of the entire population of the county, which proportion they have retained to the present time.

From the time of the first settlements made in the county and up until the year 1886, a period of about one hundred years, cattle, hogs, sheep and other live stock ran at large, the farm lands enclosed by rail fences. During this time it was a custom to burn the wood lands for pasturage, and as a result all litter and vegetable matter was consumed from year to year, thus keeping the lands impoverished.

Later, after many of the larger pines had been cut away for lumber and the custom of annual burnings of the woods had been discontinued, the undergrowth came on and the shade of the undergrowth and the accumulation of litter and vegetable matter, the uplands, formerly considered of not much value for the growing of crops, became valuable and more desirable for homes and farms, and the large river and creek plantations, in a measure, were abandoned. The magnificent homes dilapidated and in some instances entirely gone, while the farms once so productive became eroded and given over to the growth of pines and other vegetation.

The introduction and use of commercial fertilizers added quite an interest to the growing of cotton, the production in Hart County increased from 1,320 bales in 1869 to 5,094 in 1879, due in a great measure to the use of commercial fertilizers, and continued to increase at the rate of over 5,000 bales per decade until it reached a peak of over 26,000 in 1919.

The old slow process of ginning cotton by horse power gave way to more up-to-date and improved machinery driven by water and steam power. On many of the streams of the county cotton gins were operated and the work done more rapidly to meet the demands of increased production. In this connection will say that for a time during the horse-power age and for a number of years afterwards, water power was employed to operate cotton gins, flour and grist mills, and other kinds of machinery. But the water-turned mill and other machinery driven by water power, with a few exceptions, has gone the way of the covered bridge and other picturesque items of the landscape.

Our country has survived the horse-power age, the water-power age, and now in the steam-power age, which is fast passing as the electric-power age advances.

The "No Fence" or Stock Law

The method of fencing the farms and allowing the outside for pasturage continued until the year 1886. In 1885 an act of the Legislature of Georgia was passed known as the "no fence" or stock law for Hart County, which became effective on February 1, 1886, which has proven highly satisfactory. It relieved the people of the arduous task of splitting rails and building and repairing fances which required a considerable portion of the time in the winter and spring months, and was a great saving of timber which had begun to be not so plentiful. It also proved an impetus for the raising of better breeds of cattle and hogs as well as the improvement of the quality of the products.

In describing the old rail fences we reproduce some extracts from an article we have read upon the subject.

"An important springtime task of past generations was 'fixing up' the picturesque rail fences, which marked the landscape everywhere in long, rugged, zigzag lines.

"The old rail fences were the product of stalwart labor. They had in them the ruggedness of pioneer life and the sight of them brought suggestions of heroic struggle and stubborn fortitude.

"Building a new fence was an event of no small importance. Heavy rails made of some substantial timber, such as heart postoak, were selected for the foundation and if the foundation rail happened to have a large, knotty end, so much the better. This big end was placed on the ground, while the smaller end rested upon the next rail in the rear. The foundation run of the fence was called the 'worm,' and laying a fence worm properly was an art of no mean consequence. Every community had its expert worm layers who were often called upon by their neighbors.

"Rail fences could be built rapidly, the rails being placed one on top of another with interlocking corners. Each single run was called a 'course' and the standard height of a fence was ten courses."

After the passage of the stock law, many of the old fences were torn away and the site put into cultivation, and due to the decayed vegetable matter which had accumulated for years the fence rows were very fertile strips of land.

The location of the old rail fences, which have not been taken into cultivation, are now marked by hedgerows, many of them being the property lines of adjoining landowners, and being very fertile they support a luxuriant growth of oak, hickory and other trees, and along many of them there is an undergrowth of dogwood, a beauty-producing tree growing along with the others, and in the spring when they are in bloom they give a dash of sweetness and purity to the landscape and bring to the observer the suggestion of elegance and refinement as they extend along down the slope to the valleys of the streams and climb the hill beyond. Often where the old hedgerows cross the valleys there is a growth of maple trees which in the early springtime are a flame of color and bloom.

In the early days and up to not so many years ago, there was a wanton waste of the timber on the lands, as well as the erosion of the soils. The farmers used to, after clearing the land, put it into cultivation by laying off the rows for their crops, the longest distance the land would permit, without regard to the grades, and as a consequence the rows ran up and down the slopes, and in a few short years the plant food was leached out and the soils allowed to wash away to the valleys below, leaving the land bare and gullied and unfit for further cultivation.

As has been said, "these eroded slopes, like old wrinkled faces deeply furrowed with suffering, tell a tragic story. It is the story of once luxuriant forests—a home for abundant wild life, a protection to the virgin soil and a picture of beauty—ruthlessly slaughtered and the helpless earth left to the disintegrating influence of the elements."

As said by another, "Hart County, richly dowered with nature's wealth of woodland and stream, hill and dale, has been wasteful of such treasure."

However, the conditions mentioned in the foregoing paragraphs have been very much changed in the last few years. Farmers have learned the lesson of protecting the soils of their lands by terracing, better cultivation, and in many instances the growing of cover crops. We can remember when but a few years ago it was possible to see large areas of the lands, the soil of which had been allowed to wash away and presented some of the conditions already mentioned, but of late years many of these old washed-away lands have been abandoned for cultivation and left to the growth of pines and other vegetation, and it is simply marvelous how quickly nature can cover the bare and eroded areas with an overgrowth of green. Where such lands are completely abandoned and left to the tender care of Mother Nature, a change for the better rapidly takes place.

By allowing the eroded lands to grow a second forest, there is more time to be devoted to the improvement of the balance of the farm lands, and while the lands are growing another forest the lands are improved and reclaimed, and at the same time the value of the timber increases each year that it is allowed to grow. It has been estimated that lands left to the growing of timber produce as much as 300 to 500 feet board measure per acre annually, which is a clear profit, and, as stated, the fertility of the lands increasing all the while.

Another benefit derived from the reforestation of the lands is, the protection against wind and heat waves and also the conservation of moisture.

GEOLOGY OF HART COUNTY, GEORGIA

ONE of the main physiographic and geological divisions of the State of Georgia is commonly known as the Piedmont Plateau. It occupies about one-third of the area of the State lying between the Appalachian Mountains to the northwest and the Coastal Plain to the southeast. Hart County lies in the upper half of this plateau.

The present surface of Hart County is a remnant of this old plateau and has a gentle southeastern slope. It has become dissected by streams and denuded by erosion so that the old plateau is evidenced only by the level sky-line above which there are no projecting hills. The topography of the county is dominated by the deep valleys which have been carved by the Savannah and Tugaloo rivers 200 to 250 feet below the present plateau levels and by the numerous tributaries which form an intricate drainage system with gradually decreasing valleys heading into the high plateau levels. Because of such intricate dissection with attendant denudation, only scattering areas now occur at levels approximating those of the old plateau.

Such areas more commonly occur at the western side of the county more remote from the river valleys and the larger creeks, especially near Bowersville and to the north, east and south where elevations of 900 to 950 feet above sea level are common. The gentle southeastern slope of the plateau level is shown by the drop in elevation from 900-950 feet around Bowersville to 850 feet in the central part and to 750-800 in the southeastern part. Tugaloo River enters the northwest corner of the county at about 590 feet above sea level.

At its junction with the Seneca River to form the Savannah River, the elevation is 510 feet while the Savannah leaves the southeast corner at about 500 feet.

The topography of the old plateau levels varies from undulating to gently rolling but as streams approached it becomes more broken and sloping until steep slopes and narrow ridges become common adjacent to the rivers and larger creeks. There is no poorly drained upland in the county, but rather drainage is excessively free over a considerable portion of it.

The rocks of Hart County are of Archean and Pre-Cambrian age, which include the oldest rocks of the continent. The rocks include granite and gneiss, quartz-mica-schist, hornblende schist and hornblende gneiss, and small amounts of diorite and gabbro.

Quartz-mica-schist rocks and granite and gneiss rocks are about equally extensive in the county. Quartz-mica-schist extends entirely across the central part from northeast to southwest with Hartwell nearly in the center of this large area. The western boundary of this body extends from a point west of Hatton Shoals along to the west of Reed Creek School, south of New Harmony Church, west of Mt. Hebron Church, southwest nearly to Airline and then along North Beaverdam Creek to the southern county line with two radiating ridges extending off from this main body. The first ridge extends west past Cross Roads Church and Bowersville to the county line while the second extends southward past Redwine Church and Goldmine almost to Vanna. The southeastern boundary of this large body extends from a point about two miles north of Smith-McGee Bridge along to the west of Nancy Hart School to the county line near Liberty Church. Two relatively small areas of granite and gneiss occur within this large schist area: the larger one northeast of Eagle Grove School and the other south of Mt. Zion Church along Powderbag Creek.

A smaller body of quartz-mica-schist extends from Smith-McGee Bridge nearly to Cokesbury Church and Montevideo.

Granite and gneiss separate the areas of quartz-mica-schist so that Cokesbury Church, Nancy Hart School, Nuberg and Liberty Church are on one area of granite while Vanna, Royston, Canon and Airline are on another area. All the northwest quarter of the county, northwest of the quartz-mica-schist boundary from Bowersville past New Harmony Church to Hatton Shoals, consists of granite and gneiss with the exception of three con-

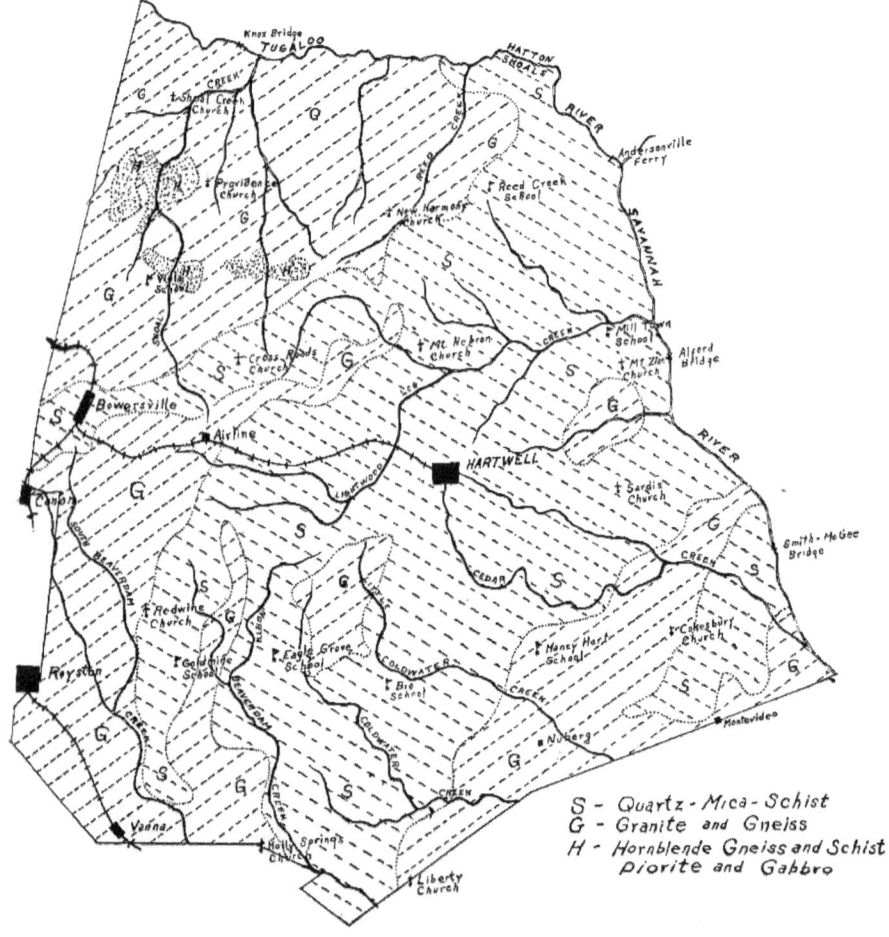

spicuous areas of ferromagnesian rocks including hornblende schist, hornblende gneiss, diorite and gabbro. One of these areas occurs west of Providence Church; another northeast of Viola School and the third about midway between Providence Church and Cross Roads Church.

In a Soil Survey of Hart County recently made by the United States Department of Agriculture and the Georgia State College of Agriculture, the following soils were found: The Cecil sandy loam and Cecil clay loam are soils with heavy, red subsoils derived mainly from granite and gneiss. The Appling sandy loam has a mottled red, yellow and gray subsoil and is also formed from granite and gneiss as are also the Durham sandy loam with a yellow subsoil and the Worsham sandy loam with a very light gray or almost white subsoil.

Davidson clay loam is a dark red soil derived from the ferromagnesian rocks in the northwest part of the county, while Madison sandy loam and Madison clay loam are soils with very friable red subsoils derived from quartz-mica-schist. Wickham sandy loam is a red soil found on the second bottoms of the rivers and larger creek, while Congaree fine sandy loam and silt loam are the first bottom soils.

History of Public Roads Being Traveled Before the Creation of Hart County—Appointment of Road Commissioners for the New County—Laying out of New Roads—The Alternative Road Law— Commissioners Appointed—Commissioners Elected—Road Supervisor Elected —Board of Commissioners of Roads and Revenues—Employment of the Chain-gang

WHEN the county was organized it was traversed by several public roads. One among the oldest to touch the territory later embraced in Hart County was the Hatton's Ford road, which crossed the Tugaloo River at said ford, leading out of South Carolina on to Carnesville, Ga.

We have seen a map dated in 1800, which describes this as a post road on a line of march through South Carolina into Georgia by Spartanburg, Greenville, Pendleton, Hatton's Ford and on to Carnesville, Ga.

In the presentments of the Grand Jury of Franklin County, July 17, 1784, the following appears with reference to the Hatton's Ford road when the "Grand Jury presented a grievance that there was not a road laid out from the Court House to Hatton's Ford on Tugaloo River."

It is very probable that the Hatton's Ford road was a trail or private way before and was laid out and worked according to the suggestion of the Grand Jury soon after the presentment was made, which was about 140 years ago.

There is a tradition that John Robinson's show once crossed the river at Hatton's Ford well over one hundred years ago, as it traveled, caravan like, over the country from and to the points of exhibition.

This road was in use long before the installation of ferries and bridges, and the only place to cross the rivers and other streams was at the fords.

Before the opening and improvement of roads, Indian trails and bridle paths traversed the country, and usually followed along the water-shed lines along the highest ground between the streams. Bridle paths were the Indian trails traveled by the traders with the Indians who carried goods upon pack-horses from the trading posts to the settlements of the Indians and exchanged their merchandise for furs, hides, blankets and other things which were transported upon pack-horses on the return trip.

The public roads laid out later, in many places, followed the route of the Indian trails or bridle paths, as they were along the most practical route and located upon the best ground suitable for roads.

Another old road that ran through the country from the mountains, and beyond, to the markets in the lower part of the State was, and is still known as the "Red Hollow Road." Its history in many ways is perhaps more interesting than any other road of the early days that traversed the country that later became Hart County. It entered that part of the country that later became Hart County at or near the place known as the Leander Hughes place, and led by the Shirley, later known as the Watson place, crossing the Carnesville road near Ford's Store, thence on by the R. D. Adams place, the William Owens place, thence on down by the Barnett Johnson place, crossing the public road at the present Goldmine School, thence on down to near Holly Springs Church where it entered Elbert County.

The name "Red Hollow Road" was applied for the reason that on this road in a red hollow near where the town of Martin, Stephens County, is located, there was a holstry or wayside inn called the "Red Hollow House."

It was the road over which all country produce of the up country, consisting of tobacco, apples, cabbage and other field and garden products were transported, and along which live stock, to wit: cattle, sheep, hogs, mules, turkeys, and geese, were driven to Augusta and other down country markets.

The tobacco "rollers" were perhaps the first to travel this road. In the northern part of the State and beyond the borders, a great deal of tobacco was raised. The tobacco, when cured, was pressed into huge and securely bound hogsheads. Around the heads of these hogsheads were pinned wooden felloes, which made a wheel at each end, and in the center of each head a large pin was inserted to serve as an axle. A hickory pole was split at one end to form shafts, which were fastened to the axle. Mules or oxen were harnessed to the pole, and as they moved they drew the hogsheads along. Many of these teams would go together for company, and the drivers were called "tobacco rollers."

The roads in the early days that ran from east to west were the arteries of immigrant travel, while those running from north to south were the arteries of commerce.

Another public road that led through that part of the country, formerly Elbert County, now Hart County, was the road leading from Dooley's Ferry on the Savannah River to Holly Springs where it intersected the Red Hollow road, just described. This road was and is still known as the Holly Springs road. After crossing at said ferry, it led on by the crossroads at the present home of L. A. Chamble, and on across the Stephenson's or Parks' ferry road near the Lit Richardson home and then by the Roebuck place near Little Cedar Creek and thence on by the crossroads near the William Myers old home, then across Big Cedar Creek and on by the home of Mr. Caswell Farmer, thence on across Little Coldwater Creek and on by the W. B. J. Norman, formerly the Betsy Teasley place, and on by Bethesda Church and by the residence of John McCurry, thence across Big Coldwater Creek on by Pleasant Hill Church, and thence on by the crossroads at the John Easten Teasley place, and on across North Beaverdam Creek into Elbert County where it intersected the Red Hollow Road, as already stated.

Another public road was the one leading from Elberton to Carnesville, which entered the county at a place known as Little Holly Springs, and thence on by the Angus Johnson place just below Royston, and which was the county line between Elbert and Madison counties, and later the county line between Madison and Hart counties up until 1863 when a small portion of Madison County was added to Hart County, and which road to day is State Route No. 17.

Another road that traversed portions of Elbert and Franklin counties before Hart County was created was the road that led from Ruckersville, Ga., to Carnesville, Ga., which entered about where Liberty Church is located and led by the present home of J. F. Olbon, formerly the J. Willis Brown place, at which was a post office known as Amandaville, thence on by the crossroads at the John Easten Teasley place, and thence on to Hon. Wm. Bowers residence at which was a post office known as Eaglegrove, thence on across North Beaverdam, and on by Hendry's Church and by the crossroads at the L. C. Brown place, and on by the George Cauthen place near where it crossed the Red Hollow Road, thence on by Redwine Church, thence on across Morea Creek by the D. H. Agnew place, and on to Bowersville, which was a post office at the home of Job Bowers, where it crossed the Hatton's Ford and Danielsville road, and thence into Franklin County to Carnesville.

There is a tradition that this road was originally an Indian trail.

Another road that was in use before the creation of Hart County led from Stephenson's, later Parks' Ferry, on the Savannah River, on across Big Cedar Creek, thence on by Cokesbury Church, and thence by the place of Barnabas Barron, commonly known as "Squire Barnes," and at which place there was a post office, a lawground and muster ground, a store, and as at all public places in those days, intoxicating liquors were sold. This road at one time was a stagecoach route leading from Anderson, S. C., to Lexington, Ga.

After the founding of Andersonville, S. C., in 1801, there was a public road that led from Andersonville up to the present site of Reed Creek Lawground where it intersected the Hatton's Ford Road, and from said lawground there was a road that led up the country parallel with Tugaloo River to Parkertown, known as the Clarkesville road, and at Parkertown there was a public road that intersected the Clarkesville road and led out by Shoal Creek Baptist Church, crossing the public road at Dr. J. H. Parker's place and on up into Franklin County. The Clarkesville road led on from Parkertown by the S. W. Thomas place near Negro's Old Store, heretofore mentioned, and on to Carnesville, Ga. The branch or fork road that led from Parkertown intersected the public road at the Dr. J. H. Parker place, as already stated, which road was known as the Cleveland's Ferry road, which led from said ferry, now Knox's Bridge, and which road is now State Highway Route No. 59, and originally was the main road from Pendleton, S. C., to Carnesville, Ga.

There was also a public road that led from Pullen's Ferry on the Tugaloo River and intersected the Carnesville, formerly known as the Hatton's Ford, road at the place known quite a while as the Aaron Risener, formerly the Reuben Harris place, and which road crossed the Clarkesville Road at the present location of Vernon Baptist Church.

In 1795 Thomas Shockley, of South Carolina installed a ferry on the Savannah River, which was later known as Brown's Ferry, and now Alford's Bridge.

The road that led from this ferry was originally known as the "Jackson Road," why so named we are not absolutely sure; however, from a statement made in a report of a committee of the Daughters of the American Revolution on old trails and roads, it appears that the Jackson Trail, or Federal Road, had been traced to Athens, and as the road from Athens, Ga., to Shockley's Ferry on the Savannah River was one of the roads in the early days and later was a stagecoach route from Athens, Ga., to Anderson, S. C., and now the Bankhead or National Highway, it is very probable that it was an extension of the "Jackson Trail," or road.

Another conclusion is that the road, known as the "Jackson Road," that led from Athens, Ga., to Shockley's Ferry, led on down through Georgia to Petersburg, formerly Dartmouth, which was at one time an Indian trading post, and from thence on to Augusta, Ga., and was in use many years before Shockley's Ferry was installed, and that when said ferry was established a road was opened up from the ferry to connect with the "Jackson Road" just a short ways below Mt. Zion Church where it now intersects.

This, of course, is mostly a conclusion, but from the best of our information it is the best explanation we can make with reference to the "Jackson Road."

There was another road in use when Hart County was created that intersected the Carnesville road at or near King's Bench that led on by Air Line Post Office, to Danielsville, Ga., by way of Daniel's Ferry and thence on to Athens, known as the road leading from Hatton's Ford to Daniel's Ferry, which intersected the "Jackson Road" at Air Line Post Office, and, as a matter of course, it and the "Jackson Road" was one and the same from Air Line Post Office to Athens, Ga.

There are, perhaps, other roads and parts of roads that were in use before the county was organized that we have not mentioned; however, the foregoing description pretty well covers the former roads so far as we know.

After the county had been created, and during the year 1854, commissioners for the several militia districts were appointed by the Inferior Court, as follows:

1112th District: Jas. T. McDonald, Littleton Skelton and Hugh McLane.

1113th District: Pressly B. Roberts, John McGarity and William Bowers.

1114th District: Solomon S. Jones, Richard Durrett and V. D. Gary.

1115th District: Lewis Bobo, Cain Estes and John Linder.
1116th District: William Bennett, James E. Henderson and James Allen.
1117th District: Joseph P. Glover, Thomas Holland and Joseph Maret.
1118th District: James E. Brown, Jabez Skelton and Reuben B. Thornton.
1119th District: David Steifle, John McCurry and Richard Brown.

The duties of the commissioners were to appoint overseers of the several roads in the various districts, and to have supervision of the road work, and they were also empowered to make changes in the district lines from time to time as occasion required.

The list above given are the names of the first commissioners and, of course, successors were appointed as the years went by, and up to the adoption by the county of the alternative road law which was enacted by the Legislature in 1890-1, which was recommended by the Grand Jury of Hart County at the September Adjourned Term, 1897, of the Superior Court, the roads were worked by the system then in vogue, which was that all male citizens between the ages of 16 and 50 years were subject to road duty and were required to work a specified number of days in each and every year, which was 15 days, yet it was very seldom that persons subject to road duty worked the full number of days.

Commissioners were appointed to review and mark out a number of new roads, after the organization of the county, as follows: (These commissioners were not the regular appointed road commissioners. but commissioners appointed for the specific purpose of reviewing and marking out new roads.)

James Carter, B. G. Stalnaker and Henry Tyler were appointed to review and mark out a road from Mt. Zion Church to intersect the Carnesville Road near Abraham Meredith's, which place was more familiarly known as the Obed Brown place.

John F. McMullan, Banister Owens and Sampson Bobo to review and mark out a road from Hartwell to intersect the Carnesville Road near Abraham Meredith's.

John A. Cameron, Henry Tyler and Thomas Hughes to lay out road from the county seat to intersect the Brown's Ferry Road between the county seat and Labon Adams.

Thomas L. Stowers, Burrell Bobo and Tinsley Powell to lay out road from the plantation of James Shiflet by way of Thos. L. Stowers, Willis Dickerson's, Burrell Bobo's, and thence the most convenient way to the county seat.

Wm. R. Poole, Wm. F. Glover and Calvin P. Sanders to lay out a road from the ford to the creek, near J. P. Glover's Millner place, thence to Hartwell.

Sterling Pinson, Chesley Scott and J. H. Vickery to lay out road from Pullen's Ferry by way of Reuben Harris' to Hartwell.

Note: The Reuben Harris place referred to is what is now known as the Risener place at the crossing of the Pullen's Ferry and Carnesville Road. The road from Pullen's Ferry, on Tugaloo River, to the crossroads was already a public road and had been for years.

Joseph Maret, Wm. Knox, and R. K. Walters to review a new road from near Wm. Knox's Bridge by the way of Shoal Creek Factory.

Jackson M. Walters, C. B. Estes and Aaron Vickery to lay out and review a new road from Hicks' and Linder's Ferry, on Tugaloo River, to Hartwell.

J. G. McCurry, Moses Roberts, Elbert J. Brown, James Allen and Moses Davis to review and mark out road, commencing near the residence of Neal Johnson on the Carnesville Road, by Wiley B. Brown's to the "Center of the World," and also to review and mark out a road leading from Hartwell to the "Center of the World," thence to Eaglegrove Post Office, thence to the bridge near Aaron Rice's, thence to the county line in the direction of Daniel's Ferry.

Thomas White, Stephen Carlton, Radford Jordan and S. Sanders to review a road leading from Hartwell to the "Center of the World," thence by Larkin Clark's, thence by Wm. Carlton's Bridge on the Beaverdam Creek, from thence to intersect with the Daniel's Ferry Road, with the reviewers appointed to review the two routes just mentioned, that all to review three routes and mark out road to answer for all three routes.

Received a report of a new public road marked out leading from near T. Evenston's by J. G. McCurry's, thence by E. R. White's, thence by the Sullivan old place, Hill's old mill, thence to Hartwell.

Abner Walters, Wm. F. Attaway and D. H. White to review a road, leading from Hartwell, thence crossing the Beaverdam Creek at the place called Brawner's Bridge, thence the most practicable route to Franklin Springs and Madison Springs to intersect with the road below Manley's, which leads to Danielsville.

The commissioners appointed to lay out the above mentioned road reported as follows: Road to lead from the "Center of the World," thence by A. C. Walters' thence by Wm. Cheek's, thence by Robert Henderson's, thence by Wm. F. Attaway's, thence by Brawner's Bridge, thence to intersect with the public road at Aaron Wooten's, leading by Franklin Springs and Madison Springs and Danielsville.

Appointed reviewers to view out a public road, to wit: Wiley B. Brown, Wm. E. Thornton and Abraham Walters, beginning at the county line near A. Mewborn's, thence on by the Presbyterian Church, Pleasant Hill, on the Dooley's Ferry Road (also known as the Holly Spring Road), thence on by Asa Duncan's plantation, thence on by O. M. Duncan's and Wm. Goolsby's, thence onward until it intersects with the new cut road leading from John G. McCurry's to Hartwell.

This road was received as a private way, but was later made a public road.

Appointed F. B. Hodges to mark out a new road from Hartwell straight to Wm. Neese's.

Received a petition for a public road leading from Lewis Stowers' by Barnabas Barron's to where said road intersects with the Elberton and Stephenson's Ferry Road.

Received a report of a public road leading from near the line of the 1119th District, and running through Mr. Obed Brown's land in a northeast and then an east direction to the Walthour house on the Carnesville and Andersonville Road. (The beginning point above mentioned was near the late residence of J. W. Sanders.)

Appointed John M. Parks, Joseph Glover, S. C. Fisher, John H. Johnson

PUBLIC ROADS — NEW ROADS — ETC.

and Jas. F. White to review, mark out and report to the court a road from Hartwell to Bowersville.

Note: The Bowersville referred to was the place owned at the time by Job Bowers and at which there was a post office by that name.

Appointed Joseph Jackson, Joseph Ellis and John Parker to view, mark out and report on a public road leading from Parker's Mills, the nearest and best way to road leading from Andersonville to Carnesville, intersecting the last named road near Joseph Ellis', a distance of about five miles, which report was made by the commissioners and the road ordered by the court to be opened.

Received a petition for a public road, commencing at or near Wm. Jones', thence by way of A. J. Haynes', J. H. Hearston's, Jas. F. White's, E. J. Brown's, T. H. White's, J. W. Jones', J. J. Ray's, B. D. Johnson's, J. A. Brown's, thence to intersect the Carnesville Road at or near the Young place, and ordered that the same be opened as a public road.

Measuring and Posting of Public Roads

After the several new roads were laid out and established, they were posted and signboards placed at the several crossroads and forks of roads.

The posts were of sawed oak lumber, about 6x4 inches, and stood about four or five feet above the ground, and on each was a board indicating the number of miles from the county seat.

For instance, the Pullen's Ferry Road, which led out by the old Line Church, had the first mile post placed one mile from the court house, and all the mile posts on this road were numbered consecutively to said ferry, a distance of ten miles. The tenth post stood near the ferry on the Georgia side of the river. In the same manner all roads were posted and numbered.

The old roads, that is, those that were established before the county was created, presumably, were already posted.

At the fork and crossroads signboards were erected pointing in the direction in which the roads led and giving the number of miles from said fork or crossroads to the place of destination indicated on the boards.

The contract, according to the minutes of the Inferior Court, was let to Daniel E. McCurry and Asa J. Haynes, who perhaps had assistants. The records show that Daniel E. McCurry received $132.51 for his part of the work, and that Asa J. Haynes received $54.04.

The method of working the public roads from and before the creation of the new county, was that all persons between the ages of sixteen and fifty years were required to work on the public roads, as herein before stated.

There were three road commissioners for each militia district, as already stated, who appointed overseers for the several roads and prescribed or gave to such overseers a list of the names of such persons as were subject to road duty.

Formerly the commissioners and overseers were entitled to pay for their services, but later the law providing pay was abolished and they were required to perform their duties without compensation.

The tools employed in working the roads consisted of shovels, mattocks, hoes, axes and plows, the overseer notifying each person at the time of warning what kind of tool to bring, each furnishing his own tool.

The new roads laid out after the creation of the county, and those already in use before, were laid out in a generally straight course, without regard to hills, grades or other conditions of the lands over which the roads passed.

The roads ran up one hill and down another, or more correctly speaking, up one hill and down on the other side of the same hill. The roads were generally narrow, or so in most places. The work done on the roads, for the most part, was of a very inferior quality and none too much at that. The ditches on each side of the roads were not, in most instances, of sufficient width or depth to carry the water, and consequently the overflow waters coursed down the middle, the lowest part of the road, and the remedy for this trouble was to build brakes, or "dead horses" as they were called, across the road to turn the water out into the side ditches, and whenever a wagon or other vehicle ran against these "dead horses," it was in many instances wrecked, and it was a hard pull for the team to make it over such places, and it was also quite a strain on the team to pull a wagon up hill even with a light load, and whenever the farmer loaded his wagon at home to make a trip he generally loaded it with the view of the condition of the road over which he was to travel. As a consequence, wagons and teams were not loaded to the capacity of the wagon to bear or the team to pull, or if they were a "breakdown" was very often the result. These conditions obtained more especially in the hilly sections of the country. As a matter of course, where the land on which the roads were located was level or reasonably so the roads were easier of maintenance, heavier loads could be transported and better time made in travel.

Stage roads and the principal market roads were kept in a more passable condition than those of less importance, while the best were very poor, and especially so when compared with the fine roads we have at the present time.

Another thing that helped to impede travel or transportation was that nearly all streams were crossed by fords, but few were bridged, and when the streams were swollen by rains they were impassable at times, and any attempt to cross was fraught with more or less danger.

At the September Adjourned Term of Hart Superior Court, November 20, 1897, the Grand Jury recommended the adoption by Hart County of the alternative road law, to become effective January 1, 1898, and authorized the Ordinary, who at that time had jurisdiction of the roads, to appoint three superintendents to assist him in the administration of the road law. James H. Skelton, A. J. McMullan and W. J. W. Moss were appointed by A. L. McCurry, Ordinary, as such superintendents.

The alternative road law provided, among other things, that all male persons subject to road duty were required to work a specified number of days in each year, or in lieu thereof to pay a commutation tax as fixed by said authorities, not exceeding fifty cents per diem for the number of days' work required.

The authorities were also empowered to buy mules, road machinery, and all necessary equipment for working the roads, and to appoint a foreman, and employ free hired labor to work the roads. They were also authorized to have roads worked, improved or repaired, by contracting for the same in such manner as they might deem fit, with private parties, companies or corporations; provided, that if the work was done by contract, the contractors should be required to employ the chain gang, if established, and the labor of those who do not pay the commutation tax, and to pay for the same.

They were empowered to work a chain gang, which was to consist of the misdemeanor convicts of the county, or of any other county in this State that might be obtained without cost for hire.

It was also provided that the Act should not go into effect in any county in the State until it was recommended by the Grand Jury of the county.

The Ordinary and superintendents proceeded to appoint overseers to superintend the working of the several roads and to receive the tax from those who preferred to pay.

This system was continued from January 1, 1898, up until December 2, 1901, when the Legislature passed an Act providing that at the regular Adjourned September Term, 1901, of said court, to be held during the fourth week in November, 1901, of said Superior Court of said county of Hart, there should be elected by the Grand Jury three citizens of said county who should, after taking the oath prescribed, constitute a board of roads and revenues for said county. The Act further provided that at the regular March Term, 1902, of said Superior Court of said county, the Grand Jury should elect one of said commissioners for a term of three years, one for a term of two years, and one for a term of one year.

The three commissioners so elected were clothed with the same authority as that of former authorities and in addition they were empowered to make the tax levy for the county.

At the September Adjourned Term, 1901, above referred to, J. D. Matheson, J. Ed. Conwell and B. Allen Teasley were elected by the Grand Jury as road commissioners.

We find no record of any election by the Grand Jury at March Term, 1902, when commissioners were to be elected in accordance with the provisions of the Act of the Legislature.

On December 17, 1902, the Act creating a board of commissioners for Hart County was amended so as to provide for the election of commissioners by the qualified voters of the county at the regular election in the year 1904, at which election D. C. Alford, W. M. Vickery and S. H. White were elected commissioners.

At the election in 1906, S. H. White, W. T. Banister and J. F. Olbon were elected for the years 1907-8.

On August 17, 1908, the Board of Commissioners of Roads and Revenues in and for Hart County, created by the Act of the Legislature, approved December 2, 1902, was abolished.

At the same session of the Legislature, on August 17, 1908, an Act was passed creating the office of Commissioner or Supervisor of Roads and Revenues, and provided that such officer should be elected by the qualified voters of said county at the regular election to be held for State and county officers on the first Wednesday in October, 1908, and biennially thereafter, and that said commissioner should enter upon his duties on the first day of January, 1909.

The Act creating the office of Commissioner or Supervisor provided that he should be clothed with the same powers and authority as the Board of

Commissioners were empowered, with the exception of making the tax levy for the county.

The Democratic Executive Committee of Hart County met in the court house on Saturday, August 15, 1908, and ordered a Democratic primary election to be held on Thursday, September 17, 1908, for the purpose of nominating a candidate for Road Commissioner, and that the two candidates receiving the highest vote make the race in a second primary to be held on September 30, 1908.

F. M. Carter, S. H. White, L. M. Vickery, Ed. T. Cason, Lit Richardson and Reuben H. Martin announced themselves as candidates for the office of Commissioner, and at the first primary election S. H. White and Ed. T. Cason received the highest number of votes and made the race in the second primary, in which S. H. White was elected.

At the regular election on Wednesday, October 7, 1908, S. H. White was duly elected Road Commissioner, which office he held until 1912, when John S. Wilson was elected for 1913, which office he held until 1916, when Judson Vickery was elected and served until the Act of the Legislature was passed August 8, 1918, by which the office of Road Commissioner for Hart County was abolished.

At the 1914 session of the General Assembly of Georgia the office of Commissioner was abolished on August 17 of said year, and at the same session the offices of County Commissioner and Board of Finance were created, the commissioner to be elected by the qualified voters at the general election for State and county officers on the first Wednesday in October, 1914, and the members of the Board of Finance to be elected by the Grand Jury at the first Superior Court of Hart County held after January 1, 1915.

John S. Wilson was elected Commissioner, and at the February Term, 1915, of Hart Superior Court, the Grand Jury elected J. R. Leard, A. N. P. Brown and L. H. Cobb as a Board of Finance.

It is proper to state here that the county employed the chain gang in the year 1908, which has been continuously employed and by which the roads of the county are worked and maintained at the present time.

By Act of the Legislature, approved August 2, 1918, the offices of Commissioner and Board of Finance in and for Hart County were abolished.

At the same session a Board of Commissioners of Roads and Revenues for Hart County was created, to be composed of five members to be elected by the Grand Jury at the August Term, 1918, of Hart Superior Court, and begin their term of office January 1, 1919.

The county was divided into four road districts, as follows:

The First Road District is composed of the 1112th and 1119th Militia Districts.

The Second Road District is composed of the 1113th and 1116th Militia Districts.

The Third Road District is composed of the 1114th and 1118th Militia Districts.

The Fourth Road District is composed of the 1115th and 1117th Militia Districts.

The commissioners provided for in the Act were one from each road district and one from the county at large.

Two of the said commissioners to be elected for a term of one year, two for a term of two years, and one for a term of three years, their terms of office to begin January 1, 1919, and the grand jurors shall elect said Board of Commissioners of Roads and Revenues annually thereafter in accordance with the Act, said commissioners to be commissioned by the Judge of the Superior Court of the Northern Judicial Circuit after their election has been certified by the Foreman of the Grand Jury electing them.

The commissioners elected in accordance with the Act were clothed with all the authority as that of the former commissioners and in addition they were empowered to make the tax levy for the county.

At the August Term of the Superior Court, 1918, the following named persons were elected commissioners for the various road districts and the county at large, to wit:

First Road District, A. N. P. Brown for a term of two years.
Second Road District, J. M. White for a term of one year.
Third Road District, L. H. Cobb for a term of one year.
Fourth Road District, W. J. O'Barr for a term of two years.
County at large, J. R. Leard for a term of three years.

The Act provided further that the Chairman of said Board of Commissioners, after the passage of the Act, should be general supervisor of all roads and bridges in the county, thus abolishing the office of Road Supervisor.

After the adoption of the alternative road law by Hart County, the roads were worked by free hired labor until 1908, when the chain gang was established. Many changes were made in routes and locations of the roadbeds. Where the roads ran up hill, the route was changed to contour the hills and thus reduce the grade. The roadbeds were widened and the right-of-way cleared of all trees, rocks and other obstructions, the hills in many places cut down and fills built across low places.

The system of contouring the hills was later, to some extent, changed and the roads laid out as nearly straight as the conditions would allow, the curves reduced to the least amount of curvature possible, thus reducing the hazard of accidents.

On August 14, 1931, the General Assembly of Georgia approved an Act providing for the election of the members of the Board of Commissioners of Roads and Revenues of Hart County by the qualified voters of said county, the provisions of said Act to become effective when after the same had been ratified by the voters of Hart County, and on March 22, 1932, a special election was held in connection with the primary election for county officers in which election a majority of the voters of Hart County voted in favor of the ratification of the Act, and at the September primary election for State officers O. G. Heaton was nominated as commissioner for the county at large, H. O. Cordell for commissioner of the First Road District, Hubert Cheek for the Second Road District, S. B. Gaines for the Third Road District and W. J. Bailey for the Fourth Road District, all said nominees were duly elected at the general election on November 8, 1932.

On the first Monday in January, 1933, O. G. Heaton, H. O. Cordell, S. B. Gaines and W. J. Bailey qualified, and Hubert Cheek who had been elected from the Second Road District failed to qualify, and C. A. Ginn, a former commissioner from said district, was appointed by Hon. A. E.

Ertzberger, Ordinary of Hart County, to fill the vacancy caused by the failure of Hubert Cheek to qualify, and they, the aforementioned, now (1933) constitute the Board of Commissioners of Roads and Revenues of Hart County, Ga.

In 1925 $200,000.00 of 5% road bonds were voted and sold for the purpose of construction and improvement of the public roads in Hart County, $20,000.00 of principal to become due at intervals of three years, the last installment to be due in 1955, with interest on all bonds payable semi-annually.

The General Assembly of Georgia, on August 25, 1931, approved an Act to reimburse the several counties of the State 10% annually until all indebtedness was liquidated due by the State, which Act was to become effective by the ratification of a majority of the qualified voters of the State.

On November 8, 1932, at the general election, the Act was ratified by a majority of the voters at said election.

The payment by the State to the counties to begin in 1936.

Ten per cent. of the amount due Hart County will amount to something over $12,500.00 per annum, and this amount, together with the fuel oil tax which amounts to about $12,000.00 per annum to Hart County, will amount to about $25,000.00 per year, and if the provisions of the Act are complied with and no diversion is made of the gas tax now being paid the counties, the tax levy for roads and road bonds for the county would be reduced to at least one-half the present levy for such purposes.

There are at present about sixty miles of State-maintained roads in the county on which the county receives fuel oil tax payments.

According to an audit made in 1931, there were approximately 745 miles of public roads in Hart County, classified and valued as follows:

Paved Highways, 20 miles @ $15,000.00 mile	$300,000.00
Graded and Topsoiled, 30 miles @ $2,000.00 mile	60,000.00
Graded and Soiled, 45 miles @ $1,500.00 mile	67,500.00
Secondary Roads, 650 miles @ $500.00 mile	325,000.00
	$752,500.00

Bridges:

Concrete, 3	10,000.00
Steel, 10	10,200.00
Various Others	10,000.00
Total Roads and Bridges	$782,700.00

The progress Hart County has made in constructing and improving her public roads is phenomenal, and it is simply marvelous to visualize the condition of the public roads at the time the county was created and compare with the present condition.

To break the monotony, we will here intersperse with the splendid poem by Edgar A. Guest, entitled "Roads."

> "Roads are footprints multiplied,
>   From little paths they grew.
> Time was the busy highways wide
>   Were traveled by the few.
>
> But one by one the footprints made
>   A line from place to place,
> Then signs were raised and pavements laid
>   To serve man's swifter pace.
>
> Thus easily I travel on
>   From town to town today,
> Reading the sign posts, one by one,
>   Which tell the certain way.
>
> Men of a hundred years or more
>   In shadowy lines I see
> Who made this journey long before
>   And left this path for me.
>
> When from my shoulders falls the load
>   And life on earth is o'er,
> My soul shall fare that last long road
>   Of all who've gone before."

Old Abandoned Roads

The old abandoned roadways, relics of the past, that ran up and down or contoured the hills, are all very fascinating items of the landscape and appeal to those who have a taste or love of nature, and to give some idea of the charm and impression these old roads produce upon the observer we will reproduce herewith extracts from an article written by Mr. James A. Hall, "Lover of Nature and Georgia Lore."

"Not far from my house there is a bit of old, abandoned road—a kind of relic of the past which the growing city has not yet swallowed. In my walks I often seek this remnant of ancient roadway and enjoy its companionship as I would that of an old friend. I feel a sense of comfort the moment my feet leave the paved street and touch the soft, responsive earth where two dim parallel trails, still marked by the tracks of an occasional vehicle, show where the ancient and the modern meet. What a feeling of safety comes with the knowledge that you can stand or walk in the middle of the road without risk of being run over, for only a wood hauler's wagon may pass that way!

"My old road winds around the slope of a wooded hill and crosses a small stream, which slips quietly away through a tangled swamp. In an open space where the sunlight falls upon the road a ribbon of short grass grows along its center between two strips of grayish brown sand, and in this sand may be seen the tracks of rabbits, birds, and occasionally sprawling toe prints of a 'possum or the flat-heeled impression of the foot of a coon.

"Numerous vines creep out of the jungle and thrust their feelers into the open roadway, but the passing of the wood wagon and the two strips of sterile sand keep these intruders back. Out here in this silent and restful old road one finds a bit of the forgotten past, which seems strangely new amid the hurry and turmoil of the present.

"The old road invites you to loiter at will, to dream and make yourself at home with its silence and peace."

Post Offices—Star Routes—Rural Free Delivery

"ON HORSEBACK AND BY STAGECOACH WENT GRANDSIRES' LETTERS"

IN WRITING of the history of post offices and star routes by which they were supplied, and later of rural free delivery, we will preface what we may say upon the subject by reproducing some paragraphs under the above quoted caption.

"Georgians of today speed letters by plane, as well as by railways that seem to outstrip the wind. But a hundred years ago conditions were such as are described in Waddy Thompson's History of the United States:

"Postage was still charged according to distance; the rate for a letter, written on a single sheet of paper, graded from six cents for distances of thirty miles or less to twenty-five cents for distances greater than four hundred miles. For every extra sheet the fee was charged again. As the letter was not enclosed in an envelope, but merely secured by sealing wax, the number of sheets could be easily counted by the postmaster. Postage stamps were not yet used. There was not a postal route west of the Mississippi, and it took almost a month for mail to go from Washington to New Orleans. Nor was the transportation altogether safe even in the older communities. On the routes between Philadelphia and Baltimore robbers frequently held up the stagecoach and rifled the mail pouch."

The oldest post road, of which we have any record, to touch the territory now embraced in Hart County was on a line of march through South Carolina into Georgia by Spartanburg, Greenville, Pendleton, Hatton's Ford to Carnesville. On this route was a post office named Hatton's Ford, which evidently was on the South Carolina side of the Tugaloo River. We have no record of any post office in Georgia on the line from Hatton's Ford to Carnesville. This information was optained from a copy of a map of the route dated 1800.

Another mail route was from Carnesville, Ga., to Pendleton, S. C.

On this route was a post office named Aquila located at the home of Samuel Knox, another on down the line was named Parker's Store. The route crossed the Tugaloo River at Cleveland's Ferry, where Knox's Bridge was later constructed.

When Hart County was created Parker's Store Post Office was included in the new county, and the old store house in which the post office was kept is still standing, though in a dilapidated condition.

There is an incident connected with the history of this old post office that will be of interest to relate.

After the close of the War Between the States there was no one eligible for the position of postmaster, the men having been in the war who were not too old, and those too old had aided by paying taxes to the Confederacy. Under these circumstances Morgan L. Parker, who was not old enough to take part in the war, was, at the age of sixteen years, appointed postmaster at Parker's Store, his commission bearing date of February 8, 1867.

This post office was later supplied by a mail route from Lavonia, which also supplied mail to the post office at Shoal Creek Factory and which was known as Shoal Creek Post Office. Both of said offices were discontinued after the establishment of the rural route from Lavonia.

Another mail route in the long ago was from Carnesville, Ga., presumably to Fairplay, S. C., though we are not sure that it extended to Fairplay. We wrote to the Post Office Department at Washington, D. C., for a description of this route, but were informed that it was not practicable to furnish the information, inasmuch as the records containing the desired information had long since been destroyed.

On this route there was a post office established at King's Bench on July 19, 1832, known as King's Bench Post Office, and William King, Jr., was the first postmaster. He was succeeded by Sterling Pinson on July 17, 1849, the latter serving until April 7, 1852, when the office was discontinued.

When Sterling Pinson was appointed postmaster, the office was moved about four miles northeast of King's Bench to the residence of Noel L. Skelton, a son-in-law of Sterling Pinson, which residence was located on the Pullen's Ferry road, a little more than two miles from said ferry.

In 1852 Noel L. Skelton sold the place to John Baker, who had recently emigrated from Lancaster County, S. C., and soon after, on April 7, 1852, as stated, the office was discontinued.

On this route, if we are not mistaken, was another post office called Ford's Store Post Office established August 30, 1851, and Henry Ford was the first postmaster. He served until June 27, 1866, at which time the office was discontinued, but re-established on July 23, 1867, with Miss Nellie Mitchell as postmistress. The office at this time, or perhaps later, was moved to the residence of Mr. Samuel White.

Along about some of the above dates this route was extended from Carnesville, Ga., to Anderson, S. C., and crossed the Tugaloo River at Andersonville, S. C., at which place there was a post office.

Reed Creek Post Office was supplied by this route and during the Civil War was located at the residence of Peter L. Fleming. During the Civil War Mr. John T. Boleman was the carrier on this route and the people used to congregate at Reed Creek Church and other points along the route and anxiously await the arrival of the mail to get tidings from loved ones who were away engaged in the conflict.

Later the Reed Creek Post Office was moved to the Col. Wm. O'Barr place, where it remained for some time, and later moved to the residence of A. B. Moore, and still later to the store house at the place where L. J. Ayers now lives, and finally to the store of Ertzberger & Co., at the crossroads near Reed Creek Church where it remained for some time after the rural route No. 2 was established by which it was supplied, and was also the distributing point for a loop route that served a portion of the country that the rural routes did not reach at the time.

For some years after the office was removed from the O'Barr place, Reed

Creek Post Office became the terminus, that portion of the route from Reed Creek to Anderson, S. C., being discontinued.

After the building of the Elberton Airline Railroad, the mail was supplied from Bowersville instead of Carnesville, as formerly, and on the route between Ford's Store Post Office and Reed Creek Post Office two other post offices were established; one at the residence of L. B. Fisher and known as Aquavia Post Office, and another at the residence of Cornelius Cleveland at the crossroads where the Hartwell and Avery's Ferry and the Andersonville and Clarkesville roads cross. This office was named "Cooper," for the sobriquet or nickname that had for some reason become attached to Cornelius Cleveland, probably during the Civil War, and by which nickname he was ever afterwards most commonly called. This office was moved to the home of Mr. Newton Isom, who was appointed postmaster, but later moved back to the original location and Mr. W. J. O'Barr appointed postmaster, he having come into possession of the Cornelius Cleveland place.

There was a post office established in Elbert, later Hart County, known as Montevideo Post Office, of which place mention has been elsewhere made, which was supplied by a star route from Ruckersville, Ga., if we are not mistaken about the route.

Later this office was kept at Rice's store, located at the crossroads near the Sinclair McMullan old homestead, now the home of Mr. C. W. Rice. The store house was destroyed by fire and for a long time afterwards, and by the older citizens of the community still is known as "the old burnt store place."

The last location of Montevideo Post Office was at the residence of Mr. D. O. Chapman and supplied by a mail route from Elberton, Ga., and was discontinued several years ago when a rural route was established out from Elberton, Ga., known at Route No. 6.

During the time of the Civil War, and perhaps for years before, there was a stage route from Anderson, S. C., to Lexington, Ga., which crossed the Savannah River at Stephenson's Ferry, later Park's Ferry, not far from the site where the Smith & McGee Bridge is now located. This route was by the Barnabas Barron place, at which there was a post office, the name of which we have never learned.

In the year 1859, a stage route for the carrying of the U. S. mail and transportation of passengers was put into operation between Athens, Ga., and Anderson, S. C. Following is the announcement as the same appeared in the *Southern Banner*, a newspaper published in Athens, Ga., at the time.

"U. S. Mail Line, From Athens, Ga., via Danielsville, Madison Springs, Franklin Springs, Bowersville and Hartwell, to Anderson, C. H., S. C.

"The proprietors of the above line would respectfully announce to the travelling public that they will run on this line the best horses and Troy coaches. Persons going to the Madison Springs, or from the West to the upper districts of South Carolina, or from South Carolina westward, will find this the shortest, cheapest, and best route.

"It will connect with the trains on the Ga. R. R., at Athens, and with the Greenville and Columbia trains at Anderson, avoiding night travel.

"A four-horse coach will leave Athens Mondays, Wednesdays and Fridays, immediately after the arrival of the cars, and arrive at Anderson next day;

leave Anderson Mondays, Wednesdays and Fridays, immediately after the arrival of the cars, and arrive at Athens next morning in time for the cars."

"Through Fare $6.00.
Laniear House, Athens.
Benson House, Anderson.
D. B. Langston & Co., Proprietors."

"D. B. Langston
J. S. Williford."

It will be seen from the above schedule that Hartwell was at the time supplied with daily mail by the above route.

The Bowersville mentioned was a post office by that name at the home of Job Bowers.

After the stagecoach services had been dispensed with, the mails were continued to be carried by buggy or on horseback, and on the route was a post office established at the home of Thomas W. Bowers, called Airline Post Office, not far from the present village of Airline, which perhaps was established before the stagecoach services were dispensed with.

This office was so named, presumably, for the reason that the route of the Georgia Airline Railroad had been located through the immediate community near where the post office was located.

The post office was kept in a small frame house, over the door of which was painted in large black letters, "Airline P. O." This small building is still standing, and the letters over the door, until recently, were faintly visible, though very much weathered by the storm and shine of the years.

On this route between Hartwell and the Savannah River was a post office called Oak Bower, which for a long time was kept in the store house of Mr. Ladwick Alford. Later it was moved for a short distance down the road and kept at the store house of Mr. W. J. Neese.

This route was continued until the building of the Elberton and Hartwell railroads, when that portion from Athens to Hartwell was discontinued, but the portion from Hartwell to Anderson, S. C., was continued for a while.

Later there was a star route established from Hartwell by the home of Mr. Thomas L. McMullan, at which place there was established a post office called Nickville, and another further on at the home of Mr. D. B. Bobo named Ryle, thence by Oak Bower Post Office to the home of Mr. Littleton Richardson, at which place there was established a post office called Dobbs. This last-named office was perhaps so called in memory of John Dobbs, Esq., who was a pioneer citizen of the community. From this last-named post office, so far as we have been able to learn, the route extended back to Hartwell.

Mr. Samuel Rowe was the carrier on this route, and for some reason the route was discontinued soon after it was established, with the exception that mail was continued to be carried from Hartwell to Ryle until the establishment of Rural Route No. 2. Satterfield Banks, colored, was the mail carrier from Hartwell to Ryle.

In November, 1877, there was a star route established from Toccoa, Ga., to Hartwell, Ga., and after first arrival of the mail the following amusing article appeared in *The Sun*, issue November 21, 1877.

"TOCCOA MAIL."

"On the 16th inst. the above mail came to town on the Yankee doodle style, riding a pony. You ought to have seen some of our citizens 'wilt,' who were looking out for a fine coach and pair of spanking bays.- We understand an enterprising citizen of Toccoa got the contract on what is called a 'star bid,' that is to carry it on foot or any other way. Eleven hours is allowed from Toccoa to the town of Hartwell. That would be very pleasant in blackberry time. Toccoa has two mails daily by railroad, and as this route was gotten up for the counties below Toccoa, where mail facilities are meagre, we hope they will be allowed some say so in the schedule of running the same."

In the following issue of *The Sun,* the following item appeared:

"HONOR TO WHOM HONOR IS DUE."

"The people of Hart County are much indebted to Mr. John S. Williford, of Athens, Ga., for the mail route from Toccoa to this place. He has been working a long time for this, and at last succeeded through Hon. B. H. Hill. Mr. Hill did the work in Washington. Mr. Williford did the work here necessary to putting the thing through."

This route was discontinued after the building of the Elberton Airline Railroad.

For a while, before the building of the Hartwell Railroad, there was a star route from Elberton to Hartwell.

Another mail route established in the early days to traverse what later became a part of Hart County was from Ruckersville, Ga., to Carnesville, Ga. On this route was a post office called Amandaville, located at the home place of Mr. J. Willis Brown, and another at the home of Hon. Wm. Bowers, called Eagle Grove, the route extending by Bowersville Post Office, at the home of Job Bowers, and thence on to Carnesville.

In later years the Amandaville Post Office was supplied by a mail route from Canon, Ga., with Mr. J. F. Olbon as postmaster, he having obtained possession of the J. Willis Brown place. This route also supplied the office at Eagle Grove and the post office at the Barnett Johnson place, known as Pay Up Post Office. This last mentioned office was moved from the original location and was last kept at the home of Mr. John R. Hayes.

For a short time prior to the year 1900, and for a part of said year, there was a short mail line from Hartwell by the home of Hon. James F. White, at which place was a post office known as Alford, and another on the same route known as Buffalo at the home of Mr. W. I. Brown, thence to Bio Post Office at the home or storehouse of Mr. B. Allen Teasley, and from thence to the home of Mr. Henry F. Hailey at which was a post office called Hale Post Office, from thence back to Hartwell.

Major Banks, colored, was the carrier on this route. When Rural Route No. 1 was established the above mentioned route and post offices were discontinued. There are at present three post offices in Hart County, to wit: Hartwell, Bowersville and Vanna, the last mentioned was established some time after the Elberton Airline Railroad was built and so named by Mr. Ezra Bowers, mail agent on said railroad, for Miss Susannah Ballenger.

Rural Free Delivery Mail Routes

The first rural free delivery mail route from Hartwell, No. 1, was established in June, 1900, and Robert H. Burns was the first carrier, with George L. Richardson as substitute. Upon the resignation of Mr. Burns, Mr. Richardson became carrier and still is the carrier on this route.

Route No. 2 was established July 1, 1902, with Mr. Joel T. Hall as carrier. Upon his retirement October 31, 1931, he received the following highly complimentary letter from the Postmaster General:

"Washington, D. C., Nov. 19, 1931.

"Joel T. Hall, Esq.,
"Rural Carrier,
"Hartwell, Georgia.

"My dear Mr. Hall: Your long and creditable record in the postal service has been brought to my attention as you close your career as rural carrier at Hartwell, Georgia, and retire with annuity as provided in Section 1 of the Act of May 29, 1930.

"It is shown by the official record that you were appointed in 1902 and have served 29 years and 4 months.

"I congratulate you upon the loyal and efficient service which you have given and which must afford you abundant satisfaction. In your future years I hope that happiness, contentment and well-being may attend you."

"Very truly yours,
"WALTER F. BROWN."

Routes Nos. 3 and 4 were established in 1903, with Irwin P. Brown as carrier on No. 3 and B. B. Webb on No. 4.

Route No. 5 was established sometime after Nos. 3 and 4 were established, with Mr. Early S. Page as carrier, and upon his retirement Mr. Fred G. Vickery became the carrier.

Route No. 6 was a loop route out from Reed Creek Post Office, and was supplied with mail by route No. 2, which delivered the mail for No. 6 at Reed Creek Post Office. Mr. C. J. Leard was the carrier on this route. Later discontinued.

Upon the retirement of Mr. Joel T. Hall, carrier on route No. 2, route No. 5 was merged with No. 2, thus eliminating No. 5.

At present there are four rural routes out from Hartwell, Nos. 1, 2, 3 and 4, with George L. Richardson as carrier on route No. 1, Fred G. Vickery on No. 2, George E. Vickery on route No. 3, and C. J. Leard on No. 4.

Parts of the county not reached by the above named routes are supplied by rural mail from Elberton, Dewy Rose, Bowman, Royston, Canon, Bowersville and Lavonia.

RAILROAD HISTORY

THE first railroad that was projected to traverse Hart County, so far as we know, was known as the Georgia Airline Railroad, chartered March 5, 1856, by Act of the General Assembly of the State of Georgia.

The original route of this road was known as the "Blount Survey," which was claimed to have been the cheapest and most practicable between the objective points, Atlanta, Ga., and Charlotte, N. C.

The original survey, in part, was from Gainesville, Ga., by Homer, Carnesville, Hartwell, Anderson, S. C., to Greenville, S. C.

At a meeting of the directors and stockholders of the Georgia Airline Railroad, held in Atlanta, Ga., in 1859, John McCurry represented Hart County, and stated in the meeting that the people of his county were exceedingly anxious to have the work go forward. He reported sixty-two thousand dollars subscribed bona fide.

Due to the approach of the Civil War all proceedings were suspended for the time being.

After the war and after the country had returned somewhat to normal conditions, the company was reorganized, new capital and new interest injected into the project and work was commenced to build the road on its present route, now known as the Southern Railway.

At a meeting held in Hartwell, Ga., June 7, 1871, an effort was made to have a survey made and stop work on the road until the question could be settled as to the route from Gainesville, Ga., via Hartwell, Ga., Anderson, S. C., to Greenville, S. C., should be adopted rather than from Gainesville, Ga., direct to Greenville, S. C., as it was then being carried out.

At a meeting held in Carnesville, Ga., June 29, 1871, it was stated that the charter provided that the route was from Gainesville, Ga., by Homer, Banks County, Carnesville, Franklin County, Hartwell, Hart County, on by Anderson, S. C., to Greenville, S. C., and that a President and Board of Directors were elected and had proceeded to locate the road by the points named and that 6% on stock had been assessed and most of it paid in, a few contracts let, and a small amount of work had been done, all of which had been suspended on account of the Civil War.

About the time of the above mentioned meetings other surveys were made and we remember in particular one, a preliminary survey, along the Carnesville and Andersonville road through Reed Creek district by Andersonville, S. C., and from said preliminary survey tangents were run and the line marked out.

However, all efforts to have the road built on the original survey failed and the road was built on its present route, which is, as described by one writer, "the crookedest on the map."

The next railroad to be projected that was to traverse the county was known as the Augusta and Hartwell Railway, chartered in 1873, and a railroad from Walhalla, S. C., to Petersburg, Ga., to intersect the projected road from Hartwell to Augusta, was surveyed in 1873, which survey crossed the Tugaloo River at Andersonville, S. C., and thence along on the Georgia side of the Savannah River through Hart County.

The last record we have of these proposed railroads was about July, 1874, when there was a meeting of the stockholders of the Augusta and Hartwell Railroad held in Ruckersville, Ga., at which Col. F. E. Harrison, of Andersonville, S. C., was made President.

The next railroad to touch Hart County was the Elberton Airline Railroad, which was surveyed from Toccoa, Ga., where it intersected the Airline Railroad, to Elberton, Ga. The survey was completed in February, 1874, the distance being 50 miles, 10 miles of which was located in Hart County.

The road was graded in 1874-5 by convict labor.

For some reason there was nothing further done towards completing the road until about the middle of the year 1878, when work was resumed and the road completed in 1879. This road at first was a narrow-gauge road, but later on was changed to a standard gauge.

The next railroad to be projected and built was the Hartwell Railroad from Bowersville, where it intersects the Elberton Airline, to Hartwell.

A railroad meeting in the interest of the Hartwell Railroad was held at Hartwell on May 7, 1878, at which Hon. W. F. Bowers made a speech in favor of the project, and which perhaps was the first meeting held to discuss, publicly, the project.

A survey was made by Isham Harrison and Charlie Magee, July, 1878, which was from Hartwell by the residence of J. R. Myers at the "Center of the World," thence on by the Hartwell Campground, by Capt. John S. Herndon's and finally to Bowersville. This route, for some reason, was not adopted and the road was located on the present route.

In 1878 a charter was granted by the Legislature of Georgia to the following named petitioners, J. L. Turner, F. B. Hodges, R. E. Sadler, John B. Benson, Lee Linder, C. W. Seidel, J. F. Craft, W. F. Bowers, E. B. Benson, J. B. Alford, W. A. Sanders, Dr. J. H. Parker, P. H. Bowers and J. W. Brown, of Hart County, to build a railroad to connect with the Elberton Airline Railroad at Bowersville and were authorized to borrow or issue bonds not to exceed $20,000, and capital stock not to exceed $60,000. Directors: Wm. F. Bowers, E. B. Benson, F. B. Hodges and John S. Herndon.

The work on the Hartwell Railroad was begun about the middle of April under the supervision of Hon. J. F. Craft, and completed in December, 1879.

"OUR RAILROAD"

Under the above caption we reproduce an article published in *The Hartwell Sun*, issue of December 10, 1879.

"On Friday, the 5th of December, anno domini, 1879, while the people of our beautiful village were each busily engaged in their respective vocations, as noiseless as a zepher, the splendid locomotive of the Hartwell Railroad, 'Nancy Hart,' glided up to the crossing and the summun bonum of long and impatiently repressed feelings of our people were realized. The day is worthy to be inscribed with a white mark and be embellished in the heart-memories of all who in the future will appreciate the growing and developing industries of our beautiful section of country. But as quietly as 'Nancy' slipped in on Friday, a brilliant ovation was in store for her on the next day when the greater portion of our populace assembled at the terminus near the contemplated location of the depot and anxiously waited her coming. After hours of waiting and restive suspense among the assembled group, at length the approaching train was seen ascending the heavy grade this side of Lightwoodlog Creek as gallantly as a ship ever plowed foaming billows of the ocean. A moment more and the shrill tones of 'Nancy's' voice went sounding through the woods and glens, always hitherto unaccustomed to such a noise, the train dashed up to the crossing amidst the smiling happy faces of our people, and Hartwell's railroad history began."

The first depot on the Hartwell Railroad was located in the fork of Franklin and West Howell streets, near the present residence of Mr. W. D. Teasley, but was after a few years moved to the present location. The first conductor on the Hartwell Railroad was Junius Aderhold and the first engineer was John Q. Snow.

The road was a narrow gauge until 1904-5, when, under the management of Mr. J. D. Matheson, it was changed to a standard gauge.

Herewith we reproduce a poem written by "Uncle Billy" Bowers about the time of the completion of the Hartwell Railroad.

"OUR NANCY HART"

By the Sweet Singer of Bowersville
Written for The Hartwell Sun

"*Time has rolled the season around,*
When in our midst we hear the sound
Of her, who is most beautiful and smart,
Whose name we call Our Nancy Hart.

Behold her as she rolls away;
Her dress how trim, how neat, how gay;
The boys all come to see her start;
Her name is called Our Nancy Hart.

The conductor is as white as snow,
The engineer—him we all do know.
Who would fail to take a part
In enjoying a trip with Our Nancy Hart?

Train hands all kind and polite
Among them none ever to be found tight.
If any do wish to ride with a dart,
Come go down with Our Nancy Hart.

Some say that Nancy cannot draft—
Dare you to say before Capt. Craft?
To see what is done by science and art,
Is to come and look at Our Nancy Hart.

Among the boys who are so merry,
None seem to be more so than our Berry;
On table he'll fix plum pudding and tart,
When rolls into Hartwell Our Nancy Hart.

Some so glad they seem almost silly,
Among such is found our Uncle Billy;
But we'll excuse him, when we think what a part
He has always taken for Our Nancy Hart.

All in the country seem to be delighted—
In praising our engine, how they are united.
The hotel-keepers, Marion and Bart,
How it does tickle them to see Our Nancy Hart.

Many in Hartwell, I guess, will rejoice
When in her streets they hear Nancy's voice;
You'll hear such a tooting wherever thou art—
The boys all mimicking Our Nancy Hart.

We admit little Nancy is very small,
Yet the work of our county, she'll do it all.
Yea, even from Elbert cotton will start
To get aboard the train of Our Nancy Hart.

Yea, many a bale she'll make quiver
Brought to her from far, far over the river.
Cotton shipped over Elberton R. R. in part
Will be furnished it by Our Nancy Hart.

Some people can't be beaten by the Jews—
For instance look at the Toccoa News.
Look out, friend Schaefer, for a firey dart,
Hurled from the battery of Our Nancy Hart."

The Hartwell and Washington Railroad

The Hartwell and Washington Railway Company was organized in 1906, and charter obtained and survey made, but nothing further was ever done.

The next and last railroad of any description to be chartered and survey located through the county was the Anderson and Atlanta Railroad, an electric line and an extension of the P. & N. from Anderson, S. C., to Atlanta, Ga.

The survey was made in about 1917 and line located from Anderson, S. C., through the city of Hartwell on the balance of the route.

Owing, perhaps, to the demoralization of conditions incident to the World War, all work on the project was suspended and never resumed.

It is hardly probable that the project will ever materialize, as we are living in such a fast and changeful age.

Since the World War, a great many of our thoroughfares have been graded and hard-surfaced and the slogan, "ship by truck," has been adopted in the transportation of freight, especially is this true of short hauls, while the automobile and the bus lines have absorbed the most of the passenger traffic.

General Assembly of Georgia 1777-1925

(Note: The General Assembly of Georgia met annually, 1777-1843; biennially, 1843-1857; annually, 1857-1877; biennially adjourned, 1878-1891; annually, 1892-1895; biennially, 1925- .)

The members of the Legislature from Hart County are as follows:

74. 1855-56 Wm. Myers
75. 1857-58 Wm. Myers
76. 1859-60 Jefferson Holland
77. 1861-62-63 Ex. James E. Strickland
78. 1863-64 Ex. 64-65 Ex. D. E. McCurry
79. 1865-66-66 E. R. White
80. 1868 Ex. 68-70 James Allen
81. 1871-72-72 Adj. James W. Jones
82. 1873 Moses A. Duncan (unseated 1-25-73)
    1873-74 Allen S. Turner (Jan. 25-....)
83. 1875-76 Jefferson Holland
84. 1877 John B. Benson
85. 1878-79 Adj. A. G. McCurry
86. 1880-81 Adj. A. J. Mathews
87. 1882-83 Ann. Adj. A. G. McCurry
88. 1884-85 Adj. B. B. Parker
89. 1886-87 Adj. B. B. Parker
90. 1888-89 Adj. John H. Skelton
91. 1890-91 Adj. James F. White
92. 1892-93 S. V. Brown
93. 1894-95 A. G. McCurry
94. 1896-97 Adj. J. R. Leard
95. 1898-99 M. M. Richardson
96. 1900-01 W. L. Hodges
97. 1902-03-04 Julian B. McCurry
98. 1905-06 A. J. McMullan
99. 1907-08-08 Ex. A. J. McMullan
100. 1909-10 Alpha A. McCurry
101. 1911-12 Ex. Alpha A. McCurry
102. 1913-14 Alpha A. McCurry
103. 1915-15 Ex.-16-17 J. B. Morris
104. 1917-18 J. Seaborn Winn
105. 1919-20 Tennis S. Mason
106. 1921-22 Tennis S. Mason
107. 1923-23 Ex.-24 W. B. McMullan
108. 1925-26 Broadus B. Zellars
109. 1927-28 Broadus B. Zellars
110. 1929-30 A. N. Alford
111. 1931-32 James H. Skelton
112. 1933-34 T. O. Herndon

State Senators

Representation in the Senate was by counties, rather than districts, until 1845, and again 1853 to 1860.

74. 1855-56 W. R. Poole
75. 1857-58 F. G. Stowers
76. 1859-60 F. G. Stowers

From 1860 Hart County was included in the Thirty-first Senatorial District, composed of the counties of Hart, Franklin and Habersham.

77. 1862-63 Ex. John B. Benson served out the unexpired term of John H. Patrick who was the senator from Franklin County and died before the expiration of his term of office.

80. 1868 Ex.-69-70 Ex. Rev. William F. Bowers
85. 1878-79 Adj. Frederick B. Hodges
88. 1884-85 Adj. John Franklin Craft (died 8-23-85)
    1885 Adj. James F. White (Sep. 28-....)
91. 1890-91 Adj. F. B. Hodges
94. 1896-97 Adj. W. Y. Carter
97. 1902-03-04 James H. Skelton
100. 1909-10 Julian B. McCurry
104. 1917 Asben Alpha McCurry (died July 1917)
    1917-18 James H. Skelton (Aug. 9-....)

In 1918 Hart County was changed from the Thirty-first to the Thirtieth Senatorial District, composed of the counties of Hart, Elbert and Madison, by Act of the Legislature passed November 5, 1918.

107. 1923-23 Ex.-24 Tennis Mason
110. 1929-30 Broadus Brown Zellars

List of County Officers of Hart County, Georgia, from Organization to the Present, 1931

Ordinaries

1854 to 1860	James T. Jones (died March 23, 1860)		1895 to 1896	A. L. McCurry, unexpired term of J. L. Johnson.
1860 to 1863	F. B. Hodges, unexpired term of J. T. Jones.		1897 to 1900	A. L. McCurry
1864 to 1867	F. B. Hodges		1901 to 1907	J. M. Thornton (died May 12, 1907)
1868 to 1895	F. C. Stephenson (died May 18, 1895)		1907 to 1908	W. B. McMullan, unexpired term of J. M. Thornton.
1895 to 1895	J. L. Johnson, part of unexpired term of F. C. Stephenson.		1909 to 1916	W. B. McMullan
			1917 to 1932	J. W. Scott
			1933 to	A. E. Ertzberger

Clerks Superior Court

1854 to 1855	Burrell Mitchell (died in 1855)		1871 to 1880	C. A. Webb
			1881 to 1896	M. M. Richardson
1855 to 1855	Thos. J. Cason, unexpired term of Burrell Mitchell.		1897 to 1899	W. T. Johnson
			1899 to 1903	D. B. Brown (died Dec. 1903)
1856 to 1856	Thomas Holland		1904 to 1904	J. Rod Skelton, Interim
1856 to 1857	F. B. Hodges, unexpired term of Thomas Holland.		1904 to 1905	J. W. Baker, unexpired term of D. B. Brown.
			1906 to 1916	J. W. Baker
1858 to 1865	Thomas J. Cason		1917 to	J. G. Richardson
1866 to 1870	James L. Johnson			

Sheriffs

1854 to 1855	William Myers		1866 to 1876	W. A. Holland
1855 to 1855	John G. McCurry, unexpired term of Myers resigned.		1877 to 1884	J. R. Myers
			1885 to 1890	J. P. Roberts
			1891 to 1894	J. R. Leard
1856 to 1857	Thomas Hughes		1895 to 1900	D. W. Johnson
1859 to 1859	Richmond Skelton		1901 to 1912	W. M. Kidd
1860 to 1861	Wm. A. Neese		1913 to 1920	A. S. Johnson
1862 to 1863	Thomas B. Adams		1921 to 1924	B. R. Brown
1864 to 1865	Wm. A. Neese		1925 to	A. B. Brown
1864 to 1865	W. A. Holland to fill vacancy by death of Wm. A. Neese.			

Tax Receivers

1854-	Wm. C. Davis	1895-1896	J. R. Hays
1855-	Jeremiah Askea	1897-1898	Sinclair Richardson
1856-	Wm. C. Davis	1899-1900	J. R. Hays
1857-	David Stiefel	1901-1902	C. L. Scott
1858-1861	Jeremiah Askea	1903-1908	W. H. Smith
1862-1863	David Stiefel, Receiver and Collector	1909-1912	Chas. A. Ray
		1913-1916	Fred B. Heaton
1864-1865	David Stiefel	1917-1924	Thomas M. Bailey
1866-1884	J. M. Thornton	1925-1932	Furman E. O'Barr
1885-1890	Geo. W. Cleveland	1933-	Tom C. Bailey
1891-1894	A. L. McCurry		

Tax Collectors

1854-1855	Richard Shirley	1864-1865	William Bowers
1856-1858	James W. Ray	1866-1868	M. M. Richardson
1859-	E. R. White	1869-1872	James Shiflet
1860-	Samuel B. Sanders	1873-1874	J. R. Hays
1861-	E. R. White	1875-1876	S. T. Fleming
1862-1863	David Stiefel	1877-1882	Jas. L. Johnson

Tax Collectors—continued

1883-1886	H. R. Anderson	1907-1908	Asa C. Cleveland
1887-1888	Jesse C. Vickery	1909-1912	J. W. Scott
1889-1890	H. R. Anderson	1913-1920	H. A. Jordan
1891-1896	Jesse C. Vickery	1921-1924	W. J. A. Cleveland
1897-1898	Geo. W. Cleveland	1925-1927	Joe Whitworth
1899-1900	Jesse C. Vickery	1927-1928	J. R. Leard, unexpired term of Joe Whitworth.
1901-1905	S. G. Bowers (died June 3, 1905)	1929-1932	Carl J. Ayers
1905-1906	Asa C. Cleveland, unexpired term of S. G. Bowers.	1933-	Columbus J. Cleveland

Treasurers

1854-1859	Samuel White	1889-1896	Thomas Burton
1860-1863	F. C. Stephenson	1897-1898	C. L. Scott
1864-1865	Elijah Chapman	1899-1900	Thos. H. Burton
1866-1868	F. C. Stephenson	1901-1904	Geo. V. Young
1869-1870	W. H. Cheek	1905-1908	J. Walton White
1871-1874	Benjamin Thornton	1909-1912	J. G. Daniel
1875-1878	John O. Bobo	1913-1914	Sam Martin
1879-1880	A. R. Brown	1915-1916	A. V. McCurry
1881-1888	John O. Bobo		Office abolished

County Surveyors

1854-1855	John A. Cameron	1899-1904	R. L. B. Shirley
1856-1859	F. B. Hodges	1905-1906	A. S. Richardson
1860-1870	Hugh McLane	1907-1920	J. H. Warren
1871-1872	L. B. Fisher	1921-1924	F. C. Gaines, resigned and J. W. Baker filled unexpired term.
1873-1878	A. S. Turner, resigned and A. J. McMullan filled unexpired term.	1925-1928	Lat Ridgway, resigned and J. H. Warren filled unexpired term.
1879-1880	A. J. McMullan		
1881-1888	S. W. Peek		
1889-1896	J. W. Baker	1929-	J. H. Warren
1897-1898	Bunyan Bowers		

Coroners

1854-1855	Richmond Skelton	1899-1902	W. E. T. Cleveland, died; E. T. Cason filled unexpired term.
1856-1857	Lemuel Scott		
1858-1863	Allen McGee		
1864-1865	C. H. Barron	1903-1906	Eppy W. Phillips
1866-1876	Allen McGee	1907-1908	John R. Bailey
1877-1882	H. K. Phillips	1909-1916	Jas. T. Nixon
1883-1884	Joseph Land	1917-1932	Robert H. Snow
1885-1896	W. E. T. Cleveland	1933-	A. D. Brown
1897-1898	Nipper Tribble		

Judges of the Inferior Court

The Act of the General Assembly, creating Hart County, provided, among other things, for the election of five Judges of the Inferior Court for the county, and at the election for county officers of the new county, which election was on the first Monday in February, 1854, as hereinbefore stated, the following named citizens were elected:

Henry F. Chandler Micajah Carter Clayton S. Webb
Daniel M. Johnson James V. Richardson

CONGRESSIONAL DISTRICT REPRESENTATIVES 87

Following is a list of others who served as Judges of the Inferior Court, to wit:

C. P. Pressnel	Wm. C. Davis	William Bowers
John Gordon McCurry	King Jasper Skelton	James M. Webb
Ransom A. Cobb	Simeon M. Scales	Wm. R. Poole
D. G. Johnson	Joel Towers	Asa H. Langston
Chesley L. Scott	Francis S. Roberts	

Representatives from the Congressional Districts to Which Hart County, Georgia, has belonged.

Congres. Dist.	Representative	Congress	Date of Term	Other Terms Served
6th Dist.	Hon. Junius Hillyer	Thirty-second	1851-1853	
		Thirty-third	1853-1855	
6th Dist.	Hon. Howell Cobb	Twenty-ninth	1845-1847	Elected by general ticket to
		Thirtieth	1847-1849	the Twenty-eighth Congress.
		Thirty-first	1849-1851	
		Thirty-fourth	1855-1857	
6th Dist.	Hon. James Jackson	Thirty-fifth	1857-1859	
6th Dist.	Hon. William P. Price	Forty-second	1871-1873	
8th Dist.	Hon. Alex. H. Stephens	Thirty-third	1853-1855	Elected by general ticket to
		Thirty-fourth	1855-1857	the Twenty-eighth Congress.
		Thirty-fifth	1857-1859	
		Forty-third	1873-1875	Elected from the Seventh District to the Twenty-ninth, Thirtieth, Thirty-first and Thirty-second Congresses. (1845-1853)
		Forty-fourth	1875-1877	
		Forty-fifth	1877-1879	
		Forty-sixth	1879-1881	
		Forty-seventh	1881-Nov. 4, 1882	
8th Dist.	Hon. Seaborn Reese	Forty-seventh	Dec. 4, 1882-Mar. 3, 1883	
		Forty-eighth	1883-1885	
		Forty-ninth	1885-1887	
8th Dist.	Hon. H. H. Carlton	Fiftieth	1887-1889	
		Fifty-first	1889-1891	
8th Dist.	Hon. T. G. Lawson	Fifty-second	1891-1893	
		Fifty-third	1893-1895	
		Fifty-fourth	1895-1897	
8th Dist.	Hon. Wm. M. Howard	Fifty-fifth	1897-1899	
		Fifty-sixth	1899-1901	
		Fifty-seventh	1901-1903	
		Fifty-eighth	1903-1905	
		Fifty-ninth	1905-1907	
		Sixtieth	1907-1909	
		Sixty-first	1909-1911	
8th Dist.	Hon. S. J. Tribble	Sixty-second	1911-1913	
		Sixty-third	1913-1915	
		Sixty-fourth	1915-Dec. 8, 1916	
8th Dist.	Hon. Charles H. Brand	Sixty-fifth	1917-1919	
		Sixty-sixth	1919-1921	
		Sixty-seventh	1921-1923	
		Sixty-eighth	1923-1925	
		Sixty-ninth	1925-1927	
		Seventieth	1927-1929	
		Seventy-first	1929-1931	

Congressional Districts to Which Hart County, State of Georgia, Has Been Attached Since Eighteen Hundred and Fifty-three

Date of Census	Congress	Session	Congressional District		Counties
1850	Thirty-fifth	First	Sixth	District	Walton, Gwinnett, Forsyth, Lumpkin, Hart, Towns, Jackson, Habersham, Clark, Madison, Union, Rabun, Franklin, and Hall. (14 counties)
1860	Thirty-eighth	First	Sixth	District	The counties named are precisely the same as they were recorded in the Thirty-fifth Congress (1857). (14 counties)
1870	Forty-third	First	Eighth	District	Columbia, Elbert, Glascock, Greene, Hancock, Hart, Jefferson, Johnson, Lincoln, McDuffie, Oglethorpe, Richmond, Taliaferro, Warren, Washington, and Wilkes. (16 counties)
1880	Forty-eighth	First	Eighth	District	The counties named are precisely the same as recorded under the Census of 1870. (16 counties)
1890	Fifty-third	First	Eighth	District	Clarke, Elbert, Franklin, Greene, Hart, Jasper, Madison, Morgan, Oglethorpe, Putnam, and Wilkes. (12 counties)
1900	Fifty-eighth	First	Eighth	District	The counties named are precisely the same as recorded under the Census of 1890. (12 counties)
1910	Sixty-third	First	Eighth	District	Clarke, Elbert, Franklin, Greene, Hart, Madison, Morgan, Newton, Oconee, Oglethorpe, Putnam, Walton, and Wilkes. (13 counties)
1920	Sixty-eighth	First	Eighth	District	There was no re-apportionment of Congressional seats under the Census of 1920. The counties remain as they were arranged under the Census of 1910.

By an Act of the General Assembly of the State of Georgia, approved August 25, 1931, to reapportion the several Congressional Districts of the State and for the reapportionment of members of the House of Representatives among the several counties, Hart County became attached to the Tenth District, composed of the counties of Clarke, Columbia, Elbert, Greene, Hart, Lincoln, Madison, McDuffie, Morgan, Oconee, Oglethorpe, Richmond, Taliaferro, Walton, Warren, Wilkes, and Franklin. (Seventeen counties.)

Hon. Charles H. Brand, who had been elected for the years 1933-4, died on Wednesday, May 17, 1933, and a special election was ordered by Governor Eugene Talmadge to be held July 5, 1933, to elect a congressman to fill the unexpired term of Hon. Charles H. Brand, at which Hon. Paul Brown, of Elberton, Georgia, was overwhelmingly elected.

When Hart County was created it was attached to the Northern Judicial Circuit, composed of the counties of Elbert, Hart, Hancock, Lincoln, Madison, Glascock, Oglethorpe, Taliaferro, Warren, and Wilkes.

The Judges who have presided over the Northern Circuit, since Hart County was organized, have been as follows:

First, Garnett Andrews, of Washington, Wilkes County, Ga.

Second, James Thomas, of Sparta, Hancock County, Ga.

Third, Thomas W. Thomas, of Elberton, Elbert County, Ga.
Fourth, William Reese, of Washington, Wilkes County, Ga.
Fifth, Garnett Andrews, of Washington, Wilkes County, Ga.
Sixth, E. H. Pottle, of Warrenton, Warren County, Ga.
Seventh, Samuel Lumpkin, of Lexington, Oglethorpe County, Ga.
Eighth, Hamilton McWhorter, of Lexington, Oglethorpe County, Ga.
Ninth, Seaborn Reese, of Sparta, Hancock County, Ga.
Tenth, Horace M. Holden, of Crawfordville, Taliaferro County, Ga.
Eleventh, Jos. N. Worley, of Elberton, Elbert County, Ga. Unexpired term of Horace M. Holden.
Twelfth, David W. Meadow, of Danielsville, Madison County, Ga.
Thirteenth, Jos. N. Worley, of Elberton, Elbert County, Ga. Unexpired term of D. W. Meadow.
Fourteenth, W. L. Hodges, of Hartwell, Hart County, Ga.
Fifteenth, Berry T. Moseley, of Danielsville, Madison County, Ga. Unexpired term of W. L. Hodges.

The terms of Hart Superior Court were originally the third Mondays in March and September, and on up until 1910 when the terms were changed to the second Mondays in April and October, and still later the terms were changed to the fourth Mondays in February and August and an additional term to convene on the first Monday in December. At the last mentioned term no Grand Jury serves.

At the 1909 session of the General Assembly of Georgia, a resolution was adopted to appoint a committee to rearrange the judicial circuits of the State and to report at the next session of the General Assembly, and by said rearrangement the Northern Judicial Circuit was reduced to four counties, viz.: Elbert, Hart, Madison and Oglethorpe, and later Franklin, by Act of the Legislature, approved August 19, 1911, was transferred from the Western to the Northern Judicial Circuit.

City Court of Hart County, Later City Court of Hartwell

The first term of this court convened Monday, December 7, 1903, with his Honor W. L. Hodges, Judge presiding, and James H. Skelton, Solicitor. The court had been constituted in accordance with the law providing for the establishment of city courts upon recommendation of the Grand Jury, and the Grand Jury so recommending at the September Term, 1903, the court was accordingly constituted under the name and style of the City Court of Hart County, under which name it operated for one year, and later the name was changed to City Court of Hartwell, the first session of which was held in December, 1904, just one year from the time of the first sitting of the City Court of Hart County.

The court was, after several years operation, discontinued by an Act of the Legislature abolishing the same. Hon. W. L. Hodges was Judge during the entire period of the existence of the court. J. H. Skelton was Solicitor for a part of the time, and J. Rod Skelton, a brother, succeeded him and continued as Solicitor until the abolishment of the court, which was by Act of the Legislature, approved August 19, 1911.

POLITICAL PARTIES

AS HAS been stated, at the time Hart County was organized Elbert was a Whig county, and Franklin was Democratic, and Hart County was so organized as to give a small Whig majority.

However, in the course of a few years, the old political lines were obliterated and the two old counties, Elbert and Franklin, as well as the new county of Hart, were all merged into the Democratic party, and which was the party of the counties up to the time of the secession of Georgia from the Union, which was on January 19, 1861.

There was a division of opinion among the citizens of the county relative to the seceding of the State, and those who opposed secession were known as the Union party; while there was no organization, yet a number of the citizens of Hart County were in sympathy with the Union and opposed to secession.

After the close of the War Between the States there was an effort made to organize, foster and keep alive the Union party in Hart County, as well as in other portions of the State. We can remember when there used to be what was termed the Union League Clubs in the different militia districts of the county, and at the election in 1868 James Allen was elected Representative to the Legislature from Hart County by the Union men and such as affiliated with the Union party. Hon. William F. Bowers was at the same time elected State Senator from the Thirty-first State Senatorial District, to which district Hart County belonged at the time.

In 1870 James W. Jones was elected on the Democratic ticket, being the first Democrat elected in Hart County after the war. James Allen ran at the same time for re-election, but was defeated, as was James L. Johnson, who was also a candidate at said election.

The election was conducted by managers appointed by Federal authority, and was of three days' duration. Georgia at that time had not been admitted back into the Union.

At the election in 1872 Allen S. Turner was a candidate for Representative and was opposed by Moses A. Duncan. Turner was a Democrat and Duncan was of the Union persuasion. Duncan was elected by one vote majority at the election, but Turner entered a contest and when the Legislature convened Duncan was unseated and Turner seated as the legally elected Representative, after eliminating illegal votes.

After this time there was no partyism, the county remaining Democratic until the year 1892.

The Third Party

The Third Party, Peoples' Party, or Populist Party, as it was variously called, loomed up in Hart County in 1892. The party perhaps had been launched some time before in other parts of the country, but up until 1892 there had not been any definite organization of the Third Party in Hart County.

When the Third Party was organized the Democrats organized in self-defense, and in the general election there was quite an interest manifested by each party in the success of their respective candidates. Excitement ran unusually and we might say unnecessarily high.

The two parties kept up their respective county organization for several years. First one side would carry the county and then the other, until in the year 1900 they came together in a joint convention, nominated a candidate for Representative and county offices, some from one party and some from the other, all of whom were elected at the general election. While there were independent candidates for some of the county offices, yet not one of them was elected.

After this the two parties ceased to keep up their party organization and never nominated candidates afterwards.

Following is an account of the various conventions, nominations and elections by the Democratic and Third Parties during the time they kept up their party organizations:

Democratic Convention

The Democratic Party met in Hartwell August 12, 1892, in convention for the purpose of nominating a candidate for representative in the Legislature.

F. B. Doyle was elected Chairman, and James M. Ussery Secretary. Every militia district of the county was represented by delegates in the convention.

Hon. S. V. Brown was unanimously nominated, and in the general election in October following was elected by 162 votes majority over W. A. Sanders, the Populist candidate, as the result of the election referred to later on will show.

At the general election, held October 5, 1892, the following was the result as to the race for Representative, Hon. S. V. Brown being the Democratic nominee and W. A. Sanders being the nominee of the Third Party.

District

District				
Town	Brown	480	Sanders	282
Ray's	Brown	49	Sanders	99
Smith's	Brown	58	Sanders	14
Reed Creek	Brown	40	Sanders	103
Hall's	Brown	43	Sanders	117
Shoal Creek	Brown	106	Sanders	52
McCurry's	Brown	92	Sanders	48
Alford's	Brown	34	Sanders	25
		902		740
Brown's majority		162 votes		

At the election in January, 1893, for county officers there were no nominations made by either party, but the party lines were pretty well drawn and the voters, as a rule, supported the candidates that were of their own political persuasion.

At a Democratic mass meeting held on July 12, 1894, A. G. McCurry was nominated as the candidate of the Democratic Party to represent the county in the next Legislature, and we might state here that he was elected in the general election by a majority of 125 votes over his opponent, Jones R. Leard, the Peoples' Party candidate of Hart County.

In the election for Congressman from the Eighth District in November, 1894, the following was the result:

Hon. Thomas G. Lawson, Democrat, received....928 votes
W. Y. Carter, Populist, received.........................790 votes

Majority for Lawson...138 votes

Democratic Nomination for County Officers

At the Democratic Convention on Wednesday, November 7, 1894, the following named persons were nominated, to wit:

For Clerk of Court	M. M. Richardson
For Sheriff	D. W. Johnson
For Tax Receiver	J. R. Hays
For Tax Collector	Jesse C. Vickery
For County Treasurer	Thomas H. Burton
For County Surveyor	J. W. Baker
For Coroner	W. E. T. Cleveland

The Populist Party of Hart County in convention nominated the following ticket for county officers Saturday, November 24, 1894:

For Clerk of Court	John C. Massey
For Sheriff	A. N. P. Brown
For Tax Collector	H. R. Anderson
For Treasurer	Jas. L. Johnson
For County Surveyor	Bunyan Bowers
For Coroner	James E. Brown

No nomination was made for Tax Receiver for the reason that A. L. McCurry, the present incumbent, had made a good and faithful officer and run in the election independent of party nomination.

At the general election on January 4, 1895, the Democratic ticket was elected all the way through.

Frederick C. Stephenson, Ordinary, died May 18, 1895, and a special election was called to elect an Ordinary to fill his unexpired term of office.

At a mass meeting of the Democratic Party of Hart County, held in the court house on June 12, 1895, A. J. Cleveland was nominated as the candidate of the party to make the race for Ordinary to fill the unexpired term of office of Hon. F. C. Stephenson, deceased.

At a meeting of the Populist Party, held June 13, 1895, in the court house, Capt. Jas. L. Johnson was nominated as their candidate for Ordinary to fill the unexpired term of office of Hon. F. C. Stephenson, deceased.

At the special election held June 25, 1895, Capt. Jas. L. Johnson was elected by a majority of 23 votes over his opponent, A. J. Cleveland, which was the first political victory for the Populist Party in Hart County.

On September 30, 1895, James L. Johnson died, leaving the office of Ordinary vacant, and a special election was ordered to be held for electing an Ordinary to fill the unexpired term of office of Capt. Jas. L. Johnson, deceased.

At a meeting of the Democratic Party of Hart County October 23, 1895,

A. J. Cleveland was again nominated to make the race for Ordinary for the unexpired term of Capt. J. L. Johnson, deceased.

At a mass meeting of the Populist Party of Hart County held on Saturday, October 26th, 1895, in the court house at Hartwell, A. L. McCurry was unanimously nominated by acclamation as the candidate of said party to make the race for Ordinary to fill the unexpired term of office of Capt. J. L. Johnson.

At the special election held on Thursday, November 7, 1895, A. L. McCurry, Populist nominee, was elected by a majority of 55 votes over his opponent, A. J. Cleveland, Democratic nominee.

A. L. McCurry received 736 votes, and A. J. Cleveland received 681 votes. This marked the second victory for the Populist Party in Hart County.

Democratic Convention

The County Convention of the Democratic Party convened in the court house June 10, 1896, for the purpose of nominating a candidate for State Senator from the 31st Senatorial District, it being Hart County's time to name the Senator. Also, to nominate a candidate for Representative in the Legislature, and for the various county officers, which resulted in the nomination of the following named persons:

For Senator 31st District	A. G. McCurry
For Representative	James H. Skelton
For Ordinary	J. M. Thornton
For Clerk of Court	M. M. Richardson
For Sheriff	D. W. Johnson
For Tax Receiver	Geo. V. Young
For Tax Collector	J. C. Vickery
For Treasurer	Thos. H. Burton
For Surveyor	L. B. Fisher

(Mr. Fisher refusing to make the race, Mr. R. L. B. Shirley was nominated.)

For Coroner	W. E. T. Cleveland

At the general election on October 7, 1896, the following was the result:

Votes received

For Senator 31st Dist., A. G. McCurry, Democratic candidate	957
For Senator 31st Dist., W. Y. Carter, Populist candidate	1137
For Representative, James H. Skelton, Democratic candidate	1058
For Representative, Jones R. Leard, Populist candidate	1081
For Ordinary, J. M. Thornton, Democratic candidate	1038
For Ordinary, A. L. McCurry, Populist candidate	1084
For Clerk of Court, M. M. Richardson, Democratic candidate	1036
For Clerk of Court, W. T. Johnson, Populist candidate	1112
For Sheriff, D. W. Johnson, Democratic candidate	1090
For Sheriff, J. M. White, Populist candidate	1036
For Tax Receiver, G. V. Young, Democratic candidate	1037
For Tax Receiver, Sinclair Richardson, Populist candidate	1090
For Tax Collector, Thomas H. Burton, Democratic candidate	1008
For Tax Collector, C. L. Scott, Populist candidate	1121

For County Surveyor, R. L. B. Shirley, Democratic candidate............1025
For County Surveyor, Bunyan Bowers, Populist candidate..................1112
For Coroner, W. E. T. Cleveland, Democratic candidate.................... 994
For Coroner, Nipper Tribble, Populist candidate..............................1134

It will be seen from the foregoing election returns that the Populist ticket was elected, with the exception of the office of Sheriff.

With reference to the race for Senator of the 31st District, A. G. McCurry received a majority of the votes in Habersham County, while W. Y. Carter received a majority in Franklin County together with his majority in Hart County, which gave him a majority in the entire district of 24 votes.

This election marked the third and last political victory for the Populist Party in Hart County.

Democratic Convention

In August, 1898, the Democratic Party of Hart County, in convention, nominated the following named persons for Representative and county offices:

For Representative	M. M. Richardson
For Clerk of Court	D. B. Brown
For Sheriff	D. W. Johnson
For Tax Receiver	Jno. R. Hays
For Tax Collector	Jesse C. Vickery
For Treasurer	Thomas H. Burton
For County Surveyor	R. L. B. Shirley
For Coroner	Wm. E. T. Cleveland

At the general election on October 5, 1898, the Democrat ticket was elected all the way through. After this, as has already been stated, there was not any more nominations by the separate parties—they in joint convention in 1900 met and nominated the candidates for the several offices, some from each party, as mentioned further on.

Democratic Nominating Convention

Pursuant to a call of the Democratic Executive Committee of Hart County, a convention composed of five delegates from each militia district of the county convened at the court house in Hartwell on May 1, 1900, and nominated the following candidates, who were declared to be the legal nominees of the Democratic Party of Hart County for Representative and the respective offices in the next October election, to wit:

Representative	W. L. Hodges
Ordinary	J. M. Thornton
Clerk of Court	D. B. Brown
Sheriff	W. M. Kidd
Tax Collector	S. G. Bowers
Tax Receiver	C. L. Scott
Treasurer	G. V. Young
County Surveyor	R. L. B. Shirley
Coroner	W. E. Cleveland

While this was known as a Democratic Convention, however, the Populist Party of Hart County was in a way represented in the convention and a part of the nominees for the offices were of the Populist Party, namely, S. G. Bowers, who was nominated for the office of Tax Collector, and C. L. Scott, who was nominated for Tax Receiver.

The ticket, as nominated in the convention, was elected all the way through at the general election in October following.

There were some who had been announced candidates for some of the offices that did not accept the action of the convention and made the race in the general election as independents; needless to say, they were not elected.

Organization of Cannon Church—Panther Lake—The Cold Saturday—When the Stars Fell—Samuel Hymer's Sawmill—The Haunted Orchard— The Peek Place—Lot's Old Field—Noel Skelton's Mill—Who Struck Billy Patterson—"Reminiscences of This Section From Away Back"

"Beaufort, S. C., September 12, 1892.

"Editor *The Sun:* On my late visit to your county, I had the pleasure of a visit to the old plantation where on the 12th day of September, 1829, I first saw the light of this beautiful world—sixty-three years ago today.

"The old place is situated five miles west of Hartwell on the headwaters of Lightwoodlog Creek, and was originally settled by William Bowers, grandfather of Hon. W. F. Bowers, of West Bowersville.

"Mr. Bowers was known by all the early settlers as Uncle Billy Bowers. This place was on what was known as the 'Big Survey,' or the 'Patterson Survey,' and belonged to William Patterson, of Baltimore, Md.

"About the year 1825 my father (John Allison) and Andrew Patterson came to Georgia from North Carolina, William Patterson having given each of them .... acres of land on condition that they come and settle the land and improve it. My father settled on the Bowers place, Mr. Bowers having moved a mile south, just across the line of the Patterson lands, and settled the place where Mr. John Herndon now lives on the head of Beaverdam Creek. Here Mr. Bowers prospered and raised a large family, consisting of seven sons and six daughters.

"Andrew Patterson settled near where Mr. John Clarke now lives.

"On the 19th of April, last, in company with Mr. S. H. White, of Lavonia, I set out to visit the old place.

"Mr. White had one of his best mules to the buggy with a well-filled basket under the seat to supply the wants of the inner man; in fact, I thought we had enough to last us two days, but late that evening when we returned, on examining into the condition of the basket it was found that our supply was about exhausted.

"On the way that morning nothing of interest occurred until we arrived in the neighborhood of Cannon Church, when my thoughts ran back to the day when that church was dedicated fifty-one or fifty-two years ago. A tremendous crowd was there on that day from the surrounding country. They came from fifteen to twenty miles, nearly all on horseback. After the services were over and the crowd began to disperse, all the roads leading away from the church was crowded with people on horseback. Buggies were unknown in those days. A few well-to-do gentlemen had carriages for themselves, wife and the small children to ride to church in on Sunday, but the young folks from ten years up went on horseback. The writer rode a spirited Indian pony on the above occasion. Among the prominent families of the community at that time were the Bowers, the Whites, the Clarkes, the Cheeks, the Sanders and Browns innumerable, and others.

"Arriving in the neighborhood of the old place, we came to a little lake of water which I at once recognized, though it is now in the open plantation of Mr. John Clarke. Sixty years ago it was in a dense forest, and there was associated with this lake a story that, whether true or not, made the place a terror to all the children of the neighborhood. It was said that there were wild panthers in the woods around this lake, and that they could be heard at night screaming in the surrounding forests. I very well remember that I would have gone five miles out of my way rather than pass that place alone, even in daytime.

"A half mile farther brought us to an old persimmon tree. From the top of this tree the Blue Ridge can be plainly seen. My first view of a mountain was from the top of this tree fifty-three years ago.

"A mile farther brought us to the old place—but how changed! Where once stood good substantial buildings and a large orchard of the best selected apples, peaches and pears, now a bare, smooth cotton field.

"Mr. Thomas Ray, an old gentleman living near by, kindly went with us to search out the old place. We went to the spring first, and from there I could easily locate every other place of interest to me. First I sat down by the spring and took a drink of water and found it to be the same pure, cold water that it was sixty years ago. While I sat for a while by the old spring my thoughts ran back to my childhood days—of how I used to romp and play around this spot. Then there was a thick, bushy swamp all below the spring; now it is all cleared up and in cultivation. On the bluff above the spring is where the old house used to stand. I easily located the spot by two objects. One was a rock that stands two or three feet above the ground near the edge of the yard, and the other the stump of a mulberry tree which stood at the opposite side of the house. This tree was planted by my mother for the leaves to feed her silk worms on, and when young was topped about ten feet from the ground, and where it was cut off four limbs grew out and spread until it made a very large and bushy tree. In looking around I found the body of the tree just outside the fence, where it had been thrown.

"Two noted events occurred while my father lived at this place, neither of them coming within my recollection. I refer to the day known as the 'Cold Saturday,' (February 7, 1835) and the night the 'Stars Fell,' (November 13, 1839) when thousands of people thought the end of the world had come. My father killed hogs on the 'Cold Saturday,' and the hogs would freeze before they could be dressed. I have an indistinct recollection of the day.

"Since the time of which I write, many changes have taken place. This was long before Hart County was formed. Where the beautiful town of Hartwell now stands was a wilderness at that time. Settlements were few and far between. Where Scott's mill on Lightwoodlog Creek stands, sixty-five years ago there was a sawmill owned by Samuel Hymer. The sawmill was burned down in the year 1838 and the place was never rebuilt or improved in any way until after the county of Hart was formed.

"About a mile down the creek from the mill, on the south side, was a large apple orchard, and as far back as I remember the houses and fencing had all been removed or destroyed on this place. Only one small house remained, and this little house stood under a large apple tree as a lone sentinel over the grave of the former settler of the place. It was a wild, lonely spot; the nearest inhabitant was two or three miles away. Thomas Sanders, two miles on the northeast, and my father, three miles on the southwest, were the nearest.

"When a small boy I often passed this place on horseback with a bag of corn going to Noel Skelton's mill about three miles lower down the creek, and I always hurried on my way home to make sure of passing this place before sundown, for it was said ghosts could be seen in that orchard after sundown.

"Peek, the former owner or settler of this place, had a tragic ending, having been killed by a charge from his own gun in the hands of a little sick boy at a place about three or four miles west of this place, which has ever since been known as the place where 'Peek was killed,' and may be located by a bare rock, about 18 feet in diameter, near the place. This rock is perhaps two hundred yards from where Peek was shot.

"About one mile south of Scott's mill, on a hillside facing southwest, gold was discovered in considerable quantities once, but was never developed. This was about the year 1834. The celebrated Brown gold mine was discovered about the year 1839 or 1840.

"A mile and a half south of the old Peek place was an old field known as 'Lot's Old Field,' where in the early settling of the country a man by the name of Lot Bramlett started to build. He had his house logs cut and hauled to the spot and the corner stones of the foundation of his house laid, but went crazy before he got his house up. If they have not been disturbed the corner stones may yet be seen on a little hill near the head of a branch two miles north of the Hartwell Campground, where they were laid about ninety years ago. Lot Bramlett spent the balance of his days chained in a log cabin near his mother's house, and he lived to be an old man.

"At the time he went crazy he had a nice crop of corn growing on this old field, and twenty-five years afterwards when some men called to see and talk with him he remarked: 'I expect my corn is getting grassy by this time.'

"The Bramlett place was on the Patterson lands, and when William Patterson heard of their condition he gave them the land where they were living. The family consisted of the mother, two daughters and the crazy son, the father having died long before.

"The world-renowned conundrum, 'Who Struck Billy Patterson?' had its origin at a district court ground near where the town of Bowersville is located, on the Elberton Airline Railroad. The court house stood about four hundred yards northeast of where the depot stands. The spot may be located by an old well on the side of the dirt road which was there long before the railroad or Bowersville was ever thought of at that place. It was when Billy Patterson was in Georgia looking after his lands. One day his business called him to this court ground. A great row was gotten up from some cause, and in the scramble some one unknown to Patterson struck him from behind. He immediately offered a reward of one thousand dollars to any one who would tell him who it was that struck him. But no one in the crowd ventured to report the guilty party, and I suppose it will forever remain unknown as to 'Who Struck Billy Patterson.' Several places have been named by different writers as the place where it occurred. Some have said it was in Carnesville, another at Manley's, near Royston, another at Social Circle on the Georgia Railroad; but near Bowersville, as above stated, is the place where the affair actually occurred.

"Billy Patterson at the time owned a large body of land lying between where Bowersville and Hartwell are located. He was a very wealthy man and owned whole blocks of brick buildings in Baltimore; large warehouses, extensive docks, and seven or eight ships, besides large tobacco plantations both in Virginia and in Maryland, all well stocked with slaves. Elizabeth, his only daughter, married Jerome Bonaparte. Jerome was made a king, and received his crown as a reward in part for deserting his American wife. Elizabeth Patterson, otherwise 'Madame Bonaparte,' died a few years ago in Baltimore at the advanced age of ninety-four years."

—*Written by John Quincy Allison.*

"Center of the World"

THE "Center of the World" is a locality about three miles southwest of the city of Hartwell, situated upon a fine plateau of ground not far from the headwaters of Cedar, Coldwater, North Beaverdam, and Lot's Creeks, the last named being a tributary of Lightwoodlog Creek.

The place was originally a Cherokee Indian assembly ground, from which Indian trails radiated in many directions. It was here the Cherokees met in their various councils, and it was here that they met the Indian traders with whom they exchanged hides, furs, blankets and other articles of Indian commerce and manufacture for such goods as the traders had for barter.

One of the trails that led down by where Cedar Creek Church is now located was perhaps a bridle path along which the traders transported their merchandise upon packhorses to the Indian settlements, and along which they carried such goods as obtained from the Indians to their places of business or trade centers located in the lower part of the State, presumably Dartmouth, Augusta, and other down-the-country markets.

At one time it was a noted pigeon roost in the days when the passenger pigeons migrated annually, in the autumn season, to this part of the country in quest of acorns, crops of which were abundant before so much of the forest lands were cleared away.

People used to gather here and shoot numbers of the pigeons from their roost in the large forest pines. It is said that the pigeons would alight upon the trees in such quantities that their weight would often break down the branches of the trees.

In a recent publication we note the following bit of history relative to the passenger pigeon:

"The Passenger Pigeon was the most numerous bird in all North America less than one hundred years ago, yet the race disappeared entirely from the earth on September 1, 1914, when the last specimen died in the Cincinnati Zoo."

The place is also historic by reason of the several meetings of a portion of the citizens of the county who desired that the county seat be located at the "Center of the World." An account of the proceedings of the meetings appears elsewhere in this history.

Marker at Center of the World

On October 25, 1923, a beautiful granite marker was unveiled at the place by the John Benson Chapter of the Daughters of the American Revolution in commemoration of the Cherokees.

On the occasion of the unveiling, Mrs. T. L. Matheson, Regent at the time, in well-chosen words, presented the marker, which was accepted on the part of the county by Mr. D. C. Alford, Chairman of the County Commissioners, in a timely speech in which he gave much interesting history connected with the place. Mr. A. N. Alford also made a speech of acceptance on the part of the Bankhead Highway, of which he was director.

The marker stands on the south side of the highway, and besides the insignia of the Daughters of the American Revolution and other parts of the inscription, in bold letters is the word, "Ah-Yek-A-Li-A-Lo-Hee," which purports to mean in the Cherokee dialect, "Center of the World."

Indian Dancing Mound

Down a short ways below where the public road crosses Little Coldwater Creek near the residence of James B. Thornton, and on the left or north side of the creek, is an old mound built by the Cherokee Indians, where they engaged in their various dances. Right near it was an excavation formed by the removal of the dirt with which to build the mound, and it is said that the excavation filled with water and formed a kind of artificial lake.

The Indians had a number of dances that they performed, not as amusements, but as religious rites. The dances were engaged in as a petition to the Great Spirit for some kind or other of blessing. They had what was known as the green-corn dance, the Buffalo dance, the war dance and many others in which they implored the aid of the Great Spirit in their enterprises or undertakings.

Powder Mill Branch

There is a large branch that flows along down about equal distance from the Rev. J. H. McMullan place and the John Snow place, a tributary of Big Cedar Creek, and known as Powder Mill Branch.

Just below where the public road crosses the branch there was once a mill that made powder for use in the War of 1812. The powder was made from willow wood, which is said to be better suited for the purpose perhaps than other kinds of wood.

The old site of the mill may yet be seen.

The David Creswell Survey

Besides the "Headright" grants to heads of families to the lands in Wilkes (later Elbert) and Franklin counties, now embraced in Hart County, there were a number of grants to large bodies of land to soldiers of the War of the Revolution in consideration of their services.

Among the lands so granted was a large tract of something over 5,000 acres granted to David Creswell on November 10, 1792, situated partly in Elbert and partly in Franklin counties, lying southwest of where the city of Hartwell is now located on both sides of Big Lightwoodlog Creek, including the "Center of the World," now traversed by the National Highway, including the Hartwell Methodist Campground, as well as the homes and farms of Mr. T. M. Myers, Mr. T. O. Herndon, the John M. Vickery place, the D. D. Dickerson place and many others.

Mr. Creswell later sold these lands to Thomas Smythe, who in turn sold same to William Patterson in 1793.

David Creswell was a brave and gallant soldier and fought under Gen. Nathaniel Greene, and held the position of Colonel.

Col. Creswell's home was in Wilkes County, and at one time he was County Surveyor of Wilkes.

He married Phoebe Talbot, daughter of John Talbot, and sister to Matthew Talbot, at one time Governor of Georgia.

The Talbot family was one of the most prominent in the early days of the State; John Talbot came originally from Virginia, and was a scion of the aristocratic Talbot family of England.

Col. David Creswell, his father-in-law, John Talbot, and his two brothers-in-law, Thomas and Matthew Talbot, are buried at Smyrna Church, on the old Lincoln Road, eight miles from Washington, Ga., in the rear of which there is an old burial ground of rare historic interest.

The Isaac Briggs Survey

There was another large body of land of over 5,000 acres granted to Isaac Briggs, January 17, 1787, while the boundary was included in Wilkes and before Elbert County was created.

Why this tract of land was granted to Isaac Briggs, we have not learned, as it does not appear that he was in the War of the Revolution, and about all we have learned of him is stated in the following paragraph:

"Isaac Briggs was a Georgian of some note and standing. He was secretary of the convention in Augusta, Ga., which ratified the Federal Constitution in 1788, and was associated with William Logstreet in his project to develop steamboating on the Savannah River long before Robert Fulton's day."

The lands granted to Isaac Briggs extended from a point, now within the corporate limits of the city of Hartwell, to the Lodwick Alford grocery house, extending on each side of the Brown's Ferry road, now the National Highway, including Lightwoodlog Creek on the one side and Powderbag Creek on the other, and the lands along said streams and their tributaries.

William Patterson also obtained ownership of the Briggs Survey, and later sold both the Creswell and the Briggs surveys to Ira Christian, with the exception of a portion of the Creswell Survey which had previously been sold to other parties, executed bond for title to Ira Christian, and before the terms of the bond were complied with both Mr. Patterson and Mr. Ira Christian died, and afterwards the sons of William Patterson, to wit: Joseph W., Edward and George, executors of William Patterson, executed deeds to said lands to the heirs of Ira Christian, deceased.

In 1873 the lands were partitioned between the Christian and McMillan heirs by Abram Walters, A. S. Turner and Chesley L. Scott, partitioners, and survey made by F. B. Hodges, Surveyor.

Tugaloo River

Men may come and men may go, but the Tugaloo goes on forever.

THE name Tugaloo in the Cherokee dialect means "rough flowing," so named on account of the various falls, cascades, rapids and shoals along the channel of the Tugaloo.

The Tugaloo is formed by the confluence of the Chattooga and Tallulah rivers, both of which have their sources in the State of North Carolina. It has been stated by one author of physical geography that the Chattooga and Tallulah in the distant past were tributaries of the Chattahoochee River, which statement reads as follows:

"The Chattooga River, at the western corner of South Carolina, was formerly the upper part of the Chattahoochee; but the Savannah had a shorter course to the sea and a more rapid fall. One of its tributaries, the Tugaloo, was able to extend itself until it tapped the Chattahoochee and robbed it of its headwaters."

The divide was thus shifted from the head of the Chattooga to its junction with the Tallulah and then along a line between the Tallulah and the headwaters of the Chattahoochee.

By reference to a map of the physical features of the locality, it is evident that along parallel with the course of the Chattooga, a ridge, known as the Chattooga ridge, extends for a long distance down the river on the east side to the junction of the Chattooga and Tallulah rivers, and that there is also a ridge, known as the Chattahoochee ridge, that extends along parallel with the course of the Chattahoochee, pretty well in line with the Chattooga ridge, and at one time the two ridges were one continuous ridge without a break. At the junction of the Chattooga and Tallulah, where they form the Tugaloo, there is a deep gorge or gap, and from an observation of the conditions it seems logical that the contention is perhaps true.

The Tugaloo River, together with its tributaries, drain a large area of country, and the upper end of the basin or watershed area, for grandeur, sublimity, beauty and picturesqueness surpasses all other parts of northeast Georgia.

Within the watershed area of the Tugaloo are a number of mountains, many, if not all, very historic on account of the Indian legends and lore connected with their history.

The Tallulah Falls

When it was apparent that commercialism was soon to grasp and mar the beautiful Tallulah Falls, the *Savannah News* said, in part, describing the beauty, grandeur and sublimity of the scenery:

"There is no such rare bit of scenery on this continent outside of the Yosemite Valley as at Tallulah, and there are critics who have pronounced the Georgia gorge and falls even more fascinating and altogether charming than those of the far-famed national park of the West.

"The rugged beauty of Tallulah has delighted generation after generation of Georgians and others, and inspired them to a higher conception of nature and of God. If there are sermons in stone, the jagged precipices of Tallulah have preached them to thousands of admirers, to the accompaniment of the music of the dashing and foaming waters rushing down the mountains. The legend of the falls, of Indian loves and tragedies are poetic in the extreme and are as numerous as the boulders of the gorge.

"These legends have been celebrated by some of the sweetest of American singers, Lanier among them. The spirit of poetry and romance characterize the place. It is one of nature's choicest scenic gifts to man."

Developments of the Georgia Railway and Power Co.

The total area covered by the different developments on the Tugaloo and Tallulah rivers, according to a report made in 1923, was 5,214 acres, more than eight square miles.

From the upper end of the developments to the lower end, the air-line distance is 21.42 miles, and the river distance is 32.94 miles.

Hydro-electric power is furnished to many municipalities with a combined population of hundreds of thousands.

The Tugaloo River is quite meandering in its course, more so in its upper reaches than further down stream, due to the character of the substance through which it has cut or plowed its channel. Along its course it passes many mountains, hills, slopes, bluffs, cliffs, ridges, saddles, gorges, ravines, hollows, valleys, vistas and confluences of many tributaries, all of which features of nature have a very significant physiographic meaning, as there is a reason for each and every phase and feature, very little of which we understand and all of which is an interesting study in nature if we would take the time and trouble to ferret out, and which perhaps, as the study of physical geography becomes more popular and receives more attention and thought, will become apparent.

The Tugaloo River enters Hart County at the northwest corner at the mouth of Gumlog Creek, where it has an elevation of about 590 feet and the distance along the river to where it joins the Seneca River is fifteen miles, at which point the elevation is about 510 feet, making the total fall from the mouth of Gumlog Creek to the mouth of the Seneca about 80 feet.

After passing the mouth of Gumlog Creek at a point about half way between the mouth of the creek and Knox's Bridge, the river makes almost an abrupt bend where the channel is deflected from the right towards the left side of the stream. Then again after flowing along for a distance of about three miles the channel is shifted at about a right angle from the right to the left, then again after flowing for about a mile and a half, there is another abrupt bend in the river where the channel is shifted towards the left side, then again in about the same distance another shift from right to left, and then after a distance of about two miles is passed there is another shift from right to left.

It is the nature of a stream to flow along the line of the greatest descent and at the same time to cut out a channel through the substance of least resistance, while at the same time it is the nature of a stream to flow in a straight line until obstructed or deflected in its direction.

There are two things that may be observed in the action of the Tugaloo at the points where the course is deflected. One is that at each turn of the channel there projects a cliff of rock and in each instance the cliff is just immediately below the mouth of a branch, creek or other tributary.

At the first turn mentioned there is a high cliff of rock just below the mouth of a branch which, perhaps, is known as the Parker Branch; the next turn is at a cliff of rock just below the mouth of the branch, known as the Goforth Branch; the next is at a rock that extends something like half way across the river, not far below the mouth of Payne's Creek; the next is at the mouth of the Gilbert Branch at a cliff; and the next is just below the mouth of Reed Creek. Why all of these several cliffs or rocks are on the same side of the river furnishes food for thought along physiographic lines.

After the river passes on down about a mile below the mouth of Reed Creek there enters from the South Carolina side of the river a large creek, known as Beaverdam Creek, which enters the river at a noted bend. The river from just below the mouth of Reed Creek makes a long, gradual bend to Hatton's Ford, a distance of about three miles. The Beaverdam Creek enters the river at about half way between the upper and lower end of the bend. There is another question with reference to the action of rivers and other streams, and that is why does a larger stream bend to meet the mouth of a smaller stream? Quite an area of the country on the Georgia side of the river opposite the bend in the river is termed "the bend."

Hatton's Shoals, of valuable water-power, heads not far from the mouth of Beaverdam Creek and terminates just below Hatton's Ford, a distance of about two miles, and has a fall of about 37 feet.

The river at Hatton's Ford is about one-fourth of a mile wide. The island in the river at Hatton's Ford is about 70 acres in area, the title granted to George W. Dyar by the State of Georgia in 1848. The island is historic for the fact that the noted Perry and Bynum duel was fought on it in 1832, a full account of which is elsewhere given in these pages.

The island about equally divides the water of the river, and it is a matter of conjecture that at one time there was but one channel of the river and that it flowed on the South Carolina side of where the island is located, and that the island, formerly, was a portion of the mainland on the Georgia side.

It is the tendency of all streams to flow in a straight direction, and it is very probable that the waters of the Tugaloo River at Hatton's Ford, during times of high water, the overflow ran down on the Georgia side of the island and each overflow deepened the channel until a part of the water ran along the Georgia prong permanently, widening and deepening all the time, and it was thus the island was formed.

It is further conjectured that in the course of time all of the water of the river will flow down the Georgia prong and that the island will become a portion of the mainland on the South Carolina side.

There are many matters of history that could be related in connection with the history of Tugaloo River, all of which would be interesting, however we are not conversant with but a very few of them and even if we were space would prohibit an account of them all, and we will have to be content with just a few.

The Tugaloo flows by Knox's Bridge, which spans the stream, an account of which we have given. It flows on down by the old site of Pullen's Ferry, where the pioneers crossed a century ago and more. It flows by the old site of Avery's Ferry which was discontinued many years ago. Thence on down by the Chandler Ferry, which still is a crossing place, and the shoals just below known as Chandler's Shoals, and an old abandoned ford just below the foot of the shoals which has a history that we have mentioned in a small way.

On down below the mouth of Reed Creek there is a large rock in the river not far from the South Carolina side, known as the "Scoggins Rock," with a more or less interesting history, but we have never learned the particulars fully, but it appears from what we have learned that a man by the name of Scoggins was drowned at or near this rock and for all the years since it has been known as the "Scoggins Rock."

The man, Scoggins, lost his life by drowning in an effort to secure a deer which he shot. Whether the deer was on the rock at the time it was shot, or whether Scoggins was on the rock at the time, we have never learned. Just above the location of the Scoggins Rock there is a shallow place in the river, and according to tradition the deer in the upper part of the country in the early springtime, before the grass and other vegetation put forth, would make annual trips down the river in search of pastures green, the verdue along down the Savannah being much earlier than in the mountainous parts of the country, and the deer followed a well-beaten path or trail, crossing the river from first one side to the other, and the above-mentioned place was where the deer crossed the river from the South Carolina side to the Georgia side, and as they later wended their way back to the mountains they would cross the river from the Georgia to the South Carolina side, and it was perhaps during some of these migrations of the deer that the drowning of Scoggins occurred.

About the middle of the river, not far above Hatton's Ford, is a noted sluice, known as "Mauldin's Sluice." The channel of the sluice is some thirty feet wide and one hundred feet or more in length, and down this sluice the water rushes at a terrific speed and it is dangerous for persons or vessels to get near the head of the sluice, especially when there is a rise in the river, as there is great danger of being carried down with fearful results. The story of the drowning of Mauldin, in consequence of which the sluice took its name, is about as follows:

This man, Mauldin, undertook to cross the river in a bateau—some say he was trying to carry two bateaus across at the same time—and as he steered too close to the head of the sluice, he and his vessel, or vessels, were rushed into the sluice and carried down, in which event he was drowned.

On the Georgia side of the river, near the high-water mark, he was buried, which was in keeping with the superstitution that all who came to their death by drowning should be buried close by the stream in which they lost their lives.

On the Georgia side of the river at Hatton's Ford there once was a flour and grist mill operated by water power supplied by the river. The mill was owned by a man whose name was Reuben Richey, and right near where the road enters the ford there is a rock in the river, shaped somewhat like the back of a huge turtle, which has for decades been called the "Reuben Rock," which derived its name for the reason it was the criterion by which Reuben Richey could determine when it was safe to cross the ford. As long as the rock remained exposed above the surface of the water, it was safe to cross the ford, but if the water was over the top of the rock it was then that the river was too high to ford.

Tugaloo River flows by many historic places, notably among others may be mentioned the Prather estate on the Georgia side just below the mouth of Panther Creek, where a large old mansion sets upon the hill overlooking a wide expanse of bottom lands along the river, and further on down on the Georgia side is the famous Jarrett Manor, and just a short ways further down on the South Carolina side located not far from the river is the tomb of Gen. Benjamin Cleveland, a soldier and an officer in the War of the Revolution and a hero of the famous battle of King's Mountain.

Not far below the old site of Pullen's Ferry, and on the Georgia side, is the site of the old home and burial place of Thomas Gilbert, one of the first settlers in the country, who was a soldier in the Revolutionary War, a pioneer Baptist preacher and prominent in the affairs of church and State in the early days of our country. His grave is on the summit of a beautiful hill overlooking the verdant valley and the limpid stream of the Tugaloo and deserves to be marked in a way appropriate with his devotion to his church and to his country.

Our country, in its primitive state, was one vast domain all hidden in the fastnesses of the forest, lapped in sylvian luxury, surrendering itself to the spell of the woods, the peace of the hills, the charm of the clouds and sky, while the limpid stream of the Tugaloo rolled along from the mountains to the sea, and as future generations read its history in story and song the Tugaloo will continue to roll along.

New Town—An Old Cemetery—Shockley's Ferry— Brown's Ferry—Alford's Bridge—Shockley Apple —Foul Murder of Three Federal Soldiers— Murder of William Pearce—Deeds from George Lumpkin to the Lands in the Vicinity of Mt. Zion Church

TRADITION has it that in Colonial days, or perhaps in the early years of American Independence, there was located on the south side of the creek on the Georgia side of the river where Big Lightwoodlog Creek empties into the Savannah River a town known as New Town.

This town was, in all probability, contemporary with Dartmouth, which was located at the confluence of the Savannah and Broad rivers, and upon the site of which Petersburg was later built.

Dartmouth was so named in honor of the Earl, to whose influence was due the concession enjoyed by a band of colonists engaged at this point in trade with the Indians. The area in question was known as the New Purchase, and to defend it against assault, there was erected in the angle between the two rivers a stronghold called Fort James. But the little settlement failed to realize the expectations of those who planted it and, after struggling somewhat feebly for existence, it met an early death.

As already stated, New Town was perhaps contemporary with Dartmouth and was at the head of navigation, or rather as far up the Savannah River as boats ran at the time, and was, perhaps, like Dartmouth, an Indian trading post, and for what few white people who lived in the community at the time.

During the Yazoo Flood in 1795, the town was entirely swept away and the foundation covered up, and remained so until the year 1852, when there was another flood in the Savannah River, known as the August freshet, when the location was unearthed, exposing to view the base of many old chimney locations and other signs of earlier habitation long hidden from the sight of man.

We might say, by way of digression, that the Yazoo Flood was so named on account of the popular indignation at the time which had been aroused by the efforts of certain parties to rob the State of Georgia of her western possessions, as well as other parts of the State.

Just a short distance down the river on a plateau of ground, slightly above high-water mark, is an old cemetery of some thirty graves marked by rough head and foot stones with no inscriptions. There is no record or tradition as to who are buried at this old graveyard, but it is a logical conclusion that this was the burying ground used by the citizens of the old town in the long ago. An old gentleman, still living in the community said that when a boy he moved to the community with his father's family and at that time there was a paling fence inclosing the old graveyard.

When we think of this old cemetery, and many others over the country located at the old residences of the pioneers and at the sites of old churches, now abandoned and gone, which are now overgrown with brier, bush, oak and clinging vine, with modest little brown stones, tilted this way and that, we are reminded of the lines of Grey:

> "*Beneath those rugged elms, that yew-tree's shade,*
> *Where heaves the turf in many a moul'ring heap,*
> *Each in his narrow cell forever laid,*
> *The rude forefathers of the hamlet sleep.*"

Hon. James M. Carter, in conversation with the editor of *The Hartwell Sun*, years ago, said that the old McCurry mansion where John McCurry, deceased, lived was removed from New Town.

Very few people now living know anything of this old town. Its site is now covered by brake and bramble, and all the sign that remains is a few hard, burnt bricks of cellars and chimneys.

About a mile and a quarter down the river from the site of this old town is Alford's Bridge, the site of which is quite historic.

From the deed records of Elbert County, which contain records of transactions of Wilkes County, later Elbert, we have gathered the following items of history relative to Shockley's Ferry and community, later Brown's Ferry, and now Alford's Bridge:

George Lumpkin, of Wilkes County, Ga., made a deed, May 3, 1790, to Thomas Shockley, of Abbeville County, S. C., conveying one-quarter of an acre of land for a ferry landing from a tract of land laid out to Samuel Foster, soldier of the War of the Revolution, consideration five pounds lawful sterling money.

Also the following deeds:

George Lumpkin and wife, Ann Lumpkin, deed dated January 22, 1792, to Elijah Owens to 100 acres of land between Powderbag and Lightwoodlog creeks, bounded south by James Greenstreet, west by land of John Tweedle, north by Nehemiah Howard, including the school house, lying on both sides of the wagon road, being part of four hundred acres of land granted to George Lumpkin, consideration six pounds sterling.

Also, George Lumpkin to Jesse Vinson, June 21, 1793, 400 acres, consideration 10 shillings. (Evidently there is a mistake in the records as to the consideration.) Two hundred acres and Savannah River and 200 acres lying on S. W. side of, first 200 acres mentioned. The first 200 acres granted Samuel Foster June 19, 1787, the other 200 acres being part of a survey granted to George Lumpkin.

Also, George Lumpkin to James Greenstreet, 178 acres of land on waters of Lightwoodlog Creek, February 9, 1795, being part of land granted to George Lumpkin April 9, 1792, consideration 10 pounds.

We give here these abstracts of deeds as a kind of historical background of the community.

It will be noted that in the deed to Elijah Owens that it is stated that the land lies on both sides of the wagon road and includes the school house. We have not been able to identify with any degree of certainty the location of the school house mentioned.

It is a matter of history that the road leading by Shockley's Ferry on the Savannah River, afterwards known as Brown's Ferry, and now Alford's Bridge, was called the Jackson Road and ran near where the city of Hartwell is situated. So far we have not learned for sure why the road was called the "Jackson Road."

The ferry established by Mr. Shockley was one of the earliest, and played a large part in the history of the country, both in South Carolina and Georgia.

At this place the famous "Shockley Apple" was named. A great freshet of the Savannah River in the late summer brought down an immense quantity of apples that were lodged in various lagoons along the river bottoms. One of these lodging places happened to be a few hundred yards below the ferry. In the spring of the year many apple scions came up and Mr. Shockley requested that some of the thrifty ones be retained to see the kind of apples they would bring. One of these brought an apple of great beauty and delightful taste. This new variety being without name was called the "Shockley Apple," by which name it is known today.

Another item of interesting history connected with Shockley's Ferry is that there was established in 1792 a Baptist church not far from the ferry on the South Carolina side and was known as Shockley's Ferry Church. In the history of the Georgia Baptist Association, Shockley's Ferry Church is mentioned as being organized in 1792, and became a member of the said association and remained a member for several years, and it is also stated in the history that no mention was made of it in the minutes after 1803. While the church remained at or near Shockley's Ferry, there was an Arm or Mission Station organized some two or three miles southwest of the present church of Sardis in Georgia, and was known as Cedar Creek Church, which sometime prior to 1811 went down and was merged into or with Sardis Church, while the church at Shockley's Ferry was perhaps merged into the Shiloh Church in South Carolina.

After Shockley's death the ferry passed into the hands of one Mr. Brown, and though well over a hundred years ago, and having changed ownership many times, it still bore the name of "Brown's Ferry" up until a few years ago when it was purchased by Mr. A. N. Alford.

Another historical incident, sad and altogether different, is connected with this famous ferry. From several accounts that we have read, we give herewith in condensed form the story of a horrible tragedy committed at Brown's Ferry.

One Sunday night in September, 1865, three young men were killed and their bodies thrown in the river. They were three young Federal soldiers who were sent there from the Yankee garrison at Anderson to guard a lot of cotton that had been placed there awaiting an opportunity of being shipped down the river to Augusta for sale. The cotton belonged to Mr.

Crawford Keys and perhaps others. The soldiers were there to prevent its being removed, as all cotton was confiscated by the United States Government.

Crawford Keys, Elisha Byrum and Robert Keys, of South Carolina, and F. G. Stowers, of Georgia, were arrested. The Carolina citizens were interested in the cotton and F. G. Stowers was engaged in boating, and they were suspicioned for the reason of their interest in the cotton and its transportation. They were carried to Charleston, S. C., and given a speedy trial by court martial, convicted and condemned to be executed in April, 1866. They were secreted away from Castle Pinckney (where they were imprisoned) the night before they were to be executed and carried to Dry Tortugas in the Florida Keys, and remained there several months until they were pardoned by President Johnson.

The bodies of the soldiers were taken out of the river on Monday and removed to Anderson and interred in the Presbyterian graveyard, where their dust remained for over thirty years. There was in Anderson one tenderhearted woman, who, for all that time, remembered those lonely graves and took care of them. She was the veteran teacher, Miss Leonora C. Hubbard. When, in 1905, the bodies were taken up and carried to the Federal Cemetery in Atlanta, Miss Nora received the official thanks of the Legislature of Maine for her humane and womanly conduct.

On May 12, 1917, another horrible tragedy was committed at Brown's Ferry, on the South Carolina side, when Mr. Will Pearce, the ferryman, was foully murdered. His skull was crushed with an axe, death being instantaneous. Robbery seemed to have actuated the murder, as both a billfold and change book used by Mr. Pearce were taken. The Sheriff and Coroner of Anderson County, S. C., as well as Sheriff Johnson of Hart County, Ga., were promptly notified and several clues were located in a short while after the arrival of the officers. Two parties were arrested that lived near the scene of the crime, but were released upon investigation, there being no evidence produced to connect them with the crime. Several other parties were later arrested and incarcerated, but nothing came of it for the want of evidence.

Mr. A. N. Alford offered a reward of $1,000 for the apprehension of the murderer, and Mr. Pearce's father added $300 to the sum, but so far the guilty party or parties have never been apprehended and brought to justice and it remains unknown today who committed the foul murder.

In 1917, Mr. A. N. Alford, single-handed, built the bridge at Brown's Ferry, and a notice of the accomplishment was written up and published in about the following language:

The bridge completed over the Savannah River, built by A. N. Alford, of Hartwell, was one of the biggest things of any nature that has occurred in this section of the State in recent years. It was an individual undertaking, Mr. Alford being sole owner.

The bridge proper is 450 feet long, with a bridge approach on the Georgia side of 270 feet long and 210 feet long on the South Carolina side, a total length of 930 feet. The bridge was built 30 feet above the water, and is 10 feet higher than the river had ever been known to reach at high-water.

The bridge accommodates two roadways, each nine feet wide, with a low partition separating them. The cost of the bridge was $40,000.

The scenery approaching the bridge on both sides of the river is decidedly beautiful and impressive, and the tourists who carry their cameras can get interesting and attractive mementoes for future reference.

At a point on the bridge, about midstream, there is to be had a long view down the river of a mile or more, and upstream for half that distance. It would be a difficult task to fully describe the grandeur and beauty of these views, however we will venture the following lines:

"The river-lines are never seen so distinctly under the foliage of summer as under the snow of winter.

"Upon this white background the dark-looking water dances and flashes, swirls and ripples; and the unbroken harmony of the lines, the continuity of the movements are things of beauty.

"The summer foliage blurs the graceful cutting of the banks, but compensates for this loss by a wealth of color. The stream sparkles between great borders of green, reflecting the blue sky where smooth, and turning to amethyst where it runs over shallows. The tree and the bank, the fern and flower are mirrored in the dark pools, the cloud shadow and the sunburst are flung across the moving surface, and the path of the moonlight weaves and ravels there as on the sea. Flexible and changeable as the sky above it, the river glides along, and chameleon-like, takes its color from its surroundings. It may be whipped with rain-squalls tonight, but tomorrow it will show the first silvery light of dawn upon its shining face, and whatever momentary effect may mar its surface, there is no pause in the smooth slipping seaward."

In 1924 Mr. Alford acquired possession of the Smith & McGee Bridge located about six miles lower down the Savannah River and operated both as toll bridges up until 1926, when he sold the two bridges to the State Highway Departments of the two states, Georgia and South Carolina, since which time they have been free bridges, the Alford Bridge being on the Bankhead Highway and the Smith & McGee Bridge being on a State highway maintained by the two states.

HISTORIC OLD ANDERSONVILLE

A HISTORY of Hart County would not be complete without giving a more or less mention of Andersonville, S. C., which was in former days a scene of commercial, manufacturing, and other business activities, but now almost forgotten among the Piedmont hills.

The spot is as sequestered as it is romantic; the soft and tender imaginable influence of woodland nymphs seem to enshroud, with magic charm, the entire scene. The overgrowth of green upon the destroyed area explains how quickly nature covers the buried cities of man, all emphasizing the assertion, "There is nothing constant but change."

A history of this old and long since abandoned town should become and form apart of Hart County history for several reasons, some of which we will enumerate.

When King George II granted to General James Edward Oglethorpe, and trustees, a charter to the territory on which to found a colony and which later became the State of Georgia, the Savannah River was designated as the boundary line between the states of Georgia and South Carolina up to the confluence of the Tugaloo and Seneca rivers, and thence up the Seneca River, the most northerly branch of the Savannah, to the North Carolina line; so thus the land upon which the town of Andersonville was later located was Georgia soil from 1732 up until the Beaufort Treaty was signed by authorized representatives from the two states, Georgia and South Carolina, by the terms of which treaty the line between the two states was shifted from the Seneca to the Tugaloo River, which treaty was entered into in 1787, and from 1784 to 1787 it was included in and formed a part of Franklin County, Ga., the county of Franklin being created in 1784, three years prior to the date of the Beaufort Treaty.

Again it is proper to include the history of Andersonville in the Hart County history for the reason that quite a number of the people who lived on the Georgia side of the Tugaloo River were so intimately identified and associated with the town in various ways, owning property in the town, employment in the stores, shops, mills, and other business carried on in the place, that they were in a way citizens of the town; many of them had their membership in the church there, while many children from the Georgia side of the river attended school at Andersonville.

The town was founded December 19, 1801, by an Act of the South Carolina Legislature, and laid out on the lands owned by Colonel Elias Earle between the two rivers, Tugaloo and Seneca, where they unite and form the Savannah River. Colonel Elias Earle was a soldier and officer in the War of the Revolution and one of the pioneer settlers of upper South Carolina.

General Robert Anderson, another soldier and officer of the War of the Revolution, and for whom the town was named, together with Col. John Baylus Earle and Col. Elias Earle, were appointed commissioners to lay off the town.

Col. Elias Earle had been an officer in the war, as already stated, and afterwards a member of Congress. He sold some of the lots in the new town, but retained the greater part for himself; later he sold a half interest to his son-in-law, James Harrison, who later became the owner, and still later Col. F. E. Harrison, his son, became sole owner of the place.

The physical features of the location of the town are unique and very interesting. A short ways up the public road leading from Andersonville to Townville, the ridge between the Tugaloo River and Little Beaverdam Creek becomes quite narrow, with the river on the left, going up the road, and the creek on the right. To the casual observer, it would appear that the creek should have entered the river at this point, however the crest of the creek is higher than that of the river and it is a well-known law of physiography that a tributary enters the master stream upon a level and never by an overfall. The creek at this point turns almost, if not quite, at right angles to that of the river and forms a semi-circle, or "horse shoe," and flows over the shoals of the creek, where once stood the dam that held back the water for use in operating the various kinds of machinery of the town, and after descending the shoals the water of the creek flows on and units with the waters of the river upon a level.

Along the creek, after passing the shoals, there arises a hill on the left side from steep to almost precipitous to a height of one hundred feet or more. On top of this hill or eminence is located the church and cemetery. The land from the summit of the hill is sloping towards the Tugaloo and Seneca rivers, which is in accordance with another pretty well established rule or condition of nature, that where there is a mountain or hill located between a large and a small stream, that the steep side is adjacent to the smaller stream, while that of a more gradual slope is adjacent to the larger stream.

Another very interesting feature of the location is that of the island in the Savannah River a short ways below the fork of the rivers, the Tugaloo and Seneca. This island was evidently at one time connected with mainland. The Tugaloo River approaches the point of confluence with the Seneca at an angle, termed the angle of incidence, and then deflects at about the same angle. The Seneca River approaches the junction of the rivers at about the same angle as that of the Tugaloo, and then deflects at an equal angle to that of approach. This is in accordance with the well-known law of physics that the angle of deflection is equal to the angle of incidence.

The contention is, that the action of the waters of the two rivers, Tugaloo and Seneca, scoured the sides of the land that formerly connected the island with the mainland, until the land was washed away and the rivers united at this point, but deflected and each followed its respective side of the island until they reached the lower point where they became permanently united.

A very logical reason for this statement is that the island formerly contained about thirty-seven acres of land, while today it contains but about twenty-three acres, proving that practically one-third of the area has been carried away from the upper end, disconnecting what remained as an island from the mainland.

The waters of the Tugaloo River are limpid, while those of the Seneca are ever turbid, and this distinction is noticeable as far down the Savannah River as McDonald's Shoals, some seven miles below the fork of the rivers.

Thus we have the Tugaloo, the Seneca—limpid stream and turbid tide— converge and form the majestic Savannah, which rolls away in classic pride; rolls on in splendor, and rolls on in might, to meet the dashing waves of the Atlantic down at Tybee Light.

Another peculiarity connected with the location of the old town is that the hills and slopes support a dense growth of spruce pines, a species of growth not, or very rarely at least, found upon the adjoining territory. Also, along the hillsides at Andersonville, on either side of the Tugaloo, and perhaps the Seneca, there grows an aromatic, perennial plant known as dittany. We know of no other place in the country where this plant is known to flourish.

At the time Andersonville was laid out, neither Anderson, S. C., or Hartwell, Ga., was thought of. The surrounding country was sparcely settled and timbered with oak, pine and other kinds of original forests. The farmers' log cabins in the woods, which abounded in wild animals, were scattered here and there over the country. The rivers teemed with fish. During the spring months, or spawning season, large numbers of shad came up the Savannah River, following up the Tugaloo and Seneca rivers.

Just a short ways up the Tugaloo River from Andersonville there were two noted fisheries, the Dyar fishery and the Bobo fishery, and from these fisheries large numbers of shad were taken each season. The spawning season was from about the middle of March to the latter part of May.

The young shad hatched in the Tugaloo and other tributaries of the Savannah made their way, in about the month of September, down the rivers to the salt water of the Atlantic Ocean.

The next year, or after maturity, as it has been claimed, the shad hatched in the Tugaloo and other tributaries of the Savannah came up the streams in which they had been hatched to spawn, as it is a well-known fact that the shad, like the salmon, return to the streams of their birth after ranging the seas.

When the dam was constructed across the Savannah River at Augusta, it ended all migration of the shad, as it was an obstruction the shad could not surmount.

The last account that we have of shad being caught in the Tugaloo River was in 1879.

Andersonville in the early days of its existence was a land office for the upper part of the State of South Carolina.

Andersonville was practically at the head of navigation, contemporary with Petersburg and Vienna lower down the Savannah River. It was the trading post for white people and the Indians as well. Here the Indians sold quantities of pink root, snake root and gensing, which was packed in large hogsheads of 600 pounds each and rolled or shipped by boat to Hamburg or other markets down the river and sold at the price of twenty-five cents per pound. The town got almost all the business of the large back country, both in South Carolina and Georgia. The people in those days did not raise cotton only on a small scale and it was for the most part brought to Andersonville and sold in the seed, where it was ginned and shipped to market. Tobacco and other produce was brought and sold here. Boats made regular trips down the river to market, Hamburg, or Augusta, carrying cotton and other produce, and on the return trip brought back merchandise for the stores at Andersonville.

Among the various kinds of industry and business conducted at Andersonville may be mentioned a sawmill of the sash, or "up-and-down," model, a grist and flouring mill, cotton gin, wool factory, tanyard, shoe shop, blacksmith shop, tailor shop, wagon shop, livery stables, a hotel of forty rooms, a number of stores—twenty or more—carrying a full line of goods needed by the trade, and it has been stated that in the earlier years of the 19th Century a gentleman living on the coast wrote to his daughter who was attending school in Pendleton that if she could not find such articles as she wished in Pendleton she could probably find them in Andersonville.

About the year 1812, there was a flourishing Female Academy located at Andersonville taught by an English couple, Mr. and Mrs. Dench, to which the wealthy people from South Carolina and other states sent their daughters. The school was in a brick building that used to stand, to the best of our information, at the intersection of the public road leading to Pendleton with the road leading out by the Seneca River ferry. This is a high point on the divide, or watershed line, between the two rivers in sight of their confluence, commanding a long, fine view for a mile or more down the

Savannah. Do not know how long the school continued. Rev. Mike McGee's mother, who was Asenath Rice, and Col. Rice's wife, who was Miss Thompson, were students there.

Col. Elias Earle served his district for five terms in the United States Congress. While in Washington he induced the Government to permit him to manufacture guns for the use of the army, proving to them that there was iron on his lands in South Carolina, which consisted of several thousand acres located on Seneca and Tugaloo rivers, and extending to Three-and-Twenty and Six-and-Twenty creeks. He had some guns made from the iron taken from his lands which he carried to Washington for inspection. The contract was given him, and he employed 32 machinists from Harper's Ferry, Va., and made guns that were used in the War of 1812. The iron was supplied by the iron works located at Centerville, Varennes and Portman, where it was smelted and transferred to Andersonville and made into guns.

In the first part of the 19th Century there was quite an exodus of emigrants from the states of Virginia, North Carolina, South Carolina and perhaps other states. There was a road known as the Old Post Road, or great southern trail, over which countless travelers migrated in the pioneer days seeking homes.

The road traversed Pennsylvania, Virginia, North Carolina, and South Carolina, over much the route now followed by the great National Highway. The old road leading by Pendleton and Andersonville was a branch of this old road, as we understand it, and the emigrants in large numbers crossed the Tugaloo River at the ferry at Andersonville, and it is said that the traffic was such that a part of the time it was necessary to operate two ferry boats to accommodate the travelers who, after crossing the river, traveled the public road leading from Andersonville on by Carnesville, Ga., which was the principal artery of emigrant travel in those days. Formerly, before the founding of Andersonville, and before the installing of ferries and bridges, the emigrants crossed the rivers at the fords. Hatton's Ford on the Tugaloo and the Cherokee Ford on the Savannah, and other fords that might be mentioned, were crossing places for emigrants. Later the ferries at Andersonville and Shockley's Ferry, now Alford's Bridge, were installed and became crossing places for travelers.

Another interesting item of history connected with Andersonville is that it was the home of a man by the name of Rusk, who by trade was a stonemason.

Hon. John B. Benson, in conversation years ago, said that when a young fellow he went from Pendleton, his home at the time, to Andersonville to fish with his friend, Frank Harrison, and there were at that time many old stores and other houses there, among them the dwelling of Mr. Rusk, who was the father of the great Rusk of Texas, for whom Rusk County in that state was named, and who was a friend of Augustus Maverick and Bonham, of Pendleton, S. C., and Davy Crockett. Bonham and Crockett were both slain in the battle of the Alamo and around them were a pile of dead Mexicans that they had slain with their knives, which calls to mind the saying with reference to Gen. Geo. A. Custer's last rally on the Little Big Horn, " 'Tis late before the brave despair."

In 1840 there was a freshet in the Tugaloo and Seneca rivers and other streams of this section, at which time the waters rose to a higher level, perhaps, than at any time before or since. The mills and other machinery located on Little Beaverdam Creek at Andersonville, and many of the business houses and other buildings on the low lands and along the river front, were swept away. In an account which we have read, describing the freshet and the great damage done, we herewith give the following paragraph:

"In 1840 there occurred a notable event in the history of this town; a great freshet visited this section of the country, inflicting great damage. The storm blew and the rain fell in torrents, increasing in intensity. The Tugaloo and Seneca rivers rose so high that practically all the buildings were rocking in the rampant waters. Finally, most of the buildings gave way, leaving ruin and desolation, especially to the cotton gin, flouring and grist mills, the wool factory and other machinery.

"They were rebuilt, but not for long—as the turbulent waters of 1852 demolished most of the settlement, which was never rebuilt. But it took more than the rush of many waters to dampen the ardor of the band of people in this town where every consideration was made subservient to progress."

In this connection will say that the mills were rebuilt and other machinery added which had not been in operation before, notable the factory for making yarn from seed cotton, described further on.

The old Earle House, which is still standing, located far back from the road, built on the stately pattern peculiar to the spacious days of the old South, and fragrant with memories of a gentler time.

In the early days there were set about this old home hedges of the beautiful Cherokee Rose, around which there clusters the beautiful and romantic love story of a brave of the Seminoles and a dusky maid of the Cherokees.

From time to time these bushes have become distributed over an area adjacent to the old home, and in the springtime, 'when the roses bloom again,' the hills and dales present a lovely scene.

For the information and entertainment of our readers we herewith reproduce the story.

The Legend of the Cherokee Rose

Once upon a time, a proud young chieftain of the Seminoles was taken prisoner by his enemies, the Cherokees, and doomed to death by torture; but he fell so seriously ill, that it became necessary to wait for his restoration to health before committing him to the flames.

As he was lying, prostrated by disease, in the cabin of a Cherokee warrior, the daughter of the latter, a dark-eyed maiden, became his nurse. She rivaled in grace the bounding fawn, and the young warriors of her tribe said of her that the smile of the Great Spirit was not more beautiful. Is it any wonder, then, though death stared the young Seminole in the face, he should be happy in her presence? Was it any wonder that each should love the other?

Stern hatred of the Seminoles had stifled every kindly feeling in the hearts of the Cherokees, and they grimly awaited the time when their enemy must die. As the color slowly returned to the cheeks of her lover and strength to his limbs, the dark-eyed maiden eagerly urged him to make his escape. How could she see him die? But he would not agree to seek safety in flight unless she went with him; he could better endure death by torture than life without her.

She yielded to his pleading. At the midnight hour, silently they slipped into the dim forest, guided by the pale light of the silvery stars. Yet before they had gone far, impelled by soft regret at leaving home forever, she asked her lover's permission to return for an instant that she might bear away some memento. So, retracing her footsteps, she broke a sprig from the glossy leaved vine which climbed upon her father's cabin, and preserving it at her breast during her flight through the wilderness, planted it at the door of her home in the land of the Seminoles.

Here, its milk-white blossoms, with golden centers, often recalled her childhood days in the far-away mountains of Georgia, and from that time this beautiful flower has always been known throughout the Southern States at the Cherokee Rose.

Almost opposite the old Earle home, on the other side of the road, stands the fine old Harrison mansion. It is set upon the top of the hill overlooking the union of the Seneca and Tugaloo into the Savannah River.

It was the dwelling of Col. F. E. Harrison, once the scene of gayety and hospitality, but is now in a state of decadence, and lies in the ruined, unpainted splendor of a vanished heyday.

In the latter business days of Andersonville, Col. Harrison established a factory there for making yarn direct from seed cotton. This probably was the only one of its kind ever operated in the South.

After the building of the Greenville & Columbia Railroad, Andersonville began to wane. Transportation by railroad supplanted river freightage and railroad towns supplanted Andersonville. Col. Harrison did everything in his power to lift the town to its former place. He tried to get a railroad through there, and although the road was surveyed, it was never built. All his efforts to make Andersonville great were in vain, and after his death in 1878 Andersonville practically went to pieces.

At the time of his death Col. Harrison was possessed of a large landed estate, consisting of several thousand acres, located on all sides of Seneca and Tugaloo rivers, and perhaps some along the Savannah River. A considerable portion of his lands, including the site of the old town, was purchased by his son-in-law, Mr. E. P. Earle. It was later owned by Dr. F. E. Harrison and Mr. L. C. Harrison, who have of recent years sold it to a corporation, looking to the development of the water power of the rivers for electrical industry.

Col. Harrison and his forefathers were relatives of the two Presidents of the United States of the same name, William Henry and Benjamin Harrison.

Col. Harrison was a man of rare intellect, possessed fine business and executive ability, was truly a master of finance and industry, prominent in the affairs of his State and county, was patriotic, serving as an officer in the War Between the States in General Orr's Company.

In religion was a Presbyterian, a scholarly, high-toned, Christian gentleman, and eminently within that class "Whose names over earth will evermore resound upon the wings of the years."

He is buried at the little church upon the hill referred to, his grave marked by a marble grave vault with the following inscription:

"FRANCIS EUGENE HARRISON
BORN APRIL 13, 1826
DIED NOVEMBER 16, 1878."

Also, the following scriptural quotation:

"Blessed are the dead who die in the Lord, that they may rest from their labors and their works do follow them."

Andersonville Baptist Church

On September 6, 1839, the Baptist Church at Andersonville was constituted. Before it was constituted it was operating as an Arm of the Baptist Church of Double Springs.

From a history of this church, prepared by Mr. D. C. Alford some years ago, we make the following extracts:

The Arm at Andersonville met on Friday before the 2nd Lord's day in September, 1839.

Ministers present, Wm. McGee and David Simmons. After preaching by Wm. McGee, proceeded to business:

1st. Appointed Wm. McGee Moderator, and H. M. Barton Clerk. Read and received the letters of the joint members composing the Arm from Double Springs.

2nd. Called for letters, when Edward Carter presented a letter for himself and wife privileging them to unite themselves with the Arm at Andersonville, which was received.

3rd. Bros. McGee and Simmons formed a Presbytery, and after having examined the members composing the Arm and having found them othodox, constituted them a Church of the Baptist Faith and Order by the name of the Baptist Church at Andersonville, S. C.

Certified this 6th day of September, 1839.

WM. MCGEE, *Moderator.*
H. M. BARTON, *Clerk.*

The following named persons were received and composed the charter members of the church:

John Smith, Elisha Dyar, Sampson Bobo, Henry Brown, Sarah Dyar, Kiziah Smith, Elizabeth Bobo, Margaret Smith, Mary Brown, Sarah Harrison, Elizabeth Reed, Rhoda Reed.

The first record found, January, 1840, is that Henry Brown was elected Church Clerk, and the 2nd Sabbath in July was set apart for the communion, and the messengers, Brethren John Smith and Sampson Bobo to Reed Creek (Ga.) and Edward Carter and Henry Brown to Double Springs, to petition the churches to commune with them.

The first deacons elected were Henry Brown and Sampson Bobo on September 11, 1841, and were not ordained until August, 1843, by the following: Rev. E. D. Simmons, Samuel Fant; Deacons F. Herrin, T. Jones and J. Bradberry, composing the Presbytery.

It seems that there was no record of business from 1846 to 1869.

Served as pastors for the church:

Samuel Fant, ... Huchens, ... Stone, Thomas Dawson, H. M. Barton, W. R. Goss, J. T. W. Vernon, Samuel Isbel, Asa Avery, Benj. Thornton, Mike McGee, J. R. Earle, L. W. Tribble, W. H. King.

As a matter of fact other pastors have served the church, but we do not have their names. Rev. Fred Fowler is the present pastor (1930), and the membership is about 85.

The original location of the church house was between the Tugaloo River and the road, or street, leading from the bridge across Little Beaverdam Creek on towards the Seneca River ferry, with the front facing the road, or street. After it had stood here for a number of years it was removed to the top of the hill, the present location, and as was said a few years ago by Prof. Solomon M. Bobo in describing the location of the church: "On the summit of a high hill, surrounded by a grove of spruce and cedar, a little church keeps vigil over the silent hills and foam-flecked rivers below. Beside it is an old graveyard. The wife of Jesse Mercer, founder of Mercer University, is buried here. A small mound with a cedar tree at the foot is all that marks her last resting place. Dr. Mercer was traveling through Andersonville in September, 1826, when his wife became ill and died at the old Earle home."

Since the above paragraph was spoken by Prof. Bobo, the grave of the wife of Dr. Mercer has been marked by a small concrete head and footstone, with the name and date of death roughly scrawled upon the headstone, and while those who placed this marker at her grave are to be commended for their humble tribute of respect, it is to be regretted that the Baptist denomination has not long since placed a marker at her grave in keeping to some extent with the great work Jesse Mercer has done for the Baptist denomination.

The name of Jesse Mercer's wife, before her marriage, was Miss Sabina Chivers. She died at Andersonville on September 23, 1826, in the 53rd year of her age, and it is hoped that the Baptists of Georgia in particular, and the Baptists of the country in general, will at no distant time mark her grave in a substantial way.

On July 24, 1889, Andersonville had its most distinguished visitor, in Henry Woodfin Grady, and the largest concourse of people that ever assembled there in its history.

After the ceremonies of the introduction were completed, in which several speakers from the two states, Georgia and South Carolina, took part, Mr. Grady proceeded to make his speech, which from start to finish abounded in lofty flights of eloquence and silver-tongued oratory. From a newspaper report of the occasion, we reproduce the following paragraphs:

After a pleasant allusion to the beautiful natural scenery amid which the meeting was held, Mr. Grady proceeded with an eloquent and elaborate discussion of the practical questions that then confronted the American people. He emphasized three important dangers that then menaced the greatness, perpetuity, and happiness of this country, to wit:

1. The building up of cities at the expense of the rural or country population.
2. The large number and enormous extent of mortgages held by Northern companies over the farming lands of the country.
3. The great danger resulting from trusts, syndicates and plutocrats, who were enabled to successfully ply their work to the injury of the people, on account of the support and acquiesence of the party then in power whose trend was toward centralization.

From the first bugle note of his clarion voice till his well-rounded peroration had died upon the air, his large audience was held spellbound. Commanding in expression, graceful in attitude, and musical in diction, Mr. Grady stood before "the sea of upturned faces before him," every inch an orator. When painting the iniquities of centralization and oppression of the people, his bright eyes flashed with indignation, his great heart swelled with feeling, and he seemed like Vulcan, in his armory, forging thunderbolts for the gods. And then the speaker would pass to the tender theme of the South's noble women and her high and exalted mission, and painted true happiness, true greatness, and true nobility as dwelling at last in the homes of the people, a smile bright as a sunbeam would light up his eloquent face, his voice would become subdued with emotion, and his eloquence float over his large audience and die out on the still summer air as the gentle wave of murmuring ocean breaks on the shore when the storm is passed.

In the course of his speech, and in line with the subject matter outlined in the foregoing paragraphs, he took occasion to repeat in his inimitable way that great production of his matchless brain, entitled, "The Homes of the People," which is as follows:

"I went to Washington the other day, and I stood on the Capitol Hill; my heart beat quick as I looked at the towering marble of my country's Capitol, and a mist gathered in my eyes as I thought of its tremendous significance; the armies and the treasury; the judges and the President; the Congress and the courts, and all that was gathered there. And I felt that the sun in all its course could not look down on a better sight than that majestic home of a republic, which had taught the world its best lessons on liberty. And I felt that if honor and wisdom and justice abided therein, the world would at least owe that great house in which the ark of the covenant of our country is lodged, its final uplifting and its regeneration.

"But a few days later, I visited a quiet country home. It was just a simple, modest home, sheltered by big trees and encircled by meadow and field, rich with the promise of harvest. The fragrance of the pink and of the hollyhock in the front yard was mingled with the aroma of the orchard and of the garden, and resonant with the cluck of poultry and the hum of bees.

"Inside the house were thrift, comfort, and the friendliness which is next to godliness. There was the old clock that had held its steadfast place amid the frolic of weddings, that had welcomed in steady measure every new-comer to the family, that had kept company with the watches at the bedside, and that had ticked the solemn requiem of the dead. There were the big, restful beds and the open fireplace, and the old family Bible, thumbed with the fingers of hands long since still, and blurred with the tears of eyes long since closed, holding the simple annals of the family and the heart and conscience of the home.

"Outside the house stood the master, a simple, upright man, with no mortgage on his roof, and no lien on his growing crops; master of his lands and master of himself. Nearby stood his aged father, happy in the heart and the home of his son. And as they started to the house, the old man's hand rested on the young man's shoulder, laying there the unspeakable blessing of the honored and grateful father and ennobling it with the knighthood of the fifth commandment.

"And as they reached the door, the old mother came with the sunset falling on her face, and lighting up her deep, patient eyes, while her lips, trembling with the rich music of her heart, bade her husband and her son welcome to their home. Beyond was the good wife, happy amid her household cares, clean of heart and conscience, the buckler and the helpmate of her husband. Down the lane came the children, trooping home after the cows, seeking as truant birds do the quiet of their home nest.

"And I saw the night descend on that home, falling gently as from the wings of the unseen dove. And the old man, while a startled bird called from the forest, and the trees thrilled with the cricket's cry, and the stars were swarming in the bended sky, called the family around him and took the Bible from the table and read the old, old story of love and faith. He then called them to their knees in prayer, and the little baby hid in folds of its mother's dress while he closed the record of that simple day by calling down God's blessings on their simple home.

"And while I gazed, the vision of the great marble Capitol faded from my brain. Forgotten were its treasure and its splendor. And I said, 'Oh, surely here in the homes of the people are lodged at last the strength and the responsibility of this government, the hope and the promise of this Republic.'"

The Perry and Bynum Duel Fought on the Island in Tugaloo River at Hatton's Ford, August 16, 1832.

WE HAVE read several accounts of the duel fought on the island at Hatton's Ford, more or less conflicting.

Major Benjamin F. Perry was a resident of Greenville, S. C., and opposed the secession of the southern or Confederate States from the Union, and also opposed nullification. He edited a newspaper called, according to one of the accounts, the *Mountaineer*. In his writings and in his speeches he did not mince words to express his opinions upon the issues which were so prominent before and up to the War Between the States, and which with other issues of a national character culminated in the war.

John C. Calhoun was an advocate of nullification and state rights, and had a large following in South Carolina as well as in the other southern states.

By Perry's attitude upon the issues he became quite obnoxious to the people of South Carolina, as it was a state that was overwhelmingly in favor of the principles advocated by John C. Calhoun, their favorite son, and other leaders in the South.

His antagonist, Turner Bynum, who was said to have been a professional duelist, was imported for the express purpose of putting Mr. Perry out of the way, and edited a rival paper called the *Greenville Sentinel*.

Following we give some extracts from the different accounts which we have read:

"These two men differed in political beliefs, and as was the custom of the times, their argument was settled at ten paces with pistols. A sandy spot under the spreading limbs of an old oak tree, on a small island in the Tugaloo River, was the scene of the tragic end of their dispute.

"'Nullification' was the issue over which they disagreed. Perry was a staunch unionist and Bynum was a fiery nullifier and follower of John C. Calhoun, one of the foremost advocates of states' rights.

"Perry, who is described as 'a bold and fearless man,' was then editing the *Greenville Mountaineer*. He opposed John C. Calhoun's views, and by his vigorous articles he began to win a following.

"At this time Turner Bynum, Esq., 'a brilliant writer,' and also 'a brave man,' and a staunch believer in nullification, became editor of the *Greenville Sentinel*. Following Bynum's arrival, Greenville voters were addressed by two of the fieriest writers in South Carolina. As each editor grew more and more personal in their remarks, it soon became evident that their dispute would take them to the field of honor.

"Finally, Perry issued a challenge, and a day, place and seconds were named.

"At the appointed time, Perry and Bynum rowed out to the island in Tugaloo River, each accompanied by his seconds. They fought at ten paces. At the signal, Perry fired first. Bynum then fired, and his ball tore a hole through the breast of Perry's coat, exposing the red lining.

"Colonel Huger, a prominent South Carolinian who stood near Bynum, exclaimed: 'He's got it.' Bynum replied: 'I have, too.'

"The ball from Bynum's pistol hit exactly where he had told his friends it would—on Perry's coat lapel. But the coat was a very loose fit and the bullet merely grazed the skin, leaving a blue streak across the body.

"Perry's missile went through Bynum's thigh, cutting the main artery and mortally wounding him. He was carried to the home of Mr. Price nearby, where he bled to death the following day. Until the home was torn down, many years later, the stains of Bynum's blood remained on the floor, a constant reminder of the tragedy."

(Note: The home referred to was at the crossroads where the Hatton's Ford and Earle's Bridge road crossed the Andersonville and Townville road, and was at one time, probably at the time of the duel, the home of Mr. Mathew Martin. Mr. Harrison Price lived there many years afterwards, and Mr. Price evidently was not born until after the time of the duel.)

"Bynum's body was buried in the graveyard of historic 'Old Stone Church,' three miles from Pendleton, S. C. There had been a very heavy rain, the streams were swollen and much difficulty was experienced by those in charge of the funeral. They did not reach the grave until about midnight, at which gloomy hour the mortal remains of this brilliant young man were lowered into a grave half filled with water.

"The two pine poles that had been laid across the grave upon which to rest the coffin were driven into the ground after the funeral, one at the foot of the grave and one at the head. These two poles grew and became large pine trees, standing as faithful sentinels to keep watch over the sacred spot. In recent years some one ruthlessly destroyed the stately pines. However, the old stumps are there today.

"The late A. C. Campbell, who lived about a mile from Old Stone Church, was present at the burial, and during the ceremony of lowering the body a valuable diamond ring slipped from his finger and fell into the grave. The ring was buried with Bynum, since Mr. Campbell had no way of recovering it from the water. Mr. Campbell, long since dead, often told the story of the duel and of Bynum's burial, stating that to his own personal knowledge the pines over the grave sprouted from the bare poles.

"Bynum, who was born in Charleston, S. C., was scarcely 28 years of age when he was killed. Although so young, he had already made a marked impression on the political history of his time. He is described as 'a young man of unusually brilliant intellect and scholarly attainments.' His friend and second, the Hon. James H. Hammond, in writing to Bynum's widowed mother of the tragic duel, said: 'I feel the full force of the affliction. His country has much to lament, for his talents were rapidly ripening into eminent usefulness. The loss will not soon be supplied.'

"Bynum was not married. He was survived by his mother and one brother, Alfred, who was a poet as well as a lawyer. Soon after the duel Alfred Bynum went to Texas and joined the army then being organized to fight for Texas' independence. His regiment was captured by Mexicans and massacred at Goliad, Texas, by order of General Santa Anna.

"Benjamin F. Perry, the survivor of the duel, had attracted little attention before he took over the *Mountaineer* in 1832. Then his virile editorials immediately aroused interest in the Greenville district, and he soon became a national figure.

"He seldom referred to his fatal duel with Bynum, and then only to express regret at the tragic outcome of that affair and to explain that he engaged in the duel only because he felt that no other course was left to him.

"Perry clung to his beliefs in a strong, centralized government up to the time of the Democratic Convention in 1860, and he gained so many followers among the mountaineers of the Greenville district that he continued as a member of the State Legislature from 1832 until the outbreak of the War Between the States.

"But when his state seceded, Perry seceded with her. During the conflict he served as Confederate Commissioner, District Attorney, and Judge of the Confederate States Court. At the close of the war a group of influential South Carolinians sent a petition to President Andrew Johnson, recalling Perry's strong union tendencies in the three decades before 1860. The President listened to the plea, and on June 13, 1865, Benjamin F. Perry was appointed Provisional Governor of South Carolina by Presidential Proclamation. He served in that capacity until October 18 of the same year, when James L. Orr was duly elected Governor.

"Perry continued to live in Greenville, and was buried at Sans Souci. His old home is standing today, and until a few years ago was used as a club house.

"In Walhalla, S. C., the county seat of Oconee County, a monument was unveiled about fifty years ago to the memory of Benjamin F. Perry, one of the South's most unusual men—gentleman, duelist, editor, unionist, Confederate, barrister, judge, statesman and governor."

Following we give, in part, another article written just a few years ago:

"The young men of Greenville imported Bynum, put him to editing a revolutionary newspaper with the deliberate intention of so insulting Perry, that according to the notions of that time, a duel between the two was inevitable—I think however that they were unsuccessful in provoking Perry to challenge Bynum, therefore Bynum had to take offense at some of Perry's newspaper articles and send him a challenge, which of course, public opinion being what it was at that time, Perry could not refuse—hence the meeting at Hatton's Ford. They met at sunset, or what would have been sunset had there shone a sun that day; but it was a very dark, rainy, miserable day. To the consternation of the real instigators of the trouble, at the command to fire it was Bynum, not Perry, who fell mortally wounded. His friends took him up dead, for he died almost immediately, and without any ceremony hustled him into a shallow grave just outside of the burial ground of the Old Stone Church near Pendleton. It is said that after covering over the grave they stuck a pine pole, part of the bier on which they had carried him, at the head and at the foot of the grave, and that both the poles, freshly cut, and stuck immediately into the wet ground, took root and grew into trees which stood for many years, marking the spot where Turner Bynum rests. Even they are gone now, though the grave is included within the cemetery walls, the graveyard having been enlarged at some period since Bynum's death. About those pines great controversy has raged. There is no man living now who was present at Bynum's interment, but for many years some one of those who bore the body to its resting place would curse and vehemently vouch for the truth of the statement.

"I was present some years ago at a meeting held by the Daughters of the American Revolution at the Old Stone Church when this very matter was under discussion. Mr. J. C. Stribling, then of Pendleton, was asked to make a talk, and he stated that several years prior to that time he was a member of a committee appointed to clean off the old graveyard—several persons interested in the cemetery petitioned that the two tall pines over Bynum's grave be cut down, as they menaced the safety of tombstones, in that in the first place they darkened the marble of the grave stones, and moreover, they were so tall that it was certain that in some storm they would fall and break the monuments on which they would fall, so as no voice was raised in protest, the pines came down. Then the question was asked whether pines could ever grow from cuttings. Dr. Brackett, of Clemson College, who had just completed a history of the Old Stone Church, was asked for his opinion. He said that in regard to those very pines, he had consulted an eminent botanist whose reply was that he would not say that a pine never would grow from a cutting, because science was constantly making new discoveries and performing undreamed of miracles, but he would say that so far, no pine has been known to grow from a cutting.

"Governor Perry lived for many years after the duel, but he would never discuss it. While opposed to secession, when South Carolina seceded he went with her, as many other of her eminent sons did. During reconstruction times, when a strong man was very necessary as Governor of South Carolina, those in authority remembered Perry's anti-secession attitude and he was appointed to the position, which he filled satisfactorily to all parties."

Note: It will be noted that in the first article which we have copied that the statement is made that Perry challenged Bynum, and in the part of the last story copied, the statement is made that Bynum challenged Perry, and from all the circumstances as recorded it is very probable that last statement is correct.

It is also recorded in the first story that Perry was buried at Sans Souci, his estate near Greenville.

It is our information lately obtained that Perry was buried in the cemetery of the Episcopal Church in the City of Greenville.

"*Hartwell Sun*, December 10, 1886.

"Hon. Benj. F. Perry Dead.

"Hon. Benj. F. Perry, of Greenville, S. C., died Saturday, last (December 4, 1886), aged 81. He has been a prominent figure in South Carolina politics for sixty years, and before the war was a strong Union man and faithfully predicted the result of secession, rendering himself for a time obnoxious to the people he loved most; but when his State seceded, stood to her with all the fervor of a loving son. Over fifty years ago he engaged in a duel against his desire and better judgment, forced to do so by the barbarious sentiment of the times, on the island at Hatton's Ford in this county, and killed his antagonist, Bynum, who was said to have been a professional duelist, imported for the express purpose of putting Mr. Perry out of the way. Mr. Perry was a man of the highest order of intellect and integrity of character."

King's Bench

AT THE place of the late residence of W. W. Wilson, on the old Andersonville and Carnesville road, there was at one time in the early days of Franklin County and up until Hart County was created, a court ground and company muster ground, and known as "King's Bench." The militia district in Franklin County, of which King's Bench was the court ground, was known as the 214th District, Georgia Militia, and was at one time known as Captain Conner's District, who was Captain of the Company. The captains were changed from time to time, and consequently the name of the district was changed to that of the captain in command of the company, though the official number remained the same.

The 214th District, G. M., of Franklin County, embraced all of the present district of Reed Creek, all of the area of Alford's and Town districts north of Big Lightwoodlog Creek, which was at that time the county line between Franklin and Elbert (formerly Wilkes) counties, and the most, if not all, of the present district of Shoal Creek.

The land upon which the court ground and muster ground were located was granted to William King by Wm. Rabun, Governor of Georgia, on November 25, 1817. The tract of land so granted contained 650 acres. Whether the court ground was located here before the land was granted to Mr. King, we do not know. We have a record that Captain Conner was Captain in 1810, and it may be that the court ground was moved to King's Bench after Mr. King became in possession of the place.

At the place was a post office, known as King's Bench Post Office, established July 19, 1832, and William King, Jr., was the first postmaster. He was succeeded by Sterling Pinson on July 17, 1849, and the office moved to a different location.

William King was a Justice of the Peace in 1832, as it appears from the record of marriages of Franklin County that Joseph Coker and Cloe Bridges were married on November 25, 1832, by Wm. King, J. P.

Why the place was called "King's Bench," we are not sure, but there is a pretty well authenticated tradition that on public days liquors were sold at the place, as was common at all public places and on most all public occasions in those days, and that a large work bench was installed upon which the wares were placed and dispensed to the customers, and for this reason the place was called "King's Bench."

Hon. James M. Carter, in a letter written many years ago, and published in the *Hartwell Sun* at the time, says in part: "There was but one settlement from my father's house to King's Bench, a distance of ten miles. (Mr. Carter's father lived near where Big Lightwoodlog Creek enters Savannah River.)

"William King lived at the Bench. I do not know why this place was so called. I do know, however, this used to be what we called company muster ground. Our battalion muster ground was near Ford's Store. Our regimental muster ground was near Sam Knox's, north of where Lavonia is now located. I remember that Calvin Sanders was a Major. Our Colonel was William O'Barr, the father of Mitch. O'Barr, J. P., of Reed Creek District at present."

It was at this place, so we have been told, that one David Ayers was killed in a horse race. He and another man by the name of Burton decided to try out the speed of their horses and Ayers' horse became unmanageable and ran against a tree, killing him.

There is a tradition, to which we attach but little credence, to the effect that King's Bench at one time was the county seat of Franklin County.

It is a matter of record that Judge George Walton, one of the signers of the Declaration of Independence, held the first Superior Court in Franklin County. When Franklin County was established there were, of course, no place for holding Superior Court, no county seat, no place of public records, and no provision for the operation of the machinery of justice. There was a Superior Court in Georgia, but there was no Superior Court Circuit.

There was a Chief Justice in Georgia whose duty it was to hold Superior Courts in conjunction with the Assistant Justices of the Peace of the county.

The Justices of the Peace were appointed regularly and at the same time the Assistant Justices were appointed. The Assistant Justices, with the Chief Justice, held the Superior Courts in the counties. This procedure was in force till 1789, when the Western Circuit was created and provisions made for Superior Court Judges.

The first Chief Justice of Georgia was George Walton. He was chosen on February 4, 1783, at a salary of a thousand pounds a year (English money). It is interesting to note when and where the first Superior Court of Franklin County was held. If we have been correctly informed, it was held on Gum Log, near the present Davis School House, at the home of one Warren Philpot. It seems that it was the custom to hold the Superior Courts at different places over the county, and probably one such court, or maybe more than one term, may have been held at King's Bench, which, if true, perhaps gave rise to the tradition that King's Bench was at one time the county seat of Franklin County.

The possession of the place passed from Mr. King to his successors in title, and at one time the place was owned by John S. Henly, who kept a store, and perhaps other stores were kept at the place from time to time. John S. Henly was a local Methodist preacher and it is a matter of record that in the early years of Hart County he made the race for State Senator from Hart County, but was defeated.

It was at King's Bench that Capt. Wm. R. Poole's Company, known as Company "H" of the 15th Regiment of Georgia, was organized July 15, 1861. A complete muster roll of the company is given in another part of this history.

At or soon after the close of the War Between the States, Sanford Barron, a son of Barnabas Barron, and a son-in-law of Kintchen Phillips, taught school at King's Bench, who later moved to Alabama.

After the election of Hon. B. H. Pearman to the office of County School Superintendent in 1904, he, together with the members of the County Board of Education, and in accordance with an Act of the Legislature providing for the same, divided the county into local school districts, and local school tax was levied in each district for the support of the schools.

One of the districts was called King's Bench School District, No. 11, and the school house located at King's Bench, and school was taught there until the school district was merged with the Mt. Olivet Consolidated School District.

Joseph S. Chambers came into possession some time after that of Mr. Henly's place and lived there for a number of years. In addition to the store, or stores, and other business carried on at the place, there was a ginhouse on the place operated by horse power, as was common on many of the large farms of the country in those days, but which have long since gone the way of other picturesque items of the country landscape.

Thomas P. Carnes

THOMAS P. CARNES, whose name for a century or longer has been referred to as Thomas Peter Carnes, but by well-authenticated proof it appears that his name was Thomas Petters Carnes, and not Thomas Peter Carnes, as will be explained further on.

From Biographical Sketches we get a brief history of his ancestry. He was born in Bladensburg, Prince County, Maryland, in 1762, of English ancestry, his forefathers having come to Maryland in the Eighteenth Century. His early schooling was received in Maryland. He no doubt received his training in law in Maryland. He saw service in the Revolutionary War, and received a bounty in Franklin County for his services. He was admitted to the practice of law in Georgia in 1786, and represented Franklin County in the Executive Council the same year, which position corresponds to our present State Senate. Served several terms in the Georgia Legislature from Franklin County, viz.: 1786-1787, 1789, 1797, 1807, 1808.

He was commissioned Judge of the Superior Courts of the Western Circuit by Governor James J. Jenkins, and again in 1799, and in which connection his name appears as Thomas Petters Carnes, and in his will his name given the same way, while in signing documents he usually signed his name Thomas P. Carnes.

That Col. Carnes was a citizen of Franklin County, is evidenced from the fact, together with a number of other facts, that in delivering the charge to the Grand Jury of Franklin County in 1800, he commented on the lax moral conditions that existed in the county at that time and added that at times it almost deterred him from acknowledging himself a citizen of the county.

Carnesville, the county seat of Franklin, and the Carnes Road in Augusta were named for Thomas P. Carnes. The name Carnesville is found first in a Grand Jury presentment of 1797 in connection with a road the Grand Jury desired laid off and established. This road would lead from Carnesville to Petersburg and Augusta.

Col. Carnes was a member of Congress from March 4, 1793, to March 3, 1795. Was Attorney-General (Solicitor-General of the Western Circuit), 1790-1791-1792. He was Judge of the Western Circuit from January 27, 1798, to May 20, 1803, when he resigned. He was Judge of the Western Circuit from December 15, 1809, to November, 1810.

As a Judge he presided over courts over the entire State for a time. He served as Attorney-General for three years, and as such he also practiced law all over the State.

In addition to the bounty he received for his services, we have a record that he bought the bounties of Joseph Braswell, Henry Beall, Penman Floyd and Henry Davis, Revolutionary soldiers, of $287\frac{1}{2}$ acres each, making 1,150 acres of land, all located on Big Shoal Creek. He was also granted a tract of 410 acres on Fork Shoal Lightwoodlog Creek in 1810.

In 1809 Col. Carnes lived on Shoal Creek on the lands of the bounties mentioned of 1,150 acres.

In the Minutes of the Superior Court of Franklin County it is of record that Thomas P. Carnes entered a suit for damages against William Guy, of Elbert County, and William Chisholn, of Franklin County, for one thousand dollars. The amount was claimed against the defendants for breach of promise in building a sawmill.

In this suit it was alleged that the mill was to be built on the upper shoal of Shoal Creek near the residence of said Thomas P. Carnes in the county of Franklin. The upper shoal mentioned is where Jacob Parker & Co. later owned and operated a wool factory, and where now there is a mill belonging to L. A. Power. The suit and the full record of same, which we do not reproduce here, gives indisputable evidence that Thomas P. Carnes lived near Shoal Creek in 1809, and leaves a pretty good reason for surmising that he lived at this place for several years previous. Tracing this lead down, it is found that there is a current story around Parkertown handed down to the effect that Col. Carnes lived at the upper shoal of Shoal Creek for many years and that his law office stood on the roadside just west of the Parker old home place. Over on a knoll in the pasture they point out a cellar which was under the Carnes house, and also it is reported that his first wife was buried near his home. For many years the grave of his wife could be located.

It was a simple grave with simple uncarved stones at head and foot. The grave has disappeared now in a cotton patch, but the two stones have been cast aside and are still mute evidence to the passer by.

Col. Carnes was twice married. His first wife was Elizabeth Bostwick, a daughter of Captain Chesley Bostwick, who lived in St. Paul's Parish near Richmond County, Georgia.

To this marriage there was born at least three children. One was Dr. Robert Watkins Carnes, who lived a long time at Sparta. He represented Hancock County in the Legislature in 1830 and 1831. He was Clerk of the House of Representatives in 1832. He died in 1852.

Quite a number of his descendents live in Sparta now, among whom are Mrs. Sarah Smith Carnes, from whom some of the information for this story was obtained. Another son by first marriage was William W. Carnes. He was Comptroller General of Georgia in 1834 and 1835. He lived in Milledgeville. The date of his death is not known. A daughter by his first marriage was Ann Low, who died at some time before his will was written. She is referred to in his will.

His second wife was Susan Crews Carnes. Their marriage was in Milledgeville within the years 1807-8-9. He married after 1806 and they executed a deed together in Franklin County in 1809. She was living at the time his will was written and is mentioned as executor of his will. To this union were born five children: Thomas P. Carnes, Peter Johnson Carnes, Nancy Clarke Carnes, Richard Stanley Carnes, and Susan King Carnes.

There is another daughter, however, not mentioned in the will of Judge Carnes. Her name was Julia Carnes. She was married in 1808 to Augustin N. Clayton, for whom Clayton Street in Athens was named. A daughter of Col. and Mrs. Clayton, Augusta, married William King. Their daughter, Julia C., married Henry W. Grady, and another daughter, Augusta, married ex-Congressman Wm. M. Howard, now living in Augusta.

Col. Clayton read law in Augusta in the law offices of Judge Carnes, and after his marriage to Miss Julia Carnes they moved to Athens.

A story about Col. Carnes, which has been current in Franklin County and other parts of the country for one hundred years or more, is the story of his connection with the Beaufort Treaty, which settled the boundary dispute of the northern boundary of Georgia and the eastern boundary north of the junction of Seneca and Tugaloo rivers. The story goes that Col. Carnes was a member of the Beaufort Commission, and that while in Beaufort, S. C., with the other members of the commission, he became infatuated with the women and wine he found at Beaufort, that in a convivial mood, he signed away Georgia's right and title to that part of Georgia and Franklin County known as the fork section which now lies in South Carolina between Seneca and Tugaloo rivers.

The fact is that Col. Carnes was not even a member of the Beaufort Commission. The commission was composed of six men, three from Georgia and three from South Carolina. The members from Georgia were: John Houston, James Habersham, and Lachlan McIntosh. Those from South Carolina were: Charles Cotesworth Pinckney, Andrew Pickens, and Pierce Butler. Only Habersham and McIntosh attended from Georgia. John Houston, for some reason unknown to the writer, failed to attend. All of which will fully appear by reference to the Beauford Treaty, a copy of which appears elsewhere. By reference to Col. Carnes' charges to grand juries, it is quite evident that he was adverse to any such discipations as referred to in the story. Col. Carnes' charges to the grand juries while he was Judge of the Western Circuit were of a high ideal and characteristic of the man he was.

Col. Carnes was a Justice of the Peace in Franklin County in 1788, and a member of the commission to settle the boundary dispute between North Carolina and Georgia in 1806, and did distinguished work for his State in the settlement of the dispute.

It was perhaps his connection with this commission which caused the connection of his name with the Commission of Beaufort and the Beaufort Treaty. There was a dispute for several years between Georgia and North Carolina about the location of the 35th degree of north Latitude, which had been decided on as the northern boundary of Georgia.

The commission appointed from Georgia, of which Col. Carnes was a member, was to survey this line across the northern border of the State. The other members of the commission from Georgia were Thomas Flourney and William Barnett. The commission from Georgia complained often and persistently about the instruments in use by the surveyors. The survey was finally completed. Many years later it was learned that the line deflected four miles too far south of the northwestern corner of Georgia, thus leaving Chattanooga in Tennessee, when it would and should have been in Georgia.

When Col. Carnes moved to Georgia he was admitted to the bar and practiced law in Milledgeville. He at one time lived in Augusta and at another in Athens, and evidently was a resident of Athens at the time of his death as his will is recorded there.

He died at Milledgeville, Ga., May 5, 1822, and to the best of our information, he was buried in the cemetery at Milledgeville.

Parkertown

THE village of Parkertown was founded in 1832 in Franklin (later Hart) County by a family of the name of Parker and from which it derived its name.

The forefather of the Parker family was Joseph A. Parker, born April 17, 1774, and moved from Virginia to Georgia and settled in Elbert (later Hart) County, as early as 1796.

He married Barbra Redwine, a daughter of Jacob Redwine. To Joseph

A. Parker and his wife, Barbra Redwine Parker, were born six sons, viz.: John D., Benjamin B., Jacob, Wm. H., Lewis and J. Hubbard Parker; and two daughters, viz.: Polly, who married Joel Ledbetter, and Miss Betty, who was never married.

Joseph A. Parker's wife, Barbra, was born June 3, 1797, and died May 19, 1845, and is buried in the old cemetery at Redwine Church.

Joseph A. Parker died November 12, 1860, and is buried at Providence Methodist Church.

Joseph A. Parker and family moved from the Redwine community and settled on Big Shoal Creek, where three of the sons, viz.: John D., Benjamin B., and Jacob, a partnership known as Jacob Parker & Co., purchased a large tract of land containing 1,400 acres, composed partly of a tract formerly owned by Thomas P. Carnes and partly of a portion of a 5,000-acre tract granted by the State to the University of Georgia. The lands included two shoals of valuable water power.

Jacob Parker & Co. built a wool factory on the upper shoal, where Thomas P. Carnes once owned a sawmill.

At the lower shoal they built a stone dam at a cost of $2,000 and had a grist and flouring mill, which was the pioneer of its kind and was the most complete in north Georgia. In addition to the grist and flouring mill, they operated a cotton gin, thresher, and perhaps other machinery. They also engaged in merchandising and farming, and in ante-bellum days owned a number of slaves.

There was a post office at the place known as Parker's Store Post Office supplied with mail by a star route from Carnesville, Ga., to Pendleton, S. C.

The homes of John D., Jacob and Benjamin B. Parker were all near each other, village like. The home of John D. Parker was located on the west side of the creek at the intersection of the public road leading out by Shoal Creek Church with the Carnesville road. The home of Jacob Parker was a short ways up the Carnesville road from that of John D., and above the mill, on the east side of the road and between the road and the creek. The mill was on the west side of the creek, between the residences of John D. and Jacob Parker, and the home of Benjamin B. Parker was on the east side of the creek about opposite that of Jacob Parker, near the intersection of the public road that led out by Providence Church with the Carnesville or Andersonville road.

These old homes are still standing, though in a much delapidated condition, while the waters of Shoal Creek which once drove the wheels of industry for a round of years now sing a requiem of a vanished splendor and a glorious past.

The three Parker brothers had all things in common, as will appear from a newspaper article published many years ago, and which we herewith reproduce in part:

Parker Brothers

"There is a firm in Hart County, known as the Parker Bros., who have conducted a business at Parker's Store for the last forty-five years. The brothers are named John D. Parker, age 79 years; B. B. Parker, Senior, age 76 years; and Jacob Parker, age 73 years.

"These brothers have during the long period mentioned had all their property in common, each one has raised large and respectable families and an unkind word or even thought has never been known among them. John D. Parker, the senior member of the firm, is now in his dotage and in declining years.

"Their names have for years been the synonym of honesty and gentlemanly bearing. The junior member of this firm was in Toccoa the other day, and although he is 73 years of age, yet he moves and attends to business like a man in his prime. The co-partnership property of these brothers consist in part of a very fine flouring mill which was burned down just after the war, but has since been rebuilt."

In connection with the mention of the mill being destroyed by fire, we will state a fact that is more or less interesting. At the time the mill was burned down there was no money in the country, or any banks or other institutions from which money could be secured. The War Between the States had just recently ended and all Confederate money was worthless and of no value.

Peter E. Burton, who had wisely held a lot of cotton during the war, sold it for a good price and received payment in gold, which he kindly loaned to Jacob Parker & Co. with which to rebuild their mill, which was quite an accommodation to them as well as to the people generally who were very much inconvenienced on account of the destruction of the mill.

For a fuller history of these three brothers, we give further on the obituary of each, written by competent writers who were familiarly acquainted with them, as from these obituaries a more complete history is to be had than if we were to undertake to weed out just certain portions and write it in condensed style.

Lewis Parker settled near Providence Church, where he engaged in farming. He was a mill-wright, being of a mechanical turn of mind, and was successful both as a farmer and machinist.

Wm. H. Parker was a teacher and moved to Fulton County, Ga.

J. Hubbard Parker settled near Shoal Creek Church, where the Knox Bridge, formerly the Cleveland's Ferry road, now the Stone Mountain Highway, and the public road leading from Parkertown on up into Franklin County cross. He owned and operated a large farm and also engaged in the practice of medicine.

For many years Parkertown was an educational center for this part of Georgia, where many of our distinguished men received their higher education.

The first school in the community was known as Pulliam's Academy, and later located at Parkertown and known as Shoal Creek Academy. The school at Parkertown was famous all over northeast Georgia. It is said that the school building was the first in this section to be fitted with glass windows. It was built in 1845 and the first teacher was C. H. Spears, a pupil of Cecil Hammond, a graduate of Yale, who taught a school at Carnesville, Ga., for years.

Spears taught the school one year and was succeeded by Morgan H. Looney, a classmate of his in Hammond's school.

After Morgan H. Looney had taught the school for several years, Hon.

B. B. Parker took charge of the school. He, assisted by his wife, successfully taught the school for many years.

Among the men who followed Mr. Parker as principal of the school were: Jno. D. Brown, F. M. Taylor, Lewis B. Gaines, R. M. Harrison, Prof. "Pet" Stribling, and others.

There were, and still are, two churches within easy reach of Parkertown. Shoal Creek, Baptist, and Providence, Methodist. Providence organized in 1815 and Shoal Creek many years before—in fact we have no date as to when Shoal Creek Church was organized.

Parkertown in its halycyon days, with its magnificent homes, stores, shops, mills and other buildings, including "The School House on the Hill," was a picturesque village and presented a very business-like aspect, and while the hum of industry was wafted upon the breezes, devotion to the service of God was of first consideration of the church people—and withal there pervaded Parkertown and community an atmosphere of culture and refinement similar in way to that of Athens of Greece in the zenith of its classic glory.

Obituary of John D. Parker

Brother John D. Parker, a venerable father in Israel, was removed from the church militant to the church triumphant, on the 29th of March, 1878, in the 80th years of his age.

In early life he professed religion and joined the M. E. Church, and from this time to the day of his death he continued to manifest the desire of salvation by doing "no harm," and "by doing good," both to the bodies and souls of men, so much so, that he was a model Christian. He loved the Church of Christ, especially the branch of it to which he belonged. He loved her institutions and ordinances.

For over fifty years he held the office of class leader, and was for the most of the time a steward. As a class leader, he was very efficient, watching closely after the spiritual interest of those committed to his care, and if any one of his class should in any way violate the laws of the church, or go astray in any way, he set himself to work at once to restore such a one; and if by prayers and exhortations he failed to restore him, he at once brought him before the church—always with the loving kindness. With dram drinkers or drunkards in the church, he had little patience. As a steward he was faithful, discharging his duty acceptably. He made it a rule for many years at the fourth quarterly conference to ask, "What is our church behind?" and if there was any deficiency, would invariably foot the bill. As a citizen he was highly esteemed. Being a man of sound judgment, his neighbors sought his counsel in almost all of their differences; and his godly counsels were almost invariably heeded and obeyed. In the pursuits of the secular business of life he was diligent and strictly honest. By the strict observance of the "golden rule," he but seldom, if ever, had a bitter feeling against him, although his business caused him to have to deal, more or less, with all classes of men. He was blessed with almost uninterrupted health, being very robust and active up to some five years past, when his physical and mental powers began to give way. For the past two years he had but little mind left; but in all of his mental deficiency he never forgot the

Church of God—would often go to the church through the week, and never failed to go on the regular church day and be in his place in due time. He seemed conscious that his time was drawing very near, and for several days previous to his death he spoke of his approaching end. The day he died, and before any one knew that he was any worse than common, the vigor of mind returned to him, and he talked with his son of his death; said he was going to heaven. Thus passed away this holy man, leaving his aged and much afflicted wife and several children, brothers and sisters, and numerous friends, to mourn their loss, all of whom have our sympathies and prayers.

W. T. N.

Obituary of Rev. Benjamin Blanton Parker

Parker.—Rev. Benjamin Blanton Parker was born in Elbert County, Ga., October 3, 1800, and died April 9, 1887.

Joseph Parker, his father, from Virginia, settled in Elbert (now Hart) County, as early as 1798, where he reared a family of eight children, six sons and two daughters. John D., Benjamin, and Jacob formed a business partnership in 1832, bought property, and settled on Shoal Creek. Their homes were near each other, village like, having a good mill and farming interest and for a number of years, sold goods. From this date the lives of these brothers were so intimate that to write of one necessarily includes, more or less, the others. The subject of this notice joined the Methodist Church in 1817, under the ministry, possibly, of Rev. Wm. Redwine. In 1832, he, with his brothers, moved his membership from Redwine to Providence Church, some twelve miles above, near their new home. This church was then in the Broad River Circuit, a small log house, erected as early, possibly, as 1815 by James and John B. Wade, local ministers and cousins; Mary and Elizabeth, sisters of James, "assisting with their own hands to raise it." At this place Uncle Benjamin had his membership for fifty-five years, during which time he helped to build two houses on the old site. The first in 1842 or 1843, the second in 1870. Here he preached and labored much; here many of his loved ones were converted and added to the church.

Here the remains of father, three brothers, and many others dear to him, sleep, and here, too, his own body, weary and worn, was laid to rest. He was thrice married, first to Miss Sarah Wilson, 1834, who died in 1835, leaving one son. Miss Letitia Glenn became his wife in 1838. She died in February, 1847; four daughters still live. His last wife was Miss Jane Tyler; they were married in November, 1848. She, too, preceded him to the grave; her death occurred August, 1870. One son and two daughters are living. In 1815, Danby P. Jones, the great apostle of temperance, was the pastor of Joseph Parker and family. It is no wonder, then, that Benjamin and his brothers became temperance advocates, by precept and example, when quite young. A drunken man at Parkertown, their home, was seldom seen. Uncle Benjamin was licensed to preach September 15, 1840, Rev. W. J. Parks, presiding elder. He was an industrious preacher. His sermons were from the Book. He read our standards, loved and taught the doctrines of his church. "A workman that needeth not to be ashamed." He always prayed like he believed in something. His care for the sick and bereaved was prompt, thoughtful and tender. As a member of the firm, he was in constant contact with the public for more than fifty years. During this time hundreds of men were in his employ, from the skilled machinist to the common laborer. Yet no man was ever known to question his piety, or fail to respect him as a minister. The relation between the brothers was of unusual intimacy. They and their families in the same church, their children in the same school, owning and enjoying their property in common—never had but one pocket book. There was a marked individuality in each; their eyes sparkled, but not in anger; never a hasty word, never the least estrangement ever occurred. The devotion of Jonathan and David was no more beautiful than that existed between these brothers during an entire lifetime—(all now deceased). Just how it was done I can not tell, but this I know, what one said the others believed, what one did the others endorsed. "Behold how good and how pleasant it is for brethren to dwell in unity." In this relation Uncle Benjamin's piety went without a question—was never at a discount.

Feebleness incident to age retired him from business. In the quiet home, without a murmur, he spent several of the last years of his life. His long pilgrimage came to its close as quietly as the evening shades come on. Too feeble to sit up, free from pain, he excused himself from further conversation because of a cough, turned slightly in bed, remarked "All's right," and in a moment the weary wheels of life stood still.

JOHN R. PARKER.

Obituary of Jacob Parker

Once more the insatiable enemy of the human race has made a demand, and Death's unerring shaft has stricken a husband, a father, and a friend.

Jacob Parker, after an illness of two weeks of typhoid fever, passed quietly and peacefully away at 10 o'clock on the morning of the 6th of September, aged 77. He was a member of the Methodist Church 60 years. The first thought that comes crashing in upon us, and absorbs every other, is our loss —our great loss. We look around and find no one to whom we can go for that wise counsel, affectionate sympathy, and liberal aid which he was ever ready to give to those around him.

None ever applied for aid in vain. His heart was ever tender, his ear attentive, his hand ever open to the appeals of religion, of benevolence, and of charity. It was a sad hour for this community when his heart ceased to beat, and his hand, that had so long administered to the poor and needy, grew cold and still in death. His place in the family circle and his seat in the sanctuary are vacant; yet we have the consolation that he is "gathered home." How sweet the thought that he has already joined those on the other shore! So, while his death tells us of loss, and reminds us of duty, it also gives brighter hope and stronger faith. Therefore, let us go forward with fresh courage and quickened zeal in the discharge of every duty, so that when life's toils are over our end may be peaceful and happy like his.

P.

Mr. Nathan P. Cox, of Atlanta, married Miss Maud Parker, daughter of Seaborn P. Parker, son of Lewis Parker, and before his wife's death they spent their summer vacations every year at Parkertown, and the following poem was composed by Mr. Cox.

> "The verdant valleys form a feast,
> Rich to the eyes of man and beast,
> In broken lines against the skies,
> The lofty hills in grandeur rise:
> And at their base the stream that flows
> In graceful curves all speak repose.
> All nature seems joined in the plot
> To spend its best on this spot.
> I could not nurse my sorrows there:
> Nor could I cling to sordid care,
> My brow could never wear a frown
> In quiet, peaceful Parkertown.
>
> Each primitive old house that seems
> So changed with cherished hopes and dreams
> Of other lives and other days—
> Speak out to me in a thousand ways,
> Of noble men whose lives were spent
> In honest toil. Thus well content
> To serve their fellow men and God.
> And I would tread the paths they trod,
> Whose names reached higher than to fame;
> Pure hearts, clean lives, and honest name,
> Proud are the names they handed down,
> And proud of them is Parkertown."

Some of the Members of the Parker Family That Attained Distinction

Hon. Blanton B. Parker

Hon. Blanton B. Parker was a son of John D. Parker and wife, Nancy Merritt Parker.

As has been said of him, he in his boyhood days did what few boys of his time did. He obtained a good education and for many years was an educator of high repute. He was principal of the famous Parkertown School for a number of years, as already stated.

He married Miss Frances A. Looney, a daughter of Judge Noah Looney, and sister to the three great southern educators and distinguished brothers, Morgan H., George C., and Martin V. Looney. She was also a fine teacher and assisted her husband, Hon. B. B. Parker, in conducting the Parkertown School, as has also been stated.

Besides teaching, Mr. Parker was also engaged in farming, merchandising and other business enterprises.

To him and his wife were born four sons: Morgan L., Edgar A., Wm. H., and George M. Parker; and three daughters: Ellen, Fannie and Mollie.

In 1884 Mr. Parker was elected Representative from Hart County to the

Legislature, and again in 1886, serving two consecutive terms. It was during his first term in the Legislature that a petition, signed by a majority of the citizens, was presented to him requesting that a local Act be passed for Hart County known as the Stock or "No Fence" Law, which was passed and approved December 3, 1885, and became effective February 1, 1886.

In religion Mr. Parker was a member of the Methodist Church, and also belonged to the order of Free and Accepted Masons.

Mr. Parker's death occurred February 11, 1907, in the 78th year of his age, a newspaper account of which we give herewith.

"Hon. Blanton B. Parker died February 11, 1907, in the 78th year of his age. His body was laid to rest in the cemetery at Providence Methodist Church in this county, of which he was a faithful member, on Wednesday morning with Masonic honors by the Lavonia Lodge, of which he was a member, and the Hartwell Lodge.

"The funeral services were conducted by Rev. Jno. B. Yarbrough, pastor of the Lavonia Circuit, to which Providence Church belongs."

Morgan L. Parker

Morgan L. Parker, son of Hon. Blanton B. Parker, like his father, and also like his illustrious uncles, Morgan H., George C., and Martin V. Looney, has for three score years or longer been a teacher of high renown, and as has been said of him as a teacher in the high school, "is the peer of any in the South," as attested by his auto-biography of his career as a teacher, which we give herewith.

"Auto-Biography of Morgan Leonidas Parker Career as Teacher.

"Shoal Creek Academy, Assistant of B. B. Parker, one year; Fayetteville High School, Fayetteville, Ga., two and one-half years; Homer High School, Homer, Ga., three months; resigned to accept Harmony Grove Academy, ten years, in five-year periods; Hartwell High School, afterwards named Hartwell Institute, fifteen years in five-year periods; South Georgia Male and Female College, Dawson, Ga., three years; Alexander Free School, Macon, Ga., three years; Clayton High School, College Park, Ga., two years; resigned to accept Waynesboro Public School, three months' unexpired term; Fairplay High School, Fairplay, S. C., three months' unexpired term; Colloden High School, Colloden, Ga., one year; Parker's Private School of Individual Instruction, twelve years. Still in harness, eighty summers young.

"Positions of Honor.

"Taught mathematics in Peabody Institute, Lithia Springs, one session; lectured on education one session, Lithia Springs; taught mathematics in Grady Summer School, Lithia Springs, Ga., one session; conducted teachers' institutes in the following counties: Hart, five years; Elbert, one year; Franklin, three years; Oconee, three years; Fayetteville, one year; Meriwhether, two years; Jackson, five years, associated with Profs. Neal and Hunt.

"Elbert Hubbard advises not to retire too soon, or you will shuffle off this mortal coil before long after retirement, so I am holding on to my vocation; that of a pedagogue."

Old Home of Jacob Parker
Old Parker's Store Post Office
Old Home of Rev. Benj. B. Parker
Old Home of John D. Parker

Howell B. Parker

Howell B. Parker, son of Benjamin B. Parker, Sr., and wife, Jane Tyler Parker, was another that made a most enviable reputation. He was also the co-laborer of Prof. O. S. Fowler as a phrenologist and delivered interesting lectures on the subject. He was a man of original thought and lived and taught a life of strict temperance, self-denial and action.

With his wife, Minnie, herself a fine teacher, he taught school in many prominent towns in Georgia, and was building up a good one here when his useful life came to an untimely end from pneumonia.

Prof. Howell B. Parker, to the best of our information, died in Lavonia, Ga. He is buried in the cemetery at Providence Methodist Church, Hart County, Ga., his grave marked by an imposing monument with the following inscription:

"HOWELL B. PARKER, AUG. 5, 1855; DIED FEB. 4, 1897.
TEACHER, PHRENOLOGIST, CHRISTIAN HELPER."

Rev. John R. Parker

Nearly all the Parkers are Methodists and of religious bent.

John R. Parker, son of Dr. J. Hubbard Parker, was one of the most prominent members of the North Georgia Conference, having filled several stations and was a presiding elder.

Many of the members of the Parker family and their descendents have occupied prominent positions and followed various avocations, professional and otherwise, and to mention them all would require a voluminous record.

The Looney Family

JUDGE NOAH LOONEY, son of Robert and Mary Looney, was born November 30, 1799, and died October 26, 1876. He married Frances McNeil, born November 17, 1802, died September 3, 1889, both buried at Shoal Creek Church, Hart County, Ga., their graves marked by a marble monument on which is inscribed the foregoing dates of birth and death.

Judge Noah Looney once live in South Carolina, not far from Cleveland's Ferry, now Knox's Bridge, across the Tugaloo River, but later moved to Franklin County, Ga., and located at Parkertown.

Judge Looney by trade was a cabinet maker, contractor and builder.

To Judge Noah Looney and wife, Frances McNeil Looney, were born three sons: Morgan Harbin, George C., and Martin Van Buren Looney; and two daughters: Frances A. and Elizabeth Looney.

Morgan H. Looney, oldest son of Judge Looney, was born in South Carolina, but came to Parkertown when a mere boy.

Morgan H., George C., and Martin Van B. Looney, all became school teachers, and might have been very appropriately termed the three great southern educators and distinguished brothers. They set the pace and were instrumental in laying the foundation of our educational interests. They taught school all the way from South Carolina and Florida to Texas, and each at one time or another taught in Hartwell, Ga. From their schools went forth many men who have touched the world in no small way: ministers of the gospel, educators, legislators, lawyers, jurists and captains of finance and industry.

Morgan H. Looney

Morgan H. Looney was the author of text books, was an orator and poet, deserves to rank with other literary and poetical celebrities who have been signally honored in different ways and at different places, and in addition there is his matchless record as an educator.

Hon. Alexander H. Stephens said of him: "As an educator, Morgan H. Looney has no equal in the South." Governor Roberts, of Texas, called him "The Blackstone of America."

John H. Magill, who so long and so ably edited *The Hartwell Sun*, said of Morgan H. Looney, "Intellectually Prof. Looney was one of the most wonderful men we ever met. His genius was most versatile. In the vigor of his manhood he was an incomparable orator; as a poet he ranked in imagery, exalted sentiment, and delicacy of expression with Father Ryan, the southern poet-priest. We never knew one with a more retentive mind than his, and as a classical writer he stood without a peer. A reveler in the classics, he was ever ready with apt quotation upon demand.

"As an educator, however, his fame rests superbly, and here he was grandly successful. The great good he accomplished for the rising generation during his long career as a teacher is beyond computation."

Dr. B. C. Smith, of Elbert County, Ga., once said, "Morgan Looney was an accomplished scholar, with fine conceptions of the beauties of nature, and a deep philosopher in general affairs of life. With poetic trend of thought he was wont to waft in the starry realms of ethereal bliss; yet his eventful life led through shades of grief. His experimental knowledge in the various phases of human existence qualified him for impressing his classes the more forceably in his lectures, which pointed out the true standard of mankind. His unique extemporaneous lectures in the school room, if preserved in book form would constitute a library of universal knowledge, and probably embrace more wholesome counsel to young men than any yet written."

Marion F. Taylor, who once taught school at Parkertown, in an article written upon the death of Prof. Looney, said, among other things:

"A splendid poet, and, I am sorry to say, was not appreciated as a poetical genius deserved. Had the poem on 'The Odd Fellows' Chain' been written by A. H. Stephens, or Wordsworth, or Irving, it would have been awarded ten or fifteen thousand dollars; and it would be quite a deserved recompense for that fraternity, even now, to remember his children in a large donation, as he received nothing for it—one of the best poetical productions in the English tongue."

Morgan H. Looney died in Hartwell June 20, 1901, and is buried in the local cemetery, and it is to be regretted that his grave remains yet unmarked.

Morgan H. Looney deserves a monument in keeping with his great achievements, all of which is a rich heritage that the citizens of Hartwell and Hart County should preserve and perpetuate, as it is a source of county pride to be the native heath of such illustrious men as the Looneys.

George C. Looney

Prof. George C. Looney, second son of Judge Noah Looney and wife, was born February 6, 1836, and died Thursday, April 28, 1927, at his home on Highland Avenue, Atlanta, Ga., in the 92nd year of his age.

At the age of 12, Professor Looney began drumming arithmetic into the heads of pupils twice his size at a little school near Hartwell, Ga., and his more than three score and ten years of teaching turned out such pupils as Judge Hugh M. Dorsey, of the city court of Atlanta; his father, the late Judge Rufus Dorsey; Dr. Frank K. Boland, prominent Atlanta physician; and Professor Otis Ashmore, of Savannah, Ga., noted astronomer.

At the beginning of the War Between the States, Professor Looney exchanged his ruler for a sword and took time out to recruit a company near Palmetto, Ga. Entering the conflict as a captain, he was promoted to a colonel before the close of the war. After the war he returned to his profession, which he followed longer than the life of the average man; located at Fayetteville, where he was associated with the late Governor Allen D. Candler.

After several years at Fayetteville, he was brought to Atlanta to take the position as principal of the Southern Military Academy.

Wishing to put into practice certain educational theories which he had evolved, Professor Looney established the Angier Terrace School for Girls, on Capitol Avenue, and operated the school successfully for a number of years after leaving the Southern Military Academy.

At his last birthday, February 6, 1927, he received congratulations from many old pupils scattered throughout the United States.

Martin Van B. Looney

Martin Van B. Looney, youngest son of Judge Noah Looney and wife, was born February 17, 1841, and died April 2, 1911, and buried at Shoal Creek Church, Hart County, Ga., his grave marked by an imposing granite monument with the following inscription:

"Sacred to the memory of Martin Van B. Looney, born Feb. 17, 1841, died April 2, 1911. Teacher and Philanthropist. His hope in Jesus was his only guide, and in this precious hope he died."

Martin Van B. Looney, like his distinguished brothers, was a teacher of high renown and taught successfully for a number of years in Texas and also in Georgia, his native State. He married in Texas, his wife a member of the distinguished Culberson family of that state, who ably assisted him in teaching. Her given name was Achsah, and was always called by her pupils and others "Miss Achsah."

Martin Van B. Looney and wife taught school in Hartwell in 1873, and again in 1875-6-7, and it was said of them that no teachers that ever taught in Hartwell were ever more generally esteemed and more professionally admired than "Bud" and "Miss Achsah."

Mrs. Looney died January 22, 1901, at their home in Atlanta, Texas. After the death of his wife, Martin Van B. Looney returned to Georgia and taught school at Martin Institute, Martin, Ga., and at other towns in the State.

History of the Sanders Family

A SHORT distance above the Hartwell Railway trestle, and on the south, or right side of Big Lightwoodlog Creek, whose waters perpetually ripple and splash in their onward journey to the sea; on a green hillside where the violets bloom in rich profusion in the early springtime and where the beautiful goldenrod bends in the autumn breezes, is the site of an old pioneer home, near which is a neglected and abandoned family burying ground in which Elias Sanders and other members of his family sleep in graves marked by rude, unlettered stones—all forgetful of the world —and by the world long since forgotten.

This man, Elias Sanders, came in his youth from Maryland to Georgia, the date of his advent into this country we do not have. To the best of our information, he was born in 1775.

Tradition says that his father was a man probably of English descent, and his mother an Indian woman of the Plumer tribe.

After coming to Georgia he married Mary Carter, born in 1775, daughter of Thomas Carter.

We have in our possession, from the Secretary of the State, a certified copy of a plot of land containing 250 acres, granted to Elias Sanders in 1808, bounded on the north by Lightwoodlog Creek, which stream at that time was the line between Elbert and Franklin counties; east by lands of Henry Sanders; south by vacant lands; and west by lands of Jonathan Payne, all of said described tract lying and being in Elbert (now Hart) County, and on which is located the site of the old home and cemetery to which reference has been made.

To Elias Sanders and his wife, Mary Carter Sanders, were born six sons, viz.: Thomas Sanders, known as "Kit," Elias Sanders, Calvin P. Sanders, Samuel B. Sanders, Lewis Sanders and Jonathan P. Sanders; and three daughters, viz.: Rachael, Mary and Patience Sanders. We do not have the date of birth of any, therefore, we perhaps have not named them in the order of their birth.

From an article printed years ago in *The Hartwell Sun*, we make the following extracts relative to the location of the old home and graveyard:

"Last Sunday was a lovely day, and after Sunday School, there being no preaching in either of the churches, in company with Hon. B. F. Hodges, Prof. Parker, and W. R. Stephenson, we took a stroll over to the trestle a mile and a quarter from town. Mr. Hodges pointed to a hill on the left of the trestle and remarked, 'On that hill used to stand the house of Elias Sanders, the father of Tom, Calvin, Prep, &c.

" 'When Elias Sanders died at an advanced age, he was buried under the kitchen—suppose we go over there and see if we can find the grave.'

"We agreed, and found four graves with rude headstones with no marks and the dismantled chimney of the kitchen."

The members of the original Sanders family, as a rule, were of remarkable longevity and we herewith quote further from the article referred to written by Mr. John H. Magill:

"Tom (Kit) is now nearly 97, and his father, Elias, was near the same age when his spirit bade the hills adieu and mounted upward. Rev. Calvin

Sanders, recently deceased, was over eighty when he died. Mr. Hudges related the following incident concerning him: A dispute as to certain boundary lines was being tried in court, Judge Pottle presiding. Calvin Sanders was on the witness stand, and the question was asked, how long the land lying just below the trestle had been in cultivation. 'Sixty-eight years this spring,' answered the witness, a tall stalwart looking man with hair as black as a raven's wing and never a streak of gray. 'What did you say?' asked the Judge, doubting if he heard aright. 'Sixty-eight years,' came the answer promptly. 'How do you know this land was in cultivation for sixty-eight years?' 'Because sixty-eight years ago this spring I helped my father clear it.' 'How old are you, Mr. Sanders?' asked the astonished Judge. 'I am 78 years old.' The Judge said he had no idea he was more than forty-five."

Thomas Sanders, son of Elias Sanders, known as "Kit," married Isabella Totman, a sister of Joshua Totman of Elbert County. Her father's name we have never learned.

To Thomas Sanders and his wife, Isabella, were born Thomas J., Benjamin, and Chandler Sanders. Thomas J. married his cousin, Rachael Sanders, daughter of Lewis Sanders. Chandler Sanders was never married. We have no record of Benjamin Sanders being married.

The daughters of Thomas Sanders and wife were Rebecca, Lavinia, Millie, Polly or Mary, and Rachael.

Rebecca married Thomas G. Cleveland, son of Reuben Cleveland; Lavinia married Cornelius Cleveland, brother to Thos. G. Cleveland; Millie married Dyar P. Cleveland, son of John Ashley Cleveland, brother to Thomas G. and Cornelius Cleveland.

Mary or Polly married William E. T. Cleveland, son of Jeremiah Cleveland, a relative of Thomas G., Cornelius and John Ashley Cleveland. Rachael married her cousin, James Sanders, son of Elias Sanders, son of Elias Sanders, and to avoid confusion will designate them as junior and senior.

Elias Sanders, Jr., son of Elias Sanders, Sr., married Julia Vickery, a daughter of Aaron Vickery. His sons were Samuel, James Monroe, Thomas, Franklin and Nathan.

Samuel married Harriett Ayers, daughter of Jedidiah Ayers. James Monroe married Frances E. Barron January 22, 1863; she was a daughter of William Barron, son of Barnabas Barron, and commonly known as "Squire Barnes." Franklin married Alpha Evans November 22, 1863. Thomas married Jane Massá October 14, 1855. Nathan married Amie Dyar.

We have no record of any daughters of Elias Sanders.

Calvin P. Sanders married Sarah Miller, daughter of Jerry Miller, and sister of Prudence, wife of Lewis Sanders, and Orpha, wife of Jonathan Sanders. Date of marriage, December 23, 1824.

To Calvin P. Sanders and his wife, Sarah, were born three sons: Thornton, Mallory and Alberry. The daughters were Mary, Rhoda, Alice and Orpha.

Thornton Sanders married Mary Burgess January 26, 1865. Mallory married a daughter of Rev. John D. Adams of Elbert County, Ga.; we do not have her given name. She died several years ago. Mallory died in 1930 at

Anderson, S. C., and was buried in Silver Brook Cemetery. We have no record of who Alberry married.

Mary, daughter of Calvin P. Sanders and wife, married A. M. Culpepper January 5, 1858, and Rhoda married A. T. Latty on the same day. They were both married by Rev. J. T. W. Veron.

Alice married James E. Scott. Orpha was never married.

Samuel B. Sanders, son of Elias Sanders, married Anne Skelton. To Samuel B. Sanders and his wife, Anne, were born seven sons: William, James, Swan H., Thornton, Thomas H., John Willis and Harrison S. Sanders; and three daughters, Elizabeth, Martha and Mary Ann.

William lived somewhere near Athens, Ga., and we know practically nothing of him or his family. He was killed years ago by a man with whom he had a difficulty.

Swan H. Sanders married Elizabeth Bailey, daughter of Joel Bailey of Hart County, Ga.

Thomas H. Sanders married Miss Martha J. McMullan, daughter of John F. McMullan, October 29, 1868, and after the death of his wife, was married a second time to Sarah Rowland. He was a soldier in the War Between the States and died several years ago and was buried at Reed Creek Church; a Confederate cross of honor marks his grave.

John Willis Sanders married Lettie Vickery, daughter of Elias Vickery. He and his wife are buried in the cemetery at Milltown Church, of which he was a member and deacon.

Harrison S. Sanders, the youngest son of Rev. Samuel B. Sanders and wife, was twice married, his second wife a daughter of B. B. Herring. We never knew who was his first wife before her marriage. He is buried at Mt. Hebron Baptist Church.

James and Thornton, sons of Samuel B. Sanders, were never married, and both killed in battle in the War Between the States.

Elizabeth Sanders, daughter of Samuel B. Sanders and wife, married John McLeskey. Martha, another daughter, married John C. Bailey, and Mary Ann married John M. Madden September 4, 1878.

Lewis Sanders married Prudence Miller, daughter of Jerry Miller, August 5, 1824, being his first marriage, and to him and his wife were born four sons: James, William H., Lewis M., and Alfred; and two daughters: Alpha and Rachael.

James married his cousin, Rachael, daughter of Thomas (Kit) Sanders. William H. married Mary F. Evans. Lewis M. married Ellen Estes, daughter of William Estes. Alfred married Martha, daughter of Thomas (Kit) Sanders. Alpha married A. H. Hall. Rachael married Thomas J. Sanders, her cousin, and son of Thomas (Kit) Sanders.

We do not know who Lewis Sanders married the second time. His sons by his second marriage were: Thomas, Phillip and Nelson. Do not know about the daughters of his second marriage.

Jonathan P. Sanders married Orpha Miller, daughter of Jerry Miller, and sister to the wives of Calvin P. and Lewis Sanders. The children born to Jonathan P. and wife were three sons: Gilbert, William Anderson and Elias Harrison Sanders; and four daughters: Martha, Mary, Jane and Caroline.

Gilbert was killed in battle in the War Between the States, unmarried.

William Anderson married Ann E. C. Carter, daughter of David Carter. Elias H. married Miss Lettie E. Smith, daughter of Jess and Elizabeth Smith, December 5, 1867, by Rev. Samuel B. Sanders.

Martha married Thomas Osborne. Mary E. married James M. Allen September, 1867, by William Vickery, Justice of the Peace. Jane Sanders married John H. McDougle December 2, 1869, by William Vickery, Justice of the Peace. Caroline Married John N. Herring January 10, 1873, by M. G. O'Barr, Justice of the Peace. After the death of John N. Herring, her first husband, she married William Bagwell.

Mary, daughter of Elias Sanders, married James Vickery, a son of Aaron Vickery, who was a son of Joseph Vickery, of Welch or Scotch descent. Joseph Vickery came either from Wales or Scotland, and his son Aaron was contemporary with Elias Sanders, Sr., that is to say, they were both of about the same age and lived at the same time and their children intermarried. James Vickery, husband of Mary Sanders Vickery, was killed accidently many years ago not far from where the city of Hartwell is now located. According to tradition, he and his brother-in-law, Calvin P. Sanders, were engaged in catching wild hogs, which perhaps were hogs that belonged to them that had strayed off into the forest, as the entire country at that time, or the most of it, was in original forest. They had a gun with them which accidently discharged and killed Vickery.

The children of James and Mary Vickery were six sons: Elias, J. Hightower, James A., John Thomas, William and J. Parker Vickery.

Elias was twice married; his first wife was a Miss Hubbard; his second wife was Miss Nellie Skelton, daughter of Noel and Margry Skelton. J. Hightower Vickery married a Miss McLeskey, daughter of Joseph McLeskey, sister to Joseph, Jr., John and B. J. McLeskey. James A. married Caroline Scott, daughter of Lemuel Scott. John Thomas married Mary Herring. William married Susan Stiefle. J. Parker married Malisa Crump, being his first wife; his second wife was Mrs. Janie Elizabeth Speer, the date of their marriage being April 4, 1910.

The daughters of James Vickery and wife were: Millie, Mary, Cynthia, and Rachael.

Millie married John McDougle, commonly referred to as "Jack McDougle." Mary married Levi Herring, Cynthia married Zenus Hubbard, and Rachael married James Stiefle.

Patience Sanders, daughter of Elias Sanders, Sr., and wife, married Joseph Hightower Vickery, son of Aaron Vickery, and brother of James Vickery, who married Mary Sanders. To this union were born one son, W. J. Vickery, and one daughter, Mary.

W. J. Vickery, who married a Miss Haynes, was a Baptist preacher and lived and died in Elbert County. Mary, the daughter, married Tinsley Powell.

Joseph Hightower Vickery lived at one time right near where the trestle of the Hartwell Railway is located. When he died he was buried a short ways east of the present public road leading from Hartwell to Airline on the south side and not farm from Lightwoodlog Creek.

After the death of Joseph Hightower Vickery his widow, Patience, married John W. Smith, and to this union were born two sons: Lindsey and

William. We do not know who either married. There were three daughters: Rachael E. married George W. Cleveland, being his second wife. Lettie E. married Judge T. Vickery, son of John Thomas Vickery, she being his second wife. Martha married Joseph F. Carter, son of Lamarcus Carter.

Rachael Sanders, daughter of Elias Sanders, Sr., married Joel H. Dyar, a son of Jack Dyar, and grandson of Elisha Dyar, who was a soldier in the War of the Revolution. He had one son named Elias Sanders Dyar after his grandfather, Elias Sanders. We have no record of any other children of Joel H. Dyar and his wife, Rachael Sanders Dyar.

Elias Sanders Dyar, son of Joel H. Dyar, was marshal in the early days of the town of Hartwell, and also served some of the time as Deputy Sheriff of the county. He was a deacon of the Hartwell Baptist Church. In the War Between the States, he enlisted in Captain J. H. Skelton's Company, known as Co. "C," 16th Georgia Regiment, as Second Lieutenant, on July 13, 1861. Died June 6, 1864, at Richmond, Va. Wounded at Wilderness May 6, 1864.

For further history of Joel H. Dyar and his son, Elias Sanders Dyar, see History of the Dyar Family.

The Sanders and Vickery families, and the families with whom they intermarried, viz.: Hubbards, Herrings, Stiefles, McDougles, and Clevelands, obtained lands either by headright titles or purchase, located along Big Lightwoodlog Creek and its various tributaries, where they settled and lived in one large community, colony like, their farms adjoining.

They were industrious, "hardy-handed sons of toil," and converted a wilderness into cleared fields and habitations of men.

As we think of them, we are reminded of a verse of Grey, though in reverse order:

"How bow'd the woods beneath their sturdy stroke!
How jocund did they drive their team afield!
Their furrow oft the stubborn glebe has broke:
Oft did the harvest to their sickle yield."

They built their homes on the hills and knolls near where crystal waters gushed forth from springs at the foot of the wooded hills. Along the streams they erected and operated mills, gins, threshers and other machinery for their own convenience and for the convenience of their neighbors.

Many of the homes of these first settlers are now delapidated or gone entirely, while some are yet standing. The farms in many places abandoned and overgrown by a second growth of trees.

Near by the sites of the residences are the family burying grounds, neglected and forgotten.

In religion, they were mostly of the Baptist denomination; many of them became ministers of the Gospel and did faithful work for the Master.

Knox's Bridge

KNOX'S BRIDGE, a wooden structure which spans Tugaloo River at what was formerly Cleveland's Ferry where the public road leading from Pendleton, S. C., to Carnesville, Ga., crossed said river, was built in the year 1854 by Col. Samuel Knox, of Franklin County, Ga., as an individual undertaking, at a cost of $10,000.

Col. Bowman, of Elberton, Ga., was the architect, and Col. Clarke Mason was foreman of the work on one end of the bridge, and Judge Noah Looney was foreman on the other.

The work was done chiefly by slave labor.

The dimensions of the bridge are as follows: 300 feet in length; 12 feet in width; 12 feet high, and rests upon four stone pillars or piers, and stands 35 feet above low, or common water.

During the freshet of 1887 the river reached a height of 45 feet above common water and was 10 feet up in the bridge.

The bridge was a toll bridge for a number of years, but several years ago was bought by the two states, Georgia and South Carolina, and made a toll-free bridge. It is now the crossing place of the Stone Mountain Highway, No. 59.

While this bridge has stood through flood and storm for more than three-fourths of a century, it is yet in a fairly good state of preservation, and has never been repaired, with the probable exception of a new roof.

In this connection, we will give a short sketch of Col. Samuel Knox. It is said that he began life in youth or early manhood as a wage hand, and with only his brain and brawn as capital accumulated what was considered in his day quite a fortune.

He was twice married. His first wife was Mary M. Reed, to whom he was married on February 10, 1829. His second wife was Mary Ann Swift, the date of their marriage being April 3, 1832.

While Col. Knox was a citizen of Franklin County, he was also identified in a very material way with Hart County enterprises. Besides being the builder and owner of the bridge, and farm and home attached thereto, he was for a number of years associated with Col. Albin Cornog in the business of the Shoal Creek Factory and mills.

Knox's Bridge

His home was located on the old Red Hollow Road near where it and the Pendleton and Carnesville road crossed, where he owned a large farm, and prior to the War Between the States he owned a number of slaves. Besides his business and financial career, he was also prominent in the political affairs of his State and County, and represented Franklin County in the Georgia Legislature. He was a delegate from Franklin County to the secession convention at Milledgeville, Ga., January 19, 1861, and with Hon. Alexander H. Stephens and others opposed the measure and voted against the ordinance of secession.

He and his wife are buried in the cemetery at Shoal Creek Church, their graves marked by a marble monument, enclosed with an iron fence, with the following inscriptions:

"COL. SAMUEL KNOX, BORN OCT. 27, 1808, DIED NOV. 5, 1870.
MARY ANN KNOX, BORN 1815, DIED MARCH 13, 1886."

The "Big Sawmill"

SOMETIME between the years 1850 and 1860, Joel Towers, who perhaps had others associated with him in the enterprise, built a sawmill on Lightwoodlog Creek just above the ford where the public road leading toward Mt. Zion Church crossed and where now a bridge spans the creek.

The dam for the mill was a short ways above the ford, and the mill, which was the first circular-saw mill to be operated in this country, stood just below the dam.

John A. Cameron, the first county surveyor of Hart County, to which office he was elected at the organization of the county, was the foreman of the work. Besides being of an engineering turn of mind, he was also a carpenter and millwright.

The dam was perhaps about twenty feet in height. The fall of the creek for a considerable ways above down to the dam was but slight and the water backed quite a distance up stream, forming a long pond or lake.

The hillsides adjacent to the creek supported a large quantity of original forest pines, which condition prevailed throughout the entire course of the creek, as well as that of its tributaries and watershed area, and by reason of which fact it derived the name "Lightwoodlog Creek."

The pines were cut down and cut or sawed into given lengths and either rolled or skidded down the hills to the pond and then floated down to the mill, where they were taken out and sawed into lumber.

After the mill had been in operation for a few years, it was swept away by a freshet. Remains of some of the logs that had been skidded down to the pond or lake, and that had not been floated down to the mill, could for years after, and perhaps may yet be seen.

The mudsills are yet intact over which the waters of Lightwoodlog Creek have poured for seventy-five years, or about so, and if not disturbed will continue to flow for an indefinite time in the future.

After the mill had been carried away by high-water, Mr. Thomas Parks, who lived on the South Carolina side of the Savannah River about opposite the Carter place on the Georgia side, who it appears was in some way interested, and perhaps very materially so, in the property, began arrangements to rebuild the mill and maybe add other machinery besides a sawmill. He had a race, or canal, dug along parallel with the creek on the north side for a long ways up the creek with the intention to turn the water from the creek into the race, or canal, and bring it down to where the mill would be built, and thus escape the hazard of the mill being again destroyed by highwater, but due to the approach of the War Between the States, which event demoralized most all projects, the work was suspended and never resumed. Signs of the race, or canal, can yet be seen.

Mr. Parks appears to have owned the lands upon which the mill stood, as it appears of record that he bought the place containing one hundred and fifty acres from James H. Strange. It also appears of record that after the death of Mr. Parks his administrator, J. L. Turner, sold the place to S. V. Milford, who later sold it to James B. Alford.

While Mr. Parks lived in South Carolina there was a ferry on the Savannah River somewhere above the Carter home and about even of the Parks home known as Tate's Ferry, and Mr. Parks procured a right-of-way for a road from the ferry to intersect the public road somewhere near Milltown Church.

While Mr. Joel Towers lived at the place he built a splendid dwelling house on the hill about opposite Milltown Church. The house was built of the best of lumber, which was plentiful at that time. It was constructed by skilled workmen and artistically finished, provided with day-doors and dormer windows and conveniently and well arranged in every respect. As stated, it was located on a prominence and could be easily seen from other parts of the country-side.

This house was destroyed on a windy day in March, 1876, and the Milltown Church house, which stood on the opposite side of the public road, and also on a hill, came near being burned. The forest near the church was burned over and much of the fencing around the fields near the church was destroyed by the fire.

On Little Lightwoodlog Creek, less than a mile north of the big sawmill, was a grist mill built by Larmarcus Carter, later owned by Thomas Murry, and still later by his son, Peter A. Murry, and to whose estate the property still belongs.

On Gum Branch, about one-fourth of a mile from the big sawmill, Hon. F. G. Stowers built a grist mill, and maybe a flour mill, and also a cotton gin.

A dam was thrown across the small branch that heads on the Stowers place and runs along down parallel with the public road leading from Mt. Zion to Milltown, and the water carried in a race that contoured the hill and emptied into the pond, or race, above the mill, thus increasing the volume of water afforded by Gum Branch for driving the mill and gin.

Signs of this old race running around the side of the hill may yet be seen by the passer-by.

Due to the proximity of these several mills, all of which appear to have been in operation contemporaneously, the church organized near by was given the name, "Milltown."

THE WAR BETWEEN THE STATES

AT THE time Hart County was created there existed, and had existed for many years prior, differences of opinion upon several questions of a national character, prominent among others was the institution of slavery. The attitude of the people of the North was that of abolition of the slaves and they entertained the hope that slavery was in a state of final extinction, while the attitude of the people of the South was to foster, perpetuate and extend the institution into new territory as time and necessity demanded. Several efforts were made to compromise and settle the question between the two sections, but as the years passed the question became more unsettled. Secession of the southern states from the Union had been advocated for quite a while, until finally on December 20, 1860, the State of South Carolina took the initiative and passed an ordinance of secession formally dissolving the Union between that state and the United States of America.

Georgia followed the example of her sister state, and on January 19, 1861, passed the ordinance of secession, being the fifth state to secede. A full account of the various meetings held by the people of Hart County with reference to the question of secession are hereinafter given, reciting the proceedings had, the election of delegates from Hart County to the Secession Convention, a copy of the Ordinance of Secession as passed at the Convention held at Milledgeville, which was then the capital of the State.

Political Meeting in Hart County.

Hartwell, December 4, 1860.

According to previous notice, the citizens of Hart County, met today at the court house en masse, for the purpose of nominating suitable candidates to represent Hart County in the State Convention, to be held in Milledgeville on the 16th of January, 1861.

On motion of P. E. Devant, Esq., Joel Towers was called to the chair, and John H. Skelton, Esq., was requested to act as secretary. The chair then announced the convention ready for action.

On motion of P. E. Devant, Esq., James E. Skelton and R. S. Hill were announced as candidates and that they be nominated by acclamation.

Col. William R. Poole moved the following as a substitute for Mr. Devant's motion: that there be three delegates appointed by each militia district to meet immediately for the purpose of selecting two suitable candidates, and report their names to the convention. After a short absence, the committee returned and through their chairman, H. F. Chandler, reported the names of James E. Skelton, Esq., and Col. R. S. Hill as suitable candidates to represent the people of Hart County in the State Convention.

On motion of P. E. Devant, Esq., the report of the committee was adopted unanimously by the convention.

Col. William R. Poole then offered the following resolution:

Resolved, That we pledge ourselves to stand to and abide the action of the State Convention, which resolution was unanimously adopted.

On motion, the proceedings of this convention be published in the *South-*

ern Banner, Athens, Ga., the *True Democrat and Constitutionalist*, Augusta, Ga.

On motion, the convention then adjourned.

JOEL TOWERS, *Chairman.*

JOHN H. SKELTON, ESQ., *Secretary.*

On the 16th day of January, 1861, the State Convention convened in Milledgeville, and the Ordinance of Secession was adopted by a vote of 208 to 89, after which the vote was made unanimous. The delegates from Hart County both voted for the Ordinance and also signed the same.

Copy of the Ordinance

"The Ordinance of Secession as Signed
"An Ordinance,

To dissolve the Union between the State of Georgia and the other States united with her under a compact of Government entitled the Constitution of the United States of America.

"We, the people of the State of Georgia, in Convention assembled, do declare and ordain, and it is hereby declared and ordained, that the Ordinance adopted by the people of the State of Georgia, in Convention, on the second day of January, in the year of our Lord, seventeen hundred and eighty-eight, whereby the Constitution of the United States of America, was assented to, ratified and adopted; and also all acts of the General Assembly of this State, ratifying and adopting amendments of the said Constitution, are hereby repealed and abrogated.

"We do further declare and ordain, that the Union now subsisting between the State of Georgia and the other States under the name of the United States of America, is hereby dissolved, and that the State of Georgia is in full possession and exercise of all those rights of sovereignty which belong to a free and independent State."

Other southern states followed the example of Georgia and the other states that had seceded. Conditions grew more turbulent, the breach between the sections grew deeper and wider, war clouds hung upon the horizon which thickened and darkened until on that fateful day, April 12, 1861, cannon boomed on Charleston main, Fort Sumter fell and war was on with all its alarms, and for four years following there was waged the most horrible and destructive war, both to lives and property, of any civil conflict in the annals of history.

On April 9, 1865, at Appomattox, Va., Gen. Robert E. Lee, that great southern chieftain, surrendered his army which had so long and so valiantly contended against fearful odds, to Gen. U. S. Grant, and to the great gratification of the people of the South, as well as to those of the North, the awful struggle was at an end.

Reconstruction

After the stirring scenes of the war had passed, then followed the stressful aftermath of the reconstruction.

For the first few years after the close of the war, there was a regime of the scalawag and the carpetbagger. It was the policy of some of the Federal authorities to add insult to injury and to trample an already subdued and humiliated people under the heel of northern despotism.

But in the course of a short time reason and better judgment prevailed and the people of the South were allowed to re-enter the Union and receive the recognition due them and peace and harmony once again prevailed.

Muster Rolls of Companies Regiment Georgia Volunteers C. S. A., Hart County, Ga.

Company "B" Organized June 9, 1861, 24th Georgia Regiment

DEVANT, PHILLIP E. Captain, June 9, 1861. Transferred to 3rd Batallion Sharp Shooters June 9, 1863, and promoted to Major of Batallion.

TURNER, ALLEN S. 1st Lieutenant, June 9, 1861. Appointed A. Q. M. May ...., 1862.

GORDON, ROBERT I. 2nd Lieutenant, June 9, 1861. Promoted 1st Lieutenant May ...., 1862. Died September 18, 1862 at............

JOHNSON, JAMES L., JR. 3rd Lieutenant, June 9, 1861. Promoted to 2nd Lieutenant May, 1862. Promoted to 1st Lieutenant September, 1862. Promoted to Captain June 9, 1863. Lost arm at Front Royal, Va., September 23rd, 1864.

MCCURRY, WILLIAM. 1st Sergeant, Aug. 24, 1861.

PRUITT, WILLIAM C. 2nd Sergeant, Aug. 24, 1861. Died in hospital, June, 1862.

HAYNES, WILLIAM H. 3rd Sergeant, Aug. 24, 1861. Died Feb. 10, 1864 at ....

STEPHENSON, W. H. 4th Sergeant, Aug. 24, 1861.

GINN, ISAAC. 1st Corporal, Aug. 24, 1861. Elected 2nd Lieutenant, 1864.

FLEMING, THOMAS J. 2nd Corporal, Aug. 24, 1861.

JOHNSON, THOMAS M. 3rd Corporal, Aug. 24, 1861. Promoted to 1st Corporal, 1863. Killed at Wilderness, May 6, 1864.

TEASLEY, WILLIAM J. 4th Corporal, Aug. 24, 1861. Promoted to 2nd Corporal, 1863. Promoted to 1st Corporal, 1864. Surrendered at Appomattox, Va.

ALLEN, JOSEPH F. Private, Aug. 24, 1861. Died of disease, 1865, at ....

ALLEN, FRANK. Private, Aug. 24, 1861. Died of disease, 1865, at ....

ALLEN, JAMES W. Private, Aug. 24, 1861. Appointed 3rd Corporal, 1863. Promoted 2nd Corporal.

ALLEN, THOMAS J. Private, Aug. 24, 1861.

BAKER, DICKSON L. Private, Aug. 24, 1861. Promoted Jr. 2nd Lieutenant, May 29, 1862. Promoted 2nd Lieutenant, Sep. 18, 1862. Killed at Deep Bottom, Va., Aug. 16, 1864.

BOBO, SOLOMON. Private, Aug. 24, 1861. Appointed 5th Sergeant, 1863. Appointed 1st Sergeant, 1864. Captured at Deep Bottom, Va., April 16, 1864.

BALLENGER, D. B. Private, Aug. 24, 1861. Died at Richmond, Va., July 15, 1863.

BOWERS, ASA. Private, Aug. 24, 1861.

BOWERS, BYRON. Private, Aug. 24, 1861.

BROWN, ASA. Private, Aug. 24, 1861.

BROWN, JAMES R. Private, Aug. 24, 1861. Surrendered at Appomattox, Va.

BROWN, MORGAN M. Private, Aug. 24, 1861. Discharged 1864.

BENNETT, M. J. Private, July, 1862. Wounded at Sharpsburg, Md., Sep. 1862, died from wound Union Point, Oct., 1862.

BROWN, THOS. D. Private, Aug. 24, 1861.

BROWN, WILLIAM B. S. A. Private, Aug. 24, 1861. Died at Richmond, Va., May 1, 1862.

BROWN, WILLIAM F. Private, Aug. 24, 1861. Surrendered at Appomattox, Va.

BRAY, JAMES C. Private, Aug. 24, 1861. Captured at Deep Bottom, Va., Aug. 16, 1864.

BOWERS, JOHN D. Private, May 7, 1862. Appointed 3rd Sergeant, March 1, 1864. Killed at Petersburg, Va., June 8, 1864.

BROWN, L. C. Private, March 13, 1862.

BUNN, W. B. Private, Aug. 24, 1861. Died at Richmond, Va., May 1, 1862.

BURNETT, WILLIAM A. C. Private, May 7, 1862. Captured at Cold Harbor, Va., June 1, 1864.

BENNETT, REUBEN K. Private, July 9, 1862. Captured at Gettysburg, Pa., July 2, 1863. Point Lookout, Feb., 1865.
BENNETT, WILLIAM F. Private, Aug. 13, 1863. Discharged, disabilities.
BOBO, MATHEW. Private, May 7, 1862. Died Feb. 10, 1864, at _____.
CALDWELL, JOSEPH W. Private, Aug. 24, 1861. Appointed 2nd Sergeant, 1863, at _____.
CALDWELL, SAMUEL W. Private, Aug. 24, 1861. Appointed 4th Corporal, 1863. Appointed 3rd Sergeant, 1864.
CALDWELL, WILLIAM J. Private, Aug. 24, 1861.
CAUTHEN, GEORGE T. Private, Aug. 24, 1861.
CROW, THOMAS L. Private, May 7, 1862.
COBB, JAMES H. Private, Aug. 24, 1861. Died Nov. 12, 1861 at _____.
CHEEK, HIRAM. Private, May, 1862. Died of disease, Dec., 1862.
COBB, WILLIAM J. Private, Aug. 24, 1861. Killed at Sharpsburg, Md., Sep. 17, 1862.
CHEEK, J. B. Private, 1862. Discharged 1864.
COLSTON, AARON. Private, Aug. 24, 1861.
CROW, CHRISTOPHER W. Private, May 7, 1862.
CALDWELL, DAVID S. P. Private, May 7, 1862. Captured at Cold Harbor, Va., June 1, 1864.
CALDWELL, BAILAS T. Private, May 7, 1862. Captured at Gettysburg, Pa., July 2, 1863. Died in prison at Fort Delaware, June 30, 1864.
COLSTON, W. A. Private, May 7, 1862. Died at Richmond, Va., July 5, 1862.
COLE, JOHN. Private, March 13, 1862. Killed at Wilderness, Va., May 6, 1864.
CULPEPPER, J. F. Private, Aug. 24, 1861. Died in Macon, Ga.
DEAN, JAMES B. Private, Aug. 24, 1861.
DAVID, JAMES V. W. Private, May, 1862. Died in hospital at Scottsville, Va.
DICKERSON, DOZIER D. Private, Aug. 24, 1861. Appointed 4th Sergeant, 1863. Captured August 16, 1864 at Deep Bottom, Va.
DICKERSON, WILLIAM H. Private, Aug. 24, 1861. Elected Jr. 2nd Lieutenant, 1864. Captured Aug. 16, 1864, at Deep Bottom, Va.
DICKERSON, JOHN C. Private, March 11, 1863.
EATON, WILLIAM A. Private, March 11, 1862.
FAIR, C. M. Private, March 17, 1862.
GAINES, JAMES R. S. Private, Aug. 24, 1861.
GAINES, WILLIAM A. Private, Aug. 24, 1861. Died Nov. 6, 1861 at _____.
GINN, GAINES B. Private, Aug. 24, 1861.
GAINES, JOHN L. Private, March, 1862. Died at Richmond, Va., April, 1864.
GINN, JAMES A. Private, Aug. 24, 1861. Appointed 5th Sergeant, 1864.
GINN, ROLAND J. Private, Aug. 24, 1861.
GOSS, JAMES Private, Aug. 24, 1861.
GRANT, WILLIAM P. Private, Aug. 24, 1861.
GINN, JAMES M. Private, March 11, 1862. Home on furlough at close of war.
GOOLSBY, WILLIAM J. A. Private, March 11, 1862.
GORDON, WILLIAM J. Private, Sep. 11, 1862. Captured at Deep Bottom, Va., Aug. 16, 1864. Died at hospital at Savannah, Ga., returning from prison, 1865.
HAYNES, JAMES M. Private, Aug. 24, 1861. Captured at Deep Bottom, Va., Aug. 16, 1864. Discharged from Elmira, N. Y., prison, April, 1865.
HENDRICKS, JESSE W. Private, Aug. 24, 1861. Died at Richmond, Va.
HANDLEY, D. P. Private, May, 1862. Died of measles at Richmond, Va., Hospital, June, 1862.
HICKS, JAMES F. Private, Aug. 24, 1861.
HERRING, M. B. Private, 1864. Captured at _____. In prison April 6, 1865.
HINTON, DANIEL C. Private, Aug. 24, 1861. Appointed 4th Corporal, 1864. Died of disease, 1864.
HOLMES, BENJAMIN W. Private, Aug. 24, 1861. Killed, May 6, 1864, at Wilderness, Va.
HUGHES, THOMAS. Private, Aug. 24, 1861.
HOLBROOK, THOMAS T. Private, March 13, 1862. Appointed 1st Sergeant, Oct. 1863. Killed at Wilderness, Va., May 6, 1864.
HAYNES, JAMES M. Private, July 12, 1862. Appointed 3rd Corporal, 1864. Captured at Deep Bottom, Va., Aug. 16, 1864.
HOLBROOK, F. C. Private, March 12, 1862.

JACKSON, MARTIN V. Private, Aug. 24, 1862. Discharged at Johnson Island, O., June 20, 1865.
JOHNSON, BENJAMIN W. Private, Aug. 24, 1861.
JOHNSON, DANIEL F. Private, Aug. 24, 1861. Wounded at Chattanooga, Tenn., Sep. 25, 1863.
JOHNSON, DANIEL G. Private, Aug. 24, 1861.
JOHNSON, GENERAL R. Private, Aug. 24, 1861. Surrendered at Appomattox, Va.
JORDAN, JOHN W. Private, July 12, 1862.
JORDAN, JAMES. Private, Dec. 12, 1861. Captured at .... Died in prison at Fort Delaware, Del., September 2, 1863.
JORDAN, H. B. Private, May 7, 1862. Died Dec. 30, 1863 at ....
KNIGHT, HUGH A. R. Private, Aug. 24, 1861.
KIMBRELL, JAMES. Private, 1861. Killed at Gettysburg, Pa., July 2, 1863.
MAXWELL, ELBERT T. Private, Aug. 24, 1861.
MAGEE, PINKNEY. Private, 1862. Died of measles, July, 1862.
MCARTHUR, JOHN L. Private, Aug. 24, 1861. Transferred Aug. 1, 1864 to ....
MCLANE, HUGH. Private, Aug. 24, 1861. Wounded at Chancellorsville, Va., May 3, 1863. Surrendered at Appomattox, 1865.
MIZE, JEREMIAH. Private, Aug. 24, 1861. Captured at .... In prison at Point Lookout, Lookout, Md., April, 1865.
MANLEY, BENJAMIN F. Private, Sep. 15, 1862. Lost eye at Gettysburg, Pa., July 2, 1863. Retired to invalid corps, May, 1864.
MCGARITY, G. Private, May 1, 1862. Surrendered at Appomattox, Va.
NELMS, NATHANIEL H. Private, Aug. 24, 1861. Lost toe at Sharpsburg, Md., Sep. 17, 1863.
PAYNE, LARKIN C. Private, Aug. 24, 1861. Surrendered at Appomattox, Va.
PARKER, J. Private, Aug. 24, 1861. Died in Richmond, Va., March 8, 1865.
PEARSON, ALFRED. Private, Aug. 24, 1861. Died in Richmond, Va., May 24, 1862.
PHILLIPS, BENJAMIN F. Private, Aug. 24, 1861.
PHILLIPS, EPPY W. Private, Aug. 24, 1861. Surrendered at Appomattox, Va., April 9, 1865.
PHILLIPS, JAMES. Private, Aug. 24, 1861. Deserted at Richmond, Va.
PRITCHETT, JOHN L. Private, Aug. 24, 1861.
PRITCHETT, POWELL. Private, Aug. 24, 1861.
PRUITT, ALONZO. Private, Aug. 24, 1861. Captured at Cold Harbor, Va., June 1, 1864.
POWELL, JOHN W. Private, March 13, 1862. Surrendered at Appomattox, Va.
ROBERTS, JOHN W. Private, Aug. 24, 1861. Died Nov. 28, 1861, at ....
RANSOM, W. B. Private, Aug. 24, 1861. Killed at Chancellorsville, Va., Aug. 3, 1863.
ROBERTS, MOSES L. H. Private, Aug. 24, 1861.
RUSSUM, WILLIAM. Private, Aug. 24, 1861. Retired May 3, 1864 to invalid corps.
REYNOLDS, SAMUEL. Private, July 13, 1861. Died June 8, 1864, at ....
SANDERS, H. S. Private, Aug. 24, 1861. Died at Richmond, Va., June 10, 1862.
SCOTT, BENJAMIN M. Private, Aug. 24, 1861. Killed at Fredericksburg, Va., by explosion of cartridge box, Aug. 2, 1863.
SEAL, H. Private, Aug. 24, 1861. Died in Richmond, Va., May 18, 1862.
SMITH, LARKIN. Private, Aug. 24, 1861. Died in Richmond, Va., June 17, 1882.

Muster Roll of Company "C" 16th Regiment, Georgia Volunteers Infantry, Army of Northern Virginia, C. S. A., Hart County, Georgia

SKELTON, J. H. Captain, July 13, 1861. Promoted Major, Sep. 14, 1863. Captured at Shenandoah Valley, Aug. 1864. Discharged from Fort Delaware prison, 1865.
MCMULLAN, H. G. 1st Lieutenant, July 13, 1861. Promoted Captain, Sep. 14, 1863. Killed at Wilderness, Va., May 6, 1864.
DYAR, E. S. 2nd Lieutenant, July 13, 1861. Died June 6, 1864, at Richmond, Va. Wounded at Wilderness, May 6, 1864.
GORDON, C. H. Jr. 2nd Lieutenant, July 13, 1861. Company physician. Absent without leave, dropped Nov. 25, 1863.

WATSON, W. H. H. 1st Sergeant, July 13, 1861. Captured at Front Royal, August, 1864. Elmira, N. Y., May, 1865.
MYERS, J. B. 2nd Sergeant, July 13, 1861. Captured, wounded, at Front Royal, Aug. 16, 1864. Elmira, N. Y., May, 1865.
MCDONALD, W. G. 3rd Sergeant, July 13, 1861. Captured at Knoxville, Tenn., Nov., 1864.
RICHARDSON, R. 4th Sergeant, July 13, 1861. Captured at Wilderness, Va., May 6, 1864.
MYERS, W. E. 5th Sergeant, July 13, 1861.
HOLLAND, J. T. 1st Corporal, July, 13, 1861.
SANDERS, S. H. 2nd Corporal, July 13, 1861. Wounded in elbow at Wilderness, Va., May 6, 1864. Wounded in shoulder at Chancellorsville, Va., May 3, 1863. Wounded in side, South Mountain, Sep. 12, 1862. Wounded in foot at Fredericksburg, Dec., 1862. Captured at Front Royal, Va., Aug. 16, 1864. Discharged from Elmira, N. Y. Prison, June 21, 1865.
PRITCHETT, N. C. 3rd Corporal, July 13, 1861. Captured at Gettysburg, Pa., July 2, 1864. Died at Fort Delaware, Pa. Prison.
OUTZ, ROBERT. 4th Corporal, July 13, 1861. Captured at Knoxville, Tenn., Nov., 1863. Prison, June 21, 1865.
ADAMS, W. M. Private, March 11, 1863. Captured at Cold Harbor, Jan. 1, 1864.
ANGLIN, WILLIS. Private, May, 1861. Killed near Richmond, Va.
BOBO, S. Private, March 4, 1862. Captured at Wilderness, Va., May 6, 1864.
BOBO, W. M. Private, July 13, 1861. Captured at Knoxville, Tenn., Nov. 1863.
BAILEY, W. T. Private, July 13, 1861.
BAILEY, H. M. Private, Sep. 5, 1861. Captured at Cold Harbor, June 1, 1864. Died in Elmira, N. Y., 1864, of smallpox.
BAILEY, J. C. Private, March 11, 1863. Captured at Wilderness, May 6, 1864. Discharged from prison at Elmira, N. Y., June 16, 1865.
BROCK, R. J. Private, July 13, 1861.
BONDS, J. R. Private, Feb. 10, 1863.
BUFFINGTON, G. W. Private, 1862.
BAGWELL, MARTIN. Private, April 21, 1864. Lost finger at Wilderness, Va., May 6, 1864. Surrendered at Appomattox, Va., April, 1865.
CRAFT, MOSES. Private, July 13, 1861.
CHEEK, J. B. Private, July 13, 1861.
CLEVELAND, W. E. Private, Sep. 13, 1863. Captured at Wilderness, Va., May 6, 1864.
CLEVELAND, GEO. W. Private, July 13, 1861.
DUMAS, J. C. Private, 1862.
DUNN, HENRY. Private, July 13, 1861. Lost three fingers, Sep., 1861 at .... Wounded June, 1864.
DYAR, ELIAS S. Private, July 13, 1861. Died May 12, 1864 at Richmond, Va., Hospital.
EDWARDS, I. J. Private, March 4, 1862. Captured at Front Royal, Aug. 16, 1864. Elmira, N. Y., June 25, 1865, discharged from prison.
EDWARDS, T. J. Private, Feb. 12, 1864. Captured at Wilderness, Va., May 6, 1864.
EVANS, A. Y. Private, May, 1862.
FROST, W. T. Private, March 4, 1864. Captured at Wilderness, Va., May 6, 1864. Discharged from Elmira, N. Y., Prison, April, 1865.
FAULKNER, T. M. Private, July 13, 1861. Died Sep. 5, 1861 at Richmond, Va.
FAIN, J. R. Private, July 13, 1861. Deserted at Wilderness, May 6, 1864.
FAIN, R. M. Private, March 4, 1863. Captured at Wilderness, Va., May 6, 1864.
FAIN, F. W. Private, July 13, 1861. Captured and died at Camp Douglas, Ill.
GAINES, W. B. Private, Sep. 5, 1861.
GAINES, T. L. Private, Aug. 10, 1863.
GAINES, L. G. Private, July 13, 1861. Surrendered at Appomattox, Va.
HILLEY, W. Private, July 13, 1861. Captured at Gettysburg, Pa., July 2, 1863. Died at Fort Delaware, Del., prison, Nov. 1, 1863.
HILLEY, T. R. Private, July 13, 1861. Captured at Cold Harbor, June 1, 1864. Discharged from Elmira, N. Y., 1865.
HERRING, LEVI. Private, Sep., 1865. Died Dec., 1863 at Chattanooga, Tenn.
HOLSENBECK, A. H. Private, Aug., 1862.
HILLEY, J. A. Private, March 11, 1862. Captured at Wilderness, Va., May 6, 1864.
HILLEY, THOMAS. Private, Sep., 1862. Died Jan., 1863 at Richmond, Va., Hospital.

MUSTER ROLLS OF COMPANIES 155

HOLLAND, S. Private, Aug. 1, 1864. Captured at Wilderness, Va., May 6, 1864. Discharged from Elmira, N. Y., Prison.
JACKSON, M. V. Private, July 13, 1861. Elected 1st Lieutenant, Dec. 1, 1864. Promoted Captain Dec. 8, 1864.
JORDAN, J. W. Private, March 1, 1862.
JESTER, J. M. Private, July 13, 1861. Captured at .... Died at Fort Delaware, Del., Nov. 23, 1863.
KINSLEY, JOHN. Private, July 13, 1861.
LANDERS, GEO. W. Private, July 13, 1861. Discharged 1863, disability.
LEWIS, DEMPSEY B. Private, June, 1862. Died Oct., 1863 in hospital at ....
MCDONALD, J. C. Private, April 4, 1864. Captured at Wilderness, Va., May 6, 1864.
MCDONALD, J. P. Private, July 13, 1861. Sharpsburg, Md., 1862.
MYERS, F. L. Private, Sep. 30, 1863.
MCCOY, HENRY J. Private, July 13, 1861.
MARTIN, M. L. Private, Aug. 30, 1862. Captured at Wilderness, Va., May 6, 1864. Discharged from prison, April, 1865.
MCDOWELL, D. B. Private, Sep. 5, 1861. Captured at Wilderness, Va., May 6, 1864.
NEESE, J. M. Private, July 13, 1861. Wounded at Chancellorsville, Va., April 5, 1863 and at Deep Bottom, Aug. 16, 1864, in hip.
NEESE, W. Private, March 4, 1864. Captured at Wilderness, Va., May 6, 1864. Died at Elmira, N. Y., 1864.
OUTZ, JOHN. Private, July 13, 1861. Captured at Wilderness, Va., May 6, 1864.
POWELL, DAVID. Private, July 13, 1861. Captured at Wilderness, Va., May 6, 1864. Discharged from prison at Fort Delaware, Del., April, 1865.
PATTON, ALLEN D. Private, Sep, 1862. Captured at .... Died in prison at Johnsons' Island, O., 1864.
POWELL, J. W. Private, July 13, 1861. Captured at Wilderness, Va., May 6, 1864. Died in Louisville, Ky., Jan. 3, 1865.
PARTAIN, J. T. Private, July 13, 1861. Wounded at Wilderness, Va., May 6, 1864.
PAGE, J. R. Private, March 4, 1862. Captured at Cold Harbor, Jan. 1, 1864. Died in Elmira, N. Y., Prison.
RUMSEY, H. M. Private, July 13, 1861. Captured at Wilderness, Va., May 6, 1864. Died at Richmond, Va., Dec. 25, 1865.
RAY, W. E. Private, March 6, 1863. Captured at Wilderness, Va., May 6, 1864. Lost Harrisburg, Pa.
ROBERTSON, W. B. Private, Aug., 1863.
SANDERS, E. H. Private, July 13, 1861. Captured at Gettysburg, Pa., July 2, 1863. Took oath Point Lookout.
SANDERS, W. R. Private, Dec. 25, 1861.
SANDERS, B. T. Private, Sep. 5, 1861. Captured at Front Royal, Va., Aug. 16, 1864. Died in Elimra, N. Y., Prison, 1865, with fever.
SANDERS, G. T. Private, March 1, 1863. Died at Athens, Ga., June, 1865.
SCOTT, J. H. Private, April 10, 1864. Captured at Front Royal, Va., Aug. 16, 1864. Discharged at Elmira, N. Y., June 21, 1865, from prison.
SANDERS, T. H. Private, April 10, 1864. At home on sick furlough, April, 1865.
SKELTON, LITTLETON. Private, March 13, 1862.
SKELTON, WILEY. Private, July 13, 1861. Elected Captain Aug. 1, 1864.
SKELTON, W. R. Private, March 4, 1862.
SISK, W. S. Private, July, 1861. Captured at .... Discharged from Fort Delaware, Del., Prison, April, 1865.
SKELTON, G. M. Private, April 6, 1864. Surrendered at Appomattox, Va.
SHIFLET, S. C. Private, July 13, 1861. Disabled at Sharpsburg, Md., Sep. 17, 1862.
SMITH, J. W. Private, Sep. 13, 1863.
SOUTH, J. B. Private, June 1, 1862. Surrendered at Appomattox, Va.
TURNER, T. A. B. Private, July 1, 1862. Captured at Bristol, Tenn., Sep. 1, 1864.
WATSON, R. I. Private, July 13, 1861. Surrendered at Appomattox, Va.
WILLIAMS, J. W. Private, July 13, 1861. Captured at the fall of Richmond, Va., March, 1865. Paroled July 10, 1865.
WRIGHT, J. P. O. Private, March 4, 1862. Killed at Gettysburg, Va., July 1, 1863.

VINING, J. C. Private, July 13, 1861. Captured at .... Died at Camp Chase, O., Feb. 5, 1865.
SANDERS, J. M. Private, July 13, 1861. Killed at Sharpsburg, Md., Sep. 17, 1862.
SKELTON, IRA. Private, April 10, 1864. Captured at Wilderness, May 6, 1864.
SATTERFIELD, W. H. Private, July 13, 1861. Discharged, disability.
STEWART, ELIJAH. Private, July 13, 1861. Killed at Sharpsburg, Md., Sep. 1862.
REED, JOE. Private, July 13, 1861. Wounded at Gettysburg, Va., July 2, 1863. Died at .... 1863.
MCDOWELL, JIM. Private, July 13, 1861. Wounded at South Mt., Md., Sep. 1862. Died 1862.
RISENER, JACK. Private, July 13, 1861. Wounded at South Mt., Md., Sep., 1862.
ADAMS, LABON. Private, July 13, 1861. Killed at Wilderness, Va., May 6, 1864.
BANKS, SIM. Private, July 13, 1861. Killed accidently at Yorktown, Va., April, 1863.
BARRON, WILLIAM. Private, March 4, 1862.
BARRON, NEWTON. Private, March 4, 1862. Killed accidently at Yorktown, Va., April, 1863.
BROWN, W. B. Private, July 13, 1861. Killed at Chancellorsville, Va., April 5, 1863.
BOND, ASBURY. 1st Sergeant. Killed at Wilderness, May 6, 1864.
DOOLEY, GEORGE. Private, July 13, 1861.
GAINES, EARL. Private, July 13, 1861. Killed at Malvern Hill, Va., 1862.
KAY, JOHN R. Private, July 13, 1861. Discharged June, 1862. Disability.
MORGAN, PERRY. Private, July 13, 1861. Killed at Knoxville, Tenn., Nov., 1863.
MASTERS, A. N. 1st Sergeant, July 13, 1861. Killed at Dam No. 1 near Yorktown, Va., April, 1862.
MCCURRY, JOHN D. Private, July 13, 1861.
MCCURRY, HORATIO. Private, July 13, 1861. Died in hospital from wound received at Fredericksburg, Va., Dec., 1862.
MARTIN, MIKE. Private, March 4, 1862. Captured at Cold Harbor, Va., June 2, 1864.
MARTIN, CHARLES. Private, March 4, 1862. Killed at Sharpsburg, Sep., 1862.
OUTZ, DALLAS. Private, July 13, 1861. Died of fever at Suffolk, Va., Oct., 1861.
REID, J. W. Private, July 13, 1861. Died at Suffolk, Va., of fever, Oct., 1861.
TEMPLES, C. W. Private, July 13, 1861. Transferred to cavalry.
TEMPLES, BEN. Private, July 13, 1861. Wounded at Sharpsburg, Md., Sep. 17, 1862. Died in hospital.
WYLEY, JOHN. Private, July 13, 1861. Killed at Wilderness, Va., May 6, 1864.
CLEVELAND, JASPER. Private, July 13, 1861. Died at Suffolk, Va., Oct., 1861.
DUNN, JACK. Private, July 13, 1861. Lost right leg.
DUNN, JIM. Private, July 13, 1861. Killed.
DUNN, JOHN. Private, July 13, 1861. Deserted in McMullan's Company.
WATSON, T. J. Private, March 11, 1863. Killed at Wilderness, May 6, 1864.

Muster Roll of Company "H" 15th Regiment, Georgia Volunteers Infantry, Army of Northern Virginia, C. S. A., Hart County, Georgia

Organized at King's Bench, July 15th, 1861

POOLE, WM. R. Captain, July 15, 1861. Resigned April 5, 1862.
LINDER, JOHN. 1st Lieutenant, July 15, 1861. Resigned Feb. 29, 1862.
JOHNSON, M. 2nd Lieutenant, July 15, 1861. Resigned Sep. 10, 1861.
KNOX, WILLIAM. Jr. 2nd Lieutenant. Resigned Oct. 17, 1861.
JACKSON, THOMAS. 1st Sergeant, July 15, 1861. Elected 1st Lieutenant.
FISHER, THOMAS. 2nd Sergeant, July 15, 1861. Elected Jr. 2nd Lieutenant 1863. Resigned April 20, 1864.
SHIRLEY, J. M. 3rd Sergeant, July 15, 1861. Captured at Gettysburg, Pa., July 2, 1863.
BURROUGHS, F. W. 4th Sergeant, July 15, 1861. Elected Jr. 2nd Lieutenant, Nov., 1861. Died July 19, 1862, in Franklin County, Ga.
ROE, SAMUEL. 1st Corporal, July 15, 1861. Killed June 20, 1864 at Petersburg, Va.
AYERS, J. W. 2nd Corporal, July 15, 1861. Died at Richmond, Va., Dec. 12, 1862.
SHIRLEY, J. D. 3rd Corporal, July 15, 1861. Died at Richmond, Va.

ASKEW, MARSHALL. Private, July 15, 1861.
ARNAM, ... Private, July 15, 1861. Died at Richmond, Va.
BUFFINGTON, J. W. Private, July 15, 1861. Appointed 2nd Sergeant April, 1862. Deserted Feb. 26, 1865.
BUFFINGTON, J. H. Private, July 15, 1861. Died May 20, 1864 at Richmond, Va.
BAILEY, PASCHAL. Private, July 15, 1861. Wounded and captured at Gettysburg, Pa., July 2, 1863.
BROWN, A. R. Private, July 15, 1861. Lost right leg, Nov., 1862 at ....
BYRUM, SAMUEL. Private, July 15, 1861. Died April 12, 1864 at Bristol, Tenn., hospital.
BROWN, NOAH W. Private, July 15, 1861.
BROWN, J. C. Private, March 4, 1862. Appointed 4th Sergeant, April, 1862. Captured at Gettysburg, Pa., July 2, 1863 .
BAILEY, J. A. Private, March 4, 1862.
BURKE, F. M. Private, July 15, 1861. Died Aug. 18, 1862 at Richmond, Va.
BROWN, S. C. Private, July 15, 1861. Died May 7, 1862 at Richmond, Va.
BAILEY, G. R. Private, 1863.
BUFFINGTON, W. W. Private, March 4, 1862. Died May 25, 1862 at ....
BAILEY, W. J. Private, March 1, 1863. Surrendered at Appomattox, Va.
BAILEY, WILLIAM. Private, July 15, 1861. Elected 1st Lieutenant, March 3, 1862. Died Oct. 5, 1864 of disease at Richmond, Va.
CARROLL, CLEMENT. Private, July 15, 1861. Discharged Aug. 10, 1864.
CARROLL, G. W. Private, July 15, 1861. Surrendered at Appomattox, Va.
CARROLL, NELSON. Private, July 15, 1861.
CARROLL, A. J. Private, July 15, 1861. Died ...., 1863 at .... Md.
CALL, JOSEPH. Private, July 15, 1861. Wounded and discharged at Ocean Pond, Fla. Feb. 20, 1864.
CARROLL, LARKIN. Private, July 15, 1861. Captured at Gettysburg, Pa., July 2, 1863.
CARROLL, THOMAS. Private, July 15, 1861. Died May, 1862.
CARPENTER, THOMAS. Private, Aug. 22, 1862. Substitute for H. L. Fisher.
ESTES, J. W. Private, July 15, 1861. Discharged Nov. 6, 1861.
ESKEW, SAMUEL. Private, July 15, 1861. Discharged Dec. 9, 1861.
FISHER, H. L. Private, July 15, 1861. Discharged Aug. 22, 1862, furnishing Thomas Carpenter as substitute.
FLEMING, LEONARD. Private, July 15, 1861. Died at Richmond, Va., Nov. 2, 1861.
FULLER, MILTON. Private, July 15, 1861. Wounded June 20, 1864 at Petersburg, Va.
FAIN, JAMES. Private, May, 1863. Killed at Farmville, Va., April 6, 1865.
GRUBBS, W. M. Private, July 15, 1861. Surrendered at Appomattox, Va.
GABLES, H. F. Private, July 15, 1861.
GULLEY, J. W. Private, March 4, 1862. Killed 1863 at ....
GULLEY, W. F. Private, March 4, 1862. Died June 22, 1862 at Richmond, Va.
GUEST, J. P. Private, March 4, 1862. Died April 1, 1863 at Richmond, Va.
GRUBBS, G. W. Private, April 15, 1862. Killed Aug. 28, 1862 at 2nd Manassas, Va.
GUEST, SPENCER. Private, March, 1863.
HOLLAND, JOHN T. Private, July 15, 1861. Captured at Gettysburg, Pa., July 2, 1863.
HARRIS, W. P. Private, July 15, 1861. Died May 25, 1862 at Richmond, Va.
HOLLAND, B. F. Private, July 15, 1861.
HENLEY, JAMES E. Private, July 15, 1861. Wounded and captured 1864 at ....
HARRIS, H. Private, July 15, 1861. Died at Richmond, Va., Sep. 26, 1862.
HARRISON, E. A. Private, July 15, 1861. Killed at Darbytown, Va., Oct. 7, 1864.
HALL, W. M. Private, July 15, 1861. Died at Richmond, Va., Aug. 1, 1862.
HUNT, W. J. C. Private, July 15, 1861. Discharged March 27, 1863, disabilities.
HALL, G. W. Private, March 4, 1862. Died June 9, 1862 at Richmond, Va.
HALL, J. M. Private, July 15, 1861. Died at Spotsylvania, Va., 1864.
HIGGINS, C. A. Private, March 4, 1862. Died May 3, 1862, at Richmond, Va.
JACKSON, JOSEPH. Private, March 4, 1862. Wounded at .... Surrendered at Appomattox, Va.
JORDAN, AARON. Private, March 4, 1862. Wounded at ....
JACKSON, T. H. Private, July 15, 1861. Elected Captain, April 25, 1862. Captured Sep. 29, 1864 at Fort Harrison, Va.
LEROY, JESSE M. Private, July 15, 1861. Killed at Sharpsburg, Md., Sep. 17, 1862.
LINDER, LEE. Private, July 15, 1861.

LAIRD, J. P. Private, March 10, 1863. Killed at Chickamauga, Ga., Sep. 19, 1863.
MADDEN, J. F. Private, July 15, 1861. Killed at Sharpsburg, Md., Sep. 17, 1862.
MATTHEWS, WILLIAM H. Private, July 15, 1861. Wounded at Petersburg, Va., July 1, 1864.
MOORE, R. F. Private, July 15, 1861. Wounded 1864 at .... Surrendered at Appomattox, Va.
MASSEY, CHARLES E. Private, July 15, 1861. Wounded Oct. 7, 1861 at ....
O'BARR, WHITNEY. Private, July 15, 1861. Wounded at Sharpsburg, Md., Sep. 17, 1862. Captured at Gettysburg, Pa., July 2, 1863. Exchanged; mortally wounded at Wilderness, Va., May 6, 1864.
OLE, PEARMAN. Private, July 15, 1861.
O'BARR, J. H. Private, March 4, 1862. Died in hospital at ....
PEARMAN, C. C. Private, July 15, 1861. Captured at Gettysburg, Pa., July 2, 1863.
PEARMAN, W. C. Private, July 15, 1861. Died April 10, 1863 at Petersburg, Va., hospital.
PRICAE, L. H. Private, March 4, 1862. Died May 10, 1862 at Richmond, Va., hospital.
PRUITT, W. H. Private, Feb. 10, 1864.
ROWLAND, WILLIAM. Private, July 15, 1861. Captured Jan. 22, 1864 at ....
ROE, C. W. G. Private, July 15, 1861. Killed Sep. 20, 1863 at Chickamauga, Ga.
RICHARDSON, J. M. Private, July 15, 1861. Discharged Nov. 10, 1861.
ROBERTSON, G. C. Private, July 15, 1861. Discharged Dec. 24, 1861.
SULLIVAN, JAMES. Private, July 15, 1861. Wounded at Sharpsburg, Md., Sep. 17, 1862.
SMITH, WILLIAM. Private, July 15, 1861. Discharged Dec. 17, 1861 at ....
THRASHER, P. J. Private, July 15, 1861. Wounded at Malvern Hill, Va., July 1, 1862. Retired July 1, 1864.
THRASHER, L. H. Private, March 4, 1862. Died June 5, 1863 at Montgomery Springs, Va., of measles.
THRASHER, CLARK T. Private, July 15, 1861. Died Oct. 1, 1861 at Richmond, Va., Hospital.
USSERY, CHARLES E. Private, July 15, 1861.
VICKERY, JAMES P. Private, July 15, 1861. Appointed 1st Sergeant, April, 1862. Surrendered at Appomattox, Va.
VICKERY, JAMES PERLEY. Private, July 15, 1861. Appointed 4th Corporal, April, 1862. Died July 7, 1862 at Richmond, Va.
WHITE, D. M. Private, July 15, 1861. Wounded at Sharpsburg, Md., Sep. 17, 1862.
WALTERS, JOHN F. Private, July 15, 1861. Mortally wounded at Wilderness, Va., May 6, 1864.
WALTERS, J. C. Private, July 15, 1861.
WALTERS, B. W. Private, July 15, 1861. Discharged Nov. 5, 1861.
WALTERS, DEAN W. Private, July 15, 1861. Died Dec., 1862 at Richmond, Va.
WALTERS, H. F. Private, March 4, 1862. Discharged Dec. 26, 1862.
WALTERS, FRANKLIN. Private, March 4, 1862. Captured at Gettysburg, Pa., July 2, 1862.
WALTERS, J. G. Private, March 4, 1862. Died at Richmond, Va.
WRIGHT, T. G. Private, March 4, 1862. Captured at Gettysburg, Pa., July 2, 1863. Surrendered at Appomattox, Va.
WADE, J. A. C. Private, Sep. 17, 1863.
WADE, W. G. Private, Sep. 17, 1863. Died May 5, 186.... in hospital at ....
YATES, ELISHA. Private, July 15, 1861.
YOW, T. A. Private, July 15, 1861. Died Nov. 1, 1861 at Richmond, Va.
WALTERS, W. R. Private, July 15, 1861. Elected 2nd Lieutenant, Dec. 4, 1862. Killed June 19, 1864 at Petersburg, Va.
ISAAC FOWLER, EZEK ELROD, JOE MARTIN, JOE BURTON, TOM FLEMING, LEVIS CORNOG, JOHN GRUBBS and W. F. PRICE, were also members of this company.

Muster Roll of Company "F" 38th Regiment, Georgia Volunteers Infantry, Army of Northern Virginia, C. S. A. Evans Brigade, Gordon's Division, Hart County, Georgia

THORNTON, JOHN C. Captain, Oct. 15, 1861. Resigned Feb. 11, 1863.
TEASLEY, JOHN H. H. 1st Lieutenant, Oct. 15, 1861. Died June 19, 1862 at ....
BROWN, BENAGER T. 2nd Lieutenant, Oct. 15, 1861. Promoted 1st Lieutenant, June 22, 1862. Died July 29, 1862 at Staunton, Va.

MAXWELL, JACKSON O. Jr. 2nd Lieutenant, Oct. 15, 1861. Promoted 2nd Lieutenant, June 22, 1862. 1st Lieutenant, Aug. 18, 1862. Captain, Feb. 1, 1863. Resigned Jan. 24, 1865.
RUCKER, WILLIAM B. 1st Sergeant, Oct. 15, 1861. Elected Jr. 2nd Lieutenant, June 22, 1862. Died Aug. 1, 1862 at ....
HUNT, REUBEN. 2nd Sergeant, Oct. 15, 1861. Appointed 1st Sergeant, 1862. Elected Jr. 2nd Lieutenant March, 29, 1863.
EAVERSON, JOHN W. 3rd Sergeant, Oct. 15, 1861. Promoted 2nd Sergeant, 1862. Wounded, 1862 at .... Promoted 1st Sergeant, March, 1863.
BROWN, WILLIAM J. 4th Sergeant, Oct. 15, 1861. Died Aug. 25, 1862, at ....
ALMOND, JOHN A. 5th Sergeant, Oct. 15, 1861. Died May 14, 1862 at ....
HARPER, JAMES W. 1st Corporal, Oct. 15, 1861. Wounded at Cold Harbor, Va., June 27, 1862. Private, June, 1863. Appointed 2nd Sergeant, Aug. 22, 1864.
PARTAIN, ROBERT P. 2nd Corporal, Oct. 15, 1861. Wounded, 1864 at ....
PARTAIN, HENRY H. 3rd Corporal, Oct. 15, 1861. Appointed Color Guard, March, 1862. Captured Sep. 19, 1864 at Winchester, Va.
FLEMING, DAVID B. 4th Corporal, Oct. 15, 1861. Discharged Dec., 1862. Disability.
HUTCHERSON, JAMES M. Musician, Oct. 15, 1861.
NELMS, WILLIAM. Dec. 1862. Surrendered at Appomattox, Va.
ADAMS, ALFRED H. Private, Oct. 15, 1861. Captured, 1864 at .... Died July, 1864 at ....,
ADAMS, LAWRENCE. Private, Oct. 15, 1861. Appointed 4th Corporal, Feb., 1863, 3rd Corporal, 1863. Died Nov. 15, 1863 at ....
ADAMS, WILLIAM H. Private, Oct. 15, 1861. Appointed 4th Sergeant, May, 1862. 3rd Sergeant, March, 1863. 1st Sergeant, Jan., 1864. Captured 1864 at ....
ADAMS, HARPER. Private, Oct. 15, 1861. Captured Sep. 19, 1864 at Winchester, Va.
ADAMS, WILLIAM M. Private, Oct. 15, 1861.
ALMOND, ISAAC B. Private, Oct. 15, 1861. Wounded Sep. 19, 1864 at Winchester, Va.
ALEXANDER, PHIL W. Private, Jan. 23, 1862. Appointed Q. M. Sergeant, April 1, 1862.
ALMOND, JOHN B. Private, March 23, 1862. Wounded Dec. 13, 1862 at Fredericksburg, Va. Died .... 1864 at ....
ADAMS, J. J. Private, Aug. 29, 1862. Wounded Jan., 1864 at ....
ADAMS, H. P. Private, Aug. 29, 1862. Wounded Dec. 13, 1862 at Fredericksburg, Va.
BENTLEY, JOSEPH A. J. Private, Oct. 15, 1861. Appointed 3rd Sergeant, Aug. 1862. 2nd Sergeant, March, 1863.
BENTLEY, JOHN D. Private, Oct. 15, 1861. Wounded 1864 at .... Surrendered at Appomattox, Va.
BROWN, WILLIAM A. D. Private, Oct. 15, 1861. Captured 1864 at ....
BROWN, BURTON. Private, Oct. 15, 1861. Wounded Dec. 13, 1862 at Fredericksburg, Va.
BROWN, JOHN A. J. Private, Oct. 15, 1861. Wounded Dec. 13, 1862 at Fredericksburg, Va.
BROADWELL, WILLIAM T. Private, Oct. 15, 1861. Appointed 4th Corporal, Jan., 1863. Private, Aug., 1863. Wounded May 6, 1864 at Wilderness, Va.
BOND, ANDREW J. Private, March 16, 1862. Captured Oct. 22, 1864 at ....
BREWER, COLUMBUS. Private, March 16, 1863. Discharged June 24, 1862, at ....
BURNES, JOSEPH. Private, Sep., 1862. Wounded at Gettysburg, Pa., July 2, 1863.
BROWN, ASA C. Private, May 10, 1862. Killed May 5, 1864 at Wilderness, Va.
BENTLEY, R. F. Private May 14, 1862. Appointed 3rd Corporal, Jan., 1864. Wounded at ....,
BENTLEY, M. A. Private, May 14, 1862. Wounded Dec. 15, 1862 at Fredericksburg, Va.
BROWN, E. W. Private, July 15, 1861. Wounded at Gettysburg, Pa., July 2, 1863. Discharged Oct. 12, 1864. Disability.
BROWN, J. C. Private, Oct., 1862. Died in Richmond, Va., July 5, 1864.
BAILEY, JOHN A. Private, May 21, 1864. Wounded and captured, Sep. 19, 1864 at Winchester, Va.
CARPENTER, FRANCIS N. Private, Oct. 15, 1861.
CRUMP, ROBERT C. W. Private, Oct. 15, 1861.
CAMPBELL, J. C. Private, Sep. 5, 1862. Transferred from Company—15th Ga. Regiment, Sep. 5, 1862. Appointed 5th Sergeant, Aug. 1864. Captured Aug. 19, 1864 at Winchester, Va. Point Lookout, Jan., 1865.
COLLINS, WILLIAM. Private, Dec. 10, 1862. Deserted Dec. 10, 1863 at ....

HISTORY OF HART COUNTY

DANIEL, WILLIAM A. Private, May, 1862. Died of Measles, July, 1862 at ....
DAVIS, HENRY B. Private, Oct. 15, 1861.
DUNCAN, JEPTHA H. Private, Oct. 15, 1861. Discharged .... furnishing .... as substitute.
DUTTON, WILLIAM J. Private, Feb. 12, 1862. Absent without leave, 1862.
DAVIS, W. H. Private, April 25, 1862. Died Nov. 9, 1863 at ....
DENING, J. M. Private, Feb. 2, 1862. Died 1864 at ....
DUNCAN, J. W. Private, Feb. 2, 1862. Wounded Sep. 19, 1864 at Winchester, Va.
EVANS, WILLIAM W. Private, Oct. 15, 1861.
EAVERSON, WILLIS J. Private, Oct. 15, 1861. Wounded 1864 at ....
EAVERSON, T. M. Private, March 10, 1862. Mortally wounded at 2nd Manassas, Va.
EAVERSON, T. A. Private, Feb. 3, 1864.
EAVERSON, J. W. Private, Oct. 15, 1861. Transferred .... Major S. W. Lee's Battalion .... Wounded 1864 at .... and disabled.
FLEMING, JOHN R. Private, Oct. 15, 1861. Discharged May 10, 1862. Disability. Re-enlisted 1863. Died Aug., 1864 at ....
FLEMING, DAVID F. Private, Oct. 15, 1861. Died Aug. 26, 1862 at ....
FORTSON, WILLIAM T. Private, Oct. 15, 1861. Appointed 5th Corporal, March 1, 1862. Wounded Dec. 13, 1862 at Fredericksburg, Va.
FORTSON, JESSE W. Private, May 10, 1862. Died July 27, 1862 at Staunton, Va.
FORTSON, G. G. Private, May 14, 1862. Discharged Dec. 10, 1862, furnishing .... as substitute.
FORTSON, S. H. Private, May 14, 1862.
FORTSON, D. A. Private, May 14, 1862.
FORTSON, E. L. Private, May 14, 1862. Killed July 1, 1863 at Gettysburg, Pa.
GULLEY, R. P. Private, May 10, 1862. Wounded at 2nd Manassas, Va., Aug. 28, 1862. Absent without leave, Aug., 1863.
GUEST, G. B. Private, Sep. 5, 1862.
GREENWAY, L. A. Private, Sep. 5, 1862. Died in Richmond, Va., Hospital, 1862.
HIGGINBOTHAM, DOZIER J. Private, Oct. 15, 1861. Discharged 1864. Disability.
HIGGINBOTHAM, JOHN T. Private, Oct. 15, 1861. Died June 15, 1862 in Augusta, Ga.
HUNT, DOZIER C. Private, Oct. 15, 1861. Captured 1864 at .... Died in Richmond, Va., Nov. 15, 1864.
HUTCHERSON, BENJAMIN H. Private, Oct. 15, 1861.
HICKMAN, BENJAMIN H. Private, Dec. 14, 1861. Killed Dec. 13, 1862 at Fredericksburg, Va.
HICKMAN, COLUMBUS J. Private, Feb. 12, 1862.
HUNT, JAMES W. H. Private, March 10, 1862. Captured 1864 at ....
HUNT, THOMAS J. M. Private, March 10, 1861. Died May 20, 1862 at ....
HUNT, J. M. B. Private, Oct. 15, 1861. Surrendered at Appomattox, Va.
HUNT, SINGLETON J. W. Private, March 10, 1862. Captured 1864 at ....
HUTCHERSON, JOHN M. Private, March 10, 1862. Died June 29, 1862 at ....
HUNT, B. T. Private, May 14, 1862. Died July 30, 1862 at ....
HUTCHERSON, J. M. D. Private, March 10, 1862. Discharged May 10, 1862 at ....
HULME, J. D. Private, Sep. 5, 1862.
HIGGINBOTHAM, E. C. Private, May 14, 1862. Lost both legs at Spotsylvania, Va., May 12, 1864.
HUNT, B. A. T. Private, Aug. 29, 1862. Died Dec. 1, 1862 at ....
HUNT, JAMES J. Private, April, 1863. Died Jan., 1864 in Winchester, Va.
HENDRICKS, W. J. Private, May 22, 1864. Captured Sep. 22, 1864 at Fisher's Mill, Va.
HOWLAND, T. J. Private, March 18, 1864. Surrendered at Appomattox, Va.
JORDAN, F. M. Private, Sep. 5, 1861. Captured, 1864 at ....
JENKINS, E. J. Private, Sep. 5, 1862. Captured Sep. 22, 1864 at Fisher's Mill, Va.
KING, THOMAS W. Private, Oct. 15, 1861.
LOFTEN, WILLIAM D. Private, Sep. 9, 1861.
LOFTEN, A. Private, May 7, 1862.
MCCURDY, JAMES D. Private, Oct. 15, 1861. Captured Sep. 22, 1864 at Fisher's Mill, Va.
MCCURRY, JOHN G. W. Private, Oct. 15, 1861. Elected Jr. 2nd Lieutenant Aug. 18, 1862. Promoted 2nd Lieutenant, March 22, 1863.
MAXWELL, THOMAS. Private, Oct. 15, 1861.

MAXWELL, WILLIAM H. Private, Oct. 15, 1861. Appointed 5th Sergeant, March 29, 1863. 4th Sergeant, June, 1863. Died June 24, 1864 at _____.
MAXWELL, B. M. Private, May 10, 1862. Killed Aug. 28, 1862 at 2nd Manassas, Va.
MAXWELL, CHANDLER. Private, Aug. 29, 1862. Wounded 1863 at _____.
MEEKS, JOHN. Private, Aug. 29, 1862. Died Sep. 7, 1862 in Richmond, Va.
MOSS, HAMILTON. Private, May 10, 1862. Captured, 1864 at _____.
MOSS, BENTON. Private, March 9, 1863. Captured 1864 at _____.
MOTES, W. A. Private, Sep., 1862. Captured at Gettysburg, Pa., July 2, 1863.
MCCURRY, W. E. Private, Nov. 1, 1862. Captured Sep. 22, 1864 at Fisher's.
MAXWELL, C. Private, Aug. 29, 1862. Wounded Aug., 1863 at _____.
NELMS, JAMES C. Private, Oct. 15, 1861.
O'BRYANT, WILLIAM. Private, Oct. 15, 1861.
POWELL, WILLIAM J. Private, Oct. 15, 1861. Appointed 5th Corporal, June, 1863. Killed July 1, 1863 at Gettysburg, Pa.
POWELL, JAMES L. Private, Oct. 15, 1861. Died Oct., 1863 at _____.
PARTAIN, BENJAMIN P. Private, Oct. 15, 1861. Wounded June 27, 1862 at Cold Harbor, Va.
PAGE, WILLIAM H. Private, Oct. 15, 1861.
PARKS, ARCHIBALD. Private, Oct. 15, 1861.
PARKS, JOHN M. Private, Oct. 15, 1861.
PEARSON, LITTLETON D. Private, Feb. 12, 1862. Captured 1864, at _____.
PARTAIN, HENRY C. Private, April 6, 1862.
PARKS, LINDSEY B. Private, April 6, 1862. Wounded June 27, 1862 at Cold Harbor, Va.
PARTAIN, L. M. Private, Dec. 27, 1862. Captured 1864, at _____.
POWELL, WILLIAM. Private, Dec. 14, 1862.
POWELL, WILEY. Private, June, 1862. Wounded Aug. 28, 1862 at 2nd Manassas, Va. Died at Lynchburg, Va., 1864 of wound.
PEARSON, G. W. Private, May 1, 1865. Wounded Jan., 1864 at _____, Captured Oct. 19, 1864 at Cedar Creek, Va.
ROBERTS, JOHN T. Private, Oct. 15, 1861. Wounded Dec. 13, 1862 at Fredericksburg, Va. Captured 1864 at _____.
RICE, A. M. Private, May 14, 1862. Wounded June, 1863 at _____ and discharged.
STAMPS, JAMES L. Private, Oct. 15, 1861. Captured 1864 at _____.
SAYER, WILLIAM T. Private, Oct. 15, 1861. Captured 1864 at _____.
SMITH, STEPHEN F. Private, Oct. 15, 1861.
SAYER, DAVID W. Private, Feb. 12, 1862.
SAYER, WILLIAM O. Private, Feb. 12, 1862. Captured 1864 at _____.
STANSEL, JAMES. Private, Nov. 17, 1862. Wounded June, 1863 at _____. Discharged _____ 1864 account of wound.
SHIFLET, W. J. Private, May 14, 1862. Killed July 1, 1863 at Gettysburg, Pa.
THORNTON, R. B. Private, May 10, 1862. Appointed 5th Sergeant, Feb. 10, 1863. Appointed 4th Sergeant, March, 1863. Died May 29, 1863 at _____.
TERRY, ELIJAH M. Private, Oct. 15, 1861.
THORNTON, THOMAS D. Private, Oct. 15, 1861. Elected 2nd Lieutenant, Aug. 18, 1862. 1st Lieutenant, March 29, 1863. Surrendered at Appomattox, Va.
THORNTON, WILLIAM M. Private, Oct. 15, 1861. Appointed 5th Sergeant, June, 1863. 4th Sergeant, Aug. 22, 1864. Surrendered at Appomattox, Va.
THORNTON, JESSE M. Private, Oct. 15, 1861. Wounded Dec. 13, 1862 at Fredericksburg, Va. Appointed 4th Corporal, Aug. 30, 1863. Killed July 9, 1864 at Monocacy, Md.
THORNTON, BENJAMIN F. Private, Oct. 15, 1861. Died Aug. 7, 1862 in Richmond, Va.
THORNTON, JAMES C. Private, Oct. 15, 1861. Wounded Dec. 15, 1862 at Fredericksburg, Va. Surrendered at Appomattox, Va.
TYNER, JAMES A. Private, Oct. 15, 1861. Discharged May 23, 1863.
TYNER, WILLIAM. Private, Oct. 20, 1861. Absent without leave, 1864.
TYNER, JOSHUA. Private, Oct. 15, 1861. Died Dec. 5, 1862 at _____.
TYNER, JOHN H. Private, Oct. 15, 1861.
THORNTON, JEPTHA M. Private, Oct. 15, 1861. Wounded at 2nd Manassas, Va.
THORNTON, ASA C. Private, Oct. 15, 1861.
TERRY, WILLIAM J. Private, Oct. 15, 1861. Wounded Dec. 13, 1862 at Fredericksburg, Va. Absent without leave June, 1865.
THORNTON, WILLIAM G. Private, Oct. 15, 1861.

THORNTON, JOHN C. Private, Feb. 12, 1862. Wounded at Fredericksburg, Va., Dec. 13, 1862, and absent until Feb. 1863. Died in Savannah, Ga., Hospital, Oct. 19, 1864.
THORNTON, WILLIAM T. Private, Sep. 5, 1862. Appointed 5th Sergeant, 1862. Died Jan. 29, 1863 of wound received Dec. 13, 1862 at Fredericksburg, Va.
TERRY, JOSEPH C. Private, Dec. 27, 1862.
WANSLEY, THOMAS M. Private, 1862.

Muster Roll of Company "D" 37th Regiment, Georgia Volunteers Infantry, Army of Tennessee, C. S. A., Hart County, Georgia

MCMULLAN, JOHN G. Captain, March 4, 1862. Killed Nov. 25, 1863, at Missionary Ridge, Tenn.
CLARK, W. M. 1st Lieutenant, March 4, 1862. Promoted Captain, Nov. 25, 1863.
GAINES, J. J. 2nd Lieutenant, March 4, 1862. Promoted 1st Lieutenant, Nov. 25, 1863. Resigned Aug. 1, 1863, Tyner Station. Joined Militia, Aug., 1864. At home on furlough, April, 1865.
RICHARDSON, M. M. Jr. 2nd Lieutenant, March 4, 1862. Promoted 2nd Lieutenant, Aug. 1, 1863. Promoted 1st Lieutenant, Nov. 25, 1863. Wounded at Chickamauga, Ga., Sep. 19, 1863, in right forearm, and at Resaca, Ga., May 15, 1864 in left elbow joint. Retired at home, April, 1865.
MCDOWELL, JAMES T. 1st Sergeant, March 4, 1862.
LATTA, M. J. 2nd Sergeant, March 4, 1862.
SHEPPERD, B. F. 3rd Sergeant, March 4, 1862. Elected 2nd Lieutenant, March 10, 1864.
GRAY, B. M. 4th Sergeant, March 4, 1862.
CHAMBERS, R. G. 5th Sergeant, March 4, 1862. Elected Jr. 2nd Lieutenant, July 4, 1864.
SKELTON, J. D. 1st Corporal, March 4, 1862.
LATTA, A. T. 2nd Corporal, March 4, 1862.
JONES, D. R. J. 3rd Corporal, March 4, 1862. Died at Knoxville, Tenn., May, 1862.
PHILLIPS, W. A. 4th Corporal, May 10, 1862. Absent without leave, 1863.
ADAMS, ALFRED. Private, March 4, 1862.
ADAMS, W. C. Private, March 4, 1862. Captured at _____. Released from Camp Douglas, Ill., April, 1865.
BROWN, JOHN A. Private, March 16, 1862. Captured at Missionary Ridge, Tenn., Nov. 25, 1863.
BROWN, R. D. Private, March 16, 1862.
BROWN, S. B. Private, March 16, 1862.
BOWERS, J. B. Private, March 4, 1862.
BROWN, NOAH L. Private, March 4, 1862. Died of disease, June 29, 1862.
BARRON, R. F. Private, March 4, 1862.
BROWN, S. M. Private, May 10, 1862.
BEGGS, THOMAS M. Private, March 4, 1862.
BRIDGES, DANIEL. Private, March 4, 1862. Died Jan. 1, 1864 in Atlanta, Ga., Hospital.
CHEEK, R. V. Private, March 4, 1862.
CLEVELAND, CORNELIUS. Private, March 10, 1862.
CLEVELAND, N. B. Private, July 1, 1862. Died Dec. 1, 1863 in Rome, Ga., Hospital.
DYAR, W. J. Private, March 4, 1862.
DYAR, R. J. Private, March 4, 1862.
DAVIS, H. W. Private, March 15, 1862.
DAVIS, W. H. Private, Oct. 18, 1863. Discharged at _____, 1864. Disability.
DYAR, F. M. Private, March 25, 1864.
EATON, FRANKLIN. Private, March 4, 1862.
ERWIN, JOHN A. Private, March 4, 1861.
FAIN, W. B. Private, March 4, 1862. Surrendered at Greensboro, N. C.
GAINES, JAMES B. Private, March 4, 1862. Died July 1, 1862 at Knoxville, Tenn., Hospital.
GARY, JOHN W. Private, May 10, 1862.
GREENWAY, T. M. Private, May 1, 1862. Died Nov. 5, 1862 in hospital at _____.
GRAY, JOHN W. Private, May 10, 1862.
HERRING, ISARIAH. Private, March 4, 1862.

HERRING, B. B. Private, 1863.
HERRING, JEREMIAH. Private, March 16, 1862.
HERRING, JAMES E. Private, March 16, 1862. Wounded at ....
HARRELL, W. J. Private, Nov. 1, 1862.
HERNDON, M. A. Private, May 16, 1862.
HAYNES, J. S. Private, March 4, 1862.
HUBBARD, ZENUS. Private, March 16, 1862. Surrendered at Greensboro, N. C.
HIGGINBOTHAM, B. T. Private, Aug. 1, 1862. Died Jan. 1, 1864 of disease at ....
HERRINGTON, M. A. Private, May 10, 1862.
HAM, WESLEY. Private, Aug. 20, 1863. Died Jan., 1864 at ....
ISBELL, A. B. Private, May 10, 1862.
ISOM, DANIEL. Private, May 10, 1862. Wounded 1862 at ....
JORDAN, J. F. Private, May 10, 1862. Died Jan., 1864 at ....
LOFTON, L. E. A. Private, March 4, 1862.
LATTY, H. T. Private, March 4, 1862. Captured Dec., 1864 at ....
LEARD, CASWELL. Private, March 4, 1862. Captured at Hoover's Gap, Tenn., June 24, 1863. Died at Fort Delaware, Del., Prison, June 10, 1863, of smallpox.
McCURRY, WILLIAM. Private, March 16, 1862. Captured at Missionary Ridge, Tenn., Nov. 25, 1863.
McCURRY, OBADIAH. Private, March 4, 1862. Captured at .... Released from Camp Douglas, Ill., Prison, April, 1865.
McMULLAN, T. L. Private, March 4, 1862. Wounded at Murfreesboro, Tenn., Dec. 31, 1862.
McDOUGLE, T. E. Private, May 10, 1862.
McCURRY, A. L. Private, May 10, 1862. Wounded at Chickamauga, Ga., Sep. 19, 1865. Retired on furlough, Feb., 1864.
McCURLEY, J. M. Private, March 4, 1862. Wounded, 1863 at ....
McHARGUE, J. H. Private, Oct. 1, 1862.
McCURLEY, L. W. Private, May 4, 1862. Wounded 1863 at ....
McCURLEY, L. J. Private, May 9, 1862. Died of fever at home.
McLANE, JAMES D. Private, March 4, 1862.
MYERS, J. R. Private, March 4, 1864. Elected 2nd Lieutenant, Dec. 15, 1863.
MULLINIX, H. J. Private, March 4, 1862. Surrendered at Greensboro, N. C.
MORRIS, RUFUS J. Private, May 10, 1862.
MORRIS, REUBEN J. Private, May 10, 1862.
McCURDY, WILLIAM. Private, March 4, 1862. Died July 14, 1862 of measles at ....
McLANE, W. J. Private, May 10, 1862.
McCOWN, B. W. Private, Nov. 26, 1863.
McDOUGLE, W. J. M. Private, May 10, 1862. Deserted Dec. 1, 1863 at ....
CRAWFORD, JOHN W. Private, March 1, 1862. Wounded 1864 at ....
CLEM, A. J. Private, March 1, 1862.
CRAFT, J. W. Private, March 10, 1862.
CHAPMAN, J. M. Private, March 1, 1862. Wounded 1863 at ....
CRUMP, E. S. V. Private, March 16, 1862.
CRAFT, DAVID. Private, March 1, 1862. Died May 1, 1862 of measles at ....
CRUMP, R. J. C. W. Private, March 16, 1862. Wounded at Chickamauga, Ga., Sep. 19, 1863.
CHASTAIN, A. Private, March 4, 1862. Died May 21, 1864 in Atlanta, Ga.
CRUMP, T. J. Private, March 4, 1862.
CASON, J. M. Private, Oct. 18, 1863.
CLARK, JAMES. Private, Oct. 18, 1863.
COOK, T. B. Private, May 10, 1862. Died Jan. 1, 1864 at home from wound.
CLEVELAND, T. G. Private, March 4, 1862. Deserted Jan. 1, 1864 at ....
CLEVELAND, D. P. Private, May 10, 1862. Deserted Jan. 1864 at ....
OWENS, A. F. Private May 10, 1862.
OWENS, ELI C. Private, March 4, 1862. Under arrest, 1863 for ....
OUTZ, J. F. Private, March 4, 1862.
PARKS, JOHN M. Private, March 4, 1862.
PAGE, F. M. Private, 1864.
PHILLIPS, A. W. C. Private, May 10, 1862. Under arrest, 1863 for ....
PHILLIPS, J. R. Private, May 10, 1862. Wounded 1863 at ....
POWELL, N. T. Private, March 4, 1862.

PARKS, M. J. Private, March 4, 1862. Wounded, 1863, at ----------.
RICHARDSON, SINCLAIR. Private, May 10, 1862.
RICHARDSON, S. W. Private, March 4, 1862.
RICHARDSON, MILTON. Private, March 4, 1862. Captured at Missionary Ridge, Tenn., Nov. 25, 1863.
ROWLAND, A. M. Private, May 10, 1862.
SKELTON, W. J. Private, March 4, 1862. Wounded 1863 at ----------.
SKELTON, JOHN D. Private, March 4, 1862. Surrendered at Greensboro, N. C.
SANDERS, ALBERRY. Private, March 4, 1862.
SANDERS, THORNTON. Private, March 4, 1862. Wounded and disabled at Kennesaw Mountain, Ga., June 27, 1864.
SANDERS, ASA C. Private, May 10, 1862.
SANDERS, JAMES M. Private, March 4, 1862.
SNOW, J. M. Private, March 4, 1862.
SANDERS, THOMAS J. Private, May 10, 1862. Wounded at Hoover's Gap, Tenn., June 24, 1863, in arm and wrist. Discharged at Macon, Ga., Oct. 4, 1863, Dec. 22, 1864.
SANDERS, T. S. Private, March 4, 1862.
SANDERS, FRANKLIN. Private, March 4, 1862.
SANDERS, J. F. Private, March 4, 1862.
SANDERS, JAMES. Private, July 20, 1862. Captured at Missionary Ridge, Tenn., Nov. 25, 1863.
SHIFLET, JAMES. Private, May 10, 1862. Lost leg at Chickamauga, Ga., Sep. 19, 1863. Retired at Augusta, Ga., May, 1864.
TEEL, W. J. J. Private, May 11, 1862.
VICKERY, G. B. Private, March 15, 1863.
VICKERY, JAMES H. Private, April 7, 1863.
VICKERY, M. W. Private, Oct. 20, 1863.
VICKERY, T. H. Private, March 4, 1862. Died May 10, 1864 in Atlanta, Ga.
VERNON, ROBERT M. Private, March 4, 1862.
VERNON, D. H. Private. Wounded at Chattanooga, Tenn., Sep., 1863.
WALTERS, L. B. Private, May 10, 1862. Killed, Franklin, Tenn.
WALTERS, J. P. Private, May 10, 1862. Died at home from wound in arm and hand.
WALTERS, JEPTHA. Private, May 10, 1862.
WOOD, W. C. Private, June 1, 1862.
WALKER, JOSIAH. Private, March 4, 1862. Wounded 1863. Died at Knoxville, Tenn., May, 1862 of measles.
WHITE, ALEXANDER. Private, March 4, 1862. Died May 1, 1862 of measles at Knoxville, Tenn.
SMITH, JAMES F. Private, Aug. 24, 1861. Died in Richmond, Va., July 2, 1862.
SMITH, WILLIAM B. Private, Aug. 24, 1861.
SEIGLER, ROBERT. Private, March, 1862. Died in hospital, Aug. ----------.
SHIFLET, G. JACKSON. Private, Aug. 24, 1861. Captured at Gettysburg, Pa., July 2, 1863. Died at Fort Delaware, Jan. 7, 1864.
STIEFEL, JAMES. Private, Aug. 24, 1861.
SHIFLET, LEWIS R. Private, May 7, 1862.
TYNER, JOSHUA E. Private, Aug. 24, 1861.
TYNER, JAMES A. Private, March 11, 1863.
TYNER, WILLIAM W. Private, Sep. 17, 1863.
VARNER, DAVID D. Private, Aug. 24, 1861.
WALLACE, MARION. Private, Aug. 24, 1861.
WALLACE, P. M. Private, Aug. 24, 1861. Surrendered at Appomattox, Va.
WOOTEN, JOHN W. Private, Aug. 24, 1861. Died in Richmond, Va., May 29, 1862.
WOOTEN, MARION. Private, Aug. 24, 1861.
WILLIS, FRANCIS M. Private, Sep. 13, 1862.
WOOTEN, AARON. Private, Oct. 8, 1863. Captured June 1, 1864 at Cold Harbor, Va. Died at Fort Delaware Prison.

Muster Roll of Company "C" of the 5th Regiment of Georgia, Enlisted at Atlanta and Macon

JOHNSON, D. G. Captain, May 25, 1864, Atlanta.
HERNDON, J. S. 1st Lieutenant, May 25, 1864, Atlanta.
BROWN, S. V. 2nd Lieutenant, May 25, 1864, Atlanta.
SUIT, J. W. 3rd Lieutenant, May 25, 1864, Atlanta.
STEPHENSON, J. B. 4th Lieutenant, May 25, 1864, Atlanta.
BARRON, J. A. 1st Sergeant, May 25, 1864, Atlanta.
TEASLEY, J. E. 2nd Sergeant, May 25, 1864, Atlanta.
ADAMS, M. H. 3rd Sergeant, May 25, 1864, Atlanta.
BRYANT, N. R. 4th Sergeant, May 25, 1864, Atlanta.
McCURRY, A. W. 5th Sergeant, May 25, 1864, Atlanta.
VICKERY, J. E. 1st Corporal, May 25, 1864, Atlanta.
BROWN, J. W. 2nd Corporal, May 25, 1864, Atlanta.
ALFORD, J. B. 3rd Corporal, May 25, 1864, Atlanta.
HILLARD, B. L. 4th Corporal, May 25, 1864, Atlanta.
ADAMS, M. F. Private, May 25, 1864, Atlanta.
ADAMS, T. B. Private, May 25, 1864, Atlanta.
ALFORD, W. M. Private, July 24, 1864, Macon.
BAILEY, J. D. Private, July 25, 1864, Macon.
BROWN, A. R. Private, July 25, 1864, Macon.
BROWN, A. J. Private, July 24, 1864, Macon.
BROWN, A. C. Private, May 2, 1864, Atlanta.
BARRON, C. H. Private, May 25, 1864, Atlanta.
CHEEK, S. H. Private, May 25, 1864, Atlanta.
COLE, W. J. Private, May 25, 1864, Atlanta.
CHAPMAN, E. Private, May 25, 1864, Atlanta.
CARNES, R. Private, July 24, 1864, Macon.
CHAPMAN, D. O. Private, July 25, 1864, Macon.
CRUMP, J. M. Private, July 24, 1864, Macon.
CARLTON, S. C. Private, July 24, 1864, Macon.
DUNCAN, M. A., JR. Private, July 25, 1864, Macon.
DUNCAN, J. F. Private, May 25, 1864, Atlanta.
DUNCAN, W. E. Private, July 25, 1864, Macon.
DUNCAN, M. A., SR. Private, May 25, 1864, Atlanta.
DAVIS, WM. Private, July 24, 1864, Macon.
DURRETT, T. I. Private, May 25, 1864, Atlanta.
FLEMING, P. L. Private, May 25, 1864, Atlanta.
FLEMING, E. B. N. Private, July 24, 1864, Macon.
FROST, L. F. Private, July 24, 1864, Macon.
GULLEY, J. P. Private, May 25, 1864, Atlanta.
GINN, W. I. Private, May 25, 1864, Atlanta.
GAINES, J. J. Private, July 24, 1864, Macon.
GARY, W. C. Private, Oct. 12, 1864, Macon.
HOLLAND, G. C. Private, July 24, 1864, Macon.
HALL, J. B. Private, July 24, 1864, Macon.
HUMAN, F. Private, July 24, 1864, Macon.
DICKERSON, B. Private, July 24, 1864, Macon.
JOHNSON, J. A. Private, July 24, 1864, Macon.
JOHNSON, J. F. Private, July 24, 1864, Macon.
JOHNSON, I. M. Private, July 24, 1864, Macon.
JACKSON, W. B. Private, July 24, 1864, Macon.
JOHNSON, M. A. Private, July 24, 1864, Macon.
MADDEN, R. A. Private, May 25, 1864, Atlanta.
MOORE, A. B. Private, May 25, 1864, Atlanta.
McGARITY, J. A. Private, May 25, 1864, Atlanta.
McGARITY, WM. Private, May 25, 1864, Atlanta.
McMULLAN, J. A. Private, July 24, 1864, Macon.
McMULLAN, J. P. Private, May 25, 1864, Atlanta.
MEWBORN, W. A. Private, July 24, 1864, Macon.

MIZE, J. L. Private, July 24, 1864, Macon.
MARTIN, S. M. Private, July 24, 1864, Macon.
MURRAY, T. H. Private, July 24, 1864, Macon.
O'BARR, M. G. Private, May 25, 1864, Atlanta.
PATTERSON, W. F. Private, May 25, 1864, Atlanta.
PRITCHETT, T. R. Private, July 24, 1864, Macon.
PICKENS, R. Y. Private, July 24, 1864, Macon.
PICKENS, A. M. Private, July 24, 1864, Macon.
PRUITT, J. E. Private, July 24, 1864, Macon.
PAGE, F. M. Private, July 24, 1864, Macon.
RAY, A. M. Private, May 25, 1864, Atlanta.
RICHARDSON, B. Private, July 24, 1864, Macon.
RICHARDSON, S. W. Private, July 24, 1864, Macon.
RAY, J. A. Private, July 24, 1864, Macon.
SNOW, JOHN. Private, May 25, 1864, Atlanta.
STIDMAN, J. Private, July 24, 1864, Macon.
SKELTON, W. J. Private, July 24, 1864, Macon.
SHIRLEY, R. B. Private, July 24, 1864, Macon.
SCOTT, J. E. Private, July 24, 1864, Macon.
TEASLEY, J. A. Private, July 24, 1864, Macon.
THORNTON, R. B. Private, May 25, 1864, Atlanta.
THORNTON, J. B. Private, July 24, 1864, Macon.
TYLER, G. P. Private, July 24, 1864, Macon.
TYNER, J. H. Private, May 25, 1864, Atlanta.
TEASLEY, O. G. Private, May 25, 1864, Atlanta.
VICKERY, J. A. Private, May 25, 1864, Atlanta.
VICKERY, WM. Private, May 25, 1864, Atlanta.
VICKERY, T. E. Private, May 25, 1864, Atlanta.
VICKERY, J. H. Private, May 25, 1864, Atlanta.
WELDON, J. Private, May 25, 1864, Atlanta.
WHITE, W. G. W. Private, May 25, 1864, Atlanta.
WATSON, J. I. Private, July 24, 1864, Macon.
WALTERS, A. J. M. Private, July 24, 1864, Macon.

Muster Roll of Captain B. D. Johnson, Company "E," 4th Regiment, Georgia Reserves, Army of the Confederate States

Colonel Richard Taylor, from 1st day of May, 1864, when last mustered into service.

Name	Rank	Where	Age	Height	Complexion	Eyes	Hair	Occupation
1. JOHNSON, BARNETT D.,	Capt.	Atlanta						
2. ROBERTS, F. S.,	1st Lieut.	Atlanta						
3. BROWN, E. G.,	2nd Lieut.	Atlanta						
4. HAYNES, A. J.,	3rd Lieut.	Atlanta						
1. STONE, W. A.,	1st Sgt.	Atlanta	47	5' 5"	Fair	Blue	Light	Farmer
2. DUNCAN, O. M.,	2nd Sgt.	Atlanta	47	5' 8"	Fair	Blue	Light	Farmer
3. STEPHENS, J. H.,	3rd Sgt.	Atlanta	46	5' 9"	Fair	Grey	Dark	Mechanic
4. GAINES, J. R.,	4th Sgt.	Atlanta	17	5' 5"	Fair	Blue	Dark	Farmer
5. SANDERS, J. M.,	5th Sgt.	Atlanta	17	5' 11"	Fair	Blue	Light	Farmer
1. PHILLIPS, A. H.,	1st Corp.	Atlanta	47	5' 11"	Fair	Blue	Light	Farmer
2. BOWERS, W. E.,	2nd Corp.	Atlanta	17	5' 6"	Fair	Grey	Dark	Farmer
3. STIEFEL, J. M.,	3rd Corp.	Atlanta	17	5' 1"	Fair	Blue	Light	Farmer
4. STONE, E. E.,	4th Corp.	Atlanta	17	5' 5"	Fair	Blue	Light	Farmer
1. ADAMS, REUBEN D.,	Private	Atlanta	45	5' 10"	Fair	Blue	Dark	Miller
2. ALEXANDER, W. H.,	Private	Atlanta	45	5' 4"	Fair	Blue	Light	Farmer
3. AYERS, ABADIAH,	Private	Atlanta	47	5' 6"	Fair	Blue	Light	Farmer

MUSTER ROLLS OF COMPANIES

	Name	Rank	Where	Age	Height	Complexion	Eyes	Hair	Occupation
4.	Askea, Benjamin, Private	Atlanta	46	5' 10"	Dark	Blue	Dark	Farmer
5.	Bailey, Joel, Private	Atlanta	47	5' 8"	Fair	Dark	Dark	Farmer
6.	Ballenger, Jos., Private	Atlanta	48	5' 8"	Fair	Blue	Grey	Farmer
7.	Baskins, Henry J., Private	Atlanta	45	5' 10"	Fair	Blue	Light	Farmer
8.	Baskins, W. J., Private	Atlanta	17	5' 2"	Fair	Black	Dark	Farmer
9.	Bailey, John, Private	Atlanta	49	6'	Fair	Dark	Dark	Farmer
10.	Barnett, D. J., Private	Atlanta	47	5' 10"	Fair	Blue	Light	Mechanic
11.	Blackmon, Josiah, Private	Atlanta	46	5' 6"	Fair	Blue	Light	Farmer
12.	Bradley, J. M., Private	Atlanta	48	5' 10"	Fair	Blue	Light	Farmer
13.	Brown, D. H., Private	Atlanta	45	5' 10"	Fair	Blue	Light	Farmer
14.	Brown, J. M., Private	Atlanta	45	5' 6"	Fair	Blue	Dark	Farmer
15.	Brace, B. F., Private	Atlanta	49	5' 8"	Fair	Blue	Dark	Farmer
16.	Brown, G. W., Private	Atlanta	45	5' 10"	Fair	Blue	Light	Farmer
17.	Carlton, S. C., Private	Atlanta	46	5' 6"	Dark	Blue	Dark	Farmer
18.	Carlton, W. S., Private	Atlanta	49	5' 6"	Dark	Blue	Dark	Farmer
19.	Carnes, Samuel, Private	Atlanta	47	5' 6"	Dark	Blue	Light	Farmer
20.	Chambler, Benj., Private	Atlanta	48	5' 9"	Dark	Dark	Dark	Farmer
21.	Collins, Wyatt, Private	Atlanta	47	5' 6"	Dark	Blue	Dark	Farmer
22.	Colston, James, Private	Atlanta	48	5' 10"	Dark	Blue	Dark	Farmer
23.	Caldwell, Hugh, Private	Atlanta	49	5' 4"	Fair	Blue	Grey	Farmer
24.	Carithers, R. D., Private	Atlanta	47	5' 10"	Dark	Blue	Dark	Farmer
25.	Eaton, James, Private	Atlanta	47	6'	Dark	Dark	Dark	Farmer
26.	Evanson, George, Private	Atlanta	47	5' 5"	Dark	Blue	Dark	Farmer
27.	Fields, Jesse, Private	Atlanta	48	5' 7"	Dark	Blue	Red	Farmer
28.	Gaines, James M., Private	Atlanta	49	5' 9"	Fair	Dark	Dark	Farmer
29.	Golden, Jesse A., Private	Atlanta	46	5' 8"	Fair	Grey	Light	Farmer
30.	Gilliland, S. W., Private	Atlanta	48	5' 8"	Fair	Dark	Dark	Mechanic
31.	Gilmer, W. H., Private	Atlanta	47	5' 6"	Dark	Blue	Dark	Farmer
32.	Glover, Jos. P., Private	Atlanta	48	6' 1"	Dark	Dark	Dark	Farmer
33.	Greenway, J. H., Private	Atlanta	46	6' 2"	Fair	Grey	Grey	Farmer
34.	Hammond, S. N., Private	Atlanta	48	5' 11"	Dark	Blue	Grey	Farmer
35.	Hammond, W. L., Private	Atlanta	47	5' 8"	Dark	Dark	Dark	Farmer
36.	Harris, W. J., Private	Atlanta	17	5' 9"	Fair	Dark	Dark	Farmer
37.	Haynes, Jacob, Private	Atlanta	47	5' 10"	Dark	Dark	Dark	Farmer
38.	Hubbard, Otis, Private	Atlanta	47	5' 10"	Dark	Dark	Dark	Farmer
39.	Hill, Dempsey, Private	Atlanta	48	5' 11"	Dark	Blue	Grey	Farmer
40.	Holland, Henry, Private	Atlanta	17	5' 9"	Dark	Blue	Dark	Farmer
41.	Hubbard, John, Private	Atlanta	17	5' 9"	Dark	Dark	Dark	Farmer
42.	Hughes, Thomas, Private	Atlanta	48	5' 11"	Fair	Blue	Light	Farmer
43.	Hagans, Thomas, Private	Atlanta	48	5' 8"	Fair	Blue	Light	Farmer
44.	Klaster, Henry, Private	Atlanta	47	5' 10"	Dark	Dark	Dark	Farmer
45.	King, A. J., Private	Atlanta	49	5' 9"	Dark	Blue	Dark	Farmer
46.	Linder, Andrew, Private	Atlanta	17	6'	Fair	Dark	Dark	Farmer
47.	McMullan, J. F., Private	Atlanta	46	5' 9"	Fair	Blue	Grey	Farmer
48.	McWhorter, M. F., Private	Atlanta	17	5' 4"	Fair	Dark	Light	Farmer
49.	Manley, J. H., Private	Atlanta	46	5' 10"	Dark	Dark	Dark	Farmer
50.	Nelms, Joshua A., Private	Atlanta	48	5' 11"	Fair	Blue	Grey	Farmer
51.	Oglesby, Drury, Private	Atlanta	48	6' 6"	Dark	Grey	Grey	Farmer
52.	Osley, W. W., Private	Atlanta	17	5' 8"	Sallow	Blue	Light	Farmer
53.	Penson, Marion D., Private	Atlanta	47	5' 8"	Dark	Dark	Light	Farmer
54.	Powell, John F., Private	Atlanta	17	5' 7"	Fair	Blue	Light	Farmer
55.	Pickens, Robert, Private	Atlanta	46	5' 8"	Dark	Grey	Black	Farmer
56.	Partain, John J., Private	Atlanta	47	5' 1"	Dark	Dark	Dark	Farmer
57.	Ray, William R., Private	Atlanta	17	5' 5"	Dark	Blue	Dark	Farmer
58.	Rice, Elbert A., Private	Atlanta	17	5' 10"	Fair	Blue	Light	Farmer
59.	Rumsey, S. R., Private	Atlanta	45	5' 10"	Dark	Blue	Dark	Farmer
60.	Scales, John W., Private	Atlanta	48	5' 10"	Fair	Blue	Light	Farmer
61.	Scarborough, D., Private	Atlanta	49	5' 5"	Fair	Blue	Light	Farmer
62.	Shelnot, Joseph, Private	Atlanta	49	5' 5"	Dark	Blue	Dark	Farmer

	Name	Rank	Where	Age	Height	Com-plexion	Eyes	Hair	Occu-pation
63.	SHIRLEY, BENJ.,	Private	Atlanta	49	5' 11"	Fair	Blue	Dark	Farmer
64.	STIEFEL, JAMES M.,	Private	Atlanta	47	5' 4"	Fair	Blue	Light	Miller
65.	STEPHENSON, WM.,	Private	Atlanta	47	6'	Fair	Blue	Light	Farmer
66.	SANDERS, JAMES M.,	Private	Atlanta	17	5' 4"	Dark	Blue	Light	Farmer
67.	VICKERY, ELIAS,	Private	Atlanta	49	5' 4"	Dark	Grey	Dark	Farmer
68.	VICKERY, THOS S.,	Private	Atlanta	47	5' 8"	Dark	Black	Dark	Mechanic
69.	WALTERS, ORVAL,	Private	Atlanta	17	5' 9"	Fair	Blue	Light	Farmer
70.	WHITE, THOMAS H.,	Private	Atlanta	48	5' 7"	Fair	Blue	Dark	Farmer
71.	WINN, DANIEL J.,	Private	Atlanta	17	5' 10"	Fair	Blue	Light	Farmer
72.	WILLIAMS, N. R.,	Private	Atlanta	47	5' 8"	Light	Black	Dark	Farmer
73.	WOOTTEN, R.,	Private	Atlanta	46	5' 8"	Dark	Dark	Dark	Farmer

74. BOWERS, NATHANIEL, July 16, 1864.
75. CRAYTON, ELIJAH, July 21, 1864.
76. CUNTRAMAN, A. B., July 21, 1864.
77. GILBERT, G. W., Aug. 28, 1864.
78. SANDERS, L. A., Aug. 25, 1864.
79. OWEN, SANFORD G., Aug. 15, 1864.
80. RICMAN, GEORGE N., July 16, 1864.
81. ROWLAND, J. A., Aug. 16, 1864.
82. TYNER, G. W., July 16, 1864.

The foregoing were all the muster rolls available. Many of the citizens of Hart County enlisted and served in the War Between the States whose names we do not have.

STATISTICS

IN 1854, the first year of the county, the tax digest showed 689 polls and 1,245 slaves. The total tax valuation of all property for the year, including the value of the slaves, was $1,534,832.

In 1866, one year after the close of the War Between the States, the tax valuation of all property, the slaves not included, as they had been emancipated, was $595,876, a decrease of $893,260, due in part to the emancipation of the slaves, and to the deterioration of the value of the property of the county on account of the devestation of the war.

In 1860, the last census before emancipation, the number of slaves in the county was 1,528.

Selected Population Statistics of Hart County

	1860	1870	1880	1890	1900	1910	1920	1930
Total population	6,137	6,783	9,094	10,887	14,492	16,216	17,944	15,174
Native white	4,603	4,841	6,206	7,930	10,429	11,094	12,291	11,261
Foreign white	0	2	6	21	38	42	29	29
Free colored	6	1,942	2,882	2,957	4,025	5,080	5,624	3,893
Slaves	1,528							
Born in Georgia		5,506	8,213					
Born in South Carolina		1,098	722					
Persons per family				5.37	5.22	5.08	4.99	4.84
White		5.34				5.19		
Negro						4.57		
Per cent. males								
White		50.4	48.3	49.3	49.6	49.7	50.6	51.3
Negro		47.9			50.7	50.7	49.5	49.2

Per cent. adults*								
White	40.5	36.9*	40.0*	39.5	41.1	42.7	43.9	
Negro	33.5			35.2	41.3	45.6	42.4	
Per cent. under 10								
White	31.5					31.9	30.3	
Negro	36.5					30.4	28.7	
Per cent. illiterate (over 10)								
White						15.7	8.96	
Negro						38.3	21.0	
Population of Hartwell		154	443		1,672	2,007	2,323	2,048
White		123						
Negro		31						

*Males only, 1870-1910

Statistics of Hartwell, June 29, 1860

The population of Hartwell in 1860 was as follows:

White inhabitants	200
Slaves	33
Free persons of color	2

	1930	1920	1910
Population of Hart County, Ga.	15,174	17,944	16,216
Dist. 1112, Town	4,720	5,822	4,468
Hartwell city	2,048	2,323	2,007
Dist. 1113, Ray's	2,100	2,240	2,112
Royston city, total	1,447	1,681	1,422
In Hart County	225	205	201
In Franklin County	1,210	1,476	1,204
In Madison County	12		17
Vanna town	158		
Dist. 1114, Smith's	1,176	1,526	1,242
Dist. 1115, Reed Creek	1,322	1,513	1,446
Dist. 1116, Hall's	1,237	1,508	1,429
Bowersville town	271	390	398
Canon city, total	568	1,132	728
In Hart County	50	119	8
In Franklin County	518	1,013	720
Dist. 1117, Shoal Creek	1,638	2,121	2,150
Dist. 1118, McCurry's	2,021	2,059	2,033
Dist. 1119, Alford's	960	1,155	1,336

Selected Agricultural Statistics of Hart County, Georgia

	1860	1870	1880	1890	1900	1910 White	1910 Negro	1920	1930
Number of farms	523	737	1,078	1,655	2,089	1,964	839	3,103	2,593
White	523				1,558	1,964		2,137	2,593
Negro					531		839	966	
Owners and part owners									
White			655	718	629	718		749	630
Negro					38		62	52	38
Managers									
White					3			3	1
Negro							1	1	
Tenants (cash and share)									
White				423	937	926	1,246	1,385	
Negro					493		776	913	

						1910			
Acres per farm	263.3	163	\multicolumn{3}{l	}{1880, 1890 and 1900}	55.9	44.7	\multicolumn{2}{l	}{Not calcu-}
Improved acres per farm	66.9	51	\multicolumn{3}{l	}{Not calculated because races not separated}	30.6	28.7	\multicolumn{2}{l	}{lated because races not separated}
Value per farm									
Land	1,411	261				1,619	1,315		
Buildings						470	191		
Implements and Machinery	94	37				84	25		
Live stock	328	225				\multicolumn{2}{l	}{Races not separated}		

Farm animals						1910			
	1860	1870	1880	1890	1900	White	Negro	1920	1930
Horses	1,058	871	747	740	809	858	133	768	239
Mules and asses	267	313	728	907	1,861	1,664	591	3,728	3,304
Milch cows	1,615	1,522	1,781	1,915		2,481	727		
Work oxen	773	735	335	678	4,922			6,624	6,005
Other cattle	3,150	1,600	2,816	2,451					
Hogs	7,044	4,529	5,666	4,696	4,164	3,725		6,095	1,619
Sheep	4,431	3,437	2,085	1,511	638	15		26	
Goats					12	64		20	
Chickens								62,719	44,826

Acreage and Production of Cotton in Hart County for Each Census Year From 1859 to 1929

Year	Acres	Bales	
1859		1,483	bales of 400 lbs. ginned
1869		1,320	
1879		5,094	(.34 bales per acre) or 162 lbs.
1889	27,007	9,632	
1899	37,097	12,835	
1909	45,058	18,622	
1919	49,805	26,412	
1924	38,208	18,109	
1929	43,056	15,907	

Hart County Cotton Acreage and Production as Reported by Census

Year	Acres	Bales
1910	45,058	18,622
1919	49,805	26,412
1924	38,208	18,109
1929	43,056	15,907

Production in Number of Equivalent 500-Pound Bales—As Reported by Census Gin Reports

Year	Bales	Year	Bales
1914	18,190	1923	11,156
1915	16,520	1924	14,845
1916	16,451	1925	7,391
1917	17,660	1926	7,351
1918	17,799	1927	13,036
1919	23,608	1928	15,640
1920	22,755	1929	14,093
1921	17,611	1930	18,236
1922	10,882	1931	19,582

In the year 1931, Mr. Rowland M. Harper, who was connected with the University of Georgia in research work, prepared a very comprehensive and instructive analytical article from the U. S. Census and other sources of information upon various subjects relative to Hart County, a part of which we give herewith:

HART COUNTY AND ITS PEOPLE

By Rowland M. Harper

The total population of Hart County and its various towns and districts by the census of 1930 has been known for about a year, but details of race, sex, age, etc., were published only about three months ago, in a 99-page quarto census bulletin on the composition and characteristics of the population of Georgia.

It contains over 200 different figures for each county, and 17 for each militia district, but these figures do not mean much until they are reduced to ratios for the purposes of comparison. That has been done by the writer for the more important statistics of Hart County, and the results are presented herewith.

As practically the whole area of the county is cultivatable, except perhaps a few steep slopes, it supports a pretty dense population, 58.1 per square mile in 1930, which is above the State average, and still more above the United States average. Counties that have a greater density generally contain manufacturing cities, and Hart County has never gone into manufacturing, except for a few small industries supplying chiefly local needs. And for this reason it maintains the best traditions of the Old South, much better than the factory communities with their heterogeneous population.

Only eight counties in Georgia at present have a larger proportion of their population on farms.

The 1930 census gives occupation statistics for each county, and shows that in the population over ten years old in Hart County 76.3% of the white males, 11.75% of the white females, 78.5% of the negro males, and 19.2% of the negro females are employed outside their homes. So the people of Hart, or most of them, evidently still believe that woman's place is in the home. In the whole State 18.2% of the white females and 42.4% of the negro females are reported as employed, and the proportions are still higher in states that have more and larger cities. The proportion of males employed does not vary so much between different counties and states, and those not working are mostly boys still going to school.

Over 80% of the workers in Hart County in 1930 were engaged in agriculture, about 4% in trade, and still fewer in various other groups. Manufacturing employed only about 3%, and none were reported in mining, foresty or fishing.

The Federal agricultural census of 1925 found 2,882 farms in the county, of which 2,144 were operated by whites and 738 by negroes. The farm population was 14,143, or about 85% of the total. For agriculture in 1930 we have at preset the farm population (discussed farther on), but nothing about the number, size and value of farms, except some preliminary statistics that do not separate the races.

The Federal religious census of 1926 showed 6,629 white and 1,869 colored church members in Hart County, representing about 58% of the white population and 42% of the negro population at that time. This does not mean that nearly half the people in the county have no religion, for a great many are children too young to join the church. (Over one-fourth of the inhabitants of the county are under ten years old.) And many people living in or near Royston and Canon may have their membership in churches across the line in other counties, where the greater part of those two municipalities are located. Among the whites there were 4,917 Baptists, 1,469 Methodists, 145 Presbyterians, and about 100 in two smaller denominations. The colored church members include 1,309 Baptists and 560 Methodists (the latter all C. M. E., instead of A. M. E., which are more common elsewhere in the South).

Among the lines of evidence that show that the people of Hart County still stick to the good old traditions are the statistics of marriage and divorce. The U. S. Census Bureau, in its annual reports on the subject, reports 611 marriages and 48 divorces in the county in the five years 1926 to 1930, inclusive, a ratio of one divorce to 12.7 marriages.

Here Mr. Harper makes a statement relative to the fact that many of the divorces obtained in the county are by parties from South Carolina, and in substance says that if the number of such divorces were deducted from the number as it appears in the U. S. Census, the ratio for Hart County would be considerably less.

In the 1930 census the population of each county is divided into that on farms and that not on farms, with a separate category for cities of 2,500 or more, where there are any. The non-farm population includes smaller cities and towns, mining and lumber camps, etc. Hartwell is not yet large enough to be classed as a city in the census tables, but it includes about 90% of the "rural non-farm" population of the county, so that the figures for that class represent it pretty well. And there are a few separate statistics for it in the 1930 census, municipalities with between 1,000 and 2,500 inhabitants being treated in the same detail as militia districts.

The other incorporated places in the county are parts of the cities of Royston and Canon, and the whole towns of Bowersville and Vanna. Adding these to the population of Hartwell gives 2,752, or considerably more than the rural non-farm population of the county. But this discrepancy is explained by the fact that there are several farms within the limits of these towns, Hartwell alone having a farm population of 174.

The condition of the population in 1920 is shown by the following table, which has four columns of figures, two for the whole county in 1920 and 1930, and two for the non-farm and farm population in 1930. Hartwell, which is not shown separately here, had 2,007 inhabitants in 1910, 2,323 in 1920, and 2,048 in 1930, if the census figures are correct. The decrease in county and city characterized the great majority of Georgia counties in the decade just past, and is due primarily to the boll weevil, and two or three exceptionally dry years, one of which was worse in Hart County than in most other parts of the State. The only thing that kept the whole State from showing a loss of population was the growth of manufacturing in some of the cities, and some army training camps which should not have been counted in the population of Georgia at all, for their occupants are not voters or taxpayers. But the people of Hart withstood the onslaught of the boll weevil remarkably well, and the writer on a visit there in 1929 traversed five of the eight districts and noticed no abandoned farms, such as are now common in many parts of the State where negroes were in the majority.

The first four lines of figures are totals, for the benefit of readers who may not have ready access to the census reports, but the rest are all ratios, which are more significant for purposes of comparison.

Blank spaces indicate data not ascertainable from the census tables.

Population Statistics of Hart County

	Whole County		1930	
	1920	1930	Non-Farm	Farm
Population	17,944	15,174	2,262	12,912
Native White	12,291	11,261	1,612	9,649
Foreign White	29	20	1	19
Negro	5,624	3,893	649	3,244
Persons per family	4.99	4.94		
White population				
Per cent. of total	68.7	74.3	71.2	74.9
Per cent. over 21	43.9	46.5	50.0	44.8
Per cent. under 10	30.3	26.2		
Children per woman	2.55	2.29	1.38	2.54
Per cent. illiterate (over 10)	8.87	5.11		
Negro population				
Per cent. of total	31.3	25.7	28.7	25.1
Per cent. over 21	42.4	43.4	51.9	41.7
Per cent. under 10	28.7	25.6		
Children per woman	2.70	2.52	1.62	2.78
Per cent. illiterate (over 10)	21.0	20.4		

As the negroes were less able to adjust themselves to boll-weevil conditions than the whites, the proportion of them in the population decreased in Hart County in the past decade; as it did nearly everywhere else in Georgia, and in Mississippi between 1910 and 1920. Some of those who left the farms found employment in Georgia cities, mines, sawmills, etc., and some migrated northward. But even before the boll weevil was ever heard of, the negroes in counties where whites were in the majority tended to congregate in cities and towns, and vice versa (for they do not seem to enjoy living far away from members of their own race), and Hart County is a pretty good illustration of that. The table shows that negroes constituted 28.7% of the non-farm population and 25.1% of the farm population in 1930. And Hartwell itself, not shown separately here, had 29.8% of negroes.

Throughout the United States, foreigners, whether few or many, generally tend to congregate in cities; but Hart County is an exception. There are only twenty in the whole county, which is less than half as many in 1910, and only a fraction of one per cent. of the total population; and only one of those is in Hartwell, and the rest on farms, 13 of them in Reed Creek District. The great majority of them are Germans, who generally make the best type of immigrants.

The number of persons per family (for both races combined) decreased during the last decade, following a nation-wide tendency which has been evident for a century or more. In 1860, which is as far back as census figures for Hart County go, there were 5.34 persons per family in the free population (the slaves not being grouped by families). Medical progress, by increasing the length of life, increases the proportion of adults, and thus automatically decreases the proportion of children and the size of families. The proportion of adults is a pretty good index of wealth, for most adults are breadwinners and most children are not. In this respect whites are superior to negroes and town people to country people, not only in Hart County (as shown in the tables) but nearly everywhere else.

The percentage of adults among whites in the country increased from 40.5 in 1860 to 46.5 in 1930, and among the negroes from 33.5 in 1860 to 43.4 in 1930. And the per capita wealth has increased at the same time, probably even more rapidly though less regularly.

The birth rate is indicated roughly by the proportion of the population under ten years old, and the ratio of children to women, and that of course varies in the opposite direction from the adult percentage. In the whole country the percentage under ten among whites decreased from 31.5 in 1860 to 26.2 in 1930, and among the negroes from 36.5 in 1860 to 28.7 in 1930. The present birth rate must be nearly 30 per thousand, for both races. In the course of a year it costs about as much to maintain and operate an automobile as to feed and clothe a child, and that helps explain why automobiles are commoner now than they were ten years ago, and commoner in town than in the country. The 1925 agricultural census told how many of the people living on farms were under and over ten years old, and classified them by tenure. And it is a curious and significant fact that in both races the proportion of young children (and therefore the size of families, for which we have no exact figures) is larger among tenants than among owners. This is a condition that the uplifters who are trying to help tenants to become owners must reckon with. We do not know all the circumstances, but it may often happen that a tenant who raises a large family can save up enough to buy a farm after some or most of his children have grown up and moved to town, and perhaps helped the old man with their earnings.

As the families become smaller and the people more prosperous, the population denser and schools closer together (or roads better), illiteracy inevitably decreases, even if no special effort is made in that direction. There are no satisfactory statistics on that point for single counties previous to 1910, but in that year the census found 15.7% of the whites and 38.3% of the negroes over ten years old unable to read and write. In twenty years those figures decreased to 5.11 and 20.4, with the aid of the schools that Hart County is proud of. The illiteracy is doubtless lower for both races in the city and other non-farm population than on the farms, though there are no such figures for places the size of Hartwell and smaller. For in the towns schools are within easy reach of every child, while in the country some children may live several miles from a school, and there are many older people who grew up before the days of compulsory education and school buses.

The 1930 figures for the eight militia districts of the county afford material for some comparisons that were never possible before, for other censuses since 1870 have told nothing about the districts except their total population. The farm population ranges from 58.8% of the total in Town District (which includes Hartwell) to 100% in Smith's and Shoal Creek districts.

The percentage of whites ranges from 57.6 in McCurry's District, at the south, to 91.1 in Reed Creek at the north, and the percentage of adults (for both races combined) from 42.1 in McCurry's to 49.0 in Town and 54.2 in Hartwell itself. The per cent. over 65 years old is 3.56 in the whole county, and ranges from 2.34 in Ray's District (adjacent to Royston) to 5.00 in Alford's, on the other side of the county; but the numbers here involved are so small that perhaps too much dependence should not be placed upon them.

The Harbour Family History

THOMAS HARBOUR came from England. His son, Talman Harbour, was born in 1718, died in 1797, and was buried in Franklin County, Ga.

His son, Esaias Harbour, has the following record: Esaias Harbour, born 1757, died 1833; married Catherine Harbour 1780; Catherine Harbour born 1762.

To them were born the following children: Talman, married Catherine Harrison; Thomas, married Elizabeth McKee, December 13, 1808; Rebecca, married John Skelton; John, married Sarah Blackwell; Sarah, married Abraham Aderhold; Catherine, married Lewis Moulder.

Abraham Aderhold, who married Sarah Harbour, was granted several tracts of land in the early part of the 19th Century, some of which was located on the Tugaloo River granted December 18, 1818. Several other tracts were granted to him along about the same time, aggregating about 500 acres.

He settled on the lands of the Tugaloo River, which place many years later was owned by Adam Kelly, and later still by Rev. Asa Avery and at which was installed a ferry, known as Avery's Ferry. Besides the dwelling house and other buildings on the place was a wheat barn in which was a threshing floor where the wheat was tramped out by horses or oxen, as in Bible times.

He was a charter member of the Reed Creek Baptist Church, originally located near his home, constituted in 1830, and a few years afterwards he was ordained a deacon of the church.

He later sold his lands on Tugaloo River and moved to Carnesville, Ga., where he died at the age of 83 years.

In the account of his death we note the following paragraph:

"Father Aderhold was, truly in every sense of the word, a good man, a pious and exemplary Christian. He had been a consistent member of the Baptist Church for sixty years, a large portion of the time one of the deacons. It was seldom during all that time his seat in his church meeting was vacant. He loved his church and brethren. In the absence of the pastor, he usually presided as moderator, which duty he discharged with ability. Father Aderhold loved to talk about heaven and heavenly things with the brethren of his church, and with the young upon religious subjects."

He was the father of Dr. Henry D. Aderhold, of Carnesville, Ga., and Dr. W. V. Aderhold, of Lexington, Ga.

He was also the father of Rev. John H. Aderhold, who was ordained to the full work of the ministry at Carnesville Baptist Church December 30, 1855. It is said of him that he was a very impressive preacher and greatly beloved. He moved to Gordon County, Ga., about 1866, where he died October 21, 1868.

Lewis Moulder, who married Catherine Harbour, daughter of Esaias and Catherine Harbour, and sister to the wives of Abraham Aderhold and John Skelton, was granted a tract of land on Reed Creek and Tugaloo River not far from the home of Abraham Aderhold, where he built a house of large, hewed logs, as was common in those early days. This old house, with more or less repairs, is still standing and occupied.

He owned and operated a sawmill on Reed Creek not far from the home, of the sashsaw model.

He and his wife were presumably charter members of Reed Creek Church.

The place, many years later, came into the possession of Robert A. Madden, who lived there for many years, and the place is yet known as the Madden place.

The Skelton Family History

JOHN SKELTON married Rebecca Harbour, daughter of Esaias Harbour and wife, Catherine, and to them were born the following children: Elijah Skelton, Wiley Skelton, Jabez Skelton, Richmond Skelton, Dicey Skelton, John Skelton, Elizabeth Skelton, Swan H. Skelton, Dianah Skelton, Littleton Skelton.

We have no record who Elijah, Dicey, John or Swan H. married.

Rev. Samuel B. Sanders married Anne Skelton, who, to the best of our information, was a daughter of Swan H. Skelton, and for whom they named one of their sons, Swan H. Sanders, for his grandfather, Swan H. Skelton; further, we have no record of Swan H. Skelton or his family.

Richmond Skelton married Nancy Garrison April 24, 1822. He was the first Coroner of Hart County, to which office he was elected in 1854 at the organization of Hart County. He also was elected Sheriff of Hart County, which office he held during the years 1858-1859.

Wiley Skelton married Sarah Huln, February 6, 1822.

Elizabeth Skelton, daughter of John Skelton and wife, Rebecca, married Thomas M. McGuire March 27, 1828.

Dianah married .... McGuire.

Littleton Skelton married Nancy Highsmith and later moved to White County, Ga. He owned a large tract of land lying on both sides of Big Cedar Creek, known today as the Reuben T. Buffington place, and it has been told to us that John Skelton, father of Littleton Skelton, is buried on the lands on the right of the public road leading from the bridge across Big Cedar Creek to the Buffington place, between the bridge and the home.

Jabez Skelton, son of John Skelton and wife, Rebecca, married Julia Davis February 14, 1823. To them were born the following children:

Frances, married Thomas Ray.

Therusa, married Thomas B. Adams April 25, 1858.

John Hamilton Skelton married Mary L. Richardson, daughter of Judge J. Van Richardson, March 26, 1867, by Rev. Benjamin Thornton.

James E. Skelton, born March 25, 1829, died March 21, 1862; married Louisa J. ——————, who, after his death, married Rev. Benjamin Thornton.

Mattie Skelton was never married.
Raiford Skelton was never married.
Elizabeth Skelton married W. B. Watson.
Rebecca Skelton was never married.
Evelyn Skelton was never married.
Bert Skelton was never married.
George Skelton was never married.

Col. James E. Skelton was a lawyer and he and his brother, J. H. Skelton, composed the law firm of J. E. & J. H. Skelton, who practiced their profession in Hartwell up to the time of the War Between the States. Col. J. E. Skelton was a charter member of the Baptist Church in Hartwell; was one of the delegates to the Secession Convention from Hart County that met in Milledgeville, Ga., and voted for and signed the Ordinance of Secession. He was an officer in the war and died on his way from home to his command in Atlanta, Ga., March 21, 1862.

Real Estate Record of the Skelton Family

On January 4, 1793, Esaias Harbour and wife, Catherine, deeded to John Skelton 400 acres of land, lying on both sides of Cedar Creek, for the consideration of 100 pounds sterling; land bounded on the lower end by Pole Bridge Branch and Joshua Slud's land; on the upper end by Wm. Daniel's land.

On June 24, 1820, John Skelton deeded to Jabez Skelton 200 acres of land on north side of small branch of Coldwater Creek. Also, on the same date, 100 acres for $100 located on north Coldwater Creek. Also, on June 10, 1820, John Skelton deeded to Wiley Skelton 460 acres on branch of Big Coldwater Creek for $225, land granted to John L. Dixon May 24, 1787.

Jabez Skelton deeded to F. S. Roberts, on April 3, 1856, 367¼ acres of land, known as the Wiley Skelton place.

Littleton Skelton, on April 2, 1850, deeded Joshua Totman 100 acres of land, traversed by an Indian trail, and on a part of which Cedar Creek Church was later erected.

Littleton Skelton later deeded the balance of the place, now known as the Buffington place, of 718 acres to Mrs. Mary L. Hunter, who became the wife of Reuben T. Buffington.

Col. John Appling once owned 1,100 acres of land, a part of which was later sold by Chas. D. Stewart, son-in-law of Col. John Appling, to J. H. and James E. Skelton, located near the town of Hartwell and extended back on Big Cedar Creek.

J. H. Skelton, acting for himself and as surviving partner of J. H. & J. E. Skelton, and Littleton Skelton, sold to Hart County a tract of land of 200 acres for a county home, being a part of a tract of land granted to Reuben Bramlet. J. H., J. E. and L. Skelton owned 360 acres of the Samuel Adams lands.

Jabez Skelton sold E. R. White a small tract of land of 7½ acres lying on waters of Little Coldwater Creek.

So it is evident that the Skelton family owned a large area of land extending from near the town of Hartwell to the E. R. White place and that they were among the first settlers and citizens of the community.

Hon. John H. Skelton

Died September 21, 1893, after a long illness, having suffered with a complication of diseases for several years.

He was born in Elbert County, now Hart, November 10, 1827. Studied law in the office of Judge Rice and his brother, Col. James E. Skelton, at Marietta, Ga., and was admitted to practice at the Hartwell bar in 1858.

In 1861, entered the service of the Confederate States as Captain of Company "C," 16th Regiment of Georgia Volunteers. At the battle of Chancellorsville he was promoted to the position of Major of his regiment, and near the close of the struggle was promoted to the colonelency of the regiment, and was shortly afterwards captured and imprisoned in Ft. Delaware. He was married on the 26th of March, 1867, to Miss Mary Lavinia, daughter of Judge J. Van Richardson.

He represented his county in the Constitutional Convention after the war in 1867. For two terms he was Reading Clerk of the Legislature in Milledgeville. He was appointed Solicitor of the County Court in 1867, and served until the court was abolished.

He represented the county in the Legislature in the sessions of 1888-9, and was a member of the Judiciary Committee. Was one time Mayor of Hartwell.

The funeral sermon was preached by his pastor, Rev. A. E. Keese, in the Baptist Church. The Superior Court, which was in session, was adjourned in respect to Major Skelton and the officers of the court attended the funeral. Pall bearers were selected from the lawyers in attendance, all of whom were personal and professional friends of the deceased.

—*The Hartwell Sun.*

McMullan Family History

JOHN McMULLAN, of Scotch-Irish descent, was born in Dublin, Ireland, about 1740, emigrated to America and settled in Virginia, in that part known as Orange County then, later Rockingham County; was married to Theodisia Beasley (first wife), Orange County, Va., about 1766 or 1767, and after the American Revolution settled in Swift Run Gap of the Blue Ridge Mountains in Orange County, Va., on a tract of land of about 400 acres patented to him by the Commonwealth of Virginia in 1796; was a private in the Revolutionary War and, as related by his youngest daughter, Lavinia Smith, to Judge Frank M. McMullan, of Orange, Va., fought on the side of the Patriots and Colonists; was a tailor by trade and cut out and made the first military suit worn by George Washington after he was made Commander-in-Chief of the Army. The tailor's chest, made of cypress, which John McMullan brought from Ireland, went into possession of his son, Patrick, at his death; from Patrick it went to his son, William; from William it went to his son, William Marion; from William Marion it went to his son, William Jesse, of Newton, Miss.

John McMullan was married to Elizabeth Stowers (second wife), born in Orange County, Va., 1763, and died in Clayton County, Ga., 1848, daughter of Mark Stowers, of Orange County, Va., about 1786.

He sold his land in Swift Run Gap in 1797 and moved to Elbert County, Ga., (that part of Elbert County became Hart County in 1853) with three of his five children by his first wife, namely: Patrick, Catherine Shiflet and John, first two married; and six of his children by his second wife, namely: Neal, Jeremiah, Lewis, Thomas, Fielding and Nancy, afterwards the wife of James Mills. He left in Virginia two children by his first wife, namely: James and Mary, the wife of Wm. Lewis Powell. Four children by his second wife were born in Elbert County, Ga., namely: Sinclair, Daniel, Elizabeth and Lavinia.

He died in 1817 in what was then known as Elbert County, Ga., later known as Hart County, and was buried in a family burying ground at the brow of the hill on the north side of Big Cedar Creek and on the east side of the public road. His grave was marked by a granite tombstone in 1896 by suggestion of Judge Frank M. McMullan, of Orange, Va., a great grandson of the Irish ancestor, who contributed thereto, the other contributions being made by local descendents.

The inscription on the monument is as follows:

IN MEMORY OF
JOHN MCMULLAN
BORN IN IRELAND IN 1740
EMIGRATED TO VA. IN 1760
WAS A SOLDIER IN THE WAR OF 1776
MOVED TO GA. IN 1797
DIED IN DEC., 1817

SINCLAIR MCMULLAN
BORN IN DEC., 1799
DIED JAN. 12, 1884

Sinclair McMullan, twelfth child of the original ancestor, was born in Georgia and lived all his life in Elbert County (Hart County after 1853) and was buried in the cemetery at Sardis Church.

His home was about a mile southeast of Sardis Church, and is now (1927) owned and occupied by Mr. and Mrs. C. W. Rice, Mrs. Rice being a daughter of Andrew Judson McMullan and a granddaughter of Sinclair McMullan.

He married Clarissa Richardson, daughter of Amos Richardson, on the 11th day of January, 1824, and ten children were born to them, as follows:
1. James Henry, married Martha Loflin.
2. Lavinia, married Moses H. Adams.
3. Susan, married Levi Burriss.
4. John G., killed in Civil War—unmarried.
5. Thomas N., married Amanda Jones.
6. Elizabeth, married Fred B. Hodges.
7. Horatio Goss, killed in Civil War—unmarried.

8. Mahlon Nesbit, died unmarried.
9. Hester A. ("Hettie"), married Mahlon M. Richardson.
10. Andrew Judson, married Sallie L. Turner.

Clarissa McMullan died November 1, 1878.

In the newspaper article written upon the occasion of the erection of the monument to the memory of John McMullan, the forefather of the McMullan family in this part of the country, reference to which has already been made, the following paragraph appears:

"Nearly every honorable vocation has been represented by a member of this great family, and it is pretty generally true that whatever they undertook, success would surely follow. Many have risen to high and honorable stations—quite a number being prominent in the ministry, some being distinguished lawyers, some being scientific farmers, and others who have labored in other fields have been equally successful."

Thomas N. McMullan

Thomas N. McMullan, son of Sinclair and Clarissa McMullan, was born in Elbert (now Hart) County, Ga., December 23, 1833; married Miss Amanda Jones, of Hart County, October 13, 1885; died May 21, 1890. Buried in the cemetery at Sardis Church.

His childhood, boyhood, and early manhood were spent in quiet on the farm, the place of his birth.

In 1858, after such preparation as he could make at home in a country school, he entered the University of the State at Athens, Ga.

In 1860, he graduated with honor. After his graduation he returned home and devoted himself to agricultural pursuits until the Civil War began, when he tendered his services to the Southern Confederacy and served the government in a civil capacity until its close.

After the war was over he returned to his farm, where he remained until September, 1866, trying to close up, as far as possible, the terrible breach which the war had left in the fortunes of the family.

At the September term, 1866, of Hart Superior Court, he was admitted at Hartwell to the practice of law.

When he came to the bar, the country had not recovered from the shock received from the war, in consequence of which all things were in confusion and nothing being done at the practice, for which reason he returned to his farm and shaped for himself the splendid fortune of which he died possessed.

His superior education and literary attainments put him early in life among the foremost of his time.

In 1872-3, the neighborhood being unable to secure a competent teacher, he himself went into the Sardis Academy and there taught for the good of his neighbors a flourishing school for two years, attending at the same time the duties of his farm.

Early in life he joined the Baptist Church at Sardis, and immediately became one of its most active members—foremost in all things pertaining to the interest of the church.

Soon after becoming a member of the church he became a teacher in the Sunday school, in which he seemed to take especial delight. He would lead the songs for the children. Some of his happiest moments were spent with his Sunday school about him, singing songs of praise. One of his distinct characteristics was his fondness for children and their innocent sports.

His farming operations, which were quite extensive, were carried on almost entirely by colored labor. The esteem in which his servants held him and the love they bore for him was unusual. Never was white master more beloved by black servants.

He was a member of the County Board of Education for many years, during which time he was an enthusiastic worker for the cause of education.

He was County School Commissioner for four years and Chairman of the Democratic Executive Committee of the county six years next preceding his death. —Extract from article in *The Sun*, June 6, 1890.

Rev. James H. McMullan

Rev. James Henry McMullan, son of Sinclair and Clarissa McMullan, was born in Elbert (now Hart) County, Ga., November 18, 1824, and received his early education at Shoal Creek Academy.

When he was about six years old, Hon. Joseph Henry Lumpkin delivered in his neighborhood a speech in advocacy of total abstinence from intoxicating drink, which, partly from its surpassing eloquence, partly from the advanced position assumed by it, created much discussion in the neighborhood. Under these influences, the stripling resolved to make the principle of the speech a rule for himself through life, and to this purpose he has adhered without a single breach of it for fifty years. His youthful morals were, in other respects also, pure; and even from early childhood he had religious tendencies, and found pleasure in attendance on the sanctuary. But he struggled against the drawings of the Spirit, disguising his feelings under a mask of indifference. The resisted influences were withdrawn and he fell into the slough of skepticism. He attempted to persuade himself that the Bible is not true, and determined, if successful in the attempt, to devote his life to an exposure of its false pretensions. He was rescued from the snare of Satan through the agency of Asa Chandler, Benjamin Thornton, and I. H. and W. R. Goss, whose public ministry was enforced by their habits of social conversation on the love of Christ, and the sweet experience of personal trust in Him. In this way his doubts were put to flight, he saw his guilty distance from God, and was enabled to rejoice in the saving power of the Gospel. On profession of his faith he was baptized, in 1844, by Rev. B. Thornton, and united with Sardis Church, in his native county.

Soon after his conversion a desire to preach the Gospel was awakened in his bosom. The grace of God had been so strikingly exemplified in his own case, that he felt a strong impulse to tell it to his fellowmen; to warn them against the temptations to which he had been exposed and the snares into which he had well nigh fallen. But his youth, inexperience and conscious unfitness for the work, caused him to "withdraw his neck from the yoke," and it was not until twenty years later that these desires ripened into a constraining sense of duty. He was ordained in 1864, at the request of Sardis Church, and became its pastor—a position which he has retained until the present time. He has preached, besides, to Line, Dove's Creek, and other churches in the Sarepta and Tugaloo associations, and to Mountain Creek Church, Anderson, South Carolina.

His labors as a pastor have been abundant, and have been crowned with abundant blessing. He possesses fine executive talent, and his administration of discipline tends to keep his churches pure.

As a preacher, he is zealous and forcible; in doctrine, sound and scriptural. As a man, he is modest in deportment, courteous in manners, and, while firm in principle, kind in spirit.

He was married in 1852 to Miss Martha V. Loflin, of Lincoln County, and two children have been given them.

The above sketch of Mr. McMullan's life is taken from the "Baptist Compendium," a historical work of prominent Georgia Baptists, published in 1881.

Since that time some of the most active years of this good man's life have been spent and blessed with great success.

The Hebron Association, of which he was the honored Moderator for many years, and which has grown from a modest and feeble organization to that of a strong and influential body, owes much of its strength to his wise and discreet direction.

The very last and crowning work of his life was here in Hartwell as pastor of the Baptist Church.

While the building of a new and better temple of worship had been contemplated, it was never commenced till he became pastor. He was never happier than when he saw the magnificent building completed just before the closing of the old year. The Baptist Church in Hartwell as long as it stands will be a monument to him, and will always keep his precious name fresh in the minds of our people.

D. C. ALFORD.

The following brief and interesting sketch was published in 1895:

Rev. J. H. McMullan's labors have covered quite an area of territory and have been very arduous and long-continued, and during the period he has been an earnest worker and instrumental in establishing and building up many churches. It is said he has planned and built more churches than any man in Georgia.

He is also a good business man, having accumulated considerable property; in this he is largely indebted to the untiring industry and executive ability of his devoted wife, who has ever been his constant support and inspiration in his ministerial labors. He is now actively engaged in preaching the Gospel and is doing the best work of his life. Their two children, Peyton S. and Emma H., now Mrs. R. S. Hill, of Anderson, S. C., are both living.

The father, mother and children are all faithful workers in the Baptist Church. —Memoirs of Georgia.

Rev. James H. McMullan died Thursday, January 28, 1897, in Hartwell. His funeral was preached in the Baptist Church on Saturday, January 30, 1897. He was buried in the cemetery at Sardis Church.

Andrew Judson McMullan
May 26, 1848—September 29, 1913.

This distinguished citizen and useful man passed away at his country home Monday evening, September 29, 1913.

He was born in Elbert, now Hart County, May 26, 1848.

As to Mr. McMullan's ancestry, will say that he was a son of St. Clair McMullan. His mother's name was Clarissa Richardson. His paternal grandparents were John and Elizabeth (Beasley) McMullan. His grandfather, John McMullan, came from Dublin, Ireland, to Virginia about 1730, and after serving as a soldier in the Revolutionary War, came from Virginia to what is now Hart County, formerly Elbert County, about 1799; so that Mr. McMullan was in the third generation in Georgia and from the settlement of the family in America.

A schoolboy when the Civil War broke out, before the end of the struggle he had grown sufficiently to enter the army, and during the last six months was in service in the trenches around Atlanta.

In 1870 he entered the University of Georgia, and was graduated in 1873 as a member of the first class graduated from the Agricultural Department.

Leaving college, he engaged in his life work as a farmer in 1873. He demonstrated great ability in this line and was one of the large farmers of Georgia, operating a plantation of 2,500 acres with more than 1,000 acres in cultivation, and was recognized as one of the best farmers in the county and State. He at one time held the position of President of the Georgia Farmers' Union. Outside of his farming interests, he owned stock in the Hartwell mills, banks, and other progressive institutions.

In 1878 Mr. McMullan married Miss Sallie Turner, daughter of Dr. Joel L. and Louisa (Jones) Turner. In 1904 he was elected Representative of his county to the Georgia Legislature, which position he filled for two consecutive terms. Was trustee of the Agricultural College at Athens at the time of his death, and was one of the first road commissioners after the county had adopted the alternative road law.

Mr. McMullan was a practical surveyor, and was once County Surveyor of Hart County.

Sinclair McMullan Old Mill

He was an active member of Sardis Baptist Church and held the office of deacon.

On Wednesday morning following his death, Mr. McMullan was buried in the cemetery at Sardis Church, after appropriate service conducted by Rev. R. A. Smith, assisted by Rev. M. H. Massey.

Chancellor Barrow, of the State University, and Dr. Soule, President of the State College of Agriculture, were present, both of whom paid the highest tribute to the noble traits in the character of Mr. McMullan.

The Richardson Family History

Amos Richardson

Born September 8, 1764
Died January 15, 1847

AMOS RICHARDSON died in Elbert County, Ga., (Hart County after 1853) and was buried in the cemetery at Sardis Baptist Church. The local (Hartwell) chapter, Daughters of the American Revolution, has placed a marker (such as is provided by the organization) at or near his grave. The exact spot where the grave was located could not be definitely determined at this late day (1926), and so the marker was put near by along side the grave of his son, James Van, at the entrance of the cemetery.

He married Susannah Smith, and the following named children were born to them:

1. Mahlon, married Sallie Self.
2. Clarissa, married Sinclair McMullan.
3. James V., married Elizabeth McMullan.
4. Willis, married Drucilla Gaines February 23, 1833.
5. Amie, married John Farmer.

The home place was later known as the "Roebuck Place" on Little Cedar Creek on the road leading from Sardis (white) to Sardis (colored) Church.

James V. Richardson

Born Sept. ----, 1809
Died Aug. 6, 1884

James V. Richardson was the third child of Amos Richardson, the original ancestor. He married Elizabeth ("Betsie") McMullan, daughter of Lewis McMullan, on the 24th day of November, 1836, (then Elbert County). Their home was on Big Cedar Creek in Hart County, Ga., (formerly Elbert County), known now as home of John G. Richardson.

He was prominent in the early history of the county of Hart, being one of the Justices of the Inferior Court charged with the duty of laying off Hart County, as well as the selection and laying out of the county site at Hartwell. He was noted for a generous hospitality. His corn crib was ample and always open to his friends and the needy.

His first wife was Milly Bobo, and the following named children were born to them. (The date of his first marriage was February 11, 1830.)

1. Sinclair W., married Sarah A. Skelton December 23, 1858; died in 1831.
2. Martha, married Amaziah Heaton, Hart County; died June 15, 1895.
3. Sallie, died in childhood.

The following named children were born to him and his second wife, namely:

1. Milton, married Sarah Smith, Anderson County, S. C.; married Ida Dollar, Hart County, Ga.; married Alberta Craft, Elbert County, Ga.
2. Mahlon M., married Hester McMullan, Hart County.
3. Frances, married Judge P. Walters, Hart County; married Angus L. McCurry, Hart County.
4. Mollie, married J. Hamp Skelton, Hart County.
5. Blackmon L., married Sarah Craft, Hart County.
6. G. Washington, married Fannie Jones, Anderson County, S. C.
7. Littleton, married Fannie L. Burriss, Anderson County, S. C.
8. Emily, married Jim Craft, Elbert County; married Columbus L. Mullenix, Hart County.

Mahlon M. Richardson
May 3, 1841—April 3, 1918
77 Years

Born in Hart (formerly Elbert) County, spent boyhood on his father's farm, attended neighborhood schools. In the beginning of the War Between the States enlisted in Capt. John McMullan's Company, which was Co. "D," 37th Regiment, Georgia Volunteers Infantry, Army of Tennessee, C. S. A., Hart County, Georgia, which he entered as Junior Lieutenant on March 4th, 1862. Promoted to Second Lieutenant August 1, 1863. Promoted to First Lieutenant November 25, 1863. Wounded at Chickamauga, Ga., September 9, 1863, in right forearm, and at Resaca, Ga., May 15, 1864, in left elbow joint.

Retired at home April, 1865, and served his country with patriotic zeal until the close of the war, carrying with him to the grave the scars on his body of a gallant soldier. For a complete war record of Mr. Richardson, see Muster Roll of J. G. McMullan's Company, which is found elsewhere in these pages.

During Mr. Richardson's life he held the following offices of his county:

Soon after the close of the war he was elected to the office of Tax Collector, which position he held until 1867. When he felt the need of a better preparation for life's duties, he went to the State University, and in 1870 graduated in law.

He was happily married to Miss Hettie McMullan in 1878.

In 1881 he was elected to the office of Clerk of the Superior Court, which position he filled for sixteen years.

In 1896 he was elected to the Legislature, which position he held for one term.

Mr. Richardson was a Mason, with membership in the Hartwell Lodge F. & A. M., No. 189, and was also a Royal Arch Mason. He formerly belonged to what was known as Ferman Lodge No. 189, and was an officer, having held different positions in the order from time to time.

His Christian or church life, if any difference, stood out more prominently than any other. Sardis, his home church, elected him superintendent of the Sunday school for thirty-seven years. He also served as deacon for thirty-five years.

He was buried in the cemetery at Sardis, after funeral services conducted by Rev. T. M. Galphin, his former pastor.

The Stowers Family History

LEWIS STOWERS, SR., was a soldier in the War of the Revolution, and came afterwards, if we are not mistaken, from Virginia to Georgia and obtained a large body of land in Elbert (later Hart) County on Big Cedar Creek, which was later owned by J. Harrison Strange, and now known as the Albert Bradley place.

From the records as to the lands obtained by Lewis Stowers, we have the following:

Land Court Records 1791-1822

April 1, 1808. Lewis Stowers, self and 13 in family, by which he was entitled to 100 acres and 50 acres each to wife and children.

April 7, 1815. Lewis Stowers, old warrant 850 acres renewed, which perhaps included the place where he lived on Big Cedar Creek.

Lewis Stowers, two draws in land lottery acquired from the Creek Indians, situated in Baldwin and Wilkinson counties.

Lewis Stowers, Revolutionary soldier, two draws in territory ceded by the Indian Springs Treaty February 12, 1825.

We do not have all of the names of Lewis Stowers' children.

Frances Stowers married Lewis McMullan June 25, 1808.

Joicy Stowers married William Hunt December 4, 1815.

Savannah Stowers married Moses McCurley February 5, 1824.

We take it that the foregoing mentioned were daughters of Lewis Stowers, Sr.

He had one son, whose name was Thomas Stowers, and known as Captain Thomas Stowers; why the title we do not know.

Captain Thomas Stowers lived at the place and owned the ferry on the Savannah River formerly owned by Benjamin Brown, who was a soldier in the War of the Revolution, and came afterwards from Randolph County, Va., to Georgia and settled the place and installed the ferry.

To Captain Thomas Stowers and wife were born the following children: sons—Lewis W., Francis Gaines, Thomas L., Richard S. and Marion C. Stowers; and two daughters—Permelia and Judatha.

Captain Thomas Stowers met a tragic death by being thrown from a spirited horse near his home.

After his death his children, above named, deeded the place to John Foster Sadler, located partly in Elbert and partly in Hart counties, consisting of 260 acres of land, including the ferry and a half interest in the fishery on the South Carolina side of the river.

Lewis W. Stowers married Katherine Dooly, daughter of William Dooly.

Francis Gaines Stowers married Mary Elizabeth Gaines. A further account of Francis Gaines Stowers is given in these pages.

Thomas L. Stowers married .... McCurley, a daughter of .... McCurley. He owned and lived at the place now known as the John Snow place.

Have no record of who Richard S. Stowers married.

Marion C. Stowers seems never to have married, as by his will of record made on his return to the war, he conveys all of his property, both real and personal, to his sister, Permelia Craft.

Permelia Stowers married William J. Craft.

Judatha Stowers married .... McMullan.

The old Lewis Stowers, Sr., estate was later known as "Cedar Crest" during the time it was occupied by James Harrison Strange, a sketch of which appears further on.

"CEDAR CREST"

Written in 1930 by May-Lilly Teasley McCurry

"Cedar Crest," one of the oldest homes in Hart County, is located not far from the Savannah River near Cokesbury Church, in a community which, in the days before the war, was noted for its families of prominence and wealth who were born and reared among the glorious traditions of the Old South. The community contained among its population the ultimate of refinement and intellectual attainment.

Major James Harrison Strange and his wife, Susan Elizabeth Jones, settled there after their marriage December 5, 1840, over ninety years ago.

Major Harrison Strange came to Hart County, then Elbert County, from Banks County, Ga., and was either born there, December 6, 1813, or in Virginia, where the founder of the Strange family in America first settled.

The house, a large frame structure with gabled roof, was bought by Joseph Henderson Jones from F. G. Stowers and presented to his daughter, Susan Elizabeth Strange, for a wedding gift. Major Strange not only furnished the interior of the house with elegant furniture, but he also beautified the grounds with trees and shrubbery, some of which he bought for the purpose in Charleston, S. C. The large cedars and other trees that were native of that locality were transplanted from the woods of the old plantation. Immense boxwood, planted nearly a century ago, surround the flower garden that is still an attractive place in the springtime. Mimosa, black walnut, and crepe myrtle, when in bloom, lend an air of enchantment to the picturesque scene, and furnish nesting places for the many songbirds that spend their summers there.

Probably the first piano that was ever owned in Hart County was the one, a Chickering, square style, bought by Major Strange for his two lovely daughters when they reached young womanhood.

Major Harrison Strange, a wealthy planter and slave owner, was a man of genteel qualities, and was noted for his dignified and distinguished personality. Uncle Newton Strange, an old slave, was the carriage driver for the family; wearing a high hat and sitting on an elevated front seat, he drove around the country in grand style the old-fashioned carriage drawn by a pair of fine horses.

Susan Elizabeth Jones, born September 25, 1827, wife of James Harrison Strange, was the sister of James T. Jones, first Ordinary of Hart County. For an account of her ancestry, see the Jones family history. She died July 22, 1889, and is buried beside her husband in the Cokesbury Churchyard. To this union were born two daughters, as follows:

1. Mary Louise Strange, born September 14, 1841, and died July 2, 1875. Married, first, Alexander (Bunk) Hunter, of Elbert County; their children were: (1) Frank, (2) Alexander, Jr., (3) Elizabeth Hunter. Mary Louise Strange Hunter married second, May 28, 1873, Reuben Tinsley Buffington, and to them one son, William Yancy, was born.

2. Frances Henrietta Strange was born September 1, 1843, and married Dunston R. Blackwell, of Elbert County. She was a noted beauty of her day, and was beloved by all who knew her for her charming manner and sweetness of character. She died at the early age of nineteen years on April 13, 1863, and left the following children, who were reared by their Grandmother Strange: (1) Frances Henrietta Blackwell (Mrs. Albert Bradley), and (2) James Dunston Blackwell, who married Mary Lou McCurley.

As Major Strange had no son to perpetuate his name, it has long ago become extinct in Hart County, but the memory of him and his excellent family is still cherished by a few of the country's oldest inhabitants who knew them.

Cokesbury was the church of which they were loyal members, and the father, mother, and two fine young daughters lie sleeping in the old churchyard together.

The Carter Family History

DAVID CARTER, SR., the forefather of the Carter family in this part of the country, was born February 20, 1752, in East New Jersey, and died in Franklin County December 16, 1849, and buried at Mt. Zion Methodist Church, Elbert (now Hart) County.

He married Mehitable Cobb, born March 12, 1756. The date of marriage not known.

David Carter, Sr., was a soldier in the War of the Revolution, and his war services are given as follows: Private in Revolutionary army; fall of 1774, three months under Col. Morgan; in Virginia June, 1775, one month; spring, 1778, four months, Col. Cleveland, N. C.; 1780, Rifle Company under Gen. Rutherford; in 1780 was taken prisoner at battle of Camden and imprisoned on prison ships Concord, King George and Fidenity at Charleston until August, 1781; November, 1781, one month under Col. Isaacs; December, 1781, two months under Col. Isaacs.

After the war David Carter, Sr., moved to Georgia and settled in Oglethorpe County, near Broad River, in what is known as Goose Pond District. Later he moved to Franklin County and settled on Savannah River, near the mouth of Lightwoodlog Creek, where it empties into the river. Lightwoodlog Creek was the line between Wilkes and Franklin counties; later, when Elbert County was organized from territory taken altogether from Wilks County, it became the line between Elbert and Franklin; and in 1854, when Hart County was created from territory taken from Elbert and Franklin, the creek was no longer a county line and the place where David Carter, Sr., once lived was included in Hart County.

The house in which David Carter, Sr., lived stood a short ways north of where the old home of Micajah Carter now stands, which is located about one-half mile from Savannah River and about one hundred yards north of Lightwoodlog Creek.

To David Carter, Sr., and his wife, Mehitable, were born two sons: Micajah and David Carter, Jr.; and one daughter, Mehitable, who, it appears, was never married.

We have no record of the amount or number of acres of land owned by David Carter, Sr. It is our information that his lands were divided between his two sons, Micajah and David Carter, Jr., both of whom obtained grants from the State to large tracts of land, and at the time lived and at the time of their deaths were seized and possessed of large landed estates bordering the Savannah River and Lightwoodlog Creek for a considerable distance and reaching back for quite a ways from the river and creek.

Micajah Carter married Mrs. Nancy Barrett, widow of Isaac J. Barrett, who was a daughter of William Goolsby, as from the Franklin County records we have the following items relative to the estate of Isaac J. Barrett, deceased:

"Nov. 2, 1818—Nancy Carter, relict of Isaac J. Barrett, now wife of Micajah Carter, claims a child's part."

"Jan. 4, 1819, Micajah Carter appointed guardian of Judge Middleton, William Madison, and Eli H., minor children of Isaac J. Barrett."

"May 5, 1828. Heirs: James H. Barrett, John C. Mangum and wife, Micajah Carter by right of his wife Nancy, and he is also guardian for Judge H. Barrett, William and Eliza H. Barrett."

To Micajah Carter and his wife, Nancy, was born one son: James M. Carter.

It appears that Micajah Carter had one daughter named Malissa C. Carter, as from the record of the will of Micajah Carter on record in the office of the Ordinary of Hart County, Ga., we copy the following item:

"Fifth—I give and bequeath unto my son-in-law, E. W. Roebuck, in trust for my daughter, Malissa C. Roebuck, four hundred dollars to be paid out of the money arising from the sale of my property."

Micajah Carter in his will makes bequests to his wife, Mornan. We are not sure, but to the best of our information, Micajah Carter's last wife was Mrs. Mornan Glenn, a widow lady. When she died, August 5, 1876, she was buried at Ruhamah Methodist Church, Anderson County, S. C., beside her former husband.

Micajah Carter was a soldier in the War of 1812, and while we have no record that his brother, David Carter, Jr., was a soldier in said war, it is a well-authenticated tradition that he also served in the War of 1812 along with his brother, Micajah.

When Hart County was organized in 1854, Micajah Carter was elected as one of the Judges of the Inferior Court, and when the streets of the town of Hartwell were laid off one of the prominent streets was named Carter Street, which name it still bears.

Micajah Carter died March 25, 1876, and was buried at Mt. Zion Methodist Church, of which he had long been a member; his funeral was preached by Rev. Henry Tyler, who had been his friend for fifty-five years. Rev. W. T. Norman assisted in the funeral services.

On the large-landed estate owned by Micajah Carter, and later by his son, Hon. James M. Carter, there was in the early days a public assembly ground at which were race paths. A few years ago when the land was cleared the old track of the paths could easily be seen. At these public gatherings the people engaged in horse-racing and such other games and amusements as were common in those days.

Intoxicating liquors were plentiful and freely imbibed, and other evils and immoralities held high carnival.

Not far from the end of the race paths which terminated on the ridge or table lands, on the hillsides adjacent to the river was an Indian burying ground where many of the Cherokee Indians are buried; signs of their graves may yet be seen. On the bottom lands between the hill lands and the Savannah River was in the early days a kind of Indian village, composed of huts, wigwams, and such other places of abode as they saw fit to construct and use for dwellings. The wife of David Carter, Jr., who was before her marriage Lavinia York, used to tell about visiting this Indian village or encampment in her youth where the Indians lived and plied their trade of making baskets and other things of Indian manufacture, gardening, hunting, fishing and other pursuits common to Indian life.

Hon. James M. Carter, son of Micajah Carter, was born in 1822. Below we give some paragraphs from an article written by him as it appeared in *The Hartwell Sun*, issue of September 19, 1902.

"The house in which I was born in 1822, still stands, near where I now reside, about a half mile from the Savannah River and one hundred yards from Lightwoodlog Creek. This creek was the line between Elbert and Franklin counties. It is a fact not known perhaps to younger people of today, that the early settlers of our State always settled near watercourses, believing the ridge land to be almost valueless. I can remember well when the ridge land in this county was thought to be high at the price the State charged for the papers.

"For twelve years I ran a boat on the Savannah River. This was our principal mode of transportation of freight, in fact the only way that freight was carried from this part of the country to Augusta, then, as now, one of the chief cities of the State. Of course you understand this was not a steamer nor sail boat, but a flat boat, and we used long poles to push with. The trip was usually made from here—I mean from the mouth of Lightwoodlog Creek—to Augusta in three days. The return trip required seven days, though it was possible to make the down trip on high water in one day.

"I remember my first trip on the boat in 1840. I think we were loaded with cotton on that trip, but oftentimes we carried flour and corn. We brought back dry goods, coffee, sugar, salt, iron,—in fact, everything except meat, flour, and corn, of which we always made more than enough for our own use.

"As I have stated above, large quantities of flour and corn were shipped to Augusta, and western corn, flour and meat were unknown to our people.

Truly a case of where 'ignorance was bliss,' and where folly came with acquired wisdom."

In connection with reference to the period in which David Carter, Sr., was a prisoner, we give herewith some of his experiences as related in an article written by Hon. James M. Carter, grandson of David Carter, Sr., which was written July 7, 1902, and published in *The Hartwell Sun*.

"My grandfather, David Carter, Sr., joined the army from Pickens District, S. C., and was taken prisoner when General Gates, who was in command of the army of the south, was defeated at Camden, S. C., August 15 and 16, 1780, by Cornwallis, who commanded the British, and was held on the British prison ship at Charleston, S. C. Upon his release, he returned to Pickens and organized a company to resist the depredations of the Tories who infested that section. Twelve Tories were caught and hanged on one pole. This put a stop to the war in this section.

"Grandfather told of an attempt of the American prisoners to capture the prison ship. The plan was for them to rush on the British guards and overpower them. David Carter was selected to lead the assault. At the given signal he did so, but was not supported by the other prisoners. Several of the guards grappled with him, and after administering a severe mauling, threw him down the hatch among the other prisoners."

"About 1830 my grandfather moved to what is now Hart County, Ga., settling on Savannah River, six miles east of Hartwell, at a place now owned by my son, Captain Yancey Carter. I knew him for 20 years. He died in 1850, and was buried at Mt. Zion Church, Hart County. David Carter lived to be 98 or 99 years of age."

"Hon. James M. Carter"

"This venerable and distinguished citizen passed from the lower to the higher life at the residence of his son-in-law, Rev. T. A. Thornton, in this city (Hartwell, Ga.) on Sunday night, May 16, 1908. Full of years and with a rich harvest of good deeds, after life's fitful fever, he sleeps well.

"We will attempt no eulogy upon this grand gentleman of the old southern school, now fast passing away, but leave this duty to one more capable to do full justice to his life and character. He was a great-hearted Christian gentleman, and perhaps there was never a more widely known and popular man in the cities of Hartwell and Elberton and the counties of Hart and Elbert.

"James M. Carter was born February 11, 1822, near Savannah River in that portion of Hart County that was cut off from Franklin County. The house in which he was born is yet standing. His father was Micajah Carter, who was a well-to-do and prominent citizen of this section in his day.

"James M. Carter joined the Methodist Episcopal Church in early life and was noted for his piety and religious zeal, being remarkably well posted in Methodist doctrines and politics.

"In 1846 Mr. Carter was united in marriage to Miss Louisa Clark, of Abbeville, S. C., and reared a large and influential family."

Here we will state in the way of parenthesis that Miss Louisa Clark, who married Hon. James M. Carter, was a daughter of Mary Alston Clark, who was a first cousin of Governor Alston, who married Theodosia, daughter of Aaron Burr. She was related to five Governors of that state.

"After a beautiful and useful life, Mrs. Carter preceded her husband to the grave a number of years ago. One of their daughters, Mrs. McAlpin Arnold, of Elberton, has also passed over the river. The surviving children are: Mrs. T. A. Thornton and Capt. F. M. Carter, of Hartwell; Captain W. Y. Carter and James Carter, of Hart County; Mrs. H. C. Mickel, of Elberton; and Mrs. Kate Grubbs, of Texas. (Mrs. T. A. Thornton and James Carter have both died since this was written.)

"Mr. Carter was an industrious and enterprising man, and before the Civil War was a large landholder and slave owner."

Here we will intersperse by saying that Hon. James M. Carter owned a large body of land in Elbert County, Ga., adjacent to the Savannah River, including the site of the bridge on the Calhoun Highway, and in consideration of the fact that the site of the bridge was located on the lands formerly owned by Hon. J. M. Carter, Miss Edna May Copeland, a great-granddaughter of Hon. J. M. Carter, was given an important part in the ceremonies opening the memorial bridge.

"Mr. Carter was elected to the Georgia Senate from Elbert County in 1859-60. He served in the War Between the States from 1862 to 1865, and was Orderly Sergeant, Co. "H," Carswell's Brigade. His last service was Officer in Charge of the Pontoon Corps that brought the pontoon boats from Augusta to Petersburg Ferry, on Savannah River, for President Jefferson Davis and his Cabinet to cross on their way to Washington, Ga.

"Mr. Carter was always deeply interested in the political affairs of his county and State and cast his last ballot in the primary election in Hartwell on the 10th instant.

"Guarded by loved ones, the casket containing the mortal remains of Hon. James M. Carter was conveyed to Elberton by rail-

Micajah Carter Home

way on Monday afternoon, and on Tuesday morning his body was laid to rest in the city cemetery in the presence of a large concourse of relatives and friends, after impressive funeral services by Dr. J. H. Mashburn, Presiding Elder of the Elberton District, and Rev. J. N. Wall, a life-long friend."

War services of David Carter, Sr., and descendents: David Carter, Sr., was a soldier in the War of the Revolution; Micajah and David, Jr., sons of David, Sr., served in the War of 1812; James M. Carter, grandson of David, Sr., served as a soldier in the War Between the States; W. Y. Carter and F. M. Carter, sons of James M., served in the Spanish-American War, W. Y. as Captain and F. M. as Quartermaster; Y. Cade Carter, son of F. M., served in the same war as Sergeant; Preston B. Carter, son of James Carter, Jr., and grandson of James M. Carter, served in the World War and was killed in action overseas.

David Carter, Sr., and descendents were patriotic and readily responded to their country's call.

Family History of David Carter, Jr.

David Carter, Jr., son of David Carter, Sr., and brother of Micajah Carter, was born January 15, 1792, died March 10, 1859; married Lavinia York, October 22, 1818, born November 11, 1796, died August 14, 1891; both buried at Mt. Zion Methodist Church, Hart County, Ga.

David Carter, Jr., to the best of our information, came from North Carolina to Georgia, perhaps with his father and other members of the family, and settled on a large tract of land adjoining the lands of his father, David Carter, Sr., later the lands of his brother, Micajah Carter, who came into possession of his father's estate.

To David Carter, Jr., and his wife, Lavinia York Carter, were born 12 children:

1. Lamarcus Carter, born August 16, 1819, died _____.
2. James Madison Carter, born March 13, 1821, died in Texas.
3. Sarah Elizabeth Carter, born October 29, 1822, died May 14, 1884.
4. Mary R. Carter, born February 12, 1824, died in Alabama.
5. Riller Harriett Carter, born February 13, 1826, died March 20, 1859.
6. David Louis Carter, born January 28, 1828, died January 26, 1859.
7. William Balus Carter, born December 29, 1829, died 1865.
8. Elias Earle Carter, born April 21, 1831, died February 12, 1834.
9. Micajah K. Carter, born October 17, 1832, died March, 1859.
10. John K. Carter, born December 18, 1834, died in Louisiana.
11. Elizabeth Ann Caroline Carter, born June 19, 1837, died February 13, 1891.
12. Amanda B. Carter, born October 23, 1839, died 1900 in Alabama.

Lamarcus Carter was twice married. To him and his first wife Frances McCurry were born three daughters: Mattie, Lou and Elizabeth.

Mattie married John Stowers, son of Hon. F. G. Stowers. Lou married Lumpkin Pritchett. Elizabeth was never married, so far as we have any record.

After the death of Lamarcus Carter's first wife, he married Harriett Poole, and to him and his wife, Harriett, were born one son: Joseph F. Carter.

Lamarcus Carter settled the place and built the mill on Little Lightwoodlog Creek, afterwards known as the Murry place. Thomas Murry owned the place from the time he came into possession of it until his death, after which his son, Peter A. Murray, became owner of the place, and it still belongs to his estate.

Lamarcus Carter also built a sawmill on Gum Branch; afterwards Hon. F. G. Stowers bought the place, where he built and operated a flour and grist mill and cotton gin.

James Madison Carter settled the place now known as the old Elias Vickery home place. He afterwards moved to Texas, where he died.

Sarah Elizabeth Carter married Richard N. Brown, son of Nicholas Brown, and they had four children: James, William, Eliza and Ada. After the death of Richard N. Brown, her first husband, she married Elihu Hall, and they had three children: Joel Turner, Anderson D., and Cora Hall.

Mary R. Carter married J. Garrison Richardson, and later moved to Alabama. We have no further record of her and family.

Riller Carter and brothers, David Louis and Micajah K. Carter, and their father, David Carter, Jr., all died of typhoid fever in the first part of the year 1859. Dr. J. L. Turner was their family physician and attended them during their sickness. All buried at Mt. Zion Church.

William Balus Carter died in the War Between the States in 1865.

Elias Earle Carter died February 12, 1834, at the age of about three years.

John K. Carter died in Louisiana in 1866. We have no further record of him.

Elizabeth Ann Caroline Carter married William A. Sanders September 15, 1859. To her and her husband were born three sons: Albert Perry, Florence Newton and John Harrison Sanders; and five daughters: Fannie Angeline, Lucy Ella, Sarah Caroline, Emma Alicia and Mornin Louisa Sanders.

Amanda B. Carter married Thomas Pritchett. To this union were born one son: Balus; and one daughter: Sallie Lou.

Obituary of Mrs. Lavinia Carter

"Mrs. Vina Carter, an aged and most excellent Christian lady, died last Friday at the home of her son-in-law, Mr. W. A. Sanders, in Alford's District.

"Aunt Vina, as she was familiarly called by everybody in the neighborhood, was nearly one hundred years old, and had been a member of the Baptist Church for many years and lived a life of great usefulness.

"By her request, sometime before she died, Rev. T. A. Thornton preached the funeral at Mount Zion Church on Saturday, after which the feeble form of this good woman was laid to rest beside her loved ones gone before."

Her grave is marked by a marble tombstone with the inscription:

"LAVINIA YORK CARTER,
BORN NOV. 11, 1796,
MARRIED OCT. 22, 1818,
DIED AUG. 14, 1891."

The John McCurry Family History

JOHN McCURRY. Family Record. Taken from *The Hartwell Sun*, issue February 8, 1901, as prepared by Julia A. Stewart and John A. Brown.

For the benefit of the Scotch families who came to this country over one hundred years ago, we have prepared this record and ask the editor to publish it; also the obituary of John McCurry, which was published years ago.

The McCurrys, Johnsons, Gordons, and McDonalds all came from the old country to North Carolina about the same time and from there they moved to what is now Hart County, Ga.

They labored under many difficulties to establish homes for themselves. The Indians were very hostile and for protection they all camped together in order that the women and children would not be alone while the men were away building their houses and clearing the land. Their camp was somewhere near where Cokesbury Church is now located.

During this time, John McCurry and Sarah McCurry were married. They established their home near where Bethesda Church is now located, a full description of the lands owned by John McCurry is herein given.

John McCurry, born August 11, 1776; died December 6, 1857. Married to Sarah McCurry, December 31, 1799, who was born October 9, 1783; died September 18, 1863.

The children to this union were:

1. Catherine; born October 5, 1828. Married to Edmond T. Penn; born March 16, 1804; died August 25, 1855.

2. Laughlin; born September 10, 1804; died August ___, 1882. Married February ___, 1832, to Eliza Brown; born ___, 1811; died May 3, 1863. Second wife, Margarette Lewis.

3. Mary; born May 2, 1807; died November 28, 1880. Married February 11, 1841, to Elbert Brown.

4. Daniel E.; born June 22, 1809; died March 7, 1894. First wife, Elizabeth Ashworth. Second wife, Arsenia Hodges. Third wife, Jane Newson. Fourth wife, Jane D. (Stewart) Bobo.

5. Duncan M.; born February 2, 1812; died August 12, 1865. Married September 18, 1834, to Elizabeth C. Chandler; born May 1, 1817; died October, 1893.

6. Flora; born August 17, 1814; died October 5, 1872. Married December 6, 1832, to James Clark. Second marriage to David Cheek. Third marriage to William Jones.

7. John Gordon; born April 26, 1821; died December 4, 1886. Married January 27, 1842, to Rachael S. Brown; born June 5, 1829; died July 6, 1899.

8. Nancy; born October 6, 1818. Married December 12, 1839, to James E. Brown; born March 27, 1814; died September 18, 1869.

9. Sarah P.; born October 11, 1824; died January 7, 1889. Married to Elbert J. Brown; born August 17, 1817.

10. Alexander W.; born November 21, 1826; died July 22, 1885. Married March 14, 1850, to Nancy Roberts; born March 1, 1831.

Obituary of John McCurry—From An Old Newspaper

Departed this life on the 6th of December, 1857, at his residence in Hart County, Ga., John McCurry, in the 82nd year of his age.

The deceased united with the Associated Reformed Presbyterian Church at Generostee, S. C., about the time the Rev. R. Irwin took charge of same.

He was for many years a regular attendant, though the church was fifteen miles distant. His connection with and attachment for this church remained unchanged, though the state of his health for many years past prevented his attendance.

While in service, during the War of 1812, his health was so impaired that he was removed home under difficult circumstances. During this trip he contracted an aversion to riding in any kind of vehicle, which never left him, so that he rarely left home unless to attend church, an election, or where he thought his duty demanded his presence, on which occasions he generally walked.

Five weeks before his decease he was attacked with a disease of the chest, at which time he expressed the opinion that this attack would put a close to his sufferings on earth and would remove him from the dangers of this life, which he esteemed greater than death. He refused to take medicine, saying that medicine could not restore youth or give a sound constitution. He seemed entirely resigned against murmuring or repining at his sufferings.

He leaves a widow, a large number of children and grandchildren, with many friends to mourn his death; but with the consoling belief that what was their loss was his gain.

John McCurry obtained possession of a large tract of land, containing 600 acres, not far from where Bethesda Church is located, lying on both sides of the old Holly Springs Road, and on both sides of Coldwater Creek. This tract of land was originally granted to Hugh McDonald, perhaps in consideration for his service in the War of the Revolution.

The memoranda on the grant and plot are as follows:

"Pursuant to a warrant under the hand of the Honorable John King, Esquire, Senior Justice, presiding at a land court held in Wilkes County, dated November 30, 1787, was surveyed for Hugh McDonald, who lives in this State, a tract of land containing six hundred acres, bounded N. W. by Ledbetter, S. W. by Patterson and surveyed land, S. E. by Thomas E. Smith, and on all other sides by Bedford Brown's land, having such form and marks as are represented in the above plot.

"Surveyed December 1, 1787, by H. McDonald, D. S., and certified by D. Creswell, Esquire, C. S.

"T. M. McCALL, *Sur. Gen.*"

At the time this land was granted to Hugh McDonald it was embraced in Wilkes County. Later, in 1790, when Elbert County was created, it was then included in Elbert County, and later, in 1854, when Hart County was organized, it was included in and became a part of Hart County.

When Elbert County was created in 1790, this tract of land was included in the 10th Militia District as originally laid off in the organization of Elbert County, and was also known as McDonald's District, Hugh McDonald being the Captain of the 10th district.

On the above described land John McCurry built his home, which, if we are not misinformed, is still standing, though changed and improved since it passed from the McCurry family.

It later became, by the provisions of the will of John McCurry, the home of his son, Alexander W. McCurry. John McCurry, by deed and also by provisions in his will, conveyed the balance of his lands to his other sons and sons-in-law. In making bequest to his son, Daniel E. McCurry, he gives and bequeaths to him his bounty land warrant. We have never learned where the land covered by his bounty land warrant was located.

While John McCurry owned the place he erected and operated a cotton gin on Coldwater Creek, and at that time the cotton press, as now used, was not known and perhaps had never been invented. The cotton was packed as the lint came from the gin into round bales. The lint was placed in holes, or excavations, in the ground near the gin, or large, planked-up cylinder-shaped boxes, lined with sufficient bagging to cover the bale of cotton when packed and tramped and packed with a crow bar or other rods or bars of iron, and when completed was lifted out of the hole or box. The bales so packed were not of such size or weight as at present, but necessarily much smaller.

During a part of the time the gin was operated, cotton seed were considered of no value other than for planting purposes, and at the gin the seed were either piled out or allowed to float down the creek so as to be out of the way.

It has come down to us by tradition that it was by accident, during this time, that cotton seed were discovered to be quite valuable as a fertilizer for wheat and other crops as well. As told to us by an old citizen who still lives in the community, some of the sons of John McCurry were hauling a load of cotton seed across a corn field, and as the wagon passed over the corn rows some of the seed fell out on to the ground. The land was sown to wheat and it developed that where the cotton seed were left on the ground the wheat grew very luxuriantly, and from this incident people began to save and use their cotton seed for fertilizing purposes.

John McCurry and his wife, Sarah, are buried south of the old Holly Springs road, about opposite the old home, their graves marked by a marble monument with the following inscription:

"JOHN MCCURRY, BORN AUGUST 11, 1776; DIED DECEMBER 6, 1857;
MARRIED SARAH MCCURRY, DECEMBER 31, 1799.
SARAH, BORN OCTOBER 9, 1783; DIED SEPTEMBER 18, 1863."

John Gordon McCurry

From a very lengthy and also a very interesting article written by Prof. George Pullen Jackson, of Vanderbilt University, Nashville, Tenn., upon the life and activities of John Gordon McCurry, musical and otherwise, we make the following extracts:

"Aldine Kieffer wrote an editorial in his Dayton, Va., *Musical Million* of 1883 (Vol. 14, p. 70) about the Social Harp, a four-shape song book compiled and in part composed by John G. McCurry, of Hart County, Ga., and published in 1859. The copy of the song book which had just fallen into the shape-note champion's hands led him to tell the *Million* readers something of the interesting old compilation of camp-meeting and revival songs and of its maker. For Kieffer had visited McCurry in the latter's northeastern Georgia home but a few months before. The information brought by this editorial was all I had until Will H. Ruebush of the Ruebush-Kieffer form lent me a copy of the book—the only one, incidentally, which I have been able to locate—and until I made a visit to Hart County, Ga., in 1931.

"Hart County is on the eastern edge of the State, and on the Savannah River, about 100 miles northeast of Atlanta. It is a stretch of hilly cotton fields tilled largely by whites. Hartwell, the county seat, has about 2,000 souls and is reached now by one good highway, and is the terminus of one very primitive spur track of the Southern Railroad.

"The search for McCurrys was not hard. I learned, immediately on my arrival, that the name was well known and highly esteemed in those parts and that nearly everybody was "some sort of kin" to the old family. So it was easy, after a day or so of inquiry among these relatives, and in conference with J. W. Baker, Hart County's Historian, to piece together the following story.

"In the latter part of the Eighteenth Century a group of Scotch-Irishmen and their families—Johnsons, Gordons, McDonalds and McCurrys—came from North Carolina to what is now Hart County. They camped in the neighborhood of where Cokesbury Church is now located some ten miles southeast of Hartwell for mutual protection against the very hostile Indians, while the men folk built their houses. Among those pioneers was Angus McCurry. And it was in 1799 that his son, John McCurry, married Sarah McCurry (a relative it seems). John became a soldier of the War of 1812. The seventh child of John McCurry and wife, Sarah, born April 26, 1821, was John Gordon McCurry, the Social Harp man. John Gordon married Rachael S. Brown in 1842, but they had no children. I met many who had known McCurry personally. And all of them agreed that he was a most unusual man. As a farmer he tilled several hundred acres. He could walk around a piece of land and then tell with great accuracy how many acres it contained. He took one of the first censuses in Hartwell. As President (Judge) of the Inferior Court during the Civil War times, he signed script that was used as currency in that county. He was a Royal Arch Mason. Although his father had been, for traditional reasons we may presume, a member of the Associated Reformed Presbyterian Church, John G. went the more popular Missionary Baptist way. He could nod, as he usually did, throughout the sermon and could still tell the rest of the church goers more than they knew of the preacher's words. He was the 'mud sill' of the Baptist Church at Bio in the McCurry's District, and is buried in its churchyard.

"McCurry's esthetic bent is well shown by the 'dream quilt' story. He dreamed one night, Mrs. T. R. Estes, his grandniece, told me, of a beautiful 'piece quilt' design. In the morning he took a stick and drew the design in the sand of the yard beside the house, and from this he cut a pattern. Two-color quilts made from this pattern soon became very popular, and today they may be found in numerous homes. They are always called 'the dream quilt.'

"Mrs. Estes told me that her 'Uncle Gordon' was also a tailor, to whom the people from miles around would bring their home-spun cloth to be cut. And she maintains that the dozen dressmakers (including herself) among the grandnieces now living ascribe their inspiration and perhaps their talent to their Uncle Gordon.

"As a man who had the reputation for knowing everything, McCurry was consulted on all imaginable subjects from song composition to horse trading.

"Aldine Kieffer tells, in the editorial of 1883 referred to above, that he, Kieffer, was one of a group who spent an evening in the McCurry home in singing and in the discussion of musical matters. Dr. Clark told me, however, that McCurry had some voice affection which almost completely prevented his singing during the last forty years of his life. McCurry died December 4, 1886. His wife survived him by 13 years.

"Representation of the first cover page of McCurry's Social Harp is on page _____ of this work. It reads 'The Social Harp, a Collection of Tunes, Odes, Anthems, and Set Pieces. Selected from Various Authors, Together with Much New Music Never Before Published; Suited to all Metres and Well Adapted to all Denominations, Singing-Schools, and Private Societies. With a Full Exposition of the Rudiments of Music. And the Art of Musical Composition so Simplified that the Most Unlearned Person Can Comprehend it with the Utmost Facility. By John G. McCurry, Philadelphia; Published by S. C. Collins, N. E. Cor. Sixth and Minor Sts. For the Proprietor, John G. McCurry, 1859.' Its back cover shows that it was for sale, wholesale and retail, by John B. Watson, Anderson, C. (ourt) H. (ouse), S. C.; H. S. and J. P. Rees, Columbus, Ga.; and W. N. White, Athens, Ga.; and that its 'traveling agents' were R. W. Waldrup, G. W. Bo——— (unreadable), Wm. C. Davis, J. H. Moss, A. N. Benton and Joseph Lawrence. These are probably singing-school teachers.

"Although the date 1859 appears on the front cover of this book as on the copy which Kieffer saw, still it is probable that this is a later printing of the book and that its first appearance was in 1855. The only information we have as to this first printing is given by J. S. James in his 1911 edition of the Original Sacred Harp, page 507. Referring there to the Social Harp, he states that its preface was signed by McCurry in Andersonville, Hart County, Ga., March 16, 1855. I can not verify James' statement from my copy, since its preface and its first six pages are gone. But a little internal evidence points to the correctness of James' observation. I refer to the fact that dozens of the songs are dated. Their composition dates run from the 1840's down to 1855. But not one song has a date later than that year.

"The 237 pages of song in this book form one of the richest storehouses of southern indigenous music and text in all the Fasola literature. For McCurry, himself a facile composer of sprightly tunes, was successful in obtaining for his Social Harp the songs of a number of his composer-friends in that remarkably pregnant northeastern Georgia and northwestern South Carolina field.

"McCurry's own songs in Social Harp number 49. They are: Glorious

News (18), The Cross (18), Mandaville (19), River of Jordan (21), Substantial Joys (28), Martin (29), Happy Children (33), To the Land (34), Hallelujah, Third (35), The Traveler (37), Better Day (47). (Here four pages are torn out of my book. Enough of them remain to show that McCurry composed at least two tunes on the missing pages.) Heavenly Meeting (60), Kay (61), Maxwell (62), A Home in Heaven (68), Hermon (70), Dove of Peace (71), Old Tory (75), Bower's, or Happy Souls (82), Hail, Ye Sons (100), Parting Friends (101), Teasley (102), Mosley (103), Burgess (106), Memphis (107), Derrett (108), The Harvest Field (135), Zion's Walls (137), Morning Star (138), Crumbly (139), Sweet Canaan (140), Slabtown (141), Bowman (143), Roll Jordan (145), Wake Up (155), Navigation (165), Wilkes (183), Hartwell (193), Birth of Christ (199), John Adkin's Farewell (200), Vanderver (201), Few Days (209), The Beggar (212), Eagle Grove (227), Marion (228), and Good By (253).

"That he was in close touch with the Sacred Harp group is indicated by his using eleven songs by B. F. White, ten of which were in the Sacred Harp, which had made its appearance eleven years before; four songs by the Sacred Harp's co-author, E. J. King; one song by J. Tom White, B. F. White's nephew; and four and three, respectively, by the Sacred Harp contributors, Leonard P. Breedlove and T. W. Carter.

"Through inquiry in Hart County, I have been able to identify a number of the Social Harp song producers as relatives and other neighbors of the compiler. Alec W. McCurry (two songs) was the compiler's brother. William C. Davis (11 songs), Henry F. Chandler (7), and E. R. White (4) were Hart Countians, as were, in all probability, J. F. and J. A. Wade (9 songs between them), Silas W. Kay (2) and Thomas Maxwell (1).

"McCurry's songs bearing local family names are Teasley, Derrett and Vanderver. Those having local place names are Hartwell, Bowman and Eagle Grove. His song, 'John Adkins' Farewell,' bears the name of a man who murdered his wife and was hanged for it in Clarkesville, Ga., so I was told in Hartwell. The song thus fits nicely into the frame of indigenous heraldy which is carrying on the immigrant traditions.

"Mixed in here and there are songs that are designated as a 'set piece.' I have examined them to find out just what 'a set piece' is. They are on pages 18, 29, 37, 68, 80, 137, 142, 194, 201, 209, and 212, and are rather unsuccessful. As to their text material, two are straightout secular pieces, two are missionary's farewell songs, one tells of the crucifixion, and the rest are songs of prayer, shouting, traveling home, etc. Seven out of the eleven 'set pieces' are the melodic product of McCurry's pen. All have sprightly tunes. That McCurry considered the metrical form when he called a song a 'set piece,' seems clear from his statement on p. 11 of his 'rudiments' to the effect that, 'set pieces have no general rule of measurement.'

"The extraordinarily large number of indigenous tunes in this book are, naturally, predominatingly of five-tone scale type. I say 'naturally' because I am thinking of the important Scotch-Irish tradition in the Hart County folk. An interesting piece of documentary evidence of the influence of this song inheritance from the old country (where the folk song in the five-tone modes) came to my observation in a letter written recently by Thomas Gibson Lewis, a descendant of the Hart County Gordons, to J. W. Baker, the Hart County Historian. In telling of his Gordon ancestors, Mr. Lewis said that his great-great-grandfather came over as a very old man from Ireland to join his younger kinfolk in Hart County, and that he spoke the Irish language and sang Irish songs to my father, who was five or six years old, which songs my father learned, sang to us children of later generation, and still sings from memory such songs as 'Pat Malloy,' etc.

"Perhaps it was Civil War conditions, coming on so soon after the Social Harp appeared, that cut the book's life short. A more considerable reason however for there being no post-Civil War printings was probably McCurry's important civic duties and his voice affection, both of which must have effectively prevented his pushing the sale of his book at singing schools and conventions as his competitors—Hauser, Walker and White, for example— were able to push the sale of theirs. Certainly the book's short life was not due to any intrinsic defects. For if ever a book grew out of its native soil, that book was McCurry's Social Harp."

Obituary

Judge John Gordon McCurry Dead

John G. McCurry

Judge John G. McCurry died last Saturday afternoon at his home, five miles south of Hartwell. He had been very sick for some time, and his death was not unexpected to his family and friends, and we learn that he himself entertained but slight hope of recovery from his first confinement.

It is sad indeed to chronicle the death of a citizen who has always made it a special feature in life to identify himself so closely with the interest of his fellowman.

Mr. McCurry has filled many prominent positions in the affairs of our county, and was perfectly intimate in detail with all the important epochs connected with the same.

He was one of our most influential men, and many of the good citizens of his neighborhood watched closely the course he pursued, and when he established himself he always had a strong following.

He was sixty-five years of age last April, and was quite different from most men of that age in keeping pace with the progress of the times. He was a man endowed with fine reason, always keeping away from extremes. He avoided exciting extravagances on the one hand and dull indifference on the other, but looked thoughtfully and devoutly upon all changes whether social, political, or ecclesiastical. He viewed the affairs of life with a great deal of consideration, but was always in harmony with the best interests of his county, both sacred and secular, believing that whatever transpired would have its effect in some way upon the peace and prosperity of the community in which he lived.

Mr. McCurry was the author of "Social Harp," a music book famous throughout the whole country for its choice selections of church music. We remember one piece especially that it contains, commencing with "I heard a great voice from heaven saying unto me, write from henceforth: Blessed are the dead who die in the Lord," which is perfectly inspiring in melody.

If we were to write many columns narrating the noble traits of character connected with our dear friend's life, there would still be something untold. And to sum it all up as far as our knowledge and observation extends, concerning his life—he lived in the interest of religion, his family, his friends, his county, and his State.

John G. McCurry is buried in the cemetery at Bio Church, his grave marked by marble tombstone with the following inscription:

"R. A. M."
J. G. MCCURRY
BORN
APRIL 26, 1821
DIED
DEC. 4, 1886.
AGED 65 YRS., 7 MO. & 8 DAYS.
"MY HUSBAND RESTS IN HEAVEN."

Daniel E. McCurry

Daniel E. McCurry, born in Elbert County, now Hart County, Ga., June 22, 1809, and died near the place of his birth March 7, 1894. These dates mark a long, and in this case, an eventful life. He, until twenty-nine years old, lived near his birthplace.

Soon after reaching his majority he was elected to the office of Sheriff of Elbert County, in which capacity he served during a period of seven years. While in this office he confronted many dangers, and in several instances narrowly escaped death.

In the year 1838, he removed to Saint Clair County, Ala., where he lived till 1856, when he returned to Hart County, Ga., and settled near his old home.

While he resided in Alabama he filled the office of Sheriff acceptably for several years. In 1863 he represented Hart County in the Georgia Legislature. Was during his residence in Alabama, about the year 1845, converted and joined the Baptist Church, in whose communion he continued his membership until 1868, when he united with the Methodist Episcopal Church, South, at Bethesda, where he remained a member until death. He was a son of John McCurry, and brother to John G. McCurry.

About the year 1859, a few years after Hart County had been organized, he was awarded the contract of measuring and posting the public roads of the county, reference of which has been made.

Was buried at Bethesda Thursday, March 8, 1894, after appropriate funeral services conducted by Rev. R. B. O. England.

The Jones Family

THE earliest record of the Jones family states that they came from King and Queen County, Va., and settled in Warren County, N. C., on Shocco Creek in the late 1600's. This section later being known as Wake County. Edward Jones, the founder of the Jones family of Warren County, was among the very first settlers in that part of the State. His wife, Abigail Shugan, a French Huguenot, was said to be the first white woman to cross Shocco Creek. How well qualified to act her part is clearly manifested in the character and record of her numerous descendants. Edward and Abigail Shugan Jones reared nine children, among whom were Shugan Jones (died 1762 in Granville County, N. C.), the grandfather of James Jones, of Elbert County (now Hart), Ga., and Priscilla Jones, who married first, Gideon Macon (born 1682, died 1761 in Granville County, N. C.), and later became the great-grandparents of Martha Dandridge Custis, the wife of George Washington. Shugan Jones reared ten children, many of whom served in the Revolutionary War.

James Jones, the founder of the Jones family in Hart County, Ga., was born December 25, 1766, in Wake County, N. C., and died December 25, 1865, in Hart County. James Jones was married about 1795 to Elizabeth Henderson (born 1770, died October 21, 1858), the daughter of a prominent family of Virginia and North Carolina. To be near his sister, Rachel Alston Jones, who married Ralph Banks in 1788, and settled on Coldwater Creek, twelve miles from Elberton, Ga., James Jones and his bride came to Georgia and settled in what is now Cokesbury community, this being only a few miles from his sister. Here he owned extensive farm lands on the Savannah River, using many slaves to till the soil.

James Jones was a devout member of the Methodist Episcopal Church. In order to have a church in the community, he gave the land on which Cokesbury Methodist Church now stands. This church was originally known as Jones' Chapel, but later the name was changed to Cokesbury in honor of two Methodist bishops, Coke and Asbury. The Jones family have been members of the Methodist denomination as far back as is known. The first annual conference of the Methodist Episcopal Church ever held in Georgia is said to have been held in the home of James Jones' sister, Mrs. Ralph Banks, who lived in Elbert County, on Coldwater Creek.

James Jones' father represented his county in the State Senate in 1777, was a member of the Provincial Congress in 1776, and during the Revolutionary War served as a captain. His mother was also descended from a long line of distinguished ancestors, among whom were: Colonel John Alston of Chowan County, N. C.; Colonel John Hinton, of Chowan County, N. C.; John Clarke; John Wallis (born November 23, 1616, died October 28, 1703), the great theologian, scholar, and mathematician of Kent, England, a professor of Oxford University; was one of the first members of the Royal Society; and Sir John Temple of Stantonberry, Buck, Kent.

The descendants of James Jones are eligible to the following patriotic organizations: United Daughters of the Confederacy, Daughters of the American Revolution, American Colonist, Sons and Daughters of the Pilgrims, Colonial Dames, Runnymead, Order of the Crown, Order of the

Garter, and many others. A descendant of James Jones' mother's brother is one of three members of the Order of the Garter in Georgia.

James Jones is buried beside his wife, Elizabeth Henderson Jones, in the Cokesbury Cemetery, six miles southeast of Hartwell, Ga.

Their children:

1. Joseph Henderson Jones; born 1796; died 1892 in Carnesville, Ga. Married, 26th February, 1822, in Elbert County, Ga., Lucy Banks; born 1806; died 1847.

2. Mary Louise (Polly) Jones; born 1800. Married, 17th August, 1824, James Patterson; born 17th December, 1786. No children. Their large Colonial home, located on Stevenson Ferry road (now Smith-McGee Bridge road), was one of the finest in this section of the State during the period in which they lived, and today is occupied by Rev. J. D. Turner and family, descendant of Mary Louise Jones, niece of Mrs. Patterson, who made her girlhood home with them. Mary Louise Jones married Dr. Joel L. Turner, one of the most outstanding physicians who ever lived in Hart County, and whose popularity among his patients is still cherished by their descendants. James and Polly Patterson were distinguished citizens of the early days of Hart County, and their home was the mecca for visitors and travelers who came from far and near. James Patterson died 25th November, 1853, and was buried in Roberts Cemetery, Anderson County, S. C. Mary Louise Jones Patterson died April, 1863, and was buried in Cokesbury Cemetery.

3. Mildred A. Jones married Neal McMullan.

4. Thomas Jones. There is no further record of him.

5. Priscilla Lee Jones; born 18th May, 1806; died 20th May, 1857, and is buried in Cokesbury Cemetery. Married, 8th January, 1824, James Robertson Sadler; born 2nd October, 1799, in York County, S. C.; died 9th June, 1874, in Hart County, Ga. For further data see Sadler Family.

6. James W. Jones; born 14th April, 1809; died 12th December, 1877, and is buried in Hartwell Cemetery. Married, first, 30th October, Delina Foster; died November, 1840. Married, second, 25th October, 1842, Mildred E. White; born 15th October, 1819; died 2nd September, 1865. Married, third, Elizabeth Thornton.

7. Simeon Jones married, 6th August, 1821, Rebecca Banks. He died prior to October, 1825.

8. Seaborn Solomon Jones; born 29th August, 1814; died 22nd February, 1889, in Anderson County, S. C. Married, first, 21st September, 1837, Mary Malinda Sadler, the daughter of Wm. Bratton and Jane Erwin Sadler; born 25th April, 1821; died 4th April, 1880. He married second, Margaret _____. By the last marriage there was one child, Walter S. Jones, of whom there is no further record.

Joseph Henderson Jones, the son of James and Elizabeth H. Jones, born 1796, married, 26th February, 1822, Lucy Banks, born 1806, died 1847, the daughter of John Banks (born 7th April, 1774, died 1838) and his second wife, Susan Tait, and the granddaughter of Thomas Banks (born 1709, died 28th June, 1789) and his second wife Betty White, of Granville County, N. C. Susan Tait was a member of the Tait family of Elbert County, Ga. After the death of his wife, Lucy Banks, Joseph H. Jones married _____. Joseph Henderson Jones was a prominent merchant of

Ruckersville, Elbert County, Ga., later moving to Parkertown, Hart County, where he operated a store for a number of years before moving to Carnesville, Franklin County, Ga. He died at Carnesville in 1892.

Children of Joseph H. and Lucy Banks Jones:

1. James Tait Jones; born 1823; died 23d March, 1860. Married Mary Louise Sadler; born 11th May, 1834; died 4th April, 1913; the daughter of John Foster and Eliza Hardy Sadler. James Tait Jones served as the first Ordinary of Hart County, Ga. For their descendants, see Sadler Family.

2. Susan Elizabeth Jones; born 25th September, 1827; died 22nd July, 1889. Married, 5th December, 1840, James Harrison Strange; born 6th December, 1813; died 27th August, 1866, in Hart County, Ga.

3. Martha Ann Jones married James Ford.

4. Emily Frances Jones married Dr. Henry Aderhold, of Carnesville.

5. Sarah Antionette Jones married Tom Stewart.

6. Russell Asbury Jones married, first, Mattie Mitchell; after her death he married Mrs. Price. During the War Between the States he served as Captain of Company "G," 34th Georgia Regiment. Captain Jones was noted for his kindheartedness, unselfishness and ready wit. On one occasion while his regiment was on board steamer on the Alabama River, the following incident occurred: The day was extremely uncomfortable and the request was sent down by the captain of the vessel for the officers to come up to more comfortable quarters. Captain Jones turned to his regiment and gave the command: "Company 'G,' fall in line. Men of Company 'G' are all officers." Thus showing his consideration for his men.

7. Mary Louise Jones; born 3d January, 1833, in Franklin County; died 20th August, 1894, in Hartwell, Ga. Married, December, 1850, Dr. Joel L. Turner; born 5th January, 1825, in Lincoln County, Ga.; died 18th March, 1897, in Hartwell, Ga.

8. John Seaborn Jones married Eliza Lattimer. They moved to Forney, Texas.

9. Delina Jones.

10. Cornelia Priscilla Jones; born 27th November, 1845; died 30th July, 1926. Married, 11th October, 1866, Joel Thomas Haley; born 9th November, 1836; died 14th January, 1894, in Chattanooga, Tenn.

11. Eliza Evelyn Jones; born 3d April, 1847; died 9th January, 1909. Married, 29th October, 1867, W. C. McEntire; born 23d August, 1836; died 8th December, 1886.

James W. Jones, the son of James and Elizabeth H. Jones; born 14th April, 1809; died 12th December, 1877. Married, 30th October, 1828, Delina Foster; died November, 1840; the daughter of John Foster, of Elbert County, who later moved to Monroe County, Ga. James W. Jones married, second, 25th October, 1842, Mildred E. White; born 15th October, 1819; died 2nd September, 1865; the daughter of Eppy White (born 16th March, 1791; died 19th September, 1854, in Hart County, Ga.) and his wife, Catherine Herndon (born 28th February, 1897; died 1st November, 1885). Mildred E. White Jones is descended from a long line of ancestors prominent in the social and military life of the colonies. Some of whom are: Captain John Martin White, a Baptist preacher and Revolutionary soldier; Joseph Ballenger, Revolutionary soldier; Rev. Jeremiah White; Edward Herndon, a captain in Revolution; William Herndon, who settled in America in 1673; James Gaines, a Revolutionary patriot; Col. James Taylor, settled in Virginia in 1667; Philip Pendleton, settled in Virginia 1674; Lieut. Gov. Drysdale, of Virginia; Dr. John Waller, of Virginia; and Edward Digges (born 1620; died March 15, 1675; the son of Sir Dudley Digges and Lady Mary Kemp, and grandson of Gen. Thomas Digges and his wife, Anne St. Leger, a direct descendant of Alfred the Great), Governor of Virginia, 1655-58; sent to England as agent of Virginia; member of Council in London for Foreign Plantations; member of Council in Virginia; and Auditor General. Gov. Edward Digges was zealous in fostering silk manufacturing, and in order to furnish the colonists with proper teaching he employed two Armenians skilled in this industry. Edward Digges married, 1650, Elizabeth Page, daughter of Francis Page, of Middlesex, England.

James W. Jones married, third, Elizabeth Thornton, the daughter of Daniel and Lucy Christian Bradley Thornton. There were no children.

James W. Jones represented Hart County in the Legislature in 1871-72, being the first Democrat elected after the War Between the States.

James W. and Delina Foster Jones' children:

1. Cornelia F. Jones; born 14th August, 1832; died 9th October, 1913, in Royston, Ga. Married, 10th March, 1853, Dickson L. Baker; born 21st April, 1830; killed in battle 16th August, 1864.

2. Martha Jane Jones; born 19th December, 1833; died 2nd May, 1905. Married Bert Rucker.

3. Jane Eliza Jones; born 18th December, 1835; died 16th June, 1806, in Royston, Ga. Married, 19th October, 1854, Allen S. Turner. He served as a member of Company "B," 24th Regiment, Georgia Volunteers; was appointed First Lieutenant 9th June, 1861, and in May, 1862, was appointed A. Q. M.

4. William Clayton Jones; born 13th May, 1837. Married Mary Lewis. Wm. Clayton Jones was a prominent lawyer of Greenville, Hunt County, Texas.

5. John Joe Jones; born 11th April, 1839; died 22nd March, 1897. Married Marietta Terrell, of Elbert County. They resided in Elberton, Ga.

6. James Warren Jones; born 26th September, 1840; died 9th April, 1900, in Hart County. Married, 5th October, 1865, Mary Elizabeth Brown; born 1st October, 1847; died 19th July, 1910.

James W. and Mildred E. White Jones' children:

7. Claudius C. Jones; born 28th November, 1844; died 4th April, 1915, in Hartwell, Ga. Married, 3d October, 1872, Mildred McCurry; born 29th November, 1856; the daughter of Alexander Washington McCurry and his wife, Nancy Roberts (born 1st March, 1831; died 9th October, 1920), the great granddaughter of Angus McCurry, Revolutionary soldier of Elbert County. Nancy Roberts McCurry was the daughter of Moses J. Roberts (born November, 1804; died 17th October, 1863, and buried at Holly Springs Cemetery, Hart County), and his wife, Mildred Tabor.

Claudius C. and Mildred McCurry Jones only had one child:

Flossie Jones married, 27th December, 1916, Waymon Belton McLeskey, son of Wm. H. McLeskey (born 23d February, 18....; died 9th May, 1921, in Hart County); married, 19th December, 1872, Ivey C. Stifle, and the grandson of John Miller McLeskey (born 18th April, 1829; killed in battle at Smithfield, N. C., 19th March, 1865); married, 5th November, 1848, Elizabeth Sanders (born 1829; died 25th June, 1877), the daughter of Rev. Samuel B. Sanders (born 22nd June, 1811; died 24th March, 1889, in Hart County) and his wife, Ann Skelton (born 22nd June, 1811; died 11th February, 1896), the daughter of Swan H. Skelton, and granddaughter of John Skelton.

Waymon Belton McLeskey is one of the most successful lawyers of Columbus, Ohio.

8. Lambert Junius Jones; born 7th August, 1847; died 13th May, 1913. Married, 3d April, 1873, Emma E. Brown; born 23d June, 1854; died 4th November, 1911; the daughter of James W. Brown (born 11th November, 1827; died 24th June, 1896); married, 5th June, 1851, Jane Burns (born 7th July, 1836; died 7th December, 1904); and granddaughter of Wiley B. Brown (born 21st February, 1807; died 18th December, 1857) and his wife, Sarah Clark (born 20th November, 1808; died 30th December, 1884). Wiley B. Brown was the son of Andrew Brown (born 22nd September, 1769); married, 4th April, 1794, Margaret Adams (born 10th October, 1780).

Their children:

1. James Pearl Jones. Married, November 3, 1903, Laura Elizabeth McDowell.
2. Joseph Blanton Jones.
3. Lon Clayton Jones.
4. Lillie Jones. Married, December 10, 1902, Cyrus Earl Hamilton.
5. Stakely Jones. Married, August 25, 1918, Mary Elizabeth Aderhold.
6. Nettie Jones. Married, May 27, 1915, James A. Gordon.

James Patterson Home

7. Eva Mathews Jones.
8. Leight Jones. Married, January 6, 1914, David Erskine Sadler.

Eliza Evelyn Jones, daughter of Joseph Henderson and Lucy Banks Jones; born 3d April, 1847; died 9th January, 1909. Married, 29th October, 1867, W. C. McEntire; born 23d August, 1836; died 8th December, 1886. W. C. McEntire enlisted in the Confederate Army from Banks County, Ga., in Allen D. Candler's Company and served four years. They resided in Carnesville, Ga.

Cornelia F. Jones, the daughter of James W. and Deliniah Foster Jones; born 14th August, 1832; died 9th October, 1913. Married, 10th March, 1853, Dickson L. Baker; born 21st April, 1830; killed on battlefield by a shot through the breast in an engagement with the enemy (Yankees) at Front Royal, Va., 16th August, 1864. Dickson L. Baker served as Lieutenant in Company "B," 24th Regiment, Georgia Volunteers. They lived in Royston, Ga.

Their children:

1. John Foster Baker; born 6th January, 1854. Married Minerva Ballenger, daughter of Joseph and Caroline Berryman Ballenger.

2. Laura A. Baker; born 14th December, 1855. Married, 28th November, 1872, Patrick H. Bowers.

3. Mary Deliniah Baker; born 16th September, 1860. Married, 12th November, 1874, Fletcher L. Brown. Their son, Dr. Stewart D. Brown, is one of the most outstanding surgeons in Georgia.

4. Ester Jane Baker; born 16th September, 1860. Married, 27th November, 1878, Dr. James Daniel Veal; born 2nd May, 1849; died 4th May, 1906; the son of Alexander and Sarah Godfrey Veal, of Madison County, Ga. Dr. Veal was a prominent physician of Royston.

5. Dickson Allen Crayton Baker; born 27th August, 1864. Married Minnie Bond.

The above sketch of the Jones family was compiled by Laura Lee Satterfield, Hartwell, Ga.

The Sadler Family

RICHARD (1) SADDLER, the founder of our Saddler family in America, was born in England in November, 1733; came to America as a young man and settled in Pennsylvania. He married Jane _____ (born November, 1736; died 5th September, 1822). They removed to York County, S. C., about 1770 and settled on Fishing Creek near the water's edge, where they would be as safe as possible from the lurking Cherokee Indians. During the Revolution some of the thickest of the fighting was done in this community.

Richard Saddler and family attended Bethesda, and later Fishing Creek Presbyterian churches in York District, S. C. The Saddler family has belonged to the Presbyterian Church for nearly 300 years. During the Revolution Richard Saddler rendered aid to the American cause. He died in York County, S. C., about 1816.

Children of Richard and Jane Saddler:

1. David (2) Saddler; born 31st August, 1762. Married Elsie Bratton.

2. Richard (2) Saddler, Jr.; born 9th December, 1764; died 1st February, 1834.
3. Joseph (2) Saddler; born November, 1766; died 4th June, 1812.
4. Eliza (2) (Ellen) Saddler; born 7th November, 1769. Married James Black.

David (2) Saddler (Richard (1)) was born in Pennsylvania, 31st August, 1762. When a small boy he removed with his parents to York District, S. C. He married, about 1784, Elsie Bratton (born 1766; died 22nd November, 1825), the daughter of Col. William and Martha Robertson Bratton, of York District, S. C. About 1812 David Saddler removed with his family to Pendleton District, S. C. (now Anderson County), and settled near Roberts Presbyterian Church, where they placed their membership. He served as an elder in this church for many years.

During the Revolutionary War, David Saddler, while residing in York District, S. C., although quite a young man, joined the Whigs and fought for American Independence, giving valuable aid to the American cause. He served in the South Carolina troops under Lieut. Hemphill, Capt. McClure, Cols. Neil, Bratton, Moffett, Samuel Watson. He fought in the battles of Mobley's Meeting House, Williams' Plantation, Rocky Mount, Fish Dam Ford, Wright's Bluff, and in skirmishes near Buckhead.

He died 13th February, 1848, and was buried in the Roberts Church Cemetery beside his wife.

David and Elsie Bratton Saddler's children:
1. Mary (Polly) (3) Saddler; born November 18, 1786; died March 30, 1869. Married, 1810, Archibald Simpson; born 1776; died October 11, 1860.
2. Martha Bratton (3) Saddler; born October 28, 1788; died January 19, 1880. Married David Simpson; born 1788; died October 21, 1849. He was the youngest son of Rev. John and Mary Remer Simpson.
3. William Bratton (3) Saddler; born December 9, 1790; died October 29, 1856. Married Jane Erwin; born 1794; died September 11, 1858.
4. Jane (3) Saddler; born November 18, 1792; died _____. Married Thos. O. Hill; born _____; died _____.
5. John Foster (3) Saddler; born April 5, 1795; died November 3, 1857. Married, March 1, 1827, to Eliza Hardy; born October 28, 1810; died May 3, 1889.
6. Malinda (3) Saddler; born August 10, 1797; died December 23, 1878. Married David Beaty; born January 20, 1792; died January 9, 1865.
7. James Robertson (3) Saddler; born October 2, 1799; died June 9, 1874. Married Priscilla Lee Jones; born May 18, 1806; died May 20, 1857.
8. Joseph Milton (3) Saddler; born December 8, 1801; died young. Unmarried.
9. Margaret L. (Peggy) (3) Saddler; born December 25, 1804; died July 17, 1894. Married Rev. William Carlisle; born May 19, 1797; died March 22, 1881.
10. Elizabeth E. (3) Saddler; born August 14, 1807; died July 11, 1846. Married James A. Gray, of Abbeville, S. C.
11. Richard (3) Saddler; born January 26, 1810; died young. Unmarried.

12. David (3) Saddler; born January 25, 1812; died August 2, 1885. Married Jane McLees; born December 14, 1813; died February 28, 1889.

David Saddler had three sons to settle in Elbert County, Ga. (now Hart County), about 1825. They were William Bratton Saddler, John Foster Saddler, and James Robertson Saddler. These three brothers bought adjoining plantations on the Savannah River not far from Cokesbury Church, where they became well-to-do planters, owning numbers of slaves.

The section in the vicinity of Cokesbury Methodist Church was known for a number of years as the garden spot of Hart County on account of the cultured families who resided there. In the homes of the Saddler brothers, who were among the first settlers of that community, sociability permeated the atmosphere and a spirit of hospitality was felt by the visitor who went there. And it was here that the boxwood grew. Some surrounded the old-fashioned gardens lovely with lilacs, crepe myrtle, and other flowers popular in that day.

John Foster (3) Saddler, (David (2); Richard (1)), born 5th April, 1795; died 3d November, 1857. Married, first, March, 1827, to Eliza Hardy; born 28th October, 1810; died 3d May, 1889. He was regarded throughout life an examplary Christian and was an elder in Good Hope Presbyterian Church in South Carolina, about seven miles from his home.

John Foster Saddler was named for Rev. John Foster, of South Carolina, who married his mother's sister, the eldest daughter of Col. William Bratton. Rev. John Foster was President of Mt. Zion College at Winnsboro, S. C. John Foster Saddler and his wife are buried in Roberts Church Cemetery in South Carolina, near the graves of his parents.

Eliza (Hardy) Saddler was the daughter of James and Mary (Wilson) Hardy, of Anderson County, S. C., and granddaughter of Thomas Hardy, Revolutionary soldier of Virginia, who later settled in Newberry County, S. C.

"The Methodist Church at Starr, S. C., is the old Bethesda congregation moved to a new location. James Hardy was the original promoter of that church, and gave the ground on which it stood for many years. Mr. Hardy was born in Virginia and came to this section early in the Nineteenth Century from Newberry County, S. C. Around the church there was, in early times, a great camp-meeting ground, said to have been the oldest in the state. The abandoned house of worship, surrounded by its ancient graveyard, stands desolate, a shade of the past."

William Bratton (3) Saddler, (David (2); Richard (1)); born 9th December, 1790; died 29th October, 1856. Married Jane Erwin; born 1794; died 11th September, 1858. In 1825 the Saddler brothers settled on adjoining plantations on the Savannah River. Here they became well-to-do planters, owning numbers of slaves. The ferry near William B. Saddler's home was known as Saddler's Ferry, and was located just below Green's Island. This ferry was used by the Saddlers and their neighbors to go to Good Hope and Roberts Presbyterian churches and other sections of Anderson County, S. C. William B. Saddler taught school during his young manhood. On April 10, 1836, he was elected an elder in Roberts Church. This office he held for many years. He also served as the foreman of the first Grand Jury of Hart County in 1854.

Children:
1. Mary Malinda (4) Sadler; born 25th April, 1821; died 4th April 1870. She married, 21st August, 1837, Seaborn Solomon Jones; born 29th August, 1814; died 22nd February, 1889; the son of James and Elizabeth (Henderson) Jones.
2. Elsie Clarinda (4) Sadler; born 1824; died 9th July, 1839.
3. Rufus Erwin (4) Sadler; born 1826; died 1880. Married, 1855, to Catherine L. Hardy; born 6th November, 1836; the daughter of Miles Hardy (born 27th November, 1803; died 6th June, 1843) and his wife Eliza Speer, and granddaughter of James and Mary (Wilson) Hardy. Rufus Sadler resided all his life in Hart County, Ga., and was buried in the Cokesbury Church Cemetery, near his home. Catherine (Hardy) Sadler, his widow, is living in Atlanta, Ga., in the 98th year of her age.
4. Seraphina (4) Sadler married .... Rice and moved to Texas.
5. Elizabeth Maria (4) Sadler; born 8th January, 1829; died 1862. Married Col. Richard Simpson Hill.
6. Salena (4) Sadler married Mr. Moore.
On this plantation was a cotton gin propelled by horse power, the last one of its kind to be operated in the county.
Children of John Foster and Eliza (Hardy) Saddler:
1. James Hardy (4) Sadler; born 29th May, 1829. He was killed in action, 14th May, 1863, in Jackson, Miss., during the War Between the States. He married, 8th July, 1858, Catherine Elizabeth Speer; born 7th October, 1841; died 11th September, 1922.
2. David Frances (4) Sadler; born 18th March, 1831; died 13th January, 1916. He married, November, 1860, Virginia Speer; born 24th January, 1843; died 22nd June, 1917. David Sadler was a consistent member and officer of the Good Hope Presbyterian Church for many years. He is buried beside his wife in the cemetery at Iva, S. C.
3. Mary Louisa (4) Sadler; born 11th May, 1834; died 3d April, 1913. She married, in 1850, James Tait Jones; born 1823; died 23d March, 1860. She is buried in Silver Brook Cemetery, Anderson, S. C.
4. John Eugene (4) Sadler; born 31st May, 1839; died 8th June, 1877. He married Mrs. Mary (Benson) Sloan, daughter of John P. and Catherine (Sloan) Benson. John E. Sadler attended Emory College, at Oxford, Ga. He joined the Confederate Army and served throughout the War Between the States. He is buried beside his wife in Silver Brook Cemetery, Anderson, S. C.
5. William Weston (4) Sadler; born 27th May, 1842; died in service in Virginia during the War Between the States 3d August, 1862. Never married. He is buried beside his parents in Roberts Churchyard in South Carolina.
6. Elsie Maria (4) Sadler; born 25th February, 1845; died 1911. Married in 1867, to Benjamin Hilliard Clarke Maybin; born 1842 in Charleston, S. C.; died 1887. They met while she was attending Spartanburg College for Women, and he was a student at Wofford College. He was the son of John Maybin (born 1799; died 1843) and his wife, Mary Clarke (born 1811; died 1871); and a grandson of William Maybin, Revolutionary soldier of South Carolina. Ben Clarke Maybin was a Confederate soldier during the

War Between the States. He is buried beside his wife in the old Ebernezer Methodist Churchyard in South Carolina.

7. Juliet Eliza (4) Sadler; born 25th January, 1848; died 20th July, 1865. She is buried beside her parents in Roberts Presbyterian Churchyard.

8. Elizabeth Jane (4) Sadler; born 17th July, 1851; died 24th January, 1931. She married, 6th February, 1879, Col. Thomas William Teasley; born 17th September, 1853; died 11th September, 1912; son of William H. and Jane Ann (Wansley) Teasley. They are buried in the cemetery at Hartwell, Ga.

James Robertson (3) Saddler, (David (2); Richard (1)); born 2nd October, 1799; died 9th June, 1874, in Cokesbury community, Hart County, Ga. He married, 8th January, 1824, Priscilla Lee Jones; born 18th May, 1806; died 20th May, 1857; and is buried beside his wife in Cokesbury Cemetery. James Robertson Saddler was a large planter and slave owner in Hart County, Ga. (formerly Elbert.) He was a consistent member of the Presbyterian Church.

Priscilla Lee Jones was the daughter of James Jones (born 25th December, 1766, in Wake County, N. C.; died December 25, 1865, in Cokesbury community) and his wife, Elizabeth Henderson (born 1770; died 21st October, 1858).

Their children:

1. Cynthia (4) Sadler; born 25th September, 1825; died 18th May, 1874.

2. Mary Elsie (4) Sadler; born 2nd July, 1826; died 3d July, 1898. Married, 1st January, 1846, Jeptha Mercer Bradley; born 20th September, 1815; died 11th December, 1897.

3. Laura Mildred (4) Sadler; born 25th October, 1830; died November 3, 1899. Never married.

4. Martha Jane (4) Sadler; born 18th July, 1835; died 19th September, 1896. Married, 19th January, 1854, Isham Asbury Teasley; born 17th May, 1832; died 3d February, 1903. They joined Cokesbury Methodist Church in 1856, soon after its removal to the new site. Their two children died in early childhood.

The Teasley Family

FOLLOWING is a brief historical sketch of the Teasley family, as prepared by Charles J. Teasley.

"The first Teasley we have any record of in this country was John Teasley, who died in Isle of Wight County, Va., sometime in the spring of 1738, for the appraisement of his estate was made on June 26th, of that year, and is recorded at the court house in the above-named county in Virginia. He was probably a wealthy man at the time of his death, considering the time in which he lived, for his estate's appraisement, as is recorded, lists, among many interesting articles, the following:

"Forty hogs, appraised at from two pounds and fourteen shillings to three pounds and nineteen shillings.

"Two cows and calves and one steer.

"One riding horse.

"Two mares, appraised at only one pound and four shillings each.

"Other things of interest included 71¾ yards of garlick (this probably accounts for the Teasleys' craving for onions), 23¾ yards blue linen (unbleached, or green linen), some Virginia cloth, 2 old brass kettles, iron pots, pot hooks, 1 set iron wedges, 3 trowels and 3 moulds, 4 peggins (pails), drawing knives, broad axes, hackles (instruments used to dress flax), 56 pounds of old iron, 1 whipsaw file and chest, 1 cross-cut saw, 1 parcel shoemaker's tools, 4 hides of leather, 2 linen wheels, 2 spinning wheels for wool, 1 hand mill, 1 pair cart wheels, 2 swords, fish hooks and drum line, 3 pieces of wool cards, 13¼ pounds wool, 25 pounds cotton, 47 pounds of new pewter, 1 pound of old pewter, 3 pewter measures, 1 mustard pot, 1 parcel of smith's tools. There were also listed 24 head of cattle besides the ones mentioned before, and the amount of cash was three pounds and eleven shillings and eleven pence.

"No one can read this list of articles without thinking of the hard times our ancestors experienced when they first came to this country. Practically all of the Hartwell people's ancestors were Virginia settlers, and this list is typical of what the average family had in those trying days.

"This first John Teasley had three sons: one named Richard, who, by the way, was executor of his estate, and another named John, and a third named George. George and Richard never married, but John did marry, and from him descended a very large family, which migrated from Virginia through North Carolina and on to Georgia, from where some went to Tennessee and other sections of the country. The name, John, was carried on down through six or seven generations, and even today there are several John Teasleys. The John Teasley, mentioned above, had two sons, one named Silas and the other, John.

"This John Teasley had nine children, one of whom was Isham Teasley, who was the father of John A. Teasley, my great-grandfather, who was the father of William H. Teasley, my father's father. To give you the marriages and dates, together with all of the children, would require a book itself.

"I failed to mention, in the beginning, that the name Teasley, a variation of Teasley was formed from Tees, the name of a river in England, and ley, meaning field. The Teasleys probably lived on leand near the river Tees.

"Marriage books in England record the marriages of several Teasleys, including a Richard, and the towns from where these Teasleys came show that they were near the Tees River."

The Teasley Family

One line of the Teasley family history, as prepared by Dr. B. C. Teasley.

John (1) Teasley; born .... ; died 1738. Married .... Lived and died in Isle of Wight County, Va.

Children:

1. Richard (2) Teasley (John (1)). Lived in Isle of Wight County, Va. No record of marriage.

2. John (2) Teasley (John (1)); born ....; died in Isle of Wight County, Va., 1759. Married Mary ....; born ....; died .... He was administrator of the estate of his brother, Richard Teasley.

Children:

1. Silas (3) Teasley; Revolutionary soldier. Married Fanny ⸺.
No record of children.
2. George (3) Teasley.
3. John (3) Teasley.
John (3) Teasley (John (2); John (1)); born 1755; died 1816 in Tennessee. Married, 1776, Lucy Hunt; born May 18, 1757; died November 4, 1846.
Children:
Isham (4) Teasley.
John (4) Teasley; born December 28, 1788; died October 20, 1852. Married Mary Hunter.
George (4) Teasley; born 1782. Married Lucretia Shearon (George (5); Plumer (5)).
Peter (4) Teasley; born November 30, 1793. Married ⸺ Clifton (John Decatur (5)).
James (4) Teasley.
Thomas (4) Teasley; born September 2, 1796. Married ⸺ Hunter. Went to Illinois.
Aquilla (4) Teasley; born 1785. Married Adam Brown.
Priscilla (4) Teasley; born 1788; died May 8, 1846. Married, first, ⸺ Parker; second, ⸺ Tyner.
Lucy (4) Teasley; born 1790. Married Henry Hunter. Went to Illinois.
James (4) Teasley (John (3); John (2); John (1)); born March 18, 1779; died February, 1849. Married Drucilla Allen; born March 4, 1782; died July 4, 1847.
Children:
1. James (5) Riley Teasley.
2. Lucy (5) Teasley. Married Lawrence Adams.
3. Pricilla (5) Teasley. Married Willis Hunt.
4. Phronie (5) Teasley. Married Malcomb Johnson.
5. Drucilla (5) Teasley. Married John Easton Teasley.
6. Patsey Martha (5) Teasley. Married Jefferson Teasley.
7. Beverly (5) Allen Teasley. Married Elizabeth Evanson February 15, 1828.
Beverly Allen (5) Teasley (James (4); John (3); John (2); John (1)).
Children:
1. Alfred (6) Teasley.
2. Priscilla (6) Jane Teasley. Married Calloway Thornton.
3. Cassie (6) Teasley. Married Martin Maxwell.
4. Frances (6) Teasley. Married James Adams.
5. Elizabeth (6) Teasley. Married W. R. Adams.
6. Emma (6) Teasley. Married Isham Brown. Went to Mississippi.
7. Adeline (6) Teasley. Married Wig Adams.
James (5) Riley Teasley (James (4); John (3); John (2); John (1)).
Children:
1. Jane (6) Teasley. Married J. Will Thornton.
2. Lucy (6) Teasley. Married Reuben Carter.
Isham (4) Teasley (John (3); John (2); John (1)); born 1776; died 1829. Married, 1801, Jane (Gency) Adams.

THE TEASLEY FAMILY

Children:
1. Benager (5) Teasley.
2. John Adams (5) Teasley.
3. Isham (5) Teasley; born July 12, 1807; died November 22, 1883. Married Mary Maxwell; born December 31, 1804; died July 22, 1851.
4. Ausborn (5) Teasley; born November 10, 1817; died August, 1864. Married, November 18, 1841, Lucy A. Crawford; born September 3, 1824; died 1867.
5. Alfred (5) Hunt Teasley; born August 14, 1819; died February 18, 1878. Married, January 9, 1840, Sarah Ann Craft; born March 9, 1821; died April 15, 1864. Married, second time, December 26, 1866, Laura Elizabeth Haygood.
6. Gency (5) Adams Teasley; born August 6, 1806.

Benager (5) Teasley (Isham (4); John (3); John (2); John (1)); born February 27, 1802; died 1836. Married, October 30, 1822, Lucy Hailey; born September 21, 1804.

Children:
1. Elizabeth (6) Ann Teasley; born November 18, 1823; died March 13, 1869. Married, June 30, 1839, Rowland Brown; born March 11, 1816; died August, 1894.
2. Mary (6) Jane Teasley; born 1833; died 1907. Married, 1858, William M. Dobbs; born 1823; died 1904.
3. John (6) Easton Teasley.
4. James (6) A. Teasley; born October 20, 1825.
5. Benager (6) Teasley, Jr.; died young.

John Easton (6) Teasley (Benager (5); Isham (4); John (3); John (2); John (1)); born December 4, 1827; died September 5, 1904. Married, December 16, 1847, Drucilla Ann Teasley; born November 10, 1827; died November 20, 1880.

Children:
1. Mary (7) Elizabeth Teasley. Married Isham Brown.
2. Isham (7) Jefferson Teasley. Married Amanda Jane Brown.
3. Benager (7) Pierce Teasley. Married Lettie Rice.
4. John (7) Easton Cone Teasley. Married, first, Sarah Margaret Brown; second, Ann Cunningham.
5. James Wm. (7) Alfred Teasley. Married, first, Lettie Burden; second, Lois Maxwell; third, Emmie Jordan.
6. Ida (7) Ione Teasley. Married Allen Jones.

Isham Jefferson Teasley (John Easton (6); Benager (5); Isham (4); John (3); John (2); John (1)); born July 25, 1852; died December 1, 1930. Married, August 27, 1871, Amanda Jane Brown; born September 1, 1851; died April 4. 1902.

Children:
1. John Easton (8) Teasley; born April 2, 1872; died August 11, 1898.
2. Wm. Early (8) Teasley; born January 7, 1874; died December 7, 1895.
3. Benager (8) Columbus Teasley.
4. Hailey (8) Isham Teasley; born October 29, 1877; died February 12, 1898.

5. Lucy Ann (8) Teasley; born June 21, 1881; died May 27, 1907.
6. George (8) Allen Teasley; born March 25, 1883.
7. Sidney Ewell (8) Teasley; born May 27, 1885; died January 27, 1908.
8. Sallie Elizabeth (8) Teasley; born July 12, 1888.
9. Drucilla Cecil (8) Teasley; born August 20, 1892; died July 3, 1913. Married Ernest L. Bacon, December 18, 1912.

Benager Columbus Teasley (Isham J. (7) Teasley; John E. (6); Benager (5); Isham (4); John (3); John (2); John (1)); born January 26, 1876. Married, December 10, 1901, Effie G. Adams; born November 12, 1881.
Children:
1. Harry Eugene (9) Teasley, M. D.; born September 29, 1902.
2. Gerald Haynes (9) Teasley, M. D.; born June 30, 1907.
3. Benager Columbus (9) Teasley; born March 16, 1913.

John Adams (5) Teasley (Isham (4); John (3); John (2); John (1)); born January 8, 1804; died July 11, 1853. Married, December 18, 1828, Elizabeth Caroll Hailey; born November 24, 1806; died February 14, 1853; daughter of William Hailey, of Virginia, Revolutionary soldier. John A. Teasley and wife are buried in family graveyard at the old homestead in Elbert County.
Children:
1. William Hailey (6) Teasley. Confederate soldier.
2. Isham Asbury (6) Teasley.
3. John Henry (6) Teasley. First Lieutenant, Co. "F," 38th Regiment, Confederate Army. Born June 2, 1842; died June 19, 1862, of typhoid fever in a hospital at Savannah, Ga., during the War Between the States. Never married.
4. Mary Jane (6) Teasley.
5. Lucy Meanda (6) Teasley. Married .... Eavenson, and moved to Mississippi.
6. Elizabeth (6) Teasley.
7. Katherine (6) Teasley. Married .... Eavenson, and moved to Mississippi.

William Hailey (6) Teasley (John A. (5); Isham (4); John (3); John (2); John (1)); born October 24, 1830; died March 11, 1907. Planter and early merchant of Hartwell; Confederate soldier in War Between the States. Married, first, January 11, 1849, Jane Anne Wansley; born May 26, 1834; died October 2, 1877; daughter of Wiley Wansley and Martha Cleveland Wansley. Wiley Wansley was the grandson of John Wansley, Revolutionary soldier. Martha Cleveland was the daughter of John Cleveland, who also served in the Revolutionary war.
Children:
1. Martha (7) Teasley; born December 6, 1849; died July 22, 1892. Married Cicero Alexander. No children. He was postmaster of Commerce, Ga. (formerly Harmony Grove).
2. John Wiley (7) Teasley.
3. Thomas William (7) Teasley.
4. Andrew J. (7) Teasley.
5. Samantha Ophelia (7) Teasley.
6. Mary Catherine (7) Teasley.

7. Isham Asbury (7) Teasley, II; born August 20, 1863; died May 6, 1890. Never married. Died in early manhood, and is buried in Hartwell Cemetery.

8. James Hailey (7) Teasley, M. D.; born September 16, 1866; died September 20, 1905. Never married. Practiced medicine and died in Sandersville, Ga. He is buried in the Hartwell Cemetery.

9. Amos Milton (7) Teasley.

10. Minnie (7) Teasley.

11. Gertrude (7) Teasley; born November 13, 1876; died July 6, 1893, and is buried in the Hartwell Cemetery.

William Hailey (6) Teasley (John A. (5); Isham (4); John (3); John (2); John (1)). Married, second time, Mrs. Martha Beaty Baker, daughter of David Beaty and Malinda Sadler Beaty, of South Carolina.

John Wiley (7) Teasley (William H. (6); John (5); Isham (4); John (3); John (2); John (1)); born August 7, 1851. Planter and faithful member of Good Hope Presbyterian Church in South Carolina for many years. Married, November 2, 1874, Leonora McAllister; born December 10, 1856; died February 18, 1904; daughter of John A. and Elizabeth Reid McAllister, of South Carolina.

Children:

1. Paul Reid (8) Teasley. Never married.

2. Leila Jane (8) Teasley. Married, January, 1905, Rev. Palmer B. Reid, of Reidville, S. C., son of Rev. Robt. Reid, minister of the Presbyterian Church. (Children: 1. Robert, II (9). 2. Palmer, Jr. (9). 3. Julia (9)).

3. Mary Hamilton (8) Teasley; died March 31, 1925. Married Clarence Gay. (Children: 1. Evelyn (9); married, December 25, 1932, E. D. Ballard, Atlanta, Ga. 2. Mary Elizabeth (9); married Quillian Toler. (Children: 1. Quillian (10); 2. Toler, Jr. (10); 3. Infant (10). 3. Clarence Gay, Jr. (9).)

4. Sumpter Ophelia (8) Teasley. Married, June 4, 1902, Benjamin Calloway Alford, son of Drury Cade and Sallie Thornton Alford, grandson of Priscilla Jane Teasley and Rev. Calloway Thornton, Baptist minister. (Children: 1. Elmer Guy (9); married, November 8, 1932, Grace Guidry, of Louisiana. 2. Sarah Louise (9). 3. Benjamin Calloway, Jr. (9).)

5. William Dewitt (8) Teasley. Married, August 23, 1927, Minnie Lou Crawford, daughter of John S. Crawford and Elvira Hayes, of Stephens County, Ga.

6. Elizabeth (Bess) (8) Teasley; died June 30, 1913. Married, January, 1913, Norton Gaston, of Reidville, S. C.

7. Lucia (8) Teasley. Married, May, 1918, Wilmer Shade, of Winchester, Va. World War soldier. (Children: 1. Elizabeth (Bess) (9). 2. Martha (9).)

8. Lois (8) Teasley. Married, April, 1924, James Moss, of Spartanburg, S. C. (Children: 1. Edward (9). T. James, Jr. (9).)

9. Floyd McAllister (8) Teasley. World War soldier. Married, June, 1918, Lantha Wood, of Reidville, S. C. (1. John Wiley (9).)

10. John Henry (8) Teasley.

Thomas William (7) Teasley (William H. (6); John A. (5); Isham (4); John (3); John (2); John (1)). Lawyer, private banker, merchant, planter, and former Mayor of Hartwell, Ga. Born September 17, 1853; died September 12, 1911. Married, February 6, 1879, Elizabeth Jane Sadler, daughter of John Foster Sadler and Elizabeth Hardy Sadler. John Foster Sadler was the son of David Sadler, a gallant soldier of the Revolutionary war, and Elsie Bratton Sadler, daughter of the Rev. Colonel William Bratton and Martha Robertson Bratton, of York County, S. C. Eliza Sadler was the granddaughter of Thomas Hardy, Revolutionary soldier. Thos. W. Teasley and wife are buried in the Hartwell Cemetery.

Children:

1. James Loyd (8) Teasley (Thos. William (7); William H. (6); John A. (5); Isham (4); John (3); John (2); John (1)). Married, November 22, 1905, Grace Turner Benson, daughter of Enoch Berry and Alice Adams Benson, granddaughter of John B. Benson, early settlers of Hartwell. (Children: 1. Elizabeth (9). 2. Alice (9). 3. Grace (9). 4. James Benson (9); died January 26, 1925, in the seventh year of his age.)

2. Ethel Eliza (8) Teasley (Thos. W. (7); Wm. H. (6); John A. (5); Isham (4); John (3); John (2); John (1)); born December 6, 1881; died July 13, 1883, and is buried in the cemetery at Cokesbury Methodist Church.

3. Carl Sadler (8) Teasley (Thos. W. (7); Wm. H. (6); John A. (5); Isham (4); John (3); John (2); John (1)).

4. Ralph Bratton (8) Teasley (Thos. W. (7); Wm. H. (6); John A. (5); Isham (4); John (3); John (2); John (1)). Married, July 14, 1920, Frances Greene, daughter of George C. and Fannie Lundy Greene, of Eatonton, Ga. (Children: 1. Ralph Thomas (9).)

5. May Lilly (8) Teasley (Thos. W. (7); Wm. H. (6); John A. (5); Isham (4); John (3); John (2); John (1)). Married, June 15, 1916, William Baird McCurry, son of Dr. William Hamilton McCurry, dentist, and Susan Oglesby McCurry. (Children: Elizabeth Sadler (9) McCurry.)

6. Charles Jones (8) Teasley (Thos. W. (7); Wm. H. (6); John A. (5); Isham (4); John (3); John (2); John (1)). Married, March 28, 1923, Anne Pollock-Royde-Smith, daughter of James Pollock and Catherine Wark Pollock, of Philadelphia, Penn.

An Old Pioneer Home, and Burton Family History

THE old Burton home, more recently known as the O'Barr place, located a short distance west of the Reed Creek court ground, on the north side of the Andersonville and Carnesville, formerly the Hatton's Ford and Carnesville road, was, to the best of our information built by John Burton, to whom the land was granted and who settled the place about the first of the 19th Century.

It was built of large, hewed logs and lumber, chopped from the virgin forests of pine, and the nails that hold it together were forged, perhaps, in a makeshift blacksmith shop. It is a two-story building with two large rooms on the first or lower floor, the upper story reached by a flight of stairs, with spacious fireplaces both down and upstairs. It has a lean-to, an annex that was common to most of the houses in the early days. The entire house was weatherboarded outside, and the two large rooms ceiled, and a brick chimney at each end of the house, up and down which, for ornamental design, ran zigzag lines of blue colored brick, crossing each other at given intervals, forming diamond-shaped spaces between.

The house is today in a fairly good state of preservation, never having been repaired, with the exception of a new roof put on a few years ago and perhaps some minor repairs.

This old house is very impressive, replete with interesting history, and fragrant with memories of a former time.

It was during the time Mr. Burton lived at the place, and also for a part of the time his successors occupied the place, a wayside inn, and oft the dusty, weary and wayworn traveler stopped here for shelter, rest and refreshment for himself and "straw and provender" for his tired beast of burden.

It was also here that the immigrants turned aside at nightfall for lodging and entertainment, dispensed by the genial landlord and his family, and who on the morrow, after having partaken of a lavish hospitality, and after the sun had leaped up from the purple east, illuminating the heavens with splendor and bathing the world in light, took leave of their host, the landlord, and resumed their westward trek in quest of better homes and broader acres.

The first of this Burton family, so far as we have learned, was Abraham Burton, who married a woman by the name of Harrison.

John Burton, son of Abraham Burton, married Mary Hudson, and it is our information that she was a relative of the family for whom the Hudson River, a tributary of Broad River, was named. Her father was Cuthbert Hudson.

To John Burton and his wife, Mary Hudson Burton, were born three sons: John H., Abram and Peter E. Burton; and five daughters: Sallie, Martha, Rhoda, Mary and Susan Burton.

John H. Burton married Nancy Harrison December 22, 1831. We have not been able, from the records available, to determine how many children were born to John H. Burton and wife. In the synopsis of the will of John Burton there is a bequest to Evelina E. Harrison, daughter of John H. Burton, a granddaughter of John Burton.

Abram Burton married a Miss Cawthon, and later moved to Arkansas. He settled and lived on Tugaloo River, adjoining lands of Thomas Gilbert and others. He moved away while his children were small, and we have never known how many he had or their names.

Peter E. Burton was twice married. His first wife was Miss Nancy Chandler, daughter of Henry Farmer Chandler. To this union were born three sons: John Farmer, Joseph J. and William P. Burton; and one daughter, Mattie C. Burton.

Peter E. Burton's second wife was Martha Chandler, and sister to his first wife. To this union were born two sons: Thomas H. and Elias C. Burton; and six daughters: Sarah A., Fannie, Eveline, Nannie, Susan and Emma Burton.

Sallie Burton married Allen Isbell January 25, 1833.

Martha Burton married a Mr. Barton. She and one child are buried at the Michael Johnson place, which was the old home of John Burton, and at which John Burton and his wife are buried near the residence.

Rhoda Burton married Jedidiah Ayers, and to her and her husband were born two sons: Cuthbert D. and Alfred Moses Ayers; and four daughters: Harriett, Eliza, Orpha, and one whose name we do not know and who married a man by the name of Reed.

Mary Burton married Sterling Pinson, March 4, 1827, and to this union were born five daughters: Eliza, Jane, Rhoda, Susan and Martha B. Pinson.

Susan Burton married Lewis Aderhold. We have no record of their children. Rhoda C. Pinson married James Cullen Baker, December 14, 1857.

At the old Burton homestead, later known as the O'Barr place, is a family burying ground in which Mary Pinson, wife of Sterling Pinson, is buried. Others, perhaps, of the Burton family are buried there, but we do not have the names of any except Mary Pinson.

After John Burton sold the above-described place, he came into possession of a large body of land located on Payne's Creek and its tributaries. It included the lands of the Mumford Ussery place, the Joel Bailey place, a part of the John Baker place, and maybe other lands not mentioned.

In 1850, November 4, Peter E. Burton sold to Michael Johnson 674 acres of land, which was perhaps the real estate owned by John Burton at the time of his death, which included the old homestead of John Burton.

The surveyor, in making a survey of this tract of land, describes it as being situate in Franklin County on Payne's Creek, waters of Tugaloo River, containing 670 acres, and being composed of part three original tracts, viz.: part of a tract purchased by John Burton of J. V. Harris, Administrator of J. Wood; part of a tract granted to John H. Burton, December 16, 1840; and a tract granted to John Thrasher, November 27, 1830.

Re-survey November 5, 1850. M. S. McCay, Surveyor.

We herewith give a synopsis of the will of John Burton as it appears in the Franklin County records.

Old Burton Home

"Wife Mary and son Peter, Exrs. Sons: Abram, John H., Peter E., Grandson Benjamin H. Burton and his father's share. To heirs of dau. Rhoda Ayers; to heirs of dau. Mary W. Pinson; to dau. Susan S. Aderhold; to heirs dau. Sarah Isbell; to Eveline E. Harrison, dau. of John H. Burton, her father's share.

"Wit: Barthsheba Burton, Robinson Adams, H. F. Chandler."

"Probated July 4, 1842."

The O'Barr Family

THE ancestor of the O'Barr family, so far as we have learned, was Michael O'Barr, of Irish lineage, as the name implies.

William O'Barr, son of Michael O'Barr, removed from Abbeville County, S. C., or it might have been known as Abbeville District at the time, in 1839, to Franklin County, Ga., and purchased the place formerly known as the Burton place, a full account of which appears elsewhere.

He married Miss Frances Adams, who was a sister to Reuben D. Adams, who lived in the upper part of Hart County on the upper reaches of Shoal Creek, and who also came from South Carolina. Further than Reuben D. Adams, and perhaps some of his brothers, we know nothing of the family history of the wife of William O'Barr.

William O'Barr was Sheriff of Franklin County, Ga., during the years 1848-9, and during his term of office he executed Joab, a slave who killed a Mr. Crawford, an overseer on the Benjamin F. Sloan farm, a full account of which also appears elsewhere.

William O'Barr kept public house a part of the time that he lived at the place for the accommodation of the traveling public, as had been done by the former owners of the place.

He was at one time Colonel of the State Militia of Franklin County, Ga., and by reason of which he obtained the title of colonel and was ever afterwards referred to as Col. O'Barr.

He deeded to the authorities of Reed Creek Church the lot of land on which the church and cemetery are located, containing four acres, more or less, for the consideration of ten dollars. The lot of land was laid off so as to include a spring for the use of the church.

Col. William O'Barr died about the year 1861-2, as it appears that his will was published and signed October 12, 1861, and probated June 2, 1862, witnessed by Aaron Risener, Daniel Isom and Peter L. Fleming, and by which he provided that his real estate remain intact during the lifetime of his wife. His wife, Frances, died about 1877, and the lands, containing several hundred acres, were divided into lots and sold at executor's sale.

To Col. William O'Barr and his wife, Frances Adams O'Barr, were born the following named children: Sons—Jonathan W., M. G., Whitney, Joseph H., and Asa O'Barr; and the following named daughters—Mary, Elizabeth, Emily, Eliza, and Caroline O'Barr.

Jonathan W. O'Barr was twice married. His first wife was Miss Martha J. Fleming, daughter of Peter Fleming, to whom he was married February 4, 1858. After her death, which occurred in 1863, he married Mrs. Jemima McConnell, Feburary 11, 1864.

While a young man he was a student of Morgan H. Looney's school, and afterwards taught school. He was a member of the first Board of Education organized in Hart County, composed of a member from each militia district. He was at one time Notary Public Ex-Officio Justice of the Peace in the 1115th (Reed Creek) District. He died about the year 1898.

M. G. O'Barr, son of Col. William O'Barr, married Frances Baker, a daughter of John Baker, December 2, 1858. He was a soldier in the War Between the States, and enlisted in the service May 25, 1864, in Company "C," 5th Regiment of Georgia, under Captain D. G. Johnson, at Atlanta, Ga. He served for a long term of years as Justice of the Peace in the 1115th District.

M. G. O'Barr was born May 5, 1833; died March 6, 1909. His wife, Frances, was born April 21, 1837; died May 28, 1917.

Whitney O'Barr, son of Col. William O'Barr, was a member of Capt. Poole's Company, known as Company "H," 15th Regiment of Georgia, organized at King's Bench July 15, 1861, and the following memoranda appears upon the muster roll of the company with reference to his war record: "Private, July 15, 1861. Wounded at Sharpsburg, Md., September 17, 1862. Captured at Gettysburg, Pa., July 2, 1863. Exchanged, mortally wounded, at Wilderness, Va., May 6, 1864."

Joseph H. O'Barr enlisted in the same company at the same time of that of his brother, Whitney, and died March 4, 1862, in hospital at _____.

Asa O'Barr married Miss Eliza Adams, February 21, 1867. He lived for the most of the time after his marriage in the neighborhood of Pleasant Hill Church in Franklin County, where he died several years ago.

Mary O'Barr, daughter of Col. William O'Barr, married James W. Leard, a son of Major W. McLeod, the name McLeod being later changed to Leard. James W. Leard owned the place on Reed Creek where he operated a grist mill, cotton gin and thresher. He also owned considerable lands and engaged in farming as well as his other interests. The place still is known as the Leard place, all machinery long since abandoned and gone.

Elizabeth O'Barr married A. B. Moore. They lived for a long time at the old home place of Alec Moore, father of A. B. Moore. A. B. Moore was for a long time Constable of the 1115th District, and was at one time Deputy Sheriff.

Emily O'Barr married Coleman Meredith. Mr. Meredith was a blacksmith by trade and ran a shop at Townville, S. C., where they made their home.

Eliza O'Barr married Franklin M. Walters January 18, 1855. They made their home either in the upper part of Hart or the lower part of Franklin County. Eliza lived several years after the death of her husband and died in Reed Creek neighborhood at the home of some of her people. She is buried in the cemetery at Reed Creek Church.

Caroline O'Barr married Capt. J. W. Suit, December 23, 1856.

Capt. J. W. Suit was born in Lancaster County, S. C., July 2, 1828, and moved to Franklin (now Hart) County about the year 1852. He was an officer in Company "C," 5th Regiment of Georgia, D. G. Johnson, Captain, in which he enlisted May 25, 1864, at Atlanta, Ga.

Mr. Suit was a fine mechanic and carpenter by profession, as well as being a successful farmer, and at the time of his death owned a large and valuable farm on Tugaloo River. Soon after he came to Georgia, in about 1852-3, he was awarded the contract to build a new church house at Reed Creek at the price of $100, which of course meant with all material furnished. In 1884 a contract was let for the building of a new church house at Reed Creek, and he, in association with Mr. N. S. Osborne, were awarded the contract at the price of $660, it being the present church and is a monument to his skill as a carpenter and builder.

He died May 8, 1898, buried in the cemetery at Reed Creek Church, his grave marked by marble tombstone.

His wife, Caroline, survived him by about twenty years, and died at the advanced age of 90 years. Born in 1828.

An item of interesting history connected with the old O'Barr place, is an account of a hat shop located on the place on the public road a short distance from the residence and on the right side of the road, going from the old home towards Reed Creek lawground.

At this shop, before and for some time after the War Between the States, hats were made by some of the sons of Col. O'Barr and his son-in-law, James W. Leard.

During the war and for a while afterwards, while the people were in straitened circumstances, many of the citizens of the country wore hats made in this shop, and to give such of our readers as may not be familiar with the history of the manufacturing of hats in our country during the early days, we herewith reproduce an article written by Mr. James A. Hall, "Lover of Nature and Georgia Lore," as the same appeared in the *Atlanta Journal* a few years ago.

"The Old Hat Maker."

"We are accustomed to buy our hats from the merchant and have no knowledge how the hats are made or from whence they come. This was not the case in the days of our great-grandfathers.

"In those primitive times practically everything was made by hand and produced by some one in the community trained by long practice to do such work. The hat shop was a familiar institution and the hat maker occupied a place of importance in the industrial scheme along with the shoemaker and the wheelwright.

"The making of hats became an important industry in the American colonies at an early date, and during the reign of George II a law was passed prohibiting the export of American hats into the other British colonies and also restricting the number of apprentices to be employed by American hatters. This law stated that its object was 'to repress the making of hats in America and to encourage and make more favorable the situation of ye hatters in Great Britain.'

"America, being well supplied with the fur of the beaver, rabbit and muskrat, was a favorable field for the rapid growth of the fur hat production. In the beginning these hats were made by a slow and laborious process.

"The fur was trimmed from the hides by hand, a crude 'bat' was formed, and this, covered by a wet cloth, was hammered down by wooden mallets until it formed a thick blanket. Covered with shellac and carried through a shrinking, dyeing, ironing and blocking process, a shapely hat was produced. It was then lined, furnished with bands inside and out, and sold to the fashionable gentry of the community.

"Most people, however, wore wool hats. They were much cheaper and of cruder workmanship, and hence political speakers seeking votes constantly glorifying 'the strong arms and the brave hearts of the wool-hat boys.' And because the wool hat was the headgear of the common people, constant effort was manifested on the part of some fastidious individuals to disassociate themselves from the herd by wearing only the best fur hats obtainable.

"Hat shops were scattered throughout Georgia in the early days, and many large slave owners produced at home the hats, shoes and clothing needed by their slaves.

"A newspaper printed in Putnam County during the Civil War advertised several cases of wool hats for sale, and stated that 'the hats are all lined and banded, suitable for negroes and white gentlemen, too, if they can't do any better.' "

Henry Farmer Chandler

HENRY FARMER CHANDLER was born in Franklin County, Ga., in 1805, and lived in the neighborhood of Poplar Springs Church until he moved down to the place on Tugaloo River. His father was Joseph Chandler and his mother, before her marriage, was a Miss Farmer, hence his middle or second given name, Farmer, by which he was commonly called.

His father, Joseph Chandler, came to Georgia from Virginia, and was one of the commissioners to locate the permanent county site of Franklin County, by Act approved November 29, 1806.

Henry Farmer Chandler married Fannie Harbin, a daughter of Thomas and Mary Harbin, of South Carolina, and settled at the place on Tugaloo River, Franklin (now Hart) County, which has so long been known as the Chandler place.

A brief abstract of the title and history of the lands composing this place may not be out of order.

The first or original tract of 176 acres was owned by Thomas Thornton, who sold the same to Mark Hardin March 7, 1805, bounded on the north by Tugaloo River; east by lands of W. Whitney; south by unknown lands, and west by lands of Job Brookes.

Mark Hardin sold the 176 acres of land to George Aderhold March 10 1818.

A tract of presumably 114 acres was bought by George Aderhold from Lewis Moulder January 17, 1812.

To George Aderhold was granted by the State 98 acres July 15, 1818.

George Aderhold conveyed to Harrison & Earle, a partnership of Andersonville, S. C., 290 acres of land December 14, 1822.

George Aderhold conveyed to Harrison & Earle 98 acres October 18, 1824.

The above tracts of land were sold by Harrison & Earle to John Crocker December 29, 1826.

John Crocker sold all of said described lands to Morgan Harbin December 28, 1831. Morgan Harbin, who was presumably a brother to the wife of

Henry F. Chandler, sold all of said lands, 388 acres, to Henry F. Chandler December 21, 1835.

Henry F. Chandler owned, in addition to the above described lands, about 214 acres, originally owned by one Mr. Wood. We have no record from whom Henry F. Chandler bought the last mentioned lands. It is now owned partly by the estate of W. H. McLeskey and partly by the estate of W. J. O'Barr.

The last mentioned tract of land extended to the Clarkesville road, and at one time the Chandler lands of approximately 600 acres extended from the crossroads at the W. J. O'Barr place to Tugaloo River, a distance of practically two miles.

To Henry F. Chandler and his wife, Mary Harbin Chandler, were born five sons: J. Newton, Thomas Callaway, Asa David Simmons, Morgan Farmer, and Elias Harrison Chandler; and six daughters: Nancy, Martha, Mary, Sallie, Ella and Fannie Chandler.

J. Newton Chandler was a Baptist preacher, ordained at Grove Level Church in Banks County, Ga. He moved to Texas in the fall of 1867. His brother, Elias, and sister, Fannie, going with him. He was instrumental in establishing a great work among the Baptists in Texas, organizing many churches and helping educate young preachers.

He was moderator of the association of the churches he helped to organize for 28 years.

During the War Between the States he was a Captain and did service for the cause of the Confederacy. He died at the age 91 years.

Asa David Simmons Chandler was named for his uncle, Asa Chandler, a brother of Henry Farmer Chandler, a prominent Baptist minister in his day. He was the first pastor of Reed Creek Church after its organization. David Simmons was pastor of Reed Creek Church for twenty years, being the longest pastorate in the history of the church.

Asa D. S. Chandler was born December 16, 1835. Joined the Baptist Church at Beaverdam, S. C., in his 16th year. He served during the full period of the War Between the States.

He married Miss Lou Roberts, a daughter of Francis S. Roberts, of Hart County, Ga. He resided at the Chandler place for many years, having bought it from his father before his death. While he lived at the place he was engaged in farming and also taught school at different times and at different places in the neighborhood. He later, together with his family, moved to Lavonia, Ga., where he spent the remainder of his life. He was an active member of the Baptist Church, was a deacon and served as superintendent of the Sunday school for years.

He died about April 30, 1894, and after funeral services conducted by his pastor, Rev. J. H. McMullan, was buried with Masonic honors, being a member of that order. His wife preceded him to the grave but a few weeks previously.

Thomas Callaway Chandler lived to the age of 66 years, lived and died in Banks County, Ga.

Elias Harrison Chandler lived to be 75 years old; was baptized at the age of 60. He served as First Lieutenant during the War Between the States.

Morgan Farmer Chandler was killed in the Battle of Gettysburg.

Nancy and Martha married Peter E. Burton. Nancy being Mr. Burton's first, and Martha being his second wife.

Mary married A. S. Stephens. Sallie married Harrison A. Teasley. Ella married John H. Oliver, a Baptist preacher, whose field of labor was mostly in South Georgia. Fannie married A. B. Sanders.

Mr. Chandler, besides a large and interesting family, owned several slaves before the War Between the States, and carried on considerable farming operations on the place. There was a large area of bottom lands along the river and also many acres of the uplands in cultivation, all producing abundant crops.

At the place was a private ferry, known as Chandler's Ferry, located a short distance above the shoals known as the Chandler Shoals. The ferry was used by Mr. Chandler and his friends. It is today a public ferry, the road leading to it maintained by the county, and still is known as Chandler's Ferry. This ferry was the scene of the unfortunate drowning of Mr. Thad Holbrook and a colored man not many years ago, the incident still fresh in the minds of the people of the community.

The shoals on the river are of considerable water-power value and have been bought up by parties looking to the project of development later, together with other shoals along the river.

In the days when Mr. Chandler lived at the place, the river abounded in fish of various kinds, and when shad run up the river at spawning season many were taken at the traps on the shoals.

At the lower corner of the place, at or near the mouth of a branch, there was a small corn mill while John Crocker owned the lands driven by water power from the river. The mouth of the branch referred to was one corner of the Chandler lands and is referred to in a deed of conveyance as being at the Guest Ford.

Many years ago a man by the name of Jake Robinson was drowned while attempting to cross the river at this ford, from the Carolina to the Georgia side of the river, on horseback. He lived at the time on a tract of land that had been granted to him, located between the lands formerly of Nathaniel Bowers and the lands formerly owned by Swan H. Sanders, and which place today belongs to the estate of Lee Jones, colored. The branch that traverses the lands was in former times known as the "Robinson Branch," taking the name of the former or original owner. Robinson's body was rescued from the river and buried in the cemetery at the original location of Reed Creek Church, which is on the Chandler place.

Mr. Chandler was quite prominent in his day in church, State and county affairs. He at one time, in 1849-50, represented Franklin County in the Georgia Legislature.

In 1854, when Hart County was organized, he was chosen as one of the Judges of the Inferior Court, the duties of which was to lay out the county into militia districts, establish a county seat, and to have general supervision of county affairs.

In laying out the streets of the town of Hartwell there was a street named for each of the Judges of the Inferior Court. There was donated to the churches, Baptist, Methodist and Presbyterian, a lot on which to erect a church house. The lot donated for the Baptist Church was located on

Chandler Street at the intersection with Howell Street. It probably did not occur to the authorities how appropriate it was to locate the lot for the Baptist Church on, the street named for one of the most prominent Baptists of the country at the time. However, it is to us of interesting significance.

In connection with the history of the Chandler place, there was a school house located at the head of the Gilbert Branch, which branch was the property line between the Chandler and the adjoining lands for a part of the way, the lower reaches traversed the property of Thomas Gilbert, from which the branch took its name. There is considerable mention made of Thomas Gilbert elsewhere in this history.

It has come down to us that Sterling Pinson, grandfather of the writer, and a kinsman of Henry Farmer Chandler, came from Virginia to Georgia at the instance of Mr. Chandler, and that he was the first teacher at this school. We are not sure as to the correctness of the statement that Sterling Pinson was the first teacher at the Chandler Schoolhouse. The school was taught before and for a few years after the War Between the States by different ones of the sons and daughters of Henry Farmer Chandler, his daughter, Sallie, being the last perhaps to teach at the place. It was a noted school in the early days and was patronized by the people for many miles around.

Henry Farmer Chandler was, as stated, prominent in church affairs and was Clerk of the Tugaloo Baptist Association for 29 years, and attended the sessions for fifty years. He was, as has been said of him, a pillar in the Baptist Church of his county and the Elijah of the denomination of his association, and a prince in Israel. He served his day and generation and served it well.

The ashes of this godly man, together with those of his companion, are

Old Home of Henry Farmer Chandler

sleeping in the family burying ground on the old Chandler homestead in graves marked by substantial headstones, while near by in a pretty fair state of preservation, approached through an avenue of aged cedars, stands the old Chandler home, keeping vigil over the silent hills and vales, with the Tugaloo rolling hard by whose waters murmur a perpetual requiem of peace.

History of the Old Linder Farm on Tugaloo River

THE lands now known as the Old Linder place on Tugaloo River, formerly in Franklin (now Hart) County, were granted to one Mr. Payne, and originally contained about 1,500 acres. Payne's Creek, which traverses the place for a distance of some two miles, was so named for the first owner of the place.

Benjamin F. Sloan came into possession of the place and lived there for a number of years. He owned a number of slaves, by which the farm was cultivated.

The place had a river frontage of two miles, with considerably more than 100 acres of bottom lands along the river, while on Payne's Creek there were 100 acres, or over, all of which were very fertile and produced abundant crops of corn and other farm products, considerably more than was necessary for consumption on the place, hence a large surplus was sold.

There were large areas of table or level lands, besides many acres of hillsides in cultivation.

On the place was a most magnificent farmhouse, perhaps the best of any in the surrounding country at the time it was built. We do not know if Mr. Sloan built the house or whether it was built by a former owner.

The house was conveniently and ideally located with reference to the farm, commodious in all departments, located right near a spring of crystal, sparkling water that gushed forth in a grove of stately oaks. A spring house built of rock through which the water from the spring trickled, keeping the milk, butter, and other articles of food in a nice, cool and appetizing condition for the use and enjoyment of the inmates of the home.

Besides the home there were barns, carriage houses, quarters for the slaves and all other necessary outbuildings, a cotton gin, thresher, and all equipment essential for successfully carrying on farm operations. There was also a tannery on the place operated commercially or as a custom business, or perhaps both, equipped with bark mill, vats and all other things usually employed in a tanning business. The house, known as the "Tanyard house," is still standing and is used as a tenant house.

There was a ferry on the Tugaloo River in connection with the place, which was a private ferry for the use and convenience of the place as Mr. Sloan had considerable interests in South Carolina. This ferry was located a few miles from Fairplay, S. C., and when Hart County was organized the road leading by this ferry was adopted as a public road by the way of King's Bench to Hartwell. Mr. Linder had come into possession of the place and the ferry was known as Linder & Hicks Ferry, Mr. Bailus Hicks owning the property on the Carolina side of the river.

Mr. Sloan moved from the place to Pendleton, S. C., where he was con-

HISTORY OF THE OLD LINDER FARM

nected with the cotton mill near Pendleton, known as "Pendleton Factory." After Mr. Sloan left the place it was managed by overseers in Mr. Sloan's employ.

An unfortunate murder was committed at the place in about the year 1848-9, which was the killing of a Mr. Crawford, an overseer, by a slave of Mr. Sloan's, named Joab. As told to us by the older citizens who lived in the community at the time, Joab and other slaves were hoeing one Saturday afternoon when they became involved in a quarrel and Mr. Crawford undertook to quell the disturbance and for some reason struck Joab with his walking cane. Joab returned the lick with a hoe, fracturing Mr. Crawford's skull. Dr. Cater, of Anderson, S. C., was called and removed the fractured part of the skull, but the wound was mortal and Mr. Crawford died in a short time. Meanwhile Joab absconded and sought concealment among the slaves of Mr. Sloan at Pendleton. Mr. Sloan, through the communication of the slaves, induced Joab to come in. He was turned over to the authorities of Franklin County and lodged in jail at Carnesville to wait his trial at the next term of court. At court he was tried, convicted and sentenced to hang. He was executed by William O'Barr, who was Sheriff of Franklin County at the time, and was among the first criminals to be executed at Carnesville.

In 1851 Mr. Sloan sold to John Linder, of Spartanburg, S. C., 1,100 acres of the place for $5,000, Mr. Sloan having previously sold Peter E. Burton 225 acres.

Mr. Linder, like Mr. Sloan, owner a number of slaves, by which the farm was cultivated on up until the close of the War Between the States. Large crops of corn were made on the place. We can remember in our boyhood days when people went from a distance to the Linder farm to buy corn, of which there always seemed to be a large supply.

After the close of the war, Mr. Linder put up a store at the place and sold goods for several years.

The family of Mr. Linder and his wife, who was Miss Eliza Bonner before her marriage, consisted of four sons: Lee, Andrew, T. J., and John C. Linder; and two daughters: Mary Ann and Susan J. Linder.

Andrew was a soldier and died in the War Between the States. Lee and T. J. Linder were also soldiers of the war of the Confederacy.

Lee Linder married Miss Lou M. Webb, daughter of Judge Clayton S. Webb, February 1, 1866.

T. J. Linder married Miss Susan Alice Peek, daughter of Capt. John Peek, February 18, 1872.

John C. Linder married Mrs. Mollie C. Swilling, October 16, 1887.

Mary Ann married J. J. Goforth. We have no record of their marriage, as perhaps they were married before Hart County was created.

Susan J. Linder married Capt. Wm. H. Rudd, December 21, 1865.

All of the sons and daughters of Mr. John Linder and wife have been dead now for many years.

Mr. John Linder was the First Lieutenant in Poole's Company, known as Company "H," 15th Georgia Regiment, organized at King's Bench July 15, 1861, which position he resigned February 29, 1862.

Mr. John Linder died December 4, 1888, his wife preceding him to the grave a few years before. They are buried in the family burying ground near where the residence once stood.

We herewith reproduce a clipping from the *Hartwell Sun* giving an account of Mr. Linder's death.

"Mr. John Linder died at his home in Reed Creek District on last Tuesday, December 4, 1888, aged 77 years. He removed from Spartanburg County, S. C., to Hart (then Franklin) County in 1850, where he has since resided, a highly honored and respected citizen. He was a genial, clever gentleman, and for many years had been a member of the Baptist Church at Shoal Creek.

"His body was interred in the family buying place."

This once large and valuable farm is now in a wretched state of dilapidation. All of the buildings of any note have been destroyed by fire or otherwise. The fine bottom lands along the river and creek are overgrown with Bermuda grass, some of which has been devoted to pastures and hay fields. The uplands eroded and gullied and much of it abandoned to a growth of pines.

The entire scenes are desolate and forlorn, especially is this feeling realized when we visualize the prosperous and happy conditions that once obtained where the people were surrounded with peace, plenty, luxury, wealth and contentment.

Montevideo — John McDonald — James Patterson — Montevideo P. O.—Montevideo Manufacturing Company—Col. Richard J. D. Durrett—Rice's Store

AMONG the first settlers on the Savannah River in what is now Hart County, formerly Wilkes and later Elbert County, was John McDonald, who emigrated from Virginia and bought or had granted to him many acres of valuable lands along the river adjacent to the shoals, known as McDonald's Shoals, so named for Mr. McDonald.

It is said of him that he was a very smart man, was a surveyor, and Amos Richardson, forefather of the Richardson family, said he learned to calculate figures from picking up papers that were thrown from McDonald's office.

This place afterwards fell into the hands of the Ruckers, of Elbert County. Tinsley White Rucker, son of Joseph Rucker, of Ruckersville, Ga., bought of James Patterson 1,000 acres, being a part if not all of the McDonald lands located on Savannah River and Mill Branch.

Mill Branch was so called for the reason that James Patterson owned a mill on the branch, which was the line between said tract of land and the lands of William Dooley; a small portion of land containing about five acres was bought by Mr. Patterson from Mr. Dooley in order to give Mr. Patterson water rights so as to raise water on the branch by means of a dam to operate his mill.

The residence and other improvements on the place were situated on a prominence from which could be had a marvelous view of the surrounding and outlying country, and for this reason the place was named Montevideo, like Montevideo, the capital of Uruguay, opposite of which there rises the

Cerro, a picturesque mountain in connection with which the name Montevideo is derived.

At the place was a store kept by a man by the name of Hughes, who came from Augusta, Ga. A post office was established at the place, called Montevideo, supplied by a star route from Ruckersville, Ga.

The name Montevideo is perpetuated by the splendid school located in Elbert County, near the line of Hart and Elbert, which is patronized by the citizens of both counties. The post office originally located at Montevideo was later kept at Rice's Store, and later at the home of John Dozier Brown, now known as William H. Pruitt place, and later still at the home of Mr. D. O. Chapman, and at all of the several locations it retained the name Montevideo.

The name Montevideo was also perpetuated for a time by a firm known as the Montevideo Manufacturing Company, composed of John M. Simpson, Rufus E. Sadler, John E. Sadler and John J. Hardie, which firm or company built and operated a plant consisting of a mill and perhaps other machinery at the shoals on Big Cedar Creek, not far below the bridge where the Cotton Belt Highway crosses the creek. Signs or ruins of the plant can yet be seen.

The McDonald place, later owned by Tinsley White Rucker, later became the property of Col. Richard J. D. Durrett, who also came from Virginia and married Martha E. Rucker, daughter of Joseph Rucker, of Ruckersville, Ga., and sister of Tinsley White Rucker. It is probably true that Col. Durrett bought the place from his brother-in-law, Tinsley White Rucker, and it is also probably true that the place was named Montevideo after Col. Durrett came into possession.

Col. Durrett, after coming into possession of the place, had a wide avenue of nearly a mile in length cleared out straight from his home to the public road leading out of South Carolina by way of Stephenson's Ferry, which served as a standing invitation to Col. Durrett's friends as well as to the traveler and wayfarer to turn in and share lavish Old Dominion hospitality dispensed by Col. Durrett, it being characteristic of the people of Virginia, who in pioneer days extended an open arm and hearty welcome to immigrants who came seeking homes in the new world.

The route of this old avenue, while it has long since been abandoned for travel, can yet be seen and easily traced.

To Col. Durrett and his wife, Martha, were born three sons: Douglas, William and Thomas Joseph Durrett; and one daughter: Fannie Margaret Durrett.

Thomas J. Durrett married Elizabeth Price.

Fannie M. Durrett married William Harper, and to this union were born four sons: Richard, William J., Thomas S. and Alston Harper; and three daughters: Ann Yancy, Mary E., and Sallie T. Harper.

William Harper, son-in-law of Col. Durrett, owned the place on Savannah River which still goes by the name of the Harper place, containing several hundred acres. It formerly belonged to John Dobbs, Esquire, and is sometimes referred to as the Dobbs place.

Thomas J. Durrett owned the place, later owned by Thomas N. McMullan, which is still known as the "Tom Joe Durrett" place.

Col. Durrett is buried near the site of the home on the old homestead.

Martha E. Durrett is buried at Van's Creek Church, Ruckersville, Ga., her grave marked by a grave vault with marble slab with the inscription:

"MARTHA E. DURRETT, DAUGHTER OF JOSEPH RUCKER, AND WIFE OF
RICHARD DURRETT.
BORN JULY 15, 1815, DIED OCTOBER 11, 1847."

In connection with Montevideo and the immediate community, we will mention some other matters of a historic nature.

In the early days Indians were plentiful and their signs still show on Cedar Creek, where they hollowed out holes in the rock to beat their corn into meal.

Near the Montevideo place is the Gordon burial ground, around which is an Indian graveyard. When the man, Gordon, located there, there were plenty of arrows and other Indian relics to be seen on the Redmen's graves.

A fort was built near where McMullan's Mill on Little Cedar Creek is located, which was known as Fort Ellis, named perhaps for Henry Ellis, the second Royal Governor of the Colony of Georgia. Signs of this old fort can yet be seen on the left of a branch, known as Fort Branch, just a short ways below where the public road crosses the branch. The fort was built by the pioneers for the protection of the women and children against the onslaught of the Indians while the men folks were off either on a hunt or clearing fields and building homes.

Obadiah Wright

OBADIAH WRIGHT was a pioneer who settled in Franklin (now Hart) County on a tract of land of about 450 acres, granted to him by the State of Georgia, lying and being on Holly Creek, a prong of Whinnery's Creek. His home was just east of Holly Creek and near a fine spring of water, on the west side of the present public road leading from the fork of the roads near the residence of Jason Sanders on by the present home of J. G. McMullan. The site of the old home can yet be seen.

Holly Creek derived its name from the numerous holly trees that grew along the hills and slopes adjacent to the stream, which presented a gorgeous display of crimson and green, a decorative universally employed as suggestive of Christmas cheer and good will at the season when we celebrate the joyous return of the anniversary of the birth of the precious Babe of Bethlehem.

To Mr. Wright and his wife, whose name we have never learned, were born four sons: Prior H., Wm. C., Thomas G. and Dillard V. Wright; and two daughters: Mary and Permelia Wright. There may have been other children that we do not know about.

Wm. C. Wright, son of Obadiah Wright, married Deliliah Bridges, March 17, 1835, by John B. Wade, M. G.

We do not have the names of the wives of Prior H. or Thomas G. Wright, or when married.

Dillard V. Wright married Mrs. Knox, widow of William Knox, and lived some of the time at or in the neighborhood of Fairplay, S. C.

Mary, daughter of Obadiah Wright, married Spencer Brown, son of Nicholas Brown. She and her husband lived on a tract of land just west of the home of Obadiah Wright, which they sold years ago. The place still is known as the Spencer Brown place.

Permelia married Joseph C. Lowery, December 10, 1830, by John Burton, J. P.

Prior H. Wright later came into possession of the lands formerly owned by his father, which he divided into three tracts and sold one tract to James McDougle, one to M. G. O'Barr, and another to George McMullan, colored. The ownership of these lands have changed several times since.

Prior H. Wright lived and died in Banks County, Ga.; was a very successful business man and became quite wealthy in his day.

Thomas G. Wright, at the time of his death, owned a tract of land on Reed Creek and Tugaloo River, which Prior H. and Dillard V. Wright, his administrators, sold to Robert A. Madden.

Wm. C. Wright obtained a grant from the State of Georgia to a tract of land in Franklin (now Hart) County, lying and being on Whinnery's Creek, where he settled and built a home, cleared a portion of the land for cultivation, and among other improvements set out a large orchard of Red June apple trees. He later sold the place to James Bridges, who in turn sold it to Mr. Winston Adams.

While Mr. Adams lived at the place, the June apple trees were in full bearing; abundant crops of the beautiful cardinal red apples were produced from year to year, and was the most noted and extensively known June apple orchard in the country. Like the fruit mentioned in the Bible that grew in the Garden of Eden, "good for food and pleasant to the eyes."

Mr. Adams and his family were generous people and liberally shared the luscious fruit with their neighbors and friends.

The orchard and other improvements are gone now, while Mr. Adams and wife and other members of the family sleep on the hill in the little cemetery not far from the site of the old home.

Adjoining the lands of William C. Wright, later owned by Mr. Winston Adams, was a settlement on Whinnery's Creek on the lands of the Isaac Briggs survey, where one Mr. Amaziah Frost had a cotton gin, thresher and furniture shop located at the shoals just above where the public road leading from Hartwell to Andersonville crosses the creek. While Mr. Frost and his sons were not engaged in operating the cotton gin and thresher, they engaged in the manufacture of spinning wheels, bedsteads and other kinds of furniture, which they peddled over the country.

While Mr. Frost lived at the place his wife committed suicide by shooting herself with a shotgun. On the hill, not far from the site of the cotton gin and other machinery, is the site of the home of Mr. Frost, and near by is the grave of the unfortunate woman.

History of the Black, Bobo, Brown and Dyar Families

THE lands at one time owned and occupied by the families mentioned, who were the pioneers and first settlers of the section, embraced practically all of the lands from Hatton's Ford, thence down the Tugaloo River to a point below Andersonville, a distance of more than three miles, and extended westward out from the river for an equal distance and at some points even much farther, including an area of several thousands of acres, most all of which was granted to them by the State, and such other portions as was granted to others, was bought by some member of the families named; so thus, as already stated, they owned practically all of the territory described, located on both the north and south sides of the Andersonville and Carnesville road, and drained by Crane's Little Lightwoodlog, and Holly creeks, and Caney, Tarkiln and Pole Bridge branches.

We have in our possession a copy of a plot of land granted to Robert Black in 1835, situate on Holly Creek, containing 551 acres.

At the time of Mr. Black's death, he owned a tract of land containing 123 acres, lying north of the old Hatton's Ford road, known as the Ussery and Crocker place, adjoining lands of Jedidiah Ayers, James Reed, and Mary Crocker. This place was later owned by James W. Leard and is yet known as the "Black Place."

From the records of Reed Creek Church, it appears that Robert Black united with the church by letter on June 21, 1835. He was a deacon, and when the property on which the church was built was deeded on the 23d day of May, 1854, by William O'Barr, he is mentioned in the deed as a commissioner of the church, along with Sterling Pinson, Michael Johnson, and Henry F. Chandler, the other commissioners.

The children of Robert Black, according to his will of record, consisted of three sons: James, Joseph and Thomas A.; and six daughters: Mary, Jane, Elizabeth, Susan, Emilee and Nancy.

We have no record who James married, but it appears that he died before his father did, as Robert Black in his will provided a legacy for Joseph William, George Washington, and James Robert Black, sons of James Black. We have no record as to who Joseph married. Thomas A. married Mary E. Smith. Mary married George W. Dyar. Jane married James L. Brown, Elizabeth married William Estes. And one of the daughters married William J. Dyar, and the other two perhaps never married.

Robert Black died in 1860 and is buried in the Black graveyard, situate on the north side of the Old Hatton's Ford road, just east of where the road crosses the Mary Ann Branch.

Bobo Family History

The forefather of the Bobo family was named Samuel Bobo, who came to Georgia from Union, S. C., during the Revolutionary War.

Tradition says that he came to the Tugaloo River, two miles above Andersonville, and swam his horse across the river and captured an Indian camp on the Georgia side. He also brought his wife with him, and that he made a canoe of poplar bark upon which he brought her across the river.

After he had located at the place where he had landed on the Georgia side of the river, he procured titles to the land, consisting of about 200 acres, more or less.

It is said that he made the trip on horseback to Augusta, which was then the capital of the State, to procure titles to the lands and that it required two weeks' time to make the trip, going and returning.

On the place, which still retains the name of the "Bobo Place," Samuel Bobo and members of the family are buried in an old family graveyard.

In addition to what we have said with reference to the "Old Bobo Place," we herewith reproduce an item that appeared in *The Hartwell Sun* years ago, which is as follows:

"One of the oldest settlers was Mr. Samuel Bobo, grandfather of S. M. Bobo. His house still stands and is in good condition yet. It was built of hewn logs, and located on the west bank of the Tugaloo River, a short distance above the old town (Andersonville). The view from this place is one of the most beautiful in the State of Georgia."

The old "Bobo House" has long since been dismantled and torn away. The view referred to in the above item is a long view down the river towards old Andersonville.

Samuel Bobo had three sons: Sampson, Dempsey and Lewis; and doubtless there were others whose names we do not have.

It is said that Lewis was scalped by the Indians while out hunting.

Dempsey Bobo married a Miss Enmond. To this union was born a large family of children. He moved, in his old age, to Alabama about the year 1875, where he died in 1882. We are not advised as to who were all of his children, but one daughter, Sarah, married Elisha M. Dyar; another, Millie, married Robert Richardson, known as "Shoe-maker Bob" to distinguish him from another by the same name. He had one son named Lewis Bobo, who also moved to Alabama in his old age.

Robert Richardson, known as "Shoe-maker Bob," was a very expert workman and followed his trade at Andersonville, and a number of young men served their apprenticeship under him and learned the trade. He moved to Alabama years ago.

The Walthour place on the Andersonville road, a part of which is now the home of Mr. O. G. Heaton, containing 200 acres was granted to Dempsey Bobo December 8, 1829.

Sampson Bobo, son of Samuel Bobo, married Elizabeth, a daughter of Burrell Bobo. To this union were born six sons: Solomon M., Jeptha, Thomas I., William, Mathew and Sampson; and four daughters: Susannah, Mattie, Mary E. and Dillie.

Sampson Bobo, at the time of his death, owned the "Old Bobo Place" of about 200 acres; also, the mill tract where he lived of about 300 acres, where he had a mill, gin and other machinery, which was destroyed by fire soon after his death. The place was later bought by Thomas L. McMullan. In addition to the two tracts of land mentioned, he also owned property in the town of Hartwell, designated as Lots Nos. 13 and 37. The property is now owned by Dr. W. I. Hailey.

Sampson Bobo was a charter member and one of the first deacons of Andersonville Baptist Church, which was organized September 6, 1839. Elizabeth, the wife of Sampson Bobo, died October 24, 1873, and he died October 26, 1873, age 67. His wife, Elizabeth, was 65 at her death.

They were both buried in the same grave in the cemetery at Reed Creek Church, the inscription on the marker as follows:

"IN MEMORY OF ELIZABETH BOBO, DIED OCT. 24, 1873, AGE 65.
"SAMPSON BOBO, DIED OCT. 26, 1873, AGE 67.
"BLESSED ARE THE DEAD WHICH DIE IN THE LORD."

In a newspaper report of their death, it is stated that they had been members of the Baptist Church for forty years, and had often expressed the wish that when one died, the other wanted to die and be buried together, and so it happened.

Nicholas Brown Family History

Nicholas Brown came to Georgia from either North Carolina or South Carolina. He was granted a large body of land on Caney Branch, about three miles west of Andersonville, and there lived and reared a large family of five sons: James L., Spencer, Jesse, Obed and Robert N.; and three daughters: Kizziah, Hannah and Catherine.

Nicholas Brown divided his lands into several tracts, which he gave to his children, and on the place, not far from the present residence of Thomas N. Madden, is the old family graveyard where Nicholas Brown, his wife and other relatives are buried.

Besides the tract of land mentioned, Nicholas Brown was granted another tract of 135 acres on December 1, 1837, which he later sold to Obed Brown, and which is now the home place of J. Willis Sanders, deceased.

James L. Brown, son of Nicholas Brown, married Jane Black, daughter of Robert Black. He lived for a part of his life on the lands given him by his father, and for a part of the time on a tract down below the Andersonville Ferry, and at the time of his death he owned both places.

James L. Brown joined the church at Reed Creek October, 1832, and remained a member, so far as we know, until his death. He is buried in the cemetery at Reed Creek Church. His wife, Jane, moved to Alabama after his death, where she died many years ago.

To James L. Brown and his wife, Jane, were born four sons: Robert N., James Thornton, Obed and Samuel; and three daughters: Catherine, Sarah and Rebecca.

Robert N. married Nancy C. Allen, daughter of James Allen. James Thornton married Mary E. Stewart. Obed married Mary Skelton, daughter of Noel L. and wife, Eliza Skelton. Samuel married Martha Grant, daughter of George Grant. Catherine married James M. Landers. Sarah married Thomas W. Bobo, son of Lewis Bobo. Rebecca married Wiley Dyar.

Spencer Brown, son of Nicholas Brown, married Mary Wright, daughter of Obadiah Wright, who lived on Holly Creek, and of whom we have written a brief sketch.

Jesse Brown, son of Nicholas Brown, married Sarah Ann Dyar, daughter of Elisha M. Dyar. He was a Baptist minister and preached to various churches in Hart and Franklin counties in Georgia, and perhaps to some in South Carolina. He moved from the community in which he was born and reared to Franklin County, where he lived for many years, and later moved to Alabama, where he died.

As to his labors as a minister, we herewith reproduce an account as the same appears in the history of the Tugaloo Baptist Association, written by Rev. J. F. Goode.

"Jesse Brown was truly a wonderful man in many respects. According to facts gathered from himself and others, his opportunities in childhood and youth were extremely limited. I think he was a native of South Carolina. If so, he came to Georgia when quite a young man. The writer heard him say he was ordained to the ministry in 1864, but at what church he did not state. He was somewhat abrupt in speech and manner, but he had a magnetism about him which made him popular, and this magnetism (whatever it was) was more manifest in the pulpit than elsewhere. He was what churches now seek after, a drawing preacher, and his congregation 'stayed drawn.' He constituted and built the church at Pleasant Hill in 1872, and continued as pastor until 1887, when he moved away to Alabama, He was pastor of a number of the churches in the Tugaloo Association: Pleasant Grove, Eastanollee, Poplar Springs and Middle River; besides some churches in South Carolina. The churches always prospered under his ministry. What part of Alabama he made his home, or the time of his death, we know nothing. He was a consecrated Christian man. All those who knew him best had the utmost confidence in his sincerity."

Jesse Brown joined the church at Reed Creek by letter, September, 1852. He served the church at Reed Creek as pastor for the years 1882-3-4.

Obed Brown, son of Nicholas Brown, and known as "Little Obe," married Mary Slater. He moved away many years ago to Cherokee County, Ga., and perhaps later moved to Alabama. He had one son, Nicholas; as to his other children we know nothing.

Robert N. Brown, son of Nicholas Brown, married Sarah Elizabeth, daughter of David and Lavinia Carter. His sons were James and William, and his daughters were Eliza and Ada. After his death his widow married H. H. Hall.

Kizziah, daughter of Nicholas Brown, married Robert M. Brown, who, if we are not mistaken, was a son of Levi Brown.

Hannah married William Richardson. The tract of land given to her by her father, Nicholas Brown, still is known as the "Hannah Richardson" tract of land.

Catherine Brown, daughter of Nicholas Brown, to the best of our information, married Peter Slater.

Levi Brown Family History

Another pioneer who settled in the community was Levi Brown, who, presumably, was a brother to Nicholas Brown.

He owned a large body of land, including what is now known as the John H. McDougle place, the C. C. Hembree place, the J. Parker Vickery place, and perhaps all of the lands between the places mentioned and the Nicholas Brown lands, all of which was granted to him December 8, 1829.

Levi Brown was the father of Obed Brown, who once lived at the place on the Andersonville and Carnesville road near where the road leading from Hartwell now intersects said road. It is still known as the "Obe Brown Place."

Obed Brown owned quite a lot of land, as we shall see further on. The place mentioned on the Andersonville and Carnesville road was formerly known as the A. Busclark lands, to whom it was granted, and contained several hundred acres.

It was here that Obed Brown lived and carried on large farming operations, owning a number of slaves, and in addition to his farming interests, he sold goods, kept a blacksmith shop, and perhaps a wood shop, had a gin house on the place operated by horse power, as was common in the early days on most all large farms, and perhaps had other machinery in connection with the gin. At the place, as was common at all public places, intoxicating liquors were sold. In those days there was no law prohibiting or restricting the making and sale of intoxicating liquors. Whisky was made from corn and other materials; brandy from peaches, apples and other fruits. Stills were common in the country and the price of liquors was quite cheap.

During the time Obed Brown lived at the place, there was quite an exodus of immigrants from east to west, the road by the place leading from Andersonville, S. C., on by Carnesville, Ga., was the main artery of immigrant travel and countless immigrants traveled this road, seeking homes further west. During those days Mr. Brown had associated with him his brother-in-law, Abraham Meredith, and son-in-law of Levi Brown, and they conducted a public shop where horses were shod and repair work done on wagons, and the immigrant custom was quite profitable. Just above the place, on the right-hand side of the road going towards Reed Creek Church, was a noted camping ground where immigrants camped for the night, and sometimes remained for several days in order to rest themselves and their stock, and to have needed repairs made to their wagons and to have their horses shod.

We remember, when a small boy, to have often seen this old camping ground, which was a cleared area with several large oak trees growing on it, and in fact the site of this old camping ground could be easily seen until the land was cleared several years ago.

In addition to the Busclark place, Obed Brown owned quite a lot of other lands, and while he lived at the place he sold a tract of land to Lewis Bobo containing 95 acres. He sold another tract of 110 acres to Dempsey Bobo. He sold another tract of 50 acres to Spencer Brown, being a part of tract of land granted to Thomas King and Alvin E. Whitten, located on Holly Creek. He sold a tract of 75 acres to William Estes, lying and being on Pole Bridge Branch. He also sold a tract of 150 acres to George Grant, lying and being on Caney Branch.

Pole Bridge Branch, mentioned in the deed from Obed Brown to William Estes, was in all probability so named for the fact that it was crossed on a pole bridge, or it might have been a kind of cause-way.

In the organization of Hart County, we have noted on the minutes of the Inferior Court an entry to the effect that commissioners were appointed to lay out a road from Mt. Zion Church to intersect the Carnesville and Andersonville road at or near Abram Meredith's, which was the same place known as the Obed Brown place. Later commissioners were appointed to lay out a road from a point near dry pond to the Walthour (or Welthour) house. The dry pond mentioned was not far from the late residence of J. Willis Sanders, and the report reads as follows:

"Received a report of a public road leading from near the line of the 1119th District, and running through Obed Brown's land in a northeast and then an east direction to the Walthour House."

The dry pond, evidently, was in the hollow or low lands just above the present public road leading from J. Willis Sanders' place to O. G. Heaton's house, which was formerly the Walthour place, and the branch over which "Pole Bridge" was built was the outlet of the dry pond, and, as stated, may have been, and doubtless was a kind of cause-way built of poles, as the land for some distance on each side was saturated by the water flowing from the dry pond.

We well remember when there was a pretty large branch that crossed the road at the present bridge. Of recent years the water dried out and at present there is no water where the road crosses, as formerly.

Pole Bridge Branch empties into Savannah River not far below the island, known as McMullan's Island, and has a number of tributaries, and by the time it reaches the river it affords sufficient volume of water to entitle it to the dignity of being called a creek.

Obed Brown later moved to Banks County, Ga., where he died, and his administrator, William Turk, sold the lands of the estate consisting of several hundred acres, and from the advertisement of the sale, which was on the first Tuesday in January, 1873, we gather the following:

The home place, granted to A. Busclark, containing	514 acres
The Walthour place, granted to Dempsey Bobo December 8, 1829	225 acres
A tract on Holly Creek, known as the Cox place	350 acres
The New Hope tract	138 acres
The Jas. P. Vickery tract, which was sold to Vickery, and reconveyed to Obed Brown	157 acres
The W. A. Phillips tract	135 acres
The Island at Hatton's Ford	71 acres
One tract granted to James Brown	40 acres
All of the above described tracts aggregating	1,630 acres

A part of the Walthour place is now known as the Joe Felton place, at which is one of the finest springs of water in the country, and the branch that flows from the spring is known as Wolf Branch, a tributary of Caney Branch.

The sons of Levi Brown, besides Obed, were: Robert M., Larkin, James and Spencer.

We have no record as to who were all of the daughters of Levi Brown. One of the daughters married Abraham Meredith, and another married Martin Guest, commonly called Captain Guest.

James Brown, son of Levi Brown, was a mechanic and made wagons and spinning wheels, at which trade he was so expert that he obtained the title "Wheelwright" Brown. In making spinning wheels, he would use a pine knot for a hub, which was turned on a lathe and given the proper shape, and when finished was literally "as tough as a pine knot."

The forty-acre tract described in the lands of Obed Brown was granted to him.

Dyar Family History

Elisha Dyar, a soldier of the War of the Revolution, was the ancestor of the Dyar family, and from historical collections compiled by the Daughters of the American Revolution we herewith give the account of his services in the war as the same appears in said collections which were taken from the records of Franklin County, Ga.

"Elisha Dyar."

"Resident of Capt. Newell's District, age 69. Entered services in Granville County, N. C., March, 1778, then 16 years of age, under Capt. Abram Potter, Col. Farrar, and was marched to Brier Creek where he was engaged in a skirmish with the British at Stono, S. C., and was shortly afterwards discharged for a three-months' tour by Capt. Carrington of Orange County, N. C. Again entered North Carolina militia in Granville about two weeks before Gates' defeat near Camden, 1780, under Capt. Peter Bennett, Col. Ambrose Ramsey of Guilford, and Gen. Butler. Marched to Cross Creek, now Fayetteville, and placed under command of Gen. Carswell and kept scouting until marched to Camden and out under Gen. Gates, at which time his father sent Jesse Gaskins to serve out the tour as it was the sickly season. Was discharged by Col. Ramsey, but again entered the North Carolina militia at Granville previous to the battle of Guilford, March, 1871, under Capt. John Henderson, Col. Malbady (sic), a French officer, and Gen. Greene.

"Was in Battle of Guilford, marched near Fayetteville and discharged for a three-months' tour by Capt. Henderson. Entered again at Hillsboro under Capt. Frederick Dubois from Caswell County (month not recollected), 1782, stationed as guard to Legislature then sitting. Was under Col. Hugh Linnon and was discharged by Capt. Dubois for a three-months' tour. Served altogether 12 months, that is four three-months' tours as private soldier, three months in addition as an express under Col. Potts at Hillsboro and found his own horse as a volunteer. Was born in Virginia near Big Falls of Potomac in May, 1763.

"Was called into service when living in Granville country, from whence he removed after the war to Rockingham County, N. C., thence to Pendleton, S. C., and finally to Georgia about 1800, has resided ever since in Franklin County, except seven years which he spent in Walton County, Ga. Was never drafted—always volunteered and never served as a substitute. His discharges were in a chest which his sister took to the western country, and does not know where she now lives. His neighbor, James Cash, a Revolutionary soldier, knew him during service. Testified to by Rev. Samuel Hymer and Jesse M. Million."

Elisha Dyar, in 1827, was granted a tract of land in Walton County, Ga., in payment for his services in the Revolutionary War. He lived in Walton County for seven years, as already stated, before moving to Franklin County. He lived, at one time, on Savannah River down below Andersonville, where he owned a tract of land, and which, according to an old deed now in the possession of W. B. McMullan, sold the place to Harrison & Earle, which tract or lot of land is described as follows: Deed dated December 1, 1822, signed by Elisha Dyar, of Walton County, Ga., conveying 45 acres of land to James Harrison and Samuel G. Earle, otherwise called Harrison & Earle, merchants of Andersonville, Pendleton District, South Carolina, consideration one hundred dollars. Said land being a part of a 250 acres, originally granted to William Lewis by patent dated July 15, 1787. The deed is witnessed by David Rusk and Hugh Rusk, members of the family of the old stone mason of Andersonville. Joel H. Dyar also witnessed the deed.

Elisha Dyar had three sons, viz.: Martin, John and Joel H. Dyar; and perhaps there were other children, but the three above mentioned are all of which we have any account.

Joel H., son of Elisha Dyar, married Rachael Sanders, daughter of Elias Sanders, pioneer and forefather of the Sanders family. He lived out some two or three miles southwest of Hartwell, and not far from the home of Elias Sanders.

Joel H. Dyar had three sons: Elias Sanders Dyar, named for his grandfather, Elias Sanders, Pressly and Joel H. Dyar, Jr. We have no further record of Pressly and Joel H., Jr.

Elias Sanders Dyar, commonly referred to as Sanders Dyar, in the early days of Hartwell was Marshal of the town. He also served as Deputy Sheriff of Hart County. Was a deacon of Hartwell Baptist Church.

He enlisted in Captain J. H. Skelton's Company, known as Company "C," 16th Georgia Regiment of Volunteers, on July 13, 1861, and was elected Second Lieutenant. Was wounded at Wilderness May 6, 1864. Died June 6, 1864, at Richmond, Va.

John Dyar, son of Elisha Dyar, was commonly called "Jack" Dyar. He had the following sons and daughters: Elisha M., George W., John, Jesse, William J., Wiley and Frank Dyar; the daughters were: Sarah, Melvina, Elizabeth, Amie and Clarissa.

Elisha M. married Sarah Bobo, daughter of Dempsey Bobo. The children of Elisha M. Dyar and wife were: Joseph, Simon, Isham, Noah, Samuel, Elias, Sarah Ann, Ellen and Cornelia.

Joseph, son of Elisha M. Dyar, married Sarah Estes, daughter of Cain Estes. He was killed in the second Manassas Battle in 1862. His widow married John Reed.

Simon was never married, so far as we know. Isham married Sarah Ussery, daughter of Mumford Ussery. Noah married Mrs. Mary Magill. Samuel died when young. Elias married Mattie Stewart.

Sarah Ann married Jesse Brown. Ellen married Archie Bowman. Cornelia married John M. Campbell.

John Dyar, son of Jack Dyar, married Dillie Bobo, daughter of Sampson Bobo. His children were as follows: Francis M., Millie, John S., Sampson, Elias Dyar, and Martina Dyar, and Sallie Dyar.

Francis M., son of John Dyar, married Mary E. Adams, daughter of Winson Adams, and after her death he married Martha Adams, daughter of Fleming Adams. John S. married M. M. Partain. Millie married E. B. Hembree. Sampson married Jane Fowler. Elisha married Ella Pinson. Martina married John Meredith. Sallie married Willis Rumsey.

George W. Dyar, son of Jack Dyar, married Mary Black, daughter of Robert Black.

To George W. Dyar and wife, Mary, were born one son: William John Dyar; and four daughters: Margaret, Aurena, Frankie and Anna.

William John Dyar married Eliza A. Bowman, daughter of William Bowman. Margaret married Edward A. Caldwell. Anna married Daniel Wright. Frankie married Lewis Bobo. Aurena married an Emerson and moved to Alabama.

George W. Dyar was a carpenter and millwright. The land where he lived and owned at the time of his death was granted by the State. He also was granted the island at Hatton's Ford, of 71 acres, January 3, 1848.

Tarkiln Branch

Tarkiln Branch traverses the lands once owned by George W. Dyar, Jas. L. Brown and others. The branch was so named, no doubt, from the large quantities of tar that was run from kilns along the banks and bluffs of the stream. The country in the early days abounded in pine timber from which tar was made. Tar was used in considerable quantities for lubricating wagons and other purposes.

That our readers may get a better understanding of the mode of making tar and the various uses to which it was applied, we herewith reproduce an article written upon the subject by James A. Hall, "Lover of Nature and Georgia Lore."

"Our grandfathers performed many kinds of work which are almost forgotten now. One of these was 'running' tar, and the tar kiln was a familiar object throughout the country.

"In the early days practically all wagons had axles made of hickory wood and the spindles upon which the wheels turned were lubricated with pine tar. This tar was carried in a bucket swung underneath the wagon.

"This tar was made from small split sticks of rich heart pine. These sticks were stacked in a slanting position in a kiln, which usually consisted of a small excavation in the side of a hill or embankment. The bottom of this excavation was hammered smooth and hard so that the hot tar would flow towards the outlet and spill itself into a vessel placed below the mouth of the opening outside which was slightly below the level of the kiln floor. When the wood was all stacked in order, it was covered with green pine brush, except a small opening at the top. At this spot the wood was lighted and the entire heap covered with soil in such a manner as to prevent a blaze. The smoke issued from the smothered opening at the top and was quite dense, hence arose the common saying 'smoking like a tarkiln.'

"As the fire progressed downward among the pine sticks, the hot resin ran down them to the hard floor of the kiln and thus found its way into the vessel awaiting it at the outlet. This new tar was a deep, dark red color and had a delightful odor. Bees and other insects were attracted to it and many of them soon found themselves stuck in the tar. Hence arose another saying often heard in the country, 'As busy as a bee in a tar bucket.'

"Tar was used for many things other than lubrication, such as medicine for both man and beast, as pitch of boats, and as a kind of crude solder for mending broken household objects."

As to the two sons of Jack Dyar, Wiley and Jesse, we know nothing. William J. Dyar, son of Jack Dyar, married _____ Black, daughter of Robert Black. He moved away many years ago, but we are not sure where to. He had one son whose name was Robert J. Dyar, who married Mattie Bobo, daughter of Sampson Bobo. He moved to Banks County years ago and was for some time Clerk of the Superior Court of Banks County, Ga.

From a newspaper account of Mr. Dyar's death, we take the following portions:

"Robert J. Dyar was born in Hart County about the year 1843, and died April 9, 1928, age 78 years, 6 months, and 6 days. (That part of Hart County where Mr. Dyar was born was embraced in Franklin County at the time of his birth.) Mr. Dyar was a son of William J. Dyar and was a great-grandson of Elisha Dyar, a soldier of the War of the Revolution. He was a soldier in the War Between the States, having entered as a private March 4, 1862, in Company "D," 37th Regiment Georgia Volunteers Infantry, Army of Tennessee, C. S. A., Hart County, Georgia, of which Company John G. McMullan was Captain, and served the full four years.

"On November 15, 1866, he was married to Miss Martha Bobo. Many years ago he moved to Banks County, settling in Homer, and for several years was Clerk of the Superior Court of the county.

"Mr. Dyar was an upright, honest, Christian man and had long been a member of the Baptist Church.

"The funeral services were conducted by Rev. S. J. Baker, pastor of Lavonia-Baptist Church, on Monday afternoon at the Presbyterian Church, and interment was in the cemetery in Homer."

Frank Dyar, son of Jack Dyar, married Mary Cleveland, daughter of John Ashley Cleveland. He was a soldier in the War Between the States, and afterwards drew a pension.

Melvinia, daughter of Jack Dyar, married Francis Eaton, more generally known as Francis Massey. Amie married Nathan Sanders, and after his death she married Wm. J. McLane. Clarissa married John A. H. Jones. We do not know who Elizabeth and Sarah married.

On a hill on the Georgia side of the Tugaloo River, near the Andersonville Ferry, is the site of the old Dyar residence, and near it in a grove of cedar trees are buried Elisha Dyar, his son, Jack, and his grandson, John, and other relatives of the family.

From this eminence is to be had a splendid view of the site of the old dismantled town of Andersonville, as well as a view of the union of the Tugaloo and Seneca into the Savannah River.

Another item of interesting history connected with the community is, that in the early days about all the lands in the territory mentioned supported vast forests of large pines, suitable for lumber and other building materials, and a number of the people in the community engaged in the making of shingles.

This was before the days of shingle mills, and all shingles were "drawed" shingles. The best of the large pines were selected and felled, and then with pole axe girdled at intervals of the length the shingles were to be; that is, girdles were cut into the logs as far as the sap extended, and then sawed up into blocks, and the sap portion removed in large chunks, called "juggles." Only the heart of the pine was used for shingles. In those days there were no sap shingles.

The blocks, after the sap part had been removed, were split up into a number of parts, called staves or bolts, and these were split into about the size that the shingles were to be, by use of a tool called a frow. Afterwards these portions were placed on the "draw horse," which was a device made of a pole 12 to 15 feet long, with two legs at one end about two feet in length, and the other end of the pole lay on the ground. To the elevated end of the pole was attached a kind of clamp which was manipulated with the foot, the shingle placed on the "draw horse," one at a time, with one end held by the clamp, and a man with a drawing knife proceeded to "draw" the shingle, which, when finished, was in very much the shape of the sawed shingles of today.

It was a slow process, but the people in those days were not in such a hurry as at the present time, and they patiently applied themselves to the task until one tree after another was made up into "drawed" shingles. After the shingles were made in sufficient quantities they were loaded on ox wagons and hauled to Anderson, S. C., or other places where there was a demand for them. It is to be remembered that in those days cotton was not cultivated very extensively and people resorted to other means to make a support, and the timber being plentiful, they utilized quantities of it in making shingles. These "drawed" shingles when placed on a building made a roof that would last for many years.

It is remarkable that so many of the former citizens of the community mentioned and their descendants moved away, and many of them settled in the State of Alabama and located in the same community. We once heard Prof. Solomon M. Bobo say that in the settlement in Alabama where a great many of the people moved to, that the church out there was composed mostly of the members who formerly belonged to the churches at Reed Creek, Andersonville and Milltown.

Historic Old Home of John Martin White

FIVE miles southwest of the City of Hartwell, Ga., and a short ways west of the Bankhead Highway, on the headwaters of North Beaverdam Creek, stands the old home of John Martin White, who was a brave and gallant soldier in the War of the Revolution.

This old home was built well over one hundred years ago on lands, a large tract of which was granted to John Martin White in consideration of his services, located in Elbert (formerly Wilkes), now Hart County, and in the 9th Militia District as originally laid off in the organization of Elbert County, which district was also known as Capt. Blackwell's District.

It is constructed of large hewed logs (this was before the day of sawmills), oblong in form with rock chimney with spacious fireplace, and is in every way a substantial building, and is today in almost a perfect state of preservation. This old house has sheltered from wind, storm and bitter cold several generations of the White family, and here it will be proper to state that the old home and the real estate upon which it stands enjoys the very rare distinction of the title never having passed from the White family.

The house was first occupied by John Martin White and his wife, who, before her marriage, was Miss Milley Ballenger. They reared a large and interesting family, among whom was a son named Eppie, and he and his wife, who was Miss Catherine Herndon before her marriage, like his illustrious father and mother, also raised a large family, among whom was a son, Thomas Henderson White, who became owner of the place. The old home today belongs to the children of Thomas H. White, they being of the fourth generation.

Not far from and just south of the old home is the family burying ground in which John Martin White, his son, Eppie, and his grandson, Thomas H. White, veterans of three wars, Revolutionary, the War of 1812, and the War Between the States, respectively, and their wives and other relatives peacefully sleep, while the slaves sleep in graves not far from those of their masters.

John Martin White, while a patriot, was also a minister of the Gospel of the Baptist denomination, and his name appears as one of the ministers constituting the presbytery that officiated in the organization of Holly Spring Church February 6, 1796, Rev. John Cleveland and Rev. Thomas Maxwell being the other ministers of the presbytery.

His Bible, purchased in the year 1803, now well worn and yellow with age, holds the annals of the White family and other families of the White connection. Besides the record of the White family it also contains the record of the following relatives of the White family, viz.: Ballenger, Cleveland, Coffee, Garland, Head, Harper, Herndon, Jones, Kidd, Mann, Morris, Rice, Roebuck and Thornton.

This old Bible is at present in the care and vigilant keeping of A. C. White, a great-grandson of John Martin White, and is a most precious and priceless heirloom and will become more so as it passes on down through the coming generations of the White family.

Ancestry of the White Family

1. Peter White, of Petersboro and Brockman, England, born about 1530, was grandson of Sir Thomas White (Sir Thomas White was one of the Judges who sat on trial of Lady Jane Grey). Peter married Mary Kebble, had five sons, all ministers, as follows: Francis, Bishop; William, Clergyman in Virginia; John, Vicar Wiltshire; Jeremiah, Cromwell's Chaplain; Thomas, Deacon.

2. William White married, first, ...; had John, William, Edward and Deborah. Married, second, Mrs. Alford; had Jeremiah. Mrs. Alford's daughter by first marriage was sometimes called Mary White. Married, third, Mrs. Brice; no children. He died 1658 in York County, Va.

3. John White, son of William, married ....; had John and others.

4. John White, son of John, married Mary, daughter of Thomas Elbert; had John, died 1720, and Jeremiah, Reuben, Daniel and others.

5. Jeremiah White, son of John, born 1695, married Mary Martin 1726; had: Jeremiah, born 1728, married, first, Esther Herndon; John, born 1730, died 1732; Lettie, born 1733, married Melton; Rachael (Mary), born 1735, married Martin; Eliza, born 1737, married Webb Kidd; Milley, born 1740, married Jacob Cleveland; John Martin, born 1743, married Milley Ballenger; Reuben, Daniel, and Anne, triplets, born 1746. Daniel married Polly Ballenger. These triplets all grew up to an enormous height—even Anne, the girl, was 6 feet. She married a Shackleford and at one time had descendants in Hart County.

6. John Martin White married Milley Ballenger May 29, 1775; had

Reuben, Sarah Franklin, Nancy Kidd, Mary Martin (Polly), Patsey Johnson (she married Mastele White of another line), Eppie, Betsey Johnson (died in infancy), Frankey (married Roebuck), Lucy, Eliza Johnson 2nd (named for dead sister Betsey), John Martin.

7. Eppie White married Catherine D. Herndon, daughter of Edward Herndon and Nancy Rucker Herndon, 1815; had: Thomas Herndon, born February 20, 1816; John Martin, born July 28, 1817; Mildred Elizabeth, born October 15, 1819; Dillard Herndon, born January 15, 1822; Edward Rucker, born April 8, 1824; James Franklin, born September 15, 1826; Ann (Nancy) Herndon, born January 9, 1829; Rachael Eliza, born April 10, 1831; Sarah Catherine, born November 13, 1833; Mary Franklin, born May 7, 1836; Malissa Frances, born November 13, 1839.

Marriages of the above named children of Eppie White and wife, Catherine Herndon:

Thomas H. White married, first, Martha McMillan; born March 15, 1819; died December 12, 1864. Married, second, Malissa C. Walters, daughter of Abram Walters, February 1, 1866.

John Martin White (moved to Alabama; don't know whether he married or not).

Mildred Elizabeth White married James W. Jones, October 25, 1842.

Dillard H. White married Mary Ann Duncan, November 9, 1854.

Edward Rucker White married, first, Elizabeth Roberts, daughter of Moses Roberts, January 8, 1846. Married, second, Charlotte H. Roberts, daughter of Francis S. Roberts, March 6, 1864.

James F. White married, first, Martha R. Johnson, daughter of Neil Johnson, April 27, 1854. Married, second, Miss Martha Cobb.

Ann Nancy Herndon White perhaps was never married, as we have no record of her marriage.

Rachael E. White married James E. Strickland, May 15, 1851.

Sarah C. White married Charles W. Christian, Jr., March 25, 1853.

Mary Franklin. Perhaps died in childhood.

Malissa F. White married, first, J. L. Christian, November 13, 1856. Married, second, Jos. S. Chambers, August 18, 1863. Married, third, Robert Hager, May 7, 1884. Married, fourth, J. J. Gaines, October 13, 1887.

Milley, wife of John Martin White, was a daughter of Joseph Ballenger and wife, Sarah Franklin, daughter of Major James Franklin, of Albemarle-Amhurst and Fluvanna Counties, Va.

Joseph Ballenger was a son of Joseph Ballenger and wife Patsey, of Goochland County, Va.

Joseph, Sr., died 1744.

Joseph, Jr., married Sarah, daughter of Major James Franklin, an officer in the Revolutionary War.

At least three of their sons settled here in early development of this section. Some of the Bowers family are descended from one of them.

The Ballengers are of English descent and were of rank of baronets.

Achilles Ballenger, a son, was living in the vicinity of now Hart County, 1805.

Descendants of Joseph Ballenger have been admitted to the Daughters of the American Revolution.

Martin

Abraham, youngest son of "House of Martin," Galway, Ireland, born 1640, came to Virginia about 1680. John, son of Abraham, married, first, Lettie _____; second, Martha Brunwell, daughter of Lewis Brunwell Mary, daughter of John and first wife, born 1703, married Jeremiah White, 1726.

Colonial Service

Rev. William White, outstanding in service to crown.
John, member assembly.
Lewis Brunwell, member of Burgesses.
Abraham Martin, member assembly, Colonial officer, Colonel.
Col. John Martin, member Virginia assembly.
Descendants eligible to Colonial Dames, American Colonists 17th Century, Revolutionary service.
John Martin White, Captain Spottsylvania, Va., Militia. Served in Continental Line.
Joseph Ballenger gave equipment, supplies and money to the services; he was physically unable to serve. His brother, Richard, was Captain Virginia Line.

Services War 1812

Eppie White, officer in Captain Patterson's Company.

Confederate Services

Thomas Herndon White and his son, Eppie Washington White. Thomas Herndon served in Company "E," of the 4th Regiment Georgia Reserves, Barnet D. Johnson, Captain. Eppie Washington White served in Company "B," 24th Georgia Regiment.
James F. White served as a Cavalryman under Gen. P. M. B. Young.

Services in the Georgia Legislature

James E. Strickland, son-in-law of Eppie White, was member of the Georgia Legislature from Hart County in the years 1861-62-63.
E. R. White, son of Eppie White, represented Hart County in the Georgia Legislature in the years 1865-66.
James W. Jones, son-in-law of Eppie White, represented Hart County in Georgia Legislature in the years 1871-72.
James F. White, son of Eppie White, served out the unexpired term of J. F. Craft, deceased, in the State Senate from 31st District, to which Hart County belonged at that time. He also served in the Georgia Legislature from Hart County in 1890-91.
E. R. White, son of Eppie White, was Tax Collector of Hart County in 1861.

William Glover

DECLARATION of William Glover, age 72. Entered service of United States at Wilkes County, N. C., in militia, about 1778-9, as private under Capt. Shepherd and Col. Gordon.

Was marched to Hamilton's Old Store, from there to Shallow Ford on the (Y) Adkin, crossed Dan River into Virginia with some prisoners at Dick's Ferry, where we met a new guard and returned to Wilkes and received a discharge from Major Lewis for a three-months' tour. Immediately re-entered the service under Col. Cleveland and remained with him under Capt. Barton and Capt. Keys scouting for six months, when again entered regular service in 1780 in Wilkes County, N. C., under Capt. Noll, Col. Isaacs and Gen. Rutherford. Marched to Salisbury by way of Charlotte, thence to Camden, where we were defeated under Gen. Gates. On the way was detached under Col. Davidson and was in a skirmish at the mouth of Rocky River, where Col. Davidson was wounded. Returned home for three days and entered army at Wilkes Court House under Col. Gordon. Marched to Shallow Ford, where defeated the Tories in battle. Had previously served three months under Col. Armstrong and Capt. Bushwick and Gen. Sumter and was in Battle of Hanging Rock near Camden. Returned to Wilkes and entered Capt. Keys and Col. Cleveland and was ordered to guard prisoner taken at King's Mountain to Virginia line. Returning to Wilkes, joined Col. Cleveland and ordered under Capt Keys to scout duty to Flower Gap and lead mines on New River on Virginia line. Placed as guard over the mines. Returned to Wilkes and was under Capt. Gordon, Capt. Keys, Capt. Bacton, Maj. Lewis and Col. Cleveland until war was over. Was in fight at King's Creek. Served three years.

Born in Prince George County, Md., 1760, and was living in Wilkes County, N. C., when entered service. Came to Elbert County in 1786, thence to Franklin County, Ga., in 1800, where has since resided. Was once drafted, but other times volunteered—was never a substitute. House burned 1801 with all papers.

Endorsed by Rev. Dozier Thornton and John Stonecypher.

William Glover is buried in the old Glover family burying ground on the lands now known as the J. P. Gulley estate in Shoal Creek District. His grave has lately been marked by a monument furnished by the U. S. Government.

As to his family history we know but little. He was the father of Joseph and James M. Glover, and four daughters, viz.: Jane, who married Edy Bowers, second son of William Bowers, Sr.; Eliza F. married William Bowers, Jr., fourth son of William Bowers, Sr.; Alpha A. married Thomas W. Bowers, sixth son of William Bowers, Sr.; and Patsey married T. P. Holbrook.

The Bowers Family History

JOB BOWERS, the forefather of the Bowers generations in Hart and Franklin counties, and other parts of Georgia, was born in Virginia in 1755, and was of Welsh extraction, and lived in Wilkes (now Elbert) County at the time of the Revolutionary War, in which he was a soldier.

While serving in the war he was granted a furlough to visit his family, and when he arrived home he found a baby boy born just a few days before.

The first night at home he was taken out of his house by the Tories and cruelly murdered, an account of which incident is related further on in this sketch.

The baby boy mentioned, born October 4, 1779, was named William Bowers. When he grew to manhood he married Polly Cox, who was born June 24, 1786. William Bowers died January 26, 1844, and his wife, Polly, died September 9, 1873, and both buried in the cemetery at Hendry's Church.

William Bowers purchased, in 1819, 150 acres of land from John Martin White and wife, Milley White, being a portion of a tract of land granted to John Martin White for his services in the War of the Revolution, located on the headwaters of North Beaverdam Creek, for which he paid $350 for 100 acres, and we do not know the price paid for the 50 acres.

He later, on the 1st day of January, 1833, bought 254 acres of land from John Karr (sometimes spelled Carr) for $100, being a part of a 300-acre tract granted to John Karr in 1813, adjoining lands of the famous Billy Patterson, originally granted to David Creswell, and others.

He settled and built his home on the above described lands, where he reared his family.

There is an item of history connected with this old homestead to the effect that there is a large sycamore tree which stands near the yard that was brought there by William Bowers, or some member of his family, as an ox hickory which was set out and lived and is today a large tree.

To William Bowers and his wife, Polly Cox Bowers, were born seven sons: Job, who was named for his father that was killed by the Tories; Edy, Joel, William, Jr., Asa, Thomas W., and Elbert Marion Bowers; and six daughters: Elizabeth, commonly called Betsey, Nancy, Polly, Jr., Letty Emily, Charlotte H., and Sarah C. Bowers.

After the death of William Bowers, Sr., the place was sold by his wife, Polly, and his eldest son, Job, nominated in his will as his executors, and was bought by Dillard H. Brown, a son-in-law of William Bowers, Sr., for the price of $400. The old house in which William Bowers, Sr., and family lived is still standing, and is today known as the Captain John S. Herndon place.

After the death of William Bowers, Sr., or perhaps before his death, so far as we know, the family lived on a small tract of land near Hendry's Church, and the right or west side of near North Beaverdam Creek, on which stream there was a mill that once belonged to William Bowers, Sr., or to his family.

The lands on which the house stood and where the mill was located were a part of a large tract of land originally granted to Dr. Charles Hendry, for whom Hendry's Church, organized in 1818, was named.

This small tract of land is still in the possession of some of the descendants of the Bowers family, retained for sentimental reasons.

The old home of Dr. Hendry stood on the west side of the public road leading from Eaglegrove out by Hendry's Church, and on the left or east side of North Beaverdam Creek. A portion of the old chimney is still standing and the house was a large two-story house, as we have been told by some who remember it, built on the style common in those days.

Besides being engaged in farming and the practice of medicine, Dr. Hendry also kept a country store, and at the time the nearest post office was Ruckersville, Ga., to which place mail came up twice a week from Augusta, Ga. Some one in the neighborhood would go down and bring the mail from Ruckersville, a distance of eighteen or twenty miles, to Dr. Hendry's store, where the people would meet to get their mail and to hear the news. It is said that Dr. Hendry was a subscriber to a number of leading newspapers and, being a good reader, would entertain the people by reading to them the news.

Job Bowers, the first born and oldest son of William Bowers, Sr., was born August 31, 1803, and was married five times; his first wife was Elizabeth Ballenger, daughter of William Ballenger, who married Mary Redwine, daughter of Jacob Redwine, born January 1, 1777.

To Job Bowers and his wife, Elizabeth, were born thirteen children, seven sons:

William Franklin; born November 23, 1825; married Christana Cheek; died January 24, 1905; buried in Canon Cemetery.

Christana Cheek, wife of William Franklin Bowers, was a descendant of William Cheek, a soldier of the War of the Revolution.

Jeptha Alexander Bowers; born February 5, 1827; died December 24, 1890; buried in the Bowers family graveyard. Married Ermine Roe, who is also buried in the Bowers family graveyard.

James Basil Bowers, M. D.; born June 20, 1832; died April 13, 1890; buried in the Bowers family graveyard. An apothecary's emblem (mortar and pestle) engraved on his tombstone.

Paris Bowers; born June 15, 1837; died in the War Between the States somewhere in Virginia.

Byron Bowers; born July 20, 1839. Married Mary Manley, June, 1878; born October 2, 1857; still living.

Byron Bowers died in Decatur, Ga.; buried in Canon Cemetery.

Noah N. Bowers; born September 23, 1841; died in the War Between the States.

John Merritt Bowers, youngest son of Job Bowers. Married Mary Duncan. Was killed in an automobile wreck near Canon, Ga. Buried in cemetery at Canon, Ga.

Susie Arminda Bowers, daughter of Job Bowers; born December 18, 1828; married James M. Glover; died in 1885; buried in Canon Cemetery.

Nancy Malissa Bowers; born September 18, 1830; buried at Job Bowers home place.

Martha Bowers; born April 22, 1835. Married, first, Asa Brown; and after his death she married Bart Weaver. Buried at the Job Bowers place.

Polly Miriam Bowers; born May 28, 1844. Married Stephen P. Bond, November 1, 1861.

Ann Judson Bowers; born ....; married Marion Cheek; died ....; buried in Canon Cemetery by her husband.

Sarah Bowers; born ....; married E. Jordan; died .... After the death of E. Jordan, first husband, she married Stephen Bond.

Job Bowers married a second time. His second wife was Rebecca Hendrix, a daughter of Jesse Hendrix; born January 6, 1818; died November 28, 1858. To her and her husband, Job Bowers, was born one child that died in infancy. She is buried in the old cemetery at Redwine Church, her grave marked by a rock vault.

Job Bowers' third wife was Mrs. Julia Alexander. His fourth wife was Mrs. Betsie Reed. His fifth wife was Polly Hendrix; born April 9, 1822; a sister to his second wife; died August 7, 1902.

Job Bowers settled in Franklin (now Hart) County, at the place near the headwaters of South Beaverdam Creek, on the old Hatton's Ford and Athens road, at the intersection with the Ruckersville and Carnesville road.

He owned a large landed estate, built a magnificent home, which is yet in a perfect state of preservation, and stands as if in a dream, remembering things that used to be.

His place was known as Bowersville, and the first place in the country to bear the name.

He engaged in farming and merchandising, was at one time County Surveyor of Franklin County, Ga., was Justice of the Peace in the 370th Militia District, known as Manley's District until 1854, when Hart County was created. When the new county was organized his place was included in Hart County, and he retained the office of Justice of the Peace, and in his old docket there is a record that the first Justice's Court held in and for the 1116th District was on August 12, 1854, at John Hall's, the district taking the name Hall's, by which it is still known and designated.

At his place was a post office called Bowersville Post Office, on the star mail route from Athens, Ga., to Anderson, S. C., and at one time was a stagecoach route, carrying mail and passengers between the two points mentioned. It was also on a star mail route from Ruckersville, Ga., to Carnesville, Ga., which two routes crossed at or near Bowersville.

The old store house in which the post office was kept is still standing and is a very interesting, historic landmark and picturesque item of the countryside.

Edy Bowers, second son of William Bowers, Sr., and wife, Polly, was born January 3, 1810. He married Jane Glover, daughter of William Glover, a Revolutionary soldier, who lived and died and is buried at the old homestead now owned by the heirs of J. P. Gulley. Further, we know nothing of the history of Edy Bowers and family.

Joel Bowers, third son of William Bowers, Sr., and wife, Polly, was born February 26, 1812. He married _____ Harris; was the father of John H. Bowers, known as "Goshen John Bowers." In a sketch of the war record of Joel Bowers, soldier in the War Between the States, it is stated that he was torn to pieces by a shell at the battle of Sharpsburg, and that his son, John H. Bowers, received a wound in the same war that he never got over. As stated in the sketch, "Bowers' blood has stained southern soil all the way down in defense of what they thought was right." Further, we have no history of Joel Bowers, or his family.

William Bowers, Jr., fourth son of William Bowers, Sr., and wife, Polly, was born February 12, 1816. He was twice married. His first wife was a Miss Haynes, and to this union was born one son, named Jefferson Bowers.

His second wife was Eliza F. Glover, daughter of William Glover, and sister to the wives of Edy and Thomas W. Bowers. To him and his wife, Eliza F., were born three sons: Patrick, who married Laura Baker, daughter of Dixon Baker; Hess, who was a physician; and Job, who married Hester Brown; and seven daughters: Victoria married Leroy C. Brown; Edna married Robert Johnson, known as "Big Robert"; Cancy married Robert Johnson, known as "Little Robert"; Florence married John Johnson; Sallie married _____ McKinney; Molly married K. Bates; and Alice married Nat Bates.

William Bowers, Jr., lived at the place known as Eaglegrove and kept the post office by that name, which was on the star route from Ruckersville, Ga., perhaps later from Elberton to Carnesville, Ga. The mail route was along, according to tradition, what was originally an Indian trail.

William Bowers, Jr., was Tax Collector of Hart County during the years 1864-65. He was also at one time a member of the Inferior Court of Hart County, by reason of which service he derived the title of Judge.

Asa Bowers, fifth son of William Bowers, Sr., and wife, Polly, was born March 12, 1818; married Elizabeth Brown. To him and his wife were born three sons: John D., William E., and Sanford G. Bowers. The last named at one time was Tax Collector of Hart County, and died while holding said office. There was one daughter, named Mary E. Bowers.

Asa Bowers was a soldier in the War Between the States, the service of which he entered as a private August 24, 1864, in Captain Phillip E. Devant's Company, known as Company "B," 24th Georgia Regiment, and died on a Virginia battlefield.

William E. Bowers, his son, enlisted at the age of 17 years in Captain B. D. Johnson's Company, known as Company "E," 4th Georgia Regiment, in which company he was Second Corporal.

Thomas W. Bowers, sixth son of William Bowers, Sr., and wife, Polly, was born May 22, 1820; married Alpha A. Glover, daughter of William Glover, and sister to the wives of Edy and William Bowers, Jr. Was father of W. Marion Bowers. We do not have the names of his other children. He bought and settled the place at the crossroads where the Hatton's Ford and Athens and the Jackson road, later known as the road leading by Hartwell to Brown's Ferry, and the Carnesville roads cross, near the present village of Air Line.

At this place was established a post office known as Air Line Post Office, so named, as already stated, for the reason that the Air Line Railroad had been surveyed through the immediate community.

Elbert M. Bowers, seventh son of William Bowers, Sr., and wife, Polly, was born October 11, 1832; married _____ Brown. Died in the War Between the States.

Elizabeth Bowers, first daughter of William Bowers, Sr., and wife, Polly, commonly called "Betsey," was born November 3, 1805; married Jesse Smith; died June 20, 1888. To her and her husband were born six daughters and one son.

The son, whose given name was Joel, met a tragic death by being killed in a run-away of a yoke of oxen that he was driving at or near the mill on the Nancy Merritt place. The mill was later known as the Cauthen & Blackmon Mill.

One daughter, Nancy, married Albert Leard, son of Major Leard. Another daughter, Letty, married Elias Harrison Sanders, a son of Jonathan P. Sanders. Martha A., another daughter, born April 22, 1832, married Joseph Hairston; she died April 16, 1884, and is buried in the cemetery at Hendrys Church beside her mother. Another daughter named Mary was never married, so far as we have any record. Malissa married .... Hulme. Eliza married E. W. Brown.

Nancy, second daughter of William Bowers, Sr., and wife, Polly, was born October 8, 1807; married John Merritt. We have no record of any children born to Nancy and her husband. In the will of John Merritt, of record, he bequeaths all his property to his wife, Nancy, during her lifetime, and at her death, to go to his nephew, Blanton B. Parker, Jr. John Merritt is buried in the cemetery at Holly Springs Church, with the following inscription on his tombstone:

"JOHN MERRITT
BORN NOVEMBER 23, 1796
DIED NOV. 20, 1843."

Beside the grave of John Merritt are the graves of Toren Merritt and wife, Priscilla Merritt, with the following inscriptions:

"Toren Merritt, born Feb. 22, 1762, died Dec. 1823. Wife Priscilla, born Oct. 16, 1781." Evidently Toren and Priscilla Merritt were the parents of John Merritt. We have no record of the death of Nancy Merritt.

Polly Bowers, Jr., third daughter of William Bowers, Sr., and wife, Polly, was born January 21, 1814; married Reuben Williford.

Letty Emily, fourth daughter of William Bowers, Sr., and wife, Polly, was born April 27, 1822; married Dillard H. Brown, son of Dozier T. Brown.

Charlotte, fifth daughter of William Bowers, Sr., and wife, Polly, was born February 8, 1824, and met a tragic death by being drowned.

While the family lived at the place near Hendrys Church and close to the millpond, the daughter, Charlotte H., went to the pond for a bucket of water and when she failed to return the family began an investigation, and as they approached to near the pond she was no where to be seen, but the waterbucket was floating on the surface of the water, which told all too true the sad story of her fate.

Another story of a drowning is related in connection with the Bowers family. A daughter of Polly, Jr., who married Reuben Williford, married Mr. Washington Wilson, and to them was born a girl which they named Charlotte, after great-aunt, who was drowned. This little girl, when some years old, fell into a large spring on the Williford place and was drowned, sharing a like fate of that of her great-aunt for whom she was named.

Sarah C. Bowers, sixth daughter of William Bowers, Sr., and wife, Polly, was born August 31, 1825; married Robert Berryman; died October 21, 1892.

William Franklin Bowers, first born and son of Job Bowers and wife, Elizabeth Ballenger Bowers, was perhaps the most noted of any other of the Bowers family, and following we reproduce a number of articles written by various writers as to his life and activities, political, religious and otherwise.

He lived for a part of the time in Hart County, about one mile west of Cannon Baptist Church, and later moved to Canon, Ga., where he spent the remainder of his life.

William F. Bowers

"William F. Bowers. There are many families in Franklin County, Ga., who may justly claim to be sprung from the 'oldest settlers,' and many persons have been born who have become distinguished. But few, if any, families can prove earlier settlement or a clearer, more reputable record— though not as conspicuous or distinguished as some— than that of the family of which Hon. William F. Bowers (familiarly known as 'Uncle Billy') is now the living head. Simple as a child in friendly intercourse or devoid of ostentation, and conscious of entire rectitude, he is always self-poised. For stern and steady, and inflexible adherence to what he deems correct principles, and conscientious conviction, he is almost without a peer. Mr. Bowers was the son of Job and Elizabeth (Ballenger) Bowers, and was born in what is now Hart County in 1825. His paternal great-grandfather, Job Bowers, was of Welsh extraction, was a soldier in the patriotic army during the Revolutionary War; and who, while at home 'on furlough,' was killed by the Tories. He was actually one of the earliest settlers on or near the Savannah River in that part of Georgia. His grandparents were William and Mary Bowers, and his grandfather was born in what is now Elbert County and lived there a farmer until he died. Mr. Bowers' father was born in Elbert (now Hart) County, taught school and farmed, and later became a merchant. For many years he was Surveyor of the county, and also served his fellow citizens as Justice of the Peace for more than a score of years. 'Uncle Billy's' mother was a daughter of William Ballenger, a farmer, and another of the oldest settlers of the territory now known as Elbert County, and was a prosperous farmer. 'Uncle Billy' was brought up on the farm, and as he expresses it, 'in the store room,' his only education being obtained at the dirt floor, puncheon-seated log school house without a nail in it, and stick-and-mud chimney. He began life as a farmer, and afterward engaged, very much to his pecuniary advantage, in merchandising. None of his family would ever own a slave, and from earliest life he was an uncompromising Union man. He claims to be, and probably is, the only man then a resident of Georgia, now living, who voted for Abraham Lincoln in 1860. He did not swerve from his Union principles during the war; was a member of the Constitutional Convention of 1868, and served on the committee on the bill of rights and other committees. Subsequently he represented his senatorial district in the General Assembly. In 1884 he established the *American Union* newspaper, still published, which reflects his political opinions, and sometimes his religious convictions. In 1890, he was a district supervisor for taking the United States census. He is remarkably intelligent, his intellect bright and clear, very robust physically, and possessing the progressive spirit and vigor of a man half his age. He enjoys the unquestioning confidence of the people of the large extent of territory in which he is known. Mr. Bowers was married in 1851 to Miss Christana— born in Franklin County in 1825—daughter of Ellis and Dorcas (Attaway) Cheek. Mr. Cheek was a native of South Carolina, a farmer, and came to

Georgia and settled in Franklin County about 1820. Of the children born to Mr. and Mrs. Bowers, six survive: Bunyan, Naomi, Pink, Ezra, Nehemiah, and Lois. He is particularly proud of his family, all of whom are strictly pious and none ever having taken a drink of intoxicating liquor. Himself and wife are devoted and working members of the Church of Christ. He is an ordained minister and goes about doing good and carrying the glad tidings of great joy, having worked in the ministry more than fifty years, and is one of the most entertaining talkers of that part of Georgia."

—Memoirs of Georgia, Vol. 1, 1895.

"UNCLE BILLY BOWERS."

Tender tribute to Rev. W. F. Bowers by his brother, John M. Bowers.

"On Tuesday, January 24, 1905, at 10 o'clock A. M., William Franklin Bowers died at his home here (Canon, Ga.), from an attack of paralysis that struck him on Sunday night previous.

"From the record found in the old family Bible, which we have before us, he was born November 23, 1825. This is no doubt correct, as we have often heard our father say that the Bible before us is the first Bible he ever owned. Uncle Billy, himself, was under the impression that he was born Christmas day, and often so stated it, but it is entirely probable that he was mistaken. We called Uncle Bill's attention to this old record not long before he died, and he said he did not know how he got the impression that he was born on Christmas day. We allude to this to try to correct this small matter among the relatives and friends.

"Judging from the tone of the press and universal expressions of eulogy that is being passed upon Uncle Billy since his death, it must be conceded he was the greatest and most useful man ever born and reared in our midst. He had the heart of a lion and of a lamb. He feared not man; but the cry of distress and suffering of the very poorest immediately melted him to tears, and he would hasten to their rescue at all hazards. There are hundreds of living witnesses to testify to this, and a thousand more dead.

"Uncle Billy had no royal line of ancestry to boast of, save his great-grandfather, Job Bowers, who shed his blood upon the altar of American freedom during the Revolutionary War.

"For the benefit of the many hundreds of Young Bowerses scattered over this country, we will put in cold and enduring type a matter of history never printed as we have any knowledge of, and but few living ones ever heard of it.

"In the dark days of the Revolutionary War, there lived a poor, honest man in Wilkes County—now Elbert—by the name of Job Bowers. The identical spot can not be pointed out, but it can not be over thirty or thirty-five miles from Canon, from the best we could learn from our father while he lived.

"This Job Bowers became a soldier in the Revolutionary War. He obtained a furlough to come home to see his family. On his arrival he found a little baby boy three or four days old. We could stop here and expatiate upon the joys of the meeting of those young parents, but we will have to desist, and leave every parent to work it out for themselves. When the sable curtain of night fell upon that joyous home—the very first night, the Tories came and ruthlessly tore away the husband and father and took him out below the house only a little way and murdered him. The young mother's heart is now torn asunder with grief that just a little while ago was so happy. The agonies of that mother's heart during the remaining drawn-out hours of that night will never be told by human tongue or described by pen. The little baby boy was her only company, while she knew full well the fate of husband and father cold in death near by.

"The mother and babe survived, and the babe was called William. This William grew to be a man—married and settled within eight miles of where we now write, and a substantial, honest and industrious citizen he was. His first-born was a boy, and they called him Job in honor of his grandfather whom the Tories murdered. This second Job was born August 31, 1803.

"Finally this second Job grew up and married and named his first-born William Franklin Bowers, who is the subject of this sketch.

"Our grandfather owned a few slaves, but said it was wrong, and that they ought to be freed. This made our father opposed to slavery, and he never owned a slave. Uncle Billy caught the same spirit, and he, too, never owned a slave.

"It seems that a love of the Union has been inherited by the descendants of this Job Bowers, who shed his blood as a victim for it, but in many cases that love seemed to weaken, especially in the dark and stormy days of secession. But not so with Uncle Billy, he loved the Union and he never did yield one inch of ground, even at the peril of his life. He was a man of convictions, and he never failed to stand bravely for those convictions.

"Religious Life

"Uncle Billy joined the Missionary Baptist Church early in life, and at once became an active worker in his church. He soon was set apart to the ministry and, we have been told, made a poor showing at the start, but by his indomitable will-power and perseverence, he soon worked his way up as an acceptable preacher.

"He became a very conspicuous figure in the Tugaloo Baptist Association, and was rapidly forging his way to the front ranks in that denomination when the war between the North and the South came. He loved the Union, and plead for it, and this caused the 'big guns' to turn the cold shoulder to him. Of course he felt this, but it only tended to spur him on to greater feats of heroism. He revolted, and had a strong and respectable following all over the country. His movement was called the Reform Church, and it grew, and began to take root far and near.

"After the war, politics were hot. Uncle Billy dived in in good earnest and was elected to the Convention of 1868 to draft a State Constitution. Later he was elected to the Senate. In connection with politics he caught on to the idea of developing the country, and became a great railroad man. He had as much to do in building the railroad from Toccoa to Elberton as any other one man, and perhaps more. When this road was built, he wanted a road from Bowersville to Hartwell. It was built against his personal interest, everybody said, as he owned pretty much all the town lots in Bowersville. In this connection, we may say, he died wanting a railroad from this place to Carnesville. He has spent about twelve or fifteen thousand dollars trying to get it.

"Some may think we have strayed from our subject, but we think not. We allude to these things to show one important sad fact, viz.: While Uncle Billy was doing these things his Reform Church scattered to the four winds. Is there not a lesson in this great man's life?

"We candidly believe that if Uncle Billy had pushed his church work for the past forty years, as he began it at the close of the war, it would have been the predominating church over a large portion of this part of the State.

"There is another thing worthy of note in the history of Uncle Billy. While he was always a busy man, for the past forty years he has made it a rule to call his family together every morning before breakfast, read a chapter, sing a song, and have prayer. He has told us that he had found this practice a sheet-anchor to him. Uncle Billy was a great believer in prayer, and was always willing to help answer his own prayers, a lesson many of us would do well to learn. He came as near returning good for evil as any man we ever knew. Whatever may have been his motive we do not pretend to say, but we do know that he was good to his enemies.

"Uncle Billy had some little petty faults of course, as all men have, but his goodness greatly overshadowed them all.

"Uncle Billy's house has been always one of plenty, and perhaps more people have been entertained there than any house in this country. The rich and influential have shared his hospitality; the poor have eaten at his table.

"Now Uncle Billy is gone, and no one will be missed more than he. He caused the building of the towns of Bowersville and Canon, and the citizens of these two towns keenly feel their loss.

"Uncle Billy and the writer differed on a few points of doctrine, but it

Job Bowers Old Home

was a friendly difference—we never ceased to love each other. Now he is gone and can not answer and I will not parade our little differences. We feel that it would be unmanly in us to do so.

"We heave a sigh and drop a tear, and journey on more lonely than before, to the same haven of rest that Uncle Billy has gone."

From the History of the Tugaloo Baptist Association, by Rev. J. F. Goode, we have the following account of William F. Bowers:

"William F. Bowers was perhaps the most widely known of any minister who ever was a member of the Tugaloo Association. He was a man of statewide reputation. He was a member of the Constitutional Convention in 1868. Upon his return home he was elected State Senator of his district, composed of the counties of Hart, Franklin and Habersham. The writer was well acquainted with the subject of this sketch, and was pleased to claim him as his friend. Anyone well acquainted with him would be impressed that he was a very conscientious man and a very devout Christian. He had the courage of his convictions under any and all circumstances. Having had the pleasure of hearing him preach one time only, if his discourse on that occasion was a fair sample of his ability in the pulpit, he would be considered a preacher far above the average. He was a man of wide information, of broad views, and far in advance of the age in which he lived. He was the possessor of a fine library, and to hear him talk on any subject, one would be convinced that he was a man of no ordinary mind. What year he entered the ministry, we do not know, and have no means of ascertaining.

"He was employed for some time as a missionary under the Domestic Mission Board. He was Clerk of the Association from 1861 to 1864; was pastor of Indian Creek, Poplar Springs and a number of churches now members of the Hebron Association. His departure from the Association on account of the ladies wearing jewelry, and more especially his violent opposition to Free Masonry, was referred to in the sketch of the life and ministry of John A. Davis. Now which led the other in this departure, the writer saith not, but there was certainly some leading done. We leave everyone to draw their own conclusions. He departed this life about 1906. Of this we are not certain, for we write from memory. (As a matter of fact, William F. Bowers died January 24, 1905.)

"His going off from the Association was a source of great grief to his brethren, who had been associated with him for so many years. They felt they had lost a wise counsellor from the deliberations of the body. The present efficient Moderator, Claude Bond, is a nephew of his."

Joseph Jackson

JOSEPH JACKSON was born December 2, 1799, died May 30, 1887, age 85 years. Buried in the cemetery at Shoal Creek Baptist Church, of which he had long been a member. His wife, Nancy Barton Jackson, sister to Rev. Henry Martin Barton, born October, 1807, died in 1858. She was also buried at Shoal Creek Church.

To Joseph Jackson and his wife, Nancy, were born seven sons: William, James, Thomas H., H. M. T., Joseph, W. B., and John L. Jackson; and three daughters: Mary A., Nancy, and Margaret.

Thomas H. married Nancy Swift; Joseph married Elvira A. Shirley; W. B. married Onah Lankford; John L. married Mary Frances Burton, daughter of Peter E. Burton.

Mary A. married Dr. William F. White; Nancy married John A. Sewell; and Margaret married James Wade.

Joseph Jackson was married a second time. His last wife was Louvicie Parker, daughter of John D. Parker.

Thomas H. Jackson was First Sergeant of Capt. Wm. R. Poole's Company, known as Company "H," organized at King's Bench July 15, 1861. Later was elected First Lieutenant.

Joseph Jackson's father was an Englishman, and his tall figure and finely formed face and forehead carried the well defined marks of his distinguished ancestors.

Some Reminiscences of Joseph Jackson

Mr. Jackson knew John C. Calhoun, South Carolina's favorite son, and the former home of Mr. Jackson was near the plantation of Calhoun, and in conversation with a representative of *The Hartwell Sun*, said that Calhoun took great interest in agriculture and spent much of his time, when not engaged in public service, on his farm personally superintending the details of farm work. He was accustomed to remain in the warmest weather through the entire day in the fields with his hands.

Pioneer Preachers

Mr. Jackson knew Cleveland, Frank Calloway and the Vandivers, and other pioneer preachers. Said that Calloway, in his opinion, the most remarkable of them all.

A Sparsely Settled Country

When Mr. Jackson located at the place where he made his home for the remainder of his life, the Humphreys were his neighbors who lived on the place owned by the Parkers and where they built the noted Parker Mills.

At that time there was no settlement between the place, later known as Parkertown and Carnesville.

Cherokee Indians

The Cherokee Indians were the nearest neighbors. They were peaceable and friendly. Game was abundant and the Indians lived and traded on furs and venison hams. When killing deer they usually took the hams only, leaving the balance of the carcass in the woods.

Wolves

These cunning and ferocious animals were plentiful, but gradually retired before the white man and his flocks, but when driven to the Currahee Mountain would often come down in gangs to Shoal Creek, taking the public road, kill a number of sheep or young cattle, and return to their far-off retreat the same night; showing their cunning instinct in getting their prey at a distance from their lair to evade detection.

Wild Cattle

There were a great many wild cattle in the range when Mr. Jackson was a boy. To protect their young from wolves they would form a ring at night by lying down in a circle, their horns pointing outward, and their young carefully herded in the center.

The Haynes Family

THE ancestors of the Haynes family emigrated from Wales and settled in Virginia and other parts of America. Many of them are named in Colonial wars, and there is a record of one Haynes who was Governor of Massachusetts for a period of six years.

Moses Haynes, a descendant of the Haynes family, was a soldier in the War of the Revolution, and some time after the war he moved from Virginia to Georgia and settled in what later became Elbert County, in the community in which Holly Springs Baptist Church was later established. He was given a large tract of land in consideration of his services in the war, and also obtained headright titles to other lands, making in all about 1,200 acres.

When Holly Springs Church was organized, he donated about three acres of land as a site for the church, and, perhaps, contributed the timber for the first church house which was built of logs, as most all churches were in those early days. The church was organized in 1796 and they worshiped there for forty years.

In 1836, seven years after Moses Haynes' death, about five acres was secured from his son, Thomas J. Haynes, for the present site located about one-half mile from the original site, for which five acres Thomas J. Haynes was paid $14.00, and who also gave about three acres in lieu of the three acres at the original site. Later about five acres were bought from the Daniel estate, formerly the Haynes place, for an addition to the new cemetery, making in the whole tract thirteen acres.

Moses Haynes was a member of the first Grand Jury in Elbert County, in 1790, the year the county was created—the year after George Washington was inaugurated the first President of the United States. Moses Haynes showed some of his capability by being chosen, not only as a Grand Juror, Justice of the Peace for years.

Some of the Haynes descendants have been members of the church since its organization—Asa J. Haynes being clerk for a number of years; Beecher Haynes, a deacon and regular attendant until death; his son, Clifford, still a member, besides the children and grandchildren of Milledge Haynes, among them Mrs. Lettie Mewborn and daughter, Miss Rose, who are still members. The church is now 136 years old.

Returning to the Haynes' history, Moses Haynes had nine children; four sons and five daughters. The sons' names were: Stephen, William, Moses, and Thomas J. Haynes. The daughters were: Nancy, Elizabeth, Polly, Sarah, and Jane.

Moses Haynes must have been a very successful business man, as he left much property, consisting of real estate, slaves and personal property to his children. His wife and his son, Thomas J. Haynes, were nominated in his will as his executors.

He died in 1829 and was buried in the cemetery at Holly Springs Church, now on the Hart County side of the line between Elbert and Hart counties. A marker furnished by the government was unveiled at his grave with appropriate exercises on Sunday, November 20, 1932, at which time a history of the Haynes family was given by Miss Delrey Adams, a great-great-granddaughter of Moses Haynes.

The inscription on the marker is as follows:

"MOSES HAYNES, REV. SOLDIER, 1829."

Thomas J. Haynes followed in the footsteps of his father in patriotism and was a soldier in the War of 1812.

He was at one time Sheriff of Elbert County, and at another time he was Tax Collector of Elbert County.

He married Lettie Duncan, one of the popular daughters of John Duncan—Leonard Rice, the grandfather of Mr. Peter Rice, also married one of the daughters—John Duncan, the father of Rev. Asa Duncan, was one of the brothers—making three families of that time—the Duncans, Rices, and Hayneses—brothers-in-law.

In 1818 Thomas J. Haynes bought from his father, Moses Haynes, 230 acres of land in the fork of Beaverdam Creek, including the Big Holly Springs, for $500.00.

The house now (1932) occupied by the Bradberry family was Thomas J. Haynes' store house. It was the only store for this territory at that time. He sent wagons and teams to Augusta for his goods. He accumulated wealth and had a large store, a two-story frame building for his home, with negro quarters extending from his store to his dwelling several hundred yards up the road.

His store was located on the old Red Hollow Road and was a stopping place for the people from the up country as they carried their apples, cabbage, chestnuts, potatoes and other field and garden products to Augusta to market, and also for the hog, cattle, geese and turkey drovers as they drove their livestock to market, and on the return trip from market.

Thomas J. Haynes and wife had eleven children: Sarah or Sallie, Thomas Jefferson, Henry, Frank, William D., James W., Moses, Milledge, Asa J., Lettie, and Mary, called Polly.

Sarah or Sallie, as she was called, never married—neither did Jeff nor Henry. Henry was killed in the War Between the States and was brought home in a metalic coffin to be buried at Holly Springs. His mother and family not knowing of his death till his body was at the door. Frank married Sallie Burns. Wm. D. married a Miss Ballenger. James W. married _____, and lived near Tallulah Falls. Moses married Linnie _____. Milledge married Nancy Brown. Lettie married William Bowers. Mary or Polly married James Allen. Asa J. married Elizabeth Clark.

John Milledge Haynes, fourth son of Thomas J. Haynes, born in 1809—named for John Milledge, a soldier of the Revolution, U. S. Senator, Governor of Georgia, and for whom Milledgeville was named—married Nancy Brown. He died February 1, 1891, at the age of 82 years, four months, and

22 days. He was in Captain Bowman's Company in the removal of the Cherokee Indians from Georgia in 1838, for which service he afterwards drew a pension. He served as Constable for fifty years, and made a faithful and efficient officer.

Mr. Haynes and his wife, Nancy, reared a large and respectable family of children. Their oldest son, Albert Haynes, was killed in the battle of Seven Pines, near Richmond, Va., in the War Between the States. Mrs. Lettie Mewborn and many grandchildren and great-grandchildren are still living. He is buried at Holly Springs Church.

Asa J. Haynes, son of Thomas J. Haynes, was born in 1816, and was 13 years old when his grandfather, Moses Haynes, died. He married Elizabeth Clark, daughter of Williamson and Patsey Clark. To this union were born ten (10) children—five sons and five daughters, viz.:

James W., who married, first, Eliza Rice; second, Mollie Johnson. Columbus, who married, first, Bettie Vaughn; second, Mollie Ginn. Calloway Beecher married Alice Whitaker. Asa Bartow married Mollie Threlkeld. William Henry was never married. Lettie Evelyn married Rev. W. J. Vickery. Sarah Ann married Wm. McCurry. Laura married Russell Hendrick. Mary Frances married Wm. Rice. Louisa married Col. T. L. Adams.

Asa J. Haynes was a well-read man, above the average in his day. At one time was a school teacher, Superintendent of Rehoboth Sunday School, Clerk of Rehoboth and Holly Springs churches, and Justice of the Peace for years. He lived to be 84 years of age, the last of his brothers and sisters. His wife, 82 years of age, died the same year, in 1900, after living together for 62 years.

His oldest son, Harrison Haynes, enlisted in Captain Devant's Company August 24, 1861, and after two and one-half years' service, contracted an illness, was granted a furlough and came home and died February 10, 1864, and was buried in the cemetery at Holly Springs.

James W. Haynes, commonly called Jim, son of Asa J. Haynes, enlisted in Capt. Devant's Company July 12, 1862—was appointed Third Corporal in 1864, captured at Deep Bottom, Va., August 16, 1864. Returning home he married Eliza Price and reared a large family of children. He died at the age of about 71 years.

C. C. Haynes, or Lum Haynes, was too young to go to the war, but he remained at home, helping to look after mother and the other children, among them Lettie Vickery and Sarah McCurry, whose husbands were also off to war.

Asa J. Haynes, himself, at the age of 49 years, was enlisted in Captain Barnett Johnson's Company, called Georgia Reserves, in May, 1864, and served at Andersonville, Ga. He was Third Lieutenant.

In every war in which the United States has engaged, unless it be the Spanish-American, this Haynes family has gone to the front.

In the World War Emmett Haynes, son of C. C. Haynes, went to France and saw active duty as a marine.

Asa Mewborn, another direct descendant, also went to France.

One child of Asa J. Haynes yet remains—a daughter—Mrs. L. G. Adams, the mother of four children, one of them the present Regent of the John Benson Chapter, Daughters of the American Revolution, Mrs. B. C. Teasley.

The Herndon Family History

WE HEREBY reproduce parts of an article in an old newspaper clipping entitled, "The Herndons of Elbert County."

"These sketches of Elbert County would not tell the story of Elbert well without mention of the Herndons—few families are as much a part of the county as they. Many Virginians came here and wrought well for a while and then passed on—the Herndons stayed and are here still. The antiquity of this name and family loses itself in the midst of nearly two thousand years. However it is not of the ancient glory of the race I wish to speak but coming nearer to the time of the Norman Conquest I will skim lightly over a few items of interest and then tell you about the Herndons of America. Armerial bearing of this family are, Arms: Argent, a heron volant azure between three escallops sable. The escallop shells were added to the shield 1193 when a Herndon journeyed to Palestine with Richard I. His escutcheon is carved on a stone gateway in the city of Rhodes. This arms is also found in stained glass in Lincoln's Inn Chapel London. The escallop shells was the emblem of pilgrims to the Holy Land, and became such a distinguished ensign that it was allowed by Pope Alexis to none but pilgrims of noble birth. The colors in the shield mean, Or, generosity. Argent, peace and sincerity. Sable, constancy. Azure, truth and loyalty. Whoever has known a Herndon will recognize the colors, and say the Herndons today are just the same Herndons they were more than a thousand years ago. The family traits have undergone very little, if any, change at all. *The Virginia Magazine of History* says: 'Among the names inscribed on the roll of Battle Abbey as having come into Britain with William the Conqueror 1066, is that Heiroun. He was the ancestor of Herons, as they were afterwards called, and which for centuries were very prominent in the affairs of their adopted country. One branch of the family, to distinguish it from the others, assumed the suffix "don," which means the "Herons on the hill." The name is very ancient both in England and France.'

"They were seated in Kent County as late as 18th Century, where Herndon Hall is still standing, but now the name is bourn only by the Virginia family and their descendants scattered all over America.

"Just before the middle of the 17th Century there came to the wilderness of the new world two young Englishmen, Benjamin and Thomas Herndon. Benjamin settled at what is now Providence, R. I., and Thomas, after spending a while in the Barbadoes, is said to have returned to England. Benjamin left numerous descendants, many of whom have been distinguished in politics, science, literature, and war. But it is of the Virginia line our sketch has to do.

"William Herndon married, in 1677, Catherine, youngest daughter of Edward Digges. Edward Digges was a son of Sir Dudley Digges, who was Governor of Virginia in 1655-1657, Auditor General 1670-1675. Sent to England as Colonial Agent. Settled on York River in Virginia 1650. His grave is at Belfield and his tombstone bears the shield of a crusader knight. Edward, the son of William and Catherine, married Mary Waller. Their son, William, married, first, Annie Drysdale, daughter of Hugh Drysdale,

Lieutenant Governor and Governor of Virginia; and second, Sarah Leftwich, daughter of a distinguished English and Colonial family. Their son, Edward, married Mary Gaines, daughter of James Gaines, a prominent Colonial family of Caroline and Orange (afterwards Culpepper) counties, Virginia. Their son, Benjamin, married Susan Ahart, daughter of Michael Ahart, of Culpepper County, Va. They came to Elbert County when Elbert County was still a wilderness, and their descendants who bear the name are here still.

"Benjamin died in 1805. A brother of Benjamin, Edward, married Nancy Rucker, daughter of Thomas Rucker, of Culpepper County, Va., and came to Elbert prior to 1805. They left descendants, among them the Browns, Whites and Adamses, but the name passed with Judge Dillard Herndon, who was born 1793 and died 1873 unmarried. The graves are on the hillside of the old homestead between Elberton and Ruckersville on what is called the James Edward Herndon Ford road (except the grave of Dillard; that one is in the old churchyard at Van's Creek Church at Ruckersville). Another brother, William, older than Benjamin, a soldier in the Revolution, when a slip of a lad came to Elbert County when Elbert was still a part of Wilkes. He returned to Virginia and married Mary Rucker, a sister of Nancy. He died in Culpepper County, Va. A carefully compiled list of the Herndons in the Revolution shows more than a score were there—nearly all officers. The records of the War of 1812 also are not lacking in Herndons, officers and privates—too many to list in a short sketch—and a Herndon was one of the last to die in the Alamo. Mr. Michael Herndon, of Elbert County, furnished eight sons to the cause of the Confederacy."

The sons of Michael Herndon were Benjamin, George, Thomas, John S., Edward, Michael and Franklin, and perhaps another whose name we do not have. The daughters were Elizabeth, Elmira, Margarett and Sarah.

Michael Herndon's home was in the neighborhood of Redwine Church, located on the west side and near Morea Creek, later known as the Agnew place.

Benjamin, son of Michael, married _____.

George, son of Michael, married _____,

Elizabeth, daughter of Michael, married Edward Brown.

Elmira, daughter of Michael, married Washington Brown.

Thomas, son of Michael, married _____.

John S. Herndon, son of Michael, married Susan Brown, daughter of Elbert Brown by first marriage. Elbert Brown's second wife was Mary McCurry, daughter of John and Sarah McCurry.

Michael, son of Michael, married Fannie Roberts, daughter of Moses Roberts.

Franklin was never married. Was killed in the War Between the States.

William married _____, daughter of Jackie Hulme first; second marriage to Sallie Clark, sister to Capt. W. M. Clark.

Margarett married Alphaus Brown first; second marriage to Barnett Johnson. Had one daughter, Cornelia, who married Jeff Dean.

Sarah Herndon married Thomas Cook first; second marriage to James Fleming.

John S. Herndon's Family

George E.; born July 2, 1855; married Catherine Brown, daughter of Jackson Brown; died January 1, 1920.

John Alpphus; born June ----, 1857; died ....; married Mollie Brown, daughter of Francis Brown.

Cornelia; born December, 1864; married Charles McCurry; died ....

Thomas Oscar; born April 22, 1867; married Sallie Jenkins, October 25, 1888.

Claud; born September 2, 1871; married Cloe Judd.

Clayton; born September 2, 1871; married Bessie Webb, daughter of Dr. C. A. Webb.

Flora; born June ----, 1869; married James A. W. Brown; died February 22, 1927.

Ida; born April 12, 1864; married S. L. Thornton.

Eula; born April 11, 1870; married T. Joe Rucker.

Captain John S. Herndon

Herndon Coat of Arms

"In the death of Capt. Herndon, a prominent landmark of Hart County has been removed.

"He was a good citizen—patriotic, public-spirited, progressive and liberal. A man of convictions—frank in their expression, and fearless in their advocacy and defense. True to his friends, generous to his neighbors, and liberal to the poor. He was an open-hearted, sunny-natured, genial gentleman—and his passing will be universally deplored.

"John S. Herndon was born near Elberton, Ga., October 5, 1825. His father, Michael Herndon, was a leading citizen of Elbert County. When quite a young man he was united in marriage to Miss Susan Ann Elizabeth Brown, a daughter of Elbert Brown, another prominent citizen of Elbert County. Shortly after their marriage they removed to Hart County and settled at the present family homestead.

"Captain Herndon made no mistake in the selection of a boon companion, and in the long years of their wedded life she was truly a noble wife and helpmate, and together they nurtured a large family of children of whom they had cause to be proud.

"For over forty years they resided at their fine old plantation home, and by industry and excellent financial management won a generous living and laid up a solid competency; and there is probably not a more popular country home in Hart County, nor one more noted for its generous hospitality.

"As an efficient officer in the Confederate Army, Capt. Herndon illustrated his patriotism and manhood upon the battlefield with bravery and distinction."

—Paragraphs from *The Sun*, issue June 8, 1900.

Capt. John S. Herndon died June 5, 1900, in his 75th year.

Tamar Escapes from the Indians

NOT long after the Revolution there lived on the banks of Coody's Creek, in the flat woods of what is now the county of Elbert, a poor but worthy man by the name of Mr. Richard Tyner. During his absence one day a party of Indians made an attack upon his home and Mrs. Tyner was killed, together with her youngest child, whose head was dashed against a tree. Another child was scalped and left for dead, while a third, whose name was Noah, succeeded, amidst the confusion, in escaping the notice of the Indians and crept into a hollow tree, which for many years afterwards was known by the name of Noah's Ark. An elder son of Mr. Tyner fled to the Savannah River and was pursued by some of the savages, but he effected his escape.

Mary and Tamar, two daughters, were carried by the Indians to Coweta Town, and here they remained for several years until an Indian trader named John Manack purchased Mary, who returned with him to the county of Elbert and became his wife. At another time he offered to purchase Tamar, but the Indians refused to sell her. The main employment of Tamar was to bring wood. One day an old Indian woman informed her that her captors, suspecting her of an effort to escape, had resolved to burn her alive. The feelings of the poor girl can be better imagined than described. She determined, if possible, upon immediate flight. The old woman obtained for her a canoe, well supplied with provisions, and gave her directions how to proceed down the Chattahoochee River. Bidding adieu to her benefactress, Tamar launched her canoe and commenced her perilous voyage down the stream. During the day she secreted herself amidst the thick swamps of the river, and at night pursued her course. She finally reached Appalachicola Bay, embarked on a vessel going eastward around the peninsula of Florida, and at last arrived in Savannah. With the assistance of some of the citizens she was enabled ere long to reach her home in Elbert, where she afterwards married a Mr. Hunt, and many of her descendants are still living in Georgia.

Tamar Tyner was born in 1760 and died in 1840. She married Major Moses Hunt, and they lived at the old homestead where Mr. Lev. S. Gaines now lives, and are buried there. Major Hunt owned a very large tract of land. He survived his wife, and met a very tragic death. When about 89 years old, feeble and nearly blind, he fell into the fireplace and his head was burned to a crisp. Very little information about him is preserved. He was a Revolutionary soldier and belonged to Major Dobbs' battalion in Elbert County.

Moses Hunt, son of James Hunt, Sr., was born June 18, 1760, married Tamar Tyner, died in 1840, as already stated.

To Moses Hunt and his wife, Tamar Tyner Hunt, were born the following children: Mary, born February 5, 1799, died April 17, 1863; married James Adams, born February 25, 1799, died April 18, 1877, in Elbert County, Ga. James; John S., married July 14, 1825, to Mary Gaines; Joel; Nancy, married to Lawrence M. Adams; Henry; Joshua; Richard; George.

Tamar Tyner Hunt was the great-grandmother of Mr. J. W. Thornton, of Nuberg community, and she and her husband, Moses Hunt, have a host of descendants in Elbert County, Hart County, and other parts of the country, viz.: Adamses, Hunts, Thorntons, and others.

The Hunt Family

Mary (Polly) Hunt, daughter of James and Jemima Carter Hunt, of Elbert County, Ga., was born 16th August, 1817, died 15th August, 1863, in Hartwell, Ga. Married, 16th August, 1838, William (Buck) Page, born 28th February, 1808, in Virginia, died 20th April, 1877, in Hartwell, Ga. William Page operated a farm in Elbert (now Hart) County before moving to Hartwell, Ga.

Their children:

1. W. J. Henry Page; born 11th September, 1837; died 26th June, 1899, in Hartwell, Ga. Never married. He entered the Confederate service and on 13th November, 1861, was stationed at Camp Kirkpatrick. On account of ill health was later sent home. He graduated from the University of Maryland 1st March, 1871. After his graduation he became a prominent physician of Hartwell.

2. James Richard Page; born 5th March, 1839; died 22nd February, 1865, a prisoner of war, in Elmira, N. Y. Never married.

3. Jemima Drucilla Page; born 6th August, 1840; died 31st May, 1909. Married, 16th February, 1864, James Wesley Williams; born 22nd December, 1839; died 21st August, 1923. James W. Williams entered the Confederate Army 13th July, 1861; was captured at the fall of Richmond, Va., March, 1865. Parolled 10th July, 1865. He was a prominent financier of Hartwell, Ga. (See Williams Family History.)

4. Mary E. Page; born 12th April, 1842; died 8th September, 1912. Married, 9th February, 1862, Ira J. Edwards. Ira J. Edwards served as a soldier in the Confederate Army. They lived in Hart County, Ga.

5. Martha Lucinda Page; born 30th May, 1845; died 1st February, 1920. Married, 1st January, 1867, William Henry Satterfield; born 11th April, 1842; died 17th May, 1880. He was a Confederate soldier. They resided in Hartwell, Ga.

6. Early Stephens Page; born 18th March, 1853; died July, 1925.

7. Alice Hunt Page; born 18th September, 1855; died 9th August, 1922, in Hartwell, Ga. Married, 30th March, 1882, Robert K. Vandiver.

8. George Jackson Page; born 28th May, 1858. Married, 2nd March, 1881, Amanda Thornton.

Noel Skelton

NOEL SKELTON settled on Lightwoodlog Creek some time prior to the War Between the States, and while the place was in Franklin County, Ga., which later was embraced in Hart County, said creek being the line between Elbert (formerly Wilkes) and Franklin counties up until the creation of Hart County, when, as a matter of course, it ceased to be a county line. His wife's name was Margarett; we do not know who she was before her marriage.

To Noel Skelton and his wife were born the following sons and daughters: Noel L., Hymer, W. J. W., and Vandiver Skelton; Anne, Mary, Millie, Nellie, Clarisa, and Rachael Skelton.

Noel L. Skelton married Eliza Pinson, daughter of Sterling Pinson. He died in the War Between the States.

Hymer Skelton married Fannie A. McCurley, daughter of Moses McCurley, on December 11, 1866.

W. J. W. Skelton married Mary Ann Walters, daughter of Abram Walters.

Vandiver met a tragic death, while yet a youth, by the falling of a tree on his father's farm.

Anne Skelton married Obadiah Cleveland, son of Reuben and Polly Cleveland. Mary married John Ashley Cleveland, brother to Obadiah. Millie married George W. McMullan. Nellie married Elias Vickery. Clarisa married Rev. J. T. W. Vernon. Rachael married O. M. Duncan.

During Noel Skelton's lifetime and while he lived at the above mentioned place, he owned and operated a grist mill on Lightwoodlog Creek. He owned a few slaves and carried on considerable farming operations.

He was awarded the contract and built the first court house at Hartwell, which was a wooden structure and was built as a temporary court house, as elsewhere mentioned.

On the old homestead is a family burying ground where Noel Skelton, his wife, and other members of the family are buried.

The inscription on the headstones at the graveyard are as follows:

"NOEL SKELTON DIED FEB. 4, 1863, AGE 66 YEARS."
"MARGRY SKELTON DIED JULY 10, 1879."
"GREN V. SKELTON DIED ----, 1840."

The name which appears to be Gren V. Skelton was a son of Noel Skelton, who was killed, as already mentioned.

The John McCurry Family History

ANGUS (1) McCURRY, SR., was born in Scotland, came to America with an expedition on the Flora McDonald ships, settled on the shores of North Carolina in 1774, and later removed to Elbert County, Ga. (now Hart County), where he became one of the first settlers of north Georgia on the Savannah River. Katherine McCurry is mentioned as the widow of Angus (1) McCurry, Sr., Revolutionary soldier, in the records at the office of the Ordinary in Elbert County. He received land grants for Revolutionary services, as follows: 65 acres on Powderbag Creek, 277 acres on Powderbag Creek, 276 acres on Lightwoodlog Creek, 300 acres on Cedar Creek, 490 acres in 1st District, Wayne County. Some of this land is still owned by descendants of Angus (1) McCurry, Sr.

Children of Angus (1) McCurry, Sr., and Katherine McCurry:

1. Margaret (2) McCurry. Married John McDonald. (Children: Nancy (3), Margaret (3), Rodrick (3) McDonald.)

2. Sarah (2) McCurry. Married John Gordon. (Children: Mary (3), Flora (3), Thomas (3), Margaret (3) McCurry, son of Daniel L. (2) McCurry.)

3. John (2) McCurry; born August, 1776. Married Sarah McCurry, first cousin, once removed. Both of them came from Virginia in a wagon in 1818.

4. Daniel L. (2) McCurry. Married _____.

5. Angus (2) McCurry, Jr. Married Elizabeth Davis, daughter of John Davis, Revolutionary soldier, and died about 1841.

On Sunday afternoon, November 13, 1932, the John Benson Chapter, Daughters of the American Revolution, unveiled a government marker to the memory of Angus (1) McCurry, Sr., Revolutionary soldier, who is buried in the old Mt. Zion Methodist Churchyard, about six miles east of Hartwell. He died, as will appear from his will, between 1836 and 1840. It is not known which church Angus (1) McCurry, Sr., and his family were members of, however, John (3) McCurry joined the Baptist denomination, since he married the daughter of a Baptist preacher. Some of his children were Baptists and some were Methodists. It is thought that Angus (1) McCurry, Sr., belonged to the Presbyterian denomination.

Angus (2) McCurry, Jr., (Augus (1) McCurry, Sr.), settled on Powderbag Creek, adding to the land inherited from his father. He married Elizabeth Davis, daughter of John Davis, Revolutionary soldier; died about 1841. Their children:

1. Lauchlin B. (3). 2. Neal M. (3). 3. Angus III (3). 4. James Alexander (3). 5. Mary (3), born November 14, 1802, died April 20, 1866; married Levi Masters. 6. Margaret (3). 7. Katherine (3); married _____ Johnson. 8. Flora M. Haynes. 9. Frances (3); married Daniel. 10. Elizabeth (3). 11. John (3).

John (3) McCurry (Angus, Jr. (2); Angus, Sr. (1)); born 1804. Married Nancy Goss, daughter of Rev. Horatio Goss. They settled on the old McCurry homestead, located on Powderbag Creek, the original land grant.

Here they reared a large family, some of whom have filled places of prominence in this section of the State. Their children:

1. Mary Elizabeth (4). Married James Herring.
2. Sarah Katherine (4). Married, first, Stephenson; second, Archibald H. Parks, August 28, 1867.
3. Eliza Frances (4). Married Isham Burriss.
4. Louis A. Antionette (4). Married, March 8, 1860, James D. Rice.
5. John Benjamin (4). Died in service during the War Between the States.
6. Horatio James (4). Died in service during the War Between the States.
7. Judge Angus Loftin (4) (John (3); Angus Jr. (2); Angus, Sr. (1)). Married, April 4, 1867, Mrs. Fannie E. Walters, widow of Judge P. Walters, who, before first marriage, was Fannie E. Richardson. When the War Between the States came on, Angus Loftin volunteered and entered the same on the 10th of March, 1862, as a soldier in Capt. John G. McMullan's Company. He was wounded in the battle of Chickamauga on the 19th of September, 1863. He held the office of Tax Receiver of Hart County for several consecutive years; also the office of Ordinary for two terms. He died at his residence in Hartwell, Ga., February 26, 1913, and was buried in the cemetery of Sardis Baptist Church, of which church he was a member.
8. William Hamilton (4) McCurry, D.D.S. (John (3); Angus, Jr. (2); Angus, Sr. (1)). Married Miss Susan Oglesby.
9. Alexander Robert (4) McCurry (John (3); Angus, Jr. (2); Angus, Sr. (1)); born November 30, 1849. Married, July 18, 1882, Ella Neese, daughter of Rev. J. C. Neese. Robert McCurry was a merchant many years in Hartwell, Ga. He died December 9, 1929, and was buried in the Hartwell Cemetery beside his wife, who preceded him to the grave many years ago.
10. Asbury Goss (4) McCurry (John (3); Angus, Jr. (2); Angus, Sr. (1)); born February 17, 1852. Was a distinguished lawyer as well as a leader in the Democratic party. He married, October 16, 1876, Fannie Norton Benson, daughter of Hartwell's pioneer merchant, John B. Benson and his wife, Elizabeth Norton. Their children:

1. Julian B. (5) McCurry; born April 22, 1879. Was an outstanding lawyer and statesman, having been honored by being elected to both legislative bodies of Georgia. He also served as Secretary to Governor Thomas Hardwick. He married, June 7, 1911, Richmond Walton, of Madison, Ga., who is the present State Regent of the Daughters of the American Revolution of Georgia.
2. Stella (5); died young.
3. Eloise Norton (5). Married Judge Walter Lee Hodges, a distinguished son of Hart County. Their daughter, Frances Elizabeth (6), married Albert F. Vaughan, Jr., of Greenville, S. C.

Dr. William Hamilton (4) McCurry (John (3); Angus, Jr. (2); Angus, Sr. (1)); born October 22, 1845, at the old McCurry homestead near the Savannah River, granted to Angus (1) McCurry, Sr., for Revolutionary service. William H. McCurry was a Confederate soldier during the War Between the States; was captured and imprisoned for six months at Rock Island, Ill., where he was released after the surrender of Lee.

Following the war he studied dentistry in Anderson, S. C., later graduating from Vanderbilt University, Nashville, Tenn., and had a wide reputation as a dentist, skilled in his profession. He married, October 15, 1872, Susan Butler Oglesby; born November 21, 1851; died in Elberton, Ga., March 26, 1926, and is buried beside her husband in Elmhurst Cemetery, who preceded her to the grave July 11, 1911. After their marriage they lived for a number of years in Hartwell, where they reared a large family, later removing to Elberton, Ga., where they spent the rest of their lives.

Susan Oglesby was a member of one of Elbert County's most prominent families, being the daughter of Adkins Oglesby; born October 10, 1810, in Elbert County, near old Stinchcomb Methodist Church. Married, August 19, 1841. Sarah Katherine Baird, born June 13, 1814, of Danburg, Elbert County, Ga. Children of William H. (4) and Susan Oglesby McCurry:

1. Luther (5) McCurry; died young.
2. Katherine (5) McCurry. Married William A. Peek. (Children: 1. Fone (6); married William Erskine Gallant. (Children: 1. William Erskine (7) Gallant, Jr. 2. Margaret Helen (7) Gallant. 3. Robert (7) Gallant.) 2. Helen (6); died young. 3. Evelyn (6) Peek.)
3. Lilly (5) McCurry. Married Stanley Matthews.
4. Nan (5) McCurry. Married George M. Carithers. (Children: 1. Amy (6). 2. Hildah (6). 3. Cornelius Whelchel (6).)
5. John Adkins (5) McCurry. Married Lucy Earl, descendant of the Earl family of historic Andersonville, S. C. (Children: 1. John Earl (6). 2. Eugene (6). 3. Thomas (6).)
6. Carl Oglesby (5) McCurry. Married Mrs. Pearl Vaughan. (Children: 1. Barbara (6). 2. William Hamilton (6) McCurry.)
7. Amy Lois (5) McCurry. Married Charles Hamilton Dodson. (Children: 1. William Hamilton (6); died young. 2. Helen Peek (6).)
8. William Baird (5) McCurry. Married, June 15, 1916, May Lilly Teasley. (1. Elizabeth Sadler (6) McCurry.)
9. Madge (5) McCurry. Married Mitchell Augustus Von Stein, of Richmond, Va. (1. William Augustus (6) Von Stein.)

Nancy, the wife of John (3) McCurry, was descended from the following:

Benjamin (1) Goss; died November 11, 1813. Married, April 14, 1764, Elizabeth Hamilton; born May 12, 1743, of Scotch descent; died May 3, 1815. They resided in Buckingham County, Va., until about 1831, when they, with most of their children, removed to Elbert County, Ga.

Rev. Horatio James (2) Goss, Baptist preacher, was born in Virginia October 10, 1788. Married, first, November 27, 1806, Elizabeth Roebuck; born September 17, 1788. Their daughter, Nancy (3) Goss, married John (3) McCurry.

Rev. Horatio James Goss married, second, Mrs. Ann Deadwyler Bradley, mother of Jeptha Bradley.

William Dooly

WE HAVE no record of the ancestry of William Dooly and his wife, Elizabeth. He obtained a large body of land of 850 acres in Elbert (later Hart) County adjoining the lands of Col. Richard Durrett, Sinclair McMullan, John McCurry, and others, located along the Savannah River, including an island of about sixty acres at or near the head of McDonald's Shoals.

He owned a number of slaves and engaged in farming, and was what might have been called a "planter," due to the size of his plantation and extensive farming operations. Besides the place on the river, he owned considerable other lands in the county, and also in South Carolina.

He operated pole boats on the Savannah River, transporting cotton and other produce to Augusta, and perhaps other markets, and merchandise on the return trips.

He owned a mill on a prong of Powderbag Creek; also the ferry on the Savannah River, known as Dooly's Ferry, where the old Holly Springs road crossed, leading out of South Carolina into Georgia, afterwards known as Craft's Ferry, Captain J. F. Craft later obtaining possession of the place.

He was what was known as a local Methodist preacher; was prominent in financial, political, social and religious affairs.

When Hart County was created his place was included in the new county, and in laying out the militia districts, the district including his home was called Dooly's District, which name it retained on up until the year 1861, when the court ground was established at Lodwick Alford's, when the name was changed to Alford's District.

The children of William Dooly and wife, Elizabeth, were as follows:

Polly Dooly, who married Barnabas Barron, February 17, 1820.

Nancy J. Dooly married Joseph M. Brantley, March 18, 1823, and after the death of Brantley she married Moses Hutchenson.

Allen D. Dooly married Letty M. Brantley, April 22, 1824, and after the death of Allen D. Dooly, his widow, Letty, married Lewis Bobo, July 7, 1829.

William W. Dooly married Mary Brantley, July 5, 1827.

Mitchell N. Dooly married Katherine Brantley, November 11, 1830.

Sarah Ann Dooly married William H. Crawford, August 20, 1832.

Elizabeth A. Dooly married Leroy Crawford, December 13, 1832.

Barnabas J. Dooly married, name and date not known.

Frances L. Dooly married Van D. Gary, February 9, 1826.

Katherine Dooly married Lewis W. Stowers, date not known.

William Dooly in his will, besides his children, makes bequests to his granddaughters, Sarepta Jane Crawford and Elizabeth Gaines, and to his grandsons, William D. Barron, Rufus Barron, and Hamilton Barron, and two dollars each to his sons-in-law, Barnabas Barron, Moses Hutchenson, Leroy K. Crawford, and William H. Crawford.

In his will he nominated William W., Mitchell N., and Barnabas J. Dooly executors.

It appears that two of his sons, Mitchell N. and Barnabas J. Dooly, came into possession of his home place, where they lived perhaps until death.

Mitchell N. Dooly lived near the ferry on the river and Barnabas J. Dooly lived at the crossroads at the place now occupied by L. A. Chamble.

Barnabas Barron

BARNABAS BARRON lived in Elbert (later Hart) County, at or near where the Stephenson's Ferry and Ruckersville roads cross, which is now in Smith's District, Hart County.

He owned a large tract of land, a number of slaves, kept a store and post office, the name of the post office we have not as yet learned. At one time Mr. Barron had in his employ a Mr. Wiley as overseer and general manager of the farm, store and post office.

The place later came into the possession of Elijah Chapman, who sold it to James W. Smith, who in turn sold a portion of it to Jink Curry, colored, embracing the old homestead of Barnabas Barron.

Barnabas Barron was a Justice of the Peace in and for the militia district in which he lived, and when Hart County was created his place was included in the new county, and he perhaps retained the office of Justice of the Peace and officiated as such in Smith's District, as was true in other instances where the residence of the Justices of the Peace were included in the new county they retained their office and acted as such for the district in which their residence was included in the new county. He was commonly referred to as "Squire Barnes," however the correct name was Barron.

Besides the store and post office, there was also a voting precinct, Justice's court ground, muster ground, and perhaps, as was common in those days, intoxicating liquors were sold at the place as at most all public places, and the people used to assemble there and engage in horse racing, foot racing, gander pullings, town ball, as it was called, similar to baseball of the present time, and such other sports as were common at the time.

According to tradition, Mr. Barron was a native of England and came direct to this part of America, and later two of his brothers, Thomas and Onias, came from England, landing at Savannah, to visit their brother, and after a month's stay returned to England.

In the same story it is related that Barnabas Barron was a soldier in the War of 1812, and fought under General Jackson in the famous battle at New Orleans, and later, in 1838, helped to remove the Cherokee Indians from Georgia to their western reservation.

Several years ago there was a report circulated in this country to the effect that there was a large estate in England awaiting distribution among the descendants of a generation of Barrons in North America, and that the Barrons in Virginia and Texas had made application, but failed to prove that they were descendants of the Barron that left the fortune. Later a similar report was circulated and some of the descendants of Barnabas Barron made more or less investigation, but so far as we know nothing came of it.

It was perhaps like other reputed estates said to be waiting for distribution among the descendants of men of colossal fortunes who died in England and other countries, which upon investigation have proven to be a deception and nothing more than a scheme of designing individuals or concerns to extort money from the unsuspecting.

The public road that leads by the place, now known as the Cotton Belt Route, was in the days of the Civil War, and perhaps before, a stagecoach route conveying passengers and mail to the different post offices from Anderson, S. C., to Lexington, Ga., crossing the Savannah River at Stephenson's Ferry, later Parks' Ferry, near where the Smith & McGee Bridge spans the river.

The approach of the stage was heralded by the sound of a clarion or bugle, which was notice to the people in waiting that they might take notice and govern themselves accordingly. The stage made regular trips between Anderson and Lexington, returning over the same route every other day. Mr. Barron's place was a relay station on the route where the horses were changed.

Barnabas Barron married Polly Dooly, a daughter of William Dooly, February 17, 1820, and to them were born the following children: Sons—James, William D., Rufus F., C. Hamilton, and Sanford C. Barron; and daughters—Elizabeth and Frances.

James Barron was a soldier in the War Between the States, in the services of which he enlisted as First Sergeant in Capt. D. G. Johnson's Company, May 25, 1864.

William D. Barron enlisted in Capt. J. H. Skelton's Company, March 4, 1862, and died soon after reaching home from the war.

Rufus F. Barron enlisted in Captain J. G. McMullan's Company, March 4, 1862.

C. Hamilton Barron was Coroner of Hart County in 1864-1865. He at one time owned the mill on Big Lightwoodlog Creek where Samuel Hymer once had a sawmill. The mill was later owned by Mr. T. J. Linder, and still later known as Scott's Mill.

Sanford C. Barnes married Rosee E. Phillips, daughter of Kintchen Phillips, August 7, 1856. He at one time taught school at King's Bench, and later moved to Alabama.

Elizabeth Barron married James B. Gaines.

Frances Barron married William J. Shiflet.

Barnabas Barron was more than once married, as in his will he makes a bequest to his wife, Lucy.

Barnabas Barron, in his will, makes bequests to his wife, Lucy, and to his sons, James, Rufus F., C. H., and Sanford C. Barnes, and to the children of William D. Barron, his son, and to the children of Elizabeth Gaines, widow of James B. Gaines, and to the children of Frances, widow of William J. Shiflet.

C. H. and S. C. Barron are nominated in his will as executors.

A Jug Factory

Not far from the Barnabas Barron place, just described, was a kaolin mine on the lands of Elijah Gunter, who constructed a factory for the purpose of making jugs, jars, churns, cups and saucers, and other vessels.

The vessels were moulded by the potter into just the shape desired, and while yet soft, the name "Gunter" was scrawled upon each vessel, after which they were burned in a kiln or furnace, after which they were glazed and were then ready for sale.

We remember, years ago, to have seen one of the jugs, and there are, perhaps, many of the vessels today scattered around over the country bearing the name "Gunter."

The deposit of kaolin is perhaps inexhaustible and in the future may be further developed.

Moses Ayers

MOSES AYERS was born at Snowdon, Wales, 1747. Came first to Virginia, and later to the Free State of Franklin, which later became North Carolina.

While a citizen of Virginia, he fought in the French and Indian War under George Washington, who was an officer under General Braddock, of the famous "Braddock Defeat." Was in the battle of Pittsburg.

Later fought in the War of the Revolution and was in the battle of King's Mountain, and was present at the surrender of Cornwallis at Yorktown, Va.

After the War of the Revolution he moved from North Carolina to Georgia and settled in the Reed Creek community, Franklin (now Hart) County.

Was several times married. His last wife was Abigail Payne, a half-breed Indian of the Cherokees.

Had quite a number of children by his last marriage, and also some by former marriages.

He was the father of Jeremiah Ayers, who settled and lived at the foot of Dick's Hill in Habersham County; his old house built of logs by the assistance of the Indians is still standing, and near by is the family burying ground where he is buried.

When the Air Line Railroad, later known as the Southern, was built, a small village and station near his old home was named Ayersville.

Moses Ayers was possibly the forefather of the Ayers families in Hart, Franklin, Banks, Habersham and other adjoining parts of the country.

Moses Ayers was the father of Jedidiah Ayers, a man of considerable note in his day, who lived in the Reed Creek section near where his father settled and lived.

Jedidiah Ayers was a large land owner, also owned several slaves, engaged in farming, operated a sawmill on Reed Creek near a hundred years ago, and in some of the old houses in the community may yet be seen building material which was sawed at this old mill in the long ago. He also had a horse gin on his farm near his residence. Was Justice of the Peace in Reed Creek District for a number of years and perhaps held said office while the territory was embraced in Franklin County before Hart County was created. One incident of note in connection with his official acts was the swearing into office the Judges of the Inferior Court of Hart County, who, after their election, were required to take and subscribe an oath of office before an officer qualified to administer oaths.

Jedidiah Ayers lived to be over 90 years of age. He is buried in the old family graveyard near his old homestead.

Many of the descendants of Moses Ayers have been and are men of distinction in various ways.

Notably, among others, is the name of Dr. W. T. Ayers, who spent twenty-five years of his life as a missionary and physician in China, and whose brother, Sanford M. Ayers, is a prominent citizen of Franklin County, always active in the affairs of his church and in all movements for the betterment and promotion of his town, county and State. He has been connected in various business enterprises in Carnesville, his home town. He was the last Pension Commissioner of Georgia.

Sanford M. and his brother, Dr. W. T. Ayers, if we have been correctly informed, are grandsons of Jeremiah and great-grandsons of Moses Ayers.

Moses and his wife are buried at the original site of Reed Creek Church, whose graves have of late been marked with appropriate markers, purchased with funds of a general donation taken up at an Ayers family reunion held at Dick's Hill a few years ago. The inscription on the marker of Moses' grave is: "Moses Ayers, 1747-1837, Age 90."

Major William McLeard

MAJOR WILLIAM McLEARD, of Scotch descent, was born in North Carolina March 14, 1792, and died March 14, 1875, at the age of 83 years. It is a noticeable coincidence of his birth and death, both occurring on the same day of the same month.

He served as a soldier in the War of 1812, and the title of Major may have been obtained while in the service, though perhaps it is more likely that he obtained the title while serving as an officer in the militia of his State.

As to his name, it appears it was originally McLeard and in later years he dropped the Mc and assumed the name of Leard. It is a matter of history that many years after the War of 1812, when Congress passed the act granting pensions to the soldiers of the War of 1812, he had Uncle "Billy" Bowers to make out and file his claim with the authorities at Washington, D. C., having signed his name as usual, Wm. Leard. Soon his application was returned with the notation that there was no such a name found on the roster of the soldiers of the War of 1812.

After puzzling over the matter, he called to memory the fact that in his younger days he went by the name of McLeard, and later dropped the Mc. He then signed the Mc to his application, accompanied by the foregoing explanation and his claim was promptly granted. At the time of this occurrence there were some discussion as to his nationality; also, as to the correct spelling of the name, which never was agreed upon. The spelling of the name "Lard" was pretty well eliminated at this time.

The name has been spelled Lard, Laird, and Leard, the last becoming more generally adopted and used by his descendants.

He married Elvey Rushing, of North Carolina, date of marriage not known. She lived to be 92 years old.

To William McLeard and his wife, Elvey, were born nine sons: James W., Jesse, Dixon, Wm. J., Albert, Caswell, Jackson, Alfred and David; and three daughters: Mary, Nancy and Harriett. There were two other children born to them, but died in infancy.

MAJOR WILLIAM McLEARD

Most of this family of boys were noted for their physical ability and strength, and had a reputation of killing more deer and other game with rocks than the other hunters who had guns.

Mr. Albert J. Owens, a grandson of Major McLeard, says that he used to listen and enjoy the stories told by his grandfather of his deer and wild turkey hunting, and his travels to western North Carolina and Tennessee, and his trips to Augusta, Ga., then, in his younger days, the nearest market for all this adjoining country.

He removed from North Carolina to Franklin (now Hart) County, Ga., and located in the Reed Creek community near Tugaloo River. Later moved to the place which in later years was known as the William Hilliard (a noted cotton farm) place, adjoining lands of Job Bowers. He sold this place, or perhaps exchanged it with Job Bowers for 100 acres located near Cannon Church, where he lived the remainder of his life. By trade he was a hatter and followed his trade at the last mentioned place.

He is buried at Cannon Church, his grave marked by a marble monument with the inscription: "Maj. Wm. McLeard, March 14, 1792, March 14, 1875."

James W. Leard, son of Maj. Leard, married Mary O'Barr, a daughter of Col. William O'Barr, and lived on Reed Creek, Hart County, Ga., where he owned a grist mill, cotton gin, thresher and other machinery, and also engaged in farming. His children were: Polk, Dallas, John, Luther, Thomas; and one daughter, Martha, who married Monroe Cleveland.

Polk was a soldier in the War Between the States, and was killed probably in the battle of Chickamauga; the shell that killed him also killed Charles Roe, father of John S. Roe, who has recently died.

Jesse married a McDougle in or near the Reed Creek settlement; moved to Texas before the Civil War.

Dixon, when grown, went to Arkansas and married there, and became a Baptist preacher.

William J., before going to North Carolina, married Samantha Phillips. He served in the Confederate Army, and was wounded four times in the battle of the Wilderness.

Jackson married a Smith, and he and his family moved to Alabama at the beginning of the war, where shortly after the war he died, leaving several descendants.

Alfred and David went to Tennessee in 1863. David was never heard from after leaving. Alfred was heard from after his death, in 1878, through his son, Byron. He married, after the war, in Tennessee and took up the profession of school teaching.

Caswell married Lonie Stiefle, and enlisted in the service of the Civil War on the Confederate side. He joined Company "D," 37th Georgia Regiment, under Captain John G. McMullan, March 4, 1862. Captured at Hoover's Gap, Tenn., June 24, 1863. Died at Fort Delaware, Del., Prison, 1863, of smallpox. Was the father of Hon. Jones R. Leard, of Hartwell, Ga.

Albert married Nancy Smith, daughter of Betsy Smith, who was a daughter of William Bowers and sister to Job Bowers.

Mary married William Owens, Nancy Married James Owens, and Harriett married Robert W. Massey.

John Gordon, Esquire

JOHN GORDON, or perhaps his full name was John B. Gordon, and familiarly known as Squire John Gordon, was born in northern Ireland, to which his parents had migrated from southern Ireland some years before the time of the insurrection in Scotland. He came from northern Ireland to Virginia when he was about twenty-one years old, and later, about 1840, came from Virginia to Georgia and located in what is now Hart County, formerly Elbert, near the Savannah River, and bought a tract of land for seventy-five cents per acre.

The place is yet known as the Gordon place, which was sold in 1871 by Miss Sarah M. Gordon to Dr. J. L. Turner for $1,500. In the division of the estate of Dr. J. L. Turner the place became the property of his daughter, Mrs. A. J. McMullan, and in the division of her estate, it became the property of her daughter, Mrs. C. W. Rice, to whom it still belongs, containing 194 acres.

John Gordon was related to the Johnsons, McCurrys and other Scotch families who came to Georgia from Virginia, as told elsewhere in these pages.

Squire Gordon was a very devout member of the Associated Reformed Presbyterian Church, and reared a very fine and interesting family of sons and daughters.

We have never learned who Mr. Gordon married. His wife's given name was Sarah, and to him and his wife were born the following children, and there may have been others that we have not learned about.

The sons were Thomas, Gilbert, Neal, John, Jr., Angus and Robert I. Gordon. The daughters were Mary, Flora, Eleanor and Sarah M. Gordon.

It is said of the sons of John Gordon, that they were so ambitious that they walked from the Gordon home, after crossing the Savannah River, to Generostee Presbyterian Church, in South Carolina, every Sunday, a distance of about seven miles, and when they wanted to go to college they had to go to Ohio by stagecoach, there being but few railroads in those days, and no colleges in the South.

Thomas Gordon moved to Kentucky and lived out several miles from Lexington, where he engaged for a part of the time in farming and cultivated a variety of crops, consisting of apples, tobacco, hay, etc., in the bluegrass region of Kentucky.

Gilbert Gordon was a Presbyterian preacher in Florida. Neal Gordon was head of the Gordon School of Lexington, Ky., John Gordon, Jr., was a business man of Louisville, Ky., Angus died and is buried at the old Gordon home, his grave marked by a tombstone with the inscription: "Angus Gordon, Born Aug. 1, 1825, Died Oct. 14, 1846, Son of John and Sarah Gordon."

Robert I. Gordon studied law and practiced in Hartwell, being one of the first lawyers of the place. He bought a small portion of Lot No. 44 in the original plan of the town of Hartwell, containing 12 feet front on Franklin Street, and running back 30 feet parallel with Elbert Street, on which he built a small wooden building as his law office, which was later used as a shoe shop, and still later by Dr. W. H. Page as an office. He was a member of the Board of School Commissioners at one time.

When Capt. Devant's Company, known as Company "B," was organized, June 9, 1861, he enlisted in the service and was Second Lieutenant. Later promoted to First Lieutenant in May, 1862. Died September 18, 1862, at ―――――.

The daughter, Mary, married Rev. I. H. Goss; and Flora married Rev. Benjamin Goss, a brother to I. H. Goss.

Eleanor married William A. Lewis, father of Gilbert and Major J. Lewis. Gilbert Lewis died in Kentucky. Major J. Lewis is still living.

Eleanor J. Lewis is buried in the family graveyard at the old Gordon home, with the following inscription on the tombstone:

"ELEANOR J. LEWIS, CONSORT OF
WM. A. LEWIS, ESQ.,
BORN SEPT. 9, 1833, DIED NOVEMBER 28, 1868."

Sarah Margarett, called Maggie, was never married. She followed teaching for a portion of her life, and died at Bowman, Ga., where, presumably, she is buried.

The father and mother of John Gordon came over to this country from northern Ireland when they were very old and lived with their son, John, in a little cabin in the yard of the Gordon home.

They talked and sang in the original Irish language.

Hon. Francis G. Stowers

HON. F. G. STOWERS was a son of Capt. Thomas Stowers, who lived at the ferry on Savannah River, known as Stowers' Ferry, formerly Brown's Ferry, and which was later sold by Capt. Thomas Stowers' heirs to John F. Sadler.

We have no date of the birth of F. G. Stowers. He married Miss Mary Elizabeth Gaines, no date of marriage known.

Mr. Stowers settled at what is now so well known as the Stowers place on the Bankhead Highway, formerly Brown's Ferry road, five miles east of the town of Hartwell.

He had erected a large and well arranged home, artistically designed and built by expert architects, and at the time was the most magnificent home in that portion of the county, located on a fine plateau of ground, shaded by stately oaks, commanding a fine view of the outlying country, and is today in a remarkably fine state of preservation.

It was the original site of the Oak Bower Post Office on the star mail route from Athens, Ga., to Anderson, S. C., and whether the post office was named in keeping with the location or not, the name very appropriately corresponds with the location. The post office was later moved about a mile up the road towards Hartwell to Mr. Lodwick Alford's place and still retained the name, Oak Bower, now long since discontinued. Still further up the road for another mile there is today the Oak Bower Baptist Church, perpetuating the original name of Oak Bower.

Mr. Stowers owned a large farm and several slaves before the Civil War, and engaged in farming. He also owned and operated a mill and gin on Gum

Branch in connection with his farm, and besides his other enterprises he was engaged in boating on the Savannah River in the transportation of cotton to Augusta, Ga., and merchandise upon the return trips.

Hon. F. G. Stowers was State Senator in the Georgia Legislature from Hart County in the years 1859-60.

To Mr. Stowers and his wife were born three sons: John, James Benjamin and M. Columbus Stowers.

John Stowers married a daughter of Larmarcus Carter. He and his wife are buried in the family graveyard at the Stowers place. James Benjamin and M. Columbus Stowers both died in Elbert County several years ago, where they had made their homes.

The daughters born to Mr. Stowers and wife were: Sallie, Mary Ann, Eliza and Fannie.

Eliza died when quite young. Sallie and Mary Ann died later, unmarried.

Fannie married James M. Bailey and died in Texas, where she had moved many years ago.

Mr. Stowers was at one time a man of considerable wealth for his day, and his family were aristocratic and of high social standing. One of his daughters, Miss Sallie, attended school at Lucy Cobb Institute at Athens, Ga., a select school for young women, and in those days it was only the wealthy that could afford to send their daughters there to be educated.

Mr. Stowers was a Mason, and when he died in 1870 was buried with the honors of the order.

His wife died several years later.

Mr. Stowers and wife and the other members of his family, John and wife, Sallie, Mary Ann and Eliza, are all buried in the family graveyard at the old Stowers home, their graves marked by unlettered stones.

This burying ground is now abandoned and neglected, and to add to the marring conditions of the place, the beautiful cedars set out by loving hands at the graves have of recent years been ruthlessly cleared away.

Hon. F. G. Stowers Home

The Peek Family

THE Peaks are of English descent, and the family can be traced back as far as the year 1284, to the reign of Edward I, and the conquest of Wales.

In 1598, in the reign of Elizabeth, we find the grant of their Coat of Arms. Sir Robert Peak was with Charles I in the Battle Naseby, and Major Thomas Peak in the Cavalry Services of Prince Rupert, nephew of the King. We find Sir John Peak, Lord Mayor of London in 1667, and Sir William Peak filling that office in 1668.

Though staunch Royalists and Churchmen, they doubted the right of the King to rule the Church as well as State; and becoming disgusted with the revolution, the younger members began to emigrate to America.

The earliest known emigrant was Robert Peak, who came to Virginia in the Ship, Margaret; and John, in 1623, aged 23 years, settled in James City County. He was granted 1,600 acres of land in James City County for the transportation of thirty-two persons into the Colony of Virginia.

The Land Patent Books in the Richmond, Va., Land Office, from 1623 to 1666, however, shows that the following Peak immigrants came to Virginia from England between the above dates: Thomas Peak to Accomack County, 1635; Matthew Peak to Accomack County, 1636; Thomas Peak to Charles City County, 1642; William Peake to Northern Neck, Va., 1643; and John Peake in 1652.

To which one of these men the Hart County Peeks descended we are not sure, but it points to Robert, because he patented or bought land all the way from James City County to Pittsylvania County, from where we have a direct line. George Peek, Pittsylvania County, Va., although an old man, furnished supplies and guns to the Revolutionary War. He had several children. Among them was William, who also fought in the Revolution. William's wife was Miss Elizabeth Shockley.

William moved from Virginia to Buncombe County, N. C., about 1788. His children were: David, James, Jesse, George, William, Zachariah, Ruth, Judy and Lizzie.

The William of this family married Miss Isabella Redmond and twelve boys and one girl were born to them, namely: George, Lewis, Garrett, Stephen, John, Minerva, William, Jesse, Osborne, Zack, Levi, Alfred—one boy died young.

This family was divided during the War Between the States, some fighting for the South and some for the North.

At the close of the war, John, William, Zach, and Levi, with their families and old father, William, moved to Hart County, Ga.

All except Zack married in North Carolina; John to Mary Woodson, William to Julia Profitt, Levi to Elizabeth de Board. John always lived in Hartwell, where he raised three children, namely: Dr. Woodson Peek, S. Walker Peek, and Mrs. T. J. Linder.

William, Zack and Levi bought land six miles from Hartwell on Powderbag Creek, where they raised large families. William's children were: Mary,

Janie, Anna, Addie, William, George, Augustus, and Lula. Levi's children were: Zach, James, Charles, Hattie, Harley, Arrie, Lillie. Grandsons of William and Levi served in the World War. William's were: Oscar, Will, and George Embler. Levi's was Julian Peek, son of Z. B. Peek, who was the first Georgia boy wounded in France and the first American soldier to lose a limb.

The following was taken from a book in a New York library:

In searching the annals of the family in this country we find no member of it occupying an enviable niche in the political world. To use the words of an old Virginian of the family, George R. Peak, of Richmond: "I have followed the name wherever it could be traced, and have yet to find the first instance of crime to be charged against it, or an arraignment in court of justice for violation of law. I have never known one ambitious of political fame, mean, cowardly, or tyrannical; none who ever lived by his wits; only one office-holder: Humphrey Peake, who was appointed Collector of Alexandria, Virginia, by General Washington, and who held that office until the time of President Jackson. I think the great merit of which the family can honorably boast is attending to their own affairs and demanding that every one else attend to theirs."

Captain John Peek, Veteran of Two Wars

Capt. John Peek, son of William and Isabella Redmond Peek, was born in Buncombe County, N. C., February 14, 1821, and died Monday, March 10, 1896, in Hartwell, Ga.

He served in the Mexican War in Payne's Regiment of North Carolina Volunteers, and was with the army when it occupied the City of Mexico.

He married Miss Mary Woodsen. Five children were born to them, to wit: Dr. W. W. Peek, Mrs. T. J. Linder and S. W. Peek; the names of the others we do not have.

When the War Between the States broke out, he raised a company and was elected Captain. The company was attached to the 16th North Carolina Regiment. Afterwards he organized a second company, of which he was elected Captain, and which was attached to the 27th North Carolina Regiment.

He was severely wounded in the arm by bushwhackers.

After the war, in 1863, he removed to Hartwell, where he resided continuously up to his death, with the exception of a short time that he lived in the country.

In 1877 he was married a second time, to Miss Ann Williford, who died in 1880. He had been a member of the Hartwell Methodist Church for many years, where his funeral was preached to a large and sympathetic congregation by Rev. Crawford Jackson, after which his remains were interred in the Hartwell Cemetery.

Many improvements in Hartwell are enduring monuments of his love for his town, notably among others are the beautiful elm shade trees, a part of which were set out at his instance and by his assistance.

The Thornton Family History

FROM Rev. J. F. Goode's History of the Tugaloo Association we have the following sketch of Dozier Thornton, the ancestor of the Thorntons in this and adjoining counties.

"According to Campbell's 'History of Georgia Baptists,' on page 244, we find it stated that Littleton Meeks and Dozier Thornton, who were then acting as missionaries to the Cherokee Indians, lost their way among the mountains, and after traveling until a late hour at night, they were compelled to take up in the woods, without fire or food, and wait for the dawning of the day. They were entertained with music by the barking of the foxes and the howling of the wolves.

"We also gather from the same source that Dozier Thornton was born in Lunenburg County, Va., April 14, 1755, and departed this life in Franklin County, Ga., in September, 1843, in the eighty-ninth year of his age. Brief but suitable and impressive resolutions were introduced and passed by the Association at the next session of the body after his death. He presided as Moderator at the time the Association was organized."

He was Moderator of the Sarepta Association 1804-1818, a period of fifteen years.

From the History of the Georgia Baptist Association, we gather the following account of Rev. Dozier Thornton:

"Dozier Thornton was born April 14, 1755, in Virginia. His father was an Episcopal and his mother a Baptist. While still young he was employed by a widow as overseer on her farm in upper North Carolina. He was converted one day while ploughing in the field. He ungeared his horse and went to the farm house, telling them what great things the Lord had done for him.

"An unusual thing about Mr. Thornton is that he began preaching even before he united with the church. After joining the church, however, he was ordained to the work of the ministry. He thus came to Georgia as a minister in 1784, and settled in Elbert County.

"Mr. Thornton was pastor of Dove's Creek and Vann's Creek for nearly forty years. As these churches soon became members of the Sarepta Association, his work in the Georgia Association was not of an active nature. He usually attended the meetings of the body, and may have had churches within its bounds.

"His death occurred in 1843 in the 90th years of his age."

Dozier Thornton was a soldier of the War of the Revolution. According to the records in the office of the Ordinary of Franklin County, Ga., Dozier Thornton testified to many of the declarations of Revolutionary soldiers who made applications for pensions.

Dozier Thornton married Lucy Hall in 1783.

He evidently was married a second time, as we have the record from the marriage records of Franklin County that Dozier Thornton married Jane Pulliam, May 4, 1826, who from the following record of his will was a widow at the time of their marriage, and further, if we are not mistaken in our information, his second wife, Jane Pulliam, was a daughter of Rev. Thomas Gilbert before her marriage to ---------------- Pulliam.

Will of Dozier Thornton

July 27, 1837—November 6, 1843

Wife Jane, place on which I live, it being the place which she owned when I married her; a note on Benj. S. Pulliam for the sale of lot she drew as a widow. Balance to my own children, amounts advanced are recorded in my "Alphan Book," in the hands of my exrs., Joseph Chandler and Reuben Thornton.

Wit: S. Hymer, David Carr, Job Brown, J. P.

April 17, 1840—As son, Reuben, has moved to Alabama, I appoint Henry F. Chandler in his place.

Wit: S. Hymer, James Attaway, Frances Pulliam.

March 14, 1842—Codicil: I give more to my wife Jane, she having lived longer than expected.

Wit: James M. Glover, Benj. R. Pulliam, S. Hymer.

Benjamin Thornton, Sr., son of Dozier Thornton; born about 1784; died 1854. Married Rebecca Upshaw; born ....; died after 1854.

Rev. Benjamin Thornton, Jr., son of Benjamin Thornton, Sr.; born August 15, 1801; died April 12, 1878. Married, first, Nancy F. Payne, September 16, 1819; born December 19, 1802; died 1864.

To this union were born twelve children.

Rev. Benjamin Thornton, Jr. married, second, to Mrs. Louisa J. Skelton, September 6, 1864.

Rev. Benjamin Callaway Thornton, son of Benjamin Thornton, Jr.; born December 13, 1827; died October 30, 1881. Married, first, Malissa Gaines, November 17, 1846.

To this union were born one son, Frank B. Thornton, April 27, 1848; married Julia A. Walters, September 27, 1868; died March 28, 1888.

After the death of Malissa Gaines Thornton, Rev. B. C. Thornton married Priscilla J. Teasley, September 4, 1851; born July 24, 1834; died May 23, 1896.

The following children were born unto them:

Thomas A. Thornton; born July 31, 1852; died May 13, 1933. Married Georgia E. Carter; born July 15, 1857; died September 18, 1929.

Sarah Frances Thornton; born January 1, 1854; died April 5, 1924. Married D. C. Alford, October 3, 1878; born February 12, 1856; died March 28, 1933.

Dozier A. Thornton; born October 30, 1855; died July 30, 1909. Married Susie Gillison.

James B. Thornton; born September 5, 1857; died March 14, 1921. Married Sallie Speed.

Janie Thornton; born October 17, 1859; died January 11, 1863.

Cornelia Thornton; born November 18, 1861; died January 7, 1863.

Amanda Thornton; born November 27, ... Married George J. Page, March 2, 1881.

John C. Thornton; born March 25, 1866; died March 25, 1899.

Rebecca Thornton; born December 30, 1869; died August 20, 1870.

Jessie Thornton; born April 20, 1871. Married J. H. Skelton, December 23, 1891.

McAlpin Thornton; born October 3, 1873. Married Claire Dodd; born January 20, 1877; died January 12, 1928.

Dunston V. Thornton; born July 2, 1876. Married Daisy G. McCurry, April 26, 1899.

Annie Thornton; born June 24, 1878. Married John P. Cash, June 11, 1908.

SHOAL CREEK FACTORY

THIS one-time famous industrial plant was founded about 1842-3 by J. J. J. Sheppard and Albin Cornog, both of whom came from Pendleton, S. C., and purchased a tract of land from R. K. Walters, including a splendid water power on Big Shoal Creek.

Perhaps it would be proper to here give a brief history of the Sheppard and Cornog families.

Albin Cornog was born December 11, 1819. He came from Chester, Pa., to Pendleton, S. C., in early manhood. He was a machinist and was an employee in the Pendleton Factory, which was located on the Three-and-Twenty Creek, near Pendleton, and was the first cotton mill to be built in South Carolina, if not in the South. It was originally a yarn mill and propelled by water power furnished by said creek. The mill has passed on down to successive owners. It now belongs to a northern corporation and has been fitted up with up-to-date machinery and converted from that of a yarn mill to that of a tapestry mill, and no longer driven by water power, but by electricity, and its output of the finest quality. The place is now known as LaFrance.

Albin Cornog married Miss Sarah Sheppard, daughter of Capt. James Sheppard, of Pendleton, and sister of J. J. J. Sheppard.

Col. Cornog, as he was commonly called, died September 6, 1893, and is buried at Providence Methodist Church, Hart County, Ga., his grave marked by a granite monument with appropriate inscription.

In the cemetery at Providence is the grave of Capt. James Sheppard, marked by a rock vault and inscribed: "Capt. Jas. Sheppard, Born Jan. 1787, died July 18, 1859." He was, perhaps, a soldier of the War of 1812.

J. J. J. Sheppard, son of Capt. Jack Sheppard, and brother-in-law of Albin Cornog, was born in Pendleton, S. C., and married Miss Mary Gunnells, of Franklin County, Ga. His home was on the Knox's Bridge, formerly Cleveland's Ferry, road. He sold his interest in the cotton mill and his other property and moved to Jackson County, Ga., and the place where he lived still is known as the Sheppard place.

Col. Cornog's home was down near the factory.

The cotton mill originally had about 250 spindles, with a daily capacity, or output, of 50 to 75 pounds of yarn.

About 1868 to 1870 the number of spindles were increased to around 600 spindles, with a production of about 200 pounds of yarn per day, put up in skeins of from $2\frac{1}{2}$ to 4 ounces per skein, and then bundled in 5-pound bundles, or bunches, and sold to merchants in Elberton, Hartwell, Toccoa, Clayton and Harmony Grove, Ga.; also the near-by towns in South Carolina.

This yarn was used as warp mixed with wool for making jeans, coverlets, balmorals and other garments. It was also used for knitting purposes and woven into homespun and counterpanes on old hand looms.

The counts, or sizes, or numbers, was 6s to 12s, mostly 8s and 10s. Later on, after the people quit buying locally, the yarn was shipped east, mostly to New York and Philadelphia.

Later on, Samuel Knox, a very wealthy man of Franklin County, Ga., obtained an interest in the property and the business was conducted for a number of years under the name of Knox & Cornog.

Some time in the 1870's the mill was incorporated by A. or W. L. Cornog, R. D. Yow, S. H. Moseley, B. B. Parker, Jr., and others. This company, or corporation, operated the mill only for a short while. They sold out to A. Cornog and T. P. Wilkerson in 1883 or 1884. Col. Cornog sold his interest to J. N. Edwards and the business was run under the name of Edwards & Wilkerson till about 1886. Mr. Wilkerson dying, J. N. Edwards bought his interest and became sole owner until his death in 1897.

When Mr. Edwards acquired the sole interest in the property he added 1,000 spindles, making a 2,000-spindle mill, with a production of about 800 pounds of yarn per day. Edwards & Wilkerson had added two frames, 400 spindles, while they were joint owners.

Yarn was now put up in 6 to 8-ounce skeins and packed in 350 to 400-pound bales, nearly all of which was shipped east, most of it going to New York, and used in the making of carpets.

The employees, or operatives, were usually from 22 to 25.

There were wool cards operated in connection with the yarn mill, and the people for quite a distance used to bring their wool here to be carded into rolls, which were spun on the old-time spinning wheels into thread and mixed with the yarn and wove into jeans, etc., as already described.

In addition to the cotton mill, there was also a fine flouring and grist mill located at the place, on the opposite side of the creek and just a short ways down the creek from the cotton mill, which was swept away by the freshet of 1887, an account of which appears elsewhere in these pages.

Shoal Creek Factory passed into history many years ago. The cotton mill, the flouring and grist mill, the store house, the splendid residence formerly occupied by Col. Cornog and later by J. N. Edwards, together with the homes of the operatives have all disappeared, and the hillsides where once stood this prosperous mill village are now bleak and bare, while Big Shoal Creek rolls on, as of yore, to join the Tugaloo.

W. L. Cornog

W. L. CORNOG was a son of Albin Cornog; born November 23, 1841; married _____, daughter of William Holland, of Anderson County, S. C.; died June 28, 1876. Enlisted in the service of the War Between the States, in Capt. Wm. R. Poole's Company when same was organized at King's Bench, June 15, 1861. Buried at Providence Church, his grave marked by a marble monument.

Mr. Cornog was a public-spirited man, a fine machinist, and was prominently identified in the construction of the Elberton Airline Railroad, of which he was a director and took an active part in building and securing subscriptions and obtaining right-of-way, at which he spent as much as one year of his time.

To Mr. Cornog and wife were born one son, W. W. Cornog, who became, and is still, a prominent physician located at Lavonia, Ga., where he has always enjoyed a lucrative practice of his profession.

One daughter, Miss Julia, who married Mr. John Mason, died years ago.

King's Mount Gold Mine

IN THE YEAR 1860, one Mr. Otho Berg, of Baltimore, Md., purchased of Mr. James L. Brown a tract of land, composed of 503 acres, upon which land gold had been discovered.

This Mr. Brown was a son of Andrew Brown, a soldier in the War of the Revolution, and is buried at Holly Springs Church. This Mr. James L. Brown was distinguished as being the father of twenty-one children.

After the purchase of the property by Mr. Berg, a corporation was formed under the name of the "King's Mount Gold Mine Company of the City of Baltimore." After organization of the company, a plant was installed for the production of gold, which was operated for a short time, but on account of the hostility between the two sections and the approach of the War Between the States, and the owners all being northern people, the strife was such that they did not deem it prudent to remain longer in the South, and for these reasons operations ceased and were never resumed after the war. We have no record of the amount of gold taken from the mine during the time it was worked.

Mr. Charles W. Seidell, who was in some way employed or connected with the company, had some kind of claim against the property, which was sued to judgment and the property was sold at sheriff's sale after the war. Mr. Seidell became the purchaser and sole owner, and many years afterwards sold the place to Mr. S. A. Ginn, retaining unto himself, heirs and assigns, a half interest in all minerals for a term of ninety-nine years.

The price paid Mr. James L. Brown, according to the deed record, was $5,291.70.

This property is located in the 1113th District, G. M., Hart County, Ga., and known as Ray's District, and on the one-time famous "Red Hollow Road."

In Hon. W. S. McCallie, State Geologist's report of minerals of the State, he refers to what is known as the Madison County gold belt which extends from a point near Comer, Ga., and terminates about three miles northeast of Bowman, Ga., and the "King's Mount Gold Mine" evidently is the northeast terminus of the belt.

The Maret Family

THE first of this Maret family was Benjamin Maret, who came from York County, Va., and settled in Hillsboro, N. C. He married Judie Harbin. All their children were born in Orange County, N. C., in which Hillsboro is, and was once the capital of the state.

His sons were: Steven, who married Lucy Walters in the territory which is now Hart County. The second son, John Maret, married Fannie Walters, a sister of Lucy. And another son, Benjamin, married Lucy Keese. Isom married Febia Walters, who was a first cousin to the wives of Steven and John.

Wyley Maret, son of Isom Maret, married a daughter of George Cleveland, who lived in the neighborhood of Parkers' Mills.

Joseph Maret, son of Isom, and brother of Wyley Maret, married Sarah Ann Holland, daughter of Robert Holland, who lived in the upper edge of Anderson County, S. C. She was a sister of Jefferson and Thomas Holland.

Isom Maret lived on Little Shoal Creek, and owned the property that was later owned by his sons, Wyley and Joseph, who divided the estate, the home of Wyley Maret being on the right and near the creek, Joseph lived on the opposite side of the creek from the home of Wyley, both homes located on the public road leading from Andersonville, S. C., to Parkertown, Ga.

To Joseph Maret and his wife, Sarah Ann Holland Maret, were born five sons, viz.: Robert W., B. Isom, Joseph William, Albine and Elijah Foster Maret. The daughters were: Margaret E., M. Fannie, Sallie J., and L. Alice Maret.

To Wyley Maret and wife were born five sons, viz.: William Isom, Joseph Franklin, George Washington, Robert Monroe and Wyley Jackson Maret. The daughters were: Nancy Jane and Sarah Frances Maret.

Near the old home place of Joseph Maret, and on the south side of the public road leading towards Parkertown, is an old family graveyard in which many of the older members of the Maret family are buried. Many of the graves are marked with substantial rock vaults.

Flood—Drought—Freeze—Quake and Storm

SOME of the events recorded in this sketch occurred while the territory now embraced in Hart County was a part of Franklin, while others occurred since the creation of the county.

The first flood, or freshet, in the Savannah River and its tributaries of which we have any account was in the year 1795, known as the Yazoo Flood, which was general throughout the country, a brief mention of which has been made elsewhere in these pages.

The next floor of which we have any account occurred in May, 1840, and has ever afterwards been referred to as the "May Freshet." It was perhaps the most destructive in its effects to property and the waters reached the highest level of any other either before or since. Following is the comparative height of the water in Augusta, Ga., for several of the floods to which reference is made. The freshet of 1840 reached the height of 37.10; 1852, 37.05; 1864, 34.04; 1865, 36.10. As to the freshets of June, 1876, and the July and August freshets of 1887, we have no figures as to the height reached.

One very noted instance of the destructive effects of the flood of 1840 was the destruction of property at Andersonville, S. C., which has also been mentioned.

Another noted instance of the result of the flood of 1840, as related to Franklin (now Hart) County, was the overflow of sand and the change of the channel along and adjacent to the Cleveland, formerly the Gilbert, plantation, or farm, on the Tugaloo River. There is a long, wide expanse of bottom lands extending from near the site of Pullen's Ferry down to the mouth of Gilbert Branch, and during the freshet of 1840 the upper portion of the bottom lands were covered up with sand, rendering it less productive, with the probable exception for the growing of watermelons. The channel of the river was diverted from towards the Georgia side towards the Carolina side a distance of the width of the river or more. The lower reach of the channel was not filled with sand, but remained open and under water for perhaps a period of twenty years or longer, and at the lower end at the mouth of the Gilbert Branch there was formed a kind of estuary of deep water which afforded fine fishing grounds, but later as the channel of the river deepened the water in the lower end of the old channel together with the water at the mouth of the branch was gradually drained off and today there is no sign to indicate that at one time the place was under water. After the water moved off, the lower end containing several acres was left sufficiently dry for cultivation and was very fertile due to the deposit of silt, and for many years produced abundant crops of corn, and referred to as the "mud row."

The next flood was in August, 1852, and known as the "August Freshet." It perhaps was not so destructive in its effects to property along the streams as that of the "May Freshet." The waters reached a level of 37.05, as already stated.

The next floods occurred in 1864 and 1865, of which we have no account, except the height to which the water reached, which has also been stated.

The next freshet of any note was in June, 1876, of which we have no record further than practically all growing crops along the streams were destroyed, and while some of the crops were re-planted they did not have sufficient time to mature and perhaps a lot of the crops were used for feed in the green stage.

The next freshets occurred in July and August, 1887, and may be termed the freshets of July and August of 1887.

In July, 1887, Georgia was swept by a flood and considerable damage to property in Hart County was sustained. The rain storm seemed to have started at the Gulf and was mostly confined to Georgia.

Following we give several newspaper accounts that appeared at the time.

The Great July and August Freshets of 1887

"The crops on the streams were destroyed and mills and bridges were swept away. The Savannah River is said to have been higher than the June or August freshets, and the damage to crops in the river bottoms was incalculable. In many places corn and cotton were swept entirely away. The surging waters broke the wire at Brown's Ferry, which was 18 or 20 feet above ordinary water mark.

Tugaloo River

"Both the abutments of Knox's Bridge washed away. River higher than the August freshet. All the bottom corn ruined. Forty-five feet perpendicular above low-water mark.

Cedar Creek

"Herring's Mill swept totally away, nothing was left but the bare site. When the dam broke the flood of water that went down carried every temporary obstruction with it.

"Hodges' Mill was fortunate, only a small break in the dam and the water wheel thrown a little out of balance. R. T. Buffington's gin house was moved down the creek a short distance.

Beaverdam Creek

"Our information is that every mill dam on the creek is washed away; also, several mills and nearly all bridges. The new bridge at Dr. W. C. Mathews' Mill (better known as Wynn's Mill) was swept away. Brewer's Mill we learn is gone. This was one of the best mills on the creek. The bridge at Heard's Mill is gone.

Lightwoodlog Creek

"Scott's (Stephenson's) Mill escaped without serious damage.

"The railroad trestle was considerably damaged. It is about 300 feet long, and in places the crossties alone were left suspended to the iron. No trains have passed over the trestle since Saturday afternoon. The damage is being repaired as fast as possible and the trains will soon be running as usual.

"The bridge at McMullan's Ford was damaged considerably. The end on the north side of the creek was washed off. Quite a number of the oldest citizens say the creek was higher than ever known before.

"A correspondent writes us that the freshet was very disastrous on Shoal Creek, Gumlog Creek and Broad River.

"Several chimneys fell down in Hartwell and Bowersville. The damage to the county will run up in the thousands, but the loss in Franklin, Elbert and Madison must naturally far exceed ours, having more and larger streams."

The Hartwell Sun, August 5, 1887.

Shoal Creek's Angry Waters Sweep Away $15,000 Worth of Property in 30 Minutes

"Last Monday morning at 8 o'clock A. M., rain began falling very steady until 10, when it began to fall in torrents. At about 12:7, fills on the E. A. L. R. R. gave way between Lavonia and Bowersville and emptied their rushing waters into Middle Shoal Creek, which raised it three feet above high-water mark. On the plantation of Benjamin Shirley, Sr., the three creeks come together, and presented a scene the oldest citizens have never seen. Ten and fifteen-foot water could be had anywhere. Six hundred panels of fence washed off of Mr. Shirley's plantation. Just below this place the hills come near together and bring the water to a greater depth, and gives it a lightning surge down the old factory shoals; trees large enough to make ten rails to the cut were uprooted and sent hurling down the streams, tearing them to atoms. Rocks that would weigh half a ton were torn from the shoals and washed several hundred feet. About 1 o'clock P. M., the new bridge at Parker's Mill was swept like so much straw, and in a few minutes the stone dam began heaving up rocks on the north side next to the mill, then the water house under the mill bursted, and the mill began to tremble, and in a minute the $5,000 mill of Jacob Parker & Co. left its old seat where it has stood 35 years, with a moan, a crash, it went backward, and buried mid the wave, carrying with it a tolling bell. Not a pillar was left of the mill and bridge, which was of solid rock. One-third of the dam was washed clean down to the shoal. A blacksmith shop which stood on the hill apparently at a safe distance from all expected floods was washed away. With all this timber and stone the water sped on.

"Reaching the Shoal Creek Factory, carried its dam and two pillars from under the factory. Picked up the mill dam and race, and in a few minutes the Cornog Mill tumbled off its seat. The miller's house was turned over and the eye could see nothing but destruction. Two weeks ago the fine crops and machinery that studded the banks of Shoal Creek would make any one feel glad his home was near the rippling waters. Tonight it is a lonely sand bar, covered with mud and rock. The estimated loss in Shoal Creek District would not fall short of $25,000."

The fall, or inclination, of the channel of Shoal Creek is much greater than that of Tugaloo River, and the large volume of water rushed down with such velocity and momentum the water of the river could not check the force and as a result the waters of Shoal Creek rushed on across the river and uprooted trees and excavated a great hole or basin on the Carolina side of the river.

Lightwoodlog Creek

"On Monday, August 8, 1887, there was another freshet in which great damage was done in Hart County. Lightwoodlog Creek rose considerably higher than during the freshet of the week before. The trestle on the Hartwell Railroad over the creek was well nigh totally wrecked. Seventeen benches were swept from under it, leaving the crossties and iron swinging in festoons. The eight-o'clock train from Bowersville crossed over alright, but when the noon train reached the trestle and started to go across the engineer saw one of the benches topple down and stopped the train.

"The bridge at McMullan's Ford was swept entirely away.

"The new mill just constructed at Flat Shoals was swept away.

The Sun, August 12 and 19, 1887.

Drouth of 1845

The most noted drouth in the recollection of the oldest citizens and of which we have any record, was in the year 1845, commonly referred to as the "Dry Year." We have often heard old people who lived at the time speak of it, and as to duration it was perhaps from early spring up to sometime in August following, and was general throughout North Carolina, South Carolina and Georgia and perhaps other parts of the country, in fact we do not know just how extensive it was.

Many of the springs and wells went dry, creeks ceased to function as streams and fish died as a consequence. Especially was this true as to South Beaverdam Creek, in Franklin (now Hart) County, as it has come down to us by tradition, and a like condition prevailed as to many of the other streams of the country.

During the summer of 1845, a school was taught at Reed Creek Church, and the spring near by which always afforded ample water supply for the church and school went dry, and those attending school were forced to bring water from the bold spring near the residence of Jedidiah Ayers, a distance of a mile from the church.

We mention this as typical of the condition that prevailed throughout the drouth-stricken section.

It is said that many of the slave owners of North and South Carolina, and perhaps other parts of the country, were forced to carry their slaves to Mississippi and other points west where they were sold, as the crop failure was such that the owners were not able to feed, clothe and care for them and were without sufficient supplies to make a crop the following year.

Another disadvantage at which the people were placed as a result of the drouth, was that there were no railroads in the country by which food and other necessary supplies could be transported to the drouth section.

At the time of the drouth in 1845, cotton was not extensively grown as in years following, and the people, as a rule, produced all necessary supplies, and in many instances the farmers had sufficient of the crop of the previous year left over which they used as a partial supply for the next year, and by means of economy to which they were forced to resort, and while hard times were experienced, however the people were enabled to live and make a crop in 1846 and no serious destitution was experienced by the people.

The Drouths of 1925-6

There have been a number of years since 1845 in which the crops suffered, more or less, for rain, but no such drouth as that of 1845 occurred until the year 1925.

To give some idea of the effect of the drouth of 1925, as related to the production of cotton in Hart County, we give herewith the figures as to the number of bales produced in the county. In 1925 there was produced in Hart County 7,391 bales as compared with 14,845 in 1924, and in the year 1926 there was produced in the county 7,351 bales as compared with 14,845 in 1924, and as compared with 13,036 bales in 1927.

The wheat and oat crop of 1925 was fairly good, as it was not affected so much by the drouth. The same was true in the year 1926. The corn crop of both years was a partial failure.

As to the water supply in the year 1925, many of the springs and wells went dry, and many of the streams almost ceased to function.

The Tugaloo River was lower during the drouth of 1925 than it perhaps had been since 1845. Ledges of rock in the river were exposed that had not been seen above the surface of the water since 1845, a period of eighty years.

We remember to have visited the river at a point near the mouth of Reed Creek where we had an unobstructed view upstream of the Chandler Shoals, and the water was so low that none could be seen about the shoals from our point of view. Of course the water was still running in places between the spaces between the rocks, and the shoals presented the appearance of a huge yellow or brown wall extending all the way across the river from bank to bank.

At Hatton's Ford the water was so low that a footman could wade across dry shod.

Another effect of the drouth of 1925, was that large areas of forest timber died for the lack of sufficient moisture, especially was this true of the timber on the hilly and table lands.

While the crop failure of the year 1926 was as great as that of 1925, yet the water supply was not so low.

The Cold Saturday

"In order to settle the date of this memorable day definitely, and explain why some people claim that Sunday was the coldest day, we give the following official information, furnished us by our good friend, Dr. B. C. Smith, of Coldwater, Ga.

"The 'Cold Saturday' of 1835 occurred on the 7th of February, the cold wave striking the northern and western portions of the State. On that day reports are on record stating that the thermometer at Athens, Ga., registered 15 degrees below zero.

"In other portions of the State, i. e., the southern and southeastern, the greatest intensity of the cold was felt on Sunday morning, February 8th, at which time the mercury at Milledgeville registered 9 degrees below zero, and at Augusta 2 degrees below." —*The Hartwell Sun*, May 26, 1905.

The Earthquake of August 31, 1886

On Tuesday night, August 31, 1886, about 10 o'clock, there was felt throughout the country perhaps the heaviest earthquake ever experienced by those living at the time. There were several shocks experienced, but no damage to the property or citizens of this part of the country. The heaviest of the quake was in Charleston, S. C., and vicinity, where the damage was very great to buildings, railroads and other property. As the greatest damage was in that community, the same has ever since been known as the Charleston Earthquake.

Below we give an account as the same appeared in *The Hartwell Sun* on September 3, 1886.

"On Tuesday night, about 10 o'clock, Hartwell experienced a series of five shocks from an earthquake, and after 1 o'clock in the morning two other shocks, making in all seven. The first one was the most severe and caused great fright and consternation.

"Houses were shaken, windows rattled, dishes clattered, and teeth chattered. The shock lasted for about a minute and a half, some say three minutes.

It was accompanied by a rumbling sound in the bowels of the earth resembling heavy thunder in the distance. The succeeding shocks were less violent and of shorter duration.

"The only damage done was a few loose bricks shaken from the chimney upon the roof of the Vickery House. Wednesday morning those who were the worst scared when they couldn't see how to dodge assembled on the square and began to tell how badly scared somebody else was. A lawyer, it is said, brought out the Georgia code and form book to find a form of prayer suitable to the occasion. Parties who were fishing in the Savannah say the water in the eddy places became agitated and splashed and foamed like the shoals."

The Big Sleet Storm of 1858

In 1858, and on or about the 10th day of February of said year, our country was visited by the greatest and most destructive sleet storm in the annals of history.

Our country at that time was, for the most part, in original forest, and the excessive weight of the sleet broke off the tops of many of the pines and other timber.

After the storm the forest presented the appearance as if some Ajax or Hercules, mythological gods of strength, had stalked through and snapped out the tops of the towering pines which had so long held undisputed sway as monarchs of the forest.

In our boyhood days we remember that there were many pines and other trees still standing with the tops gone, and at the present time an occasional tree may be observed with the top broken off as a result of the sleet storm in the long ago.

Hon. William Myers

HON. WILLIAM MYERS was born in Edgefield County, S. C., May 29, 1812, and came in his boyhood to Georgia and settled in Elbert (now Hart) County.

He was twice married; his first wife, who he married February 21, 1833, was Miss Sarah Highsmith, daughter of John Highsmith, who owned and lived at the place now known as the Henry F. Hailey place, situate on both sides of Boyd's Creek, more generally known as the north prong of Little Coldwater Creek.

To him and his wife, Sarah Highsmith Myers, were born seven sons and three daughters, to wit: James Robert Myers, J. Bruce Myers, Lewis B. Myers, Ira F. Myers, W. C. Myers, Thomas Myers and Ezekiel Myers; and the daughters were: Mary E. Myers, Sarah F. Myers, and Elizabeth Myers.

Sarah, his first wife, is buried in an old family burying ground on the Highsmith estate.

The lives of Thomas and Ezekiel Myers were sacrificed on the altar of their country in the War Between the States.

Mr. Myers' second wife was Mrs. Sarah Neal, who before her first marriage was Sarah Hamilton.

Marriages

J. Robert Myers married Susan Richardson, October 22, 1857, by J. Van Richardson, Justice of the Inferior Court.

J. Bruce Myers married Mary Ann Farmer, daughter of Caswell Farmer.

Lewis B. Myers married Emma Obrey, of Lincoln County, Ga.

Ira F. Myers married Mary E. Perryman, December 23, 1875, by Rev. J. H. McMullan.

W. C. Myers married N. C. Neal, December 4, 1879, by Rev. J. H. McMullan.

Nancy E. Myers married William E. Tiller, March 8, 1873, by Rev. J. H. McMullan.

Sarah F. Myers married N. J. Tiller, December 3, 1874, by Rev. J. H. McMullan.

Elizabeth Myers married James L. Fain, October 28, 1858, by J. Van Richardson.

Marriages of Second Set of Children

E. E. Myers married Martha Cash, January 18, 1900, by Rev. T. J. Rucker.

W. Thos. Myers married Hortensey Sanders, December 10, 1905, by Rev. T. R. Wright.

Laura E. Myers married L. H. Cobb, May 13, 1896, by Rev. T. J. Rucker.

Leila Myers married L. H. Cobb, May 14, 1899, by Rev. T. J. Rucker.

Lilla Myers married C. M. Sanders, December 14, 1899, by Rev. T. J. Rucker.

As will appear from the foregoing, ten children of the first and five of the second marriage.

Mr. Myers was the first Sheriff of Hart County, to which office he was elected at the first election held for county officers. He resigned before the expiration of his term of office and was elected Representative to the General Assembly of Georgia, being the first Representative, which position he filled for two consecutive terms, 1855-1858.

Mr. Myers died January 16, 1897, and his wife, Sarah N., died May 25, 1910, both buried in the cemetery at Sardis Church.

James Robert Myers

James R. Myers, son of Hon. William and Sarah Highsmith Myers, was born January 21, 1835, and died January 15, 1918, at the age of 83 years.

As stated in his obituary, "For one to have lived from 1835 to 1918—eighty-three years—there must have come to his observing mind many startling changes, material and otherwise. We would not think of enumerating them if we could, but only mention them that the living may, if they will, assume for a little while in their silent meditations something of what this splendid citizen could have told us of his experience if we would have taken time to listen.

"Even in the great rush of things, would it not be well to stop occasionally and hear what the aged citizen might tell us that would help us?"

Mr. Myers married Miss Susan Richardson, daughter of Mahlon and Sallie Richardson, October 22, 1857—sixty years before his death.

A short time after his happy marriage this heroic man heard the call to arms and promptly enlisted in Captain John McMullan's Company, which was Company "D," 37th Regiment, Georgia Volunteers Infantry, Army of Tennessee, C. S. A., on March 4, 1862, as a private. Later, was elected Second Lieutenant, December 15, 1863. For four and a half long years he freely subjected himself to the life and death grapple. Near the close of the war he was taken a prisoner and carried to Johnson's Island in Lake Erie.

The writer of the obituary of Mr. Myers, in speaking of the location of the prison where Mr. Myers was retained, said: "The writer several years ago had the privilege of visiting this famous prison ground and the resting place of many brave fellows whose bodies sleep beneath the low green tents whose curtains never outward swing till the dead are called to live again."

Mr. Myers held the office of Sheriff of his county for several terms, and during the time the unfortunate murder of Thomas V. Skelton by Henry Hill occurred, a notice of which appears elsewhere.

He joined the church at Sardis in early life and remained a devoted and worthy member until a few years before his death he moved his membership to Bethany Baptist Church, which was nearer and more convenient in his declining years, and where he was buried after appropriate funeral services conducted by his pastor, Rev. John B. Brown, assisted by Rev. T. M. Galphin, a friend of many years' acquaintance.

To James Robert Myers and wife, Susan Richardson Myers, were born the following children:

T. Mahlon Myers; born November 2, 1867. Married, first, Sarah M. Pruitt, January 26, 1887, who died February 24, 1907.

Married second time to Miss Cancy Smith, daughter of Moses D. Smith and wife, of the Holly Springs community.

Sarah E. Myers, daughter of James Robert and wife, Susan; born September 26, 1858. Married W. A. Ray, October 18, 1877, who died September 5, 1901.

Lou Ella Myers, daughter of James Robert and wife, Susan; born October 24, 1870. Married A. N. P. Brown, December 22, 1886.

Clara Mabell Myers, daughter of James Robert and wife, Susan; born January 8, 1879. Married T. E. V. White, October 9, 1898; died August 22, 1901.

Hon. F. C. Stephenson

HON. FREDERICK CHAPMAN STEPHENSON, Ordinary of Hart County, died May 18, 1895, after a week's lingering sickness.

Mr. Stephenson was born November 7, 1825, in Elbert County, now Hart, in the Cokesbury settlement.

He was married to Miss Mary A. Pritchett, January 8, 1851.

In 1854, when Hart County was organized, he was elected Clerk of the Inferior Court. After his election, in 1854, he moved to Hartwell, and in addition to his duties as Clerk, he taught school for some time, being the first school ever taught in the town. Mr. Stephenson held the office of Clerk until 1868, when at the general election in that year he was elected

Ordinary, which office he held continuously from that time till his death. When Judge Stephenson moved to Hartwell, Hon. John B. Benson was postmaster, and he at once turned the office over to the former, who held that office in connection with that of the others for nearly twenty-five years.

When about ten years of age, Judge Stephenson united with the Methodist Church and remained a valued member until his death.

In all the walks of life—as citizen, as official, and as Christian gentleman —he measured fully up to the high standard of duty. Physically disabled by sickness when young, yet the amount of work accomplished by him during his life will rarely be excelled. From the time he was called to public station by the voice of his fellow citizens he literally dedicated his life to the interests and welfare of his county. As fair and impartial magistrate, as incorruptible citizen, and as wise counsellor, peacemaker and friend, he has left a record behind him that is a priceless legacy to his friends and fellow countrymen.

F. C. Stephenson

His funeral was preached by Rev. Crawford Jackson, assisted by Rev. J. R. Earle, in the Hartwell Methodist Church. He was buried in the cemetery at Hartwell, where an appropriate monument marks his last resting place, with the following inscription:

"To the Memory of Frederick C. Stephenson, Born Nov. 7, 1825. Gave himself to Christ and the M. E. Church in early life. Was loved and honored by all who knew him. Passed the furnace of affliction, he represented Christ in his life. Was conqueror to the end. Died May 18, 1895."

Mrs. Stephenson, his wife, preceded her husband to the grave a little over a year, having died April 27, 1894.

To Judge Stephenson and his wife were born two sons and two daughters: William R. Stephenson married Miss S. A. Pressnell, February 24, 1872. F. L. Stephenson, the younger son, married Miss Matilda Ida M. Taylor. Miss E. C. Stephenson, the older daughter, married John Q. Snow, May 4, 1881. Miss Frances Alice Stephenson married John Q. Donald, January 12, 1881.

Two children of Judge Stephenson and wife died in infancy.

Ransom A. Cobb, 1824-1892

DIED at his residence in Hart County, January 12, 1892, (Tuesday). He was born in Pickens County, S. C., October 19, 1824, and came with his parents to Georgia in the year 1839.

He was the oldest son of James and Mary Cobb. His mother's maiden name was Sullivan, sister of Kelly Sullivan, well known in Anderson County, S. C.

Married Lucy E. Brown, daughter of G. W. and Elmira Brown, of Elbert County, May 22, 1856. Served as one of the Judges of the Inferior Court during the war, and did much in aiding the soldiers who were in service and their wives and children who were left at home.

He was the first Steward of the County Pauper's Home of Hart County. Served as Notary Public—Ex-Officio J. P., after the war in the 1118th District. Joined the Baptist Church at Hendry's in the year 1871 or 1872. When the church was organized at Bio he withdrew from Hendry's to become a member at Bio.

Was buried at Bio on January 14, 1892, where a large congregation met to pay the last tribute of respect to one whom they loved and respected when living and one whom they mourned when dead.

The funeral services were conducted by the pastor, Rev. P. F. Crawford, assisted by Rev. L. W. Stephens and Rev. J. H. McMullan, both former pastors of the church.

Elijah Chapman

ELIJAH CHAPMAN died November 21, 1893, in the 71st year of his age. He was converted, about the age of 12, and joined the M. E. Church at about the age of 18. He was class leader about 45 years, and superintendent of the Sabbath school for many years; and it argues well for his Christian character, that he never had a church difficulty during his membership.

He was widely and favorably known as a zealous and indefatigable Christian worker.

In his younger days he was a most excellent songster and taught sacred music extensively, with beneficial results. He was a peaceable and loyal citizen, a good neighbor, and a bright and shining light as a Christian, and beloved by a host of friends and acquaintances.

He served as County Treasurer of Hart County, 1864-5.

Rev. J. T. W. Vernon, Pioneer Preacher

REV. J. T. W. VERNON, who is one of the pioneer Baptist preachers in this section of the country, was recently interviewed by the writer for the purpose of obtaining a brief history of his life work in the ministry.

Mr. Vernon, though now in his eighty-fifth year, is an active man, mentally and physically. He has perhaps done more hard work than any man in Georgia of his age and calling. Many years ago the lamented Hon. J. B. Benson, who was a life-long friend of Mr. Vernon, in speaking of him, said: "Brother Vernon can push the jack plane all the week and then preach a better sermon on Sunday than most of the D.Ds."

Mr. Vernon's convenience in life for an education and his opportunity of applying what little he gathered from observation have been very limited. His father and mother died when he was under ten years of age, leaving him to fight the battles of life without the benefits of parental help or guidance.

He was born in Abbeville County, S. C., in 1821. Said he never heard a Methodist preacher before his father and mother died. Also said he had never heard but one Baptist preacher till he was 21 years old, and that was the noted Dr. Spalding, who passed away many years ago. Said that his parents were Presbyterians, and in the neighborhood where they lived there were very few Christians except Presbyterians.

Mr. Vernon has been married three times and raised twelve children. He moved to Georgia in 1859.

A brief summary of his ministerial life, as told by himself in his own way, is about as follows:

"I was baptized on Saturday before the fourth Sunday in April, 1853, by I. H. Goss, into the fellowship of Generostee Baptist Church in Anderson County, S. C.

"Was licensed to preach in June, and ordained to the ministry October 22, 1853. Was called to supply Neals' Creek and Andersonville churches in Anderson County, S. C., for the year 1854. Continued as pastor of Neals' Creek twelve years. Eight years of the time I received a salary of fifty dollars a year, and four years at one hundred dollars per year. During my labors at Neals' Creek Church I baptized about two hundred and forty.

"I served Andersonville Church as pastor twenty-six years, on a salary of thirty to forty dollars per year, and baptized about two hundred and sixty.

"To the church at Double Springs, in Anderson County, I served as pastor twelve years, on a salary of thirty to thirty-seven dollars per year, and baptized about two hundred and fifty.

"To the church at South Union, in Oconee County, S. C., I was pastor four years, on a salary of seventy-five dollars a year, and baptized about eighty-five.

"To the church at Beaverdam, in Oconee County, S. C., four years, at a salary of seventy-five dollars a year, and baptized about ninety.

"To the church at New Prospect, Anderson County, S. C., four years, on salaries of seventy-five to one hundred dollars, and baptized about one hundred and ten.

"To the church at Shiloah, in Anderson County, S. C., eighteen months; received fifty dollars; no baptisms.

"Reed Creek, in Hart County, two years; salary twenty-two dollars; baptized about ten.

"Cannon, in Hart County, two years and six months; salary fifty dollars; baptized sixty-five.

"Pleasant Grove, in Franklin County, ten years; salary fifty dollars; baptized about three hundred.

"Line Church, in Hart County, fifteen years; salary about thirty-five dollars a year; baptized about two hundred and fifty.

"Cross Roads, in Hart County, one year; salary twelve dollars; baptized about twenty-two.

"Cedar Creek, in Hart County, one year; salary sixty dollars; baptized ten.

"Constituted the following churches in Hart County:

"Milltown in 1857, under a brush arbor, where the church now stands. There were about thirteen members. I was called as pastor and preached to them about twenty years, on a salary ranging from twenty-five to seventy-five dollars, and baptized about one hundred and fifty, including a good many colored people, as many as eight since the war.

"The church in Hartwell, in the spring of 1859, was constituted in the court house, as the Baptists had no house of their own. I was serving the church as pastor when the war clouds began to gather over our sunny South. Many of the young members went to the post of duty, leaving but a few to do work for the Master; but the Lord was gracious, and protected them in war, permitting all to return home alive except Col. James E. Skelton, who died on his way to his command in Atlanta. I continued as pastor at Hartwell till the close of the war. Do not now remember how much the church paid as salary, but for the years of 1859 and 1860 the Home Board paid me two hundred dollars each year.

"The amount paid by the Home Board I have always thought was well expended, as this church has many times paid back the principal, besides large dividends. Owing to the great immorality and confusion incident to the excitement of the war I was not permitted to baptize more than a half dozen into the fellowship of the Hartwell church. I hope I will be pardoned for saying so much about the Hartwell church, but I rejoice at the record of the church in the past and look forward with much interest to her future fullness. May the work that was begun be continued to the end of the Mastor's glory.

"The church at New Prospect was constituted in 1884. I was chosen as pastor on a salary of fifty dollars per year, but the church is now paying seventy-five to one hundred dollars a year. Have baptized thirty-five to forty into the fellowship of that church.

Death of Rev. J. T. W. Vernon

"Rev. J. T. W. Vernon died Saturday, November 25, 1905, at his home in Hartwell, where he had been living for several years.

"Only a few months before his death that scholarly and widely esteemed divine, Rev. J. R. Earle, of South Carolina, life-long friend and co-worker, spent a day or two with Mr. Vernon, during which time they reviewed much of their past interesting and pleasant experience together. Finally, before they separated for the last time, the subject of their final departure came up, and Mr. Vernon made the request of Mr. Earle in a very pathetic way that, if he passed away first, he wanted him to conduct the funeral services. They then together selected the scripture to be read, which was the 14th chapter of John's Gospel. This was read Sunday afternoon at the beginning of the services by Rev. T. M. Galphin, pastor of the Hartwell Baptist Church. Rev. J. R. Earle, as requested, preached the funeral sermon, using as a text a part of the 13th verse of the 14th chapter of Revelation: 'I heard a voice from heaven saying unto me, Write, Blessed are the dead which did in the Lord from henceforth: Yea, saith the Spirit, that they may rest from their labors; and their works do follow them.'

"The funeral sermon was a very impressive one, and listened to by an unusually large number of people who gathered at the house to pay their last testimony to the memory of one whom they had known to love and respect so long.

"Mr. Vernon was a very enthusiastic Mason, never having found within the threshold of that oriental order anything that conflicted with the duties he owed to himself, his family, or his God. At the conclusion of the funeral services, the Masonic fraternity took charge of the services and with loving arms bore the body of this good man to the Hartwell Cemetery, and after the imposing ceremonies of this ancient order were concluded the congregation of people dispersed, feeling that thus ends the earthly career of another patriot and pioneer minister of great Christian activity."

Peter Fleming

PETER FLEMING was born May 5, 1771, in the Colony of Virginia, five years before the declaration of American Independence. He later moved to Lancaster County, S. C., where he lived a number of years.

He married Frances Suit, who in her youth moved with her parents and other members of the family from a neighborhood somewhere near Neuse River, N. C.

To Peter Fleming and his wife, Frances Suit Fleming, were born one son: Peter Lewis Fleming; and five daughters: Charlotte, Sarah Dianah, Martha Jane, Rachael Lenora, and Frances Ann.

Peter Lewis Fleming married Margaret Elizabeth Cauthen, Charlotte married John Mickle, Sarah Dianah married Monroe Cauthen, all of Lancaster County, S. C.

Rachael Lenora married Dillard Williams, and Martha Jane married Jonathan W. O'Barr, all of Hart County, Ga.

Peter Fleming, in his old age, moved from Lancaster County, S. C., to Franklin (later Hart) County sometime in the early 1850s, and purchased a home and farm located on the Andersonville and Carnesville road. He owned several slaves and engaged in farming.

In religion he was a Presbyterian, and also belonged to the order of Free and Accepted Masons.

In 1857 he made his will, disposing of lands, slaves, and all other property.

He died June 19, 1858, at the age of 87 years, one month and 14 days, and was buried near his residence.

Peter Lewis Fleming

Peter Lewis Fleming, son of Peter Fleming, was born in Lancaster County, S. C., November 7, 1831, and, like his father, moved to Georgia in the early fifties. As already stated, he married Margaret Elizabeth Cauthen, of Lancaster County, S. C.

To him and his wife were born five sons: Andrew Jackson, Wade Hampton, William Cauthen, P. L. Fleming, Jr., commonly called Luke, and Michael T. Fleming; and six daughters: Nancy (who died young), Janie, Elizabeth E., Martha Lenora, Sarah D., and Myra F. Fleming.

After the death of Peter Fleming, father of Peter L. Fleming, he came into possession of the home, farm, and slaves, and engaged in farming. After the War Between the States, and after the slaves were set free, he continued to live and farm on the place the remainder of his life, with the exception of a few years that he lived on Savannah River, on the farm known as the Bowman place, which, for the time he lived there, belonged to Michael Johnson, an uncle by marriage of the wife of Peter L. Fleming.

In the War Between the States he enlisted as a private in Company "C," of the 5th Georgia Regiment, under Capt. D. G. Johnson, on May 25, 1864, at Atlanta.

He held the office of Justice of the Peace in the 1115th District, G. M., and was at one time during the war postmaster of Reed Creek Post Office, which was located at his home.

He was a member of the Board of Education of Hart County for a while, to which office he had been duly elected by the people. At one time after the war he taught school at what was then known as the Weldon School House.

He died March 14, 1917, and was buried in the family burying ground. His grave, as well as that of his father and other members of the family, marked by marble tombstones with appropriate inscriptions.

Judge William R. Poole

IN WRITING a history of Judge Poole, we will state that we are under many obligations to Mrs. Nelle Poole Hamer, a granddaughter of Judge Poole, for a most excellent and well-written article upon his life and character, which we reproduce herewith and incorporate as a part of this sketch.

"Captain William Roach Poole was born in Spartanburg County, in July, 1811. His parents were William (?) Poole and Polly Coleman Poole. He was the seventh child of a large family.

"Tradition says the progenitor of this Poole family was from Poole, a village on the coast of England. The father of the progenitor of this family was a sea captain. He and his twelve-year-old son came to America and liked the new country so well that he returned for his family, leaving his twelve-year-old son with friends in America. He and his family left England and have never been heard of. It is supposed that they perished in a storm at sea.

"When only nineteen years of age, William Roach Poole visited relatives in Franklin County, Ga., and met Miss Susan Stovall; soon afterwards she became his wife. They made their home in Spartanburg County for several years after their marriage. They had one son, LaFayette Stovall Poole. In 1838-1840, or 1839-1841, William R. Poole represented Spartanburg County in the Legislature. Soon afterwards several brothers went to Mississippi, and William R. Poole, wife, and son, decided to go to this new state.

"On their way, they went by to tell his wife's parents good-bye. They found her parents so feeble that they changed their plans and stayed with them. They settled at the old Stovall home, on what is now known as Poole's Creek, about two miles southeast of Lavonia.

"Soon after coming to Georgia he was elected to the House of Representatives, and afterwards became State Senator.

"While in office, the movement that Hart County be made from what

JUDGE WILLIAM R. POOLE

was then Franklin County was agitated. William R. Poole was very much interested in this plan, and was very active in getting the bill passed. At this time Milledgeville was the Capital of Georgia.

"While in the Senate his wife became very ill. His friends becoming very much alarmed, went to Milledgeville to carry the sad message. When he reached his home, after driving for days and nights, he found his wife dead, and his son so ill that they never told him of his mother's passing. La-Fayette Stovall Poole died a few days later. He had just passed his twenty-first birthday. This was about the year 1852.

"He continued to live at his home in Georgia a few years, always busy with a large plantation, many slaves, and always vitally interested in public affairs.

"While at court in Carnesville, Ga., he met Miss Martha Vashti Cunningham from Abbeville, S. C., who in 1855 became his wife. They built the old Poole home, which still stands, located one and a fourth miles southeast of Lavonia.

"Their children were: Rosanna Coleman Poole, deceased; Mrs. Mollie Poole Black, Montrose, Ga.; Mrs. Rebecca Poole Lee, of Weatherford, Tex.; and Robert Toombs Poole, deceased.

"When war was declared between the states, William R. Poole volunteered and at King's Bench organized the first company in Hart County, known as Poole's Volunteers. William R. Poole was captain of the company, and soon they were in the midst of the great war.

"When the War Between the States was over, General Robert Toombs took refuge from the Federal authorities in Captain William R. Poole's home. This was while General Toombs was trying to escape to England. He spent about a week in Captain Poole's home. Captain Poole recognized him when at a distance. He was riding his famous saddle horse, 'Nelly Gray.' Capt. Poole had his horse taken and cared for down in a ravine in a thick woodland back of the family cemetery.

"This was the middle of September, 1865. A day or so before the General's visit a son was born to Captain and Mrs. Poole. During the General's stay, Captain Poole took his young son in for the General to see. General Toombs took him in his arms and asked if he might be permitted to name the child. Captain Poole gave his consent. Then the General said, 'I christen thee Robert Toombs Poole.' I intend to be a godfather to this boy. Afterwards saying, 'When my star was bright I had many namesakes, but since I am an exile this is my first.'

"About 1874 Captain Poole and family moved to Jefferson, Ga. They lived there for four years because of the educational advantages offered by Martin Institute at that place. About 1879 Captain Poole and family returned to his home in Hart County. On March 20, 1882, he died of apoplexy. He is buried with his first wife and son at the Poole family burying ground about two miles south of Lavonia. The monument is of granite, and the family graves are enclosed by an iron fence, and outside this there are posts and chains marking off the old cemetery. His second wife died in 1899 and was carried back to Abbeville to the Cunningham burying plot in the Long Cane Cemetery.

"Captain Poole was vitally interested in education. He built a school on his plantation. Here his children and all the neighboring children attended school. The teacher lived in his home. He served on various school committees in the county. He served as Judge of the Inferior Court."

In addition to the foregoing interesting article, we herewith give some paragraphs relative to Judge Poole's activities, political, military, and otherwise.

Judge Wm. R. Poole served as State Senator from Franklin County, Ga., during the years 1853-1854, and Jefferson Holland was the Representative at the same time. At that time, each county in Georgia bordering on the Savannah River, except Lincoln County, was entitled to one Senator, regardless of population of the county, and also one or more Representatives, according to population.

The same rule applied after Hart County was created, and Judge Poole was the first Senator from Hart County, serving during the years 1855-1856. It was due to the foresight and fine judgment of Judge Poole and Hon. Jefferson Holland, while in the Legislature in 1853-1854, that Hartwell, the county seat, has wide and capacious streets, an account of which is related in the history of the streets of the town.

Judge Poole was elected as one of the Judges of the Inferior Court, which position he held from January, 1857, for a term of four years, and by reason of his services as such, he obtained the title of Judge.

Judge Poole was Captain of Company "H," 15th Georgia Regiment, organized at King's Bench July 15, 1861, which position he held until April 5, 1862, when he resigned. This company, however, was not the first company to be organized in the county, as Company "B" and "C" had been organized June 9, 1861 and July 13, 1861, respectively.

The death of Judge Poole was accidental, as appears from an account given in *The Hartwell Sun,* issue March 25, 1882.

It appears from the account that Judge Poole came to Hartwell on Monday, March 20, 1882, and on his way home at the Herring hill near Lightwoodlog Creek, he fell from his buggy and his neck was broken.

The home of Judge Poole was a splendid ante-bellum home, located on a large and valuable farm, which was a part of a 5,000-acre lot of land that was donated by the State to the University of Georgia as an endowment, which lot was divided into farms of about two hundred acres each, and was and still are known as "Academy Lands."

After the home and farm had passed from the Poole descendants, unlike many of the old homes of other prominent citizens and first settlers of our country, which have been in a great measure abandoned and allowed to become delapidated, it has by its present owner, Mr. J. E. Conwell, been very much improved and is today a magnificent home of Colonial style, while the farm has been brought up to a high state of fertility and cultivation, located right under the shadow of the prosperous City of Lavonia, a little more than a mile away.

However, the name Poole, the former owner, the family burying ground in which Judge Poole and members of his family sleep, the visit of Gen. Robert Toombs in the days of his exile, together with the other incidents that cluster around and about the old homestead will ever make the place interestingly historic, and in the years to come it will continue to be known as the "Poole place."

Solomon M. Bobo

SOLOMON M. BOBO, son of Sampson and Elizabeth Bobo, was born in Franklin County, Ga., on December 30, 1842.

His grandfather, Samuel Bobo, came from Union, S. C., at the close of the War of the Revolution, and crossed the Tugaloo River not far above where Andersonville was later established, swimming his horse across the stream and dispersing a group of Indians, and took possession of the premises, to which he later obtained a grant from the State for something over two hundred acres of land, where he built his home, lived and reared his family, and when he died was buried near his home.

Sampson Bobo, his son, came into possession of the place and lived there for many years. The place is yet known as the old Bobo place.

Solomon M. Bobo was converted and joined the Baptist Church at Reed Creek, August, 1858.

He enlisted as a private, August 24, 1861, at the beginning of the War Between the States, in Captain P. E. Devant's Company, which was organized in Hartwell, Ga., June 9, 1861, and known as Company "B," 24th Regiment of Georgia. He was appointed Fifth Sergeant in 1863. Appointed First Sergeant in 1864. Captured at Deep Bottom, Va., April 18, 1864.

He was in the hottest of the conflict, and none were more brave or patriotic. He was one of the few who went through and came out alive in that great slaughter, the battle of Gettysburg.

When taken a prisoner he was subjected to the severest ordeals. The prison was near the coast in New York and subject to overflow during great tidal waves. He was stricken with smallpox in the coldest of winter in that northern prison and suffered untold hardships.

At the close of the war he came home determined to be and to do. After seeing that his father and mother were properly cared for, he went to Mercer University, which was then located at Penfield, Ga. He was unable to take a full course and complete his education. As soon as he felt able to teach in the common schools he took up teaching, in which he soon built up a reputation second to none in many respects. He taught the fourth school that was taught in Hartwell after the Civil War.

He was one of the outstanding school men in the State. Together with Morgan H. Looney, George C. Looney, Martin V. Looney and Morgan L. Parker, he put Hart County on the map as a school center. Was member of the Board of Education of Hart County for several years.

He was co-principal with S. W. Peek of the Hartwell High School in 1879-80. Many are living today who cherish and revere the memory of this good man for lighting the spark of inspiration in their lives.

He married Mrs. Mary E. Webb, widow of Dr. James M. Webb, October 15, 1874, Rev. Henry Tyler officiating clergyman.

His hotel, the "Bobo House," where high-class service and old-time hospitality were dispensed, played an important part in the advertisement and development of the town and county. He was at one time associated with The Hartwell Publishing Company, which edited and published one of the best weekly newspapers in the State.

He was, likewise, a leader in church work. He served his church conspicuously for many years as superintendent of the Sunday school. Served as clerk of the church for many years, and in April, 1883, the church increased her board of deacons and he was chosen as one.

He was elected Moderator of the Hebron Baptist Association in 1889, when that body met with the church at Reed Creek, and served as moderator for three terms, and again in 1896, when the association met with the Church at Harmony, and continued as moderator for seven consecutive terms.

He died at the Confederate Veterans' Home in Atlanta, Monday morning, February 11, 1923.

On Tuesday, February 12, 1923, the funeral services of Prof. Bobo were conducted by his pastor, Rev. G. J. Davis, at the Baptist Church in Hartwell. Following several songs, favorites of the deceased, and appropriate remarks by Rev. Davis, a number of citizens gave expression, in which they expressed their highest esteem for Prof. Bobo.

Interment was in the Hartwell Cemetery. His grave is marked by a marble monument with the following inscription:

"S. M. BOBO
DEC. 30, 1842
FEB. 12, 1923."

The Samuel White Family History

SAMUEL WHITE, son of William White, was born in South Carolina, March 2, 1808. He married Nancy Murrell, daughter of David and Elizabeth Harlan Murrell, in 1832. Nancy Murrell was born May 12, 1804, and died March 22, 1888.

Mr. White moved from South Carolina to Georgia and settled in Franklin (later Hart) County.

To Samuel White and wife, Nancy Murrell White, were born the following children:

Dr. William Franklin White, who married Mary A. Jackson, daughter of Joseph Jackson.

Dr. David Monroe White, who married .... Gilliland.

Madison White, killed in the War Between the States.

Martha A. E. White, never married.

Samuel White was the first County Treasurer of Hart County, which office he held for six years, 1854-1859, inclusive.

He was a member of Pleasant Grove Baptist Church. He died September 12, 1895, and he and his wife are buried in the cemetery at Pleasant Grove.

Elizabeth Murrell, wife of David Murrell, and a daughter of George Harlan and wife, Anna Breede Harlan, was born in 1778, and died in 1841.

George Harlan, son of Aaron Harlan, Jr., and wife, Sarah Hollingsworth Harlan, was born in Chatham County, S. C., in 1756, and died in 1813. George Harlan was a soldier in the War of the Revolution, serving as a private in Captain Henry Keys' Company, Chester County (Pa.), Militia in Pennsylvania. He also served as a private in the 6th Company of the

8th Battalion of Chester County (Pa.), Militia, under Colonel Patterson Bell, 1778.

George Harlan was a direct descendant of Valentine Hollingsworth, Sr., a member of the famous Hollingsworth family, widely known and honored in the United States. A brief, yet very interesting and highly entertaining sketch of the Hollingsworth family history is given herewith.

"Descendants of Valentine Hollingsworth, Sr."

"The Hollingsworths have held their own all along the ages. They were an old Saxon family said to have settled in the northeastern part of Cheshire, as early as 1022, in which year the ancestral estate, Hollingsworth Manor, in Cheshire, was purchased. The name represents a locality, from the estate of that name, near Mottram, in the county in question. The name comes from the two words, 'holly' and 'worth,' a farm, meaning a farm of holly trees. Annals dating from the Norman conquest, speak of 'the hundred of Macclesfield or Maxfield,' known in the Damesday survey as 'The hundred of Hamstan,' and one of the Manors mentioned in these ancient books is that of Hollingsworth Manor, situated on the edge of the great woods of Macclesfield. The visitation of Cheshire by the official herald in the year 1850 includes 'John Hollingsworth, Gent,' and 'Robert Hollingsworth,' among the gentry residing in the hundred of Macclesfield.

"A further record speaks of Robert Hollingsworth of Hollingsworth Hall, from whom the family is descended, and who was Magistrate for the counties of Chester and Lancaster. The church of the family and the hall, both several centuries old, are still standing, and upon both are emblazoned the family Coat of Arms. The late owner, Captain Robert Hollingsworth, the last representative of the English branch of the family, died in 1865. The estate is said to include 625 acres and to be valued at 20,000 pounds. Picturesque red-berried holly trees abound upon the estate, and when one realizes its nearness to the edge of the Macclesfield woods, the arms and crest handed down for generations acquire a picturesque significance. The tinctures of the shield are azure, suggestive of the blue sky, argent, of the silvery streams that flow through the woodlands, and vert, of the green leafage of the forest trees.

"The virtues of these colors are equally beautiful, expressing loyalty, innocence and love. The Crest is a stag, recalling the Saxon Earl of Cheshire and merry hunting scenes, and three glistening holly leaves suggest Christmas in merry England. Motto, 'Learn to suffer what must be borne, or, bear patiently what must be borne.' The usurpation of that Saxon shire by the Norman Earl, Hugh Lupus, no doubt suggested the motto. At any rate, the records state that these freemen of Hollingsworth and the seven other manors that make up Macclesfield, paid their yearly tax to the usurping Earl and held their manors in undisturbed possession.

"It is probable that the Hollingsworths went over to Ireland from England with other planters early in the 17th Century.

"The name Hollingsworth, so widely known and honored in the United States, is spelled severally: Hollingworth, Hollinsworth, and Hollingsworth. The last spelling has been clung to by a large majority of the descendants of the founder of the family in America, who was Valentine Hollingsworth, and who came to the New World from Ireland in 1682, the year in which William Penn arrived in the Delaware, in front of which is now the city of Philadelphia, Pa. The Hollingsworth family was noted for its enterprise and industry, and many of its members were largely engaged in the manufacture of flour, and were the owners of a number of mills on the branches of the Elbe River in Cecil County, Md., New Castle County, Del., also in Virginia, South Carolina, and in other states, and later of shipyards, steel mills, etc."

The Pearman Family

WILLIAM PEARMAN was born in Virginia, before 1757, did in Halifax County, February, 1788. His residence before and during the Revolution was Halifax County, Va.

William Pearman married Betty Hanks (Mrs. Weldon, a widow) in 1785. His wife died in 1815.

Weldon Pearman, the youngest son of William Pearman and his wife, Betty Hanks (Mrs. Weldon), was born 1786; died 1868.

Weldon Pearman married Lettia Shirley 1806. Lettia Shirley was born 1789, and died 1841.

Jonathan Pearman, son of Weldon Pearman and Lettia Shirley Pearman, was born October 28, 1807, and Leta Wakefield to whom he was married, in 1827. Jonathan Pearman came from South Carolina to Georgia in about 1853 or 1854.

Weldon C. Pearman, son of Jonathan and Leta Wakefield Pearman, was born November 18, 1830; died March, 1863. Married Nancy Kathryn Parker, daughter of Lewis and Matilda Swann Parker, in September, 1856.

The Parker Family

LEWIS PARKER, son of Joseph Parker and Barbara Redwine Parker, and father of Nancy Kathryn Pearman, wife of Weldon C. Pearman, married Matilda Swann. The Redwine and Parker families came from Virginia to North Carolina, and later to Georgia, settling in the community in which Redwine Church was later established.

The children of Weldon C. Pearman and wife, Nancy Kathryn Parker Pearman, were: Benjamin Howard Pearman, born August 31, 1857, and Leta Matilda Pearman, born September 17, 1862.

Benjamin Howard Pearman married Dora Gloer, December 17, 1889. Their children are: Hayden, Howard Gloer, Clifton and Sarah Pearman.

Benjamin Howard Pearman died September 9, 1909.

Leta Matilda Pearman married Samuel Harrison White, son of Dr. William Franklin White, and grandson of Samuel White, February 23, 1886.

Samuel Harrison White was born March 8, 1860.

The children of Samuel Harrison White and wife, Leta Matilda Pearman White, are:

Lois Claire White; born March 13, 1887. Married Samuel Robert Patton, October 24, 1909.

Wallace Edmund White; born August 24, 1889. Married to Julia Leland Kendall, June 26, 1917.

Belle Parker White; born December 21, 1891. Married Philip Edwin Adams, October 22, 1913.

Fred Seaborn White; born September 28, 1894. Married, October 1, 1919, to Elsie M. Duncan.

Monroe Howard White; born October 25, 1898. Married Allie Gaines, daughter of Robert L. Gaines, of Bowersville, Ga., October 27, 1927.

William Pearman's Service in the War of the Revolution

William Pearman was one of the pioneers of Virginia, Halifax County. Received a patent of land from King George II. In 1857 he owned several hundred acres of land along the Banister River, near the center of Halifax County. Lived there till death in 1788. During the Revolution he (Wm. Pearman) served as a private in Captain Philip Richard Francis Lee's Company, Virginia Regiment, known as Captain Valentine Peyton's Company—commanded by Col. Wm. Heth. He enlisted February 14, 1778 for one year. Was discharged March 4, 1779.

Rev. Samuel B. Sanders

REV. SAMUEL B. SANDERS was born in Elbert County (now Hart) June 22, 1808. Joined the Baptist Church at Sardis in May, 1828, at the age of 20 years. Was ordained a deacon at Line Church, May 18, 1844, the same day the church was constituted, he being one of the charter members; was licensed to preach by the same church December 11, 1847. On July 29, 1849, by request of Line Church, he was ordained to the full Gospel ministry by the following noted ministers: Revs. Phillip Mathews, Benjamin Thornton, Pleasant B. F. Burgess, and Albert T. Vandiver.

During his ministry he served the following churches as pastor: Rehoboth in Elbert County 12 years. The membership when he was called was 16, and 160 when he was called to another field. For a number of years he served Union Church in Clarke County. Pleasant Grove and Clarke's Creek in Franklin County, and Reed Creek and Cannon in Hart County.

He served Reed Creek Church as pastor for 18 years in all, being the second longest pastorate in the history of the church. It was during his pastorate that more members were added to the church than that of any other pastor. He was pastor before, during, and after the War Between the States. The name Samuel B. Sanders and Reed Creek Church were so interwoven that to speak of one naturally suggested the other.

He was a man that really loved the souls of the people, and by his faithful warning many were made to think upon their ways and turn from their sins and accept Jesus as their Saviour.

It was quite appropriate that he and his companion were buried in the city of the dead at Reed Creek, where they peacefully sleep along with the fathers and mothers in Israel, who for so long a time sat beneath the sound of his preaching and were reassured, edified, spiritually uplifted and furthered on to the glory world.

Jefferson Holland

From The Hartwell Sun

"HON. JEFFERSON HOLLAND, who was stricken with paralysis week before last, mention of which was made in our last issue, died at his home in Shoal Creek District on Saturday last, at the age of eighty-one years, and had played an important part in the history of the county.

"Mr. Holland represented Franklin County in the Legislature before Hart County was organized, and afterwards was elected to the House for two terms from Hart County, in 1860 and again in 1873, was Justice of the Peace in the county. Was at one time Tax Collector of Franklin County.

"He was an acceptable member of the Masonic Lodge at Hartwell, Ga., which was known as Hermon No. 189, until the charter was surrendered several years ago.

"The funeral services were conducted by Rev. W. J. Purcell, pastor of Shoal Creek Church, who stated during his discourse that he had conversed with Mr. Holland during a series of meetings held at that church, and he expressed himself as being ready for the change when the time should come.

"While Mr. Holland never united himself with any church, yet he attended religious services, was a good friend to the church and always on the side of morality and religion on any question that arose involving such.

"His remains were laid to rest at Shoal Creek Cemetery on Monday, 9th inst., by loving hands in the presence of a large concourse of relatives and friends, and we have no doubt but that our friend has entered upon that rest that remains for the faithful and true."

Jefferson Holland was born in South Carolina, a son of Robert Holland. He was a brother of Thomas Holland, who in the early days of the town of Hartwell was prominent in the town and county, engaging in the mercantile business, and was at one time Clerk of the Superior Court of Hart County.

To Jefferson Holland and wife, who before her marriage was Matilda Barton, and sister to Rev. H. M. Barton, were born the following children: W. R. Holland, Henry M. Holland, John T. Holland, James Holland, Thomas Holland, Misses Sue and Sallie Holland, and Mrs. Frances M. Price, wife of T. S. Price. Probably there were other children whose names we do not have.

As already stated, Mr. Holland was buried in the cemetery at Shoal Creek Church, his grave marked by a granite headstone, with inscription as follows:

"JEFFERSON HOLLAND
MAY 28, 1812
OCT. 7, 1893
"AN HONEST MAN'S THE NOBLEST WORK OF GOD."

Engraved on the headstone is the insignia of F. & A. M. (Square and Compasses).

Rev. Asa Avery

REV. ASA AVERY was born October 25, 1821. To the best of our information, the state of his nativity was South Carolina, and in Laurens County of said state.

In the latter part of the year 1873, or the first part of the year 1874, he, together with his family, consisting at that time of a wife and one son and two daughters, moved to Hart County, Ga., and lived for a number of years at Avery's Ferry on Tugaloo River, which ferry was established sometime after he obtained possession of the place. In about the year 1887, he sold the place and moved up into the neighborhood of Bethany Baptist Church, where he continued to live to the time of his death, which occurred on August 8, 1906.

Following is a brief sketch of Rev. Asa Avery as the same appears in Rev. J. F. Goode's History of the Tugaloo Baptist Association:

"Of Asa Avery the writer knows comparatively little. He was a citizen of Hart County, Ga., and I think a member of Reed Creek Church. In 1883 the church of which he was a member, together with a number of other churches, withdrew from the Tugaloo to go into the organization of the Hebron Association, and if he ever attended another association of the Tugaloo, I have no recollection of his presence. Where he lived at the time of his death, or what date he passed away, we know absolutely nothing. He was a very affable man. As to his ministerial gifts, nothing is known. His work in the ministry was in Hart County, and perhaps in Elbert County. We think there is no doubt that he was a good and faithful minister of Jesus Christ."

As to Rev. Asa Avery's labors, we wish to say that he was the founder of the church at Cedar Creek, Hart County, Ga., which was organized in the year 1878. Prior to that date he had regular appointments to preach in a school house at the place where the church was later established. The community was a bit remote from other churches at the time, and after he had preached at the place for perhaps a few years the people decided to organize a church at the place, which they did on the fifth Sunday, 31st day of March, 1878, and at which time Rev. Asa Avery was chosen as pastor for the remainder of the year 1878, and was re-elected in the following October and served the church as pastor faithfully until the close of the year 1880.

Sometime prior to the year 1886, Rev. Asa Avery had regular appointments to preach in the community in which Bethany Baptist Church was later, in 1886, organized.

The place where he first conducted services was under a brush arbor something like a mile east of the present site of the church, and was for a time called "Piney Grove."

He was called as the first pastor of the church after organization, but we have no record as to how long he served the church as pastor.

So it may be said that the churches of Cedar Creek and Bethany are abiding monuments to Rev. Asa Avery's labors, and they, together with his other labors while he lived, "are his works that do follow him," while he rests from his labors.

Rev. Asa Avery is buried in the cemetery at Bethany Church, his grave marked by a tombstone with the following inscription:

"REV. ASA AVERY, BORN OCTOBER 25, 1821, DIED AUG. 8, 1906."

Hon. F. B. Hodges

HON. FREDERICK B. HODGES was born in Clarkesville, Ga., November 29, 1827. Spent his boyhood days on the farm, and in his young manhood taught school successfully in the country.

In 1854, when Hartwell was laid out, he came to Hartwell and engaged in the mercantile business. In 1856, being a practical surveyor, he was elected County Surveyor of Hart County, which position he held until 1860, when he was elected Ordinary, which office he held until 1868.

When the War Between the States broke out he was appointed by Col. Thomas W. Thomas Commissary of the 50th Georgia Regiment and received a Captain's commission. This place he was compelled to resign at Pine Creek Camp, Va., in the fall of 1861.

In 1863, when Governor Brown made a call for the officers of the State, he volunteered and raised a company in this county, which was afterwards known as Company "A," of Gen. Toombs' Cavalry Regiment.

After the war he studied law and was admitted to the bar and at once entered upon a lucrative practice, which he held until 1888.

In 1877 he was elected State Senator of the Thirty-first District. He was, therefore, a member of the body which tried Georgia's famous impeachment case, and introduced the second bill in the first Senate under the present Constitution of the state, viz.: "A bill to regulate and restrict the rate of interest in this State," which rate was fixed at seven per cent. and eight per cent. by contract. Prior to the introduction and passage of the bill, exhorbitant rates of interest were charged and collected.

In 1890 Col. Hodges was again nominated as Senator for the Thirty-first Senatorial District of Georgia by the voters of Hart County in a primary election and was duly elected at the general election.

In 1857 Mr. Hodges was appointed Clerk of the Superior Court of Hart County to fill the unexpired term of office of Col. Thomas Holland, who had died before the expiration of his term of office.

Mr. Hodges was twice married. His first wife was Miss Martha J. Holland, daughter of Col. Thomas Holland; and after her death, which occurred August 6, 1858, he married Miss Elizabeth McMullan, daughter of Sinclair McMullan, on May 10, 1859.

To this union were born four sons: Toombs T. Hodges, John H. Hodges, Walter L. Hodges and Albert Sidney Hodges; and two daughters: Anna Hodges and Clara Hodges.

Mr. Hodges was quite a prominent member of the Methodist Church, serving as trustee and member of the board of stewards, and was superintendent of the Sunday school for a number of years.

Mr. Hodges was an honored member of the Masonic fraternity, and held important positions in the lodge, including the presiding office of Worshipful Master, and his life was as near "plumb, square, and level," as any man of our country who belonged to that noble order.

Col. Hodges died February 26, 1899, and is buried in the cemetery of the City of Hartwell; his grave marked by an imposing granite monument with the following inscriptions:

"HON. F. B. HODGES, BORN NOV. 29, 1827, DIED FEB. 26, 1899.
"MARY J. HOLLAND, WIFE OF F. B. HODGES, BORN AUG. 29, 1834, MARRIED AUGUST 2, 1853, DIED AUGUST 6, 1858."

Mrs. Elizabeth Hodges, second wife of F. B. Hodges, died June 5, 1910. No inscription to her birth has as yet been engraved on the monument.

In the issue of June 10, 1910, there appears an article in *The Hartwell Sun*, written upon the death of Mrs. Hodges, a small part of which we herewith reproduce.

"MOTHER IN ISRAEL GOES TO HER REWARD"

"On Sunday morning, June 5, 1910, at eight o'clock, after an illness of a few days, Mrs. F. B. Hodges passed from earth to heaven.

"Perhaps the death of this grand woman will cause more widespread and universal regret than would that of any woman in this entire section, for perhaps more people knew and esteemed her for her Christian character and labors. Of her it might be said she was a 'mother in Israel.' She had passed the allotted span of life, being in her seventy-fourth year, and for fifty years of that time she had been an active Christian worker, and her noble deeds of charity, benediction and love can not be overestimated. Modest and unassuming as she ever was, yet she was always recognized as a leader in church work, and as a power for good she has left an impress upon her community that will never be forgotten.

"But it is not our purpose to eulogize this grand dame, that should and will be done by one better fitted for the duty, and with a more specific knowledge of her life's history. But this we will say, that Mrs. Hodges in the article of death might well have looked back on a long, well-rounded life of usefulness and good deeds and exclaimed with a happy consciousness—'It is finished.'"

John R. Kay

JOHN R. KAY was born in Abbeville County, S. C., June 4, 1828, and died in Hartwell, Ga., Friday, February 5, 1897, after a long and painful illness. At the age of eleven years he joined the Baptist Church, later he united with the Methodist Church.

On November 15, 1853, he was married to Miss Lucinda Pickerell, of Anderson County, S. C.

Mr. Kay was a pioneer settler of Hartwell. He was by profession a carpenter, and when the town was laid out, in 1854, he built the first dwelling house erected in the town for John B. Benson. And from that time up to his appointment as postmaster he industriously plied his vocation.

He was postmaster at the time of his death. He helped to build the Methodist Church in 1859, and from its organization he was an active, consistent, and leading member. He was deeply pious, and his words of exhortation, and his godly example were a source of encouragement and inspiration to the members.

In the War Between the States he was a brave soldier and served his country faithfully.

His funeral was preached at the Methodist Church by his pastor, Rev. C. A. Jamison, after which his remains were carried to the cemetery, followed by a large cortage. At the grave the pastor read the burial services, after which Rev. J. T. W. Vernon lead in a fervent prayer, and the benediction was pronounced by Rev. L. W. Stephens, after which all that was mortal of John R. Kay was tenderly consigned to the tomb. A government tombstone marks his grave.

A window of the M. E. Church was dedicated to him and is known as the "John R. Kay Memorial Window."

James Wesley Williams

James W. Williams

JAMES WESLEY WILLIAMS was grandson to grandparents of four nationalities—American, English, Dutch and Welsh. His father's father was William Williams (born 1750), a Welshman. William Williams was a Rebel in the Revolution, was captured by the English at the fall of Savannah, taken to England and held a prisoner for eighteen months.

When released he came back to America and married a Miss Lovingood (born 1760), of Dutch descent. They first lived in Pickens County, S. C. In this family were five girls and two boys, one of whom was William Williams II (born 1790), the father of James Wesley Williams.

His mother's father, William White (born 1750), English, was also a Revolutionary soldier. He married Mary Earle (born 1760), of Virginia. They settled in Georgia near Alford's Bridge. Mary Earle was a cousin of Bishop John Earle, a noted Methodist. In 1800, Sara White was born, who was the mother of James Wesley Williams.

The Williams and Whites gave their children Bible names. They were "Campmeeting Methodists." Also these families were born mechanics, building grist mills, sawmills, spinning wheels, looms, farming implements and any other machinery used in that day which was made of wood or iron.

In the year 1839, on a snowy morning of December 22nd, was born to William and Sara White Williams, baby number eight, a boy. They called him James Wesley. These parents, native Georgians, had moved to South

Carolina about five years before this, and settled on the Harrison lands, between the Tugaloo and Seneca rivers, in Anderson District, where they continued to live for fifteen years until 1850. The boy, James Wesley, grew to "plowboyhood" with a few spare weeks in a country school where he learned to spell and read. This constituted the only schooling he ever had. In 1845, another baby came to William and Sara White Williams, and a young son of eighteen years died. In 1850 the father, William Williams, bought a small farm up the Tugaloo river a few miles, where he finished bringing up the family of six sons, William, David, Harmon, Warren, James and Jesse, and two daughters, Martha Ulissia and Lydia Katherine.

In his early teens James Wesley came to Hart County, Georgia, with cash capital of thirty cents, a small bundle of clothes, and a burning desire to make a place for himself in the world. This he did. He selected the carpenter's trade for his profession, and that, with his diligent study by candle light at night, was the first stepping stone in his successful career as business man and Christian gentleman.

When the war cry sounded in the Southland in 1861, he laid aside his leather apron, and the following is his own account of his share in the struggle that followed:

"I was a volunteer in the first company formed in Hart County, Ga., Company "C," 16th Georgia Regiment—which was brought together at Big Shanty in June, 1861. We were returned, reorganized, and marched away to Virginia in time to see the wounded being brought in from the first battle of Mannassas, as we entered the city. We camped near Richmond and drilled until October, then my regiment was moved to the Peninsular. At that time I was in the hospital with typhoid fever, and it was not until March, 1862, that I was able to join my regiment then stationed at Yorktown.

"In April, 1862, we were in our first real battle with the Yanks, which was fought at Warwick Run. Soon after, we retreated from the Peninsular, fighting as we made the backward march. By then our rations were running low, and our quartermaster commandeered corn, which was issued to us on the cob. We parched it ourselves. We took up camp near Richmond, and did picket duty in and around Richmond until July. It was at this time General Joseph E. Johnson was wounded in the battle of Seven Pines, and General Robert E. Lee was put in command of the Confederate Army. After the Seven Days battle I was detailed in August to drive a mule team on the raid into Maryland. I was held on the job forty days. While a teamster I saw the most gruesome sights my eyes fell upon during the war. Driving through the second Mannassas battlefield three days after the fight, I saw many corpses—to the right, to the left, in the road,—all black as any African. Only by the hair could one tell they were of the white race.

"Our regiment then marched to head off Burnside's Army at Fredericksburg, in the late fall. We gained a signal victory over the enemy at Stone Fence in December, and drove those living back across the river. The winter of 1862-63 was the worst during the war. There were heavy snowfalls often two feet deep. I was on picket duty there and palleted in the open, on the ground, and frequently woke up to find myself completely snowed under. Here too, I had the race of my life, off picket duty line for a quarter of a mile, through the open field, with some dozen Yankees in pursuit, sniping bullets around me. None hit me, however, and I reached cover safely. The remainder of the winter we rested in winter quarters, picketing, fighting snow battles and doing other stunts for amusement.

"In April, 1863, we encountered and fought the Yankees under "Fighting Jow" Hooker, for three days. The second day I was made prisoner, held in Washington, D. C., a week, then exchanged and returned to my regiment within ten days from my capture. Shortly after my return from prison I was sent to the hospital with a bad foot. Gangrene developed, and it was only through earnest pleading with the doctors that I kept them from cutting my foot off.

"I went home on a furlough in January, 1864. On February 16th, I was married to Jemima Drucilla Page, we having been engaged since 1861. Later, I returned to the army, and was made to mark time for several days for staying at home too long. Soon we were rushed to meet Grant's Army in the Wilderness, where we spent two days in bloody, drawn battle. Both armies flanked Spottsylvania Court House, and we fought desperately there for a week. The advantage rested with our army, but there was no decisive victory. By another flanking maneuver, we warded Grant off from Richmond. He circled around Petersburg and sat down to the siege.

"On account of my yet lame foot I was again sent to the hospital at Richmond, and was there captured at the fall of our capital. I remained a prisoner until July. I was released and arrived home July 18, 1865. With good will to all old 'Vets' let us strive to be found on the right, at the final roll call up Yonder."

To resume the story of the life of James W. Williams—at home in Hart County he found poverty on all sides. Not he alone, but the whole of the remaining, outnumbered Confederate Army limped back to loved ones to find desolation on all sides. But never yet has the Southern spirit been crushed, and these men picked up the threads of life as well as they could, to make the best of a dire situation. Mr. Williams went to his carpenter's trade, and he and his wife, Jemima Drucilla Page, whom he had married while at home on furlough in 1864, set up housekeeping in a one-room shanty. Mr. John B. Benson helped him in starting a small grocery business. There was an adjoining room to the store which Mr. Williams used as a shop and did all kinds of repair and cabinet work.

This was the start of his furniture and undertaking business, and which led to the present firm of the Hartwell Furniture Company, William C. Page, a nephew, having taken training under him, and eventually succeeding him in this concern. By his attention to business he made his way steadily up, broadening the field of his pursuits until he became one of the most successful business men of Hartwell.

He was a director of the Hartwell Bank from its organization and succeeded Mr. E. B. Benson as president, which position he held a number of years. He was honorary president at his death.

In August, 1908, his wife, who had been in feeble health for a number of years, passed on into the Great Beyond. She left three grown children: Haidee Williams Carter, Warren Hafed Williams and Mary Nimqui Williams Smith.

The subject of this sketch was a devout Christian. He was a member of the Methodist Church from early manhood. There was no guile in this man; no desire for the limelight. He found joy and content in the living of a simple life. Never once did a deserving person in distress ask aid from him without getting help of some sort. Truly this man's life was spent in making the way less rocky for fellow beings. He passed out quietly as he wished to go, August 21, 1923.

NELL SMITH NICHOLS, a granddaughter.

Judge Clayton Stribling Webb

WAS born in Pendleton District (now Anderson County), S. C., January 6, 1804, and died June 28, 1889, being at the time of his death over 85 years of age. In 1852 he moved to Georgia and located at his well known place on Shoal Creek, where he was living at the time of his death.

When Hart was organized, Judge Webb was elected as one of the first board of Judges of the Inferior Court, and he along with his associates, Judges J. V. Richardson, Micajah Carter, Daniel M. Johnson and Henry F. Chandler had the task of locating the county site, over which there arose quite a famous law suit, but which resulted in confirming the selection made by the Justices. After the Justices had rambled over a considerable portion of the county, hunting for the most eligible site, and divided in opinion, Judge Webb, at the very spot where the court house is located, but which was then in the wild woods and only prominent as a deer stand, drove down a stake and said, "Here's the place—as many of you as will, come to me." Judges Carter and Chandler at once acquiesced and Hartwell was chosen.

In the death of Judge Webb, another prominent landmark of the county is removed. Throughout his long life he possessed the utmost confidence of not only his neighbors and friends, but the entire people of his county. In all the relations of life he was honest, faithful and true, fulfilling in an eminent degree the following beautiful language of Mr. Wirt: "His disposition was indeed all sweetness—his affections were warm, kind and social—his patience invincible—his temper even, unclouded, cheerful and serene—his manners plain, open, familiar and simple—his conversation easy, ingenious and unaffected, full of entertainment, full of instruction and irradiated with all those light and softer graces that flowed from a splendid and noble character." Indeed,

> *"He was a man, take him for all in all,*
> *We rarely shall look upon his like again."*

After a long and useful career he rests well, by the side of his wife who preceded him to the tomb but a short while. His remains were interred in the cemetery at Shoal Creek Baptist Church, of which he had long been a prominent member. His long, useful and honorable life, however, will be a bright example for his relatives and friends. Standing beside his newly made grave, let us hope that we, too, may

> *"So live that when our summons comes to join*
> *The innumerable caravan that moves*
> *To the pale realms of shade, where each shall take*
> *His chamber in the silent halls of death,*
> *We go, not like the galley-slave of night,*
> *Scourged to our dungeon, but sustained and soothed*
> *By an unaltering trust, approach the grave*
> *Like one who wraps the drapery of his couch*
> *About him, and lies down to pleasant dreams."*

Warm friendship for the deceased prompts us to drop this small flower on his bier, with the regret that we have not sufficient time and data to do fuller justice to his memory.

Written by A. G. McCurry.

Leroy C. Brown

MR. LEROY C. BROWN died at his home in Hartwell, Wednesday morning, November 1, 1922, age 79. He had lived at his home near Hendry's Church for a considerable part of his life after the Civil War where he was engaged in farming, owning and operating, successfully, a large and valuable farm, which he still owned at the time of his death. He also at one time sold goods at his country home for several years. Several years prior to his death he had made his home in Hartwell and was engaged in the life insurance business, at which he was very successful.

Mr. Brown was a very prominent figure in the life of Hart County for many years. He is said to have been the first citizen in Hart County to advocate the stock law, and the building and maintenance of the public roads by taxation, having written many articles upon the two measures which may yet be read by reference to the files of *The Hartwell Sun.*

He was a Confederate veteran and served with distinction in this capacity during the 60s, which service he entered as a private in Company "B," 24th Regiment, Georgia Volunteers, under Captain Phillip E. Devant, March 13, 1862. He was the last member of a family of seven other brothers and three sisters, and was born and reared in Hart (formerly Elbert) County.

He is survived by two daughters, Mrs. Texie Zellars and Miss Berta Brown, and four sons. He was the grandfather of Col. B. B. Zellars.

Mr. Brown was a member of the Baptist church. He was buried in the Hartwell cemetery, after funeral services conducted by Rev. G. J. Davis, pastor of the Hartwell Baptist Church. His wife preceded him to the grave, having died March 12, 1922, who, before her marriage, was Miss Victoria Bowers, daughter of Judge William Bowers who lived at Eaglegrove.

Vanna

THE village of Vanna, located in the southwestern portion of Hart County, on the Elberton Southern, formerly the Elberton Air Line Railroad, and on state route No. 17, was incorporated in 1912.

D. M. Denney was the first mayor of the town, and E. J. Moore is the present mayor. The population, according to the census of 1930, was 158. There are three stores, a ginnery, depot, warehouse, post office, a church, consolidated school, and about forty or fifty residences in the place.

In about 1893, while Mr. Ezra Bowers was mail agent on the Elberton Air Line Railroad, there was a post office established at the place, and Mr. Bowers had it named Vanna for his cousin, Miss Vanna Ballenger, which name the town assumed.

Mr. Ira M. Brown once lived at the place and owned the property, consisting of about 140 acres of land. The adjoining landowners at the time were C. C. Tucker, W. B. Scarborough, Matilda Smith, presumably the widow of Isham Smith, and W. B. Winn.

Mr. Brown was Justice of the Peace of Ray's district for a number of years. Was Clerk and prominent member of Holly Springs Baptist Church. Was the father of J. J. Brown, who was Commissioner of Agriculture of Georgia for several terms. Mr. Brown moved to Stephens County where he died several years ago.

Mr. C. C. Tucker, commonly called "Kit," to the best of our information, came from Franklin County, was a brother to Dr. Tucker who lived at Carnesville, Ga. Mr. Tucker owned and operated a large tannery, was a shoemaker and dealt in leather and shoes. He owned and operated a farm of some two hundred acres; he also owned a tract of land on Hill Shoal Creek where he owned a mill. He was a soldier in the War Between the States, a prominent member and officer of Fellowship Methodist Church. He died many years ago and is buried at Fellowship.

Other former citizens of the community of Vanna were the McGaritys, Smiths, Winns, Ginns, Ballengers and others.

A short distance south of the town is a place, long known as Little Holly Springs, and before a portion of Madison County was added to Hart County, was the corner of Elbert, Madison and Hart Counties.

In connection with the history of Vanna and community, we herewith reproduce an article written in 1890 by John M. Bowers, a surveyor, which should prove highly interesting to the people of today, as well as to those of future years.

"BETHEL"
"A VISIT TO THE SITE OF AN ANCIENT CHURCH"
For The Hartwell Sun

"On August 27, 1890, while making a survey one and a half miles west of Fellowship Church in Hart County, amid old fields and rugged forests, I ran a line through rather a dreary, rocky woods, when one of the crowd spoke of the Old Bethel Church place. This awakened in my mind drowsy recollections of what I had heard my father say years ago. When we were opposite the old stand we stacked our surveying apparatus and went to the old site. Having learned from an aged member of the party that my own mother, who had long ago passed on to the higher life, had worshipped there when a gay young woman, sixty or seventy years ago, I felt deeply impressed as I stood upon the sacred spot.

"I found one post oak standing that I judged was there in those gone-by days. There were three rock pillars remaining, I suppose in their place; and one was gone. The house was 22x28 feet, judging from the present location of the pillars. My aged friend told me the walls of the house were hewn logs.

"I had heard my father tell of a Methodist preacher, when I was a boy, that he once knew when he was young, that would start to meeting soon Sunday morning in chinquapin time in his shirt sleeves and bare-foot, and going through the chinquapin thicket, fill his pockets and go on to church in due time, and would get up in the pulpit and eat his fruit like a squirrel. My old friend told me here was the place the preacher ate the chinquapins. His name was Malcom Smith. Another preacher that labored here was Oliver Powell.

"There are two graves here; one is the chinquapin preacher's son; the other an old Revolutionary soldier by the name of William Glasgow, who was 80 or 85 years old when he died. Joseph Ballenger and Asa Smith shaved him and dressed him for burial. The former is now an aged man living in our country, and the latter having quit these mortal shores within the last year.

"There was once a great revival at the church. Old Man Glasgow was greatly blessed at said meeting. He desired to be buried under a large oak in the churchyard where the meeting was held. Accordingly his grave was dug at the root of the oak, and his remains were there put to rest. Signs of the roots of the tree are yet to be seen.

"Finally the Bethel house went down, and the church was removed some two or three miles south from the old site, and was called 'Philadelphia.' From there some 35 or 40 years ago the church was removed to the place where it now stands on the Elberton A. L. R. R., and was called 'Fellowship.'

"This being the center around which my maternal ancestry swung for almost a century, excites solemn reflections that are easier felt than expressed."

"Surveyor."

Bowersville

THE town of Bowersville, in Hart County, Ga., is located on the Elberton Southern, formerly the Elberton Air Line Railroad, 26 miles from Toccoa, and 24 from Elberton, and on State Highway No. 17.

The altitude of the place is practically 934 feet, being the highest or near the highest point in the county, the highest point, however, is a short distance southeast of the town. The town is on the watershed line between the tributaries of the Tugaloo River on the east, and those of Broad River on the west. Incorporate limits one mile in every direction from the center of the town. Population in 1930 was 398 according to the U. S. Census of that year.

Historic Items—Old Salem Methodist Church

Old Salem Methodist Church, now abandoned and gone, stood right near where the cemetery of Bowersville is located. Besides the name and the site, we know practically nothing of its history. Rev. J. C. Neese, a local Methodist preacher, was pastor of the church some of the time of its existence. Samuel W. Gilliland, Dock Ellis and others were some of the members, and when the Methodist Church in Bowersville was organized, the membership was merged with it.

An Old Lawground—"Who Struck Billy Patterson?"

As related in a story written by a man who was born more than one hundred years ago in the territory now embraced in Hart County, there was a Justice's Court Ground located about four hundred yards northeast of where the depot in Bowersville stands, which was the lawground in the 370th Dist. G. M., of Franklin County, and probably known as Manley's lawground.

The world renowned conundrum, "Who Struck Billy Patterson?" had its origin at this courtground, according to the story, which is fully written up in another part of this history.

The town was laid out on Saturday before the 4th Sunday in May, 1878, by William F. Bowers, his sons Bunyan and Ezra, Marion Cheek, John O'Dean and others. The lands belonged to William F. Bowers, formerly known as the James Phillips place.

Mr. Bowers, for whom the town was named, had the property surveyed into lots and streets. Part of the streets were laid off parallel with the railroad right-of-way and cross streets at right angles. Mr. Bowers proceeded to sell lots to those wishing to purchase and improve the property, and in the deeds of conveyance inserted a clause that no intoxicating liquors were ever to be sold on the property conveyed, and in case of the violation of the clause, the title reverted to W. F. Bowers, heirs and assigns, which clause read as follows:

"Provided, That the said conveyance is made by the said party of the first part on the expressed condition that no intoxicating liquors shall ever be sold, given away or otherwise disposed of on said bargained premises by said party of the second part, his heirs, executors, administrators, privies or assigns. And in case of a violation of the foregoing last recited condition of this deed, in the selling, giving away or otherwise disposing of intoxicating liquors on said bargained premises by said party of the second part, his heirs, executors, administrators, privies or assigns, the title hereby conveyed shall be thereby forfeited, and the said bargained premises shall revert to said party of the first part, his heirs, executors, administrators on the payment by said party of the first part, his heirs, executors or administrators to said party of the second part, his heirs, executors, or administrators, privies, the original amount of the purchase money for the same without computing any interest or allowing anything for improvements made thereon."

One of the cross streets was named Linder Street for Mr. T. J. Linder who operated a sawmill in the vicinity and sawed the crossties of the Hartwell Railroad, built in 1879. The next cross street above or north of Linder Street, was named Schaefer Street for Mr. Edward Schaefer, who established a large cotton and fertilizer business in the town at the beginning of its business activities. The next cross street above Schaefer Street, was named Benson Street, E. B. Benson & Company having obtained property in the place, built the first storehouse and opened the first store in the town.

In the latter part of the year 1878 or the first part of the year 1879, the Elberton Airline Railroad was completed to Bowersville and later finished the balance of the way to Elberton.

During the year 1879, and before the Hartwell Railroad was built, Bowersville was the only depot in the county, and quite a large fertilizer business was carried on during the spring and a large cotton business in the fall. It was probably during this year that there was a greater volume of business transacted at Bowersville than any year afterwards, as the completion of the Hartwell Railroad detracted to some extent the business which had formerly gone to Bowersville, however, there continued to be a thriving business in the town. The fertilizer and cotton business of Edward Schaefer was carried on under the management of Mr. F. B. Doyle for a number of years.

Among the other business firms as well as that conducted individually may be mentioned the following: J. W. Holbrook, general merchant and cotton buyer; J. M. Cannon & Sons, merchants; S. T. Fleming, merchant; T. R. & H. Cheek, merchants; Alex White, Lee Mason and Perry Hilliard, merchants; John A. Reese, jeweler; Oscar Moore, livery stables; J. B. Blackmon, merchant; Williams Brothers, merchants; J. Fred Hilliard, merchant; A. Linton Neese, groceries, and a number of others not mentioned.

Doctors

The doctors, or perhaps a partial list, who have lived and practiced their profession in Bowersville and community, have been elsewhere mentioned in these pages and are as follows: J. T. Cook, T. B. Cunningham, W. L. Hanie, John W. Starr, J. W. Waldrip, Dr. Spinks, Dr. Parson and son, James Parson; H. F. Shields and Franklin Sanders.

Bunyan Bowers, farmer, carpenter and surveyor. Was one time mayor of the town. Phil Weaver, meat market and veterinarian.

Armistead Hilliard and Joe I. Bennett were two prosperous farmers who lived on the outskirts of the town. B. C. McLane, manufacturer of the famous "Town Talk" cigars.

Robert L. Gaines, who recently died, was mayor of the town, justice of the peace, member of the Board of Tax Equalizers of Hart County, prominent member and leader in the Methodist Church.

Joe H. Scott was the first depot agent at Bowersville. John A. Reese was at one time postmaster. Later Thomas M. Holland occupied the position and Mr. B. M. Holland, a nephew of Thomas M. Holland is the present postmaster.

The foregoing is only a partial list of the various businesses and avocations, made up at random, and does not include all the names of those who have from time to time lived and conducted business in the town.

Among the citizens of Bowersville and community, formerly as well as at present, may be mentioned the Bowerses, Bennetts, Cheeks, Hilliards, Holbrooks, Floyds, Fords, Adamses, Usserys, Johnsons, Fishers, Weavers and others.

Bowersville Hotel

The hotel business at first was conducted by Marion Johnson, and later by Mrs. E. W. Roberts and later still by Mr. F. W. Weaver and wife, Jenney, and was for many years the most popular hotel in the country and the drummers and travelling public made it a point to make Bowersville for dinner as well as for the night.

The table was always laden with the best of food, prepared in the most appetizing manner, and the courtesy of the host, agreeable and obliging.

The conductor on the Elberton Airline Railroad, when approaching Bowersville on the down train at noon would announce, "Bowersville next stop—change cars for Hartwell—twenty minutes for dinner."

The hotel was burned in 1888 when there was a very destructive fire in Bowersville.

A story is told further on with reference to the popularity of the hotel at the time it was destroyed by fire and an account of the conflagration is also related.

FIRE AT BOWERSVILLE

"HALF OF THE BUSINESS PART OF TOWN DESTROYED BY THE FLAMES"

"Saturday, 20th inst., (October 20, 1888) at 3 o'clock P. M., fire broke out at Schaefer's warehouse. Burned 372 bales of cotton, mostly insured. Residence of T. H. McLane burned—loss $300; no insurance. Store of J. A. Reese burned—loss $1,000; no insurance. Store and residence of S. T. Fleming burned—loss $3,000; insurance $1,400. New Hotel of E. W. Roberts burned—loss $2,500; no insurance. Residence of J. W. Holbrook burned—loss $1,500; no insurance.

"Mr. Doyle saved, at some risk, the books and papers in office at warehouse. Most of E. W. Roberts' household goods were saved in a damaged condition. Mr. Fleming saved but little as to household goods and stock in store, but his money and papers in safe were intact. John A. Reese saved most of his jewelry and watches, together with the post-office books and papers; but his loss in stock of goods was heavy. J. W. Holbrook saved most of his household goods in a damaged condition.

"The following persons had cotton stored in warehouse, and this cotton is a dead loss: John H. Bowers, 8 bales; S. T. Fleming, 5 bales; W. C. & J. B. McIntire, 4 bales; J. W. Holbrook, 3 bales; M. R. Brown, 2 bales; Mrs. Johnson, 2 bales.

"The fatal spark is supposed to have blown from an engine at Phillips' gin, located within 200 feet of warehouse. In one hour's time from commencement of fire all was over. New buildings will go up at once."

"The Drummer—The average commercial drummer is a jolly fellow, full of pranks and playful mischief. He is omnipresent; go where you may you will meet him. Never a railroad smash-up but he is there; but he rarely ever gets killed—he doesn't sit still long enough. He is 'up to snuff;' knows the best hotel, and puts up there. If he doesn't like anything, his frankness is amazing. His cheek is something stupendous, and if there is a pretty girl around he is sure to form her acquaintance if she is not deaf, dumb, and blind; and if she needs a protector she can 'bank' on the drummer every time. His good humor is proverbial, and unreasonable hours, the wear and tear of travel, nor aught else spoils his happy disposition. And talk! why he'd make a phonograph blush with envious shame. Exaggerate?—well some—his house is always the best, and the number of sales he makes in a 6 store town is startling.

"But with all of his peccadillos, the drummer is intensely human—humanely human, and he is the personification of chivalrous charity—of free open-handed generosity.

"A sample in point from his gripsack: A crowd of drummers met at Toccoa Monday. The shocking news met them that the Roberts House at Bowersville had been burned to the ground. "What shall we do boys?—we can't get accommodations at Bowersville," cried one. But one who was better acquainted with the pluck and energy of Mrs. Roberts replied: 'You just bet we can. Mrs. Roberts will find a place to stow us away for the night and give us a good supper in the bargain. Let's go down and help the little woman out.' And every hoof of them went down to Bowersville, and eating a meal fit for kings and drummers, each of them handed her a five dollar bill, remarking that the supper was worth that sum, and refused any change. And it is said that all of the drummers are imposing upon the good little lady in that same way."

The insurance company paid for the loss by fire on all the property destroyed that was insured, and then instituted suit against the railroad company, claiming that the fire originated from sparks from the engine on the railroad, but failed to make sufficient proof that the railroad was responsible for the origin of the fire, and as a matter of course failed to recover.

Bowersville School

Prof. Solomon M. Bobo taught school at Bowersville along during the first years. The noted Morgan H. Looney opened school at Bowersville on December 31, 1889 and taught the following year. One of the twelve splendid consolidated schools of Hart County is located at Bowersville.

The Bowersville Baptist Church

The Bowersville Baptist Church was constituted on the 3rd day of October, 1886, with twenty members. Rev. L. W. Stephens was moderator and A. H. Strickland clerk of the presbytery. When the church was constituted, the church had no meeting house, and services were held in the academy.

On January 2, 1887, Rev. J. H. McMullan was called to the pastorate and paid the sum of $75.00 for his services, which he gave back to the church to start a building fund.

February 6, 1887, a Sunday school was organized, with S. M. Bobo of Hartwell, as superintendent.

Rev. J. H. McMullan continued to serve the church as pastor in a most profitable and acceptable manner for nine years, and to him, more than anyone else, is due credit for the erection of the meeting house, which was begun in 1887 and finished in 1888 at a cost of $700. He seldom failed to give back to the church part of his salary, and some times he gave it all back, until the house was paid for.

It is but simple justice to Brother S. M. Bobo to state that, next to Rev. J. H. McMullan, there was no one who worked more earnestly and effectually toward the completion of the house for worship, and his name, together with those of Revs. L. W. Stephens and J. H. McMullan, two pioneer preachers of Hart County who have already gone to their reward, will ever be held in the most sacred remembrance in connection with the history of this church.

After the expiration of Rev. J. H. McMullan's nine years service, the church has been supplied as follows: In 1896 by Rev. J. T. W. Vernon, another pioneer Baptist preacher and worker; in 1897, Rev. D. B. Waite; in 1898, Rev. L. Carlyle Branyan; in 1899 and 1900, Rev. T. J. Rucker.

In 1891 the church elected Mr. B. M. Holland clerk, which position he has faithfully filled ever since. The present membership is fifty-five.

The foregoing interesting history of Bowersville Baptist Church was prepared by Mr. J. T. Williams and published in the minutes of the Hebron Baptist Association in the year 1900.

We are not familiar with the history of the church since that date. Revs. T. M. Galphin, E. H. Collins and others have served the church since 1900. Rev. D. C. Williams is the present pastor. Total membership reported to Association 1932, 134 and value of church house and grounds placed at $1,500.

We have no history of the Methodist Church at Bowersville. It was organized many years ago and is now on the Canon Circuit, with Rev. G. T. Shell pastor, and is one of the prominent churches of the circuit. The church house, built years ago, will compare favorably with the meeting houses of the country.

A Partial List of the Names of the Doctors Who Have Lived and Practiced Their Professions in Hartwell and in Hart County

Dr. Joel L. Turner

DR. JOEL LOCKHART TURNER, born in Lincoln County, Ga., Jan. 6, 1825. Died in Hart County, Ga., March 18, 1897.

B. A. Degree from University of Georgia, Class_____. M. D. Degree from University of Philadelphia, Class_____.

A country doctor of high character and service to humanity.

Inscription on monument of Vermont marble in the cemetery at Cokesbury Church in Hart County, Ga.:

JAN. 6, 1825.
MARCH 19, 1897.
"THE RIGHTEOUS HATH HOPE IN HIS DEATH."

Dr. J. L. Turner volunteered during the War Between the States and was elected First Lieutenant in Captain F. B. Hodges' Company, under Gen. Toombs. While they were in camp at Athens, a petition numerously signed by the people of the doctor's neighborhood was sent to General Toombs, praying for the discharge of Dr. Turner, as he was their only practicing physician. Gen. Toombs knowing that the Doctor was not physically able to do army service, kindly remarked to him, "Doctor, if you will resign, I will accept your resignation." The doctor resigned and another man was elected to his office, and his successor swapped him an unabridged Webster's dictionary for his sword.

Dr. George Eberhart

Dr. George Eberhart died Monday, May 8, 1893. Born in Madison County, Ga., May 18, 1832. Attended Medical College at Augusta, Ga., and graduated in 1854, at the Medical College of Philadelphia, and also, at the Chirurgical College, and began the practice of Medicine in Elbert County immediately after graduation.

Was married at Elberton, Ga., May 6, 1856, to Sarah Hellen, daughter of Ira Christian by Rev. Benjamin Thornton.

Entered the Confederate army at the inception of the war and was Captain of Company "G" North Georgia Batallion.

Moved to Hartwell in June, 1873, where he resided (except a few years residence at Harmony Grove, Ga.). Was a Royal Arch Mason.

In religious faith was a Baptist, and became a communicant of Antioch Church, Elbert County, Ga., in 1859. At the time of his death he was a member of the Baptist Church at Hartwell, Ga. His funeral was conducted at the Baptist Church by Rev. A. E. Keese, assisted by Revs. L. W. Stephens and J. H. McMullan. Funeral text "The last enemy that shall be destroyed is death." 1st Cor. XV, 26."

Dr. Charles A. Webb

Was born March 25, 1833, and died June 23, 1912. He was one of the old landmarks of the town, as a boy he was one of the first clerks. At the beginning of the War Between the States, he was living in Texas where he volunteered and fought through the war as a Confederate soldier. At the close of the war he returned to Hartwell.

He studied medicine, attended lectures at the Medical College, Augusta, Ga., and graduated in 1870, and for years had a good practice in Hartwell and Hart County.

He served the county as Clerk of the Superior Court for ten years, 1871-1880, inclusive.

Dr. Webb was a member of the Presbyterian Church, and his funeral was preached by Rev. J. D. McPhail, Presbyterian minister of Athens, Ga., assisted by Rev. H. F. Branham, the Methodist pastor at Hartwell. He was buried in the Hartwell cemetery by the side of the wife of his young manhood, who before her marriage was Miss Myra Benson, daughter of Hon. John B. Benson.

F. M. Payne

Born in Franklin, now Hart County, Ga., Jan. 1818. Died July 3, 1892. Practiced his profession in Hart County for a number of years.

Dr. C. M. Lowe

Doctor C. M. Lowe was a native of Tennessee, was a Surgeon in the Confederate Army. His command was disbanded at Washington, Wilkes County, Ga., at the close of the War Between the States. He was with the detachment of soldiers with President Jefferson Davis evacuating Richmond, all being captured near Washington, Ga. As above stated, he was a native of Tennessee. He stopped in Hartwell, liked the place and remained here several years. Later he located in Reed Creek district where he died about the year 1870, and was buried at Reed Creek Church.

He was considered a good physician. He was a bachelor and never married.

Dr. William Henry Page

Born and reared in Elbert County, Ga. Studied medicine after the Civil War—attended Medical College in Atlanta and Baltimore, Md., where he graduated about 1870.

He at one time had a drug store and had associated with him in the business, Dr. J. L. Turner. Later practiced medicine and had a drug store alone. He also at one time had a drug store in Townville, S. C., and practiced medicine in the community for a short time.

He was noted for his painstaking care and interest in his patients. He was born September 11, 1837 and died June 2, 1899.

Dr. W. T. Stoddard

Dr. W. T. Stoddard came to Hartwell about 1884. Practiced in the town and county for several years. Was connected with W. J. Harper for a part of the time in the drug business. Died in Hartwell several years ago. His wife before her marriage was Miss Lillian Bauknight of Walhalla, S. C.

Dr. .... Snow

Dr .... Snow lived in Hartwell where he practiced his profession for a short time. Do not know from whence he came. He died in Hartwell.

Dr. .... Neal

Dr. .... Neal moved from South Carolina to Hartwell about 1861, and practiced in the town and county.

Dr. A. J. Mathews

Dr. A. J. Mathews came from Elberton to Hartwell about the year 1871. Lived in Hartwell and practiced his profession in the town and county for many years. While a citizen of the county he was elected to the Legislature and served one term 1880-81 as representative from Hart County. Finally moved back to Elberton where he died many years ago.

Dr. W. C. Mathews

Dr. William C. Mathews, son of Dr. A. J. Mathews, after graduation at Medical College, practiced for a short time in Hartwell and then moved to Amarilla, Texas. Died several years ago.

Dr. James M. Webb

Dr. James M. Webb moved to Hartwell from Anderson County S. C., and was the first doctor to live and practice in the town and county. Came to Hartwell about the year 1854. He was killed in Hartwell about May, 1865, by some of the men of Brown's Raid as they passed through the town.

Dr. J. Walter Eberhart

Dr. J. Walter Eberhart, son of Dr. George Eberhart, practiced medicine in Atlanta, Ga., and later moved to Hartwell, Ga., and practiced in the town and county for a number of years. He died several years ago.

Dr. Isham L. McCurry

Dr. Isham L. McCurry, son of John McCurry, was born in Elbert (now Hart) County, February 8, 1848.

Attended Medical College, University of Georgia, at Augusta, Ga., 1872. Practiced his profession at Fairplay, S. C., from 1872 to 1891.

Practiced in Hartwell and the county 1891 to 1912.

Married Miss Nancy Henrietta Jarrard, daughter of Dr. J. D. Jarrard and Mary S. nee Dorsey Jarrard, White County, Ga., July 23, 1876. Died in Hartwell, Ga., November 8, 1917.

Nancy Henrietta Jarrard, wife of Dr. Isham L. McCurry, was born May 8, 1854.

A list of the names of some of the doctors who lived in Bowersville, Ga. from time to time, and practiced medicine in the town and community:

Dr. J. T. Cook

Dr. J. T. Cook, from Anderson County, S. C., from the community of Roberts Church, and lived and practiced his profession for many years. He died a few years ago at Bowersville.

Dr. T. B. Cunningham

Dr. T. B. Cunningham was reared in the State of Georgia. Attended Medical College in Atlanta, Ga. Did practice for several years. He died several years ago in Bowersville where he had lived for many years.

Dr. W. L. Hanie

Dr. W. L. Hanie moved from South Carolina to Bowersville. Practiced his profession for several years, later moving to South Georgia.

Dr. John W. Starr

Dr. John W. Starr, born and reared in Franklin County, Ga. Attended Medical College either at Charleston, S. C., or Augusta, Ga. Practiced his profession in Bowersville and community for several years. He was a Confederate Veteran and died at the soldiers' home in Atlanta, several years ago.

Dr. J. W. Waldrip

Dr. J. W. Waldrip practiced medicine at Bowersville for many years, later moving to Athens, Ga., where perhaps he still lives.

Dr. _____ Spinks

Dr. _____ Spinks moved to Bowersville a few years ago, and after practicing for a short while died at Bowersville.

Dr. Parson and son James Parson

Dr. _____ Parson and his son James Parson who were both doctors, moved to Bowersville from the lower part of the state. The older Parson died in Atlanta, and his son James moved back to South Georgia.

Dr. H. F. Shields

Dr. H. F. Shields came to Bowersville from Chickamauga, Ga., and after living in Bowersville a few years where he practiced his profession, he moved back to Chickamauga where, so far as we know, he still lives.

A list of the names of some of the doctors who lived in the country and practiced their profession in the county.

Dr. John K. Sewell

Dr. John K. Sewell lived in the county many years ago and did practice and was perhaps a specialist in the treatment of some diseases. He was a son-in-law of Washington Ray, and lived in the Goldmine neighborhood. He later moved to Banks County, Ga., where he perhaps died several years ago.

Dr. J. M. Sorrells

Dr. J. M. Sorrells lived in the neighborhood of Eaglegrove about the year 1880, and practiced his profession.

Dr. Hess Bowers

Dr. Hess Bowers, son of Hon. William Bowers, lived at the same place as that of Dr. Sorrells, but we have no date of when he left or to where he moved.

Dr. G. W. Sewell

Dr. G. W. Sewell lived in Hartwell where he practiced his profession. Was a brother to Dr. John K. Sewell. Do not know where he moved to from Hartwell.

Dr. L. C. Rhodes

Dr. Lindsey Crawford Rhodes lived in the county in the neighborhood of Eaglegrove and was located at the home of Mr. Reuben Williford, and practiced in the community. Do not have the date of the time he came or where and when he left.

Dr. J. Hubbard Parker

Dr. J. Hubbard Parker lived in the Shoal Creek neighborhood not far from the village of Parkertown. He was a licensed physician and practiced in the county. Died many years ago.

Dr. Samuel N. Holland

Dr. Samuel N. Holland moved from Anderson, S. C., to Georgia and lived in the neighborhood of Parkertown where he practiced his profession. He died several years ago.

Dr. J. Basil Bowers

Dr. J. Basil Bowers, son of Job Bowers, lived and died in the community near where the town of Canon, Ga., is now located. He practiced his profession for many years, and if we are not mistaken, was a specialist in the treatment of cancer.

A Brief History of Hartwell Schools

HON. F. C. STEPHENSON was the first teacher, beginning in 1855; he taught in a one-room log cabin but soon removed to the Presnell house before it was completed and taught on a dirt floor. Mr. Stephenson was one of the first citizens of Hartwell and held public office until his death some thirty-eight years ago.

Miss Ellen Holland was the next teacher and taught in a new frame building, commencing her school before the house was completed or had a chimney.

The heads of the Hartwell Schools from now on are as follows: David Stiefel, Jackson Brown, Miss Martha Monteith, John L. Mize, who closed his school to go to the war about 1862; Weston Hays, Miss Prince, Mrs. E. G. Murrah, closing her school as General Brown's raid was crossing the Savannah River.

The first school after the war was taught by Mrs. J. M. Webb, whose husband, Dr. J. M. Webb, was murdered on the public square in Hartwell, May 3, 1865, by a squad of brutal ruffians who posed as northern soldiers. This was doubted as most all regular soldiers who passed through the county at the close of the war conducted themselves in a fairly respectable manner.

Mrs. Webb, whose maiden name was Miss Ellen Holland, and mentioned as the second teacher, continued to teach a private school at intervals for several years, supplementing her meager income from her hotel; being left a widow with three small boys she, as all other widows, was left at the close of the war confronting grave problems and much hardship in rearing their children.

In 1874, Mrs. Webb married Prof. S. M. Bobo, which happy companionship was ended November 8, 1912, by the death of Mrs. Bobo. No woman ever lived in Hartwell that had more friends or was respected more highly than Mrs. Bobo.

Col. P. E. Devant was the teacher from 1865 to 1868.
Dr. James W. Earle in 1869.
S. M. Bobo in 1870-1-2.
Martin V. Looney and wife in 1873.
Rev. A. L. Campbell in 1874.
Martin V. Looney and wife in 1875-6-7.
Mrs. Capers and Mr. Scott in 1878.
S. M. Bobo and S. W. Peek in 1879 and 1880.
Morgan H. Looney in 1881.
Morgan L. Parker in 1882 to 1886.
J. P. Mathews in 1887.
S. M. Bobo and M. S. Stribling in 1888-9 and 90.
S. M. Bobo and Miss Rosa Neson, 1891.
S. M. Bobo and J. S. Foster, 1892.
Morgan L. Parker, 1893 to 1897.
George C. Looney, 1898-99-1900.
Morgan L. Parker, 1901 to 1906.
John P. Cash, 1907 to 1910.
E. A. Montgomery, 1910-11.
W. A. Ariail, 1911-1912.
C. G. Power, 1912-1920.
J. I. Allman, 1920-1927.
R. I. Knox, 1927-1928.

Mr. Knox could only serve the fall session on account of affliction. The spring session was completed in a most satisfactory way by Miss Ida Mc-

A BRIEF HISTORY OF HARTWELL SCHOOLS

Gukin. Mr. Knox's illness resulted in his death in June, soon after the spring session closed. He was universally popular and highly esteemed by all.

It will be observed that a scholastic year is a part of two calendar years.

Prof. Grover G. Maughon commenced the fall session of 1928 with the people's assurance that Hartwell's past educational history will be kept up to the highest standards.

The first school house erected in Hartwell was a one-room hulled-in frame building, located on Lot No. 113 in the original plan of the town of Hartwell, which had been donated by the town authorities in laying out the town as a lot for a female academy, on which is now the C. I. Kidd residence.

Later an addition was made to the house, consisting of a long, large room with chimney at each end, with side facing Howell Street, with the first school building attached as an ell to the new part. This building was used up until 1888. This house was moved to the east side of the lot intact, and now faces Franklin Street and is used as a residence.

In September, 1887, a movement for a new school building for the town of Hartwell was launched; subscriptions to funds, selection and an election for a site, and purchase of same, and other matters pertaining thereto, were commenced and finally carried through to successful consummation.

The election for the site was voted upon by the citizens of the town, and the respective sites voted for were the "Old Site," and the "Benson lot." The result of the election was the choice of the "Benson lot," the result of the election declared in the following terms: "Old Site," received seven hundred and eighty-five dollars, or seventy-eight and one half votes; the "Benson lot," received fifteen hundred and seventy-eight dollars, or one hundred and fifty-seven and one eighth votes.

In 1887, a very commodious wood school building was erected on the "Benson lot," at a cost of about $7,500.00, Mr. Homer Mickel being the architect and contractor.

It served well until Thursday, January 24, 1907, when it was accidently destroyed by fire while school was in session. This was a great loss, as there was only a normal amount of insurance.

However, the fire left a good, clean place to erect a much larger and more up-to-date structure. The best architects were soon employed to submit plants. A $20,000.00 bond issue was voted, which was the sum to be expended.

This building, when erected, was thought to be large enough for many years to come, but not so; for several years it had not met the demand for the continued growing school interests, so the citizens of Hartwell said conditions must not hinder the school interests, it must not suffer. A bond election was called for a $40,000.00 bond issue and was carried with so little opposition it was not noticeable.

The bonds were validated and sold at a very satisfactory price.

As in the first instance in 1907, architects were given a chance to submit plans for a $40,000.00 building, and C. D. Griffin was the lucky architect and contractor. This house is a much larger and more commodious building than the one built in 1907.

It would be hard to find a better natural location for any school building, with nearly four hundred feet frontage on Hodges Street and running clear through to Cleveland Avenue, a distance of some eight hundred feet, with streets and avenues on all sides. The buildings are about one hundred feet apart with no hazards in case of fire.

In a newspaper item announcing the official opening on Thursday night, January 26, 1922, of the new school building, among other things stated is: "It has 16 class rooms, an auditorium seating 800, and has been declared by State school authorities to be one of the most modern school buildings in Georgia. It was occupied during the spring term (1922). In addition, there are the library, laboratory, shower bath, and every other convenience for a real school."

MURDER MOST FOUL!

Henry Hill Kills T. V. Skelton, the Jailor, and Escapes Jail!

Wonderful Ingenuity of a Desperate Negro!

ON THE night of the 23d ultimo (Wednesday, February 23d), just after sunset, Mr. Thomas V. Skelton, the jailor of Hart County, went into the jail to feed and water Henry Hill, alias Henry Turner, colored, who was the only occupant, and who had been confined therein for some months under a charge of burglary, preferred against him by the Grand Jury at the last term of Hart Superior Court. Mr. Skelton had left his store just about sunset, remarking to Mr. J. L. Snipes, his co-partner, that he was going to attend to the prisoner and go home early, as his wife was in great distress, having just heard of the death of her brother, Mr. N. K. Sullivan, of Anderson, S. C. Mr. Snipes thought nothing strange of his not returning to the store, and Mrs. Skelton, supposing that her husband was at the store, suffered no great uneasiness. About eight o'clock at night Mr. Snipes needed a key which Mr. Skelton had, and sent a note up to Mr. Skelton's requesting him to send the key, when it was ascertained that Mr. Skelton was not at home. This caused considerable uneasiness, and after search had been made at the various stores in town, Mr. Dobbins, the clerk of Mr. Skelton, and others, went to the jail and found the outer door open. They entered and ascended the stairway to the inner door, which opens into the hall fronting the cells. They found that open, and just inside the hall door lay the dead body of poor Tom Skelton, his head horribly and cruelly mangled, and Henry Hill gone. Next morning Mr. Allen McGee, the Coroner, summoned an inquest, and after hearing the evidence the jury rendered a verdict, that Thomas V. Skelton was murdered by Henry Hill, alias Henry Turner, and recommended that the Governor offer a reward of five hundred dollars for his apprehension. The manner in which the prisoner succeeded in accomplishing his hellish scheme seems to have been as follows: During last fall he attempted to make his escape by burning the jail but was detected before he succeeded. After this he was put in another cell and chained until a short time ago. He got to limping and complaining so much that Mr. Skelton, through his kindness of heart, removed the chains from his limbs, but still kept him confined in the cell.

The chain was left in the cell, fastened to the floor, which Henry succeeded in breaking off, the portion of the chain link where it was broken being left as sharp as a dull pocketknife. There is a small wicket, or trap-door, large enough for an ordinary man to squeeze through, which is used for passing food, water, etc., into the cell without opening the door (both the wicket and cell door are made of large iron bars). The wicket is fastened by a strong lock to a large bolt staple driven ten inches into the huge side timbers of the door. With the piece of chain he went to work, and by degrees tediously cut out the wood across the inner framing of the cell door so that he could drive out the large staple, lock and all, that confined the wicket. As his work progressed he would fill the trench with cotton and carefully smooth it over with the lime that had been put in his cell for disinfecting purposes so there would be no danger of being detected, hiding his work from the outside of the cell. Having cut around the staple sufficiently, he pushed it out and that enabled him to crawl out of the cell into the hallway in front of the cells through the trap-door.

He was then in position to plan fully his purpose. He armed himself with pieces of plank torn from his bunk, and from the appearance of the surroundings it is likely that he took his position in the corner of the cell between the door entering the hall and the door of the cell, the one he occupied being the first one on the right as you enter, and quietly awaited the approach of his victim. Mr. Skelton unlocked the hall door, and with a bucket of water in his hand entered to approach the cell door, and doubtless as he took his first step into the hall received the merciless blow of the concealed assassin who, throttling him with his left hand, dealt the blows with his right.

There were marks on the murdered man's neck as if he had been choked, and ten distinct gashes on his head, which was crushed most fearfully, and indications showed that while Mr. Skelton was partially stunned by the first blow he had not met his death without a desperate struggle, but he could not cope with the infuriated negro, who had immense strength. And there the poor man lay in death with his face resting in a large pool of clotted gore. The staple that had been forced out to enable the prisoner to open the trap-door had been carefully pushed back, and no sort of caution or prudence could have enabled Mr. Skelton to detect the terrible preparations of the assassin.

If he had taken the precaution to have peeped through the bars of the hall door he would have seen the cell door fastened just as it usually was, and the form of the crouching murderer in the corner could not possibly be observed from the outside of the hall door. And thus, without any means of suspicion, the poor murdered man went right into the villain's horrible clutches and violently perished by his murderous hands.

The Murderer

Henry Hill, alias Henry Turner, is a notoriously desperate character. For the last few years he has been addicted to gambling and stealing. In 1876, he was confined in the Hartwell jail under a charge of larceny, and in company with Dan Burriss succeeded in escaping therefrom. At the last September term of Hart Superior Court the Grand Jury found a true bill against him for burglary, and under that charge he has been confined in jail since. A short time after said term, during the early part of November, he again attempted to escape jail by burning out, but was detected. He is about six feet two or three inches high, dark ginger-cake color, pock-marked, about 45 years old, quick spoken, walks erect, has double thumbs, and is rather rawboned. The citizens of the town and community are terribly shocked at the murder.

The Victim

Mr. Thomas V. Skelton, the unsuspecting jailor who was mangled to death by this desperate scoundrel, was one of the best citizens. He was a noble, generous, upright, Christian gentleman, and faithfully discharged his duties in all the positions of life. He was 29 years of age. His death is a great loss to our community. He was married twice, and by his first wife he leaves a little girl about 10 years of age. About three years ago he married Miss Sadie Sullivan, an estimable lady and devoted wife, to whom the blow is rendered still more overwhelming because she had just received news of the death of a brother, which occurred a day or two before. His funeral was preached at the Baptist Church on Friday morning by Rev. L. W. Stephens to a large assembly of people, and his remains deposited in the Hartwell Cemetery, the Knights of Honor, of which order he was a worthy member, acting as pall bearers. He was also a Master Mason in good standing.

The Murderer Caught!

The honor of Henry Hill's capture is due mainly to Messrs. J. F. Coker and Joel Seymour, of Elbert County. On last Sunday, while walking through the woods in Goshen looking for some "good timber," they saw a smoke a short distance from the road. They approached and saw a negro man sitting by the fire roasting potatoes, with a large piece of pine bark on his head to keep off the rain. They approached nearer, and Henry's double thumbs led them to believe that he was the man that had killed Mr. Skelton. They asked him what he was doing. He said that he was under arrest, and that Mr. Teasley and Mr. Brown had arrested him for whipping a woman, and had left him there and had gone off with some dogs after a rabbit, telling him to remain until they returned.

Coker and Seymour told him he must go with them down to a house near by, that a woman there had a dollar stolen, and they wanted to see if he was the man who got it; that if she did not recognize him they would release him. By this stratagem they got in the house, where they captured him and tied him. Henry was entirely unarmed and made no resistance. The gentlemen who captured him were also unarmed, having nothing about them but small pocketknives.

The whole country for many miles was thoroughly aroused and determined upon the criminal's arrest, and a large troop had pressed him close the day before. Henry is now safely lodged in jail and awaits his trial at the approaching assizes. The manly and prudent course of our people in exercising such forbearance and allowing the law to take its course is eminently praiseworthy, and deserves the highest commendation.

Statement of The Prisoner

On last Monday morning a *Sun* reporter visited the jail and interviewed Henry Hill, who made substantially the following statement:

"I had been working to get out of jail about one day. I commenced cutting Tuesday morning. I wrapped the chain around the outside of the bolt, or staple, and drove the sharp end with a plank. The wood was brittle and I got it off very fast. I got it completed Tuesday evening. I drove out the staple Wednesday. Mr. Skelton brought me my dinner Wednesday, last, about 3 o'clock. I only ate part of the dinner. Mr. Skelton came to the jail before sundown a while Wednesday evening; when he came he brought a bucket of water. He only came to the jail one time. I got into the hall through the trap-door about half an hour before Mr. Skelton came. I did not want to kill him, and I did not intend to kill him. Mr. Skelton unlocked the hall door and set the bucket of water down and turned and fastened the hall door. He picked up the bucket with his left hand and had the keys in his right hand and was rising to go to the cell door. I was standing in the right-hand corner, and he could not see me. The first lick stunned him, and he grabbed me on the leg with his right hand. I struck him another lick, and he fell in the corner next to the cell. I only struck him two licks, and did not intend to kill him, but did not see how I was to get out without doing something to him. I then went down and opened the door. I saw Mr. Harrison Sanders, Mr. W. W. Scott, and Mr. Fletcher Kay. I waited until they left. I then went out by the calaboose, across Mr. Powell's lot. I went down to the Carter place. I went to Hank's Ferry. I thought I heard somebody coming, and I went up the river and sat down by a log-heap fire. I did not sleep a wink that night. I struck out again a few hours before day; I went on down the river, and ate dinner Thursday at Jack Craft's. I then lay in the big woods near Dr. Turner's Thursday evening; and late that evening I went to a log fire where Ben Jones' folks had been at work. I stayed all night by the log-heap fire. Next day, Friday, I went down to Mrs. Terrell's, in Elbert County, and stayed that night with Uncle Mose Oliver, who lives on Joe Jones' place. I ate supper with him and slept until before day, and then I concluded to come back and go up the country. I came up in the neighborhood of Judge Richardson's Saturday. I saw Blackstone Richardson. The crowd got after me that evening, and I dodged down in Coldwater Creek. I lay in woods out in Goshen Saturday night. I had stopped in the woods and built up a fire, and was roasting potatoes when I was taken."

At the regular March Term, 1881, of the Superior Court of Hart County, Ga., Henry Hill was indicted, tried and convicted of the murder of Thomas V. Skelton, and was sentenced by the court, Judge E. H. Pottle, presiding, to hang on Friday, April 22, 1881.

The Black Cap!
Henry Hill Pays the Penalty of Murder
Thomas V. Skelton's Death Avenged

Yesterday was a day long to be remembered in the annals of our county. It was the day appointed for the execution of Henry Hill for the murder of Thomas V. Skelton. The day was calm and serene, the fields blooming beneath the gentle influences of spring, and the birds carroling their songs of joy in the groves, unconscious of the terrible work to be performed by mortals. At an early hour streams of people came pouring into town, and soon the entire public square was filled with heaving, anxious, restless and impatient throng awaiting the hour when the criminal should be brought forth from his cell and carried to the place of his horrible doom.

Just before 11 o'clock, Sheriff Myers, attended by a suitable corps of assistants, entered the jail to commence preparations for the discharge of the solemn duty before him. As the shackles were taken from the limbs of the prisoner he seemed completely unnerved. He was deeply affected, grasping the coarse clothes of his bed to wipe the tears profusely streaming from his eyes. It was indeed a sad spectacle to stand and behold a human being prepared and dressed for his coffin, and he in the vigor of health; and sadder still, that a human being should commit a great and dastardly crime as that such a scene should be rendered necessary. Revs. W. A. Farris and B. C. Thornton visited the cell while the preparations were going on, and conversed with him a short time on religious topics. He said he was willing to go, and after he was dressed, having become calm, he quietly asked Mr. Milton Richardson for some tobacco. At length, everything else being ready, the black cap was placed upon his head, the rope adjusted around his neck, the jail doors thrown open, and the stairway descended, where the wagon awaited with his coffin to bear the prisoner to the gallows.

At 12 o'clock the guards, numbering perhaps 200, armed with guns, under the command of Hon. John G. McCurry, repaired to the jail, and formed in open column, and a wagon drove up with a neat coffin. Henry Hill was then brought out, and seated upon the coffin securely pinioned. Here ensued a most affecting scene, the parting of the doomed man with his family. The hardest heart could not but feel sad to hear the poor man's farewells and the agonizing shrieks of his children.

At 12:07 the procession filed its way through the press toward the scaffold, with guards in front, upon each side, and in the rear. First came the wagon with Henry, then a buggy with Rev. W. A. Farris, and following a number of reporters from different newspapers.

The procession arrived at the scaffold at 12:17. The prisoner, Sheriff, Deputy Sheriff, Revs. W. A. Farris, B. C. Thornton, Drs. Eberhart, Mathews, and Page, ascended the scaffold at 12:20. The prisoner was then informed that he could make any remarks that he desired. Henry then excitedly exclaimed:

"Let my children come where they can see me; let them come!" They were brought inside of the rope enclosure, and one of the children cried out: "Is that my papa?—he looks so thin!" Henry then said: "Children, honey, you see where I am! Did you think you would ever see me here? What brought me here? Regard yourself; keep under guard—stand under guard. Jehovah is not far from me. Don't allow yourself to leave your guard. Look at my head" (pointing at the black cap). "My boy, look at your father. Don't let yourself come here. Remember me, children. Live in the fear of God. Take care of your mother and the little children. Go from this place where your father was brought with a rope around his neck. This time tomorrow I will be climbing the hills of Calvary. I will put on a crown in place of these bloody clothes. Come and meet me, children. Your father has done a crime. If I had listened to my dear wife, I would not have a rope 'round my neck. She told me before I killed him: 'Henry, pray; Mr. Skelton will be good to you!' " He then advised his children to stay with those with whom they were working, and deplored the evil effects of gambling. Motioning to his son, he said: "Keep out of your pocket, and a flask of whisky out of your side pocket. Be good to the white people. God bless you all! I must now talk to my color. I have been well treated by these men," (meaning the authorities). "I am sorry that I did what I did. I did do it. But not because he did not treat me right. I am guilty of the crime." He then turned thanks to Deputy Sheriff Vickery for his kind treatment, and resumed: "Farewell to you all. Remember me in your prayers, and meet me in Heaven. My soul is going up. If I was going to hell I would say so. I have been pardoned of my sins. I have felt this for five weeks. Remember poor Henry Turner, my name is not Henry Hill. Never take the route I have taken. The devil followed me all the time and brought me back here. White people, I bid you all farewell. Don't be mad with me. I did do the deed. I am guilty. I think it is just and right that I should hang; but it is so hard. I would rather you would take me right out and shoot me. Mr. Skelton's wife was good to me. She sent me something good from her table every day. I have looked around to see her, but can't see her face."

Here he stopped, and Rev. B. C. Thornton gave out the hymn, "Alas, and did my Saviour bleed." Henry then cried out: "Come back, children, and listen to me, I am going to sing. All of you sing. People, all of you sing." He appeared greatly excited, and the tears coursed down his cheeks. He then in a most pathetic voice cried: "I want to see my baby! I have not seen it yet. If it is in the crowd hold it up." Some one held up a child, and he said, with a voice husky with emotion: "That is not my child. If I can't see it, God bless it." Just then his child was brought and held up to his gaze, and he seemed greatly effected, crying: "There is my child, God bless it." He then nervously shook hands with the Sheriff and others on the scaffold while the song was being sung. Afterwards Rev. W. A. Farris led in a most solemn prayer.

After this Henry stepped upon the platform at 12:50, all the while bidding those in the crowd farewell, and asking those who wanted his soul saved to bow their heads. At 12:55 the drop fell, and his body fell with a thud. While there was considerable twitching of the muscles, there were no violent movements of limbs and body. Until 1:03 his pulse remained strong, but commenced going down until 1:06, when it ceased to beat. At 1:08 he was dead. He remained hanging until 1:27, when the physicians pronounced him dead, and his body was cut down and turned over to his friends, and was buried at Cedar Springs last night. His neck was not broken, and he died from strangulation.

Thus ended a scene, a repetition of which we hope may never occur in our county again. Notwithstanding the tremendous crowd, the very best of order was observed, and too much praise can not be awarded the people of their decorous behavior, and to the barkeepers for voluntarily closing their saloons.

The crowd must have been between eight and ten thousand.

Apropos of the spirit of law and order of the citizens of Hart County, exhibited in connection with the foul, atrocious, and unprovoked murder of Thomas V. Skelton, a white man, a noble, true-hearted citizen, by Henry Hill, a negro, a most lawless and desperate character, we herewith reproduce an article written and published in *The Hartwell Sun* at the time:

Law and Order in the South

We are truly glad that the period has arrived when the unjust charges of lawlessness can no longer be laid at the doors of the Southern people. Nothing perhaps has done so much to influence the North against us and to keep alive sectional hates as the many acts of imprudence in the past in those cases where the people aroused by some atrocious deed have taken the law into their own hands and inflicted summary punishment on the transgressor.

True enough there was mitigation for the acts and noble motives prompting them, but they were unauthorized by law, and cool subsequent reflection condemned them. By great exaggerations of such occurrences, especially where the colored race were involved, an impression has been created abroad that the South are a lawless people and will not give the colored race justice. We repeat we think that the time for such charges are past and we are happy to note that right in our own midst the people of Hart have exhibited a spirit of law and order that challenges the admiration of all. A great crime is committed in the town of Hartwell, a noble, true-hearted citizen who has not an enemy in the world and whose whole life has been characterized by quiet and unostentatious discharge of duty and kindness to everybody, while in the discharge of his duty is stricken down and slain in a barbarous manner by a colored criminal confined in jail. The county is frenzied with indignation and troops of armed men search in every quarter for his apprehension. He is detected and quietly lodged in jail without a single outburst from our law-abiding citizens. This exalted, patriotic, law-abiding example set by our people was a grand refutation of all such charges as we have mentioned. And we are extremely gratified that the good people of the county of Hart have set an example of patient forbearance under circumstances of such an aggravated and atrocious character. We hear sometimes of the law's delay, but in this enlightened age and high southern civilization the law is administered wisely and well. We have a high type of the judiciary and our jury system is as nearly perfect as it has ever obtained in the history of the world. Our people can afford to wait in all cases the due administration of the law, believing that while "the mills of the gods grind slowly they grind exceedingly fine."

INTOXICATING LIQUORS

BEFORE the War Between the States, there were no laws or restrictions governing the manufacture of intoxicating liquors in Hart County. All persons were at liberty to distill their corn and other grain into whisky and their fruits into brandy, however there were some legal regulations as to the sale of intoxicating liquors.

Before any person was allowed to retail spiritous and intoxicating liquors, they were required to register with the county authorities and obtain a license for a term of twelve months and for such license they were required to pay a nominal fee of five dollars to cover recording fees, etc., and in addition they were required to take and subscribe an oath not to sell, bargain, or give or in any way to furnish liquors to minors, or to persons of color without the consent of the owner of such person of color. After the war, and after the negroes were set free, the oath only applied to minors.

Where licenses were issued to persons keeping a regular barroom or public house where liquors were sold, the keeper was required to take the same oath, and in addition to give bond with security for their faithful performance in the conducting of their business as such, and in this event the license was twenty-five dollars.

From the creation of the county and up until the close of the war, a number of persons in all parts of the county obtained licenses and engaged in the sale of intoxicating liquors.

In the town of Hartwell there were barrooms, and the keepers were required to pay such license as the town authorities fixed from time to time. Some years the license was as high as two hundred dollars per year, and at other times a less amount was fixed and charged by the town authorities.

The town, under and by virtue of its charter, had the right either to allow or to prohibit the sale of liquors inside the corporate limits. Why the authorities allowed liquors sold at all within the corporate limits was perhaps for the reason that in case the sale of liquors were prohibited inside the town limits, there perhaps would have been barrooms located just outside the limits on some or all of the public roads leading into town, and in which case the town would have been menaced with the evil influence and consequences just the same, and so the authorities perhaps decided that of two evils they would choose the lesser, which from our view point of reasoning is a mistake, as the wise course to pursue is, that of two evils, reject both.

So licenses were granted to persons to sell liquors in barrooms and the revenue derived from the sale of such licenses were applied to the expenses of the government and upkeep of the town.

LICENSED FOR WHAT?

"Licensed where peace and quiet dwell,
To bring disease, want and woe!
Licensed to make this world a hell,
And fit men for a hell below."

The people in the early days did not consider the manufacture, sale and drinking of intoxicating liquors to be of much, if any harm, nor did they realize the awful consequences to which it would eventually lead, and so they sowed the decanter on their mantelpieces and sideboards and reaped the barrooms later on.

After the war there was imposed by the U. S. Government a revenue upon the manufacture and sale of intoxicating liquors and barkeepers had to obtain licenses from the government before they could legally sell liquors, and in the towns and cities the barkeepers were required to pay such licenses as imposed by the town or city authorities in addition to that imposed by the government.

From time to time Acts of the Legislature of the State were passed prohibiting the sale of intoxicating liquors within certain limits of churches and schools, and other acts of a local nature were enacted until finally the barrooms in the towns were about all the places where liquors were legally sold. As a matter of course, all along there has ever been the moonshiner, blindtiger, and the bootlegger, who have made and sold liquors in violation of the laws of county, State or national government.

While barrooms were kept open in Hartwell they were the favorite rendezvous of the rowdy and the sot, and drunken brawls were of common occurrence, especially was this true on public days.

Ladies could not pass barrooms without the danger of being intimidated and embarrassed by vile oaths and the sight of reeling, drunken men. There were other immoralities, due in a great measure to the influence of intoxicating liquors, that were practiced in the town and county, which today would not be tolerated or allowed, which is evidence that our morality has in a way kept pace with our civilization, and while the morals of our county are not by any means what we would have them be, nor what the better element of our people hope they may yet be, yet it is a great consolation to know that we are so far removed from the baneful conditions that formerly obtained in our town and county.

Local Option in Hart County

An Act of the Legislature of Georgia was passed and approved on September 4, 1883, allowing the people of Hart County to vote on the question of prohibiting the sale of intoxicating liquors in the county. A lively campaign ensued and many speakers of note canvassed the county and made speeches in all parts in favor of prohibition. Notably among others was Rev. J. C. Wingo, a preacher and citizen of Hartwell at the time, who was perhaps the most prominent among the advocates of prohibition. Many other preachers of different denominations took an active part and the majority of the citizens were for prohibition and so voted on the day of the election, which was held on the 3d day of November, 1883, with the following result:

```
For Prohibition .................................... 805 votes
Against Prohibition .............................. 456 votes

    Majority for Prohibition.................. 349 votes
```

The prohibition law for Hart County went into effect February 6, 1884. At the time prohibition was voted in, there were three barrooms in Hartwell, kept by J. H. Vickery, H. C. Allen and Foster Butler.

HISTORY OF THE CLEVELANDS

IF THE reader will examine Middlesbrough's "New International Encyclopedia," he will find the derivation of the name Cleveland and the country from which they originated to be as follows:

Clif, Clef, Pl. Clives, Cleves, Cliffs plus land equals Cleveland.

A hilly region with some picturesque fertile valleys forming the eastern part of North Riding of Yorkshire, England, between Whity and the Tees. Some of the heights are marked by mounds called "houses." Many archeological relics have been found among the hills. It has become a populous mining district, owing to the discovery of limestone.

In 1851 an eminent English antiquarian wrote to Bishop A. Cleveland Coxe, of Buffalo, N. Y., that the Clevelands of America were descended from William Cleveland, who removed from York to Henckley in Leichestershire, where he was buried a very old man in 1630. His son, Thomas, became Vicar of Henckley, the family estate. One of his sons was John Cleveland, the poet; another son, Thomas, may have been the father of Moses Cleveland, the emigrant, who came in 1635 from Ipswich, Suffolk County, England, to Massachusetts.

John Cleveland (1613-58). An English Cavalier poet. He was born at Lougborough, Leicester, and educated at Cambridge, where in 1634 he became a fellow of St. Johns. Six years later he strenuously opposed Cromwell, and in consequence lost his fellowship in 1645. Joining the Royalist, he was appointed Judge Advocate in the King's Army in 1655, he was sieged at Norwich and imprisoned at Yarmouth for three months; when he was released by Cromwell after that he lived in retirement.

Cleveland had a great reputation as a wit, satirist. A volume of his poems in circulation before 1656 was reissued in that year. In 1687 appeared his collection entitled Clevelandi Vindicial, which attempts to combine several of his preceding publications.

The bibliography of Cleveland is too complicated for treatment here. Cleveland still awaits a competent editor; Thomas Fuller describes him as: "A General Artist, Pure Latinist, Exquisite Orator and Eminent Poet."

—From "New International Encyclopedia."

There is also a tradition that a Cleveland of Henckley came over to Virginia, with Skepworth and Herrick. He was later, 1653, at Salem, Mass. His coat of arms gave proof that he was a very distinguished gentleman of England.

The Cleveland family have to their credit many illustrious names, both in England and the United States. The most celebrated on this side of the water was Grover Cleveland, three times a candidate and twice elected President of the United States. James B. Cleveland, of Oneonta, N. Y., published a book in three parts in 1881 about the Cleveland family. We have had access to part I, and from this we glean the following information:

"From the year 1200 A. D. up to the present, the family have spelled the name in a variety of ways, sometimes the same individual in the family spelling his name at different times in his life in more than one way."

It is Clyveland and Cleveland. The last was one adopted by the members of the family who came to this State. There used also to be "de" before the name, but that was dropped when they emigrated to this country as being undemocratic. Sir Guy de Cleveland was knighted at the siege of Boulogne by the King and was therefore entitled to have a coat of arms, a crest and motto. (For description of crests and coat of arms see J. B. Cleveland's book about the Clevelands.)

The Clevelands seem to have had rather more than their share of mottoes, claiming two as belonging to them, "pro deo at patrio"—"For God and Country." Showing them to be both patriotic and a religious family. Another motto, "semet et semper"—once and always, meaning, "Once a Friend Always a Friend," or opposite. Both mottoes, I think, have been somewhat characteristic of the family.

For given names, the Clevelands used Bible names or abstract qualities, as, Faith, Hope, Perseverance, Justice, Mercy, Answer to Prayer, Abigail, Sarah, Ephraim, Abraham, Benjamin, Jacob, and by no means were Joseph and Gypsy wife, Asenath, forgotten. James B. Cleveland deals mostly with part of Cleveland family descended from Moses Cleveland, who came to Massachusetts in 1635. Many counties and towns are named for them. Cleveland, Ohio, one of the most noted and largest cities in the world named for a citizen of the United States.

—"New International Encyclopedia."

D. A. R. Magazine, 1719:

All Clevelands, except the New England stock, descended from Alexander Cleveland, Sr. He settled in Virginia and had at least one son, Alexander, Jr., born 1667. He married Margaret McMinn, and they had the following children: John, Alexander, Micajah, Elizabeth, Jeremiah, Jacob, Martha, Reuben, Daniel, Larkin. Jeremiah, Jr., had at least two children: Reuben and Jacob. My ancestor, Jacob, was born in Culpepper County, Va., May, 1739. He married Milly White, October 10, 1756. She was a sister of Rev. John White, Baptist minister of Virginia, and also Ruckersville, Ga., Elbert County.

From Colonial records of North Carolina, a letter from M. K. Cleveland, Secretary to Admiralty, dated February 28, 1757, we learn that about the year 1790 the churches, composing a certain conference, formed a distinct association, and that the ministers belonging to this were: George M. Neal, John Cleveland, William Pitty, William Stone, Cleveland Coffee, Andrew Baker and John Stone.

John Cleveland, son of Alexander, Jr., and Margaret McMinn Cleveland, and father of Benjamin, John, Robert and Jeremiah, died about 1778. He settled early in 1700 in Orange County, Va.

Robert Cleveland was father of sixteen children. Jeremiah, one of his sons, was grandfather of Marietta, Ga., Clevelands.

Wheeler, in his history of North Carolina, page 462, has this to say of Benjamin Cleveland: "Col. Benjamin Cleveland, hero of King's Mountain, after whom Cleveland County is named, lived and died in Wilkes County, Cleveland County was formed in 1841 out of Rutherford and Lincoln counties. He was a brave and meritorious soldier. A serious impediment in his speech prevented his entering political life. However, he was a Senator to

General Assembly from Wilkes County in 1779. In 1775 he was appointed ensign in second regiment of troops and served in battle at Kings Mountain. Hero of one hundred fights with Tories. Surveyor of Wilkes County. Capt. Robert Cleveland was little less distinguished than his brother, and was with him in a majority of his campaigns.

—From V. Magazine, Vol. 7.

Letter written to Dr. Draper from Maj. Red:

"The Clevelands, or the grandparents of Col. Cleveland, died about 1770. I do not know their given names. The father of Col. Cleveland was named John. He and his wife were living in 1774. How much longer they lived, I do not know. I never knew the Clevelands claimed descent from Oliver Cromwell. Claxby and Smith, who married two of Col. Cleveland's sisters, were men of but little note. Franklin, who married the other, was a man of very fine standing in the county.

"I do not know what became of Claxby. Smith moved to Kentucky. Franklin moved to Surry County, N. C., settled on Mitchell's River and lived there until his death. He raised a large family of children, some of whom became men of distinction. Jesse was a member of the United States Senate, and afterwards Governor of North Carolina. Meshac, the younger brother, was a member of Congress from the same state several years. Abednigo, the youngest, emigrated to Georgia and became a man of considerable distinction.

"Col. Benjamin Cleveland and Martin Sumpter were the best of friends in their youthful days. Col. Cleveland was born and reared in the southern part of Orange, Va., six or eight miles from the mouth of a north-side branch of the Rapidan River, called the Blue Run. John Cleveland, the father of Benjamin Cleveland, lived and died at this place. In my first recollection the father and mother, as well as grandfather and grandmother, lived until they were one hundred years of age, and what is very remarkable, they died very suddenly and within two or three days of each other. Col. Cleveland had four brothers and three sisters.

"Benjamin was the eldest. Col. Cleveland and John Cleveland and wives were members of the Baptist Church, and doubtless members of the Blue Run Baptist Church. There is a stream about a mile northeast of Barboursville, Va., called Cleveland's Run. It was probably named for the Clevelands, as they lived near it."

History of Spartanburg County, by Landrum, mentions Benjamin, John and Robert. John, the second son, Baptist minister of good standing, influence and ability. Robert Cleveland, Captain in his brother's regiment in the battle of King's Mountain. Among his children were Jeremiah and Jesse. Jesse emigrated from Wilkes County, N. C., in 1810, merchandising business. His son, Robert Easley Cleveland, graduated from Charleston Medical College, interested in the affairs of the town, successful in the treatment of typhoid, man of extensive reading and information. He was hospitable in home, social in nature, store of anecdotes and conversational qualities caused to be much sought after. He was survived by Hon. John B. Cleveland and Dr. Jesse F. Cleveland.

We learn from the State records of North Carolina, 1781, that Captain

John Cleveland, probably the son of Benjamin Cleveland, was appointed by the House of Commons to command troops.

John Cleveland, father of Rev. John Cleveland, was born about 1667 and died about 1778. He left a will in which he mentions daughters Mary, Franklin, Betty Claxby, Patty Smith; sons, Benjamin, John, Robert, Reuben (deceased), Jeremiah; and grandchildren, Betty and Austin Smith. No mention is made of his wife. In 1779 a short appraisement was made of John Cleveland.

From James B. Cleveland's book on the Clevelands, I glean the following: "John Cleveland, the second son and third child of John Cleveland and Martha Coffee Cleveland, was born about 1740 in Orange County, Va., and died about March, 1825, at Cleveland's Ferry, S. C., about ninety years of age. He and three brothers are said to have been at the Yorktown surrender. The children of John Cleveland were: John, Neal Cornelius, William, Fanny, Elizabeth, Jeremiah, Mary, Larkin and Benjamin. Rev. John Cleveland and one of his brothers went from Virginia about 1772-75, journeyed on pack horses, and cut their way through brush as they traveled. When he would preach the wicked people would take him out and beat him seriously, but he would preach on, and when they let him go, would mount a stump or log and finish his sermon. They came to Pickens District, S. C., and were of the first settlers. They lived in Pendleton District at Cleveland's Ferry. The Clevelands lived mostly in what is now Oconee County. He was one of the very first settlers of Franklin County, Ga., about 1785 (then inhabited by Indians). His home was on Tugaloo River, where he dwelt many years and reared his family, who settled at various points along the river. He was kind to his neighbors and the poor, and to his many darkies, who thought their master better than any other man.

"He was living with his daughter, Elizabeth, at the time of his death. Elizabeth was born at Cleveland's Ferry, and married Benjamin Harrison, of Carnesville, Ga."

J. F. Goode, in his "History of the Tugaloo Baptist Association," has this to say of John Cleveland: "John Cleveland was one of the delegates from the church by the name of Tugaloo River when the Association was organized in 1818. According to Campbell's History of Georgia Baptists, he was at that time a very aged man.

In his brief outline of the Tugaloo Association, held at Eastonollee in 1819, he speaks of John Cleveland as one of four aged ministers who were present. He was a delegate from Tugaloo River at each succeeding session until 1822; after that date his name is not mentioned again until the session in 1825, when the following resolution was passed: "We make this statement to commemorate the death of our father, John Cleveland, who passed this life on Friday before the fourth Sunday in March last, after being a preacher of the gospel for about fifty years. He died in full hope of being received to God through Christ, being in the eighty-seventh year of his age."

Albert Henry Newman states in *Christian Index*, printed September 6, 1895, that he has in his possession the roughly printed history of the travels of John Asphland, who was employed to gather material for a history of Baptists in this country, which states that in 1789 Tugaloo River was the only Baptist Church in Franklin County; that John Cleveland was pastor, and membership was 108 persons. It is not certainly known who was founder of this church, but the most reasonable conclusion is that it was founded by John Cleveland. It may not be amiss to state in this connection that Franklin County, in 1789, embraced in her territory what is now Hart, Madison, Oglethorpe, Clarke, Oconee, and a large territory in the forks of Seneca and Tugaloo rivers in South Carolina. The territory in South Carolina was in dispute at this time, but held by Georgia. This statement is made for the purpose of showing that in all probability John Cleveland was the first man who lifted the Standard of the Cross in the territory now or formerly embraced by the Tugaloo Association. From the little vine planted by him in the late years of the Eighteenth Century, arms have spread out east, west, north and south. And whatever may be said to the contrary, it is now a well-established fact that John Cleveland was the father of Baptist principles in the vast territory embraced by Franklin County, in 1789, and Tugaloo is the mother church.

In the biography of Thomas Gilbert, a statement is made that in all probability he and John Cleveland were intimately associated in establishing the church known as Tugaloo River, both being delegates to the first association, 1818, and continuing as delegates from same church until 1823.

John Cleveland, Francis Calloway, John Sandridge, John Bramlett, ministers, helped compose a Presbytery for the Clark's Creek Church, Franklin County, Ga., seven miles northeast of Carnesville, which church was constituted on the tenth day of December, 1824.

The Poplar Springs Church was constituted in May, 1815. According to statement made by Brother Henry Stovall, Joseph Chandler, Thomas Wilkins, John Nail, John Mullins, and James Jackson were some of the first members. John Cleveland, Thomas Gilbert and Francis Calloway, Jr., supplied the church until 1826. John Cleveland's name is again mentioned in connection with Francis Calloway, Nancy Meeks, John D. Terrell and David Barton, as composing a Presbytery September 8, 1810, for the Eastonolle Church.

At the 9th annual session of the Tugaloo Association held at Beaverdam Church, Pendleton District, S. C., on Saturday before the third Sabbath in September, 1826, the death of old Father Cleveland is mentioned in very touching language with the statement that he had been a minister for fifty years, and was eighty-seven years of age at the time of his death."

Among the old records at Carnesville is a book containing the names of persons entitled to draws in the land lottery of 1825, and its continuancy taken by Joseph Chandler and H. M. Payne. John Cleveland's name is mentioned as a Revolutioner, being entitled to two draws, and whose name had been given in for draws in the contemplated Land Lottery under Acts of the Legislature of the 9th of June, 1825, and of 24th of December, 1825, and of the 14th of December, 1826, in Col. John H. Patrick's Regiment, composed of Major Shackleford and Chandler's Battalion, January 3d, 1827, signed Joseph Chandler, Maxfield H. Payne, L.L.C.

Thomas Gilbert and John Cleveland were usually associated in their work. The families were connected, we know. There is a record of a will made by Thomas Gilbert in the County Clerk's office at Carnesville, Ga., made in 1810. He wills all his estate to Polly and Betty and he states a wish that his other children will be satisfied as he has given them what he could afford. He says Polly and Betty have helped him accumulate his property and have taken care of him and his wife in their infirmities, weakness and old age. Witness: John Cleveland.

Polly and Betty willed same estate to their nephews, Cornelius and Thomas Cleveland. Reuben Cleveland was the father of Cornelius and Thomas, and the son of one John Cleveland. By the will we see he had to be the son of one of Gilbert's five daughters. Doubtless his father was the John Cleveland who was the son of Rev. John Cleveland. I have read that John was his eldest child.

Thomas Gilbert was born in Orange County, Va. He was of English descent. He married Ann Farneyho, of Virginia and Maryland.

Thomas Gilbert was a Revolutionary soldier and obtained large grants of land from the government. It has been said that at one time he owned one hundred thousand acres of land in north Georgia and Tennessee, and that he had many slaves. He was one of the first to go to Louisville, Ga., to frame a Constitution for the State of Georgia.

Dozier Thornton married Thomas Gilbert's granddaughter, Mrs. Pulliam. George Stovall married Mrs. Pulliam's daughter. Thomas Gilbert's daughters, Betty and Polly, were known as the English Aunts, and were noted for their cooking and immaculate housekeeping. They were fond of growing flowers.

Thomas Gilbert died at the age of ninety, about 1820-25.

About ten miles north of Hartwell, Ga., on the summit of a beautiful hill overlooking the verdant valley and the limpid stream of the Tugaloo, lie Thomas Gilbert, his wife, and Polly and Betty, peacefully sleeping in what used to be their flower garden. Their graves marked with rough, unlettered stones, and covered with tomb vines. Between this hill and the river is another burial ground. About sixty years ago Reuben Cleveland was buried here. After spreading joy and sunshine for nearly a century, for his was a happy nature, he has gone to rest, and the Tugaloo will forever sing to him about the good that he has done, while the tall pines above his grave will always look after him by each year covering his grave with a soft blanket of needles.

Reuben Cleveland married Nancy Bryan, and to them were born the following children: John Ashley, Obadiah, Thomas and Cornelius, boys; and Rebecca, Alpha, Elizabeth and Hannah, girls. Hannah married a man by the name of Farr. Ashley married Mary Skelton.

In 1837 Reuben Cleveland purchased from Joshua Carpenter a plantation situated on Whinnery's Creek on the Reed Creek highway, about four miles from Hartwell, Ga. This plantation is now owned by T. J. Cleveland, grandson of Reuben Cleveland.

Obadiah, the son of Reuben Cleveland, married Ann Skelton in 1840. She died March 16, 1885. There were five other daughters included in his wife's family, namely: Mary, Nelly, Rachael, Milly and Clarissa. There were four boys in this family: Wesley, Hymer, Larkin and Vandiver.

Obadiah served in the War Between the States, and was killed in the battle of Griswold Mill, ten miles south of Macon, Ga. His grave is unknown.

No shroud or coffin was allowed his mutiliated body. There is a marker in the National Cemetery at Macon, Ga., with O. Cleveland on it.

About 1851, Obadiah bought from his father the above mentioned plantation, and while living there the following children were born: George Washington, Jasper Marion, Andrew Jackson, King David, John Wesley, and Thomas Jefferson, who all lived to be grown men. Two sons and one daughter died in infancy. G. W. Cleveland married Martha Allen, who was the daughter of James Allen, a member of the Legislature directly following the war. After her death, he was married again to Evelyn Smith, who is still living near Hartwell, Ga. G. W. was wounded in the Civil War and died in 1902.

Jasper Cleveland died in Virginia, 1862, at the age of 18, while serving in the same war.

A. J. Cleveland, also a Confederate soldier and a Baptist minister, died, 1921, at the age of 80. He was married to Mary Ann Vickery.

K. D. Cleveland, now living at Gadsden, Ala., is the fourth son of Obadiah who fought for the cause of the Confederacy. He was married to Jane Vickery, who died in 1928

J. W. Cleveland married Nancy Dyar. He died in 1929, a few years after his wife's death.

T. J. Cleveland married Lou A. Boleman. The following is an extract from Lucian Knight's History of Georgia, Volume V, page 2541, written about the year 1914:

"Professor Thomas Jefferson Cleveland is known as a prominent educator, whose life has been spent in the advancement of humanity and progress along educational lines. His ability and knowledge have found a medium through which to reach the people of recent years in the position of County Superintendent of Schools in Elbert County, where his untiring labors have accomplished wonders in advancing, elevating and developing the school system.

"Professor Cleveland was born in Hart County, Ga., May 18, 1860, and is a son of Obadiah and Ann (Skelton) Cleveland, natives of Franklin County, Ga. His father, who was engaged in agricultural pursuits in Franklin County, enlisted for service in the Confederate Army during the War Between the North and the South, and met a soldier's death on the battlefield at Griswold Mill, in 1864, being then forty years of age. The mother survived until 1885, and was sixty-two years old at the time of her death.

"The youngest of his parents' nine children, and growing up at a time when the country was just recovering from ravages of an invading army, Thomas Jefferson Cleveland's education was of a somewhat ordinary character, although his instruction was of a practical nature, and as such was of much general value to him when he came in contact with a life's work that has required all his energies. Having received the rudiments of his education in the public schools of Hart County, he further advanced himself by attending the high school, and taught his first school at the age of nineteen in the county of his birth. After several years thus spent, he accumulated the means with which to enter the University of Georgia, which he left in his sophomore year. Before going to the University his worth as a teacher had been established, and upon his return he was employed to teach in Marshall County, Ala., where he remained two years; it was his constant aim to elevate the character of the schools of the county, and he accomplished much in that direction, many of his former students today figuring prominently in places of trust and responsibility. After two years in Marshall County, Ala., Professor Cleveland spent eight years in Hart County, and then came to Elbert County, where for a quarter of a century he has continued to be one of the most popular educators this section has known. Notable is the fact that eighteen years of this period were spent at Montevideo, both as teacher and principal, his work always recommending him for a call to the same position.

"When the Board of Education of Elbert County commenced to look around for a Superintendent of ability, well versed in the system of public schools, and splendidly equipped as an educator and disciplinarian, Prof. Cleveland was elected by the people to fill the laborious and important place. This was in 1912. Since that time he has labored continuously at his post, giving that satisfaction which can be given only by a man whose soul is in his work. His proficiency is best attested by the satisfaction he has given. Having supervision over thirty-eight colored and forty-four white schools in Elbert County, his duties are many and laborious, yet he is a tireless worker, and has won his way through his unremitting exertions to a front rank and has among the foremost educators of Georgia. His ideas are progressive and unusual and their working out has been attended with excellent results.

On January 21, 1883, Professor Cleveland was married at Hartwell, Georgia, to Miss Lou A. Boleman, daughter of the late W. H. Boleman, who was well known in Hart County. Six children have been born to this union: Mrs. Anna Crawford, born in Marshall County, Alabama, who is the mother of five children and resides at Elberton; Mrs. Maggie Higginbotham, born at Hartwell, Georgia, who resides in Elbert County, and is the mother of two children; Mrs. Pearl Myers, born in Elbert County, and is the mother of two children; D. M., born in Elbert County, who is engaged in teaching and agricultural pursuits, in this county, is married and has two children; Miss Dixie, who was born in Elbert County, is now the wife of Dr. J. L. Cooley of Bellaire, Kansas, and Miss Opal, born in Elbert County, who is a student at the Elberton High School."

Written and compiled in 1929 by Mrs. Dixie Cleveland Cooley, 305 Mount View Drive, Chattanooga, Tenn.

Redwine Family—Redwine Church—Mrs. Corra Harris at Redwine—Maj. Durkee—Families of Redwine Community

JACOB REDWINE was born in Pittsburg, Pa., in 1751, and was the son of Frederick Redwine, who was born in Prussia, 1699. Jacob moved to Montgomery County, N. C. He married Rowena Rhineheart. To Jacob Redwine and his wife, Rowena Rhineheart Redwine, were born, all in Montgomery County, N. C., the following children:

1. Mary; born January 7, 1777; married William Ballenger of Franklin County, Ga.
2. Elizabeth; born June 21, 1778; married John W. Carroll, March 26, 1811; died January 19, 1859 at Palmetto, Ga.
3. Jemima; born February 17, 1779; died June 8, 1779 in Montgomery County, N. C.
4. Jemima (Second); born May 26, 1783; married McGee; died June 27, 1848 at Palmetto, Ga.
5. Sallie; born August 29, 1793; married Larimore; died June 11, 1842 at Palmetto, Ga.
6. Katie; born April 12, 1781; married Hearn; died August 15, 1836 at Palmetto, Ga.
7. Barbara; born June 3, 1797; married Joseph Parker; died May 19, 1845, Elbert County, Ga.
8. Nancy; born October 23, 1799; married Underwood; died October 19, 1873, Newnan, Ga.
9. Lewis; born December 26, 1791; married Mary Merritt; died February 28, 1870, Coweta County, Ga.
10. Jacob; born September 15, 1783; married Trible; died March 12, 1866, Ben Hill, Ga.
11. Michael; born August 11, 1789; married Hart; died September 15, 1855, McLemore, Ga.
12. John; born February 9, 1795; married Crawford; died November 25, 1841, Palmetto, Ga.

Jacob Redwine was a soldier in the Revolutionary War. He moved to Georgia and settled in Elbert County, and as stated by some historical writer, drew land in District 12, Section 4, Lot 119; Bowers' District, Elbert County, Georgia. Also, his name is listed in the Cherokee Lottery under the head of "Revolutionary Soldiers and Widows."

His wife, Rowena, died at the Redwine home in Elbert County, July 4, 1831, and was buried there, possibly in the old cemetery at Redwine Church.

In 1832, after the death of his wife, Jacob Redwine moved to the home of his son, Lewis Redwine, in Coweta County, Ga., where he died in 1840 and was buried at Concord Church in the northern part of Coweta County. This church has since been abandoned.

There was a mill on Morea Creek, known as the Redwine Mill, built by Lewis Redwine, who also had a rice mill in connection with it.

Why this creek was named Morea we have never been able to learn. We have made extensive investigation as to the origin and meaning of the name Morea. We had an inquiry from the State of Oregon to know what the name signifies.

Redwine Church was founded with the co-operation of the Redwines who lived there at the time, and William Redwine, who was perhaps a nephew of Jacob Redwine, was among the first preachers to serve the church.

Among the former citizens and first settlers in the community, may be mentioned William Fleming, Benjamin Higginbotham, Jesse Hendrix, Berrin Holbrook, James Cook, Mike Herndon, Jacob Hays, Franklin Cunningham and others.

Several of the above named, together with a number of others, are buried in the old cemetery near the site of the first church house, located several hundred yards from the present church house. Their graves, many of them marked by large stones, the inscriptions upon which are now almost obscure due to the weathering of the years.

We have no date as to when Redwine Church was organized, but it is safe to say that it has been a church for considerably more than one hundred years. It was organized back in the early days when church houses were improvised log cabins in the wilderness. There have been four church houses built at Redwine. The first, a log house, located at the old cemetery mentioned, several hundred yards west of the present church. The next, a log house, near the present house. The third, a frame house erected in 1878. Rev. A. G. Worley, Presiding Elder, preached the dedication sermon, and at which meeting Capt. A. S. Turner was licensed to preach. The present church house, being the fourth, erected in 1906, at which time Rev. W. A. Maxwell was pastor and Rev. John Mashburn preached the dedication sermon.

The church is now, 1932, on the Canon charge, with Rev. Carl Stanley, pastor, and a membership of one hundred and thirty-eight. It was originally on the Royston, and still later on the Hartwell Circuit.

Reverting to the history of the early days of Redwine Church and community, will state that Joseph Parker, who came from North Carolina to Georgia, married a daughter of Jacob Redwine and lived in the community. To him and his wife were born several sons and daughters. The sons were: John D., Jacob, Lewis, William, Benjamin B. and J. Hubbard.

It is noticeable that the name of Jacob Redwine, the grandfather, and two of his sons, who were uncles, were perpetuated in the naming of three of the sons of Joseph Parker, viz.: Jacob, John and Lewis.

John D. and Benjamin B. Parker at one time owned the place known as the Cunningham place, which they sold to Franklin Cunningham. The Parker family later moved up into Franklin County and located on Big Shoal Creek, where they founded the village of Parkertown, a history of which will appear elsewhere in these pages.

Benjamin B. Parker was a Methodist preacher, and, if we are not mistaken, we have heard it said that he probably was converted under the preaching of his kinsman, William Redwine.

Franklin Cunningham, who bought the place, as stated, died September 25, 1856, at the age of 72 years, and is buried in the old cemetery at Redwine. We are not advised as to a complete family history of Franklin Cunningham, any further than he had one son, James Stewart Cunningham, who married Miss Elizabeth Henderson. He died during the War Between the States at Macon, Ga., survived by his wife and several children.

The Cunningham family played a very important part in the affairs of Redwine Church. Mrs. Elizabeth Cunningham donated the four acres of land upon which the church is located. She had two daughters, Misses Eliza and Lavonia, who died unmarried, and to the church was given a memorial window which was dedicated to their memory.

Lorenzo Dow at Redwine Church in the Early Days

In an article which was printed in the *Canon Echo* in May, 1909, by John M. Bowers, the editor, we clip the following very interesting history of

Redwine Church and of the visit of Rev. Lorenzo Dow, an itinerate and independent evangelist of the Methodist Church.

"On last Sunday quite a crowd from here visited this old church to attend a quarterly meeting. They report a pleasant and profitable day, as Dr. Mashburn, the Presiding Elder, was present and delivered an uplifting discourse.

"While the editor was not present, yet the occasion wakes up many memories in his mind. We remember attending a quarterly meeting at this old church, nearly fifty years ago; and have attended a number since. We do not remember a single preacher of the olden times who preached at this church, who is living today.

"Rev. George Yarborough, who was elder on the circuit some time in the seventies—then quite a young man—as far as we know, is yet living, but now an old man.

"Our grandmother, who was born in seventeen hundred somewhere in the eighties, went to this old church near 125 years ago to hear Lorenzo Dow preach. She was then a little girl, but large enough to ride horseback behind her mother.

"The church, at the time alluded to, was then a little pine-pole house, and stood over near the old graveyard, a quarter of a mile, perhaps, from where the church now stands. Dow was a very peculiar fellow anyway he was taken. He would send his appointments on a year ahead, and would be there on the hour promptly. On this notable occasion, the people gathered at the little pine-pole church, from many miles around, forming a large concourse of people. Promptly at the hour appointed, there suddenly appeared at the door of the crowded little church, a little, long-haired, dusty and way-worn stranger, who peeped in at the door, and turned away. There was a large fallen chestnut tree, legged upon some of its large limbs, near the church house. To this tree the stranger went and mounted upon its inclined trunk. He pretty soon selected a place on the fallen trunk, and fell astride it, and began to sing lustily. This was a signal to the waiting and expectant throng, who soon gathered around the strange and clownish preacher. He sang, he prayed, he preached. Sometimes he was astride the log, sometimes he sat sidewise and sometimes he was standing on the log. When this strange preacher got through with his exercises, he disappeared about as suddenly as he appeared.

"We have now written of this incident in connection with the history of old Redwine Church as nearly as our memory serves us of what we heard our old grandmother say about it forty or more years ago. We will state that our memory is very vivid, as well as many other things that we have heard when only a stripling of a boy.

"This church was named for Old Billy Redwine. In some way Billy Redwine was related to our people, we think, but we are sorry to say that we can't write on this relationship for lack of information.

"When Uncle Billy Bowers was born, in 1825, this old Uncle Billy Redwine stole his way to the door of the humble cottage by night where the newcomer was and placed on the doorsteps a new cradle to rock the stranger in. We have often heard Uncle Billy Bowers' father tell this. Perhaps it is well to say that a long time ago—we do not know the date—this little pole church was abandoned, a new log church was built on the present site. A good many years ago this old log church was torn away and a frame building erected in its place. This house stood till just a few years ago, when it was removed and the present splendid structure was erected.

"It may be of just a little interest to a few to know that the writer of this was a pretty regular attendant at the services held in the old log church when a boy and afterwards a young man.

"We remember seeing a young lady in the congregation one day within the walls of this old log church that 'pleased us well.' We did not know who the young lady was, and asked a chum if he knew who that—pointing her out—little dark-skinned, black-headed girl was, dressed in white.

"Later on this same little dark-skinned, black-headed girl became Mrs. Bowers, and the writer has been intimately acquainted with her ever since."

Corra Harris at Redwine

In 1887, Rev. Lundy Howard Harris was sent by the North Georgia Conference to the Royston Circuit as his first charge. The churches of Redwine, Fellowship, Macedonia and Royston composed the circuit at that time.

On February of that year he married Miss Corra White, of Elbert County, who became, and still is one of the most noted of present-day novelists.

Mrs. Corra Harris wrote one book, "The Circuit Rider's Wife," and another, entitled, "My Book and Heart," and in the two she gives a complete record of the Redwine Church period. As stated in her letter, a copy of which we reproduce, in the two books mentioned and others that she wrote, she laid many of the scenes at Redwine, in the churchyard, in the church, and among the people.

All of the writings by Mrs. Harris relative to Redwine Church and community will ever occupy a prominent place in their history.

Several years ago there was a movement made by the Daughters of the American Revolution, the John Benson Chapter, to erect and unveil a monument to Major Nathaniel Durkee, a Revolutionary soldier, who was buried in the old cemetery at Redwine, and which project was eventually carried out. Mrs. W. L. Hodges, Regent of the John Benson Chapter, at the time, addressed a letter to Mrs. Corra Harris inviting her to be present on the occasion and take part in the exercises, to which letter Mrs. Harris made the following reply:

CORRA HARRIS
In the Valley
Rydal, Ga., Nov. 10, 1921.

"Dear Mrs. Hodges:—Your letter has just reached me, having gone far and wide before it was sent to the right address.

"I should like nothing better than to be at Redwine Church upon the occasion of the unveiling of the monument to Maj. Nathaniel Durkee, and I should be honored above everything to even speak to the congregation, if only I might see one face after all these years that I knew when I came into it on a certain Sunday morning in 1887, a bride yet eighteen, to take up the blessed duties of 'Circuit Rider's Wife.' I remember the revival when three young men and two young women were converted, and how they came to me in the Amen Corner afterwards to tell me that I had helped them. How many times since have I thought of them. My husband and I nursed the sick there that summer around Redwine Church. It was a sort of plague. There was a widow who lived not far from Mr. Ben T. Fleming's, where we usually stayed, who lost her son, and I helped nurse her daughters and the Agnew children. So many died!

"In all three of my Circuit Rider stories I had laid many scenes at Redwine, in the churchyard and in the church, and among the people. Of course my heart has never left them. I see myself so young and happy among them. So confident of God and His great mercies, which in the deepest sorrows have never failed me. I loved the people every one, and the leaning tombstones in the churchyard, and the very grass that grew and waved in the wind above them. I could have wished that my husband and I might have lain together at last in that quiet place where he began with such ardor the practice of His Beatitudes.

"I entreat you to remember me to them with all my love. Assure them that my years have served me well. I have eaten the bread of sorrow and found strength. I am now old and tired and bereaved, yet I have not lacked for anything that the Lord has promised. I have suffered much and been blessed far beyond my merits with so much love from all the ends of the earth. I have learned not only to believe in God, but in men and women. And I have found it easy to do what I learned in old Redwine Church—to love them and never to fail in love.

"Some day I wish to make a pilgrimage there, in the spring, when all the leaves are young and green, and white flowers bloom close to the sod —on a Sabbath day when the old church door stands open and the people go in and sit in the sweet brown gloom.

"There was one man who was mighty in prayer in that church. He used to backslide. It was a business to get him straight with his Lord in time for the revival! But how he could pray! I should like to kneel and feel the rafters shake above his voice. But I suppose he is gone long ago. God bless him!

"Just tell them some day I shall come, but I can not come now. I shall be in Washington on the 20th of this month.

"Thank you again for doing me this honor.

"Faithfully yours, CORRA HARRIS."

Extracts from letters written by A. J. Neal, of Carnesville, Ga., to *The Hartwell Sun* and to Hon W. L. Hodges, relative to the history of Redwine Church and community and with reference to the erection of a monument to the memory of Major Nathaniel Durkee, a soldier of the War of the Revolution, buried at Redwine.

"I notice in an issue of *The Sun* of several weeks ago, an article in regard to erecting a monument on the grave of a Revolutionary officer, Major Nathaniel Durkee, buried at Redwine Church in your county.

"Redwine Church has long been known as a place of historic interest on account of its intimate connection with the early settlement of this part of your county.

"One of the first and most noted schools ever taught in the county in those early days was taught by Benjamin King, who came down from Virginia in Revolutionary times.

"In those days a large per cent. of the people were unable to read or write, as indicated by many of them from that section signing their names to Revolutionary papers by mark. I have the roll call of the Revolutionary soldiers of this section and many of their original autographs, my Grandfather King having been Pension Commissioner for the soldiers of this part of the State.

"I am in correspondence with the Daughters of the American Revolution in regard to erecting a monument on the ground in memory of this official hero of the Battle of Kettle Creek, and other Revolutionary soldiers buried in the vicinity.

"It seems that there will be no difficulty about erecting the monument and having a patriotic meeting on the ground some time this year if the people of Hart and adjoining counties will manifest their patriotic interest and friendly spirit of co-operation by contributing local and preliminary expenses.

"Respectfully, A. J. NEAL, Carnesville, Ga."

Extracts from letter of A. J. Neal to Hon W. L. Hodges.

"Maj. Nathaniel Durkee was a nephew and namesake of Gen. Nathaniel Green, who commanded the Southern Division of the American Army during the Revolution. As you recall it was Mrs. Green, wife of Nathaniel Green, who really conceived the first idea of the invention of the cotton gin—explained it to Eli Whitney, and got him to construct the mechanical parts, so as to get it in practical operation. Before the invention was patented there arose a contention in regard to the patent rights in some way. So about the time of Mrs. Green's death, Nathaniel Durkee became involved in the lawsuit about the gin in some way and contributed a thousand acres of land to the final promotion of the invention of the cotton gin. Durkee's friends and relatives claim that he is entitled to at least first honor in promoting and giving to the world the greatest invention known to civilization. I have a typewritten life of Nathaniel Durkee that gives an account of all this that I will get up and send to the patriotic ladies of your city sometime before the erection of the marker.

"Yes, my first foreparents were buried at Redwine. When a youth I visited with my parents the graves of our ancestors, and recall that they showed me the grave of Nathaniel Durkee and his wife, Malinda Durkee. Mr. Byron Bowers, who is still living, was present and saw Mrs. Durkee buried. I think we will have no trouble in locating the grave. I have written Mr. Bowers to get all necessary information.

"Yes, my first ancestor came down from Maryland in the first settlement of the country and established a school at Redwine. Some members of the Bowers, Browns, Cheeks, Rays and others prominent of the section attended his school, a school of great prominence in that early day. Benjamin King, the teacher, and the ancestor I refer to, was afterward a county officer for many years and was buried in the old graveyard."

EXERCISES IN HONOR OF MAJOR DURKEE

Large Crowd Gathered at Redwine to Hear Program Honoring Revolutionary Hero

"The exercises at Redwine Methodist Church last Sunday afternoon, December 20, 1921, honoring the memory of the only Revolutionary officer buried in Hart County, Major Nathaniel Durkee, whose remains were interred in the old cemetery there 98 years ago, were largely attended, proving both educational and interesting.

"Mrs. W. L. Hodges, Regent of the John Benson Chapter, Daughters of the American Revolution, under whose direction a marker was recently placed at the grave of the distinguished soldier, opened the exercises with a most appropriate talk telling of the reason for the exercises; she very ably presided during the program.

"Following prayer, Rev. Thompson, pastor of the Hartwell Methodist Church, told of 'The Spirit of '76,' of the unselfish motives that actuated our foreparents in the great war years ago that set the country free, appealing especially to the young people for the reverence for God and country that every American citizen owes.

" 'America' was heartily joined in by the crowded house, following which Mrs. Hodges read a letter from Mrs. Corra Harris, noted writer, written in answer to an invitation to be present for this occasion. Here at Redwine Church came Mrs. Harris as a bride in 1887, the first appointment of her husband after their wedding. Her letter is full of pathos; she recalls many old faces, and hopes some day to visit the historic church and community. Many of the stories written by Mrs. Harris and read by millions in the *Saturday Evening Post* have their settings at Redwine Methodist Church, in Hart County.

"Mrs. R. E. Matheson then most fittingly told of the work of the Daughters of the American Revolution, the oldest patriotic and one of the noblest organizations in the world.

"A song by Mrs. T. D. Johnson, Mrs. Mc. L. Brown and Mrs. Louie L. Morris was beautifully rendered; Mrs. R. E. Holland playing for all the songs.

"Following an interesting talk by Prof. J. I. Allman, he read a history of the life of Major Durkee, written by Col. Nathaniel Durkee Russell, of Brunswick, which proved very interesting. The paper will probably appear in an early edition of *The Sun*. Major Durkee was a very prominent citizen of Georgia in his day, and old newspaper files in Augusta tell of his life and activities there. He died while living in what was then Franklin County, later a part of Hart.

"After 'The Star Spangled Banner,' the large crowd wended its way with many flowers to the grave of the hero of '76. The grave is in the cemetery at the first church erected at Redwine, long since gone to decay.

"Many people from far and near attended the exercises."

The marker referred to, of marble material, bears the following inscription:

"NATHANIEL DURKEE, REGT. Q. M. 7 CT. MILL. REV. WAR."

Corra Harris at the time she wrote "A Circuit Rider's Wife."

Redwine Methodist Church

A History of Some of the Families That Lived in the Neighborhood of Redwine Church

William T. O. Cook

Bible in possession of Mrs. J. O. McCrary, Royston, Ga.

Marriages

William T. O. Cook; born May 30, 1809; died May 11, 1902. Married, first, September 16, 1828, Nancy T. Ridgway; born June 17, 1803; died February 25, 1885. Married, second, October 28, 1885, Mrs. Amanda M. (Almond) Scarborough; died November 16, 1917.

William J. Cook; born July 8, 1829. Married, August 17, 1848, Martha ―――――.

Benjamin T. Higginbotham. Married, December 13, 1849, Frances E. Cook; born May 24, 1831.

Fleming B. Cunningham. Married, November 22, 1852, Mary A. Cook; born June 3, 1835.

Thomas B. Cook. Married, September 6, 1857, Sarah J. Herndon.

John W. Gary. Married, July 12, 1858, Effy J. Cook; born August 6, 1842.

Francis M. Cook; born October 4, 1837; died February 19, ――――. Married, December 15, 1859, Sarah L. Ray.

G. F. H. Ray. Married, May 15, 1860, Rebecca A. Cook; born January 16, 1840.

Daniel H. Agnew. Married, November 18, 1866, Rebecca A. Ray.

Births

Frances E. Cook, May 24, 1831.
Thomas B. Cook, April 2, 1833; died January 5, 1864.
Mary A. Cook, June 3, 1835.
Francis M. Cook, October 4, 1837; died February 19, ――――, killed on railroad.
Rebecca Ann Cook, January 16, 1840.
Effy Jones Cook, August 6, 1842.
Francis Marshall Cook, September 30, 1872.
Elizabeth Cook, April 27, 1771.
William T. Cook, July 17, 1777; died March 18, 1814.
Fanny Cook, February 25, 1781; died November ――, 1849.
Mary A. Cook, October 24, 1803.
Francis Independence Cook, July 4, 1813; died August ――, 1814.
James Ridgway, July 20, 1770; died September ――, 1840.

Deaths

Frances E. Cook Higginbotham, February 20, 1915.
Elizabeth Cook Burch, formerly Elizabeth Cook, July 2, 1855.
Mary Ann Burch, formerly Mary Ann Cook, November 14, 1863.

Higginbotham

Bible owned by Mrs. Will Turner, Greenville, S. C.

Marriages

John G. Higginbotham; born March 3, 1807. Married Eliza Jane Baxter, August 25, 1872, who was born September 11, 1836.

Jane Elizabeth Higginbotham; born February 14, 1834. Married Dickerson; Ray and Scott.

Births

Hester Lorene Melving Higginbotham, August 23, 1873.
Bailey Joseph Dearly Higginbotham, February 1, 1875.
Lola Julia Caroline Stanton Higginbotham, January 2, 1878.
Sarah S. Higginbotham, 1811.
Sarah Ann Higginbotham, November 5, 1828.
Benjamin Thomas Higginbotham, June 6, 1830.
John Thornton Higginbotham, June 16, 1832.
Mary London Higginbotham, November 20, 1835.
Elijah Benson Higginbotham, December 16, 1838.
Dosia James Higginbotham, March 28, 1841.
Prissiler Frances Higginbotham, July 2, 1843.
William Green Higginbotham, January 14, 1845.
Reuben Crumbley Higginbotham, March 16, 1846.
Jeptha B. Higginbotham, October 26, 1847.

Higginbotham

Bible owned by Mrs. William B. Higginbotham, Royston, Ga.

Marriages

Benjamin T. Higginbotham; born June 6, 1830; died January 7, 1864. Married, December 19, 1849, Frances E. Cook; born May 24, 1831; died February 20, 1915.

William Carlisle Agnew. Married, February 15, 1866, Mary Jane Higginbotham; born February 17, 1851.

William Bowers Higginbotham; born March 9, 1858. Married, January 20, 1881, Mary M. Glover.

Coda McDonald. Married, February 23, 1893, John C. Higginbotham; born May 4, 1864.

Births

Martha E. Higginbotham, June 24, 1853.
Thomas B. Higginbotham, April 21, 1855.
Sarah Thornton Higginbotham, October 27, 1860.

Deaths

Martha E. Higginbotham Phillips, October 4, 1899.
Sallie T. Higginbotham Ridgway, March 31, 1898.

Higginbotham

Bible owned by Mrs. Sue Higginbotham, Lavonia, Ga.

Marriages

Thomas B. Higginbotham; born April 21, 1855. Married, November 17, 1874, by Rev. W. T. Norman, Sue N. J. Ledbetter; born May 24, 1854.

Annetta Higginbotham; born December 22, 1875. Married, December 22, 1896, E. R. McMurray, by Rev. M. A. Simmons.

Providence Methodist Church

TO THE best of our information, Providence Church was constituted about the year 1815, as we have a record to the effect that John B. Wade and his cousin, James Wade, both of whom were local Methodist preachers, and Polly Wade, who perhaps was an aunt of John B. Wade, and Elizabeth, or Betty as she was called, sister to John B. Wade and wife of Tarvner Rucker and perhaps others, on Christmas eve, 1815, erected a log house which was the first church building at Providence, and that Polly and Betty were so anxious that the house be built that they with their own hands carried up one corner of the house when it was raised.

Perhaps it would be as appropriate here as elsewhere to give some kind of a historical sketch of Rev. John B. Wade and his activities as a pioneer preacher in the early days of our country.

He was a son of Anne Wade, as it appears from the old records of Franklin County that during the year 1825, and perhaps before and after, she drew a pension as the widow of a Revolutionary soldier, in which connection John B. Wade and others are mentioned as her children.

Anne Wade and children, and perhaps others of the Wade connection, came from Virginia and settled in what was then Franklin, later Hart County.

Anne Wade is buried in the cemetery at Providence and her grave is marked by a splendid rock vault, which bears the following inscription: "Anne Wade, Died June 18, 1849, age 84 years." It is evident from this inscription that she was born in the year 1764.

John B. Wade lived in the community at the time Providence Church was organized and on up until about the year 1854, when he sold his land and bought other lands down in the neighborhood of Macedonia Church, which was constituted in 1854, he being perhaps the moving spirit in the organization and constitution of the church at Macedonia. He and others were the trustees to whom the land on which the church was located was deeded by Job Bowers, August 23, 1854.

Along about the 1840s, or early 1850s, there was a Methodist Church called New Hope, which stood about a mile south of where Reed Creek Church is located, at which John B. Wade at one time preached. He also preached at a number of places in the country and was perhaps the leader in the constitution of other churches besides those named. It was usual in the early days, when the country was but sparsely settled and churches were few and far apart, to hold religious services at central points, which were called preaching centers or stations, and where there were houses in which services were held, they were called "Meeting Houses." At many of these centers, churches were later constituted.

John B. Wade was quite active as a pioneer preacher, did quite an amount of work along religious lines, and in consideration of his many labors for his Master, it may be truly said of him, as was once said of another pioneer preacher of our country, "Rude temples of worship in many places sprang into existence at the call of this good man, blooming like wild flowers along the woodland paths."

Rev. John B. Wade is buried at Providence. We do not have the date of his death.

The next church at Providence was built in 1832 by the Parker brothers. It was located between the present church and the spring and had board shutters. The present church was built in 1875-6. The first sermon in the present church was preached by Jake Neese from the text, "Praying always with all Prayer and Supplication to all Saints."

The steps of the present church, which are of stone, were put up by Col. Cornog and the church cost $800 or $900.

In this connection we will state by way of digression that the steps at Shoal Creek Baptist Church were built by Col. Cornog, or perhaps rather by an old stone mason by the name of Weaver who was for many years in the employ of Col. Cornog, and who also perhaps was the builder of the steps at Providence. When the new church house was built at Shoal Creek the steps were moved from the old church to the new, where they remain.

The first person to be buried in the cemetery at Providence was a man by the name of John Hutchinson, who died near the church. He was brought to the graveyard for burial on a sled, it being in time of a snow and the ground covered so that it was not practicable to use a wagon or other vehicle other than a sled.

In the early days of Providence Church there was a band of Indians who lived on Tugaloo River, or on Big Shoal Creek near where they join, and an Indian of this band once occupied the pulpit at Providence, after the regular minister had finished the services, and preached in his, the Indian language.

An infant of this band of Indians is buried in the cemetery at Providence.

At Providence, before the War Between the States and perhaps on up to the time of the war, there were annual camp meetings held at the place, where people from a distance came and tented during the sessions. At these meetings glorious revivals of religion were experienced and enjoyed by the Christian people, and sinners were happily converted and saved.

Following is a partial list of the pastors who have served the church, which list was furnished *The Lavonia Times* by Mrs. Moss several years ago.

Date	Pastor or Pastors	Date	Pastor or Pastors
1847	Rev. Anthony	1854	Cotter and Worley
1848	Rev. Henry Cranford	1855	Brady and Howell
1849	Rev. Moss	1856	Brady and Walters
1850	Rev. Henry Cranford and McGuffy	1857	Jack Deavors and Parks
1851	Cone and Steward	1858	W. P. Norman and Jack Neese
1852	Either Moss or Sligh	1859	W. P. Norman and Levi Neese
1853	Parks and Harris	1861	Chambers and Jno. P. Guess

No names given till 1868. The War Between the States must have caused cessation of pastors for a while.

1868—Put on Hartwell Circuit.	1891-2—M. D. Smith
1869—Brit Sanders	1893-4-5—F. D. Cantrell
1869-70—Amicus Williams	1896-7—W. A. Simmons
1871-72—Rev. Baker	1898—W. T. Hamby
1873-4-5-6—W. P. Norman	1899—Rev. Mr. Dimon
1877—W. P. Smith	1900-1—Rev. A. C. Cantrell
1878-9-80-81—W. A. Farris	1902-3-4—Rev. Mr. Lowe
1882—Put on Lavonia charge with G. W. Yarbrough, Elder.	1905-6-7-8—J. F. Yarbrough Put on Hart Mission.
1882—Ab Quillian	1910—Rev. Pace
1883-4—W. J. Norman	1911—Rev. Talkington
1885—A. D. Echols	1912—Rev. Maxwell
1886—W. A. Cooper	1913-14-15-16—Rev. Stephenson
1887—Rev. Lankford	1917-18—Rev. Elrod
1888-9-90—A. D. Echols	Put on Lavonia charge.

Among those who composed the membership of Providence, in other days, may be mentioned the Parkers, Pearmans, Crafts, Ledbetters, Carneses, Pruitts, and others.

George M. Ledbetter

SOME paragraphs from a notice published in *The Hartwell Sun* upon the death of George M. Ledbetter, issue of May 13, 1904.

George M. Ledbetter was born near old Providence Church in Anderson County, S. C., March 26, 1825, and was converted and joined the Methodist Church in early boyhood.

It is related of him that he gave eight acres of the land on which now stands Providence Church, Anderson County, S. C.

He was married to Sarah Jane Martin, of Fork Section, on April 27, 1848, and later moved to Georgia in 1860, where he lived till his death, which occurred April 17, 1904.

His wife preceded him to the tomb, having died February 4, 1903; both are buried at Providence Church, Hart County, Ga.

Mr. Ledbetter had been a member of the Church at Providence, Hart County, Ga., for over forty years, and had held various official trusts in the church.

Mr. Ledbetter served as a private in the War Between the States in Company "B," 2nd Georgia Regiment, State Troops, under Captains John H. Patrick and Samuel H. Moseley until the surrender.

The funeral services of George M. Ledbetter were conducted by Rev. J. T. Lowe, his pastor, assisted by Rev. W. A. Cooper. Amid a large assembly of loved ones and sorrowing friends, his remains were laid away in the cemetery of Providence Church beside his precious wife to await the roll call of the resurrection.

Ledbetter

Bible owned by Mrs. Addie Clodfelter Ledbetter, Tallulah Falls, Ga.

Marriages

George M. Ledbetter; born March 26, 1825; died April 17, 1904. Married, April 27, 1848, Sarah J. Martin; born September 23, 1829; died February 4, 1903.

Caleb M. Ledbetter; born March 4, 1849; died March 31, 1924. Married, November 16, 1871, Mary E. Parker.

Sue N. J. Ledbetter; born May 24, 1854. Married, November 17, 1874, Thomas B. Higginbotham.

W. F. Ledbetter; born October 4, 1857. Married Lizzie Black.

George R. Ledbetter; born June 22, 1868; died March 4, 1908. Married, December 8, 1892, Addie L. Clodfelter; born March 24, 1866.

Births

David A. G. Ledbetter, June 13, 1852; died August 19, 1852.
John M. Ledbetter, July 11, 1861; died August 31, 1864.
Children of George R. Ledbetter and Addie Clodfelter:
Allice C., September 18, 1893.
George F., March 25, 1895.
David T. Henry Baxter, May 22, 1896.
Wallas Smith, October 10, 1905.

Ledbetter-Verner

Bible owned by Mrs. Sue J. Higginbotham, Lavonia, Ga.

David Verner; born February 20, 1760; died June 10, 1852; was a soldier of the Revolution.

Marriages

Mary Verner, daughter of David Verner; died September 24, 1860, age 77 years. Married, April 15, 1803, John Ledbetter; died January 25, 1831, age 54 years.

James Verner Ledbetter; born February 21, 1807. Married, July 14, 1829, Martha Sisk.

John Ledbetter; born February 7, 1809. Married, December 30, 1830, Susan Williams. He died August 2, 1856.

Joel Ledbetter; born July 27, 1811; died October 25, 1873. Married, February 27, 1834, Mary Parker.

Esther Ledbetter; born June 3, 1816. Married, March 13, 1845, John Martin. She died November 23, 1885.

David T. Ledbetter; born February 4, 1819. Married, November 5, 1840, Nancy Tilly.

George Montgomery Ledbetter; born March 26, 1825. Married, April 27, 1848, Sarah Jane Martin.

George Richardson Ledbetter; born October 16, 1864; died March 6, 1908. Married, December 8, 1892, Addy L. Clodfelter.

Caleb Martin Ledbetter; born March 4, 1849. Married, November 16, 1871, Mary Elizabeth Parker.

Susan Nancy Jane Ledbetter; born May 24, 1854. Married, November 17, 1874, Thomas Benjamin Higginbotham.

William Franks Ledbetter; born October 4, 1857. Married, November 24, 1891, Lizzie Black.

Births

Children of John Ledbetter, Sr., and Mary Verner:
Henry, May 10, 1805.
James, February 21, 1807; died April 25, 1863.
John, February 7, 1809; died August 2, 1856.
Joel, July 27, 1811; died October 25, 1873.
Catherine, December 24, 1813; died March 15, 1875.
Esther, June 3, 1816; died November 23, 1885.
David T., February 4, 1819.
Mary Caroline, February 2, 1821; died June 19, 1881.
Daniel Lewis, April 1, 1823.
Children of George Montgomery Ledbetter and Sarah Jane Martin:
Caleb Martin, March 4, 1849.
Susanna N. J., May 24, 1854.
William Franks, October 4, 1857.
George R., October 16, 1864; died March 6, 1908.
David A. G., June 13, 1852; died August 19, 1852.
John M., July 11, 1861; died August 31, 1861.
James, June 22, 1868; died September 27, 1868.

Deaths

David Lewis Ledbetter, August 28, 1844, age 21 years, four months, 28 days.

Fisher

Bible in possession of Mrs. Levi B. Fisher, Lavonia, Ga.

Marriages

Samuel C. Fisher; born February 23, 1809. Married, January 8, 1829, Rhoda Wakefield; born August 23, 1806.
W. F. Price. Married, April 24, 1855, Anna Fisher; born October 8, 1835.
Thomas Fisher; born August 20, 1837. Married, February 9, 1864, Elizabeth Walters.

Births

Hezekiah Little Fisher, December 2, 1829; died January 27, 1864, in Maryland, prisoner of war.
Mary Ann Elizabeth Fisher, September 8, 1834; died September 15, 1846.
Eliza Fisher, October 22, 1833; died October 16, 1846.
Levi Branson Fisher, June 10, 1840.
John Samuel Fisher, November 8, 1842; died July 2, 1848.

Fisher

Bible owned by the late Mrs. Levi B. Fisher, Lavonia, Ga.

Marriages

Levi Branson Fisher; died February 14, 1915. Married, October 12, 1865, Cordelia Shirley.

Ulysses Sherman Brown. Married, December 15, 1887, Effie Udenia Fisher; born March 25, 1868.

Hezekiah Wakefield Fisher; born July 28, 1866; died May 26, 1892. Married, January 27, 1889, Lena W. Walters.

J. A. W. Brown. Married, February 25, 1894, Annie Cordelia Fisher; born November 29, 1874; died January 30, 1895.

Loomis Edgar Fisher; born July 20, 1870. Married, December 23, 1894, Susie Cook.

Thomas Brock Fisher; born October 24, 1878; died March 25, 1918. Married, February 15, 1905, Annie Dallas Cheek.

Curtis Eugene Fisher; born April 30, 1881. Married, February 22, 19___, Rubie Gilmer.

Thomas Orr Fisher. Married, July 28, 1913, Bessie Ayres.

Loomis E. Fisher. Married, July 28, 1915, Zettie Spears.

Births

Idris Levi Fisher, August 22, 1872; died April 16, 1881.
Infant son, August 12, 1887; died September 10, 1887.
Lois Eunice Fisher, November 19, 1883.
Samuel Boyce Fisher, November 18, 1888.

Deaths

Effie Udenia Brown Fisher, died April 24, 1899.

To the foregoing record, we add the following sketches relative to the Fisher family.

Death of Samuel C. Fisher

Samuel C. Fisher, Esq., one of Hart County's oldest and most highly esteemed citizens, was found dead in his bed Monday morning last at his residence in Shoal Creek District.

Mr. Fisher was born in Abbeville County, S. C., February 23, 1809, and died February 16, 1891, and was therefore 82 years of age.

He removed to Georgia about forty years ago, and held the responsible office of Justice of the Peace in this county for over thirty years.

Mr. Fisher was a gentleman of the old school; honest and upright in his dealings with his fellowmen. He leaves a large and influential connection in the county to cherish his memory. His remains were interred in the family burying ground on Tuesday.

—From *Hartwell Sun*, issue February 21, 1891.

When Mr. Fisher moved to Georgia he purchased a large and valuable farm, which was formerly owned by Mr. Tarvner Rucker, where he made his home to the time of his death.

We have a record to the effect that Samuel C. Fisher was a soldier in the Seminole Indian War in Florida. The company was mustered into service and marched away from Anderson Court House on February 10, 1836, under Captain John J. Pickens. Mr. Fisher at that time was 27 years of age. The company had 76 members and was attached to the Fourth South Carolina Regiment.

He is buried in the family burying ground, as stated, which is located east of his old home, near and on the north side of the old Carnesville road. His grave is marked by a marble tombstone.

Thomas Fisher

From *The Hartwell Sun*, issue of April 13, 1917.

"Mr. Thomas Fisher, one of Hart County's oldest and most respected citizens, died in Hartwell last Friday morning, April 6, 1917. He had been in declining health for some time.

"As his custom had been for several years, he was spending the winter in Florida, when stricken with apoplexy a few weeks ago. As soon as he was able to travel he was brought home, where he lingered some ten days before passing away.

"Mr. Fisher was about 80 years of age, and had been a citizen of Hart County from early manhood. He proved a gallant soldier during the Civil War and was maimed for life, carrying the scars of the conflict to the grave.

"He had been married twice, his first wife, the mother of three children, preceding him to the grave twenty years; also two children, his son, Crayton, and Mrs. T. G. Craft, died several years ago. One child, Mrs. A. N. Alford, and his last wife, together with many grandchildren, survive him. He was a kind husband, loving father and grandfather.

"Mr. Fisher had been a member of the Baptist Church for many years and was faithful in discharging his duties as a Christian.

"The funeral was conducted from the residence of his son-in-law, A. N. Alford, by his pastor, Rev. M. H. Massey, in the presence of a large gathering of relatives and friends. The body now rests in the Hartwell Cemetery beside that of his first wife.

"The relatives have the sympathy of many friends in the going of this good citizen."

Mr. Thomas Fisher enlisted in Company "H," 15th Regiment Georgia Volunteers Infantry, Army of Northern Virginia, C. S. A., Hart County, Ga., organized at King's Bench July 15, 1861, Wm. R. Poole, Captain. Mr. Fisher was Second Sergeant of the Company July 15, 1861. Elected Junior Second Lieutenant 1863. Resigned April 20, 1864.

As stated, he was twice married. His second wife, who is still living, was Miss Mattie Lou Martin before her marriage to Mr. Fisher.

Mr. Fisher's first wife, who was a daughter of Mr. Elijah Walters, was a most excellent and high-toned Christian woman, and in the history of Cross Roads Church we give a brief account of her labors in connection with the Sunday school work at Cross Roads.

As already stated, Mr. Fisher and his wife are buried in the cemetery at Hartwell, their graves marked by imposing monuments with the following inscriptions:

"THOMAS FISHER,
AUGUST 20, 1837
APRIL 6, 1917."
"ELIZABETH FISHER,
BORN NOV. 16, 1841

DIED DEC. 22, 1899.
"SHE WAS A KIND AND AFFECTIONATE WIFE, A FOND MOTHER, AND A FRIEND TO ALL."

Cokesbury Methodist Church

COKESBURY METHODIST CHURCH is one of the old landmarks along the road to higher realms above. We have no date as to when it was organized, but evidently considerably more than a century ago. It was first called Jones' Chapel, or perhaps Jones' Meeting House, as all churches were called in the early days, so named for an old citizen of the community and who was perhaps a leading member of the church.

The name was later changed from that of Jones' Chapel to Cokesbury, blending the names of the first Bishops of the Methodist Church in the United States—Coke and Asbury.

Cokesbury Methodist Church, before the Civil War, was one of the wealthiest in northeast Georgia. The Turners, Chapmans, McCurleys, Gaineses, Teasleys, Joneses and Bradleys were among the leaders in the early history of the church.

In 1911 a splendid brick church house was built at Cokesbury, and in 1922, if we are correct as to dates, the roof and interior were destroyed by fire, but soon repaired and is today one among the imposing church houses of the country.

The cemetery at Cokesbury is interestingly historic, where many of older and former citizens of the community and members of the church calmly sleep in graves marked by beautiful monuments of marble and granite with appropriate inscriptions, and is truly hallowed ground and a "beautiful silent city of the dead."

Mount Zion Methodist Church

IN WRITING with reference to this old and long-established church, we herewith give in part an article that appeared in *The Sun*, 1886.

"Mt. Zion is one of the oldest landmarks. A gentleman 84 years old, in conversation with John H. Magill, said that it was established before his recollection and that it was first known as 'White's Meeting House.' It was torn down and replaced by a more substantial structure, built of hewed logs, which was consumed by incendiary fire, and the present building was erected."

The last mentioned was evidently the one that preceded the present church house.

With reference to the first name, "White's Meeting House," will say that it appears that all churches in the early days of our country were referred to as "meeting houses," perhaps for the fact that in England, from which many of our forefathers came, the church, presumably the church of England, called the mother church, was called the church, while the meeting places of the dissenters were called "meeting houses," and which name was brought over from the old country by the Pilgrims and also by the

Puritans and other protestants and applied to the places of religious worship established in America.

We well remember that in our boyhood days to have heard the old people frequently refer to the church as "meeting house," and very seldom as church.

The church at Mt. Zion, from our best information, appears to have been organized in 1820.

In a deed of record in Hart County, dated 1849, Reuben Tyler conveyed to Lewis Shiflet the lands adjoining the church property, "reserving for the use of the Mount Zion Methodist Church, about two acres of land, including the site whereon said church stands and the graveyard, and privileges of water at the lower spring."

The church is located on the Bankhead Highway a little more than five miles east of the City of Hartwell at the intersection of the public road leading down by Milltown Church to Mt. Zion. The Bankhead Highway was formerly known as the Brown's Ferry road, and prior to the time that it was called the Brown's Ferry road, it was known as the "Jackson Road," leading to Shockley's Ferry, later Brown's Ferry, and now Alford's Bridge, where the Bankhead Highway crosses the Savannah River.

Some of the old citizens and first settlers of the Mt. Zion community were the Carters, Tylers, Shiflets, Masteres, McDonalds, Whites, McCurrys, and others, many of whom and their families were at one time members of the church at Mt. Zion.

Due to the long period of time that the cemetery at Mt. Zion has been a burying ground, its history is very interesting.

In this old churchyard sleep the ashes of Angus McCurry and David Carter, Sr., soldiers of the War of the Revolution, and who after the war settled in the community.

On Sunday, November 13, 1932, markers were unveiled at their graves with appropriate exercises, at which the Carter family history was outlined by Mrs. Z. W. Copeland, of Elberton, Ga. A history of Angus McCurry was given by Mrs. Eloise McCurry Hodges, of Hartwell, Ga.

Micajah Carter and his brother, David Carter, Jr., soldiers of the War of 1812, are buried here, while several of the soldiers who served in the War Between the States rest beneath the green sod in Mt. Zion Churchyard.

This church was never very strong in the way of numbers, and today is composed of a membership of 42 members. Rev. John H. Baker is the present pastor.

Rev. Henry Tyler

IT IS quite appropriate to follow the foregoing history of Mt. Zion Methodist Church with a brief sketch of Rev. Henry Tyler, who was a member and we might say the pillar and leading light of the church for many years.

Rev. Henry Tyler, son of Henry Tyler, was born December 25, 1812; died October 4, 1876, at the age of 64 years.

Following is an article written by John B. Benson and published in the *Southern Watchman*, Athens, Ga., on April 18, 1876.

"Hartwell, Ga., April 18, 1876.

"Twenty-one years ago Rev. Henry Tyler preached here in the old wooden court house. Most of the men present had no coats on, and wore wool hats; the ladies wore calico dresses and sun bonnets.

"One old man who seemed very much affected, and had no handkerchief, walked up nearly to the pulpit, picked up a piece of greasy newspaper and wiped his 'weeping eyes.'

"Today he preached in as large and comfortable a church as there is in northeast Georgia, and to as elegantly dressed and well behaved congregation as can be found in the State.

"Mr. Tyler has been preaching nearly half a century in this county, and a few days ago, assisted by Rev. W. T. Norman, preached the funeral of Hon. Micajah Carter, who had been his true friend for fifty-five years. If Henry Tyler had have had the educational advantages that some bishops have, he would have been a head and shoulders above any of them. The sermon he gave today had more good, sound, common sense and better doctrine than we ever heard from any preacher.

"Mr. Tyler preached his first sermon at Bethlehem, in Walton County, Ga., November 21, 1833, from Matt. 5:16, 'Let your light so shine before men, that they may see your good works, and glorify your Father which is in heaven.'

"His last sermon was preached in Hartwell July 15, 1876, from Heb. 2:3, 'How shall we escape, if we neglect so great salvation; which at the first began to be spoken by the Lord, and was confirmed unto us by them that heard him.' This last sermon was considered by many as the ablest sermon of his life. During his 43 years in the ministry he preached 2,506 sermons.

"Though nearly twenty years have passed since this great and good man's death, each succeeding year only makes stronger the holy declaration, 'the righteous rest from their labors and their works do follow them.' "

Rev. Henry Tyler married Miss Patience Reeves, date of marriage not known.

To Rev. Henry Tyler and his wife, Patience, were born one son: James Tyler, who was killed in the War Between the States; three daughters: Mary A. Tyler married James D. Conwell, November 26, 1867; Sarah Tyler married William G. McDonald; Fannie Tyler was never married.

Rev. Henry Tyler and wife are buried in the cemetery at Mt. Zion Church, their graves marked by a marble tombstone with inscription:

"REV. HENRY TYLER,
DEC. 25, 1812
OCT. 4, 1876."
"PATIENCE, WIFE,
FEB. 9, 1812
NOV. 20, 1888."

Hartwell Methodist Church

HARTWELL Methodist Episcopal Church, South, was instituted in 1854 (Conference year 1854-55). Rev. Howell Parks being senior pastor, and Rev. Wm. S. Turner, junior pastor, then Elbert Circuit, Elberton District, North Georgia Conference.

The charter members were Mr. and Mrs. John B. Benson, Colonel and Mrs. P. E. Devant, Mr. and Mrs. John R. Kay, Mr. and Mrs. F. B. Hodges, Mr. and Mrs. James T. Jones, Mr. and Mrs. Thomas M. Holland, Misses Ellen and Caroline Holland, Mr. and Mrs. C. L. Scott, Mr. and Mrs. F. C. Stephenson. Having no church building then, services were held in the temporary court house, a wooden building on the northeast corner of the public square on the ground now occupied by the Matheson and Kidd brick building. When the brick court house was ready for use, the court room was used for a while for Sunday school and preaching.

Before the completion of the church building, the school house on the lot now occupied by the residence of Mrs. C. I. Kidd was used for church services. A great revival was held there, Rev. John Knight conducting the meeting. A number of members were added.

Mr. James T. Jones was the first Sunday School Superintendent.

The lot on which the first church was built and present one, stands at the corner of Howell and Webb streets, and was deeded to the following church trustees: John B. Benson, John R. Kay, F. B. Hodges, and James T. Jones, from Wm. Marris, on the 8th day of August, 1859. The church building, a frame one, was built by J. R. Kay. It was large and comfortable, well lighted with spacious windows, and tall steeple—a notable church for its day. This being the only church building in Hartwell until after the Civil War, the courtesy of its use was extended to other denominations.

The Baptists held regular services each month.

The Presbyterians held occasional services, though no church organization for several years.

The present splendid brick structure was erected in 1897. Rev. C. A. Jamison, pastor; E. B. Benson, chairman of the building committee.

The large bell, which, with its euphonious tones, people are called to worship, is responded to with grateful hearts.

The following is a list of members of the Hartwell Methodist Church licensed to preach:

E. G. Murrah, J. D. Turner, James Guest, Geo. A. Teasley, M. D. Smith, all became members of the North Georgia Conference; J. H. Baker, licensed to preach, and is pastor of Hart Circuit, as supply.

The Hartwell Camp Ground

By E. B. Benson

THE Hartwell Camp Ground, property of the Methodist Episcopal Church, South, Hartwell charge of the Athens-Elberton District, is situated on the paved National Highway, three miles southwest of Hartwell, Ga., and contains 56 acres. The land is a part of lands formerly known as the David Creswell Survey, property for many years in litigation between Ira Christian and Robert McMillan, and continued after their deaths and finally settled by partition between the Christian and McMillan heirs.

At the sale of these lands early in the year 1875, J. B. Benson bought this tract for the location of the Hartwell Camp Ground.

Soon thereafter a committee, composed of John B. Benson, F. C. Stephenson, F. B. Hodges, E. B. Benson, W. R. Stephenson and D. D. Dickerson, went over the ground and located the square around which the tents were to be erected, and in the center the arbor, or tabernacle (perhaps more properly called), was to be located.

This location was known as "Ben's" patch, so called from a small clearing in the woods where Ben Patterson had lived, nephew of William Patterson, of Baltimore, Md., who had owned the large body of land called the "Creswell Survey" many years before Hart County was formed. He sent his brother, Andrew Patterson, to occupy for him, the claimant, and it was said to get him away from Baltimore. Benjamin and Fielding were his sons; each married in this community and reared families.

William Patterson, of Baltimore, was a wealthy merchant of high social standing, whose daughter, Elizabeth, married Jerome Bonepart, brother to Napolean Bonepart.

Napolean Bonepart was a social climber as well as conquering general, making himself Emperor and his brothers Kings—forced Jerome Bonepart to divorce his wife to marry into royalty. Well, William Patterson wanted no common kin around to interfere with his family's social life. Those here could have been provided in lands of their own, but were merely squatters. Ben Patterson abandoned this. Some of these lands are now the highest priced farming lands in the county.

The first tent holders were: John B. Benson, E. B. Benson, F. B. Hodges, F. C. Stephenson, W. R. Stephenson, J. C. Dickerson, D. D. Dickerson, Rev. W. T. Norman, Elijah Chapman, D. O. Chapman, Mrs. Betsy Teasley, T. W. Teasley, T. Jeff Teasley, M. M. Mewborn, Dr. A. J. Mathews, J. B. Alford, C. L. Scott, J. H. Winter, W. H. Stephenson, Rev. Sinclair Richardson, S. M. Bobo. Others have filled the places of those dropping out and built new tents along.

The last camp meeting had a greater number of tenters than ever. The second and third generations are well represented in the present tenters. Since the number of those tenting at the last camp meeting was 300, the list of names can not be given.

The meetings are always pleasant occasions where friends meet and Christian fellowship is enjoyed by every one.

Hartwell Camp Ground News

An interesting, illustrated newspaper, gotten out by Charles J. Teasley, of Philadelphia, Pa., visiting his home town and the camp meeting, was enjoyed by our people this year.

History of the Presbyterian Church of Hartwell, Georgia

By Mrs. Ophelia C. Norris

IN THE fall of 1881 a small number of Presbyterians met in the parlor of Mrs. Emily Cater for the purpose of organizing a Presbyterian Church in the town of Hartwell. On January the first, at eleven o'clock, 1882, at the Baptist Church, Rev. R. W. Milner, Presbyterian evangelist, preached on, "The Church, It's Principles and Agencies." After his sermon, the Presbyterian Church was organized with the following charter members: Mrs. H. N. Ayers, Mrs. Emily Cater, Miss Maude Cater (Brown), R. P. Doyle, Thomas Cater, Miss Fannie Doyle, R. W. Gilliland, Miss Belle Johnson (Meredith), D. W. Johnson, Capt. J. L. Johnson, Mrs. J. L. Johnson, Miss Lizzie Johnson (Strickland), Mrs. Rease Johnson, B. F. Morrow, Miss Emily Morrow (........), Miss Maggie Morrow (........), Mrs. Kate Sadler, M. D. Smith and Mrs. W. H. Teasley.

B. F. Morrow, R. P. Doyle and J. L. Johnson were elected Elders, and M. D. Smith and Webster Johnson, Deacons. These officers were ordained and installed at the evening service of the same day, with the exception of J. L. Johnson, who was prevented from being present on account of illness in his family. He was ordained on the fifteenth of April following.

The first Lord's Supper was celebrated the first Sabbath of February in 1882.

When the town of Hartwell was incorporated, Lot No. 94, on Carolina Street, was set aside for the Presbyterian Church building. Later this was sold and on March the twenty-fifth, 1891, the lot of the present location on Carter Street was purchased from Mrs. Fannie N. McCurry for the price of $100.00.

The little handful of Presbyterians, struggling against poverty, worshipped in the Hartwell Methodist Church for 8 or 9 years. During these years the following ministers supplied at different times: Dr. G. H. Cartledge, Rev. Hugh McLees, Eugene P. Mickel and Archie Simpson.

The church building was begun in 1890, during the pastorate of Dr. H. F. Hoyt. Rev. R. E. Telford next came to the pastorate in July of 1891, and through his efforts the building was completed in January of 1892. Mr. James W. Williams, of the Methodist Church, gave much needed help in the way of money and work. He took the building in charge, gave his personal supervision, and when the building was completed made no charge for his valuable services. Messrs. J. B. and E. B. Benson, also Methodists, subscribed larger amounts to the erection fund than any others outside the church membership.

Rev. Archie Simpson, of Toccoa, Ga., preached the dedicatory sermon on the fifth Sabbath of January of 1892.

The following ministers have served as pastor or State supply: Dr. H. F. Hoyt, Revs. R. E. Telford, John L. McBride, T. H. Newkirk, G. M. Howerton, M. E. Peabody, Fritz Rauschenberg, James Bradley, L. K. Martin, and J. B. Nelson.

Mr. J. E. Dendy joined the church in 1890 and served as Superintendent of the Sabbath School for several years. He was elected Elder on the 24th of August, 1894.

Mr. W. T. Johnson was elected Elder on the 29th of March, 1897, on the 18th day of May, 1897, he was elected Clerk of the Session, and on the 23d of December, 1897, he was elected Superintendent of the Sabbath School, all three offices he has held until the present time. Few men can boast of such a record of faithfulness and loyalty.

This church has entertained the Athens Presbytery twice, in ...., and in April of 1923.

The women entertained the Athens Presbyterial in April of 1913. During the days of the saloons the minutes record much "churching" for indulging in "intoxicating spirits" and record congratulations "in abstaining from drink" as requested.

To Mrs. Maggie Adams and her sister, Miss May Anderson, much credit is due for the maintenance of the church.

The following ministers are sons of this church: Revs. H. B. Dendy, Marshall Dendy, Willie Dendy and Emmet McGukin.

The following are the present officers: Elders—W. T. Johnson since 1897, J. E. Dendy since 1894, Guy H. Norris since 1920, C. D. Griffin since 1922; and Deacons—W. D. Teasley and H. L. Kenmore.

The church has never had more than 68 members at any time. Its present membership is 58.

The Daniel M. Johnson Family History

DANIEL M. JOHNSON, of Scotch-Irish extraction, moved to Georgia from North Carolina more than one hundred years ago and settled on Big Coldwater Creek in Elbert (formerly Wilkes) County.

His home stood on the west side of the public road leading by where the Bio Consolidated School is located to Pleasant Hill Church, and was right near and on the east side of said creek.

He married Miss Nancy Highsmith, daughter of John Highsmith, of Elbert County, born November 19, 1801, and died November 30, 1884.

Mr. Daniel M. Johnson and wife were both buried in the cemetery at Pleasant Hill Presbyterian Church. Mr. Johnson's grave was marked by a monument of concrete material which has disintegrated and partly fallen down, and the inscription destroyed, therefore we were not able to get either date of his birth or death.

Mr. Johnson was a hat and cabinet maker, a trait inherited by some of his sons, some of whom were mechanics, contractors and builders.

When Hart County was created Mr. Johnson was elected as one of the five Judges of the Inferior Court, whose duty it was, among other things, to locate the county seat, and divide the area into streets and lots, and one of the main streets in the original plan of the town of Hartwell was named Johnson Street, which name it bears today.

To Mr. Daniel M. Johnson and wife, Nancy, were born the following named children: Sons—John A., Daniel Gilmore, James Lachlin, and Angus Johnson; and daughters—Sarah C., Margarett, and Mary Johnson.

John A. Johnson; born July 18, 1826; died June 5, 1913. Married Miss Amanda Cartledge, sister to Rev. Groves Cartledge, May 9, 1854; born March 20, 1832; died July 7, 1912.

Daniel Gilmore Johnson; born November 9, 1833; died March 9, 1907. Married Mary C. Brown, daughter of Dillard H. Brown, November 17, 1864; still living.

James Lachlin Johnson; born January 4, 1829; died September 30, 1895. Married Miss M. M. Jones, daughter of William Jones, June 17, 1866; born ....; died ....

Angus Johnson was never married.

Sarah C. Johnson married John A. Gentry, December 23, 1866.

Margarett Johnson married Martin White.

John A. Johnson and D. G. Johnson lived on Big Coldwater Creek a short distance above the home of their father, their homes on opposite sides of the creek, the home of John A. Johnson on the right and the home of D. G. Johnson on the left side of the creek. They jointly owned and operated a mill and gin on the creek located between their homes. They also engaged in farming.

John A. Johnson was a contractor and builder, and built the second jail in Hartwell after the first jail had been destroyed by fire.

In religion, Mr. Johnson, as well as all of the Johnson family, was a Presbyterian, and at the organization of Pleasant Hill Presbyterian Church, in 1848, he was called into the eldership and served his church and his Lord faithfully to the end of his life.

In the Civil War he enlisted in the Confederate Army as a private under his brother, Captain D. G. Johnson, in Company "C," of the 5th Regiment of Georgia, July 24, 1864, at Macon, Ga.

In the year 1859, he joined the old Hermon Masonic Lodge of Hartwell, which went down during the reconstruction days. On the fourth day of August, 1904, he became a member of the Hartwell Masonic Lodge, No. 189, F. & A. M.

He died on June 5, 1913, at Mountain City, Ga., at the home of his son, D. W. Johnson; was brought to Hartwell where the funeral sermon was preached by Rev. G. M. Howerton in the Presbyterian Church, after which he was carried to old Pleasant Hill Church and there buried beside his wife, Amanda, who had preceded him to the grave on July 7, 1912. Their graves are marked by a marble tombstone with inscription as follows:

"JOHN A. JOHNSON
JULY 18, 1826
JUNE 5, 1913."
"AMANDA, MARCH 20, 1832
DIED JULY 7, 1912."

Daniel Gilmore Johnson died March 9, 1907, in the 73d year of his age, and was buried on the day following at Pleasant Hill Church, Rev. M. E. Peabody, pastor of the church, conducting the funeral services.

As already stated, Mr. Johnson was a farmer and was at one time co-partner with his brother, John A. Johnson, in the operation of a mill and gin on Big Coldwater Creek.

He at one time served as one of the Judges of the Inferior Court of Hart County.

In the War Between the States he enlisted in Company "C," of the 5th

Regiment of Georgia, on May 25, 1864, at Atlanta, Ga., and was elected and served as Captain of the Company.

From the newspaper article chronicling his death, we reproduce the following paragraphs:

"He was what might be termed the highest type of a high-toned Christian gentleman, as is attested by all who know him and, indeed, he was one of those rare characters who stood the test of intimacy, for those who knew him and loved him most were loudest in their praises of his most excellent traits and consistency of life.

"He was unique in that while he was strong in his convictions and never under any circumstances compromised the truth, yet if he had an enemy, nobody knew of it."

Captain J. L. Johnson

Capt. J. L. Johnson died Monday, September 30, 1895. He had recently been elected to the office of Ordinary to fill the unexpired term of Hon. F. C. Stephenson, and had only served since June 25, 1895.

James Lauchlin Johnson was the son of Daniel M. and Nancy Johnson, and was born near Bethesda Church, in that portion of Elbert now embraced in Hart County, on January 4, 1829. He was a contractor and builder by occupation up to the war, and was Justice of the Peace of McCurry's District. Near the beginning of the war he volunteered as a soldier and was elected Third Lieutenant of Company "B," 24th Georgia Regiment, McLaw's Brigade, Longstreet's Corps, Army of Virginia. He was afterwards promoted to Captain of the Company. In an engagement in the Shenandoah Valley, while resisting a cavalry charge, he received a wound which necessitated the amputation of his left arm at the shoulder. This, of course, ended his military career.

On June 17, 1866, he was married to Miss Malissa Jones, daughter of Mr. and Mrs. William Jones, of McCurry's District, with whom he happily lived until his demise.

In 1866 he was elected Clerk of the Superior Court of Hart County, and served two terms. He was afterwards elected Tax Collector, which office he held from 1877-1882.

He afterwards held the office of postmaster at Hartwell for eleven years.

His funeral was preached in the Hartwell Presbyterian Church, of which he was an official member, on Wednesday, by Rev. R. E. Telford.

Old Pleasant Hill Presbyterian Church

AMID the picturesque items of the country landscape, on a prominence among the Coldwater hills, beside the old Holly Springs road, along which the pioneers treked well over one hundred years ago, stands the old Pleasant Hill Church House, abandoned and fast going to decay. The scenes are, more or less, sad and forlorn as we think of the happy days gone when the people gathered at this sacred shrine to engage in praise and adoration of the Giver of every good and perfect gift, and where eminent divines of the Presbyterian faith proclaimed the unsearchable riches of grace with unction from on high.

Near by is the little cemetery beneath whose green sod the ashes of many of the members peacefully sleep, awaiting the resurrection when the Lord shall come to gather His jewels home.

Long after this old structure is demolished and gone and remains but a name and a memory, the good accomplished here will live on to bless the world.

Old Pleasant Hill Presbyterian Church

History of Old Harmony Presbyterian Church

IN THE latter 1840s and early 1850s there was quite an influx of people from Lancaster County, S. C., to what was then Franklin, now Hart County, Ga.

Among the citizens who came we might mention the Bakers, Baileys, Bowerses, Usserys, Robertsons, Flemings, Isoms, Johnsons, and others.

Among the names mentioned, Mumford Ussery, Nathaniel Bowers, John Bailey and Joel Bailey were of the Presbyterian persuasion, or denomination, and at the time of their moving to this country, there were no churches of the denomination in the community, and they organized a church and built a church house near where Vernon Baptist Church is now located.

This at the time was a central point and quite an ideal location for a church. The church house was a wooden structure built just west of where the Clarkesville, Andersonville, Pullen's Ferry and King's Bench roads crossed. At that time, as already stated, this community was in Franklin County, Hart County not yet having been created, and so the road now leading from said location on to Hartwell only led to the intersection of the Pullen's Ferry with the Carnesville road, near the present location of New Harmony Methodist Church.

It perhaps would not be out of place and also be of interest to give the names of some of the former citizens of the community in which the church was built, and who were living here at the time the people from South Carolina moved here. In so doing we will mention the names of Ayers, Burton, Chandler, Oswalts, Miller, Robertson, Sloan, Cleveland, Pullen, and a number of others which we don't happen to think of at present.

The church house was erected on the lands of Joel Bailey, but no deed was ever executed to the property where the church stood. Years later Mr. Bailey sold his land and some preparations were made to move the house on to the lands of Mumford Ussery, but the project was never carried out.

The membership of the church was composed mostly of Mumford Ussery, Nathaniel Bowers, John Bailey and Joel Bailey and their families. As a matter of course others joined from time to time.

Among the preachers that supplied the church during the time it remained a church, which in round numbers was about forty years, we will mention the following: Rev. Groves H. Cartledge, who lived in Banks County, Ga.; Dr. Pearson, who lived in South Carolina, probably at Greenville; and they two were perhaps the most able and prominent preachers that served the church. Others whose names we can recall were: Revs. Grady, Cleveland, Hugh McLeese, Young, John Cartledge, Eugene Mickle, Hyde and Hoyt.

The last sermon at this church by a Presbyterian minister was by Rev. R. E. Telford, on August 10, 1892. At this time the church was practically disbanded, some of the members having died, others having moved away or joined other churches, and some of the membership joined the Methodist when New Harmony Church was organized at the place about 1892 or perhaps a few years before.

During the life of Harmony Presbyterian Church, there was a Sunday school carried on during the spring and summer months of the year, the house not being sufficiently adequate for services during the winter months.

Mumford Ussery, who was an Elder and leading member, was usually the Superintendent of the Sunday school.

At the Sunday school, as conducted from year to year, very little literature was used. There was what was termed a catachism, and for the younger children, cards of various colors on which was a verse of scripture printed that the children were supposed to commit to memory and recite on the following Sunday. This was before organs or pianos were introduced in the churches, and song service was all the music had. Some of the songs which were sung at the Sunday school are of hallowed and sacred memory to the writer, and when we hear any of them sung now, at this late day in life, we are reminded of the happy days of our youth when we attended Sunday school at old Harmony Church, while fond memory paints the scenes of other years.

In connection with the history of old Harmony Church, we might mention that a day school was taught at the church occasionally, part of the time in the church house and some of the time in an improvised school house that stood near the church. The first school attended by the writer was at this place, which was taught by Miss Sarah Chandler, daughter of Henry F. Chandler. Others who taught at the place were: William J. Bailey, son of Joel Bailey; Charles E. Ussery, son of Mumford Ussery; Miss Rachael Ussery, daughter of Mumford Ussery; A. D. S. Chandler, T. P. Harris, Rev. Hyde, and others.

Old New Hope Methodist Church

IN ABOUT the years of 1850 and later, there was a Methodist Church located in what is now Reed Creek District, near the headwaters of Little Lightwoodlog Creek, at or near the present residence of Peter C. Robertson, which was known as New Hope Church. The building, like all churches of former days, was built of large hewed logs, and in our boyhood days we remember to have seen a part of this old dilapidated building which was then still standing, but torn away many years ago.

At this church Rev. John B. Wade, a pioneer Methodist preacher, was pastor, and perhaps others in those first years of our country. This church was located on lands that once belonged to Obed Brown and in the division of his large landed estate in Reed Creek District, it was designated as the "New Hope" tract.

The Browns, Guests, Owens, and others of the old settlers of this part of the country, attended services at this place and some of them were members of the church.

If the history of this old church could have been preserved it would be interesting to the people of the present time, and we are sorry that we have so meager information relative to its history.

Following is a copy of the obituary of Mumford Ussery, an elder in the Harmony Presbyterian Church, written by his pastor, Rev. Hugh McLeese.

Obituary of Mumford Ussery

"The wheels of weary life
At last stand still."

Died at his residence in Hart County, Ga., June 14, 1888, Mr. Mumford Ussery, aged eighty-six years, one month and four days. In the deceased went down a high type of Christian manhood. For seventy years he had been a member of the Presbyterian Church, and for forty years of this time an Elder. He was consistent as a member and highly efficient as an Elder. One of the most tender and watchful of undershepherds that the writer has ever been privileged to meet with in the ranks of the militant church. The spiritually troubled rarely or never hesitated to communicate to him their perplexities and hinderances. We know that brethren who have from time to time statedly ministered to the church where his last service of thirty-one years of eldership was spent, will bear us out in saying that often depression in some individual member was discovered through his efficiency, when otherwise it might not have been reached at all.

He lived, as a rule, with his lamp trimmed, his light burning, his loins girt about and himself as one waiting for the coming of his Lord. Kindly affectionate, and genial in all the relations of life. We do not always see his equal when we look at what is called a man. The upper temple has gained a priest unto God. The church militant has lost the prayers and the tireless sentinelship of a vigilant soldier. Peace to his ashes and hail to his perfected sainthood above. —McLeese.

Historical Sketch of The Hartwell Baptist Church

THE Hartwell Baptist Church was organized in the court house in the spring of 1859. Interest began in 1858. Services were continued to be held in the court house for a while, and later in the Methodist Church.

Rev. J. T. W. Vernon was a leading minister at that time and was most active in the organization and was its first pastor, continuing through the war, Baptists and Methodists worshipping in the same house until about 1869 or 1870, when the Baptists built them a house of worship, which continued to be used until the summer of 1896, when the present building began to be erected. The work was started in June and was finished in October.

The following Building Committee was chosen by the church: D. C. Alford, J. D. Matheson, S. M. Bobo, D. A. Perrett, T. P. Harris and C. I. Kidd. D. C. Alford and J. D. Matheson were empowered by the committee as a special committee to take charge of all the details connected with the construction and submit the same, if necessary, to the church for action and approval. This plan was fully carried out to the entire satisfaction of the church and, as before stated, the house was occupied in October. Rev. J. H. McMullan was the beloved pastor while the building was being erected. He counseled during the progress of the work and when finished the pastor and church humbly meditated together in thanksgiving for the privilege of worshipping the Master in a respectable building at the expense of gifts and service to the delight of all. The honored pastor, Rev. J. H. McMullan, was called to his heavenly home in January, 1897, which greatly grieved the church, as her pastor had the privilege of preaching but a few times in the house he was so interested in seeing finished. Many felt that the Master must have said, "It is enough well done good and faithful servant."

Pastors of the Hartwell Baptist Church, named in their order:

J. T. W. Vernon, 1858.
Isham H. Goss, 1865.
Benj. Thornton, 1869.
H. M. Barton, 1871.
L. W. Stephens, 1876.
C. A. Stakeley, 1881.
J. C. Wingo, 1882.
J. R. Earle, 1885.
G. M. Campbell, 1887.
E. R. Carswell, 1888.
M. L. Carswell, 1889.

T. A. Thornton, 1890.
A. E. Keese, 1891.
J. H. McMullan, 1896.
B. W. Collier, 1897.
T. M. Galphin, 1903.
H. M. Massey, 1910.
G. J. Davis, 1918.
W. A. Duncan, 1924.
D. A. Howard, 1928.
S. H. Bennett, 1931.

Pastors didn't always commence their service with the calendar year and some would represent parts of different years.

The last church service that Rev. Benj. Thornton engaged in was the organization of the Sunday school in April, 1878, a few days before he died. C. P. Presnell was the first superintendent.

The dedication of the new house was unavoidably delayed until April, 1900.

Rev. S. Y. Jamison preached the dedication sermon, using as a text, 1st Timothy, 3d chapter, and part of the 15th verse, "But if I tarry long, that thou mayest know how thou oughtest to behave in the house of God, which is the church of the living God, the pillar and ground of truth."

The following members have served the church as deacons since the church was organized:

C. P. Presnell	W. M. Vickery
Jas. E. Scott	J. P. Cash
Jas. E. Skelton	L. L. Stapleton
Zenus Hubbard	R. H. Burns
J. Wesley Skelton	A. S. Skelton
T. W. Ayers	E. M. Anderson
S. M. Bobo	J. B. Jones
D. C. Alford	A. N. Page
W. I. Adams	Z. P. Barron
T. E. Vickery	C. G. Campbell
J. R. Meredith	Isham P. Vickery
Harrison Teasley	McLester Brown

There have been others ordained since the above list was made.

Revivals held in the church from 1893 to 1928 by the following visiting ministers assisting the pastor:

1893—S. Y. Jamison; A. E. Keese, Pastor.
1894—H. W. Williams; A. E. Keese, Pastor.
1895—Dr. Pearson; A. E. Keese, Pastor.
1896—No Meeting; J. H. McMullan, Pastor.
1897—B. D. Ragsdale; B. W. Collier, Pastor.
1898—H. W. Williams; B. W. Collier, Pastor.
1902—Phil W. Davis.
1904—W. F. Hauser; T. M. Galphin, Pastor.
1906—J. C. Solomon; T. M. Galphin, Pastor.
1908—R. A. Smith; T. M. Galphin, Pastor.
1909—R. C. Buckholtz; T. M. Galphin, Pastor.
1911—W. L. Walker; M. H. Massey, Pastor.
1912—J. W. Millard; M. H. Massey, Pastor.
1913—W. P. Price; M. H. Massey, Pastor.
1914—C. W. Daniel; M. H. Massey, Pastor.
1916—J. H. Dew; M. H. Massey, Pastor.
1917—L. R. Christie; M. H. Massey, Pastor.
1919—R. L. Bolton; G. J. Davis, Pastor.
1921—T. F. Calloway; G. J. Davis, Pastor.
1922—J. H. Haymore; G. J. Davis, Pastor.
1923—J. E. White; G. J. Davis, Pastor.
1924—Meeting held by W. A. Duncan, Pastor.
1925—No Meeting; W. A. Duncan, Pastor.
1926—Jno. R. Jester; W. A. Duncan, Pastor.
1928—Meeting by D. A. Howard, Pastor.

Where blanks appear there were no revivals held, or the pastors held their own meetings.

Total membership reported to Hebron Association 1932, 540.

Holly Springs Baptist Church
By J. S. Christian, 1900

HOLLY SPRINGS CHURCH is situated in the extreme northwestern portion of Elbert County, about two and one-half miles north from Bowman, and only a few hundred yards from the line separating Elbert from Hart County, a part of the cemetery lying in Hart County. This is the second oldest church in the Hebron Association, and probably the third oldest in Elbert County, having been first organized as an arm of Dove's Creek Church on May the 9th, 1795, and composed of the following members:

Members Present

Males	*Females*
Henry Duncan, Deacon	Joanna Duncan
Daniel Parker, Deacon	Ruth Rucker
Leonard Rice	Sarah Harbin
Pearson Duncan	Priscilla Merritt
John Duncan, Sr.	Betta, a black woman
John Rodgers	

The above members sat in conference and: (1) Received by baptism three members, Daniel White and Martha White, his wife, and Martha Nelms. (2) Made choice of Bro. John Doss (minister) as our supply and Barnabas Pace, Clerk.

Holly Springs, Saturday, January 3, 1796.

Met in conference; Bro. Doss, Moderator.
On motion, agreed to petition a presbytery to aid in our constitution, as we think it expedient to organize ourselves as a regular church at this place.
Resolved to petition Brethren John Cleveland, John White and Thomas Maxwell.

Saturday, February 6, 1796.

Met in conference, and Brethren John Cleveland, John White and Thomas Maxwell, according to request of the members present, formed a presbytery to aid them in forming a constitution, which they did as expressed in the following certificate.

Georgia, Elbert County, February 6, 1796.

This is to certify that whereas an Arm of Dove's Creek Church collected on the waters of Beaverdam at Holly Springs Meeting House, having agreed to keep house together. Called a presbytery to look into their standing and the presbytery having met according to request and after making all necessary inquiry, finding them ripe for constitution, we give them to the Lord and each other, their number being 21, with an ordained minister and one deacon and other strength sufficient with the help of God to carry on discipline.

The presbytery pronounced them a church and proceeded to give them the right hand of fellowship.

JOHN CLEVELAND,
JOHN WHITE,
THOMAS MAXWELL,
Presbytery.

Males		*Females*	
John Doss, Minister	1	Joanna Duncan	12
Henry Duncan, Deacon	2	Ruth Rucker	13
Daniel Parker, Deacon	3	Sarah Harbin	14
Pearson Duncan	4	Priscilla Merritt	15
John Duncan, Sr.	5	Martha White	16
Wm. Harbin	6	Martha Nelms	17
Leonard Rice	7	Elizabeth Guttery	18
Daniel White	8	Hannah Guttery	19
Wm. Guttery	9	Mary Nelms	20
John Ginn	10	Sarah Parker	21
Benjamin Springer	11	Sarah (a colored member)	22

There were but few churches in this country in those early days, and almost all of them were what people now call "hard-shell" churches. Indeed, they were all of the primitive type, and those that were not distinctly antimissionary were ignorant of the need of missions and missionaries, and Holly Springs was no exception to the rule. Their first house for worship was a log house, and built on a lot secured from Thomas Haynes. Some unmistakable signs of the old church and burying ground can still be seen on lands now owned by one of the present members, Mr. C. W. Christian, which is about three-fourths of a mile southwest from the present site, and is said to be the spot where the old church stood. This location is said to have been selected on account of a spring, which afforded an abundance of pure water, which gushed out from beneath a large holly tree. This fact is supposed to have suggested the name for the church.

Some time in the early part of the present century, the exact date can not now be ascertained, the church was moved from the first location to the present one, the exact cause of which can not be determined, but the change was made and a new house built, also of logs, on the present site, which affords one of the finest springs to be found in this whole country. There can be no evidence now secured to prove that there ever stood a holly tree near this spring, but the church has seen fit to retain the old name.

Friday before the first Sunday in March, 1804, was observed as fast day, and was the first to be kept by this church. It was considered necessary on account of the apparent decline in spirituality among the members. In 1802 and 1803, almost every meeting day a number of members were received on profession of faith, and even in October, November and December, 1802, and January and February, 1803, from six to ten persons were baptized at each meeting, but from then on to about 1818 but few members were received, except an occasional one by letter. September 1, 1804, was set apart for fasting and prayer, and again on November 2, 1805, the same kind of religious services were held, and continued at intervals of a few months until the church again showed indications of spiritual prosperity.

Like most other churches in those days, Holly Springs admitted negroes to membership the same as white people, as they had no churches of their own, and footwashings were observed at every communion service, and followed immediately thereafter.

In 1814 the question of the church expenses was discussed in conference, and in 1816 the pastor, Rev. Thomas Maxwell, received $16.00 for his services.

One custom prevailed with this church, in its early days, which seems especially worthy of note here: Whenever it became necessary for the church to call a new pastor, the day before the one on which the election was to take place was spent in fasting and prayer. This custom was inaugurated in November, 1833, when the pastor, Rev. Samuel Hymer resigned. Friday before the fourth Sunday in November was spent in fasting and prayer, and on Saturday following Rev. Asa Chandler was unanimously elected, and served the church continuously for twenty-three years. During the winter of 1833-4, the beginning of Rev. Asa Chandler's pastorate, about twenty members were received on profession of faith and were baptized, most of them in December.

In 1836 the church lot was enlarged and a new house built. This was the third house these pioneer Christians built, and this one is still being used for public worship, although in 1850 it was enlarged by about one-third its original size and otherwise improved.

About the year 1836 a contention arose in the church in regard to missions. The same trouble arose in other churches, and some of them were hopelessly divided, but, in order to preserve fellowship and prevent any internal disruption, Holly Springs, on July 21, 1838, unanimously resolved "that differences of opinion or practice, relative to denominations for the support of missionary operations, shall be no hindrance to fellowship." So the question was finally settled, and from that day to the present the members of this church have been free to think and act as they pleased on this great question which has so revolutionized the Christian world.

Holly Springs had four ways of receiving members, viz.: by baptism, by letter, by restoration, and recantation. The record shows that the church excluded one Joel Butler, and February 23, 1839, after being convinced that the brother had been wrongfully accused and excluded, the church declared void the action which excluded him, and he was restored to fellowship.

For about three years, or from 1839 to September, 1842, the church neglected the custom of observing fast days, and no members were received.

One of the most wholesome rules, it seems to the writer, and one calculated to raise the standard of church membership, possibly, higher than any other, was the one that required its members to pay their debts and keep promises. This rule was rigidly enforced by Holly Springs Church in its earlier days, so much that a failure to keep a promise or pay a debt was sufficient cause for expulsion. A member of this church was not allowed to sue, or otherwise go to law with another member, without first getting permission from the church, and before such permission was granted the church used every possible means to effect a settlement, which was in almost every case successful.

Early in the year 1846, there arose a contention in regard to holding temperance meetings in the church, and allowing church members to join the temperance society, but, be it recorded to the honor of the church, the sister who sought to have the temperance people shut out, and denied the use of the house, and members excluded for joining the temperance society, was herself excluded, and the cause of temperance encouraged and upheld. There will probably be no more appropriate place in this sketch than in this connection, to state that probably three-fourths of the members excluded from this church from the date of its constitution to the present, were excluded on a charge of drunkenness.

On June 26, 1852, a letter of dismission was granted to a sister who stated in her application that she desired to join the Presbyterians.

During the August meeting in 1853, forty-seven members were received on profession of faith and baptism, which was the first to be added in this way for several years. At this time the church had 364 members—310 whites and 54 blacks.

August 25, 1855, the church resolved to have the pastor, Rev. Asa Chandler, preach a missionary sermon on the following day, and take public collection for missions. Slowly, but surely, the spirit of missions had grown, but now, for the first time, began to take its place at the front.

Holly Springs Church was a member of the Tugaloo Association until 1840, and from 1840 to 1883 was a member of the Sarepta Association, at which time the Hebron was organized, with Holly Springs one of the first members.

In 1877 there arose another contention in the church, which was finally settled by calling in the deacons of four other churches, which formed themselves into a council. The cause of the contention was about as follows: Mr. W. F. Bowers, who had been a Baptist, but at this time called himself a "Reformer," was preaching his new doctrine in the church, having an appointment once a month. "Uncle Billy," as he was more familiarly known, found a few followers, but a large majority disbelieved his doctrine and objected to his preaching it in the church, so the house was locked in order to keep him out. The opinion handed down by the council of deacons was, in effect, as follows: That "Uncle Billy" should not have preached in the house without first getting permission, but they did not approve of the locking up of the house.

A number of personal difficulties arose between members, but the church was able, in every case, to effect a satisfactory settlement.

From 1795 to date the church records show that 480 members have been baptized, but from about 1862 to 1897, or about thirty-five years, no mention is made of receiving members except by letter and restoration. It is known, however, that during these years quite a number were baptized, their names only being recorded on church roll, and it is thought that it would be perfectly safe to say that eight hundred or more have been baptized by this church. The books show that one hundred and seventy-five have been excluded.

Holly Springs has ordained five preachers, as follows: Thomas Maxwell, date not mentioned; Daniel White, in 1802; Elijah Moseley, in 1807; Asa Duncan, in 1852; and W. J. Brown, in 1864. And has given permission to preach, licensed: Elijah Moseley, David Roberts, Elisha Rodgers, Daniel

Montgomery, Hiram Brown, Asa Duncan and J. T. Higginbotham, two of whom were ordained.

Holly Springs is now (1900) one hundred and six years old, and has been served by eleven pastors, twenty-one deacons and fifteen clerks, as follows:

Pastors—Rev. John Doss filled out first year, 1795, then Rev. Thomas Maxwell served thirty years. Rev. John Bramlet five years, Rev. Samuel Hymer four years, Rev. Asa Chandler twenty-three years, Rev. Benjamin Thornton five years, Rev. Asa Duncan seventeen years, Rev. W. J. Vickery fifteen years, Rev. A. A. Duncan one year, Rev. J. B. Herron four years, and Rev. E. R. Goss, the present pastor, is serving his first year.

Deacons—Henry Duncan, Daniel Parker, Daniel White, Luke White, Thomas Horton, Pearson Duncan, _____ Landers, Leonard Rice, William Moss, Hiram Brown, W. T. Maxwell, A. Mewborn, Stephen W. Jordan, Adam Brown, J. T. Higginbotham, A. H. Brown, E. G. Brown, J. M. Parks, S. M. Mewborn, W. F. Brown, W. C. Roberts, I. M. Brown, J. U. Colvard and C. B. Haynes.

Clerks—Barnabas Pace, William Kelley, Larkin Coker, William Moss, Burnet Dooley, Archie Mewborn, Hiram Brown, John Brown, Asa J. Haynes, W. F. Attaway, Singleton A. Maxwell, J. E. Brown, I. M. Brown, P. V. Rice, and John W. Roberts, the present clerk, was elected in 1898.

At the regular conference in May, 1889, the church Resolved, That excessive use of intoxicating liquors is the use of same for other than medical purposes.

The same conference, by unanimous vote, decided "that it will take one or more drams to make a man drunk."

Holly Springs can truly claim to be a mother church, for five other churches were first operated as arms of Holly Springs, and were afterwards constituted as independent churches, the names of which are as follows: Double Branch, in Franklin County, in 1801; Wilson's Meeting House, in Elbert County, in 1802; Hendrys, in Hart County, in 1818; Rehoboth, in Elbert County, in 1827; Mill Shoal, in Madison County, in 1856; and Harmony, in Elbert County, in 1854.

Holly Springs has had a Sunday school under control of the church since 1881, but it has not met during the winter months until a few years back. Prior to 1881 there was a school, but not under control of the church.

The present membership of Holly Springs (1900) is one hundred and fifty-six. The numerical strength has, perhaps, a few times been a little less than at present, but, with the exception of two or three years, the total membership has reached more than two hundred, and has at times reached four hundred.

The average church expenses for a number of years has been about $75.00 per annum; about $4.00 of which went for missions and minutes, the remainder to the pastor.

Holly Springs Church owns about eight acres of land, which, with the present house, might be valued at $150.00 to $200.00, and no incumbrance whatever. At the June conference, this year, the church decided to build a new house, and the work of construction is being rapidly pushed to completion. The new house with cost, when completed, between $800.00 and $1,000.00, and no debt will be incurred.

Statistics of Holly Springs, according to the minutes of the Hebron Association, 1931, held at Deep Creek Church, Elbert County, Ga.

Pastor, Rev. J. D. Matheson; Clerk, S. P. Jordan; Superintendent of Sunday School, H. H. Roberts.

Membership, 285; value of church house and grounds, $4,000.00; total for local church work given by church and all organizations, $619.37.

Hendrys Baptist Church

HENDRYS BAPTIST CHURCH, located formerly in Elbert (later Hart) County, was organized in 1818. It was an offspring of Holly Springs Church, which was the mother of several other churches in Elbert, Madison, Franklin and Hart counties, and was perhaps an arm of Holly Springs Church before organization. It was named Hendrys for Dr. Charles Hendry, who lived in the community and owned a large body of land and on a part of which the church was located.

In 1818, when the Tugaloo Baptist Association was organized at Poplar Springs Church in Franklin County, Hendrys became a charter member and was the only church in the association at the time located outside of Franklin County in Georgia. There were several in South Carolina.

Later Hendrys Church withdrew from the Tugaloo and united with the Sarepta Association, and still later, in 1883, it became a member of the Hebron Association, which was organized at Hendrys in that year.

Hendrys at one time was the church at which the people for a considerable radius had their membership before the organization of Bio and Bethany churches. At the time of the organization of these last named churches many of the members withdrew membership from Hendrys and became members of Bio and Bethany.

Rev. L. W. Stephens was the pastor of Hendrys Church continuously from 1855 to 1884, a period of twenty-nine years, and which, so far as we know, was the longest pastorate in the history of the church. Later he was recalled and served the church again for a number of years.

The church house was destroyed by fire in 1925 and never rebuilt.

Among the former citizens of the community, and members of Hendrys church, were the Bowerses, Browns, Clarks, and others.

At the site of the church there is a large cemetery in which many of the former citizens are buried, and which will ever make the spot sacred and hallowed ground.

History of Sardis Baptist Church

By A. J. McMullan

IN GETTING up the history of Sardis Church, it is to be regretted that we are unable to find records concerning its organization.

The first minutes we have state that some of the old records were lost, and the church, in conference in May, 1811, re-wrote the articles of faith and church covenant.

In referring to the old minutes, we find them neatly recorded, from 1811 to 1850, in a well-bound book; and we remember hearing Brother J. H. McMullan state that all of the old records which could be obtained were collected and transcribed by Walter M. Gibson, the best scholar of the times. This man, Walter M. Gibson, was not a member of Sardis Church, but a school teacher residing in the vicinity, who soon afterwards left this country and later made his appearance in the Hawaiian Islands as a Mormon missionary from Utah, and eventually became Prime Minister of the Hawaiian group.

But, returning to the church history proper, we find in the old minutes, transcribed by Gibson, that the church was first located on Cedar Creek, about three miles southwest of the present site, and then called Cedar Creek Church.

For the convenience of the pastor, Casper Burnett, who resided in South Carolina, the church was moved to the present site and called Sardis. The first pastor was John Cason, who was greatly aided in his work by such members as Bram Parks, Burrell Bobo, Robert Skelton, ... Dunnaho, Samuel Self, James Prather, Patrick McMullan and Dozier Thornton.

Horatio J. Goss was received into the church in 1820, and served a number of years as clerk; and his name appears as one of the most useful and consecrated members.

In 1827 Rev. William Morning was elected pastor, and he was succeeded by the following illustrious list: Samuel Hymer, John Harris, Willis B. Jones, Asa Chandler, Benjamin Thornton, James Goss, Wm. E. Walters, Martin H. Barton, Calloway Thornton, James H. McMullan, J. R. Earle, B. M. Pack, M. L. Carswell, Bryan W. Collier.

While writing this history we find prominent the name of a noble woman, Ann Goss, wife of J. H. Goss, who united with the church in 1828. About the same time we find uniting with the church Lewis Sanders, Calvin Sanders, Samuel Sanders, John and Nancy McCurry, and Sinclair McMullan. A number of colored people also appear in the list of members, among them was Charles, the property of James Patterson.

October 5, 1849, James V. Richardson and Caswell Farmer were ordained deacons. This occasion, as related to us by our friend and brother, W. J. W. Skelton, who, having married the night before, attended the ordination, bringing his bride behind him on horseback.

In 1844 a number of letters were granted to members to constitute a church which was known as the "Line Church."

Letters were granted to forty-six members, who organized themselves, in March, 1878, into a church called "Cedar Creek Church."

In 1879, while Rev. James H. McMullan was pastor, our present beautiful and commodious church house was built on a seven-acre lot donated to the church by Sinclair McMullan. Many other beautiful church buildings of this country owe their existence to that true philanthropist, J. H. McMullan.

This grand old church is still actively engaged in the Lord's work, with a flourishing Sunday school under the management of M. M. Richardson, who has been superintendent of the school for twenty years, and who has not in these twenty years been absent but a few times. Noble record! Our present pastor is Bryan W. Collier, and among the long list of noted pastors his name will ever be held in high esteem. He is loved and honored, not only for his excellent sermons, but also for his noble, unsullied, Christian character.

May the name of Sardis Church, made sacred by the lives of so many glorious saints, long live as a synonym of righteousness and truth.

Since the foregoing history of Sardis Church, written by A. J. McMullan in 1900, many changes have taken place in the personnel of the membership. Many of the members living at that date have since passed away, among them many of the leading members.

Among the preachers who have served the church as pastor since Rev. B. W. Collier, may be mentioned Revs. Robert A. Smith, Thomas M. Galphin, Milo H. Massey, Thomas J. Espy, and others.

In 1923 the people of Sardis Church built a new church house at a cost of about $40,000, commodious in all of its departments, of beautiful architectural design, and reputed to be the most imposing church edifice in this part of the State. The membership, reported in 1932, was 408.

Walter M. Gibson

From Carriage Driver to Prime Minister of Hawaiian Islands

WE HEREWITH give extracts from several newspaper articles written about Walter M. Gibson, and published in *The Hartwell Sun* in 1888.

Mr. John B. Benson, in talking about him said, in part: "When I was selling goods away back in the forties at Old Pendleton, S. C., Walter M. Gibson came out from New York, a young man, and was employed by William Van Dyck as a carriage driver. On one occasion while he was driving the carriage, Mr. and Mrs. Van Dyck, desiring to discuss matters of a strictly private nature, began conversing in French. Gibson took the hint, and although a carriage driver, was a gentleman as well. Quickly turning to Mr. Van Dyck he remarked in a respectful manner: 'I presume you do not desire me to know what you are talking about—I understand the French language perfectly.' That gave them a good opinion of Gibson."

"The Hawaiian monarchy, of which Kapiolani, who is visiting the United States, was Queen, has been practically overthrown by a popular uprising of the people. The Prime Minister of the kingdom, who is an American named Walter Gibson.

"We saw him on a visit to the city of Anderson probably fifteen or twenty years ago. He was accompanied by his daughter, who was said to be Princess. Gibson was the Bismarck of the Sandwich Islands. This man— Walter Gibson, as he was known here—got his start by teaching an old field school in Elbert (now Hart) County.

"He lived in a one-room cabin at the old 'Burnt Store Forks' of the road on A. J. McMullan's place. While there he added to the comfort of his family by building a kitchen with dirt floor. Afterwards he sold goods, carrying only a very small stock. He interested his neighbors with stories of his travels and adventures; but they could not swallow all of his yarns. Little did his Hart County auditors think that their garrulous Munchausen would ever become Prime Minister, High Executioner, et cetera, of the Hawaiian kingdom.

"After the death of his first wife (we presume he had another), and which is said to have been from cold contracted on the dirt floor of the kitchen, Gibson left this county and was not heard of until he turned up as Prime Minister at Honolulu."

"Rev. J. H. McMullan showed us a photograph Tuesday of Hon. Walter M. Gibson, the lately deceased Premier of the Hawaiian Islands, sent him by Gibson's son-in-law, Mr. Fred Hazelton. Mr. Gibson was certainly a commanding, noble-looking gentleman. Mr. McMullan was a pupil of Gibson's when he taught school in Elbert (now Hart) County in his early manhood. Mr. McMullan says Mr. Gibson had abilities of a very high order, and that if he had remained in Georgia would undoubtedly have been a conspicuous figure among our most prominent men."

"Messrs. J. B. Lewis and Moorhead, of Anderson, S. C., and Mr. Hazelton, of Honolulu, Hawaii, visited relatives in our town and county on Friday and Saturday last. Mr. Hazelton is a son-in-law of Hon. Walter M. Gibson, deceased, late Prime Minister of the Hawaiian kingdom. Mr. Hazelton paid *The Sun* a brief call, and we found him to be a pleasant and very intelligent gentleman. He speaks, we learn, fifteen different languages fluently, has figured prominently in affairs of State, and owns valuable property on the islands. He conducts two daily newspapers, one printed in the native language and the other in English. Mr. Hazelton is a native of London, England, but has resided in Hawaii for many years and has become thoroughly identified with the interests of the country.

"One of his objects in visiting Hart County was to gather data for a biographical sketch of Mr. Gibson, who once taught school and ran a country store in the neighborhood of Sardis Church. Mr. Hazelton's wife was born in Hart County. He will probably visit the country again in a few weeks, together with his wife. Mrs. H. J. Goss is a relative of Mrs. Hazelton."

WALTER M. GIBSON

A complimentary write-up by Mr. D. C. Alford. *The Hartwell Sun*, 1920.

"A bit of history relative to Walter M. Gibson.

"The musical given at the college here last Thursday night by the Hawaiian Quartette brings to mind a little unwritten history of which Hart County contributed a small part of the prestige of the Hawaiian Islands.

"About seventy-five years ago there lived near Sardis Church, in the eastern part of what is now Hart County, a man by the name of Gibson—Walter M. Gibson. He was a school teacher, and for that day was considered a highly educated and a very scholarly man.

"Sardis Church was organized in 1811. The records of the church had not been as well kept as they should have been, and in looking for some efficient person to complete and bring them up to modern ideas, Gibson was chosen to do the work, and from statements regarding it given by those living at that time, it was considered a splendid job. (Gibson was not a member of Sardis Church.)

"Very soon after he had completed the work, some time about 1840, he left the community and was not heard from for a long time. Finally, news came that he was in Hawaii, had gone there as a Mormon missionary from Utah. Things seem to have gone well with him, as the next news was that he was Prime Minister of the Hawaiian Islands.

"It must have required a heroic and venturous spirit to go to these far away islands in the Pacific Ocean, which are said to be about 2,100 miles from San Francisco, and mix with a people who were semi-cannibal in their social and religious life.

"The Hawaiian Islands have made great progress in the last thirty years. Queen Lilinockalani was deposed in 1893 and a provisional government formed. The Queen tried hard to re-establish despotism but failed. By an Act of Congress in 1898 the Hawaiian Islands were annexed to the United States, and now known as the Hawaiian territory. The population is about 200,000, consisting of Chinese, Japanese, Portugese, Americans, British and Germans, with about one-fourth the population native Hawaiians."

Shoal Creek Baptist Church

SHOAL CREEK BAPTIST CHURCH, located in the northwestern part of Hart County, is, so far as we have any record, the oldest church in the county.

It was organized before 1798, as there is a record to the effect that the Georgia Baptist Association met at Shoal Creek Church in May, 1799, and formed a new association and called it "Sarepta," named for the city of Bible times where Elijah, after the brook Cherith went dry, spent the balance of the time of the drouth in the home of a widow woman.

The first session of the Sarepta Association convened with Van's Creek Church, of Ruckersville, Ga., in the month of October of that year.

Shoal Creek Church had evidently belonged to the Georgia Baptist Association, the first organized in the State of Georgia up until the organization of the Sarepta, and afterwards belonged to the Sarepta until it became a member of the Tugaloo Association.

In the history of the Tugaloo Association by Rev. J. F. Goode, there is a record that the Tugaloo met with Shoal Creek Church in the year 1835, at which session Lewis Ballard was Moderator and Henry F. Chandler, Clerk. The Tugaloo again met with Shoal Creek Church in 1857, at which session Rev. H. M. Barton was Moderator and Henry F. Chandler, Clerk. The Tugaloo again met with Shoal Creek Church in 1880, at which session Rev. T. G. Underwood was Moderator and T. A. McFarland, Clerk.

When the Hebron Association was formed in 1883, Shoal Creek Church became a member of the Hebron, and in 1891 the Hebron Association met with Shoal Creek, at which S. M. Bobo was Moderator and J. R. Stephens,

Clerk. The Hebron met with Shoal Creek Church again in 1905, at which session M. M. Richardson was Moderator and S. L. Thornton, Clerk.

So there have been at least five sessions, three of the Tugaloo and two of the Hebron, held at Shoal Creek, and perhaps there may have been sessions of the Georgia and Sarepta held there while the church was a member of those bodies.

We regret that we do not have the names of the pastors who supplied Shoal Creek in its early history. It appears from a record which we have that Rev. Benton Starke was called in 1823, and served as pastor for three years.

From 1826 to 1854 we have no record as to who was the pastor, or pastors, during the intervening years.

Rev. H. M. Barton was called as pastor in 1854 and served four years, Rev. D. H. Payne three years, Rev. H. M. Barton again two years, Rev. Simmons three years, Rev. H. M. Barton again seven years, Rev. Thomas H. Crymes five years, Rev. H. M. Barton again five years, Rev. J. H. McMullan two years. Rev. H. M. Barton was called again in 1884, which was the fifth time he was called to the pastorate of Shoal Creek Church, and served one year, making in all nineteen years. It was during his pastorates that the church enjoyed great spiritual prosperity.

Entreating the indulgence of our readers, we will here intersperse with a brief sketch of Rev. H. M. Barton, as the same appears in Rev. J. F. Goode's history of the various preachers, given in connection with his history of the Tugaloo Baptist Association.

"H. M. Barton was a native of South Carolina, and spent his long and useful life at Fair Play, in that State.

"According to Garrett's History of the Saluda Association, he was actively engaged, in the earlier years of his ministry, as a pastor in that body, and quite prominent in the deliberations of the Association. His name first appears in the minutes of the Tugaloo Association about 1850. At the session in 1856 he was elected Moderator, which position he filled, first and last, for 18 years. When Beaverdam Association was organized in 1881, he, with the church of his membership, left the Tugaloo and became a member of that body. He was both an able and earnest preacher of the Gospel, and was pastor of several churches both in Georgia and South Carolina.

"We have no knowledge of the exact date of his death, but writing from memory, we think his death occurred about 1889."

We visited Fair Play several months ago, and while there observed, among other things, the old home of Rev. H. M. Burton, standing, presumably, as he left it, a relic of the past, fraught with sacred memories of its former owner and occupant, who years ago passed away at the end of a long and well-spent life in the service of his Master and for the good of his fellowman.

Among the pastors who have served Shoal Creek Church since Rev. H. M. Barton may be mentioned Revs. L. T. Weldon, W. J. Purcell, E. L. Sisk, B. W. Collier, J. F. Goode, George W. Hulme, R. M. Maret, A. H. Holland, the present pastor, and others.

Among the names of those who formerly composed the membership of Shoal Creek Church, and whose descendants are members at the present time, may be mentioned the Burtons, Shirleys, Walterses, Hollands, Marets, Webbs, and others.

At the last session of the Hebron Association, in 1932, Shoal Creek Church reported Rev. A. H. Holland as pastor. Total membership, 264. Value of church property, $2,500.

The church property consists of six acres of land and church house that will compare favorably with many of the church houses of the country.

Since writing the foregoing history of Shoal Creek Baptist Church we have learned from an old copy of the minutes of the Sarepta Baptist Association that the third session of that body was held with Shoal Creek Church in 1801, at which Rev. Thomas Gilbert served as Moderator, and William Davis served as Clerk and also preached the introductory sermon.

Again the Sarepta Baptist Association met with Shoal Creek Church in 1807, when Rev. Dozier Thornton served as Moderator, and Rev. Thomas Carrington preached the introductory sermon.

History of Reed Creek Baptist Church, 1830-1930

AT THE centennial of Reed Creek Baptist Church, celebrated in May, 1930, we prepared a history of the church, which was read at the exercises, and from which we reproduce several paragraphs.

At the time the church was constituted the territory was embraced in Franklin County.

The original site of the church was on lands owned at the time by John Crocker located on the east side of the road leading from the crossroads, now known as the W. J. O'Barr place, to the Henry F. Chandler place on Tugaloo River, and about one-half mile from said crossroads. At the old site of the church is a small cemetery where several of the former citizens and members of the church are buried.

At the time the church was organized, the nearest Baptist church up the country was Shoal Creek; the nearest down the country was Sardis. Across the Tugaloo River in South Carolina were the churches of Double Springs and Beaverdam, while on the south was Hendrys Church, some 12 miles distant. So it is easy to see that there was a large area in which there was no Baptist church, and it was very necessary that a church should be established in the community for the convenience of the people, many of whom belonged to the church, but lived quite remote from a church.

On Friday, May 7, 1830, the people met at the place and a presbytery was formed composed of Rev. Asa Chandler and Rev. Samuel Hymer, Ministers, and Deacons Joseph Chandler, James Isbel and Jesse Bradbury, and the church was duly constituted.

After the constitution of the church, Isaac Aderhold was presented and ordained as a deacon by the same presbytery, being the first deacon ordained by the church.

After the constitution of the church and the ordination of Isaac Aderhold, the door of the church was opened for the reception of members, when Polly Gilbert was received by letter and was the first member, outside of the charter members, to be received by letter.

On Saturday, May 8th, the church met and, after divine services, unanimously elected Rev. Asa Chandler as pastor.

The door of the church was opened and Mary Ann Farrow and Sarah Farrow were received by experience and were the first members to unite with the church by experience and baptism.

On Sunday, May 9th, Rebecca Brown was received by experience.

At the August meeting, Isaac Aderhold and John Crocker were elected delegates to the Tugaloo Baptist Association, to which body the church had resolved to become a member. The Association met that year with New Liberty Church in Habersham County, Ga.

At the October meeting Lewis Aderhold was elected clerk of the church and was the first clerk of the church.

Some Statistics

From the constitution of the church to the present the church has had 30 pastors. Five of its members have been ordained to the ministry, viz.: Elias Brown, B. J. McLeskey, F. M. Estes, L. T. Weldon and A. R. Brown. Twenty-eight of the members have been ordained and set apart as deacons. It has received into its membership nine deacons from other churches. It has had up to date fourteen church clerks. Has received by experience and baptism, in round numbers, 1,500, and by letter 500, making a total of 2,000.

David Simmons served the church as pastor for 20 years, the longest pastorate in the history of the church. Rev. Samuel B. Sanders served as pastor for eighteen years in all, being the second longest pastorate.

After the church had stood for about twelve years at the original site, a committee was appointed to select a lot of land and to superintend the building of a new church house.

The lot selected was the present site, but there is no record that a new church building was erected at that time. It is our information that the old building was dismantled and moved to the present site, where it was reassembled. The church house at the original site was constructed of large hewed logs, with slabs for seats, and a large wooden box for a pulpit, and presumably the ground for a floor. After it was moved to the present location and reassembled it served as a church house until about the year 1852 or 1853, when the committee appointed to build a new house awarded the contract to J. W. Suit for the price of $100, which of course meant with all material furnished. The house was located on the north side of the road. This was a frame building, hulled in, but not ceiled. It stood with one side fronting the public road, with a door on the right side of the east end for the entrance of the older women, and the door on the left for the older men. Just inside the house, between these two doors, was the pulpit, which was a large, clumsy planked-up affair, and at the back of the pulpit were a couple of windows for light, air and ventilation for the benefit of the preacher. On the side of the house fronting the public road was a wide door with double shutters. Along each side of the house were several narrow windows with wooden sash, and in the west end was a door which was used for the most part by the young people as an entrance. There was no lighting system as we have at the present time, but rung around the walls of the house were wooden pedestals on which were placed tallow, or wax, candles, and when they were lit up they "gave light to all who were in the house."

The preacher at the close of the day services, when to be followed by services at night, did not announce that "there will be services here this evening at 7, 7:15 or 7:30, but said instead, "there will be services here tonight at early candle light."

The darkest chapter in the history of the church, and the entire country as for that matter, was the period covered by the stirring scenes and stressful aftermath of the War Between the States.

A number of the members of the church were called into service, but so far as my knowledge extends, all but two who entered the war, fortunately, were allowed to return home after the conflict.

During these dark and troublous times the church did not cease to function, but met regularly in their monthly meetings as before or after the war, however the ingatherings during those years were small. Several joined by experience and a few by letter.

Just here we might mention a few of the prominent members of the church to whom we have not already referred.

John Crocker, who was a charter member, seems to have been a man of means, prominent in his community, serving as Justice of the Peace, was active in the affairs of the church, serving on important committees, was often a delegate to the meetings of the association, and was several times elected as clerk of the Association. In 1855 he was granted a letter of dismission and there is no further record of him. It is a matter of tradition that he moved to a western state, presumably Arkansas.

Sterling Pinson, who was another charter member of the church, appears to have been prominent and active in the work of the church. He was at one time clerk of the church. Was for a number of years a delegate to most every session of the association, was a trustee of the church, and variously mentioned in connection with the affairs of the church.

Perhaps the most prominent member of the church during his day was Henry Farmer Chandler, who was formerly a member and deacon of Poplar Springs Church in Franklin County, but about the year 1835 bought the place down on the river which has so long been known as the Chandler place. A fuller account of Henry Farmer Chandler appears elsewhere in this history.

Another one of the members that belonged to Reed Creek Church, and entitled to special mention, was Robert A. Madden, who joined the church by letter from Rock Branch Church, Elbert County, in 1859. He was a deacon, and as such was received at the time he united with the church at Reed Creek. Everyone had explicit confidence in his piety and in the sincerity of his Christian life.

In 1884 the church decided to build a new church house and a committee was appointed by the church to have supervision of the work. The contract was awarded to J. W. Suit, who built the church then in use in about 1852-3. Mr. Suit, who had Mr. N. S. Osborne associated with him, bid off the contract to furnish all material and build the church for the sum of $660. The church was completed in 1885.

From the constitution of the church on up to and for a few years after the war, a number of colored people united with the church. In February, 1869, all the colored people who were members of the church obtained letters of dismission and formed a church of their own. At the time they withdrew from the church they had no place of worship and the church at Reed Creek very generously granted them the privilege of the use of their church until they could procure a place of worship. Their first pastor after they withdrew from Reed Creek Church was William Parker, commonly called Bill Parker, who lived in South Carolina in the neighborhood of Fairplay, and who before emancipation belonged to the Parkers of Parkertown, Ga.

Two sessions of the Tugaloo Association and three of the Hebron were held at Reed Creek Church.

The 37th session of the Tugaloo Association was held with Reed Creek Church in September, 1854, with John A. Davis, Moderator, and H. F. Chandler, Clerk. The 60th session was held with Reed Creek Church in October, 1877, with Rev. T. G. Underwood, Moderator, and A. W. Brawner, Clerk.

The 7th session of the Hebron Association was held at Reed Creek Church in 1889, S. M. Bobo, Moderator, and J. R. Stephens, Clerk.

The 27th session held at Reed Creek in 1909, T. M. Galphin, Moderator, and J. Cullen Wright, Clerk.

The 33d session held at Reed Creek in 1915, M. H. Massey, Moderator, and D. C. Alford, Clerk.

One outstanding event in the life of Reed Creek Church was a revival conducted there in 1911 by Rev. W. L. Walker, an evangelist.

It was a most glorious meeting, in which the membership of the church was greatly stirred and revived, and a large ingathering was the result. The meeting was perhaps more largely attended than any ever held in the his-

Reed Creek Baptist Church

tory of the church. It was estimated that at the evening services as many as 1,500 people attended the services.

Rev. Walker passed away several years ago, but the meeting that he conducted will ever stand out as a prominent peak in the history of the church.

Old Line Baptist Church

LINE CHURCH was so named for the reason that it was located near the line between Elbert (formerly Wilkes) and Franklin counties. Lightwoodlog Creek, which flows near by, was the line, the church located on the Elbert County side.

To the best of our information, Line was originally a preaching station, or center, which were common in the early days when the country was sparsely settled and churches were few and far between. At these stations, or centers, religious services were held as opportunity afforded. Preachers of different denominations would preach at these places occasionally. It is our information that Rev. John B. Wade, a pioneer Methodist preacher, a sketch of whom appears elsewhere in these pages, preached at Line.

In the course of time a Baptist church was constituted at the place on May 18, 1844, and continued until 1884, a period of forty years, when the church was disbanded, the majority of the members united with Mt. Hebron Church and others moved their membership to other churches.

We are not sure as to who was the first pastor, however Rev. J. T. W. Vernon was one among the first pastors. Others were: Revs. Benjamin Thornton, Samuel Isbel, Calvin P. Sanders, Isom H. Goss, James H. McMullan and others, Rev. B. M. Pack being the last pastor to serve the church in 1884, when the church was disbanded.

Samuel B. Sanders, who joined the church at Sardis in May, 1828, at the age of twenty years, was one of the charter members, and on the day the church was constituted, he was ordained a deacon. He later, on December 11, 1847, was licensed by the church to preach, and on July 29, 1849, by request of the church, was ordained to the full gospel ministry by the following noted ministers: Revs. Phillip Mathews, Benjamin Thornton, Pleasant B. F. Burgess and Albert T. Vandiver. A fuller sketch of Rev. Samuel B. Sanders appears elsewhere.

When Hart County was organized in the year 1854, the first election for county officers was held at Line Church on the first Monday in February, 1854, it being a central point in the new county.

The membership during the life of the church was composed of the families of the Vickerys, Sanders, McMullans, Walters, Powells, Skeltons and many others who were citizens of the community at the time.

One very noted and interesting item of history connected with Line Church is an account of a revival held at the church in its earlier years while Rev. J. T. W. Vernon was pastor. He was assisted in the meeting by John R. Kay and James T. Jones, both of whom were devoted and consecrated lay members of the Methodist Church. At this meeting four young men were converted all of whom later became Baptist preachers, to wit: B. J. McLeskey, W. J. Vickery, James P. Vickery and A. J. Cleveland. The friendship and brotherly love of Vernon, Kay and Jones continued through life.

The spot where the old church house stood will always remain precious in the memory of a vast number of Christians scattered throughout this country, who there first experienced the truth of the Christian religion.

Near the old site, on the opposite side of the old public road, now abandoned, there is a small cemetery which will ever serve as a pointer to mark the location of the church.

A Prayer for Rain That Was Answered

Sometime soon after the War Between the States, there was a fearful drouth in the summer time of nine weeks duration and the crops were badly suffering for rain and the outlook was beginning to be very distressing, when on a Sunday, which was meeting day at Line Church, Rev. Henry Tyler, a Methodist preacher was present and led in prayer and among other things in his petition was an earnestly expressed request for rain. It may be imagined that he wrestled, like Elijah of old at Carmel, with the Lord to send rain.

That night as the people began to gather for the evening services, the thunders began to peal, the lightnings to flash, the clouds to thicken and darken, and presently there was a copious downpour of rain, so much so that there was a rapid rise of the waters of Lightwoodlog Creek, and people who lived beyond the creek from the church could not return to their homes until the waters abated.

This story was told to us by an old man who is still living in our county and who was present on the occasion and heard the prayer for rain by Rev. Henry Tyler, and was also present at the meeting at night and witnessed the rainfall, which greatly revived the crops as well as the people.

History of Bio Baptist Church

Organization of Bio Church and Name Changed from Damascus to Bio

January 15, 1881.

THE members proposing to be organized into a church, on Saturday before the fifth Sunday in January, met at the church on Saturday, January 15, 1881, and appointed R. A. Cobb, temporary moderator, and W. M. Clark, clerk.

1. Changed the name of the church from Damascus to Bio. Called L. W. Stephens to preach to us for the present year, 1881.

Approved the covenant of the church and the articles of faith and the rules of decorum as gotten up by a portion of the members.

Elected W. M. Clark, Clerk; W. B. Higginbotham, Treasurer.

R. A. COBB, *Moderator Pro Tem,*
W. M. CLARK, *Clerk.*

January 29, 1881. Baptist Church of Christ at Bio. After preaching by Rev. I. H. Goss, the following elders and deacons formed themselves into a presbytery for the purpose of organizing a church at the above stated place, viz.: Rev. L. W. Stephens, Hartwell; Rev. I. H. Goss, Bowman; Rev. J. H. McMullan, Sardis; Deacons W. G. W. White and J. V. Richardson, Sardis; Deacon E. G. Brown, Holly Springs; Deacons E. J. Brown, S. V. Brown and R. S. Williford, Hendrys. Having the presbytery formed, called Rev. L. W. Stephens to act as moderator and requested W. M. Clark to act as clerk for the presbytery.

Then called for the church covenant which was read by the clerk, with some touching remarks by Rev. I. H. Goss and Rev. J. H. McMullan, then the covenant was unanimously approved.

Articles of faith were then read and approved, and as to gospel order we approve that:

On motion of the presbytery approved all that had been presented to them and in token of which the right hand of fellowship was given after which Rev. J. H. McMullan led in prayer.

On motion the presbytery adjourned.

The church, after organization, held conference. On motion it was unanimously agreed to dedicate the church house on Sunday.

L. W. STEPHENS, *Moderator*,
W. M. CLARK, *Clerk*.

Sunday morning, January 30, 1881. Held prayer meeting after which the dedication sermon was preached by Rev. J. H. McMullan to a large congregation, exhortation by Rev. I. H. Goss. Took up collection for missions, raised $6.60.

W. M. CLARK, *Clerk*.

Charter Members of Bio Church

Male members: John G. McCurry, William Jones, O. M. Duncan, R. A. Cobb, W. M. Clark, John A. Brown, Allen McGee, James E. Brown, James Steadman, James A. Davis, W. B. Higginbotham, Chandler Maxwell, J. L. Vickery; female members: Rachael S. McCurry, Kate E. Clark, Lucy A. Jones, Rachael Jones, Jane McGee, Lou M. Brown, Elizabeth Cobb, Nancy E. Brown, Milly A. Davis, Milly Steadman, Mollie H. Maxwell, Amanda Fore, Rosa Branham, Sallie Teasley, Fannie Johnson, Georgia Teasley, Martha C. Vickery, Martha A. Johnson, Annie B. Maxwell, Sallie C. Brown, Julia A. Norman, Amanda P. Maxwell, Lou Bond, Nancy Norman, Rachael Duncan. Total membership, 38.

The present church house at Bio was built in 1921, which was the 40th anniversary of the church, and on January 30, 1921, a very interesting program was carried out in the dedication of the new building, with Rev. T. M. Galphin preaching the dedication sermon.

One of the most fitting and appropriate parts of the preliminary program was the reminiscent story of the history of the church. This was given by Rev. T. J. Rucker, who was ordained as a deacon in the life of the church and then subsequently ordained to the full gospel ministry. His references to the worthy and noble Christian workers who had gone on and now known by the good works that follow them were tributes highly endorsed by the great congregation. He made especial mention of L. W. Stephens, the first pastor of the church, also J. H. McMullan, E. R. Goss and E. L. Sisk, who served their generation so well, and who now rest from their labors.

Milltown Baptist Church

MILLTOWN Baptist Church, located six miles northeast of the City of Hartwell, Ga., was constituted August 22, 1858, under a brush arbor where the present church now stands.

Minutes of the presbytery called to constitute Milltown Church. Georgia, Hart County, August 22, 1858.

The presbytery organized for the purpose of constituting Milltown Church.

(1) Proceeded to read the Constitution, which was received.
(2) Proceeded to read the Articles of Faith, which were received.
(3) Received the following members by letter, viz.:

> Joel Towers from church at Anderson, C. H. S. C.
> Lamarcus Carter from the church at Andersonville, S. C.
> John R. Carter from the church at Andersonville, S. C.
> Alexander Stalnaker from the church at Andersonville, S. C.
> Wm. R. Latham from the church at Andersonville, S. C.
> Harriett Carter from the Church at Andersonville, S. C.
> Elizabeth Carter from the church at Andersonville, S. C.
> Zilphey Latham from the church at Andersonville, S. C.
> Susan E. Findley from the church at Andersonville, S. C.
> Nancy Carter from the church at Andersonville, S. C.
> Harriett R. Carter from the church at Andersonville, S. C.
> Caroline Carter from the church at Andersonville, S. C.
> Amanda Carter from the church at Andersonville, S. C.

(4) Adopted the Constitution and Articles of Faith.

(5) The presbytery then extended the right hand of fellowship to the above named brethren and sisters, after which public prayer was made by Brother Jones.

J. T. W. Vernon, Moderator	William Dollar, Deacon
James C. Jones, Minister	Henry Brown, Deacon
Francis Hubbard, Deacon	J. V. Richardson, Deacon, Clerk
Abraham Walters, Deacon	William C. Davis, Assistant Clerk

A church house was later erected on the site on a lot of land containing five acres, conveyed by Micajah Carter for the use of the church. In the immediate community where the church was located there were at the time several mills, hence the name Milltown was applied to the church.

The church house is situated on a ridge which is the dividing line between the watersheds of Big and Little Lightwoodlog creeks, and calls to mind the many sacred places mentioned in the Bible where God met with his people upon the holy mount.

There is something inspiring and uplifting that we experience as we ascend a mountain and get away from the hurry and turmoil of the lower levels; so it is when we assemble at the church on the hill and, for the time being, dismiss the things of the lower world and receive spiritual blessings from God, and rededicate and reconsecrate our lives and ourselves to the things that will promote His kingdom in the world.

Following is a list of the names of the preachers who have served Milltown Church as pastor:

Rev. J. T. W. Vernon, who served the church as pastor for twenty years. Revs. Jesse Brown, B. C. Thornton, I. H. Goss, M. L. Carswell, J. C. Wingo, B. M. Pack, J. R. Earle, T. A. Thornton, E. R Goss, J. C. West, J. B. Brown, R. M. Maret, Rev. ___ Burrell, W. C. Moore, T. J. Rucker, L. M. Herndon, D. C. Williams, J. J. Hiott, L. M. Smith, Marshall Nelms, and D. C. Williams who is the present pastor.

James P. Vickery was licensed to preach by the church and was later ordained at Mt. Hebron Church to which he had moved his membership.

During the month of September, 1900, John B. Brown was licensed to preach, and later, on January 11, 1902, he was ordained to the full work of the gospel, which will fully appear from the following record:

"Ordination of Rev. John B. Brown to the ministry at Milltown, January 11, 1902.

"Preaching by Rev. T. A. Thornton, after which the following named brethren: Revs. T. A. Thornton, A. J. Cleveland, W. G. Dudley, J. P. Vickery and Deacons: J. W. Chastain, Henry Allen and T. A. Booth, composed the presbytery to ordain Brother John B. Brown to the work of the ministry.

"1st—Heard report of the church of his Christian character and general deportment.

"2nd—Heard his Christian experience and call to the ministry.

"3rd—Examined him on Bible doctrine, which was given in entire satisfaction.

"4th—After examination the presbytery proceeded with the ordination.

"5th—Rev. T. A. Thornton led the ordination prayer, after which followed laying on of the hands of the presbytery.

"6th—Rev. A. J. Cleveland delivered the charge to Brother Brown and Rev. W. G. Dudley the charge to the church.

Milltown Baptist Church

"7th—The presbytery extended the right hand of fellowship to Brother Brown.

"The benediction pronounced by Rev. John B. Brown."

Milltown may justly be accredited as the "mother" of the Hebron Baptist Association, as she invited all sister churches friendly to the forming of a new association to meet with her in July, 1882. Not only did she invite churches friendly to the project, but any of contrary opinion were also invited. The result of that conference of churches, though different opinions were freely expressed, was the formation of the Hebron Association.

The Hebron Association was organized at Hendrys Church in 1883, and the meeting of 1884 was held with Milltown Church.

Among the names of hallowed memory who composed the membership of Milltown Church, formerly, may be mentioned the Carters, Sanderses, Vickerys, Vernons, Murrays and others, who have passed on and now rest from their labors, while their works do follow them.

Many of the descendants of the former members compose in part the present membership.

The church has of late been enlarged to about double its original size, freshly painted and will compare favorably with many of the splendid churches of the country.

Cross Roads Baptist Church

THE Cross Roads Baptist Church, situated six miles west of Hartwell, in Hart County, Ga., was constituted February 25, 1871. Rev. I. H. Goss was moderator and W. G. White, clerk of the presbytery.

Before the constitution of the church, it was operating as an arm of old Canon Church.

Following are the names of the charter members, all of whom were formerly members of old Canon Church:

1. Peter A. Wood
2. Mrs. Martha Wood
3. Jeff H. Phillips
4. Mrs. Lula Phillips
5. L. H. Phillips
6. Mrs. Mary A. Phillips
7. Major John G. Watson
8. Mrs. John G. Watson
9. D. M. Watson
10. Mrs. D. M. Watson
11. R. F. Morris
12. Rebecca Morris
13. Reuben J. Morris
14. Amelia Morris
15. Thad. T. Holbrook
16. Mrs. Thad. T. Holbrook

Major John G. Watson and R. F. Morris were later ordained as deacons of the church. Rebecca Morris is the only charter member now living (1933).

The name of the church at first was Miller Old Field, so named for the reason that it was located in an old field that was once the property of Jerry Miller, a pioneer who emigrated from Virginia to Georgia and settled and lived at the place. Signs of the old Miller home may yet be seen right near where the present church house stands, and some few of the old field pines, that have been spared, are now stately trees. The name was changed in 1880 from that of Miller Old Field to Cross Roads.

CROSS ROADS BAPTIST CHURCH

Services were held under a brush arbor for some time before the church was constituted, and was continued till a house could be built.

The following preachers have served the church as pastors: Rev. Calvin P. Sanders, son-in-law of Jerry Miller, was elected as first pastor and served the balance of the year 1871. Rev. I. H. Goss, 1872; Rev. B. C. Thornton, 1873; Rev. J. T. W. Vernon, 1874; Rev. I. H. Goss, 1875-6; Rev. John D. Adams, 1877-1883; Rev. B. M. Pack, 1884; Rev. W. J. Vickery, 1885-6; Rev. B. J. McLeskey, 1887-8; Rev. L. W. Stephens, 1889-90; Rev. F. M. Estes, 1891-94; Rev. E. R. Goss, 1895-1900; Rev. F. M. Estes, 1901-1904; Rev. W. T. Mitchell, 1905-1908; Rev. L. Fields, 1909-1911; Rev. R. M. Maret, 1912-13; Rev. L. T. Weldon, 1914-1916; Rev. Geo. W. Hulme, 1917-18; Rev. G. J. Davis, 1919-1922; Rev. S. S. Mathis, 1923; Rev. G. J. Davis, 1924-25; Rev. E. C. White, 1925 to the present.

The following brethren have served as clerks: W. G. White, 1871; James E. Vickery, 1872-1879; W. O. McKinney, 1880-1893; J. T. Williams, 1894-1913; A. E. Ertzberger, 1914 to the present.

The church at Cross Roads after constitution, united with the Tugaloo Baptist Association, which body held its session of 1883 with the church at Cross Roads and at which the church, together with other churches, members of the Tugaloo Association, withdrew from the Tugaloo Association, and united with the Hebron Association when same was organized at Hendrys Church in 1883.

Two of the sessions of the Hebron Association have convened with Cross Roads Church, 1903 and 1920.

In 1919, the members of the church and people of the community built a new brick church house, at a cost of $30,000, which is one of the most imposing church edifices in this part of the State.

Cross Roads Baptist Church

The first services were held in the new church on the 5th Sunday in May, 1920, at which time Rev. G. J. Davis preached to an audience, estimated to be 3,000 people.

The church maintains a flourishing Sunday school, and in this connection, we wish to state that many years ago Mrs. Thomas Fisher, commonly called "Betty" Fisher, was elected superintendent of the Sunday school and while it was not the first Sunday school organized at the place, she conducted it in a manner that built up and advanced the interest. At the time Mrs. Fisher was superintendent there was no Sunday school literature or helps as at the present time. The Bible was the only book used.

The present flourishing Sunday school at Cross Roads is due in a great measure to the influence of the labors of this devoted and consecrated Christian woman.

Church and Sunday School Officers

Rev. E. C. White, pastor; A. E. Ertzberger, church clerk; J. T. Williams, Sunday school superintendent.

Present Board of Deacons

J. Frank Williams, chairman; J. T. Williams, D. M. Shiflet, Wilton C. Moore, T. L. Holbrook, T. P. Holbrook, L. D. Gurley, P. P. Gurley, Sr., John R. Vassar, Lee Gray, A. E. Ertzberger.

Cedar Creek Baptist Church

FOR several years prior to 1878, religious services were held at a school house, near where Cedar Creek Church is now located. At this place Revs. J. H. McMullan, J. D. Adams, Calloway Thornton and Asa Avery and perhaps others held services for the people of the community from time to time. Sabbath school services were also held regularly at the place.

On the fifth Sunday, March 31st, 1878, a presbytery composed of Revs. Benjamin Thornton, I. H. Goss and Asa Avery and Deacons T. N. McMullan, J. Van Richardson, James E. Scott and Caswell Farmer met at the school house for the purpose of organizing what is now Cedar Creek Baptist Church.

The names of forty members of the church of Sardis were presented in a letter by F. S. Roberts.

Asa Avery was chosen as pastor for the remainder of the year 1878, and was reelected in the following October, and served the church as pastor faithfully until the close of the year 1880, when Rev. I. H. Goss was chosen pastor. A house of worship was erected on a site given to the church by F. S. Roberts, within a few yards of where the present house of worship stands, and which in June, 1883, was burned to the ground.

Rev. I. H. Goss died in April, 1882, and the church called in his place, Rev. J. H. McMullan. Under his masterly guidance a new and more costly building was erected in the fall of 1883, to take the place of the one destroyed by fire, and which is the present church house.

Rev. J. H. McMullan was continued pastor until October, 1890, when Rev. T. J. Rucker was called by the church to serve them the following year.

Caswell Farmer and T. P. Tiller came as deacons from Sardis Church and were accepted as such. Since that time J. B. Myers, H. F. Hailey, N. J. Tiller, L. O. Reid, Ira F. Myers, John P. Cobb and B. A. Cash have served as deacons. P. C. Cash was received as deacon from Banks County. We do not have the names of the other deacons who have served the church.

After constitution, the church united with the Sarepta Baptist Association in 1878, when that body met with the church at Fork Broad River. Tiller and Hailey were delegates to the association. Myers and Lewis were the alternates.

In 1883, when the Sarepta Association met with the church at Rock Branch, Cedar Creek withdrew from that body and united with the Hebron Association when it was organized at Hendrys Church in 1883, and became a charter member. H. F. Hailey and F. S. Roberts were the delegates.

An item we gather from the minutes of the church is, that on October 12th, 1884, J. T. Durham was ordained to the ministry by the following presbytery: Rev. J. H. McMullan and Rev. J. C. Wingo and Deacons E. J. Brown and S. V. Brown from Hendrys Church; J. W. Thornton, R. A. Cobb and Willie Higginbotham from Bio; W. Myers from Sardis; James E. Scott from Hartwell Church; P. C. Cash, H. F. Hailey and J. B. Myers from Cedar Creek Church.

Another item is, that on June 22, 1889, John B. Saylors was ordained to preach by the following presbytery: Revs. Asa Avery, Jas. H. McMullan and T. J. Rucker. No deacons' names given.

Another item from the minutes of the church is, that at the July meeting, July 21st, 1883, granted Brother Frank Estes authority to receive members at the school house near Scott's mill as an arm of Cedar Creek Church, which presumably was later constituted as Flat Shoals Church in 1885.

During the period of 55 years, 1878 to 1933, in which Cedar Creek has functioned as a church we gather the following statistics.

Twelve pastors have served the church during the period mentioned: Asa Avery from March 31, 1883, the date of organization to close of 1880. I. H. Goss, 1881 and till April, 1882; J. H. McMullan from then until the close of 1890; J. T. W. Vernon for the year 1891; T. J. Rucker, 1892 to 1904, and again in 1909, making a total of fourteen years, the longest pastorate in the history of the church; R. A. Smith, 1908 and 1913-14, three years; John B. Brown, 1910-11-12, and again 1915 to close of 1921, a total of ten years; T. M. Galphin, 1905-6-7, and again 1925-26-27, six years in all; J. C. West, 1922; S. B. Jordan, 1923; J. J. Hiott, 1924; E. R. Broadwell from 1928 to the present, 5 years and a part of the present year.

M. J. Lewis served as clerk for many years, being the first clerk, and A. J. McMullan in writing the history of Cedar Creek Church in 1900, paid him the following high compliment:

"We are indebted to Brother M. J. Lewis for this history of Cedar Creek Church, and in connection we want to state that Brother Lewis was about 18 years clerk of the church at Cedar Creek, and a more faithful and consecrated officer the church has never known."

John P. Cobb served as clerk for two years; F. M. Hailey, two years;

W. J. Bell about twenty years as best we can get it from the records; G. C. Lewis for the last fourteen years.

The church was organized with 40 members and the number reported to the last meeting of the Hebron Association in 1932, was 210, a gain of 170 members in 55 years.

The 1895 session of the Hebron Association met with the church at Cedar Creek at which J. H. McMullan was moderator and T. J. Rucker, clerk.

The 1932 session was also held with Cedar Creek Church.

Oak Bower Baptist Church

BY request the following brethren with others, met at Oak Bower Academy on Saturday, March 21, 1891, and formed a presbytery for the purpose of organizing "Oak Bower Baptist Church." Revs. T. A. Thornton, E. R. Goss, J. B. Saylors and J. P. Vickery.

Rev. J. P. Vickery was elected moderator with John Lewis as clerk. Letters were presented by twelve worthy members, and after reading articles of faith, they constituted The Oak Bower Baptist Church.

The church then called Rev. E. R. Goss as their pastor. Also, elected J. M. Bailey, church clerk. Meeting days, 4th Sunday and Saturday before.

The membership reported to the Hebron Baptist Association in 1932 was 136. Rev. E. R. Broadwell, who has served the church for several years, is the present pastor.

History of Hart County Board of Education

THE public schools of Hart County were organized February 7, 1871. Prior to this time there were no public school funds to support education. Until 1874, our schools were maintained entirely by tuition system. Under this system each community had the kind of schools as the people would support by private funds.

The first Board of Education under the Public School System of Hart County was composed of John G. McCurry, president; J. H. Skelton, John S. Herndon, J. W. O'Barr, John Brown, Peter L. Fleming, Allen S. Turner, Jeptha Bowers and J. F. Craft.

J. W. O'Barr was secretary of the first meeting. Since that time many excellent men have served on the County Board of Education.

The executive officer of the Board of Education was called the County School Commissioner. It was his duty to act as secretary at board meetings, to keep the accounts and pay out the school funds under the direction of the Board of Education.

Below we give a brief history of the men who have served in this capacity:

The first County School Commissioner in Hart, was C. W. Seidel, who served from 1871 to 1882 with exception of one year. He was an Englishman, who came here from the North. He operated the old gold mine in Hart County, and practiced law in Hartwell until the War Between the States. He joined the Confederate Cause and served honorably through the war. He was interested in education and rendered valuable services in organizing the first schools of Hart County. He was also secretary of Governor Alex. H. Stephens. He spent his latter days in Atlanta.

Dr. C. A. Webb served as commissioner from 1875 to 1876. He was a practicing physician and for a number of years was clerk of the Superior Court. He was prominent in the affairs of the county.

Thomas N. McMullan served as commissioner from 1882 to 1888. Mr. McMullan was a farmer by profession, and did a great deal for the advancement of the schools in Hart County.

The office was occupied by J. C. Neese from 1888 to 1889. Mr. Neese was a native of Hart County and a local preacher of the Methodist church. Having been a teacher, he understood school problems.

J. R. Stephens, a native of Elbert County, was commissioner from 1889 to 1904. Mr. Stephens was also a teacher for a number of years. By his familiarity with school conditions and his business ability he was able to render valuable services to the county.

B. H. Pearman, a native of Hart County, from Shoal Creek section, served as commissioner from 1904 to 1909. Mr. Pearman was a zealous worker and did faithful conscientious work.

After the election of Mr. B. H. Pearman, as county school commissioner, he by the aid of the Board of Education, in accordance with the Act of the Legislature providing for the same, divided the county in Local School Districts, as follows: District No. 1, Viola District; District No. 2, Bowersville District; District No. 3, Duncan District; District No. 5, Shoal Creek District; District No. 6, Cross Roads District; District No. 9, Goldmine District; District No. 12, Flat Shoals District; District No. 13, Campground District; District No. 15, Beulah District; District No. 19, Cedar Creek District; district No. 20, Nuberg District; District No. 24, Liberty Hill District; District No. 26, Sardis District; District, known as Thomas District. Notice: Nos. 4, 7, 8, 10, 11, 14, 16, 17, 18, 21, 22, 23 and 25 to be supplied. Trustees were elected for each district, and local school tax was levied in each district for the support of the school in addition to the taxes received from the State and county.

Mr. B. H. Pearman died September 8, 1909, and an election was ordered to be held for the election of a county school commissioner to fill the unexpired term of office of Mr. Pearman. W. E. Meredith, Thomas G. Craft and W. B. Morris were candidates for the position and at the election, Mr. W. B. Morris was elected.

This was the first election held in the county for county school commissioner by the people. Before the Act was passed providing for the election by the people, the school commissioner was elected by the members of the Board of Education.

Mr. W. B. Morris began his term of service as superintendent in 1909, and to his efficient work the people of Hart County are indebted for the splendid progress the schools made during his incumbency of twenty-three years.

The present school system of Hart County is the result of a movement inaugurated in 1921 to consolidate and grade the several schools in Hart County.

In 1921, there were thirty-seven one, two and three teacher schools in Hart County. The majority of these schools were of the one and two teacher type. The equipment was poor, and in many of the schools as many as ten grades were attempted. The buildings were also not well arranged for efficient work. Thorough school work could not be expected under conditions that existed at this time.

Consolidation

As a new day to the then existing school difficulties a program of school consolidation was submitted to the people. This was endorsed by the people in elections on school consolidation and school bonds. Twelve new and modern brick buildings were erected to take care of the educational needs of the county. Transportation was supplied to transport the children to and from school.

The first consolidation was King's Bench and Midway schools, this was effective on petition of the school trustees of said school districts to the County Board of Education, February 3, 1920, however, the consolidation was not completed until later when Mt. Olivet school building was erected.

Reed Creek Consolidated School

The first consolidation of a school district, actually effected, was Reed Creek Consolidated School District, ordered by the County Board of Education, April 23, 1921. The territory of Reed Creek School District, Sanders, a greater portion of Eureka and a part of Vernon School District, submitted the question of whether or not the territory mentioned should be consolidated into a consolidated school district, April 15, 1921. Returns of the election resulted in the overwhelming vote for the consolidation of the territory. Following this election the County Board of Education officially consolidated the territory into a consolidated school, known as Reed Creek Consolidated School District, April 23, 1921.

Then followed immediately an election on school bonds to build and equip a school building for the new district. A $12,000.00 bond issue was approved and a building erected and equipped, located near Reed Creek Church. Prof. Lee Frye was the first teacher at Reed Creek. The school employs four trucks for the transportation of the children. Prof. O. E. Gay is the present principal.

Sardis Consolidated School

Sardis Consolidated School District is composed of Sardis, Riverside, part of Oak Bower and a portion of Liberty Hill school districts. A $7,500.00 bond issue was approved for the building and equipment of the school. The school uses two trucks for the transportation of its pupils. Prof. C. M. Reid is the present principal.

Mt. Olivet Consolidated School

Mt. Olivet Consolidated School District, composed of Mt. Olivet, Midway, King's Bench, Flat Shoals, portions of Rock Spring and Cross Roads school districts. Bond issue of $11,000.00. Employs four trucks for transportation. Prof. R. H. Smalley is the present principal.

Goldmine Consolidated School

Goldmine Consolidated School District includes the territory formerly included in Goldmine and Sandy Grove and a portion of Duncan School Districts. Bond issue of $6,500.00. Employs two trucks for transportation.

Air Line Consolidated School

Air Line Consolidated School District is composed of the territory formerly included in Air Line, Union Hill, and most of Cross Roads school districts. Bond issue, $12,000.00. Employs three trucks for transportation. Prof. W. A. Moss is the present principal.

Shoal Creek Consolidated School

Shoal Creek Consolidated School District is made up of what was formerly Shoal Creek, part of Thomas, part of Rock Spring and part of Viola school districts. Has a bond issue of $6,500.00. Employs two trucks for transportation. Prof. G. T. Gard is the present principal.

Alford's Consolidated School

Alford's Consolidated School District, composed of Mt. Zion, Milltown and a small portion of Oak Bower school districts. Has a bond issue of $3,000.00. Prof. Denver W. Cleveland is the present principal.

Bowersville Consolidated School

Bowersville Consolidated School District is made up of what was formerly Bowersville, Adams and parts of Viola and Duncan school districts. Amount of school bonds, $10,000.00. Prof. W. C. Jones is the present principal. The school employs two trucks for transportation.

Vanna Consolidated School

Vanna Consolidated School District, located at Vanna, Ga., is composed of what was formerly Vanna and Rice school districts. Amount of school bonds, $7,000.00. Prof. R. B. Carter is the present principal. One truck is employed for transportation.

Eaglegrove Consolidated School

Eaglegrove Consolidated School District is composed of Eaglegrove and part of Beaulah school districts. Amount of school bonds, $7,000.00. Two trucks are employed for transportation. Prof. Peter Herndon is the present principal.

Bio Consolidated School

Bio Consolidated School District, composed of Bio, part of Beaulah and part of Liberty school districts. Amount of school bonds issued, $10,000.00. Prof. R. F. Wagkins is the present principal. Two school trucks are used for transportation.

Nancy Hart Consolidated School

Nancy Hart Consolidated School District is composed of territory formerly included in Nuberg, Cedar Creek, Cokesbury and part of Liberty Hill school districts. Amount of school bonds, $12,000.00. Three school trucks are employed for transportation. Prof. E. H. Thomas is the present principal.

High Schools

By consolidation the schools were graded, and high school work was placed on an accredited basis. Eleven of the twelve schools now have junior high schools and do nine grades of work. By co-operation with the Board of Education of the City of Hartwell the county school authorities have secured high school facilities for all county pupils at Hartwell for the tenth and eleventh grades. Rural students are admitted at Hartwell on the same fees as are paid by resident pupils. Thus every boy and girl in Hart County have the opportunity of a first class high-school education at the lowest cost possible. Students who graduate from the Hartwell High School may enter any college in the State of Georgia without examination.

Vocational Education

All of the schools of Hart County have opportunity of placing vocational agriculture and home economics in their course of study. There are at present ten teachers of vocational agriculture and five teachers of home economics working in the schools of the county. These teachers are a great asset to the educational forces and are giving several hundred students very valuable training in vocational subjects. Vocational agricultural teachers are in the county for the entire year, and their services are not only available to the school, but to the community as well.

Teaching Force

The county schools are fortunate in having a most excellent corps of teachers. Some thirteen teachers are four-year college graduates. Fifty-two teachers have had as much as two or more years in college. The qualifications of the other teachers are high. This accounts for, to a great extent, the high quality of work that is being done in the county schools.

Co-operation

Effective work in the schools is built on mutual co-operation among the forces that go to make up the schools—teachers, children, parents and school officials. The splendid progress that has been made in school work in Hart County during the past years has been due to a fine spirit of co-operation among the teachers, parents, children and all forces affecting the school. Parent-Teacher Associations have been a strong factor in the development of schools in Hart County. The P. T. A.'s have been in the past and are destined to be in the future a most helpful adjunct to the school organization.

While much progress has been made in the school work of the county, and while Hart enjoys the distinction of being the banner county of the State along educational lines, there remains much that can be done toward school improvement. No doubt these problems will be solved from year to year, until we have one of the best school systems in the State.

Prof. B. B. Mason was elected county school superintendent at the election in 1932, and began service January 1, 1933, and is successfully carrying on.

The present Board of Education of Hart County is composed of the following members: M. M. Norman, chairman; Dr. B. C. Teasley, T. B. Whitworth, J. T. Williams and C. H. Denney.

Total number in school for the past scholastic year was 2,431.

William Anderson Sanders Family History

WILLIAM ANDERSON SANDERS, son of Jonathan and Orpha Miller Sanders was born January 24, 1834; baptized at Milltown Baptist Church, October 23, 1859; married Ann E. Caroline Carter, daughter of David and Lavinia Louise Carter, September 15, 1859, by Rev. James T. W. Vernon; died March 26, 1925; buried at Milltown Baptist Church.

Ann E. Caroline Carter, daughter of David Lewis Carter and Lavinia Louise York Carter, born June 19, 1837; joined the Baptist Church at Andersonville, S. C., and was baptized in August, 1857; married William Anderson Sanders, September 15, 1859, by Rev. J. T. W. Vernon; died February 13, 1891; buried at Milltown Baptist Church. Eight children.

Fannie Angeline Sanders, oldest child of W. A. and Caroline Sanders, born August 7, 1860; baptized at Milltown Baptist Church, August 13, 1880; married John W. Baker January 24, 1884, by Rev. J. T. W. Vernon; died July 15, 1891; buried at Reed Creek Baptist Church, Hart County, Ga. Three children. Lillian Estelle, born February 7, 1886; Eugene Baker, born May 26, 1888; Cullen Baker, born December 18, 1890; died October 1, 1914.

Lucy Ella Carter, second child of W. A. and Caroline Sanders, born October 12, 1862; baptized at Milltown Baptist Church September 6, 1874; married William Yancey Carter May 18, 1884, by Rev. J. T. W. Vernon. Nine children. Gibson, Lucile, Yancey, Ethel, Caroline, Clarence and Claude, twins; Sybil, Sarah.

Sarah Caroline Sanders, called Sallie, third child of W. A. and Caroline Sanders, born September 23, 1865; baptized at Milltown Baptist Church August 21, 1881; married Eugene Hutchinson December 26, 1889, by M. G. O'Barr, J. P.; died June 28, 1929; buried at Anderson, S. C., in Silver

Brook Cemetery. Eugene Hutchinson died November 10, 1924; buried at Milltown Baptist Church. Seven children. William Arney, born December 12, 1891; Tom Watson, Arthur Burr, Clyde Macy, Jim Marrell, born September 23, 1902; Ethel Dorothy and Estelle Dorris, twins, born September 23, 1904.

Albert Perry Sanders, fourth child of W. A. and Caroline Sanders, born March 2, 1868; baptized at Milltown Baptist Church August 21, 1881; married Conie Carlton February 5, 1891, in Wilkes County, Ga. Two children. Annie Ruth, born March 3, 1892; died December 16, 1895; buried at Milltown Cemetery, Hart County, Ga., beside Sanders grandparents; Lucy Belle, born March 28, 1893.

Emma Alicia Sanders, fifth child of W. A. and Caroline Sanders, born July 15, 1870; baptized at Milltown Baptist Church August 25, 1884; married Lawrence C. Chamblee September 9. 1894. by Rev. T. A. Thornton; died April 12, 1912; buried at Milltown Baptist Church. Five children. Norman Fred, born September 3, 1895; Nellie Lucile, born July 29, 1899; Opal Vesta, born November 7, 1901; Hazel Louise, born August 14, 1904; James Anderson, born May 11, 1907.

Lawrence C. Chamblee was born July, 1851; died April 25, 1909; buried at Mountain Creek Baptist Church, Anderson County, S. C.

Florence Newton Sanders, sixth child of W. A. and Caroline Sanders, born July 31, 1873; baptized at Milltown Baptist Church September 11, 1887; married Adria London November 3, 1907; home at Georgetown, Tenn. Four children. London Anderson Sanders, born August 26, 1908; Guy Meadows Sanders, born November 30, 1910; Paul Carpenter Sanders, born October 5, 1912; Neal Sanders, born April 11, 1916.

Mornin Louiza, called Lou, seventh child of W. A. and Caroline Sanders, born December 20, 1875; baptized at Milltown Baptist Church August 17, 1890; married Dozier A. Hilley January 29, 1893, by Rev. T. R. Wright; home now Macon, Ga. Eleven children. Ruby Cameron, Carl Newton, Dean Alexander, Swain Anderson (dead), Omer (dead), Emma Louise, Raymond Doyle, Henry Grady and Winnie Grace, twins; Evelyn Juhan, Jasper Earl.

John Harrison Sanders, eighth child of W. A. and Caroline Sanders, born June 12, 1878; baptized at Milltown Baptist Church August 23, 1891; married Lola Brown December 25, 1905; home in Atlanta, Ga. Four children. Maude Caroline, born October 18, 1906; died July 11, 1907; Emily Cater, born July 3, 1911; John Frederick, born July 3, 1913; Nell, born July 21, 1916.

William Anderson Sanders enlisted in the service of the War Between the States, July, 1863, and served in Co. B, 23rd Georgia Infantry from which service he was discharged during April, 1865.

He lived for many years on the old home place of his father-in-law, David Carter, where his family was reared and where he carried on extensive farming operations. For a part of the time, in addition to his farming interests, he engaged in the bee and chicken business. His apiary was the largest and most noted in the country. He raised thorough bred chickens of various kinds which he sold and shipped to different parts of the country.

His home was always a place of cordial welcome and hospitality to visitors and a favorite stopping place for the preacher.

He served as Justice of the Peace in and for the 1119th (Alford's) G. M. District for many years.

He served as deacon and clerk of Milltown Baptist Church of which he was an active and leading member.

After the death of his first wife, he married Miss Fannie Vaughters of Elbert County—no children born to the Sanders-Vaughters union.

We give herewith the newspaper article notice of his death and funeral:

Mr. W. A. Sanders

"Mr. W. A. Sanders, a pioneer citizen of Hart County, but who removed to Elbert County some twenty-five years ago, died at his home on the 26th of March, 1925, in his 92nd year. His body was brought to Hart County last Friday and buried at Milltown, his old home church where he had been an honored deacon for many years.

"Rev. T. A. Thornton, who had been his pastor in the years gone by, conducted the funeral services assisted by Rev. J. C. West, his Elbert County pastor Mr. Sanders was always highly esteemed by all who knew him. 'He was a good man,' and there is consolation for his relatives and friends that his body now sleeps beside his first devoted wife near the church to which he was so devoted.

"Several children and a devoted wife keenly feel the departure of an affectionate father and lovable husband."

John C. Bailey

JOHN C. BAILEY, son of Richard Bailey, was born in Lancaster County, S. C., September 20, 1826; removed to Georgia at the age of sixteen years; married Martha, a daughter of Rev. Samuel B. Sanders, and to this union were born three sons and seven daughters, viz.: James H., William and John B. Bailey. The daughters were Vina A., Frances, Louisa, Martha J., Mary, Emma and Myra Bailey.

After the death of his wife, Martha, he married Miss Frances M. Madden, daughter of Robert A. Madden on August 8, 1893, Rev. B. J. McLeskey performing the marriage ceremony. After the death of his second wife, he was married to Miss Julia Olbon.

Mr. Bailey was a soldier in the War Between the States, which service he enlisted on March 11, 1863, in Company "C," 16th Georgia Regiment, as a private under Captain J. H. Skelton. Was captured at Wilderness, May 6, 1864, and imprisoned at Elmira, N. Y., from which he was discharged June 16, 1865. Mr. Bailey died April 16, 1916, at the advanced age of 90 years and was buried in the cemetery at Reed Creek Church, after funeral services conducted by Rev. Robert M. Maret.

In connection with Mr. Bailey's war record we herewith reproduce an article which appeared in *The Hartwell Sun*, April 9, 1886:

"A captured Canteen Returned After a Lapse of 23 Years. Mr. W. Y. Holland left at this office on Monday an old wooden Confederate canteen that he had brought from Atlanta where it had been forwarded by its captor.

The inscriptions upon it give its history. On one side, cut with a pocket knife was the following: 'J. C. Bailey, 16th Ga.' On the other side: 'Taken from a prisoner from the 16th Ga., May 3rd, 1863, at Chancellorsville.' 'Col. D. C. Bingham, 24th N. Y. Vols.' Mr. Bailey, who is a citizen of Hart County, came in to get it Tuesday, and it was curious to note the emotions depicted upon the rugged face of the veteran soldier when he looked upon his old army comrade for the first time in 23 years. What a floodtide of memory came with the sight. The circumstances attending the capture of the canteen as told by Mr. Bailey were as follows: He was a member of Company C, 16th Ga., of which Major J. H. Skelton, our worthy townsman, was Captain. On the 3rd of May at Chancellorsville his regiment was advanced under a heavy fire up to within ten or fifteen feet of the enemy's lines and ordered to hold their position at all hazards. Bailey with a small squad secured a tolerably safe position in a road behind a huge log. By some means the line of soldiers on either side was withdrawn before they knew it, and when they found this fact out they discovered that they were in a serious dilemma. To retreat across the open field in plain view of the enemy was certain death, and to remain where they were, worse than foolish. The only reasonable alternative was surrender. One of the squad held up his haversack on a stick as a flag of truce. It was acknowledged by the enemy and they were ordered to 'come over.' The Colonel of the Regiment asked Bailey to let him see his canteen, and by some means the prisoners were removed to the rear before the canteen was returned. Last year at the reunion of Federals and Confederates in Atlanta the canteen was brought there by S. W. Johnson, of Ellicottesville, N. Y., where it remained until it was brought to Hartwell by Mr. W. Y. Holland on last Friday. Mr. Bailey was exchanged, but recaptured again at the battle of the Wilderness.

"He was captured both times by the 6th army corps. Mr. Bailey is 58 years old and bids fair for many years of useful living yet. He prizes his returned canteen, and it will prove a precious heirloom to the descendants of the gallant Confederate."

Captain J. F. Craft

CAPTAIN J. F. CRAFT was born at Craftsville, Elbert County, Ga., March 4, 1838. He was the oldest son of Willis Craft, who during his life had represented Elbert County in the Legislature, and who was careful in the training of his sons to business and industry. In early life Capt. J. F. Craft was sent to school at Parkertown, B. B. Parker being his tutor. After leaving Parkertown he went to Elberton, where he attended school under the famous John A. Trenchard as his tutor. He afterwards engaged in teaching. While yet young he quit the schoolroom to take charge of his father's farm. He embarked early in the Civil War as a member of the 15th Georgia Regiment. Soon after F. B. Hodges resigned as captain at Halifax, Va., Capt. J. F. Craft became his successor.

For many years during his lifetime he lived at and owned the large plantation on Savannah River, formerly the home of William Dooley, where he engaged in farming, operating a flouring and grist mill, also the ferry on the river, formerly known as Dooley's Ferry, and engaged in boating on the Savannah River, transporting cotton to Augusta and merchandise on the return trips.

He later moved to Hartwell and engaged in business, and in the year 1879 superintended the construction and equipment of the Hartwell Railroad.

He married Miss Ellen Goss, daughter of Rev. I. H. Goss and wife, Mary Gordon Goss.

In 1884 he was elected State Senator from the 31st Senatorial District, and died before the expiration of his term of office.

He died August 23, 1885. His wife, Ellen Goss Craft, born December 13, 1841, died September 7, 1916.

Julius D. Matheson

J. D. MATHESON was born in Clay County, N. C., December 28, 1857. He came from Toccoa, Ga., some 35 years before his death, to Hartwell, Ga., where he engaged in the mercantile business, in which he remained until his death, which occurred July 29, 1916.

Besides a general mercantile business, he was at different times engaged in many industrial pursuits. From the very beginning, though young in manhood, the impress of his sterling qualities was noticeable to the observing and it was not long before he was classed among the leading business men of northeast Georgia, an honored distinction he carried to the end of his life.

Not long after he became a citizen of Hartwell he was married to the eldest daughter of the lamented Hon. J. M. Thornton, on February 23, 1882.

He was a man who lived close to his friends. While he was never a candidate for any office in his county, he usually took a great interest in the politics of his county and wielded quite an influence along political lines. He was at one time Mayor of the City of Hartwell. Was a member of the Baptist Church and a Mason.

John H. Magill

JOHN H. MAGILL was born in Abbeville County, S. C., March 7, 1849, and at the age of 13, and before of military age, enlisted as a volunteer to help fight the battles of the War Between the States, in which service he received a wound on the cheek, leaving a scar that he bore to the grave. He was in the battle of Gettysburg.

He, together with one Mr. Belcher, established a newspaper in Hartwell, August, 1876. The paper at first was issued as *The Sun*, later the name was changed to *The Hartwell Sun*, which name it retains at the present time. He edited *The Sun*, later *The Hartwell Sun*, for 35 years. The paper during these years contributed more to the development of the county on all progressive lines than any other factor employed.

On April 12, 1877, he was married to Miss Laura L. Eberhart, daughter of Dr. George and Mrs. Hellen Eberhart, who preceded him to the grave by several years. He died in an Atlanta hospital on Saturday, January 20, 1923. After appropriate funeral services at the Methodist Church in Hartwell, of which he was a member, conducted by Rev. J. H. Barton on Monday, January 22, 1923, he was buried in the cemetery at Hartwell.

W. L. Hodges

WALTER LEE HODGES was born in Hartwell, Hart County, Ga., May 25, 1867. He was the son of Frederick B. Hodges and Elizabeth McMullan Hodges. He graduated from the University of Georgia in 1887, and later, in 1888, graduated from the Department of Law in this institution. Was admitted to the bar at Hartwell, Ga., and practiced his profession for several years. He had quite a brilliant career.

When quite young he was elected Mayor of Hartwell, which position he filled acceptably.

In 1900 he was elected to the General Assembly of Georgia, serving one term.

When the City Court of Hart County, later the City Court of Hartwell, was created he was unanimously recommended by the Grand Jury and the citizenry of Hart County to Governor Hoke Smith to fill the judgeship of this court, which position he held during the entire life of the court.

On January 1, 1917, he was elevated to the Judgeship of the Superior Courts of the Northern Circuit, to which position he had been elected by the people of the circuit in the fall of 1916. Was elected for three consecutive terms to this important position without opposition, which position he was occupying at the time of his death.

He was recognized as one of Georgia's leading jurists, and frequently was called into service in Fulton and other counties of the State. His judgments were rarely reversed by higher courts.

He joined the Methodist Church early in life and at the time of his death was teacher of the largest class in the Sunday school, which place he had filled admirably for several years.

On January 23, 1907, he married Miss Eloise Norton McCurry, a daughter of Hon. A. G. and Frances Benson McCurry.

Judge Hodges died October 21, 1930, at Elberton during the September Adjourned Term of Elbert Superior Court.

His funeral, which was largely attended, was conducted at the Methodist Church in Hartwell on October 23, 1933, by his pastor, Rev. Frank E. Jenkins, assisted by the pastors of the other churches of the city and visiting ministers.

Drewry Cade Alford

DREWRY CADE ALFORD was born in Anderson County, S. C., February 12, 1856. He was the son of Lodwick and Alsie Snipes Alford. married Sara Frances Thornton, daughter of Reverend Benjamin Calloway Thornton, October 3, 1878. His death occurred March 28, 1933.

In early childhood his parents came to Hart County, and in early manhood he made his home in Hartwell, where he spent the remaining years of a long, useful life.

"Cade" Alford, as he was universally known and loved, had such a varied experience in his struggle to attain the pinnacle of mankind he so fittingly occupied; contributed so much in spirit and of his means to the beginning and advancement of the business, educational and religious life of his town and county, it is humanly impossible to properly appraise his worth.

Joining the Milltown Baptist Church in early life, he added his part toward making the Christian religion the beautiful garden of love in which sage and savant have found refuge since time immemorable. Serving as a deacon in the Hartwell Baptist Church for over fifty years, he also was superintendent of its Sunday school for a quarter of a century.

His was such a retentive mind he could refer to sermons preached by different ministers over a period of fifty years, remembering the salient features of each sermon and the exact wording of texts different preachers used.

As a country boy, Cade Alford walked into the office of the local newspaper at Hartwell and inquired of John Magill, its editor: "How much money is required to own and operate a newspaper?" As the same boy, he would ride by a farm on the river road in Hart County and admire the broad fields of abundant crops—even the hand-made doors in the farm house thereon.

As a man, he had his newspaper and acquired the plantation he admired as a dreaming, working lad. He was a successful business man; acquired by close application and clear foresight a position in the business world of his section second to none, and occupied many positions of honor in the affairs of his town and county.

He was a devoted husband and father, a true friend and a most highly cultured gentleman. As a church member, he came as near walking in the footsteps of Jesus Christ as anyone who ever walked the face of the earth.

While the articulate, if not intelligent!—stand in the roadway and question; this man, possessing a God-like sense of justice, the power of love and heavenly aspiration and a soul for endless service, went down to death with faith undimmed.

Brief History

ALFORD.—The name is Saxon origin, and is derived from Alfred, the Saxon King of England.

Looking backward—Drewry Cade Alford was the son of Lodwick, the son of Drewry, the son of Lockhart, the son of Green, the son of James Wm. Zion, the son of James, the son

D. C. Alford

of Benjamin, the son of William, who was born in London in 1608. Moved to Massachusetts in 1635. Benjamin was born the same year. James was born in 1691. Zion was born in 1730 and moved to North Carolina, and made a record for bravery in the battle of Cowpens and Guilford Courthouse. Lodwick Alford, father of Drewry Cade Alford, was born in Wake County, N. C., May 30, 1802, and died in Hart County, Ga., April 25, 1877.

Drewry Cade Alford was born in Anderson County, S. C., February 12, 1856, and died March 28, 1933.

The John Benson Chapter, Daughters of the American Revolution, and the Hartwell Chapter United Daughters of Confederacy

WE HAVE been favored with quite an elaborate history of the John Benson Chapter, Daughters of the American Revolution, and the Hartwell Chapter, United Daughters of the Confederacy, but due to the prohibitive cost of publishing these articles in full, we regret that we have been forced to leave out the greater part of the accounts, however most of the more important achievements of the two orders have been more or less prominently mentioned in this history.

History of John Benson Chapter, Daughters of the American Revolution

Written by May Lilly Teasley McCurry

"Sociologists tell us there are many influences that tend to make a criminal, one of the potent ones being the lack of an individual definitely associated with a surname. While no claim is being made that back in 1890, when the group of prominent Washington, D. C., women organized a society, membership to which was contingent on having an ancestor who had aided in the cause of American independence, that the said group were showing, at the time, their interest in sociology; nevertheless, they were giving to a large number of American mothers a lever with which to hold their children in that high moral class which holds itself responsible for civic good. A child reared in a home atmosphere which regards, with pride, descent from a line of men and women who were willing to serve a just cause, is being given a mighty aid in character development.

"However, it should be a matter of pride to any one whose family has been composed of people who have left records in the communities in which they have lived, written witness of the fact they were honorable and worthwhile people. Membership in the Daughters of the American Revolution does not require this proof."

The John Benson Chapter, Daughters of the American Revolution, was organized March 12, 1913, by Mrs. Julian B. McCurry in Hartwell, Ga., she having been appointed organizing regent by Mrs. S. W. Foster, regent at that time of the Georgia Society. Mrs. Henry L. Mann, Vice-President General, was in charge of the organization of the chapter.

The following is a list of the charter members:

95436—Benson, Myra Edna		Treasurer
95437—Herndon, Elizabeth Webb	(C. M.)	Secretary
95438—Hodges, Eloise McCurry	(W. L.),	Registrar
95439—McCurry, Daisy Norton	(Wm. E.)	
94199—McCurry, Frances Benson	(A. C.)	Cor. Secretary
75181—McCurry, Richmond V. W.	(Julian)	Regent
95440—Matheson, Ethel Benson	(C. E.)	
99085—Mickel, Janie Conwell	(A. G.)	
99086—Neese, Mary Benson	(A. L.)	
99087—Peek, Mattie Benson	(S. W.)	
95441—Teasley, Grace Benson	(James L.)	
99088—Thornton, Rachel C. D.	(McAlpin)	Vice Regent

The next three members were:

100695—Lily Cloud Bradley (R. P.), transferred from at large, February 28, 1914.
123243—Juliet L. Maybin, admitted through Chapter, April 15, 1916.
114657—May Lilly Teasley (Mrs. W. B. McCurry), admitted through Chapter, April 17, 1915.

The chapter was named in honor of John Blassingame Benson, the ancestor of nine of the charter members, who was Hartwell's pioneer merchant, and gave many years of service to the upbuilding of the town and community in which he lived. John B. Benson was a native of South Carolina, and was a descendant of Thomas Benson, Revolutionary soldier of Virginia. Other members of the Benson family served their country during the Revolution.

History of the Hartwell Chapter, United Daughters of the Confederacy

Written by Nell Smith Nichols

Organization

The Hartwell Chapter, United Daughters of the Confederacy, number 490; was organized February 28, 1901, by Mrs. McAlpin Thornton, at the home of Mrs. Jas. T. Magill. Mrs. Magill was the daughter of Major John H. Skelton, ranking officer of Hart County. Charter members were: Mrs. S. M. Adams, Miss Mai Anderson, Mrs. R. P. Bradley, Miss Annie Conwell, Mrs. Jas. T. Magill, Mrs. G. B. Pledger, Mrs. A. N. Alford, Mrs. Winslow Becker, Mrs. W. A. Cason, Mrs. J. W. Eberhardt, Miss Helen Magill, Mrs. M. M. Richardson, and Mrs. McAlpin Thornton. Miss Conwell, Mrs. Becker, and Mrs. Pledger, moved away from Hartwell. Only Mrs. Cason, Mrs. Richardson, and Mrs. Thornton remain, the others having finished their life's work and passed on.

The chapter was composed entirely of new members for the purpose of perpetuating the ideals and memories of the Confederacy. A committee composed of Mrs. Jas. Magill, Chairman, Mrs. McAlpin Thornton, and Miss Susie McMullan, was appointed to prepare constitution and by-laws. These were read at the third meeting and adopted as they stood. The constitution and by-laws were revised in 1909. Meetings were at first held twice each month. The plan of holding one meeting each month, for ten months of the year, was later adopted. The chapter met with the members in alphabetical order. Dues were first eighty cents per year, per member. This was paid in installments of five cents at each meeting. In 1919 an increase of twenty cents was made. Now dues are one dollar and ten cents, paid annually.

Literary programs were introduced as part of each meeting in 1908. The charter was granted July 30, 1901. The first press reporter was elected by a nominating committee in 1913. Year books have been published in 1925, 1926 and 1927.

The first officers of the Hartwell Chapter, United Daughters of the Confederacy, were: Mrs. R. P. Bradley, President; Mrs. A. N. Alford, First Vice-President; Miss Mai Anderson, Second Vice-President; Mrs. McAlpin Thornton, Recording Secretary; Miss Susie McMullan, Corresponding Secretary; Mrs. Winslow Becker.

Monuments

The Hartwell chapter has erected one monument honoring Hart County's veterans. This monument stands in the court-house square, facing the National Highway. This undertaking was financed by soliciting, holding bazaars, having dinners, plays, and by using numerous other money-making schemes. The monument was unveiled by Little Wilma Skelton (Mrs. Willie Brown), granddaughter of the late Major John H. Skelton, who organized the first company to leave Hart County in the War Between the States. The unveiling took place July 23, 1908, at which time appropriate exercises were held and dinner served to the veterans. The total cost of the monument was $1,350.00. Mrs. C. D. Turner was president of the chapter that year.

World War Veterans—Hart County.
Army

EXTRACTS from diary on Company "F," Hartwell's Military Company in the World War. This diary was started at Camp Wheeler, Ga., in October, 1917, the events covered before that time being recorded from memory, with exceptions of muster rolls, etc., which are copied from official papers.

The National Guard Company at Marietta, Ga., having been disbanded the year 1913, it was suggested that Hartwell organize another to fill vacancy created. Several meetings were held and, after correspondence with proper authorities, permission was received to organize. Capt. J. C. Reese, of Co. "I," 3d Sep. Bn. Ing., Ga. N. G. (Elbert Light Infantry), and Lieut. H. B. Payne, Bn. Adj., both of Elberton, came to Hartwell during the last weeks of December, 1913, to enlist the men. Enough having been secured, the State of Georgia accepted the Company in January, 1914, and assigned it as Co. "F," 3d Sep. Bn. Inf., Ga. N. G., under Major H. P. Hunter, Elberton. The rest of the battalion was composed of Co. "E," at Lindale, Co. "H," at Winder, and Co. "I," at Elberton, named respectively the Lindale Rifles, Winder Guards, and Elbert Light Infantry.

The Hartwell Rifles was selected as our Company name. The upper story of the T. W. Teasley building was secured as an armory. Lieut. H. B. Payne was detailed as temporary Company Commander pending election and commissioning of a Captain.

After due process of election (by members of the company) and examination, J. L. Stapleton, J. L. Massey and J. Cullen Wright received commissions as Captain, First Lieutenant and Second Lieutenant, respectively. P. A. Leard, J. B. Magill, E. W. Leard, C. W. Dooley, M. M. Parks, and Leon Morris received warrants as Sergeants. P. A. Leard and J. B. Magill was detailed as First and Quartermaster Sergeants. C. W. Dooley, after a few months, requested and received a discharge on account of "business interests with military duty."

Equipment was received and drills begun as soon as possible.

Sgt. W. H. Stamper, of the Regular Army, detailed as Sgt. Instructor for the Georgia National Guard, spent several months in Hartwell organizing and instructing the Company.

The Company attended a ten-day encampment at Camp Wheeler, near Augusta, in July, 1914, the very period of time in which international affairs in Europe reached the crisis which terminated in the "World War."

In 1915 Capt. Stapleton and Lieut. Massey resigned. First Sgt. P. A. Leard and Sgt. E. W. Leard were elected and, after standing examinations, received commissions as Captain and First Lieutenant, respectively.

J. B. Magill was detailed First Sergeant.

The second story of the Horton building was rented as armory.

No encampment in 1915 or 1916.

All the original enlistments ran out in December, 1913, and January, 1914. A great many of them were renewed. The following received Sergeant warrants on re-enlistment: J. B. Magill, Leon Morris, Fred S. White, M. M. Parks, C. L. Johnson, and W. E. White. J. B. Magill and C. L. Johnson were detailed as First and Quartermaster Sergeants, respectively.

In June, 1916, all Georgia troops except Coast Artillery Corps, and 3d Separate Battalion, of which Co. "F" was a part (left in the State for riot duty), were called to Camp Harris, Macon, Ga., and from there were moved to the Mexican border.

Capt. P. A. Leard, First Lieut. E. W. Leard, First Sgt. J. B. Magill, Q. M. Sgt. C. L. Johnson, Corporals A. B. Brown and J. Elbert Estes, and Privates Walter W. Ayers, J. B. Thornton, J. Robert Webb and T. Burrell Harris were mustered into Federal service in July, 1916, for recruiting duty. Sgt. Magill could not rank as First Sergeant on this duty so Fred S. White was detailed in his stead.

While on this duty Lieut. Leard took examination for the Regular Army and received a commission as Provisional Second Lieutenant in November, 1916.

The whole detail was mustered out of service in November and December and Lieut. Leard left for Fort Leavenworth, Kas., for a three-months period of instruction, after which he was assigned to the 17th Infantry, then stationed in Atlanta. After a few months he received a commission as First Lieutenant in the same organization. (He remained in the Regular Army after the war and at the time of writing, February, 1933, this extract, was a Major at Fort Benning, Ga.)

W. E. White was elected First Lieutenant in his stead January 29, 1917. Congress declared war on Germany, April 6, 1917.

Notice was received that Co. "F" would be "drafted" into Federal service on August 5, 1917.

Co. "E," at Lindale, having disbanded during 1917, the Battalion was disbanded as a unit. Major Hunter and his staff were placed in the Reserve and three remaining companies were designated "Separate Co. "F," Georgia Infantry, National Guard," etc.

General Orders No. 7, A. G. O. Ga., was received August 2, 1917, ordering the company to assemble at the company rendezvous Sunday, August 5, 1917, for examination and muster.

The company assembled August 5, 1917, Sunday morning, with 100 men and three officers on the roll, five of them A. W. O. L. (absent without leave). Capt. Roscoe H. Hearn, 48th Infantry, was mustering officer, and Lieut. Thomas V. Woodring, Medical Officers Reserve Corps, was the examining surgeon.

During the afternoon men whose examination had been completed hauled the equipment to the school grounds and pitched camp. The City of Hartwell had already donated the use of the grounds and had built a kitchen and had put in water connections. Electric lights were added later.

Monday, August 6th, the work of getting ready for muster, including passing on applications for discharge on account of dependent relatives, was completed and the muster roll was made out. The organization was mustered in a light drizzle.

Preston B. Carter was enlisted on this date, making 101 men on the roll, less nine discharged on account of dependent relatives and 16 on physical examination, and one under age. This left 75 enlisted men and two officers, Second Lieutenant J. Cullen Wright having been discharged on physical disabilities.

Out of this company of 77, officers and men, all came home alive except two, Preston B. Carter and Yancey J. Wilson, both of whom were killed in action. Lieut. J. Cullen Wright died of "flu" while the company was away.

The camp was named Camp Hart and the company remained here until Sunday, September 16, 1917, on which date it moved to Macon, Ga., Camp Wheeler. The three companies at Hartwell, Elberton and Winder, were put in the old Second Georgia Infantry, a regiment mainly from south Georgia, to fill vacancies caused by taking Companies "B," "C" and "F" out to form a Machine Gun Battalion in the Rainbow Division, being organized to go directly to France. Co. "F" retained its old designation of Co. "F" but the other two were changed, the company from Winder becoming Co. "B" and that from Elberton Co. "C." The Regiment was changed a little later to the 121st Inf., making the Hartwell company from that time on Co. "F," 121st Inf.

The company remained in Camp Wheeler until Sunday, September 15, 1918, during which time there were many changes in its personnel. A number of Hart County boys who were called to the colors were sent to the company, together with others from Georgia and surrounding states.

In the spring of 1918 numbers of the men were taken out and sent ahead, many of them reaching France many months before the company got there as a unit. Their places were filled with more drafted men, mainly from the North and West.

Many of the original enlisted men were promoted to Sergeant and Corporal. Two of them, Fred S. White and W. T. Johnson, Jr., received commissions as Second Lieutenants after attending an Officers' Training Camp in Texas. Fred S. White was assigned back to Co. "F" after getting the commission and went overseas with the company. Lieut. Johnson was sent to Camp Pike, Ohio. He remained in the Regular Army after the war. Boyce D. Power, of Vienna, Ga., whose father, Prof. C. G. Power, was Superintendent of the Hartwell Public Schools, and T. Burrell Harris, one of the men mustered in on August 5, 1917, both received commissions as Second Lieutenants after attending a school at Camp Gordon in October, 1918, after the company had gone to France.

On Sunday, September 15, 1918, the company entrained for Camp Mills, Long Island, New York, arriving there Tuesday night.

On Friday, October 4, 1918, the company left Camp Mills, went to Hoboken, N. J., by train and ferry boat, and there embarked on the S. S. Orizaba, which, however, did not leave the harbor until Saturday night about midnight.

The company landed at Brest, France, on Tuesday, October 15, 1918. At Brest they saw the "Pontanezen Barracks," said to have been built and occupied by Napolean Bonaparte's army.

Monday, October 21st, left Brest for LeMans, arriving there during the night.

Tuesday, October 22nd, when the company was marced from the railway station to the "Classification Camp," orders were issued disbanding the company as a unit and making "casuals" of all officers and men. This was being done with all organizations coming across at that time on account of the fact that a big drive—the last of the war—was on and no new, untried units were needed at the front, but great numbers of individual officers and men were needed to replace casualties. Later the units were placed back in existence—on paper—each company being represented by one man, usually the First Sergeant, and these skeleton units came home in that fashion.

The officers and men of our company were sent out from LeMans to LaBazoge, a very small village, to be attached to the 49th Infantry for a short course of intensive training in rifle practice and gas-mask defense. After about a week there the majority of the men were sent on out, most of them eventually getting up to the front. About 25 or 30 of the original Hartwell and Hart County boys were kept in the 49th Infantry, came back to the States and went to Fort Leavenworth, Kas., with the regiment and were discharged from there. The others came home singly as they were sent back from overseas and discharged. Some few stayed in the Regular Army. Thomas W. Chastain is at this time a non-commissioned officer in the 3d Infantry, at Fort Snelling, Minn.

The following list of men of Separate Co. "F," Georgia Infantry, National Guard, later Co. "F," 121st Infantry, was taken from *The Hartwell Sun* of September 21, 1917, and is the list of men that left Hartwell with the company on Sunday, September 16, 1917, for Camp Wheeler, at Macon, Ga., after an error or two:

LEARD, PEYTON A., Captain.
WHITE, WALLACE E., First Lieutenant.
WHITE, FRED S., First Sergeant, later Second Lieutenant.
MAGILL, JULIAN B., Supply Sergeant, later First Sergeant.
JOHNSON, COLUMBUS L., Mess Sergeant, later Supply Sergeant.
MORRIS, LEON, Sergeant.
PARKS, MCCURRY M., Sergeant.
PEARMAN, HOWARD G., Sergeant.
BROWN, ARTHUR S., Sergeant.
ESTES, JAMES E., Corporal, later Sergeant.
HODGES, WALTER G., Corporal, later Sergeant.
CARLTON, ANK D., Corporal.

BAILEY, LLEWELLYN, Corporal.
JOHNSON, WILLIAM T., JR., later Sergeant, and then Second Lieutenant.
PARKS, ASBURY H., Corporal.
COBB, DALLAS R., Corporal, later Sergeant.
PULLIAM, BEN H. W., Corporal.
CHASTAIN, THOMAS W., Corporal.
MAGILL, DANIEL H., Corporal.
WEBB, WILLIAM T., Mechanic.
SEAWRIGHT, RYAN H. Cook.
NEESE, JOHN L., Cook.
VICKERY, CLEO D., Musician.
WILCOX, JEOL T., Musician.

Privates

ADAMS, BUFORD
ANDERSON, TOM S.
BAILEY, WILLIAM L. J.
BOOTH, JAMISON V.
BOOTH, THOMAS M.
BRADY, THOMAS L.
CLEVELAND, FRED D.
CRAFT, CLAUD F.
CRAFT, BERNICE A.
CARNES, JULIUS C.
CHASTAIN, GEORGE J.
CLARK, STILES E.
CASON, J. T.
CARTER, PRESTON B., Killed in Action.
CLEVELAND, EMIL J.
DAVIS, HARVEY R.
DOVE, DILLARD L.
ELMORE, LESTER
EAVES, CHARLES S.
EUBANKS, EDWARD B.
ELLIOTT, LEWIS D.
FRYE, JESSE C., later Corporal.
GREENWAY, CLIFFORD I.
GUEST, LUTHER W.
GALLOWAY, REUBEN E.
GOODWIN, RICHARD G.
GULLEY, JIM
HOLBROOK, BURT D., later Corporal.
HARRIS, THOMAS B., later Second Lieutenant.
HAYES, B. C.
HANSFORD, WILLIAM E.
HARPER, NOAH L.

HANCOCK, QUINCY M.
HOWELL, ARTHUR B.
JORDAN, GORDON L.
KING, GUY A.
LEWIS, JAMES T.
LEWIS, LOONEY A.
MOSS, JULIAN S.
MEREDITH, FORD M.
MACIJEWSKI, JOHN M.
MAGILL, HARRY E.
NEESE, ALPHA O., later Corporal.
OLIVER, VIRGIL L.
OSLEY, GROVER C.
OLIVER, D. L. C.
ROPER, EARL
ROPER, WILLIAM P.
REYNOLDS, ISHAM W., later Corporal.
ROBERTSON, CARL REXFORD
RHODES, WALTER
SNOW, FRANCIS J.
SCOTT, MCDANIEL
SULLIVAN, PIERCE C.
SAYLORS, OLLIE L.
SANDERS, ARTHUR R.
SCHULTZ, OTTO H., later Cook.
STEPHENS, JOE
THORNTON, JAMES B., later Corporal.
THORNTON, DON H.
TUCKER, CLYDE M.
WINN, FRANK G.
WEBB, JOHN R., later Sergeant.
WILSON, YANCEY L., Killed in Action.
WRIGHT, LEWIS A.

(Note—Looney A. Lewis, Gordon L. Jordan, Harry E. Magill and Joe Stephens, had not had their physical examination and were rejected on reaching Camp Wheeler.)

Members of Separate Co. "F," Georgia Infantry, National Guard (The Hartwell Rifles), discharged August 5, 1917, on account of dependent relatives or on Surgeon's Certificate of Disability, these being discharged prior to the company's being mustered into Federal service:

WRIGHT, J. CULLEN, Second Lieutenant.
CONNALLY, HENRY G., Corporal.
CARTER, JAMES M., Corporal.

OGLESBY, MAC, Corporal.
EAVES, GEORGE R., Mechanic.

Privates First Class

BROCK, JOHN W.
BROWN, BYRD C.
MARETT, KARL E.

MARETT, WILLIAM I.
SCHULTZ, OTTO H., later re-enlisted and went to France with the Company.

Privates

AYERS, WALTER W.
BAILEY, WILLIAM E.
CAMPBELL, CHARLES W.
CLEVELAND, BODE M.
CLEVELAND, ROSCOE F.
KING, PAUL
McGILL, JAMES
SANDERS, ALVIN M.
TEMPLES, WALKER W.

WHITE, JOHN H.
WILSON, JOHN H.
CARY, BONNEAU H.
BAILEY, JAMES W.
BAILEY, JERRY W.
HERRING, SLOAN R.
POOLER, FRED E.
REID, HUSKIN J.

List of additions to Co. "F," 121st Infantry, at Camp Wheeler, Macon, Ga., up to November 16, 1917:

Second Lieutenants

BURKHALTER, EDWIN A.
HAGAN, THOMAS W.

HAMILTON, ROBERT F.
McLARIN, WILLIAM S.

(These Reserve Officers, graduates of the Training Camp at Camp Gordon, Atlanta, Ga.)

The following were selectmen, from Hart or adjoining counties:

ANKERICH, LEO N.
BOND, HOYT
BROWN, JOHN H.
BUFFINGTON, CARL R.
CARLTON, HENRY E.
CHITWOOD, OTIS C.
COOK, CLAUD S.
CRAFT, GEORGE L.
FINLEY, RUFUS F., Franklin County.
FRANKS, JOHN D., Franklin County.
GREER, FERMON N., Stephens County.

HERRING, LEV
IVESTER, GEORGE H., Stephens County.
JONES, ROBERT L., Lavonia.
LEARD, MYRON
LEWIS, HUBERT
PEACE, BENJAMIN H., Franklin County.
PIERCE, MANSON C., Lavonia.
RICE, THOMAS W., Lavonia.
STEPHENSON, BARTOW L., Royston.
TEASLEY, LEE C.
VANDIVER, FRED R.

World War Veterans—Hart County

ACKER, FOSTER (col.)
ADAMS, ALBERT B.
ADAMS, CHARLES S.
ADAMS, GRADY (col.)
ADAMS, LEO (col.)
ADAMS, LONNIE (col.)
ALEWINE, ALBERT T.
ALEXANDER, LARKIN (col.)

ALEXANDER, WILLIAM (col.)
ALLEN, ERNEST (col.)
ALLEN, GRADY (col.)
AYERS, WALTER W.
AYERS, COLLEY
AYERS, JACK H.
AYERS, JOHN H.
AYERS, WILLIE G.

Ayers, Newland J.
Bailey, James W.
Bailey, Jerry W.
Bailey, Llewellyn
Bailey, William Eber
Baker, Curtis P.
Banks, Leo (col.)
Banks, William (col.)
Bannister, Otis Ford
Bannister, Earnest
Barnes, Henry (col.)
Barnes, Walter (col.)
Bell, Alvin F., Jr.
Bell, Robert (col.)
Bennett, Buel J.
Benson, Enoch B.
Blackmon, William D.
Blackwell, Arthur (col.)
Blalock, Barney G.
Bobo, Lewis S.
Bobo, William M.
Bonds, Jeffie (col.)
Bowers, Columbus E.
Bowers, Undona
Bowie, Grady L.
Bowman, Nathan (col.)
Bray, Hubert L.
Brock, John W.
Brock, Robert L.
Brown, Arthur
Brown, Byrd C.
Brown, Claud (col.)
Brown, Edgar J.
Brown, John Robert
Brown, Julian E.
Brown, James H. (col.)
Brown, Thomas M.
Brown, Willie L. (col.)
Burch, Roy (col.)
Burch, Taylor (col.)
Burns, Robert H.
Byrum, James
Campbell, Charles W.
Campbell, John P.
Carlton, Ank D.
Cash, Russell G.
Cason, James M.
Chastain, Claude I.
Chastain, John L.
Cleveland, Bode M.
Cleveland, Fred E.
Cleveland, Roscoe F.
Conally, Henry G.
Cook, Homer A.
Cordell, Charlie J.
Cowan, Ulysses (col.)
Craft, Elmer (col.)
Craft, Otis (col.)
Craft, Thomas F.
Crider, James M.
Curry, Linder (col.)
Dooley, Arthur (col.)
Dooley, Conway (col.)
Dooley, Johnnie B. (col.)
Durrett, Richard (col.)
Eaves, George R.
Elrod, Jud M.
Feaster, Erwin (col.)
Ferguson, Joseph R.
Fleming, Levis T.
Fortson, Earnest (col.)
Fuller, Morris (col.)
Gaines, Early (col.)
Gaines, Homer W.
Gaines, Lige (col.)
Gaines, William (col.)
Gaines, William Hamilton
Gaines, Willie (col.)
Galphin, George C.
Gary, Otis (col.)
Gear, Charley (col.)
Ginn, Earnest Watson
Goforth, Clinton W.
Greenway, Leonard
Grizzle, Arthur H.
Guest, Oscar
Gunter, Will
Hailey, Isham B.
Hall, Charlie T.
Hall, Charles S.
Hall, Homer Hamilton
Hall, Joel S.
Harper, Cooley (col.)
Harper, Elbert (col.)
Harper, Mack (col.)
Harris, Karl Pinkney
Harris, Lensey (col.)
Heard, Fred (col.)
Heard, Jesse (col.)
Heard, Lewis (col.)
Heard, T. B. (col.)
Heaton, Arthur N.
Herring, Sloan R.
Highsmith, Albert (col.)
Hill, William F.
Holbrook, Lonnie
Holland, Alton B.
Holland, Ferd T.
Holmes, John
Howell, Gordon
Huckleby, Eugene (col.)
Hunt, Lue (col.)
Hutchinson, Will (col.)
Isbell, Alexander Clyde (col.)
Isom, Landon (col.)
Isom, Tom
Johnson, Albert (col.)
Johnson, Dennis (col.)
Johnson, John (col.)
Jones, George (col.)
Jones, Jesse (col.)
Jones, Jettie (col.)
Jones, Lon (col.)
Jones, Willie (col.)

WORLD WAR VETERANS

KAY, GEORGE H.
KING, PAUL (col.)
LOCKE, IRVING G.
McCURLEY, EDGAR B.
McDOUGAL, SNOW
McLESKEY, JONES J.
McLEES, BENJAMIN T.
McLANE, BROOKS
McMULLAN, THOMAS L.
MADDEN, EUGENE T.
MANCE, HODGES (col.)
MARTIN, JAMES E.
MARTIN, JUSTUS
MASON, THOMAS W.
MORRISON, THOMAS (col.)
MURRAY, JOHN H.
NELMS, JOSEPH H.
OGLESBY, MACK
OWENS, DALLAS J.
PAGE, FLORENCE A.
PAGE, RICHARD L.
PARKS, FRED (col.)
PASS, TOM (col.)
PATTERSON, ARTHUR S.
PATTERSON, ELYARD (col.)
PATTERSON, LUTHER (col.)
PEEK, JULIAN
PHILLIPS, ISAAC J., JR.
PIERCE, BARNEY NORTHERN
POOLER, FRED E.
POWELL, CARL B.
POWELL, THOMAS C.
REEDER, LARRY A. (col.)
REED, WILLIAM
REID, HUSKIN J.
REID, WILMER E.
RIDGWAY, PAUL J.
RICHARDSON, JOHN W.
RICHARDSON, WILLIAM A.
ROBERTSON, HOWELL B.
ROEBUCK, EUGENE (col.)
RUCKER, LUTHER (col.)
SADDLER, RUFUS (col.)
SANDERS, ALVIN M.
SANDERS, CLIVIS H.
SANDERS, HENRY S.
SCOTT, BLEN M.
SCOTT, BOYCE C.
SCOTT, CHARLIE C.
SCOTT, JIMMIE (col.)
SCOTT, PENIC
SCOTT, QUINCY G.
SEAWRIGHT, TOM J.
SHEARER, DEWEY H.
SHIFLET, EARLEY B.
SHIFLET, JUDSON M.
SHIFLET, SELL (col.)
SIMPSON, ULIS (col.)
SMITH, JOHN S.
STINSON, JAMES I. (col.)
STOWERS, CLAUD (col.)
STRANGE, BLANK (col.)
STRANGE, PULLIAM (col.)
SORRELLS, CLAUD E.
STARK, PETER (col.)
SUIT, MAC L.
SWIFT, HENRY (col.)
TEASLEY, ISHAM (col.)
TEASLEY, MAJOR (col.)
TEASLEY, OSCAR A.
TEMPLES, WALKER W.
THOMPSON, LONNIE
THORNTON, ACE (col.)
THORNTON, GEORGE S.
THORNTON, JIMMIE LEE (col.)
THRASHER, JOEL W.
TUCKER, ROBERT J.
VANDUZER, FRED T.
VASSER, JOHN R.
VERNON, WILLIAM HAILEY
VICKERY, FRED G.
VICKERY, IRA C.
WAKEFIELD, ROBERT (col.)
WALTERS, JESSE G.
WEBB, EUGENE (col.)
WEBB, WILLIAM T.
WHITE, BEN H.
WHITE, JOHN H.
WHITE, MONROE H.
WILLIAMS, EUGENE
WILLIAMS, IRA
WILLIAMS, LEONARD WALKER
WILLIAMS, USHER (col.)
WILSON, HAMLIN E.
WILSON, JOHN H.
WILSON, JOHN N.
WINN, NILE
WINTERS, CLAUDE E.
WRIGHT, LEWIS A. (col.)
YOUNG, JOEL (col.)

Deceased

ADAMS, JOHN W.
ALLEN, ERSKINE (col.)
CARPENTER, MAT (col.)
CARTER, PRESTON B.
GAINES, HENRY (col.)
HARRIS, ANDERSON (col.)
HEATON, JOHN R.
PATTERSON, GEORGE W.
THOMPSON, GILBERT
WILSON, YANCEY J.

Officers

BARTON, DAVID JUDSON
BOWIE, JOHN C.
DOOLEY, WILLIAM G.
FOOTE, WALTER W.
GAINES, THOMAS R.
HARRIS, THOMAS BURRELL
JOHNSON, WILLIAM T.
LEARD, EMIL W.

LEARD, PEYTON ALEXANDER
MCCURRY, WILLIAM EDGAR
MEREDITH, ALBERT OWEN
MORRIS, JOHN BRAZE
SKELTON, JAMES HOWARD
WHITE, FRED SEABORN
WHITE, WALLACE EDMOND

Navy

ALFORD, HAROLD B.
AYERS, WILLIE EARLY
BRADBURY, FRED EDISON
BROWN, WILLIAM LEIGHTON
CARTER, LONNIE ELMER
CASON, GEORGE THOMAS
CHEEK, THOMAS ROLAND
DEAN, LUCIUS LOVIC
ESTES, THOMAS HERNDON
HAILEY, RUCKER MARION
HAILEY, WILLIAM HOWARD
HEMBREE, PHILIP SAMUEL
HAILEY, NORMAN L.
JOHNSON, JOHN A.
JORDAN, WILLIAM MURRAY

MCCURLEY, ISHAM LIGON
MCCURRY, RAYMOND SPEED
MOORHEAD, JOHN ROBERT
MOORHEAD, WILLIE THOMAS
NELMS, JOHN GREEN
PAGE, HOWARD
SKELTON, EMMETT ARNOLD
SMITH, FREDERICK BUREAN
SNOW, WILLIAM ANDY
SOKOL, CHARLES
VASSER, TOM WATSON
WADE, JESSE
WHITE, JAMES OLIVER
YATES, HERMAN LYNN

Deceased

ALFORD, OWEN JUDSON
ESTES, JAMES BROWN

DODD, CHARLES P.
VICKERY, OSCAR THOMAS

www.ingramcontent.com/pod-product-compliance
Lightning Source LLC
Chambersburg PA
CBHW020636300426
44112CB00007B/128